The Roaring Nineties

The Roaring Nineties
Can Full Employment Be Sustained?

Alan B. Krueger and Robert M. Solow, Editors

The Russell Sage Foundation ◆ New York
The Century Foundation Press ◆ New York

Library of Congress Cataloging-in-Publication Data

The roaring nineties : can full employment be sustained? / Alan Krueger, Robert Solow, editors
    p. cm.
    Includes bibliographical references and index.
    ISBN 0-87154-817-8
    1. Employment forecasting—United States. 2. Labor market—United States. 3. Full employment policies—United States. 4. United States—Economic conditions—1981–
    I. Krueger, Alan B. II. Solow, Robert M.

HD5724.R56 2002
339.5'0973—dc21 2001041787

RUSSELL SAGE FOUNDATION
112 East 64th Street, New York, New York 10021
10 9 8 7 6 5 4 3 2 1

Contents

CONTRIBUTORS   vii

FOREWORD   xi
Richard C. Leone and Eric Wanner

ACKNOWLEDGMENTS   xv

INTRODUCTION   xvii
Alan B. Krueger and Robert M. Solow

PART I   MACROECONOMIC PERSPECTIVES   1

Chapter 1   PRICES, WAGES, AND THE U.S. NAIRU IN THE 1990S
Douglas Staiger, James H. Stock, and Mark W. Watson   3

Chapter 2   PRODUCTIVITY GROWTH AND THE PHILLIPS CURVE
Laurence Ball and Robert Moffitt   61

Chapter 3   THE FABULOUS DECADE: MACROECONOMIC LESSONS FROM
THE 1990S
Alan S. Blinder and Janet L. Yellen   91

PART II   FLEXIBLE, OPEN LABOR MARKETS   157

Chapter 4   COMPARATIVE ANALYSIS OF LABOR MARKET OUTCOMES:
LESSONS FOR THE UNITED STATES FROM INTERNATIONAL
LONG-RUN EVIDENCE
Giuseppe Bertola, Francine D. Blau, and Lawrence M. Kahn   159

Chapter 5   HAVE THE NEW HUMAN-RESOURCE MANAGEMENT PRACTICES
LOWERED THE SUSTAINABLE UNEMPLOYMENT RATE?
Jessica Cohen, William T. Dickens, and Adam Posen   219

Chapter 6   THE EFFECTS OF GROWING INTERNATIONAL TRADE ON THE
U.S. LABOR MARKET
George Johnson and Matthew J. Slaughter   260

PART III   INCREASING LABOR SUPPLIES AND THEIR LIMITS   307

Chapter 7   LABOR AND THE SUSTAINABILITY OF OUTPUT AND
PRODUCTIVITY GROWTH
Rebecca M. Blank and Matthew D. Shapiro   309

Contents

Chapter 8   CHANGES IN UNEMPLOYMENT DURATION AND LABOR-FORCE
ATTACHMENT
Katharine G. Abraham and Robert Shimer   367

Chapter 9   THE SPUTTERING LABOR FORCE OF THE TWENTY-FIRST CENTURY:
CAN SOCIAL POLICY HELP?
David T. Ellwood   421

PART IV   THE BENEFITS AND PITFALLS OF TIGHT LABOR MARKETS   491

Chapter 10 ANOTHER LOOK AT WHETHER A RISING TIDE LIFTS ALL BOATS
James R. Hines Jr., Hilary W. Hoynes, and Alan B. Krueger   493

Chapter 11 RISING PRODUCTIVITY AND FALLING UNEMPLOYMENT: CAN
THE U.S. EXPERIENCE BE SUSTAINED AND REPLICATED?
Lisa M. Lynch and Stephen J. Nickell   538

INDEX   579

Contributors

ALAN B. KRUEGER is the Bendheim Professor of Economics and Public Affairs at Princeton University, research associate of the National Bureau of Economic Research, and editor of the *Journal of Economic Perspectives*.

ROBERT M. SOLOW is Institute Professor Emeritus at the Massachusetts Institute of Technology and a Nobel laureate in economics.

KATHARINE G. ABRAHAM is commissioner of the U.S. Bureau of Labor Statistics.

LAURENCE BALL is professor of economics at Johns Hopkins University and research associate of the National Bureau of Economic Research.

GIUSEPPE BERTOLA is professor of economics at the University of Turin, currently on leave as full-time professor at the European University Institute. He is also research fellow of CEPR (London).

REBECCA M. BLANK is Henry Carter Adams Professor and dean of the Gerald R. Ford School of Public Policy at the University of Michigan. She served as a member pf the Council of Economic Advisers under President Clinton.

FRANCINE D. BLAU is the Frances Perkins Professor of Industrial and Labor Relations and Labor Economics at Cornell University. She is also a Research Associate of the National Bureau of Economic Research (Cambridge, Mass.) and a Research Fellow of the CESifo (Munich, Germany).

ALAN S. BLINDER is the Gordon S. Rentschler Memorial Professor of Economics at Princeton University. He was a member of President Clinton's original Council of Economic Advisers and was vice chairman of the Federal Reserve Board from 1994 until early 1996.

JESSICA COHEN is a graduate student in the Department of Economics at the Massachusetts Institute of Technology.

WILLIAM T. DICKENS is senior fellow at the Brookings Institution.

DAVID T. ELLWOOD is Lucius N. Littauer Professor of Political Economy at the John F. Kennedy School of Government, Harvard University.

Contributors

JAMES R. HINES JR. is professor of business economics at the University of Michigan and research associate of the National Bureau of Economic Research.

HILARY W. HOYNES is associate professor of economics at the University of California—Davis and research associate of the National Bureau of Economic Research.

GEORGE JOHNSON is professor of economics at the University of Michigan.

LAWRENCE M. KAHN is professor of labor economics and collective bargaining in the School of Industrial and Labor Relations at Cornell University. He is also research fellow of CESifo (Munich).

LISA M. LYNCH is the William L. Clayton Professor of International Economic Affairs and academic dean of the Fletcher School of Law and Diplomacy at Tufts University. She is also research associate at the National Bureau of Economic Research.

ROBERT MOFFITT is professor of economics at Johns Hopkins University and research associate of the National Bureau of Economic Research.

STEPHEN J. NICKELL is School Professor of Economics at the London School of Economics and member of the Bank of England Monetary policy Committee.

ADAM POSEN is senior fellow at the Institute for International Economics.

MATTHEW D. SHAPIRO is professor in the Economics Department and senior research scientist in the Survey Research Center at the University of Michigan. He is also research associate of the National Bureau of Economic Research. He served as a senior economist on the staff of the Council of Economic Advisers under President Clinton.

ROBERT SHIMER is associate professor of economics at Princeton University and faculty research fellow at the National Bureau of Economic Research.

MATTHEW J. SLAUGHTER is associate professor of economics at Dartmouth College and faculty research fellow at the National Bureau of Economic Research.

DOUGLAS STAIGER is associate professor of economics at Darthmouth College and research associate of the National Bureau of Economic Research.

JAMES H. STOCK is the Roy E. Larsen Professor of Political Economy at Harvard University.

JANET L. YELLEN is the Eugene E. and Catherine M. Trefethen Professor of Business and professor of economics at the University of California, Berkeley. She served as a governor of the Federal Reserve from 1994 until 1997 and then as chair of the Council of Economic Advisers from 1997 until 1999.

MARK W. WATSON is professor of economics and public affairs at Princeton University.

Foreword

A s recently as 1995 it would have been difficult to find a single macro-economist at a top university who would have thought it possible that, five years later, the rate of unemployment would be below 5 percent, month after month, with only the most modest pressure on prices. So deep was the orthodoxy put forward by so many economists concerning the potentially dangerous relationship between low unemployment and high inflation that even most political leaders seemed to have embraced the notion. Almost no one, it seemed, was prepared to endorse policies that might permit such a situation to arise. The conventional wisdom was that "full employment"—an unemployment rate that could be sustained without unacceptable acceleration of the rate of inflation—was 6, 5.5, or maybe 5 percent. Advocates of a rate as low as 4.5 percent were scoffed at; those who proposed 4 percent were simply seen as economically illiterate.

The Federal Reserve today is the agency expected to seek a healthy balance between total demand for goods and services and the capacity of the economy to meet that demand. In 1995, too, there was little reason to dream that the Fed would permit an experiment in which the unemployment rate dropped far below consensus full employment. But of course, as we all know, the Fed turned out to be willing to take that particular gamble. And, in no small measure because the risk was taken, unemployment dropped to and stayed at the lowest levels in decades.

The changes in the nation in the past year or so—the emergence of terrorism as a real threat; the radical changes in tax, budget, and debt management polices; the slowdown in growth; the softening of the labor market; and fall in stock prices—are threatening to make the 1990s seem a strange and distant era. All the more reason, then, that we should look closely at the U.S. economic experience during that decade to see what we can discover about what happened and to determine what to do in the future.

It was in this spirit that The Century Foundation and the Russell Sage Foundation created the project that has resulted in this book. We were convinced that this was a moment when we might find some new and challenging views, learning from the remarkable period the economy had just experienced. We were extremely fortunate that our first choices to lead this effort agreed to do so. Robert Solow, Nobel Prize winner and sage among American economists, working closely with Alan Krueger, one of the brightest and most productive young scholars of American labor markets, put together a set of topics and authors, looking for insights into how labor markets worked at the microeconomic level and how they combined to produce the remarkable national macroeconomic outcome. The teams that wrote most of the papers are, like the project directors, a combination of an author (or two) with microeconomic expertise and perspective with someone who works mostly as a macroeconomist.

No single overriding explanation for the successes of the "roaring nineties" emerges from these papers, but—as Krueger and Solow discuss in their introductory chapter—the papers do identify a number of likely suspects. One possibility, of course, is that one or more exogenous *dei ex machina* took the economy on a wonderful, if temporary, ride. A plunge in energy prices, an unsustainable demand for dollar-denominated wealth, and a temporary surge in productivity growth might account for a period of low unemployment with stable, low inflation. A steadier surge in productivity growth, due perhaps to advances in information technology, could give the economy a more sustained boost. But several of the volume's authors warn us that unemployment cannot remain as low as it was in the late 1990s, even if productivity growth remains high, because people will begin to act with this in mind. Surely one old lesson of economic analysis is reinforced by these papers: productivity growth is a key force, not only for increasing the standard of living but for extending employment and training opportunities to more people. If this volume does no more than give greater urgency to the search for explanations for the variability of productivity growth, it will have made a contribution. Much obviously depends on healthy capital investment and the continued growth of a skilled workforce, a trend that several contributors to this volume see in serious future jeopardy in the United States.

Another important message to emerge from these chapters is that a period of low unemployment can be good for less-skilled, low-wage workers as well as better-off workers. But the message is somewhat mixed. Toward the end of the 1990s, low-wage, low-skill workers did realize rapid increases in employment and significant real wage gains. But these improvements did not occur until late in the period, and only after unemployment remained below 5 percent for some months. As several papers in this volume argue, much of the relative health of the U.S. employment figures may well have been purchased at the expense of low-skill workers, who were the first to suffer declining wages and employment during the structural adjustments of the 1980s and remain most vulnerable to the "flexibility" of U.S. labor market institutions. If the denouement of the 1990s has taught us that extremely low unemployment rates are difficult to sustain, then addressing the predicaments of low-skill workers may ultimately return us to the problem of productivity. In a labor market that achieves high-volume employment via rapid wage adjustments, increasing the productivity of low-skill workers may be the only lasting way to lift wages at the bottom.

A central question raised by these papers concerns the usefulness of the non-accelerating inflation rate of unemployment (NAIRU) as a guide to macroeconomic policy. It is hard to disagree with the notion that excessive aggregate demand eventually will trigger inflationary pressure. But whether it is useful to identify the capacity of the economy with a specific level of unemployment, a priori, is a very different matter. If the "time-variant NAIRU" looks to all the world like a smoothed version of the actual unemployment rate (barely different from a moving average), then policymaking based on the NAIRU comes perilously close to a formalized version of the simple rule of thumb: "keep the unemployment rate near its average of recent quarters." These papers are intended to take us beyond such conservative homilies as guides to policy.

In one sense, the success of this enterprise ultimately will be determined by the extent to which these papers stimulate productive and provocative discussion about how to improve labor market policy. They also offer fresh thinking about the utility of macroeconomic interventions to increase employment and incomes. We are confident, in fact, that other economists and perhaps policymakers as well will find their understanding enriched by these essays.

We extend our heartfelt thanks to Alan Krueger and Robert Solow. It has been an unusual pleasure to work with them; indeed, without them the project simply would not have been possible.

Richard C. Leone for The Century Foundation
Eric Wanner for the Russell Sage Foundation

Acknowledgments

The editors would like to thank Katy Herrmann, Suzanne Nichols, Eric Wanner, and David Weiman of the Russell Sage Foundation and Greg Anrig, Richard Leone, and Bernard Wasow of the Century Foundation for their stimulus, help, and encouragement throughout the planning, execution, and publishing of this volume. At the beginning, we were well advised by a committee that included George Perry, as well as several of the authors of chapters in this book, and others already named.

Alan B. Krueger
Robert Solow

Introduction

Alan B. Krueger and Robert Solow

A s Frank Sinatra might have said: "Those were very good years." Table 3.1 (from Blinder and Yellen, chapter 3 this volume, 92) offers a capsule version of the events that led to this project and this volume. During the five years 1995 to 2000, the U.S. economy grew faster, maintained a lower unemployment rate, and generated less inflation than in the whole of the 1970s or the 1980s. Even considered overall, the decade of the 1990s looks pretty good, but its second half was eye catching.

Table 3.1 also shows that the macroeconomic performance of the 1960s was just as strong on all three counts. That is an important fact, especially for true believers in the new economy. But the 1960s were a long time ago, and, anyway, the last few years of that decade were already strongly influenced by inappropriately financed and unsustainable spending on the Vietnam War. Suppose that, in a year like 1990, any knowledgeable student of the U.S. economy had been presented with a projection of the basic facts for the period 1995 to 2000 as they in fact turned out, including an unemployment rate of 4.0 percent for 2000 itself. The actual course of events summarized in table 3.1 would, in 1990, certainly have been considered a pipe dream—and with good reason. And that period seems even more remarkable when it is remembered that it was preceded by more than fifteen years of deficit in the federal budget, rising to almost 6 percent of GDP in 1992, by which time the federal debt held by the public was almost half of GDP. Not much room for maneuvering remained.

The consensus view at the time presumed the existence of two constraints on macroeconomic performance. The first constraint was the trend-growth rate of potential GDP, which was widely believed to be somewhere near 2.0 to 2.5 percent per year, held down mainly by the fact that, at the time, the productivity growth rate was slow—only 1.0 to 1.5 percent per year. Of course, the economy could grow more quickly than that after a recession had opened some slack that could be made up in the next upswing. But fast growth could be only temporary.

The second constraint was a lower limit to the unemployment rate of 6.0 to 6.5 percent before inflation rose. (An occasional rash adventurer was willing to hold out for a lower limit to the "inflation safe" unemployment rate of 5.5 percent.) And a good sign that the economy had reached its potential output, and was thus on the verge of tipping over into ever increasing inflation, was considered to be a reduction of the unemployment rate to that level. One did not have to accept the whole theory of a "natural rate of unemployment"—although most macroeconomists did so—to believe that too much pressure of the economy against its capacity (measured, for instance, by too low an unemployment rate) would cause wages and prices to soar upward.

The 1995 to 2000 episode clearly violated both of these two constraints. The inevitable questions then arise: Why were these constraints ineffective? Were there identifiable changes in economic institutions or behavior patterns that relaxed these earlier constraints or nullified them? Were there instead some favorable random events that improved economic performance beyond normal expectations? Must the events of 1995 to 2000 be regarded as a one-time, non-repeatable episode, a single piece of good luck, or have the rules of the game changed more nearly permanently? Are there policy choices that would make it possible to sustain the performance of 1995 to 2000 for the long term?

The research reported in this volume aims to answer these questions, at least as far as the second of the two basic macroeconomic constraints—the location of the inflation-safe unemployment rate—is concerned. As for the first, the growth of potential output, we take the faster productivity growth of the late 1990s (the fact that the productivity trend accelerated from around 1.5 percent per year in 1970 to 1995 to something like 2.5 percent per year in 1995 to 2000) as a given. Of course, we would like to know why that happened, not least because such knowledge would permit an educated guess as to whether faster trend-productivity growth will continue into the future or give way to another slow-down. But we do not attempt an explanation here (Blinder and Yellen, chapter 3 in this volume, do in places address this issue).

There are two main unresolved questions about the recent behavior of productivity: the extent to which the acceleration of productivity is a business-cycle effect related to the recovery from the 1990 recession and the extent to which that acceleration, obviously very strong in the computer-producing industries, has diffused to the computer-using industries, especially in the service sectors. Resolving these two questions is a difficult task, requiring different skills and different methods from those deployed in this volume. There is a large literature on that subject that seems to accept the existence of at least some structural, information-technology-related, broadly based acceleration (see, for example, Baily and Lawrence 2001), but we do not have to take any position on it. The facts about productivity growth play a central part in the employment-inflation connection (see especially Ball and Moffitt, chapter 2 in this volume). But we chose to focus on the employment story itself, which is complicated enough.

Naturally, then, the papers collected in this volume are primarily investigations into one or another aspect of the labor market. In every case, however, it is the macroeconomic implications of labor-market developments that are the main concern. Remember that we want to know how best to sustain a high-employment economy. To that end, whenever it seemed reasonable to do so, we assigned each of the topics to be covered to a team consisting of (at least) one microeconomically and one macroeconomically oriented person and asked that the resulting paper be a true collaboration, not an artificial welding together of, say, a microeconomic part I and a macroeconomic part II.

The notion that a high-employment economy can be sustained has overtones. There was a time within living memory when one would have said, not "sustaining high employment," but "maintaining full employment." During the 1970s, the interplay of facts and theories led to a shift in focus from full employment to the inflation-safe unemployment rate (or natural rate, the NAIRU). The difference is that the idea of full employment evoked an unemployment rate low enough to leave little more than the minimal amount of inevitable frictional unemployment necessary to lubricate a labor market in which people and firms can hire and fire, quit and take jobs, and enter and exit the labor force at will. The inflation-safe unemployment rate does what it says; it looks only for an unemployment rate just high enough to keep inflation from worsening. That is what *high employment* tends to mean nowadays. The experience of the years 1995 to 2000 suggests a reexamination of the view that rising inflation sets in well before unemployment reaches anything like the frictional minimum.

The task is special in another way. Economic analysis ordinarily aims to account for or understand some observed or observable regularities: we have just been talking about one such. But this volume is devoted to the study of a single episode, and that is not what social science normally does. Of course, part of the exercise is to determine whether the episode falls easily into some standard category. In any actual case, however, there are bound to be historical peculiarities, chance events, identifiable one-time deviations from the norm, and other such factors whose influence is hard to understand and evaluate. Certainty about conclusions is probably too much to expect, and that will be seen to be the case here. But we can provide a better sense of where to look to understand what made the decade so successful.

The Douglas Staiger, James Stock, and Mark Watson; Laurence Ball and Robert Moffitt; and Alan Blinder and Janet Yellen chapters (chapters 1, 2, and 3, respectively) are the most explicitly macroeconomic in character. It is interesting to see where they reinforce and where they contradict one another, or at least where they need to be reconciled if possible.

Staiger, Stock, and Watson find that they can give a unified account of the whole period since 1960 using a conventional Phillips curve with the natural-rate (NAIRU) property, provided that they allow for one element of flexibility. To begin, they calculate a "trend unemployment rate" using a sophisticated sort of two-sided moving average. This procedure uses only the unemployment-rate series itself and rests on no specifically *economic* theory; it is in that sense purely mechanical. The resulting trend unemployment rate is no bland construct (see their figure 1.4). It has a minimum of almost 4 percent around 1970, reaches a maximum of nearly 8 percent around 1980, and then falls steadily and dramatically until it is well below 5 percent at the end of 2000.

Staiger, Stock, and Watson then estimate a Phillips curve with a NAIRU that is also allowed to wander. They find that their calculated NAIRU series hugs the trend unemployment rate very closely, as can be seen in their figure 1.00; in fact, it is statistically just about indistinguishable from the trend rate. The statistical reason for this is connected with the logic of the Phillips curve. There cannot be large, systematic deviations of the unemployment rate from its trend; that is what is meant by a trend. If there were large, systematic deviations of the NAIRU from the trend, then there would have to be large, systematic movements in the dependent variable, the change in the inflation rate. But there are not; the change in inflation is roughly a stationary series with little or no persistence.

One conceivable explanation for the remarkable coincidence between the NAIRU and the trend rests on targeted policy. Suppose that the NAIRU is falling for whatever structural reason; then, if monetary policy tries to keep the unemployment rate near the NAIRU on average and succeeds, the observed unemployment rate must also follow a falling trend. This is, in effect, Staiger, Stock, and Watson's argument; if monetary policy failed to keep the unemployment rate near the NAIRU on average, there would have to be large, systematic movements in the change in inflation, contrary to fact. This argument allows for large fluctuations in the unemployment rate, as indeed there are. It is only on the trend time scale that things have to come out right. Of course, this reasoning is conditional on the truth of the underlying theory.

It is very important to understand this econometric finding because it has an important implication: the very good years could afford to be very good because the trend unemployment rate was already below where it had been in the 1970s and 1980s and was still falling. Staiger, Stock, and Watson need invoke no other causal factor.

Staiger, Stock, and Watson also make use of panel data across states and time to probe structural factors that could plausibly influence some of the determinants of the Phillips curve. States may exhibit much greater differences in demographic, industrial, and other characteristics than are likely to appear in national time series for such slow-moving factors. Such differences can be used to test hypotheses about the Phillips curve itself. The panel data suggest the existence of a fairly stable state-based Phillips curve, but the analysis does not come up with statistically significant statements about the underlying determinants of the NAIRU. There is some evidence that a larger prime-age working population reduces the NAIRU and that larger retail, wholesale, and service sectors may tend to increase it. But these conclusions are not robust.

Blinder and Yellen (chapter 3) do, however, attach a good deal of importance to favorable supply shocks. On the wage side, they point to the deceleration of benefit costs. The main components of this deceleration were the slower growth of employers' health-care costs, believed to result from the introduction of managed care, and the rise in asset values, which temporarily enabled many firms to reduce or eliminate required current contributions to their employees' pension funds. On the price side, Blinder and Yellen emphasize the appreciation of the dollar after 1995, the consequent fall in non-oil-import prices, and the fact that world oil prices fell by half between 1996:4 and 1999:1. Finally, they note that adjustments in the way in which the CPI measures improved product quality had the effect of (correctly) lowering the reported rate of inflation. Blinder and Yellen offer the possibility that, depending on the model utilized, these "four supply shocks either explain . . . or overexplain . . . the drop in inflation" (126).

All this sounds as if we can account for the combination of low unemployment and low inflation twice over, once without supply shocks, and once with nothing but supply shocks. Then the puzzle about 1995 to 2000 would be to understand, not why inflation was so low, but why it was not even lower. There is obviously more work to be done on this question. But one position to take that would avoid any inconsistency is to note that favorable supply shocks have the effect of lowering the inflation-safe unemployment rate. When the world price of oil is falling, for example, it is possible to live with a tighter, more fully employed economy without inflation picking up. Higher wage costs could be offset by lower energy costs, leaving prices more or less insulated. Then, if opportunistic policy (or chance again, for that matter) keeps the economy close to the new, lower inflation-safe unemployment rate, the observed trend unemployment rate will also be lower. Once the favorable supply shocks have pushed the NAIRU down, they have no more work to do. The Staiger, Stock, and Watson accounting and the Blinder and Yellen accounting are, then, two ways of describing the same phenomenon. One would have to examine timing and other factors before this way of reconciling the two findings can be accepted, but it is a reasonable possibility.

There is another, more complicated way in which this interaction between shocks and the NAIRU can be formulated. The most interesting modern ways of modeling the labor market—"insider-outsider" theory is an example—suggest intrinsic mechanisms that can make for strong persistence in the unemployment rate and perhaps the wage rate too, quite apart from the determination of equilibrium values of these things. Via this route, a string of favorable shocks could, in principle, generate a continued fall of the immediate NAIRU.

General Westmoreland's memoirs of the Vietnam War were once described as being like an account of a bullfight told by the bull. Blinder and Yellen have a much more satisfying task: compiling a detailed narrative of a memorably successful episode in monetary and fiscal policy as told by active participants who are academic economists in real life. They aptly describe the Federal Reserve's stance in the years 1996 to 1998 as "forbearance." The Fed decided not to push the unemployment rate down into territory that everyone had learned to associate with breakaway inflation. What it did instead was to wait and see, to go with the flow, instead of reacting automatically to the breach of the consensus NAIRU by deliberately pushing the unemployment rate up. That was a truly experimental attitude to take, and it worked. The expert play-by-play account is fascinating and educational.

Blinder and Yellen distill from their account a number of "lessons for policymakers" that speak to the conduct of both monetary policy and fiscal policy.

These are clearly and convincingly stated, and only one requires further discussion here.

Blinder and Yellen argue that what we normally consider to be contractionary fiscal policy *can* also be seen as expansionary. The issue arises because the two major fiscal-policy actions of the 1990s—the budget agreements of 1990 and 1993—both centered on the control and reduction of federal spending. Both moved budgetary prospects from chronic deficits toward the burgeoning prospective surpluses whose proper disposition was the main partisan issue in Washington in the summer of 2001. The paradox is that these "contractionary" actions did not, in fact, interfere with the prolonged expansion and, indeed, appeared to contribute to it. Blinder and Yellen are insistent that they do not wish to generalize from this episode. After saying that contractionary fiscal policy need not harm economic growth, they go on to remind the reader that "*need not* is not synonymous with *will not*. We argued earlier that a particularly fortuitous set of circumstances, market psychology, and design features of the budget agreement [meaning its ability to put an end to the perceived prospect of chronic deficit finance] combined to ignite the 1993 bond-market rally. We would not bet that this constellation can be replicated regularly, and, hence, we would not bet that *all* (or even most) fiscal contractions will be expansionary" (146–7).

One could go further. It seems likely that pulling off this trick once makes it less likely that it can be pulled off again. When might the trick work? If a history of chronic budget deficits has made lenders lose confidence in the government's ability to service debt without inflating it away, then they may require very high interest rates before they are willing to absorb federal debt. Those interest rates could be high enough to crowd out private expenditures. Under those circumstances, a credible commitment to federal-budget stringency could lead to a rally in the bond market, a substantial fall in long-term real interest rates, and the crowding in of a private-investment boom. Similarly, if households lose confidence in the government's ability to meet scheduled future entitlement spending, they may choose to fill the anticipated gap with private saving. The restoration of confidence could induce additional consumer spending. In that way, once again, the end of chronic deficits could conceivably be expansionary.

Other ways in which to construct similar "psychological" scenarios are explored by Blinder and Yellen. Some are more plausible than others; as with psychological scenarios generally, none is really verifiable. All such rationalizations seem to require the backdrop of chronic budget deficits, persistent enough so that they are initially projected into the future. It is the potential reversal of that expectation that creates the possibility of paradox. But, then, exploiting the paradox even once will very likely cancel the necessary condition for doing so again. This is not a repeatable policy option.

It has gone unmentioned so far that Blinder and Yellen consider the surprise acceleration of productivity after 1995 as the most important of the favorable supply shocks that, in their accounting, made the very good years possible. That is surely among the most secure conclusions that has come from this study. It is tautological to say that higher productivity means higher output for given employment. What needs analysis is the causal chain along which faster productivity growth permits or encourages high employment *without inflation.*

Figure 1.9, drawn from Staiger, Stock, and Watson (chapter 1 this volume, 54) sends a clear message and offers a broad hint about one possible story. The upper curve repeats the mechanically smoothed univariate trend unemployment rate already described. The lower curve is a similarly smoothed trend rate of productivity growth. The negative correlation practically leaps off the page, with productivity growth apparently leading unemployment by a little at the turning points. It should be kept in mind that these time series have been smoothed to within an inch of their lives, so there are practically no effective degrees of freedom left for subtle statistical inferences. Nevertheless, the two series are derived completely independently, and their comovement is not, therefore, simply preordained. It is certainly safe to say that the figure offers cold comfort to those alarmists who expect mass unemployment to follow from rapid technological progress.

More to the point in the present context is the possibility of joining figure 1.9 to a story that associates fast productivity growth with slow cost growth and, therefore, with low inflation. Such a story is provided by Ball and Moffitt (chapter 2). Leaving aside refinements of expectations, Ball and Moffitt start from a "real-wage Phillips curve." If productivity were not increasing, the proportional growth of the real wage would depend (negatively) on the unemployment rate. Conventionally and plausibly, when productivity is on a rising trend, workers will insist on a real wage that grows with productivity, not necessarily year by year, but at least matching productivity growth on average; employers will be driven by competition to go along. (This is just another way of saying that the share of wages in total income is trendless.) If, as a first approximation, the price level is determined by a more or less constant markup on unit labor cost, it is easily seen that the rate of inflation is independent of the rate of productivity growth.

Here, Ball and Moffitt introduce a new concept. They want to model an inertial component in wage aspirations; they do so by defining an "aspiration" standard for real-wage *growth.* There is more than one way to do this; they choose to make the aspiration standard a weighted average of past rates of real-wage growth, extending into the distant past with geometrically decaying weights as one looks further and further back. Wage increases are habit forming, or at least expectations forming. Then they go back to the wage Phillips curve itself, and, where previously the productivity-growth rate had appeared, feeding one-to-one into real-wage growth, they substitute an average of the productivity-growth rate and the aspiration standard. The more conventional model says that what drives real wages upward in the long run is the growth of productivity; the Ball and Moffitt model says that it is a mixture of productivity growth and customary real-wage growth. (In the empirical work, the weight on the aspiration standard is somewhere around 0.5, ranging between 0.3 and 0.6, depending on details.)

When carried over into the price Phillips curve, the model says that about half of any excess of productivity growth over the wage aspiration standard translates into lower inflation, given the other determinants. If, in a steady state, real wages grow in line with productivity, then the aspiration standard will grow at the common rate, and so will any average of the two. Then the refinement makes no difference; but, in all other cases, it appears to make just the right difference.

The Ball and Moffitt mechanism tells a story. (The relevant equations in chapter 2 are 2.3 and 2.5. Econometric estimates are given in tables 2.1, 2.2, and 2.3.) Start from a steady state, and imagine that the rate of productivity growth experiences a bulge, as it did in the period 1995 to 2000. Faster productivity growth feeds into real wages, but not one-for-one—in fact, only about one-half-to-one in the short run. This is because the aspiration standard is sluggish; it just looks back over past wage increases. So real wages lag behind productivity, unit labor costs slow down or fall, and inflation does the same. As long as this slack lasts, it can be used either to run the economy at a lower unemployment rate and at the old rate of inflation or at the old unemployment rate and with falling inflation. (In other words, the NAIRU falls temporarily.)

On reflection, one sees that a closely analogous effect can be produced in other ways. Economic theory suggests, for example, that an exogenous reduction in benefit costs should eventually lead to an offsetting wage increase. This is because the key market price is the total cost of an hour of labor. In practice, however, cash wages will respond only slowly and gradually. During that period of adjustment, the economy has some extra protection against inflation.

As applied to our period, the implication is that, by running ahead of the aspiration standard, the unexpected acceleration of productivity beginning in 1995 allowed the unemployment rate to fall while inflation continued to hover around 2 percent. A conventional Phillips curve would have translated the low unemployment rate—which fell from an already dangerous 6 percent at the beginning of 1995 to 4 percent at the end of 2000—into a forecast of runaway inflation. A forecast making use of the Ball and Moffitt aspiration standard gets the inflation forecast more nearly right and without bias. (See the top left-hand panel of Ball and Moffitt's figure 2.6.)

Another implication of this model is worth recording. The effect of the aspiration standard should have been working in reverse in the second half of the 1970s. The much-discussed productivity slowdown, often dated from 1973, would have left wage aspirations unrealistically high. Conventional Phillips curves underpredicted the ensuing inflation because, one could say, the NAIRU was temporarily higher on account of the inherited, exaggerated wage aspirations. That is what happened, of course. The further point is that estimates of conventional Phillips curves for periods that include the 1970s would estimate a NAIRU that was biased upward; the temporary increase would pull the overall estimate up. Within the Ball and Moffitt model, one should mean by *the* NAIRU the inflation-safe unemployment rate when the aspiration standard is fully adjusted to the rate of productivity growth. The authors estimate that this NAIRU is about 5.1 percent. This is a whole point higher than the 4 percent that was achieved in 2000, but it is a whole point lower than the 6.0 to 6.5 percent figure that was the consensus estimate as of 1990. The suggestion is that mid-1997 is about as good as it gets—if we are looking for sustainable situations.

The ambiguity about favorable supply shocks arises in this context too. The aspiration model works relatively well without any appeal to supply shocks; as we saw, however, the supply-shock story works relatively well on its own. When the data are allowed to choose between the two hypotheses, both retain statistical significance. The weight of the aspiration standard in the explanation of price inflation is reduced by about 40 percent, so this aspect of the story plays a reduced role. (For the regression statistics, see Ball and Moffitt's table 2.3, and, for the forecasts with and without supply shocks, see their figure 2.6.) This is not the kind of issue that is ever likely to be resolved on the basis of one or two episodes, partly because there are always going to be one or more "special factors" that can be called on as explanatory variables, and partly because one cannot rule out the possibility that the special factors appear only because they are exerting their influence *through* the parameters of the more routine model.

Anyone thinking about the possibility of sustained low unemployment has to be struck by the comparison between the United States and the large European economies, especially France and Germany. In the 1950s and 1960s, and even in the early 1970s, unemployment rates in the United States were habitually 2 percentage points or more higher than were those in Europe, even in relatively good years. By the 1980s and 1990s, the situation had been reversed, by an even larger margin. (See table 4.1 in Bertola, Blau, and Kahn, chapter 4 in this volume.)

The natural question to ask is whether the nature of labor-market (or other) institutions, which can easily differ among countries, can be at the root of this remarkable contrast. It is at least possible that European labor markets once operated in a way that favored low unemployment, relative to the United States, but that they have evolved in a direction that tends to produce higher unemployment than is at least currently experienced in the United States. There must be something to this, but simple reasoning along this line has not been very successful. One reason is that high unemployment has persisted in Europe even after, to take just one example, unemployment insurance was made less generous (that is, more like unemployment insurance in the United States) in the 1980s. A more subtle argument has begun to emerge. It asks whether different styles of labor-market and other institutions are important mainly because they respond differently to disturbances. If that is in fact the case, the place to look for an explanation of comparative unemployment rates is in the interaction of shocks and institutions. That is the point of view taken by Giuseppe Bertola, Francine Blau, and Lawrence Kahn (chapter 4 in this volume). This way of thinking may not resolve the ambiguity surrounding the role of supply shocks, but it is worth considering here.

There are of course many differences between the way labor markets are organized in the United States and the way they are organized in Europe. (And, of course, labor markets differ among European countries.) The deeper source of such differences may be in the higher incidence of trade unionism in Europe and the larger role that European governments play in labor markets, both as direct demanders of labor and as regulators of labor-market practices. The immediate contrast between Europe and the United States can be summed up for many purposes in the greater up-and-down flexibility of American wages as well as in the wider wage differentials tolerated by American labor-market institutions. One look at the data is to be found in Bertola, Blau, and Kahn's table 4.3. And their figure 4.2 plots unemployment rates for various countries in various years against a corresponding measure of the degree of inequality in the lower half of the wage distribution. (Systematic time and country effects have been removed from both variables.) There appears to be a robust relation—a wider wage spread being associated with lower unemployment—even within Europe.

This correlation represents a strong hint that wage flexibility has something to do with unemployment performance. Bertola, Blau, and Kahn dig deeper into the possibility that the correlation is produced by the interaction of labor-market institutions with external shocks. The underlying thought is that different labor-market institutions cope in different ways with economic and demographic disturbances and that some ways of coping produce more unemployment than others. The particular institutions that can be roughly measured or indexed are listed in the fifth section of the paper, and the "shocks" considered are described in the third. (These "shocks" are clearly endogenous to the economy. The hope is that they can be safely treated as exogenous to the labor market, and a partial check comes out favorably.) The limited way in which shocks and institutions are allowed to interact is exhibited in equation 4.1; drastic restriction is necessary to conserve degrees of freedom.

The authors find that, between 1970 and 1995, the United States faced a more favorable set of shocks than did Europe but that these more favorable shocks can explain only a small fraction of the reversal in unemployment rates that occurred. The interaction between shocks and institutions provides a much more effective explanation; identical shocks would evoke higher unemployment in the relatively rigid labor markets of Europe than in the more flexible labor market of the United States. It is interesting, however, that Bertola, Blau, and Kahn find that, while their analysis does a good job of capturing the broad differences in the unemployment experience of Europe and the United States between 1970 and the mid-1990s, it does not have much explanatory power when it comes to the last few years of the 1990s.

Bertola, Blau, and Kahn come to the pessimistic conclusion that "the same flexibility that allows the U.S. labor market to absorb macroeconomic shocks with smaller changes in unemployment than occur in other countries also makes for more flexible real wages and relative wages" (207). In this context, *flexibility in relative wages* means the easier achievement of and greater tolerance for widening wage inequality.

Someone who accepts this argument and finds the current amount of inequality to be indefensible should be looking either for ways to improve the underlying distribution of earning capacity in the society or for extramarket ways—like an expanded earned income tax credit—to improve the distribution of disposable income. The "European" option of buying lower earnings inequality at the expense of higher unemployment is not obviously more attractive.

These considerations can tell us something about the difference between Europe and the United States, but their bearing on the years 1995 to 2000 is more complicated. Labor markets in the United States did not suddenly become more flexible in 1994. Moreover, European labor-market rigidities—wage floors, job protection, extensive social insurance—should matter more in response to contractionary shocks than in response to inflationary shocks. (The partial exception is restrictions on firing, which could inhibit firms from hiring freely when sales are good.) The possibility remains, however, that, even if identical shocks had hit the United States and Europe in the second half of the 1990s, European labor markets would have responded in ways that guaranteed continued high unemployment, whereas U.S. institutions were able to convert the same shocks into low unemployment without inflation.

Policy reactions could have been part of this process. The restrictions imposed on monetary policy by the European Monetary System and on fiscal policy by the Maastricht criteria made it difficult for European countries to react in a timely way to macroeconomic shocks, and this may have allowed high unemployment to become entrenched.

The labor-market institutions whose effects are analyzed in chapter 4 are those that would be expected to affect wage flexibility over time and across occupations, like the strength of unions and the generosity of the unemployment-insurance system. There are other institutions or practices that are more likely to affect the efficiency of the labor market in matching unemployed workers with available jobs. They are the subject adressed by Jessica Cohen, William T. Dickens, and Adam Posen (chapter 5 in this volume).

The tool of choice for measuring and analyzing efficiency in this sense is the "Beveridge curve," which plots the unemployment rate at a given place and time against the vacancy rate (the number of unfilled jobs as a fraction of the labor force). The reference is to Sir William Beveridge, whose *Full Employment in a Free Society* (1945), a famous tract written at the end of the Second World War, defined *full employment* as a situation in which the number of unemployed workers equals the number of unfilled jobs, with the result that any remaining unemployment arises from a geographic, a skill, or some other mismatch between the unemployed workers and the available jobs, not from any overall shortage of jobs. One expects a downward-sloping relation: any increase in the demand for labor should increase the number of vacancies and decrease the number of unemployed. An "inward" shift of the curve signifies a gain in matching efficiency; a better labor exchange, for example, would match some unemployed workers with unfilled jobs, reducing both the unemployment and the vacancy rates.

The United States does not collect statistics on the number of unfilled jobs. The custom has been to use instead an index of the volume of help-wanted advertising in newspapers. This device is open to obvious biases—biases that have grown worse with the advent of Internet job sites like monster.com and hotjobs.com—but there is no alternative. In Cohen, Dickens, and Posen's figure

5.1 is displayed a Beveridge curve plot for the years 1960 to 1998. The points are dated, allowing one to see a possible interpretation: an initial curve for the 1960s shifted outward (in the "inefficient" direction) in the early 1970s and then formed another Beveridge curve for the years 1973 to 1985; an inward shift in the late 1980s led to another stable Beveridge curve for 1989 to 1995. At the very end of the period, the curve appears to be shifting further inward, but the data end before a new stage has begun.

Cohen, Dickens, and Posen put a lot of weight on the existence and timing of these two inward shifts. Their interpretation is that each shift corresponds to an innovation in human-resource-management practices in American manufacturing. The earlier one reflects the adoption of a set of reforms known generally as *high-performance work organization* (HPWO), the later the widespread outsourcing of many peripheral functions of the firm and the use of temporary-job agencies as a way of handling short-run fluctuations in the firm's demand for labor.

Why should these developments improve the job-matching efficiency of the labor market? In the case of temporary workers, the answer is more or less obvious: vacant jobs are more quickly filled; and the search efforts of unemployed workers are vastly more effective when carried on through a temporary-help agency.

The other two developments are part of a more complicated story, according to Cohen, Dickens, and Posen. The story begins with the shortening of product cycles in many manufacturing industries, sometimes, but not always, occasioned by new applications of computer technology. Shorter product cycles translated into a greater need for workers who have more general skills and are more adaptable to new tasks and a corresponding decreased demand for workers with "firm-specific human capital," that is, those who are very good at doing one thing. HPWO and its focus on team production and job rotation was the result.

An economic consequence of this change would be the erosion of worker "rents," that is, the high returns to very specific skills that cannot be learned and supplied quickly when the need develops. (This outcome is nonetheless compatible with rising average wages.) When these rents to specific skills are high, workers with the requisite skills will often—rationally—remain unemployed for a while, waiting for a high-rent job to turn up or for recall from a layoff, rather than take an inferior job and search for a better one less efficiently. This kind of unemployment will diminish or disappear when rents are eroded because the reward for successful search is smaller. Thus, the unemployment rate will be lower at any given state of the demand for labor, and this amounts to a favorable shift of the Beveridge curve.

It is easy to see how the spread of outsourcing can have a similar effect. In addition, because the erosion of specific skill rents pushes workers into a lower-skill segment of the labor market, where vacancies are more common, the vacancy rate is directly lowered.

Cohen, Dickens, and Posen argue cautiously that these developments are consistent with the timing of the observed inward shifts of the Beveridge curve and are thus capable of accounting for the fact of lower unemployment at any given state of the demand for labor. The authors find some confirmation of their hypotheses in the parallel timing of observed reductions in interindustry wage differentials for similar jobs, another symptom of eroding rents. Unlike some of the other mechanisms and forces uncovered in various parts of this project, this one has every prospect of being permanent. It reflects an improvement in matching efficiency that need not go away. This particular conclusion depends only on the reality of the inward shift of the Beveridge curve, not its timing.

It is important to realize that a "better" Beveridge curve has macroeconomic significance beyond labor-market efficiency per se. One very natural measure of overall inflationary pressure is the ratio of the vacancy rate to the unemployment rate (or the difference between them). So any given degree of inflationary pressure is represented in a Beveridge curve diagram by a ray from the origin (or by a positively sloped line if it is the difference that matters). This will intersect a "better" Beveridge curve at a lower unemployment rate. In other words, a better Beveridge curve allows a lower unemployment rate to be compatible with any fixed "safe" degree of inflationary pressure.

Lisa Lynch and Stephen Nickell (chapter 11 in this volume) estimate a Beveridge curve for the United States that shifts—first out, then in—smoothly, along a cubic time trend (see their figs. 11.5 and 11.6) instead of discretely. The shortness of the sample period and the difficulties with the help-wanted index may make it difficult or impossible to discriminate between these two hypotheses, but the effort should be made.

Other relevant conclusions emerge from the work of Lynch and Nickell. They argue that the United States may have been better positioned than other countries to convert technological progress in the production and use of computers into aggregate productivity gains, and they attribute part of this advantage to the weakness of the regulatory barriers faced by U.S. firms. They also cite evidence that various workplace innovations, including HPWO (discussed by Cohen, Dickens, and Posen in a different context), play a role in productivity improvement. (The precise parsing of these putative new-economy gains has been the subject of much research and controversy in the literature. In the other papers in this volume, the productivity story has just been taken as given.)

Lynch and Nickell go on to suggest that "the capacity of the U.S. economy to ensure that the skills of its workforce keep pace with the demands of IT [information technology] and new workplace practices seems suspect—unless we see drastic changes in business practices" (554). They find it "unlikely," however, "that the skills of American workers will be able to keep pace with the demands of IT and new workplace practices unless current education and training practices are radically overhauled in the face of the needs of the new economy" (569). This is an important observation.

Lynch and Nickell work with a somewhat different model of unemployment and inflation from the Phillips curve-based exercises in the Ball and Moffitt and the Bertola, Blau, and Kahn papers, but they come to a similar conclusion: the "equilibrium"-unemployment rate (not quite the same thing as the NAIRU) could have fallen by as much as 1.5 points since the mid-1980s. This is smaller than the nearly 3 points estimated by Staiger, Stock, and Watson but closer to the figure implicit in the work of Ball and Moffitt. Lynch and Nickell attribute this reduction to a mix of factors, including the fall in the fraction of young workers in the labor force, the rise in the prison population, the growth of temporary-job services (as in Bertola, Blau, and Kahn), and, of course, the surge in productivity growth. Some of these factors, they point out, lower the equilibrium unemployment rate only temporarily.

Lynch and Nickell make the interesting observation that, even as the unemployment rate has been falling, the inactivity rate (that is, those unemployed or out of the labor force) has been fairly stable. This suggests the continued existence of a reservoir of labor that could be available to support further growth of output. But, as does Ellwood (chapter 9 in this volume), Lynch and Nickell find that this potential supply of labor is very difficult—and perhaps impossible—to mobilize effectively.

Up to this point, the spotlight has been on one important and surprising aspect of those very good years: the successful coexistence of low unemployment and low inflation for a substantial period of time. The question of whether the good times can be sustained—that is, prolonged or repeated—boils down to the question of whether the factors that made coexistence possible were temporary or permanent.

But now a different, although closely related, question arises: Can the growth of employment be sustained? One may wonder what the relation between inflation and unemployment is: in principle, an economy could experience continued noninflationary prosperity with stable or even falling employment. One possible connection is that the existence of a fringe of potential workers—who are not now in the labor force but could and would actively seek work given adequate incentive (more attractive vacancies, higher wages, the loss of welfare benefits)—may be a force that keeps wages from rising excessively even in a fairly tight labor market. Lynch and Nickell suspect that this favorable environment may not be sustainable. In addition, they worry about the economy's capacity to provide the range of skills needed for a high-technology world and modern services.

David Ellwood (chapter 9 in this volume) provides an exhaustive analysis of the sustainability of employment growth. One disturbing finding is that demography does not favor an elastic supply of capable labor. In particular, the labor force will grow slowly. Most of the increase will be in older workers and little, if any, in prime-age workers. Even more disturbing is the finding that the pace at which the average education attainment of the labor force can be expected to improve will be much slower than it has been in the past.

Ellwood then goes on to investigate whether social policy could change this picture by altering incentives to work. One fundamental limit to change brought about in this way is that most social policies target the less-skilled and less-educated part of the working-age population. Thus, any increase in the labor force generated by social policy would not improve the skill mix and might, in fact, worsen it.

In many cases, the use of social policy to increase the supply of labor would entail substantial social costs. For example, the largest available pool of prime-age workers is probably married women with children. Inducing them to enter the labor force in greater numbers would presumably require expanded support for child care, an expensive proposition. On the other hand, prolonging the average working life by changing the incentives for earlier retirement implicit in social security regulations could add substantially to the number of older workers, many of whom are skilled and educated. Some such changes have already been legislated, but this whole issue is politically sensitive—and rightly so because of the consequences for the welfare of the elderly population. (It would be different if policy changes simply made more choices available to the elderly, but that is not usually the case.)

Ellwood concludes that a serious attempt to expand the size and improve the quality of the U.S. labor force through changes in social policy will have to focus on immigration and education, both of which are contentious issues with many ramifications, or on increasing the participation of married women with children and older people, also a politically touchy subject. One comes away from these chapters with a reinforced conviction of the importance of providing American workers with more effective training and education.

Katharine Abraham and Robert Shimer (chapter 8 in this volume) invest most of their effort in an analysis of the observed increase in the duration of unemployment spells in the United States over the past thirty years. One very interesting result of that analysis bears on the fringe-of-potential-workers issue. At any moment, people of working age can be identified as employed (E), unemployed (U), or not in the labor force (N). Between two successive observations, there are nine possible transitions, which can be abbreviated as EN, EU, EE, and so on (note that no change in status—in this case, EE—counts as a transition). The changing frequencies of such transitions are clearly informative about processes in the labor market; for example, a lengthening duration of unemployment spells must be associated with a higher frequency of UU transitions at the expense of UE and UN transitions. (The relative frequencies of, for example, UE, UN, and UU must obviously sum to 1.)

One interesting finding is that, since 1976, the frequency of NE transitions has trended up for women (but not for men) and the frequency of EN transitions has trended down for women (but slightly up for men). Abraham and Shimer interpret these observations as a confirmation of the increased commitment of women to working. For example, employed women are less likely to leave the labor force directly. There is inevitably some cyclic element here, but it is clearly riding on twenty-five-year trends. There is a further possible implication, however. The rise in NE transitions may signal that women are now more likely to belong to that fringe of potential workers who can be attracted into employment when jobs are easily available and wages rise. Women's role as an elastic supply of labor may, therefore, help restrain wage inflation.

On the question of unemployment duration, Abraham and Shimer come to a surprising conclusion. After a number of technical adjustments, they find that all or more than all of the observed drop in short-term unemployment can be attributed to the aging of the baby-boom generation. Young workers have a high incidence of short spells of unemployment, presumably voluntary or exploratory. The aging of that cohort would, then, naturally reduce the incidence of short-term unemployment in the economy as a whole. Abraham and Shimer suggest that the current short-term unemployment rate is actually higher than normal. This is a favorable turn of events in the sense that it contrasts sharply with the development in Europe of a class of long-term unemployed with deteriorating skills, diminishing employability, weakening contact with the labor market, and, thus, little capacity to restrain wage inflation. The fact that the pattern in Europe is opposite that in the United States is often thought to be one reason for the apparent rise in the NAIRU in Europe. Abraham and Shimer find no evidence that observed shifts in duration have had any measurable effect on the NAIRU in the United States.

Rebecca Blank and Matthew Shapiro (chapter 7 in this volume) consider the sustainability of the prosperity of the 1990s from a different, but still important, standpoint. The focus of the papers discussed so far has been mainly on the unusual combination of low unemployment and slow inflation that characterized the Roaring 90s and the factors that brought it about or allowed it to happen. Blank and Shapiro look instead at the growth of real output and earnings, asking whether the combination of input growth and productivity change is so unusual as to suggest a nonrepeatable pattern. Their answer is, on the whole, no, and, on the way to reaching that conclusion, they produce some interesting observations.

For instance, Blank and Shapiro's figure 7.9 shows that, in the 1990s, as in the (more cyclic) 1982 to 1990 expansion, aggregate real labor income increased at about the same rate as aggregate output and the aggregate stock of business fixed capital. This pattern is not necessary for sustained growth, and it is not to be expected year by year in view of the findings of Ball and Moffitt (chapter 2 in this volume) and other, similar studies. But the fact that earnings increased in step with productivity and without a rise in the capital-output ratio suggests a certain balance. Blank and Shapiro's figure 7.10 modifies this view, however. The 1990s were not uniform; in the key period after 1995, earnings grew faster than output, and output per unit of capital actually grew substantially. What makes this pattern possible is the acceleration of productivity—particularly total factor productivity—that has played such a large part in many of the papers collected in this volume. Much evidently hinges on the future of productivity growth.

Blank and Shapiro's figure 7.9 offers another hint. The whole of the decade of the 1990s was characterized by a steady increase in the ratio of fixed investment to GDP. By 2000, this ratio was higher than it had been at any time since 1960. Even so, as just seen, the capital-output ratio was falling in the second half of the decade. This fortunate conjunction of sustained high investment and increasing productivity per unit of capital is another consequence of rapid growth in total factor productivity. In an indirect way, this suggests the importance of sustaining a high rate of capital investment. Otherwise, continued rapid growth of productivity will have to depend too much on the mere hope of even more rapid growth of total factor productivity, which cannot be counted on.

Blank and Shapiro look at the productivity story from yet another angle, attempting to isolate the contribution of interindustry shifts in employment. They conclude that the typical worker in the 1990s took a step down in level of productivity, but more than compensated for this step down by rapid growth. In other words, the reallocation of labor across industries in the decade was not to higher-productivity industries but rather to industries with faster productivity growth. The details of this process cannot be studied because of data limitations. But Blank and Shapiro's analysis provides additional evidence that industry composition shifted in ways that do not bode well for the longer-run prospects of the least-skilled workers and that, indeed, the continuation of high prosperity may depend on the ability of the economy and society to increase the supply of skilled workers.

One of the virtues of the Blank and Shapiro paper is the attention paid to industry and demographic detail. As we have seen, demographically adjusted rates of unemployment play a significant role in several of the papers collected in this volume. Blank and Shapiro suggest that the industry composition of employment may also have implications for the sustainability of high employment with low inflation. A detailed analysis along those lines remains on the research agenda.

There is little danger of dismissing as minor the question of whether periods of combined low unemployment, low and stable inflation, and satisfactory growth can be sustained and repeated. Nevertheless, James Hines, Hilary Hoynes, and Alan Krueger (chapter 10 in this volume) attempt to confirm and quantify some of the social benefits that come along with such intervals of prolonged prosperity.

One of Hines, Hoynes, and Krueger's findings, for example, is that the experience has tended to reduce extreme inequality. The unemployment rate of African Americans fell to a new low during the second half of the 1990s, and the average real income of the poorest 20 percent of households gained on the income of the middle group. (The top 20 percent did best of all.) Hines, Hoynes, and Krueger's table 10.5 shows that outcomes for lower-skill groups are more sensitive to the business cycle than are outcomes for higher-skill groups. It is interesting that this effect is the result, not of fluctuations in relative wages, which tend to be weak, but (more likely) of the fact that better-off families can buffer the effects of recessions by sending additional family members into the labor market or at least by not losing what jobs they do have.

Hines, Hoynes, and Krueger provide at least suggestive evidence that workers take advantage of tight labor markets by shifting toward jobs in which earnings increase faster with years of tenure than they did in the jobs being abandoned. A job with a flat earnings-tenure profile is precisely a dead-end job, so this is unambiguously a desirable development. The magnitude of this effect is small in the aggregates, however, and appears to be confined to lower-paid workers.

The expansion of the 1990s was accompanied by a reduction in crime rates, especially among young people, and also by a broadly based decrease in work-related injuries. The first of these developments is no surprise; it has been known for some time that crime rates fall with unemployment and with rising wages. The reduction in workplace injuries is a surprise, however. The standard observation is that injury rates rise as unemployment falls, presumably because less-experienced workers are employed and because a longer workday and attempts to increase production rates both contribute to fatigue-related accidents. Hines, Hoynes, and Krueger's figure 10.1 shows that, by 1998, injury rates were dramatically lower than the standard model would have predicted. The source of this discrepancy is an intriguing puzzle; it may have nothing to do with sustained prosperity, being related instead to the computer-related technological advances that led to faster productivity growth. This subject needs further investigation.

Hines, Hoynes, and Krueger also trace another route by which sustained prosperity affects the quality of life and the lot of the disadvantaged. In good years, the tax revenues at the disposal of state and municipal governments naturally rise. The authors document, first, that the capital expenditures of state and local governments are especially sensitive to prosperity-related revenues. Capital expenditures include those on health and education infrastructure, which may be especially beneficial to disadvantaged groups. Hines, Hoynes, and Krueger also reach a surprising new conclusion: that spending on income-maintenance programs is greater in prosperous periods. There is an appearance of paradox here: presumably the need for income maintenance diminishes in prosperous times. If the perceived capacity to satisfy income-maintenance needs is limited by revenue, however, then the easing of that constraint could result in the increases that are actually observed.

The general conclusion of the Hines, Hoynes, and Krueger paper is that sustained prosperity tends to narrow extreme inequality, lower crime rates, and improve social conditions in still other ways. The broad payoff to achieving what used to be called *stable full employment* is therefore very great. That leaves only the policy problem of in fact achieving that goal.

Much of the analysis in this volume is focused on the U.S. economy, treated more or less in isolation from the rest of the world. There are exceptions: Blinder and Yellen discuss the appreciation of the dollar in the period 1995 to 2000 as an exogenous factor holding down the dollar price of imports and, thus, helping stabilize the domestic price level; and Bertola, Blau, and Kahn present an exhaustive discussion of the implications of international differences in labor-market and other institutions. George Johnson and Matthew Slaughter (chapter 6 in this volume) focus on the direct effects of international trade on the relative wages of skilled and unskilled workers in the United States. They follow the normal practice in the theory of international trade of assuming that labor markets clear; domestic employment at every level of skill is, then, determined mainly by the domestic supply of labor.

Events in the international sphere have their effects on the relative prices of produced goods and, thus, on the industry composition of domestic output. Some industries employ mostly skilled labor, others mostly unskilled labor. The demands for different categories of labor are generated in this way, and relative wages adjust to match them to the available supplies. From this perspective, any force—like education or immigration—that changes the relative supply of skills embodied in the U.S. labor force is like a shift in comparative advantage; it will change the industry composition of domestic production.

If relative wages are inflexible (because of inertia, custom, or policy), the result is likely to be unemployment in some parts of the labor market (and possibly excess demand in others). Failures of interindustry mobility are another possible interference in the mechanism described by Johnson and Slaughter. Both of these, of course, would have consequences even in a closed economy.

Johnson and Slaughter conclude that the role of international trade, especially the entry of low-wage countries into the world market for unskilled-labor-intensive goods, has been real but probably of secondary importance. Their reasoning is that any such effect must be mediated through the prices of traded goods. Low-wage workers abroad compete with unskilled workers here by pushing down the world price of unskilled-labor-intensive goods. Then their American counterparts must either accept lower wages, so that American firms can break even, or open themselves up to displacement. If this process is strongly at work, it should show itself in a falling relative price of textiles, simple clothing, and other unskilled-labor-intensive tradable goods. Since this is not notably the case, a large literature concludes that trade with low-wage countries makes only a small contribution to the widening of wage inequality in the United States (and some other rich countries). The finger is then pointed mainly at skill-biased technological change, the notion that evolving technology has skewed the demand for labor in favor of skilled and educated workers and against the unskilled and uneducated. (Of course, there are other possibilities, like the decline of trade unions and the relative decay of the statutory minimum wage, but they fall outside the scope of this volume.)

There is yet another route by which international competition can help answer the central question, What made low unemployment and low inflation so surprisingly compatible in the period 1995 to 2000? And here we go back to the appreciation of the dollar discussed by Blinder and Yellen. Those authors emphasize the pure price-index effect of the lower dollar price of imports. Beyond this point, it is worth noting that the appreciation itself came about mainly because of the large flow of capital into the United States, not because of anything on the trade side. (Indeed, the United States was running a large trade deficit throughout.) So the appreciation of the dollar meant ongoing pressure on the dollar prices of U.S. goods; foreign producers found it easier to compete in the U.S. market and in other markets as well. Intensified foreign competition kept a lid on prices charged by U.S. firms. The business press was full of complaints to the effect that American firms had "lost control" of their own prices. Depreciation of the dollar was not an option, for the reason already mentioned. So there was back pressure against inflation, and some of this was probably passed back to wages.

A SUMMARY VIEW

There are three good reasons why one should not expect a clear, crisp, unambiguous story to emerge from the research reported in this volume. The first reason is simply that any event that is remarkable enough to figure as an "episode" is likely to be atypical. If it were straightforwardly understandable, no one would notice it. The second reason is that two dozen independent scholars, each tackling a different aspect of a very complex reality, are unlikely to converge instantaneously on a unified view. Indeed, the fact that we arranged for shotgun cohabitation between micro- and macroeconomists on many of the papers makes it all the more impressive that each team was able to converge on a single set of conclusions. The third reason, already mentioned in passing, is that the causal thread underlying a single macroeconomic episode is bound to have many strands. Partially or wholly exogenous events are always coming and going, and alternative models will weave them into the story in different ways. Keep in mind, however, that what appears as an exogenous shock from one angle may be described as an endogenous response when seen from another. For example, lower health-care costs might be taken as exogenous, or, alternatively, they might result from a deterioration of the bargaining power of labor.

Compare the answers given to certain straightforward questions by the two perfectly respectable macro-forecasting models used by Blinder and Yellen. The gap between them is sometimes so wide as to be qualitative in character. Yet the two models must fit approximately equally well in the data that give rise to them. The conclusion to be drawn is, not that one is right and the other wrong, but that minor differences in structure and parameter values can lead two such models to major differences in the interpretation of a single episode. This may even be a general characteristic of dynamic many-equation models, not just of these two models or of economic models. Despite these difficulties, there are some broad conclusions that seem to emerge from the mix of research topics and strategies to be found in the following pages.

The authors of the papers included in this volume are, broadly speaking, all mainstream economists, although they are not dogma bound. So it is only to be expected that the basic question, to which the whole study is directed, is framed as current mainstream macroeconomics would frame it. How was it possible to reconcile low (and falling) unemployment, rapid growth, and low (and stable) inflation in the years 1995 to 2000? In the standard jargon, how did the NAIRU—the stable-inflation unemployment rate—get to be as low as perhaps 4 percent when only a few years earlier it was generally thought to be 6 percent or even higher? The events themselves (and the results of this study) might eventually suggest reconsideration and modification of the standard model, but that is where this project takes off.

Indeed, the possibility emerges that the fall of the NAIRU in the late 1990s was not just an isolated event, but a stage in a longer-term process. One careful estimate presented in this volume suggests that the NAIRU peaked near 8 percent in 1980 and then fell smoothly to close to 4 percent at the end of 2000. This time pattern would certainly have implications for our understanding of the underlying cause of this shift.

Probably the most striking and important candidate for the role of underlying cause is the acceleration that suddenly lifted the annual growth rate of productivity from under 1.5 percent in the twenty-five years after 1970 to some 2.5 percent in the five years after 1995. An extra 5 percent of productivity meant a direct 5 percent contribution to the general standard of living; there is no mystery in that. The indirect effects, however, are especially interesting. There is some reason to believe that real wages adjust only slowly to such an acceleration of productivity; before that adjustment is complete, real wages grow temporarily less rapidly than they eventually will. That gap keeps unit costs from rising much, and, by that route, part of the payoff from faster productivity growth appears in the form of lower inflation and higher employment than otherwise expected.

This way of telling the story is not without problems. The acceleration of productivity in 1995 was a sudden event. According to Staiger, Stock, and Watson, however, the NAIRU—and, with it, the trend unemployment rate—peaked in 1980 and fell fairly steadily until 2000. The year-by-year path of the NAIRU implicit in the Ball and Moffitt model follows a similar but much-attenuated path. There are at least two possible fixes for this gap, and they are not mutually exclusive. One is to feed a smoothed productivity-growth rate into a reestimated Ball and Moffitt model, instead of the year-by-year growth rate. The other is to look for whatever exogenous shocks might have caused the NAIRU to fall in the 1980s and early 1990s. There are doubtless other possible lines of thought. This is too good a lead to miss, in any case.

The reality and expectation of faster productivity growth also tends to induce higher rates of investment. (That is not a conclusion of this study but a commonplace of macro models generally.) Increased investment, also characteristic of the second half of the 1990s, has two kinds of effects. On the demand side, it helps keep an expansion going. On the supply side, it helps prolong the productivity acceleration, all the more so because new technology is often embedded in new capital equipment. And, by helping fend off the danger of inflation, this, in turn, allows the expansion to continue and to achieve unexpectedly low rates of unemployment and higher rates of investment. The exploitation of this virtuous circle requires a combination of good luck, skill, and courage in monetary policy, and these were present in the second half of the 1990s.

There is a downside, however. This mechanism works only because an unexpected acceleration of productivity leaves habitual targets for wage growth lagging behind. Even if the higher rate of productivity growth persists, targets for wage growth will eventually catch up, at which point the NAIRU will revert to its previous level. The only way to avoid this is by repeated accelerations of productivity. But that is simply not realistic, even in a high-investment economy; one is more likely to fear an eventual deceleration to something nearer the old rate of productivity growth. To the extent that this mechanism accounts for the fall in the NAIRU, it clearly provides only a temporary advantage.

The very same mechanism, operating in reverse after the productivity slow-down in the early 1970s, could account for the rise in the estimated NAIRU from about 5 percent in 1970 to about 8 percent in 1980. But then there is a problem: as Ball and Moffitt's figure 2.7 shows, the reduction in the estimated NAIRU after 1980 was continuous. How is the fall after 1980—which brought the NAIRU down to about 6 percent by 1990 without accelerating productivity—to be explained?

The mechanism just outlined is not the only one. Several distinct lines of explanation emerge from the papers collected in this volume. They are different, but not mutually exclusive, ways of accounting for the excellent macroeconomic performance of the second half of the 1990s. Having too many explanations is better than having too few, but it is not an ideal circumstance.

As discussed earlier, an alternative account can also be built out of *favorable supply shocks*. This is jargon for external—but not necessarily very external—events that independently hold inflation below what it might normally have been. The supply shocks usually invoked as favorable in our period are falling import prices, lower oil prices, reduced (or more slowly rising) health-care costs, savings on pension contributions by business firms, and even improvements in the ability of price indices to account for quality improvements in consumer and capital goods.

It is almost always possible to reformulate such events as reductions in the NAIRU; since they represent a downward force on inflation, they allow a lower unemployment rate to be compatible with steady inflation. Of course, what supply shocks give they can also take away. For the end of the 1990s, however, the net effect was favorable. This factor could have accounted for one half of the apparent fall of the NAIRU, with the surge in productivity growth accounting for the other half.

Yet another way of doing the accounting makes use of the Beveridge curve, discussed in two papers in this volume as a way of describing the efficiency of the labor market in assigning workers to available jobs. The schematic diagram presented in figure I.1 the point clearly. It shows two Beveridge curves that summarize the combinations of vacant jobs and unemployed workers that the operations of a particular labor market can generate. The innermost curve represents in a clear sense a more efficient labor market. At any given vacancy rate, it gets along with less unemployment than the outer curve; somehow, it has matched more workers to jobs. It is worth noting that an improved match of the skills demanded by firms and those supplied by workers will also shift the Beveridge curve inward. Large numbers of vacancies suggest a skill (or geographic,

FIGURE I.1 / Schematic Beveridge Curves

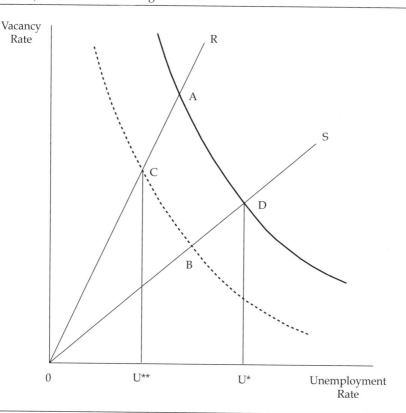

or some other) mismatch. There is evidence presented in this volume that the Beveridge curve for the United States did indeed shift inward in the second half of the 1990s.

Where on its Beveridge curve a particular economy will end up at any particular time depends on all the macroeconomic forces at work. With the NAIRU in mind, however, we can ask what combinations of vacancy and unemployment rates are consistent with steady inflation. A natural presumption is that there is a critical ratio of vacancy rate to unemployment rate that fills the bill: with a higher ratio of vacancies to unemployment, wage inflation will accelerate. The diagram in figure I.1 shows two such critical ratios, the rays OR and OS; OR corresponds to a lower NAIRU, in the sense that it stabilizes inflation with a higher ratio of vacancies to unemployment.

Suppose that the initial situation is at point D, with the less-efficient Beveridge curve and the higher NAIRU. Inflation is under control, the labor market functions as best it can, and the NAIRU is u^*. An inward shift of the Beveridge curve, like what actually happened, allows the inflation-safe unemployment rate to fall to that at point B. If, in addition, favorable supply shocks or a surge in productivity reduce the inflationary pressures in the economy, C becomes a viable situation for the economy, with even lower unemployment than at B and inflation still under control. The combination of macroeconomic and labor-market forces (like the prevalence of outsourcing and temporary-job agencies) has reduced the NAIRU from u^* to u^{**}. The research reported in some papers in this volume provides some evidence that a combination of such factors was at work in the second half of the 1990s.

Much of the research reported in this volume aims to give some rough quantitative dimensions to this framework. It does not provide a complete picture for several reasons. One of them is that proper job-vacancy data do not exist for the United States. Another is that we do not know exactly how to translate the observed and ongoing changes in the demographic and skill composition of the labor force into shifts of the Beveridge curve. Qualitatively, however, more can be said. David Ellwood's chapter can be read as showing that continued growth of employment will likely entail composition changes that move the Beveridge curve outward. Other papers, notably those by Dickens, Posen, and Cohen, Bull and Moffitt, Binder and Yellen, and Lynch and Nickell, provide insights into factors that influenced the position of the curve during the key period 1995 to 2000. Dickens, Posen, and Cohen identify the favorable shift of the Beveridge curve with the efficiency gains that came with the movement for outsourcing some service functions of business firms (thus improving the utilization of the workers providing those functions) and with the growing use of temporary workers.

The Beveridge-curve framework illustrated in figure I.1 would appear to offer a richer model than does one based only on the NAIRU. When tests have been made, the vacancy/unemployment ratio appears to be a better indicator of inflationary pressure than the unemployment rate alone. The fundamental obstacle is the absence of data on vacancies in the United States (Europe is a different story.) A new survey just launched by the Bureau of Labor Statistics should go a long way toward filling this void in coming years.

There is very little discussion of prospective policies in these papers. (The main exceptions are Lynch and Nickell's and Ellwood's papers.) The fact that the extraeconomic benefits of sustained high employment are so valuable, as measured and discussed by Hines, Hoynes, and Krueger, underlines the importance of public and private efforts to make those very good years a more typical occurrence. *Analysis first, policy second* is a good rule, even if it seems to be losing its political appeal these days.

THE VIEW FROM 2001

When the galleys for this book were being set in the summer of 2001, pundits were debating whether the Roaring Nineties came to an end in 2000. By late autumn when it came time to proofread the galleys, the terrorist attacks of September 11th made painfully clear that an era had ended. The economic expansion had already slowed beginning in the second half of 2000. Real-GDP growth, for example, fell from 4 percent per year in the second half of 1992 to under 2 percent per year in the second half of 2000, and just 1 percent per year in the first half of 2001. The advance estimate for the third quarter of 2001, which reflects the beginning of the economic fallout from the terrorist attacks, is that GDP *fell* by 0.4 percent. The terrorist attacks accelerated and exacerbated a slowdown that was already underway. The National Bureau of Economic Research Business Cycle Dating Committee had received so many inquiries from the press regarding whether the United States had entered a recession that its chairman, Robert Hall, saw fit to issue a statement on May 15, 2001, announcing that the committee had not yet met to consider whether the economy had slipped into a recession. A meeting would be premature, according to Hall, although he acknowledged that "the data normally considered by the committee indicate the possibility that recession began recently." After September 11, the popular debate among pundits concerned when the recession started, and how long it will last and how deep it will be, not whether the National Bureau will eventually declare a recession.

The employment situation was just as bleak as GDP growth, although the turning point occurred later, around April 2001. Employment declined by 223,000 jobs in the second quarter of 2001, the largest quarterly drop to that point in a decade. Between September and October of 2001, it fell by an astonishing 415,000 jobs. The unemployment rate soared to 5.4 percent in October 2001, up from 4.2 percent in the first quarter of 2001. The economic slowdown that began in the second half of 2000, and accelerated after September 11, 2001, was clearly affecting the job market.

Ordinarily, the kind of destruction wrought by the terrorist attacks, horrific as they were, would have only a small and fleeting impact on the national economy. For example, one-off events such as hurricanes and earthquakes typically register no more than a blip on the national income scales. But in this instance, the effectiveness of the allied nations' military response to the terrorist attacks, the will and ability of terrorists to conduct further acts of terror (possibly involving weapons of mass destruction), and heightened consumer anxiety significantly raise the level of economic uncertainty, at least in the short term. In addition, the economy was in a precarious state to begin with when the attacks occurred. The full impact of the terrorist attacks on the economy and the effectiveness of the United States' response to the elevated threat is anyone's guess right now.

Nevertheless, it is timely to evaluate the performance of and prospects for the U.S. economy in the early years of the new millenium in light of the questions addressed by this volume, Indeed, resuming and sustaining economic growth in the future takes on even greater urgency in light of the current contraction and terrorist threat to American society. Can the stellar performance of the 1990s be sustained after the current downturn ends? If it can be, what combination of policies will return us to (and sustain) rapid growth?

If nothing else, an evaluation at this stage provides a catalog of some of the predictions generated by explanations for the Roaring 90s that can be tested against the future course of the economy, and an early scorecard on how well the explanations have fared so far.

As mentioned, a central factor in most explanations for the success of the 1990s is the increase in productivity growth from around 1.0 to 1.5 percent to 2.0 to 2.5 percent per year. Most analysts would agree that a permanent increase in productivity growth is necessary to sustain the rapid output growth and perhaps also the low unemployment and low inflation of the 1990s. Blinder and Yellen (chapter 3 in this volume) conjecture that the faster productivity growth of the late 1990s was the result of a structural shift, not a temporary blip due to cyclic factors. Much hinges on whether this is correct. So far, the evidence has been mixed. It is reassuring that the initial estimate of productivity growth in the third quarter of 2001 was strong (2.7 percent), especially in light of the economic contraction, but the flat productivity growth in the first quarter of that year was discouraging. It is still too soon to know how much of this brief record is related to the business cycle and how much reflects more durable factors. The economic performance of the new century will depend on whether productivity growth resumes the rapid pace of the late 1990s or reverts to some slower rate.

If Ball and Moffitt's (chapter 2 in this volume) lagging-aspirations explanation is correct, and if productivity growth returns to the 1.5 percentage point rate, then one would expect wage growth to exceed productivity growth for some time to come. And the early indications are that wage growth has, in fact, continued apace. The employment cost index, for example, accelerated from about 3 percent growth in total compensation per year in 1996 to 1998 to around 4 percent per year in 2000 and early 2001. The increase in compensation growth might be a result of expectations catching up with faster productivity growth, just as productivity growth is slowing down. If that is the case and productivity growth does return to its lower trend—a big if—then the United States would be in for a period of more rapid inflation. Under this scenario, *That '70s Show* may be, not just the title of a popular television sitcom, but also an accurate description of the economy in this first decade of the twenty-first century.

Recall that one view of economic performance in the 1990s attributes much of the success to *special factors,* or negative price shocks, that are unlikely to be sustained in the future. Prominent examples are the favorable oil-price shocks and slower growth rate of employee benefits. As tends to happen with favorable special factors, these shocks have been less favorable in the early years of the current decade. The price of oil, for example, rose considerably before September 11th and then fell because of the slowdown. And employee benefits again are growing faster than wage and salary costs. The stock-market nosedive in 2000 also raised the cost of employee pensions, not to mention its potential effect on consumption, via the wealth effect, and on government revenue, via reduced capital-gains taxes.

Despite these less propitious special factors, inflation remains relatively in check. The personal-consumption-expenditure deflator, for example, increased by 2.2 percent over the most recent twelve-month period (2000:1 to 2001:1), only slightly faster than the 1.8 percent increase registered in 1999. The continuation of moderate inflation provides a hint that "special factors" may be less special (or more permanent) to the story than is commonly appreciated. If price shocks continue to be unfavorable in the coming years without much increase in inflation, then the rapid employment growth and low rates of inflation experienced in the 1990s would appear to be a more sustainable condition than those who argue for the importance of special factors acknowledge.

This historical experiment is not perfect, of course. Other factors also changed. The cooling off of the labor market, for example, would be expected to reduce inflation if the Phillips curve relation remained stable the last few years. The Fed's aggressive rate-cutting stance, on the other hand, would be expected to support aggregate spending, improve expectations about the future, and, thus, perhaps favor inflation. Experience seldom generates perfect experiments in macroeconomics. With mildly faster wage growth, subdued price growth, and at least temporarily slower productivity growth, profits naturally have been squeezed. Along with a recovery from "irrational exuberance," weaker profits contributed to the stock-market correction in 2001.

Another related development since the end of the 1990s is a precipitous fall in the growth of business investment. After growing at breakneck speed in the 1990s, nonresidential investment, particularly in equipment and software, came to a standstill at the end of 2000 and the beginning of 2001. Shipments of such capital goods as aircraft were contracting at a 20 percent rate in April 2001; the decline was 30 percent for high-tech durable goods. Even the dominant manufacturer of Internet equipment, Cisco, experienced a 30 percent decline in sales in the first quarter of 2001, provoking its CEO, John Chambers, to claim, with some justification, "This may be the fastest any industry our size has ever decelerated" (quoted in Leonhardt 2001). The April 2001 Durable Goods Report indicated a 5 percent decline in orders for all durable goods and a much-steeper decline for high-tech equipment, which portends a further weakening in investment. The situation reached the point that, in May 2001, the headline on the front page of the Goldman Sachs economics unit newsletter read: "Investment Bust Undermines Growth."

What does the sharp reduction in investment imply about the 1990s success story? The 1990s were, in large measure, an era of investment-led growth. It has become commonplace to argue that deficit reduction caused lower interest rates and thus spurred investment, as noted by Blinder and Yellen (chapter 3 in this volume). Yet the recent crash in investment occurred when the U.S. budget reached record levels of surplus. This is not strong support for the universality of any simple "crowding out" hypothesis. Evidently, high public saving and low interest rates are not always sufficient to keep private investment strong. The sustainability of investment growth bears close scrutiny in future booms.

Another way in which investment is believed to have spurred growth is by facilitating technological change. Much of the investment was in high-tech capital. Computers are believed to have finally turned up in the productivity numbers. If this view is correct, then the slowdown in investment portends substantially slower growth in productivity, as Michael Mandel (2000) has predicted.

It goes without saying that the central role assigned to investment will be put to the test in the coming years. If investment remains low and productivity growth nonetheless rebounds, then investment was probably less essential to the 1990s success story than previously believed, while, if productivity growth mirrors investment growth (either up or down), then the emphasis placed on investment will have been vindicated. So far, it looks like investment growth is a big part of the story.

With a short lag, the economic slowdown has led the labor market to cool down. The civilian unemployment rate increased from a seasonally adjusted low of 3.9 percent in September and October 2000 to 5.4 percent in October 2001. The slowdown was typical of earlier business cycles in that manufacturing was hit particularly hard. Industrial production peaked in September 2000 and declined by 2.6 percent over the next seven months—about half as much as it declined during the 1990 to 1991 recession. Manufacturing employment declined by 700,000 jobs, or 4 percent, from September 2000 to July 2001. Also, as is typical when the labor market slackens, unemployment increased by more for teenagers, African Americans, and Hispanics than for prime-age whites.

In contrast to past slowdowns, however, the increase in the unemployment rate was about the same—0.4 percentage points from May 2000 to May 2001—for college graduates and high school graduates. And unemployment fell 0.4 points for high school dropouts. Because unemployment usually rises more for the less skilled in a softening labor market, this latter development surprised most analysts. Moreover, many analysts were expecting many less-skilled workers who found jobs because welfare reform pushed them into the labor force to be the first to lose their jobs in this downturn. Data on labor-force participation and the employment-to-population rate also point in the same direction—the labor market is weakening at least as much for more highly educated workers as it is for less highly educated workers. In particular, the erosion in the labor market for college-educated, white-collar workers may be related to the dotcom bust and the slump in the financial services industry.

The temporary-help-supply sector was hit particularly hard in 2001, after years of continual expansion. Employment in that sector peaked in September 2000 and contracted by 10 percent in the ensuing seven months, after growing at an annual rate of 11 percent in the 1990s. Because temporary help is a leading indicator of future employment growth, this forebodes further weakening in the labor market. Moreover, a sustained contraction in this sector should lead to an outward shift in the Beveridge curve—if Cohen, Dickens, and Posen's story in chapter 5 is right. Conversely, if the vacancy-unemployment relation does not shift despite a contraction of the temporary-help-supply sector in the future, then, presumably, improved job matching via this sector had less to do with the 1990s success story than Cohen, Dickens, and Posen have argued.

Although it is perilously early to evaluate the effect of changes in the policy regime since the end of the 1990s—and the election of November 2000 certainly does signal a shift in policy—there has been one striking change of direction that can be evaluated so far: the effect of a "Keynesian" tax cut on current interest rates. President Bush's arguments for a tax cut shifted with the winds of the economy and political expedience, but, in the end, he and his advisers settled for an argument based on the need to stimulate the economy. In May 2001, Congress passed a $1.3 trillion tax cut. The fiscal discipline achieved by the Clinton administration was shattered. About $40 billion of the tax cut will be delivered retroactively, as a rebate in late summer 2001, in an attempt to stimulate the economy, although most of the cuts—which, unlike the expedited rebate, are highly tilted to the wealthy—are not fully phased in until five to ten years later.

The rhetoric surrounding fiscal policy has changed. One of us, Solow, was fond of making the point, "I'll believe that economists truly believe that a budget surplus has an expansionary effect when they advocate a tax increase during a slowdown." That time has not yet come. More important, short-term interest rates fell, and long-term rates held steady, in the period leading up to, and just after, the passage of the tax cut. The Federal Reserve Board's rate cuts obviously had a lot to do with the fall in interest rates in this period, but the bond market sent a clear indication that it did not view the short-term expansionary fiscal policy as crowding out private investment or driving up future inflation. That may change if foreign investors run for the exit doors, but, so far, the expedited portion of the tax cut has been viewed as a needed stimulus by the markets. The fact that long-term rates did not fall, however, could be due to the backloaded portion of the tax cuts. Politics certainly makes for odd ideological bedfellows, and the Bush administration's endorsement of Keynesian arguments for the tax rebate is a good example.

The Bush administration's initial budget submission leaves little hope that much will be done to develop the skills of the workforce in the near future. An increased emphasis on training and education was identified by the authors of many papers in this volume as an important policy thrust. Expanding the skills of the workforce and increasing the supply of qualified workers would provide an essential basis for sustained growth. The Bush administration's first budget submission, however, would cut half a billion dollars (almost 10 percent) from the federal job-training budget. And, although the Bush administration has made education a priority and has attracted bipartisan support for an education bill, it adds very little in the way of resources relative to what had previously been allocated (see Kogan 2001) and makes few structural reforms other than requiring an ill-defined and noncomparable system of statewide annual testing for third through eighth graders. The economic slowdown that began in 2000 has reduced state and local revenues, which at least in the short run appears likely to contribute to slower growth in investment in human capital as well (see, for example, Moore 2001). With an already tight budget and intensified demand for funds for homeland security, it seems likely that an undertrained workforce will be a major impediment to sustained employment and wage growth for some time to come.

REFERENCES

Baily, Martin, and Robert Lawrence. 2001. "Do we have a New E-Conomy?" NBER working paper #W8243 (April). Cambridge, Mass.: National Bureau of Economic Research.

Kogan, Richard. 2001. "Under President's Budget, Education Funding Would Grow 5.3 Percent: The Claimed 11.5 Percent Increase Is a Distortion." Unpublished manuscript. Washington, D.C.: Center on Budget and Policy Priorities, April.

Leonhardt, David. 2001. "The Rate Cut: The Impact; Just in Time, or Too Late?" *New York Times,* April 19, p. A1.

Mandel, Michael. 2000. *The Coming Internet Depression.* New York: Basic Books.

Moore, Martha. 2001. "States Struggle with Budgets as Money Drips in Economy Force Legislators to Face Hard Choices for Fiscal Year 2002." *USA Today,* July 6, p. 4A.

Part I

Macroeconomic Perspectives

Chapter 1

Prices, Wages, and the U.S. NAIRU in the 1990s

Douglas Staiger, James H. Stock, and Mark W. Watson

O ne of the most salient features of the U.S. expansion in the second half of the 1990s was the combination of low price inflation, strong real-wage growth, and low and falling unemployment. Seemingly, this runs counter to the postwar U.S. experience that periods of low unemployment and strong wage growth are associated with rising rates of inflation. This paper undertakes an empirical investigation of the extent to which changes in price-setting behavior, changes in wage-setting behavior, and fundamental changes in product and labor markets led to this happy coincidence.

The facts are summarized in figures 1.1 and 1.2. Figure 1.1 is a scatterplot of the change in the annual rate of price inflation, as measured by the GDP deflator, against the unemployment rate in the previous year, from 1960 to 1999; for example, the point labeled *98* indicates the unemployment rate in 1998 and the change in the rate of inflation from 1998 to 1999. Figure 1.2 is a comparable scatterplot, except that the series on the vertical axis is the annual percentage growth rate of real wages, as measured by compensation per hour in the non-farm-business sector, deflated by the GDP deflator. A regression line estimated using data from 1960 to 1992 is plotted in both figures. These regression lines are simple estimates of the price and wage Phillips curves. The NAIRU (nonaccelerating inflation rate of unemployment) is defined to be the value of the unemployment rate at which the price regression predicts no change in inflation, which corresponds to the intersection of the regression line and the horizontal line in figure 1.1. Alternatively, the NAWRU (nonaccelerating wage rate of unemployment), the wage-based NAIRU, is the value of the unemployment rate at which the wage-regression line predicts real-wage growth that coincides with the growth in labor productivity, which is given by the intersection of the regression line and the horizontal line in figure 1.2.

Three features are evident from these scatterplots. First, both the wage and the price Phillips curves reflect a negative correlation between the unemployment rate in one year and inflation in the next: the correlation for the 1960 to 1992 sample is -0.55 in figure 1.1 and -0.65 in figure 1.2. Second, the data for 1993 to 1999 (highlighted in the figures) are peculiar, relative to the earlier data:

FIGURE 1.1 / Price Inflation and Unemployment

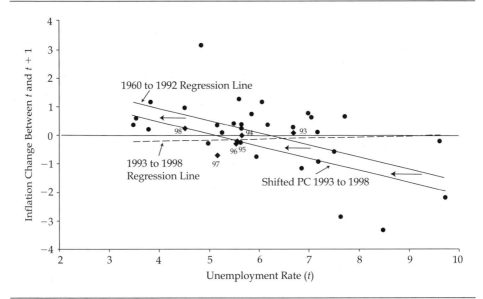

Sources: Bureau of Labor Statistics and authors' calculations.

Note: PC = Phillips curve.

FIGURE 1.2 / Real-Wage Inflation and Unemployment

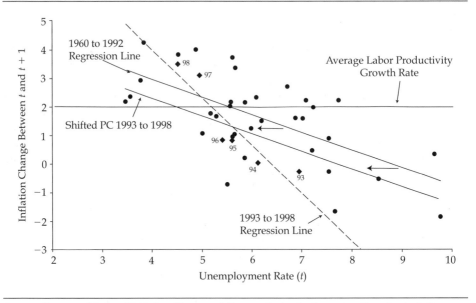

Sources: Bureau of Labor Statistics, Bureau of Economic Analysis, and authors' calculations.

Note: PC = Phillips curve.

although unemployment fell from 7.5 percent in 1992 to 4.1 percent in 1999, the rate of price inflation was essentially constant over this period (it fell by an average of 0.1 percent per year). Third, from 1993 to 1999, real wages increased substantially: real wages grew by an average of 1.5 percent over this period, consistent with little, if any, shift in the NAIRU in this wage scatterplot and, if anything, a steeper regression line for the wage Phillips curve.

The theories that have been proposed to explain these events fall into two groups: those proclaiming that "the Phillips curve is alive and well but . . ." and those proclaiming that "the Phillips curve is dead." Most of the proposed theories are in the "alive and well but . . ." group. According to these theories, the price Phillips curve–the regression line in figure 1.1–continues to have a negative slope but has been shifting inward. Such a shift is indicated by the arrow and new line in figure 1.1. Similarly, the strong growth of real wages in the late 1990s in figure 1.2 is attributed to the surge in productivity: workers are reaping the rewards of using more powerful tools. The differences among these theories arise in the particulars of their explanations of the inward shift of the price-inflation Phillips curve: some focus on the price-setting behavior of firms, others focus on labor markets, while still others suggest that we have simply been the lucky recipients of favorable supply shocks (falling energy prices and favorable terms-of-trade shocks).

The theories that focus on pricing behavior have several variants. One is that globalization has increased competition in the product market, thereby squeezing markups and yielding one-time reductions in markups and prices (for example, Brayton, Roberts, and Williams 1999). Similar arguments can be made about the possible effect of the Internet on price competition for some goods. A different argument is that the credibility of the commitment of the Federal Reserve Board to controlling inflation has increased and that this has had the effect of reducing expected inflation, which in turn moderates actual price increases posted by producers.

The theories that focus on labor markets suggest that the source of the inward shift in the Phillips curve lies in a decline in the natural rate of unemployment. Several such theories are surveyed and analyzed empirically in Lawrence Katz and Alan Krueger (1999). Some emphasize changes in how people look for work (using temporary-help firms, the Internet, etc.). Others emphasize changes in the composition of the workforce, including the aging of the workforce as the baby boom enters an age traditionally associated with high degrees of labor-force attachment, the entry of "welfare mothers" into the workforce as a consequence of welfare reform, and the removal of many marginal workers from the workforce either because of incarceration (Katz and Krueger 1999) or because of relaxed social security disability insurance provisions (Autor and Duggan 2000).

Finally, some of these theories stress the role of good luck. For much of the 1990s, energy prices were declining, and the United States enjoyed a strong dollar. Robert Gordon (1998) explored these sources in detail, concluding that they explain part, but far from all, of the price-inflation–unemployment puzzle of the 1990s.

In contrast, "the Phillips curve is dead" theories interpret the 1990s, not as an inward drift in the Phillips curve, but rather as a fundamental change in the relation between unemployment and inflation. According to these theories, it is the slope of the Phillips curve that has shifted, not the intercept: the Phillips curve now is the dotted line in figure 1.1, which was fit to the data from 1993 to 1999. This curve has a slope of 0. This more radical interpretation requires more radical theories.

The popular-press versions of these theories stress that increased price competition in the new economy prevents firms from responding to market tightness by increasing prices, thereby eliminating any relation between measures of aggregate activity, such as unemployment, and changes in the rate of price inflation. Subtler versions of these theories involve nonlinearities in firm behavior when inflation is low. George Akerlof, William Dickens, and George Perry (1996) suggest that reluctance by firms to give negative nominal-wage cuts means that steady-state hiring depends on the rate of inflation; in particular, the equilibrium unemployment rate falls when inflation falls. John Taylor (2000) develops a different theory of the state dependence of the NAIRU; in his model, low inflation itself leads firms to expect reduced pricing power, which in turn contributes to reduced inflation and reduces the sensitivity of inflation to growth in demand. Akerlof, Dickens, and Perry (2000) provide a model of price setting in which some firms find it convenient to predict no inflation as long as inflation is low, permitting the unemployment rate to be persistently low without igniting inflation. Empirically, this is the same thing as the NAIRU falling when the inflation rate gets low. In all three of these models, the NAIRU is not *permanently* low; rather, its low value is contingent on the monetary authority holding down inflation.

This paper has two objectives. The first, more modest one is to document the shifts in figures 1.1 and 1.2. To a considerable extent, this entails updating earlier estimates of Phillips curves and NAIRUs along the lines of Staiger, Stock, and Watson (1997a, 1997b) and Gordon (1998). The second, more ambitious objective is to provide new evidence, based on quarterly macro data and on a panel of annual data for U.S. states from 1979 to 1999, that will help us parse the theories outlined in this introductory section or, at least, rule out some families of theories.

We address these two objectives by asking three specific questions. First, did the Phillips curve break down in the 1990s, or did it simply shift with a new and evolving NAIRU? That is, which class of theories—"the Phillips curve is dead" or "the Phillips curve is alive and well but . . ."—has more empirical support? We conclude that the weight of the evidence suggests that the price Phillips curve has shifted in, not flattened out, supporting the "alive and well but . . ." group.

This leads to the second question: Why has the price Phillips curve shifted in? That is, does the empirical evidence help distinguish between the many theories of the inward drift in the price Phillips curve? In our view, the weight of the empirical evidence points toward explanations that involve special features in labor markets. The macro evidence suggests that changes in price-setting behavior cannot explain the broad stability of the relation between price inflation and measures of economic activity. Rather, the explanation for the shifting unemployment Phillips curve seems to lie in declines in the univariate trend rate of unemployment.

The third question, then, is whether labor-productivity gains during the 1990s can explain the apparently aberrant recent behavior of real wages in figure 1.2. That is, is the wage Phillips curve as resilient empirically as the price Phillips curve once we have accounted for productivity? Our answer is yes: adjusting for trend labor-productivity gains accounts for the discrepancies that otherwise appear between the price and the wage Phillips curves.

In short, once one allows for the *univariate* trends in the unemployment rate and the rate of productivity growth, the 1990s present no wage or price puzzles. Backward-looking price Phillips curves are stable when the unemployment rate is specified as a gap, that is, as a deviation from its univariate trend value. Similarly, wage Phillips curves are stable when wages are adjusted for changes in trend productivity growth and when the regressions are specified using activity gaps. This implies that theories of the 1990s that focus on favorable supply shocks, changes in the pricing power of firms and markups, or changes in the negotiating power of labor all miss the mark, for they imply persistent errors and/or coefficient instability that we fail to find. Rather, the evidence points to underlying economic forces that change the univariate trends of the unemployment rate and the growth rate of productivity. Unfortunately, our regressions using the state data fail to isolate any economic or demographic determinants of the trend unemployment rate.

The plan of the paper is as follows. The first four sections analyze quarterly U.S. macro data from 1960 to 2000. We begin in the first section by estimating the long-run trends in the macro data and discussing how we estimate output gaps. The second section addresses issues of econometric specification and estimation of the price and wage Phillips curves and associated time-varying NAIRUs (TV-NAIRUs). These Phillips curves are specified using output gaps, which are the difference between the output measure and its low-frequency univariate trend component. As Robert Hall (1999) and T. Cogley and T. Sargent (forthcoming) argue, the low-frequency trend component can be thought of as an estimate of the natural rate of unemployment; thus, this approach allows separate identification of the NAIRU and the natural rate. The third section reports empirical price Phillips relations estimated both with the unemployment-rate gap and with gaps based on other measures of economic activity. Consistent with the findings reported in Douglas Staiger, James Stock, and Mark Watson (1997b), Stock (1998), and Stock and Watson (1999b), we find stability and predictive content in these broader measures, which suggests that "the Phillips curve is dead" theories are premature. In the fourth section, we turn to wage Phillips curves and examine the role of productivity gains in explaining the recent rise in real wages.

The next four sections focus on the state panel data. The use of state-level data has been limited (for notable exceptions, see Katz and Krueger (1999) and Lerman and Schmidt 1999), and we are able to consider a large number of new variables and, accordingly, use the state data to examine the various theories. Specifications and econometric issues, including our instrumental-variables (IV) method for alleviating errors-in-variables bias arising from using the state data, are discussed in the fifth section. The data set is described in the sixth section, and benchmark results are presented in the seventh section. The eighth section reports the results of using additional variables to explore the stability of the Phillips curve and to examine theories about sources of shifts in the NAIRU. Conclusions are summarized in the final section.

A remark on terminology is in order before proceeding. In conventional usage, the *NAIRU* is the rate of unemployment consistent with price inflation remaining constant; the *NAWRU* is the rate of unemployment consistent with wage inflation remaining constant; and the *NAIRCU* is the rate of capacity utilization consistent with price inflation remaining constant. In this paper, we consider both wage and price inflation as well as other activity indexes, including building permits and demographically adjusted unemployment. We could, then, report TV-NAWRCUs, TV-NAIRBPs, TV-NAWRDUs, and so on. But we do not find these acronyms helpful. Instead, we shall call them all *TV-NAIRUs* and, when needed, add specificity through the use of adjectives.

TRENDS IN THE MACRO DATA

Method for Estimating Univariate Trends and Constructing Gaps

Let y_t be a quarterly time series, and let y_t^* denote its trend. Unless explicitly noted otherwise, y_t^* is estimated by passing y_t through a two-sided low-pass filter, with a cutoff frequency corresponding to fifteen years. Essentially, this estimates y_t^* as a long two-sided weighted moving average of y_t with weights that sum to 1. Estimates of the trend at the beginning and the end of the sample are obtained by extending (padding) the series with autoregressive forecasts and backcasts of y_t, constructed from an estimated AR(4) model (with a constant term) for the first-difference of y_t. The "gap" value of y_t, y_t^g, is defined to be the deviation of y_t from its trend value; that is, $y_t^g = y_t - y_t^*$. Thus, the trend value of the unemployment rate is the value of the unemployment rate resulting from the low-pass filter, and the unemployment-rate gap is the difference between the actual unemployment rate and the long-run trend in unemployment.

Description of the Aggregate U.S. Data

The U.S. data are quarterly from 1959:1 to 2000:2. The primary price measure is the GDP deflator, but, in our sensitivity analysis, we also consider the personal-consumption-expenditure (PCE) deflator, the CPI, and the deflator for the nonfarm-business component of GDP. All rates of inflation are computed as π_t $= 400 \ln(P_t/P_{t-1})$, where P_t is the level of the price index in quarter t.

Several measures of wages are used. Our primary measure is compensation per hour in the nonfarm-business sector. For sensitivity checks, we also consider the employment cost index (ECI)—both total compensation and wages and salaries only—average hourly earnings of nonagricultural production workers, and compensation per hour in manufacturing. Wage-growth rates are computed as ω_t $= 400 \ln(W_t/W_{t-1})$, where W_t is the level of the wage index.

Labor productivity is measured by output per hour of all workers in the nonfarm-business sector, except when we consider compensation per hour in manufacturing, in which case labor productivity is measured by output per hour of all workers in manufacturing.

Economic activity is variously measured by the total unemployment rate, a demographically adjusted unemployment rate, the rate of capacity utilization, and housing starts (building permits). The demographically adjusted unemployment rate was constructed as a weighted average of the unemployment rates for fourteen age-gender categories (ages sixteen to nineteen, twenty to twenty-four, twenty-five to thirty-four, thirty-five to forty-four, forty-five to fifty-four, fifty-five to sixty-four, and sixty-five and over, each by gender), weighted by the shares of each age group in the 1985 labor force.

Supply-shock variables in the Phillips curve regressions are Gordon's (1982) price-control series, the relative price of food and energy, and exchange rates.

Data sources for all series are given in the data appendix.

Low-Frequency Properties of the Data

Figure 1.3 presents quarterly time-series data and their estimated trends for (a) price inflation (the GDP deflator), (b) wage inflation (compensation per hour), (c) real-wage growth (compensation per hour deflated by GDP-deflator inflation), (d) labor-productivity growth, (e) the unemployment rate, (f) the demographically adjusted unemployment rate, (g) building permits (housing starts), and (h) the rate of capacity utilization. The "gaps" of each of these variables are the difference between the quarterly data and their estimated trends. Table 1.1 shows the sample mean of each of these series over each of the four decades in the sample and, as a measure of persistence in the series, a 95 percent confidence interval for the largest root in a univariate autoregression with six lags.

Figure 1.3 and table 1.1 show several important features of these data. First, consider wages, prices, and productivity. Figures 1.3a and 1.3b show substantial low-frequency (trend) variability in price and nominal-wage inflation. As shown in table 1.1, this low-frequency variability leads to confidence intervals for the largest AR root that range from 0.90 to 1.02 (intervals that, notably, include a unit AR root). Nominal-wage growth less productivity growth is also persistent: the confidence interval for its largest AR root is 0.81 to 1.00.

In contrast, real-wage growth and, especially, real-wage growth less produc-

FIGURE 1.3 / Macro Series and Their Trend Values

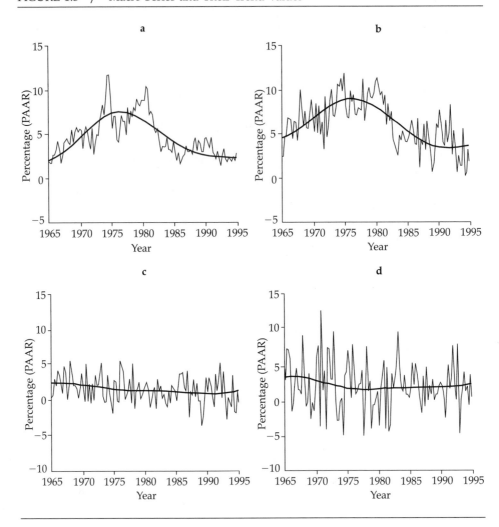

tivity growth are considerably less persistent, and 95 percent confidence intervals for their largest AR roots do not include unity. Still, the decade-long averages in real wages show considerable variability, and the ratio of the largest to the smallest decadal average varies by a factor of more than 2.5. Table 1.1 shows that these decade-long changes in real-wage-growth rates are broadly consistent with movements in the growth of labor productivity: real-wage growth and labor-productivity growth were both high in the 1960s, low in the 1980s, and so on. The relation is stronger when wages, prices, and productivity all pertain to the nonfarm-business sector than when the GDP deflator is used to construct

FIGURE 1.3 / (Continued)

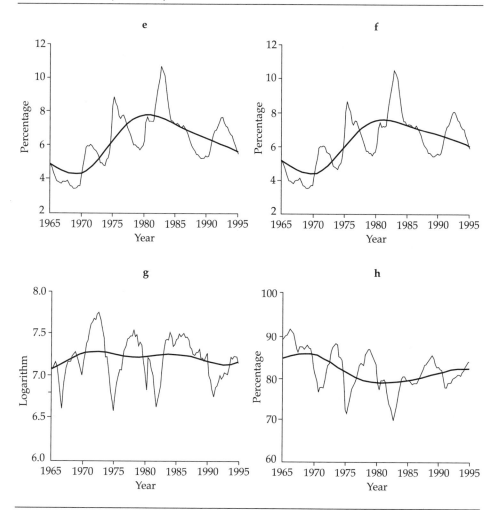

Sources: Bureau of Labor Statistics, Bureau of Economic Analysis, and authors' calculations.

Notes: a, Price inflation; b, Wage inflation; c, Real-wage inflation; d, Productivity growth; e, The unemployment rate; f, The demographically adjusted unemployment rate; g, Building permits; h, Capacity utilization.

real wages. Average real-wage growth adjusted for productivity changes little over the decades in the sample.

Formally, the hypothesis of a unit root in productivity is rejected, which, taken literally, indicates that productivity growth is stationary. This characterization, however, does not allow for the possibility of slowly changing mean productivity-growth rates that lie at the heart of the new-economy debate. From a sta-

TABLE 1.1   /   Descriptive Statistics for Trend Characteristics of the Data

| | Sample Mean | | | | 95 Percent CI for the Largest AR Root |
Series	60:1– 69:4	70:1– 79:4	80:1– 89:4	90:1– 99:4	
Price Inflation	2.47	6.50	4.46	2.23	.90 to 1.02
Nominal Wage Growth Rate	4.95	8.05	5.36	3.72	.91 to 1.02
Nominal Wage-Productivity Growth Rate	2.22	6.09	3.94	1.70	.81 to 1.00
Real Wage[1] Growth Rate	2.48	1.55	.90	1.49	<.93
Real Wage[2] Growth Rate	2.86	1.81	1.15	1.71	<.89
Real Wage[1]-Productivity Growth Rate	−.25	−.40	−.52	−.52	<.77
Real Wage[2]-Productivity Growth Rate	.14	−.15	−.27	−.30	<.77
Productivity Growth Rate	2.72	1.96	1.42	2.02	<.80
Real Wage[1]/Productivity (log)	−.029	−.067	−.080	−.138	.97 to 1.03
Real Wage[2]/Productivity (log)	−.014	−.010	−.012	−.052	.91 to 1.02
Unemployment Rate	4.78	6.21	7.27	5.76	.89 to 1.02
Demographically adjusted unemployment rate	5.04	6.06	7.26	6.11	.86 to 1.01
Building Permits (log)	7.07	7.31	7.24	7.17	<.89
Capacity-Utilization Rate	85.0	81.6	79.0	80.9	<.93

Note: Columns 1 to 4 show the sample means of the series listed in the stub column over the sample period indicated. The final column shows the 95 confidence interval (CI) for the largest root in a univariate AR(6) model (including the constant). The sample period for the regression was 1960:1 to 2000:2. The confidence interval was computed using the approximation developed in Stock (1991), for highly persistent series. Several of the series were not very persistent, and Stock's method could be used to compute only an upper confidence bound. Real Wage[1] uses price inflation computed from the GDP deflator, and Real Wage[2] uses price inflation computed from the price deflator for the nonfarm business sector.

tistical point of view, if there is a highly persistent component of productivity growth but its variance is small relative to variations induced by cyclical movements and measurement error, then it will be difficult to detect, and the series can spuriously appear to be stationary.

These results are consistent with price inflation and nominal-wage inflation adjusted for productivity growth sharing a common stochastic trend that disappears from real-wage growth adjusted for productivity growth. In the terminology of integration and cointegration, this suggests that price inflation is I(1) (that is, is integrated of order 1), wage inflation less productivity growth is I(1), and real-wage growth less productivity growth is I(0); that is, price inflation is cointegrated with wage inflation less productivity growth, with a cointegrating vector of $(1, -1)$.[1]

Consistent with this specification, the *level* of productivity-adjusted real wages (equivalently, the "markup" or "labor's share") appears to be I(1). When real wages are computed using the GDP deflator, there is a marked downward trend in the markup, but, when the GDP deflator is replaced by the nonfarm-business deflator, much of the trend disappears. In either case, the series is very persistent, and a unit autoregressive root cannot be rejected.

The unemployment rate, building permits (housing starts), and capacity utilization are shown in figures 1.3e to 1.3h. The unemployment-rate trend exhibits great variability (figure 1.3e), most of which remains in the demographically adjusted unemployment rate (figure 1.3f). In contrast, the trends in building permits and capacity utilization (figs. 1.3g and 1.3h) show much less variability. Table 1.1 indicates that the unemployment-rate series are much more persistent than the building-permits and capacity-utilization series: unit autoregressive roots cannot be rejected for either unemployment series, but they can be rejected for both building permits and capacity utilization.

In summary, these statistics suggest that price inflation and nominal-wage inflation, adjusted for productivity growth, are cointegrated. Real wages and productivity growth move together at low frequencies, although these movements are small in magnitude compared with the noise and cyclical movements in these series. The unemployment rate and the demographically adjusted unemployment rate appear to be I(1), but capacity utilization and building permits are I(0).

SPECIFICATION AND ESTIMATION OF MACRO PRICE AND WAGE EQUATIONS

Specification

Our specifications and estimation methodology follow along the lines of Robert Gordon (1982), Robert King, James Stock, and Mark Watson (1995), Douglas Staiger, James Stock, and Mark Watson (1997a), and Robert Gordon (1998), with some modifications.

Because prices and wages are codetermined, and because we will examine both price and wage Phillips curves, it is useful to consider these curves as a system. Our discussion of trends in the last section suggests that it is fruitful to treat wage inflation and price inflation as a cointegrated system, with each variable being integrated of order 1 and having the single cointegrating vector implying that real-wage growth net of productivity growth is integrated of order 0.

MOTIVATION FROM A SYSTEM WITHOUT LAG DYNAMICS Let π_t denote the rate of price inflation, let ω_t be the rate of nominal-wage inflation (the growth rate of nominal wages), and let θ_t be the growth rate of labor productivity (all expressed in units of percentage annual growth rates). Let x_t be a demand-gap variable, for example, the output gap or the unemployment gap constructed using the method outlined earlier. Let Z_t be a vector of mean 0 variables representing observable supply shocks (such as shifts in the relative prices of food and energy) that might affect wage and price setting and thus might enter either the wage or the price equations.

The price equation relates the deviation of future inflation from its expectation to the activity gap and supply shocks. Ignoring lags for the moment, this is

$$\pi_{t+1} - \pi^e_{t+1} = \mu_\pi + \beta_\pi x_t + \gamma_\pi Z_t + v_{\pi t+1}, \tag{1.1}$$

where π^ε_{t+1} is the inflation in period $t + 1$ that is expected as of period t, μ_π, β_π, and γ_π are unknown coefficients, and $v_{\pi t+1}$ is an error term.

Implementation of equation 1.1 requires specifying inflationary expectations. Following an old convention (see Gordon 1990, 1998; and Fuhrer 1995), we restrict attention to the random-walk model of expectations, with the result that $\pi^e_{t+1} = \pi_t$ and $\pi_{t+1} - \pi^e_{t+1} = \Delta\pi_{t+1}$, where $\Delta\pi_{t+1} \equiv \pi_{t+1} - \pi_t$. Making this modification, we have

$$\Delta\pi_{t+1} = \mu_\pi + \beta_\pi x_t + \gamma_\pi Z_t + v_{\pi t+1}. \tag{1.2}$$

The wage equation is obtained similarly. Again ignoring lags, we have

$$\omega_{t+1} - \omega^e_{t+1} = \mu_\omega + \beta_\omega x_t + \gamma_\omega Z_t + v_{\omega t+1}. \tag{1.3}$$

Various approaches are available for modeling expected nominal wages. We model expected wage inflation as the sum of expected price inflation and expected productivity growth, that is, $\omega^e_{t+1} = \pi^e_{t+1} + \theta^e_{t+1}$. As in the price equation, we suppose that $\pi^e_{t+1} = \pi_t$. If productivity growth is a random walk, then we can let $\theta^e_{t+1} = \theta_t$. However, productivity growth has a cyclical component, so an alternative method used by Gordon (1998) is to model $\theta^e_{t+1} = \theta^*_t$, where θ^*_t is trend productivity growth. We will use this latter approach as the base specification, but we will also report results that are based on the alternative specification in which $\theta^e_{t+1} = \theta_t$. This leads to a specification of the wage equation of

$$\omega_{t+1} - \theta^*_t - \pi_t = \mu_\omega + \beta_\omega x_t + \gamma_\omega Z_t + v_{\omega t+1}. \tag{1.4}$$

INCORPORATION TO LAG DYNAMICS   The specifications 1.2 and 1.4 omit lag dynamics. Our treatment of dynamics is motivated by the observation, made earlier, that nominal-wage growth less productivity growth, or less trend productivity growth, appears to be cointegrated with price inflation. That is, $\omega_{t+1} - \theta^*_t$ and π_t are arguably cointegrated. This leads to the triangular representation of cointegrated variables in which x_t and Z_t are treated as exogenous variables:

$$\begin{aligned}\Delta\pi_{t+1} = {} & \mu_\pi + \alpha_{\pi\pi}(L)\Delta\pi_t + \alpha_{\pi\omega}(L)(\omega_t - \theta^*_{t-1} - \pi_{t-1}) + \beta_\pi x_t \\ & + \alpha_{\pi x}(L)\Delta x_t + \gamma_\pi Z_t + v_{\pi t+1},\end{aligned} \tag{1.5}$$

$$\omega_{t+1} - \theta_t^* - \pi_t = \mu_\omega + \alpha_{\omega\pi}(L)\Delta\pi_t + \alpha_{\omega\omega}(L)(\omega_t - \theta_{t-1}^* - \pi_{t-1})$$
$$+ \beta_\omega x_t + \alpha_{\omega x}(L)\Delta x_t + \gamma_\omega Z_t + v_{\omega t+1},$$

$$(1.6)$$

where μ_π, β_π, and so on are coefficients, and $\alpha_{\pi\pi}(L)$ and so on are lag poly-nomials. Specifications 1.5 and 1.6 allow lagged effects of x_t but, following the literature, not of the supply-shock variable Z_t.

These two specifications form the basis for our time-series analysis. The price equation differs from most Phillips curve specifications because it includes a term allowing feedback from real wages net of productivity to future price changes. The wage equation also allows for feedback from price changes to fu-ture wage changes. Our motivation for these equations has been to move from the static system equations 1.2 and 1.4 using the tools of cointegration theory. Note, however, that our resulting equations are the same as the general specifi-cation considered by Gordon (1998, equations 7 and 8).[2]

An alternative specification that we explore in the empirical section adds a lag of the *level* of productivity-adjusted real wages $(\ln[W_{t-1}/P_{t-1}] - \ln[\text{productivity}_{t-1}])$ to the right-hand side of equations 1.5 and 1.6. This specification, a version of which goes back to the classic paper by Sargan (1964), is appropriate when this term is I(0). As the analysis in the last section suggested, this assumption seems at odds with the data used here, but versions of the specification have been used for both wage and price equations using data from the United States and other countries (see Barlow and Stadler, n.d.; Blanchflower and Oswald 1994; Brayton, Roberts, and Williams 1999; and Holden and Nymoen 1999). Olivier Blanchard and Lawrence Katz (1997) (and the references cited therein) contains a useful discussion of this specification as it applies to the wage Phillips curve, and we will discuss this issue more in the context of the state Phillips curves specified in our fifth section.

Estimation of TV-NAIRUs

Specifications 1.5 and 1.6 use the "gap" variable x_t, constructed as the difference between the activity variable and its univariate trend, but what should appear in the Phillips curve is the deviation between the variable and the NAIRU. So, if the univariate trend and the variable's NAIRU are different, then 1.5 and 1.6 should include another term that captures this difference. We model the differ-ence between the NAIRU and the univariate trend as a time-varying intercept in these Phillips curves and estimate this difference from estimates of the time-varying intercept.

To make this clear, consider the system in which the activity measure is the rate of unemployment, u_t, and let u_t^N denote the possibly time-varying NAIRU. If the NAIRU does not equal the univariate trend u_t^*, then equation 1.5 is prop-erly specified as

$$\begin{aligned}
\Delta\pi_{t+1} &= \mu_\pi + \alpha_{\pi\pi}(L)\Delta\pi_t + \alpha_{\pi\omega}(L)(\omega_t - \theta^*_{t-1} - \pi_{t-1}) \\
&\quad + \beta_\pi(u_t - u_t^N) + \alpha_{\pi u}(L)\Delta(u_t - u_t^N) + \gamma_\pi Z_t + v_{\pi t+1} \\
&\cong (\mu_\pi + \beta_\pi[u_t^* - u_t^N]) + \alpha_{\pi\pi}(L)\Delta\pi_t \\
&\quad + \alpha_{\pi\omega}(L)(\omega_t - \theta^*_{t-1} - \pi_{t-1}) + \beta_\pi u_t^g + \alpha_{\pi u}(L)\Delta u_t \\
&\quad + \gamma_\pi Z_t + v_{\pi t+1},
\end{aligned}$$
(1.7)

where $u_t^g = u_t - u_t^*$ is the unemployment gap, and the second equation makes the approximation that, because U_t^N is slowly varying, the term $\alpha_{\pi u}(L)\Delta u_t^N$ is negligible. Thus, to the extent that the univariate trend in unemployment u_t^* differs from the NAIRU u_t^N, the gap specification 1.5 will have a time-varying intercept. An identical argument applies to the wage equation 1.6.

This reasoning leads to a modification of the system equations 1.5 and 1.6, in which the intercepts are allowed to vary over time:

$$\begin{aligned}
\Delta\pi_{t+1} &= \mu_{\pi t} + \alpha_{\pi\pi}(L)\Delta\pi_t + \alpha_{\pi\omega}(L)(\omega_t - \theta^*_{t-1} - \pi_{t-1}) + \beta_\pi u_t^g \\
&\quad + \alpha_{\pi x}(L)\Delta x_t + \gamma_\pi Z_t + v_{\pi t+1},
\end{aligned}$$
(1.8)

$$\begin{aligned}
\omega_{t+1} - \theta_t^* - \pi_t &= \mu_{\omega t} + \alpha_{\omega\pi}(L)\Delta\pi_t + \alpha_{\omega\omega}(L)(\omega_t - \theta^*_{t-1} - \pi_{t-1}) \\
&\quad + \beta_\omega u_t^g + \alpha_{\omega x}(L)\Delta x_t + \gamma_\omega Z_t + v_{\omega t+1}.
\end{aligned}$$
(1.9)

If the slope coefficients are stable, any intercept drift in these equations arises from a departure of the NAIRU from the trend unemployment rate.

Our method for estimating the intercept drift follows King, Stock, and Watson (1995), Staiger, Stock, and Watson (1997a), and Gordon (1997, 1998) and adopts an unobserved-components model for the intercept, in which the intercept follows a random walk:

$$\mu_{\pi t+1} = \mu_{\pi t} + \eta_{\pi t+1}, \quad \text{where } \eta_{\pi t+1} \text{ is i.i.d. } N(0, \sigma^2_{\eta_\pi});$$
(1.10)

$$\mu_{\omega t+1} = \mu_{\omega t} + \eta_{\omega t+1}, \quad \text{where } \eta_{\omega t+1} \text{ is i.i.d. } N(0, \sigma^2_{\eta_\omega}).$$
(1.11)

The random-walk specification is a flexible way to track smooth changes in the intercept. The initial condition for the random walk is identified by the unconditional means of the regressors, so we construct the regressors to have mean 0 and initialize the random walk at 0.

According to the system 1.8 and 1.9, time variation in the wage- and price-equation intercepts arises from changes in $u_t^* - u_t^N$, and this means that the innovations $\eta_{\pi t+1}$ and $\eta_{\omega t+1}$ should be the same. We shall examine this by estimating the intercept drift separately for the price and the wage equations and comparing the results. In addition, we shall (separately) test the hypotheses that $\sigma^2_{\eta_\pi} = 0$ and $\sigma^2_{\eta_\omega} = 0$ using the QLR or sup-Wald test (Quandt 1960; Andrews 1993). The parameters $\sigma^2_{\eta_\pi}$ can be estimated by maximum likelihood, but the maximum likelihood estimator has a distribution that piles up at 0 when these are small and is thus unsatisfactory. Instead, we construct confidence intervals and median-unbiased estimates of $\sigma^2_{\eta_\pi}$ and $\sigma^2_{\eta_\omega}$ using the methods in Stock and

Watson (1998), as discussed in Staiger, Stock, and Watson (1997a) and Stock (1998, in press).

The estimate of the NAIRU $\hat{u}_t^N$ based on one of these estimated equations is obtained by combining the univariate drift and the intercept drift. Because $\mu_{\pi t} = \beta_\pi(u_t^* - u_t^N)$ (with mean 0 regressors), we have the estimator,

$$u_{t|T}^N = u_t^* - \frac{\eta_{\pi t|T}}{\hat{\beta}_\pi}, \tag{1.12}$$

where $\hat{\beta}$ is the estimator of β_π, and $\mu_{\pi t}|_T$ is the estimator of $\mu_{\pi t}$ obtained from the Kalman smoother implemented with the estimated parameters of the system.

We have motivated this treatment of the parameter drift by observing that we want a consistent framework that is flexible enough to handle activity measures with quite different trends. However, this formulation has two additional advantages. First, it allows separate identification of the univariate trend and the NAIRU. Second, since much of the time variation in the NAIRU is likely to be associated with changes in the trend unemployment rate, the method can be viewed as a device akin to prewhitening to obtain more precise estimates of the TV-NAIRU.

MACRO ESTIMATES OF PRICE PHILLIPS CURVES

Benchmark Price Regressions

Benchmark estimates of regressions of the form 1.8, using various activity gaps, are reported in table 1.2. The specifications include standard supply-shock variables (Gordon's [1982] series for wage and price controls and the relative price of food and energy). For comparability to conventional specifications, these specifications do not include the error-correction term (real wages less trend productivity, $\omega_t - \theta_{t-1}^* - \pi_{t-1}$) or its lags as regressors; these are included in results reported in the next section. The first row reports the estimated value of the coefficient on the level of the activity gap (which is the sum of the coefficients in a specification that uses the current and lagged gaps), its standard error, and the p-value for the sup-Wald statistic testing the stability of this coefficient. The second block of entries reports the trend value of the activity measure, and the third block of entries reports the estimated TV-NAIRU (the sum of the univariate trend and the estimated deviation of the trend arising from intercept drift). Standard errors for the NAIRU, and for its change since 1992, are computed using the Kalman smoother standard-error formula and do not incorporate estimation error, which would increase them. The final row reports the median-unbiased estimate of the standard deviation of the change in the intercept; if the population counterpart of this coefficient is 0, there is no parameter drift, so the TV-NAIRU for that activity measure equals its univariate trend.

Four results are notable. First, the slope coefficient shows the procyclical nature of the change in inflation and is statistically significant in each of these

TABLE 1.2 / Phillips Curve Estimates from Macroeconomic Data: Price Inflation Equation

$$\Delta\pi_{t+1} = \beta_\pi(u_t - u_t^N) + \alpha_{\pi\pi}(L)\Delta\pi_t + \alpha_{\pi x}(L)\Delta u_t + \gamma_\pi Z_t + v_{\pi t+1}$$

	Civilian Unemployment Rate	Demographically Adjusted Unemployment Rate	Capacity Utilization	Building Permits
Phillips curve	− .28	− .26	.09	2.18
slope (SE) [sta-	(.10)	(.09)	(.03)	(.44)
bility *p*-value]	[.06]	[.13]	[.02]	[.16]
Trend values				
1970	4.33	4.39	85.51	7.27
1980	7.79	7.55	78.74	7.23
1990	6.40	6.66	80.84	7.18
2000	4.48	4.83	81.02	7.31
Change 1992				
to 2000	− 1.60	− 1.59	− .57	.17
NAI trend values				
(SE)				
1970	4.62	4.66	84.86	7.23
	(.41)	(.44)	(1.25)	(.05)
1980	7.73	7.50	79.11	7.25
	(.39)	(.42)	(1.20)	(.05)
1990	6.38	6.65	80.86	7.18
	(.41)	(.44)	(1.25)	(.05)
2000	4.49	4.84	80.67	7.33
	(.54)	(.58)	(1.65)	(.07)
Change 1992	− 1.60	− 1.59	− .88	.18
to 2000	(.47)	(.48)	(1.39)	(.07)
SER	.92	.93	.94	.91
TVP SE	.026	.023	.024	.028
(90% CI)	(.000 to .114)	(.000 to .106)	(.000 to .107)	(.000 to .115)

Notes: Results for the first colmn use the civilian unemployment rate as *u* in the estimated equa-tion. The row labeled *Phillips curve slope* shows the estimates of β_π, with the standard error in pa-rentheses and the *p*-value of the QLR stability test in brackets. *Trend values* are the (univariate) low-pass estimates of trend unemployment rate, and *NAI trend values* are the estimated values of the NAIRU computed using the Kalman smoother, as described in the text. *SER* is the standard error of the regression, and the *TVP SE* is the median-unbiased estimate of the standard deviation of the change in the equation's constant term. The equation was estimated using 4 lags of $\Delta\pi_t$ and 2 lags of Δu_t; the vector *Z* contained Gordon's (1982) wage- and price-control variable, 2 lags of the relative price of food and energy, and 2 lags of the exchange rate. The sample period is 1960:1 to 2000:2. Results in the remaining columns replace *u* with the demographically adjusted unem-ployment rate, capacity utilization, and building permits.

specifications. The estimated value of the slope coefficient in the unemployment specification is comparable to estimates obtained elsewhere in this literature using different sample periods and different series (see Staiger, Stock, and Watson 1997a, table 1), although those other estimates are approximately half the size of the coefficients in Gordon (1998, table 3).

Second, the TV-NAIRU is estimated to have fallen by approximately 1.6 percentage points from 1992 to 2000; the decline is only slightly less if it is measured using the demographically adjusted unemployment rate. In contrast, the NAIRU for capacity utilization and building permits is relatively stable; for example, the decline in the capacity-utilization TV-NAIRU is only two-thirds of the Kalman smoother standard error of the estimated decline.[3]

Third, for all practical purposes, the estimated NAIRUs are simply the univariate trends in the various activity measures. This can be seen by comparing the selected univariate trend values with the estimated TV-NAIRUs shown in table 1.2 or by comparing the sample paths of these values for the specification plotted in figure 1.4. The reason why the TV-NAIRU and trend values are so similar follows from the data analysis presented in the first section. Neglecting lags and the supply shocks, the Phillips curve is

$$\Delta \pi_{t+1} = \beta_\pi(u_t^g) - \beta_\pi(u_t^N - u_t^*) + v_{\pi t+1}. \tag{1.13}$$

From the data analysis in the first section, $\Delta \pi_{t+1}$ is I(0), and, by construction, so is the unemployment-rate gap, u_t^g. This means that there cannot be large persistent deviations of u_t^N from u_t^*: if there were, these would be transmitted to $\Delta \pi$, but, since $\Delta \pi$ is I(0), it does not contain large persistent movements. Mechanically, this means that, in all the specifications, the median-unbiased estimate of the standard deviation of the intercept drift is very small; indeed, it is nearly the same value in each specification, between 0.023 and 0.028. This corresponds to a change in the intercept between 0.046 and 0.056 percentage points per year, which is nearly two orders of magnitude less than the standard deviation of the dependent variable, the quarterly change in inflation at an annual rate. In all the specifications, the 90 percent confidence interval includes 0, so the hypothesis of no parameter drift in these equations cannot be rejected at the 5 percent significance level.

While the TV-NAIRU and the univariate trend are very similar, figure 1.4 does show some differences between u_t^N and u_t^*. The deviation in the 1960s and early 1970s is associated with the trend increase in inflation over this period, and the deviation in the early 1980s is associated with a decline in the trend rate of inflation.

The fourth result from table 1.2 concerns the time variation in the slope of the Phillips curve. The p-values for tests of no slope change range from 0.02 to 0.16, suggesting possible time variation in the slope. To investigate the magnitude and timing of this variation, we estimated a model that allowed the slope coefficient to vary but held the intercept constant. Specifically, β_π was modeled as a random walk with innovation variance estimated using the method described in Stock and Watson (1998). Figure 1.5 shows the estimates of the time-varying slope

FIGURE 1.4 / The NAIRU from the Price Phillips Curve

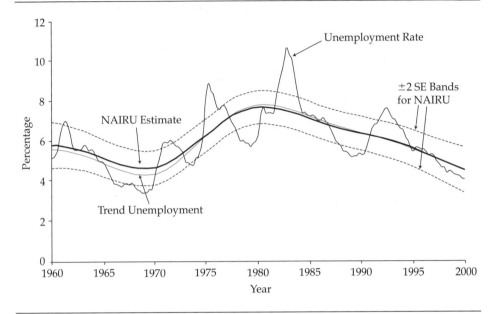

Sources: Bureau of Labor Statistics and authors' calculations.

FIGURE 1.5 / Slope from the Baseline Price Phillips Curve

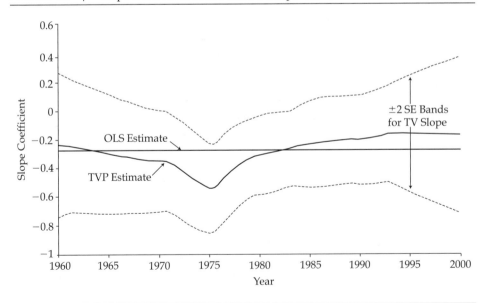

Source: Authors' calculations.

Notes: TV = time varying; TVP = time varying parameter.

coefficients for the specification using the unemployment rate obtained by the Kalman smoother together with ±2 standard-error bands and the OLS slope estimate. Most of the time variation evident in the slope occurs in the mid-1970s, and the estimated slope remained essentially unchanged during the 1990s. Similar results obtain using the other variables (capacity utilization, building permits, and the demographically adjusted unemployment rate). These results are consistent with some small amount of time variation in the Phillips curve slope over the entire sample period but little time variation in the past dozen or so years.

Sensitivity Analysis

Table 1.3 summarizes thirty-six alternative Phillips curve regressions that examine the sensitivity of the benchmark results presented in table 1.2. These regressions differ by the price index used to measure inflation, the activity measure used, whether supply-shock control variables are included, whether the error-correction term and its lags are included, whether the log level of the productivity-adjusted real wage (the "markup") is included, and how many lags are included in the specifications. The statistics reported in the table are the same as those reported in table 1.2, except that, to save space, the values of the level of the trend activity measure and the associated TV-NAIRU are not reported; rather, only the change in the TV-NAIRU from 1992 to 2000 (and its Kalman smoother standard error, ignoring estimation uncertainty) is reported.

These results suggest eight conclusions.

First, the specifications in which the unemployment-rate gap is the activity variable are robust to these changes. The coefficient on the unemployment-rate gap is fairly stable, with estimates ranging from −.25 to −.37 across specifications and all the estimated coefficients within a standard error of −0.3. The TV-NAIRUs estimated with the unemployment-rate specifications are all estimated to have declined substantially from 1992 to 2000, with almost all the estimated declines being approximately 1.4 to 1.7 percentage points.

Second, in virtually all the specifications with alternative activity gaps, the activity-gap coefficients are significant at the 5 percent level (usually at the 1 percent level). Thus, the evidence is consistent with there being a generalized Phillips relation, where the unemployment rate is only one of several possible indicators that can be used in this relation.

Third, in virtually all the specifications, the median-unbiased estimator of the drift in the intercept term suggests that there is very little drift in the intercept in these regressions. In almost all specifications, the null hypothesis of no parameter drift is not rejected at the 5 percent significance level.

Fourth, there is also little evidence of substantial time variation in the slope of the Phillips curve. Only a few of the test statistics for time variation are significant at the 5 percent level (six of thirty-six), and, when time variation is allowed,

(Text continues on p. 26.)

TABLE 1.3 / Alternative Phillips Curve Estimates from Macroeconomic Data: Price Inflation Equation

$$\Delta\pi_{t+1} = \beta_\pi(u_t - u_t^N) + \alpha_{\pi\pi}(L)\Delta\pi_t + \alpha_{\pi x}(L)\Delta u_t + \alpha_{\pi\omega}(L)(\omega_t - \pi_{t-1}^* - \theta_{t-1}^* - \pi_{t,t-1}) + \alpha_{\omega\omega}(L)\Delta\omega_t + \gamma_\pi Z_t + \nu_{\pi t+1}$$

Price	Activity	Np	Na	Ng	Nr	Nx	Ne	Nw	Nm	PC Slope	SER	TVPSE	ΔNAITV: Median UB	ΔIntercept: Median UB	ΔNAITV: 5%	ΔIntercept: 5%
A. Baseline specification (table 1.1)																
GDP def.	Civ. unemp.	4	2	1	2	2	0	0	0	-.28 (.10) [.06]	.92	.026	-1.60 (.47)	-.00 (.13)	-1.62 (.68)	-.01 (.19)
GDP def.	Dem adj. UR	4	2	1	2	2	0	0	0	-.26 (.09) [.13]	.93	.023	-1.59 (.48)	-.00 (.12)	-1.62 (.75)	-.01 (.19)
GDP def.	Cap. util.	4	2	1	2	2	0	0	0	.09 (.03) [.02]	.94	.024	-.88 (1.39)	.03 (.13)	-1.19 (2.14)	.06 (.19)
GDP def.	Bldg. perm.	4	2	1	2	2	0	0	0	2.18 (.44) [.16]	.91	.028	.18 (.07)	-.02 (.14)	.20 (.09)	-.05 (.19)
B. Different price indices																
PCE def.	Civ. unemp.	4	2	1	2	2	0	0	0	-.28 (.11) [.20]	1.08	.017	-1.61 (.33)	-.00 (.09)	-1.59 (.71)	.00 (.20)
PCE def.	Dem adj. UR	4	2	1	2	2	0	0	0	-.26 (.11) [.29]	1.09	.015	-1.60 (.31)	-.00 (.08)	-1.58 (.75)	.00 (.20)
PCE def.	Cap. util.	4	2	1	2	2	0	0	0	.10 (.03) [.49]	1.07	.020	-.70 (1.08)	.01 (.11)	-1.05 (1.95)	.05 (.20)
PCE def.	Bldg. perm.	4	2	1	2	2	0	0	0	2.02 (.54) [.19]	1.08	.021	.18 (.05)	-.01 (.11)	.19 (.10)	-.03 (.20)
CPI	Civ. unemp.	4	2	1	2	2	0	0	0	-.39 (.14) [.16]	1.34	.000	-1.60 (.00)	.00 (.00)	-1.57 (.53)	.01 (.20)

CPI	Dem adj. UR	4	2	1	2	2	0	0	0	-.37 (.14) [.19]	1.35	.000	-1.59 (.00)	.00 (.00)	-1.56 (.55)	.01 (.20)
CPI	Cap. util.	4	2	1	2	2	0	0	0	.15 (.04) [.19]	1.34	.000	-.57 (.00)	.00 (.00)	-1.04 (1.40)	.07 (.20)
CPI	Bldg. perm.	4	2	1	2	2	0	0	0	3.63 (.71) [.05]	1.37	.028	.18 (.04)	-.01 (.15)	.18 (.06)	-.03 (.20)

C. Adding lags of wage inflation and error-correction term

GDP def.	Civ. unemp.	4	2	1	2	2	1	4	0	-.25 (.10) [.07]	.91	.026	-1.67 (.55)	-.02 (.14)	-1.75 (.77)	-.04 (.19)
GDP def.	Dem adj. UR	4	2	1	2	2	1	4	0	-.23 (.10) [.16]	.92	.024	-1.65 (.56)	-.01 (.13)	-1.76 (.84)	-.04 (.19)
GDP def.	Cap. util	4	2	1	2	2	1	4	0	.09 (.03) [.02]	.94	.025	-.74 (1.49)	.02 (.13)	-.83 (2.21)	.02 (.19)
GDP def.	Bldg. perm.	4	2	1	2	2	1	4	0	2.05 (.44) [.20]	.91	.030	.20 (.07)	-.04 (.15)	.21 (.09)	-.07 (.19)

D. Increasing lag length

GDP def.	Civ. unemp.	8	4	1	2	2	0	0	0	-.34 (.12) [.34]	.89	.052*	-1.71 (.68)	-.04 (.23)	-1.66 (.55)	-.02 (.19)
GDP def.	Dem adj. UR	8	4	1	2	2	0	0	0	-.31 (.12) [.27]	.91	.050*	-1.70 (.74)	-.03 (.23)	-1.66 (.62)	-.02 (.19)
GDP def.	Cap. util.	8	4	1	2	2	0	0	0	.10 (.03) [.00]	.94	.043	-1.15 (1.95)	.06 (.20)	-1.10 (1.83)	.06 (.19)
GDP def.	Bldg. perm.	8	4	1	2	2	0	0	0	2.29 (.50) [.23]	.92	.042	.19 (.09)	-.05 (.20)	.19 (.08)	-.04 (.19)

(Table continues on p. 24.)

TABLE 1.3 / Continued

Price	Activity	Np	Na	Ng	Nr	Nx	Ne	Nw	Nm	PC Slope	SER	TVPSE	ΔNAITV: Median UB	ΔIntercept: Median UB	ΔNAITV: 5%	ΔIntercept: 5%
GDP def.	Civ. unemp.	8	4	1	4	4	0	0	0	-.34 (.12) [.42]	.89	.044*	-1.67 (.60)	-.02 (.21)	-1.65 (.56)	-.02 (.19)
GDP def.	Dem adj. UR	8	4	1	4	4	0	0	0	-.31 (.12) [.33]	.91	.041	-1.65 (.65)	-.02 (.20)	-1.65 (.62)	-.02 (.19)
DGP def.	Cap. util.	8	4	1	4	4	0	0	0	.11 (.03) [.01]	.94	.036	-1.06 (1.69)	.05 (.18)	-1.11 (1.81)	.06 (.19)
GDP def.	Bldg. perm.	8	4	1	4	4	0	0	0	2.25 (.51) [.38]	.92	.043	.20 (.09)	-.05 (.20)	.19 (.09)	-.04 (.19)
E. Eliminating the relative price of food and energy, exchange rates, and wage- and price-control variables																
GDP def.	Civ. unemp.	4	2	0	0	0	0	0	0	-.37 (.10) [.08]	1.00	.048	-1.55 (.61)	.02 (.23)	-1.56 (.53)	.01 (.19)
GDP def.	Dem adj. UR	4	2	0	0	0	0	0	0	-.34 (.10) [.17]	1.02	.048	-1.53 (.67)	.02 (.23)	-1.55 (.57)	.01 (.20)
GDP def.	Cap. util.	4	2	0	0	0	0	0	0	.11 (.03) [.05]	1.02	.050*	-1.40 (2.09)	.09 (.23)	-1.17 (1.74)	.07 (.20)
GDP def.	Bldg. perm.	4	2	0	0	0	0	0	0	1.78 (.44) [.24]	1.03	.031	.18 (.09)	-.01 (.16)	.18 (.11)	-.01 (.20)
F. Adding markup variable																
GDP def.	Civ. unemp.	4	2	1	2	2	0	0	2	-.27 (.09) [.09]	.91	.035	-1.43 (.65)	.05 (.17)	-1.41 (.72)	.05 (.19)

Price series	u											TVPSE				
GDP def.	Dem adj. UR	4	2	1	2	2	0	0	2	−.24 (.09) [.19]	.92	.035	−1.40 (.73)	.05 (.17)	−1.38 (.80)	.05 (.19)
GDP def.	Cap. util.	4	2	1	2	2	0	0	2	.09 (.03) [.02]	.93	.023	−.96 (1.41)	.03 (.12)	−1.36 (2.24)	.07 (.19)
GDP def.	Bldg. perm.	4	2	1	2	2	0	0	2	2.08 (.44) [.26]	.90	.025	.16 (.06)	.02 (.13)	.16 (.09)	.03 (.19)
GDP def.	Civ. unemp.	8	4	1	2	2	0	0	2	−.32 (.12) [.34]	.89	.043*	−1.44 (.64)	.05 (.20)	−1.45 (.60)	.05 (.19)
GDP def.	Dem adj. UR	8	4	1	2	2	0	0	2	−.28 (.12) [.27]	.90	.040	−1.43 (.69)	.05 (.19)	−1.43 (.68)	.05 (.19)
GDP def.	Cap. util.	8	4	1	2	2	0	0	2	.10 (.03) [.01]	.93	.036	−1.18 (1.80)	.06 (.18)	−1.25 (1.94)	.07 (.19)
GDP def.	Bldg. perm.	8	4	1	2	2	0	0	2	2.20 (.50) [.28]	.91	.032	.16 (.07)	.03 (.16)	.16 (.09)	.03 (.19)

Notes: This table contains alternative estimates of the price Phillips curve (PC) equation and the TV-NAIRU. The stub column shows the price series used to construct π, and the first column shows the activity variable used for u. the next columns show a set of parameters that described the specification: Np = number of lags of inflation; Na = number of lags of activity variable; NG = a binary variable indicating inclusion(1)/exclusion(0) of wage and price variable (Gordon 1982); Nr = number of lags of the relative price of food and energy; Nx = number of lags of exchange rates; Ne = a binary variable indicating inclusion(1)/exclusion(0) of the wage/price/productivity error-correction term ($\omega_t - \theta^*_{t-1} - \pi^*_{t-1}$); Nw = number of lags of $\Delta\omega$; and Nm = number of lags of markup variable described in the text. The next three columns are described in the notes to table 1.1. An asterisk in the column labeled *TVPSE* is significantly different from zero at the 5 percent level. the columns labeled $\Delta NAITV$ show the change in the NAIRU (or the NAI trend value) from 1992:1 to 2000:1, and the columns labeled $\Delta Intercept$ shows the implied in the equation's constant term over the same period. These are presented for two values of the standard error of the change in the constant: the median-unbiased estimate and a value of .039 (which implies a standard deviation of the change in the constant of 5 percent over the sample period). The sample period is 1960:1 to 2000:1 for all estimated equations.

the estimated sample path of the time-varying slope shows little movement over the past decade.[4]

Fifth, the estimate of the 1992 to 2000 change in the TV-NAIRU is largely unaffected by how supply shocks are treated. For example, in the benchmark specification (which includes the supply-shock variables), the NAIRU is estimated to decline by 1.60 percentage points, whereas, if the supply-shock variables are omitted, the NAIRU is estimated to decline by 1.55 percentage points. However, the regression standard errors of the specifications with supply shocks included are significantly smaller than those with the supply shock omitted. Evidently, these variables are important for explaining one-off changes in inflation but not the kind of persistent changes that could be confused with a change in the NAIRU.

Sixth, the estimated recent decline in the TV-NAIRU is essentially unaffected by whether the total unemployment rate or the demographically adjusted unemployment rate is used. This is consistent with the discussion in Gordon (1998) and Stock (in press) concluding that, although demographic shifts might be associated with increases in the NAIRU in the 1970s, the timing of demographic shifts is not aligned with this sharp recent decline.

Seventh, these results confirm the finding in columns 3 and 4 of table 1.2 that TV-NAIRUs estimated using the rate of capacity utilization and building permits have been relatively stable; for capacity utilization, the change from 1992 to 2000 is less than its Kalman smoother standard error.

Eighth, adding the error-correction term to the benchmark specification decreases the standard error of the regression slightly but does not change the estimates of the slope coefficient of the TV-NAIRU. This suggests that the estimated decline in the NAIRU is not a spurious consequence of neglecting feedback from wages to prices. Table 1.3 also shows results for a specification in which the markup of prices over productivity-adjusted wages (or, equivalently, the log level of the productivity-adjusted real wage) is included. Including this variable reduces somewhat the estimated decline of the unemployment NAIRU, from 1.60 percentage points in the base specification to 1.43 in the specification including this term. Thus, this term is estimated to contribute perhaps 0.2 percentage points to the decline in the NAIRU. Taken together, these results suggest that there is limited or no evidence that feedback from wages to prices has served to hold down prices during the 1990s.

Summary of Main Findings

The regression results reported in tables 1.2 and 1.3 indicate a stable and statistically significant relation between future changes in price inflation and current economic activity as measured by various activity gaps. In addition, in these gap specifications, there is very little evidence of drift in the intercept or the slope, either in terms of statistical significance or in terms of the point estimates of the drift from 1992 to 2000. Finally, including supply shocks does not change substantially the estimates of the declines in the NAIRU.

We interpret these findings as being inconsistent with "the Phillips curve is dead" theories of the 1990s. They are inconsistent with theories that place considerable weight on changes in price-setting behavior in the 1990s, for these theories would imply important drift in the intercept or slope of the Phillips curve. They are also inconsistent with theories that place great weight on sustained "good luck" in the form of favorable supply shocks. Said differently, once the Phillips curves are specified in gaps, there are no price-equation puzzles to explain. Because trend capacity utilization and trend building permits are approximately flat, the only "puzzle" about the price Phillips curve is why the univariate trend in the unemployment rate has fallen. Once we have accounted for the univariate trend in the unemployment rate, these price-inflation Phillips curves fit quite nicely throughout the decade and, indeed, throughout the entire sample period, 1960 to 2000.

MACRO ESTIMATES OF WAGE PHILLIPS CURVES

This section presents empirical estimates of wage Phillips curves and TV-NAIRUs using the unemployment rate and other indicators of economic activity. The discussion parallels that presented in the previous section: first, we present some benchmark estimates; next, we examine the robustness of these estimates to alternative specifications; and, finally, we summarize conclusions.

Benchmark Wage Regressions

BENCHMARK REGRESSION ESTIMATES   Benchmark wage regressions are reported in table 1.4, using the same format as in table 1.2.

The most striking result to be seen in table 1.4 is that these specifications are very similar to the benchmark price regressions reported in the corresponding columns of table 1.2. The slope coefficients are larger in table 1.4 than in table 1.2, but so is the standard deviation of the dependent variable. The slope coefficients are all statistically significant at the 5 percent level. Although the levels of the TV-NAIRUs are different in table 1.2 than in table 1.4 (because the variables have different means), the *changes* in the TV-NAIRUs are almost the same.[5] For example, on the basis of the total unemployment rate in the price equation in column 1 of table 1.2, the TV-NAIRU is estimated to decline by 1.60 percentage points from 1992 to 2000; on the basis of the labor-share specification in table 1.4, this decline is estimated to be 1.52 percentage points. The quantitative declines in the TV-NAIRUs are the same for the other activity variables in the two tables.

A key similarity between the price results in table 1.2 and the wage results in table 1.4 is that the intercept drift is negligible in both tables. Although the me-

TABLE 1.4 / Phillips Curve Estimates from Macroeconomic Data: Wage Inflation Equation

$$\omega_{t+1} - \theta_t^* - \pi_t = \beta_\omega(u_t - u_t^N) + \alpha_\omega\pi(L)\Delta\pi_t + \alpha_{\omega\omega}(L)(\omega_t - \theta_{t-1}^* - \pi_{t-1}) + \alpha_{\omega u}(L)\Delta u_t + v_{\omega t+1}$$

	Civilian Unemployment Rate	Demographically Adjusted Unemployment Rate	Capacity Utilization	Building Permits
Phillips Curve	−.42	−.39	.11	2.00
Slope (SE)	(.19)	(.18)	(.05)	(.78)
[stability *p*-value]	[.10]	[.10]	[.29]	[.99]
Trend values				
1970	4.33	4.39	85.51	7.27
1980	7.79	7.55	78.74	7.23
1990	6.40	6.66	80.84	7.18
2000	4.48	4.83	81.02	7.31
Change 1992 to 2000	−1.60	−1.59	−.57	.17
NAI trend values				
1970	3.75	3.72	88.61	7.40
	(.46)	(.49)	(1.37)	(.10)
1980	6.98	6.67	81.92	7.41
	(.43)	(.46)	(1.34)	(.09)
1990	5.39	5.58	84.09	7.40
	(.46)	(.49)	(1.37)	(.10)
2000	3.54	3.80	84.26	7.52
	(.58)	(.61)	(1.43)	(.12)
Change 1992 to 2000	−1.52	−1.52	−.59	.16
	(.43)	(.43)	(.45)	(.09)
SER	1.81	1.81	1.82	1.81
TVP SE (90 percent CI)	.034	.031	.009	.034
	(.000 to .186)	(.000 to .182)	(.000 to .150)	(.000 to .187)

Notes: The equation was estimated using four lags of $\Delta\pi_t$, four lags of $(\omega_t - \theta_{t-1}^* - \pi_{t-1})$, and two lags of Δu_t. For a description of the table entries, see the note to table 1.1.

dian-unbiased estimate is larger in table 1.4 than in table 1.2, the dependent variable in table 1.4 is more variable, and the standard error of the wage regressions is twice that of the price regressions, so the relative variability in the intercept is virtually identical in the price and wage specifications. In all specifications in table 1.4, the 90 percent confidence interval for the standard deviation of the change in the intercept includes 0; that is, the hypothesis of no parameter drift cannot be rejected in any of these specifications at the 5 percent significance level.

Figure 1.6 plots the estimated TV-NAIRU for unemployment on the basis of the specification in column 1 of table 1.4, where the TV-NAIRU is adjusted so

FIGURE 1.6 / The NAIRU from the Wage Phillips Curve

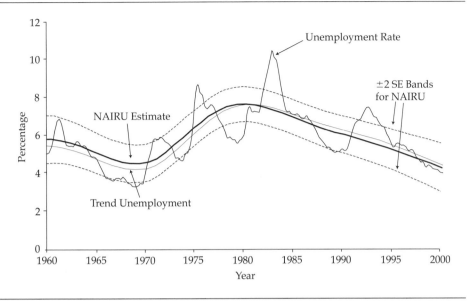

Sources: Bureau of Labor Statistics and authors' calculations.

that it has the same sample mean as the univariate trend in the unemployment rate (see note 5). Inspection of this figure underscores that there is effectively no difference between the TV-NAIRU and the univariate trend in unemployment. This is the same conclusion as was drawn from the price TV-NAIRU plotted in figure 1.4. Comparison of figures 1.4 and 1.6 reveals that the TV-NAIRUs estimated from the price Phillips curve in column 1 of table 1.2 and the wage Phillips curve in column 1 of table 1.4 (shifted per note 5) are essentially identical. The reason for this is that, in both specifications, the median-unbiased estimate indicates negligible intercept drift.

Table 1.4 indicates that there is little evidence of changes in the slope of the wage Phillips curve. The *p*-values for the test of the null hypothesis of no change in the slope range from 0.10 to 0.99. Figure 1.7 shows the estimated values of the time-varying slope in the unemployment-rate wage Phillips curve using a specification that parallels the results for the price Phillips curve shown in figure 1.5. The point estimates suggest a slight steepening of the wage Phillips curve over the past decade (consistent with the scatterplot in figure 1.2), but the standard-error bands make it clear that these changes are far from statistically significant.

Sensitivity Analysis

Table 1.5 summarizes results for forty-eight variations of the wage Phillips curve. Some of these variations are similar to the sensitivity checks reported in

FIGURE 1.7 / Slope from the Baseline Wage Phillips Curve

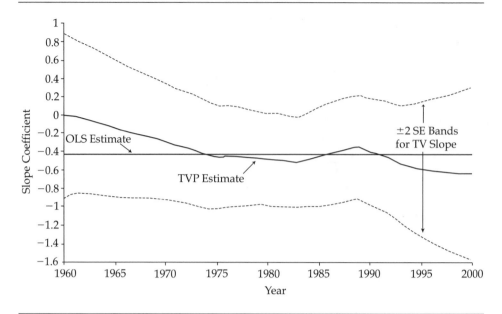

Source: Authors' calculations.

Notes: TV = time varying; TVP = time varying parameter.

table 1.3, for example, changing the definition of the wage series, changing the number of lags, and so on. Inspection of table 1.5 reveals that the main conclusions to be drawn from table 1.4, particularly the lack of intercept and slope drift in the gap specifications, are robust to these changes. However, there are some important differences among these specifications.

Most notably, these wage specifications are less stable than the price specifications are to changes in definitions of the variables. For example, the slope coefficient is often insignificant in specifications in which the GDP deflator is replaced by the PCE deflator or the CPI as well as in specifications in which wage growth is measured using the ECI (total compensation or wages and salaries only) or average hourly earnings. (The sample period for the specifications using the ECI data was limited to 1982 to 1999.) The results using compensation per hour are, however, consistent with the benchmark results. Overall, however, these results suggest that the estimated Phillips curve using trend unit labor costs is rather delicate.

An important result to be seen in table 1.5 is that replacing trend productivity growth with its sample average growth rate results in coefficients on the activity variable that are essentially unchanged but induces intercept drift that is both economically large and, now, statistically significant. In contrast to the bench-

(Text continues on p. 36.)

TABLE 1.5 / Alternative Phillips Curve Estimates from Macroeconomic Data: Wage Inflation Equation

$$\omega_{t+1} - \theta^*_t - \pi_t = \beta_\omega (u_t - u^N_t) + \alpha_{\omega\pi}(L)\Delta\pi_t + \alpha_{\omega\theta}(L)(\omega_t - \theta^*_{t-1} - \pi_{t-1}) + \alpha_{\omega u}(L)\Delta u_t + \nu_{\omega t+1}$$

Wage	Price	Activity	Nw	Na	Np	Pr	PC Slope	SER	TVPSE	Δ NAITV: Median UB	Δ Intercept: Median UB	Δ NAITV: 5 percent	Δ Intercept: 5 percent
A. Baseline specification (table 1.3)													
Comp./hr	GDP Def.	Civ. unemp.	4	2	4	2	−.42 (.19) [.10]	1.81	.034	−1.52 (.43)	.03 (.18)	−1.49 (.50)	.05 (.21)
Comp./hr	GDP Def.	Dem adj. UR	4	2	4	2	−.39 (.18) [.10]	1.81	.031	−1.52 (.43)	.03 (.17)	−1.47 (.54)	.05 (.21)
Comp./hr	GDP Def.	Cap. util.	4	2	4	2	.11 (.05) [.29]	1.82	.009	−.59 (.45)	.00 (.05)	−1.18 (1.93)	.07 (.21)
Comp./hr	GDP Def.	Bldg. perm.	4	2	4	2	2.01 (.78) [.99]	1.81	.034	.16 (.09)	.03 (.19)	.15 (.10)	.04 (.21)
B. Alternative productivity trends													
Comp./hr	GDP Def.	Civ. unemp.	4	2	4	1	−.42 (.19) [.14]	1.86	.102*	−.76 (1.10)	.35 (.47)	−1.42 (.50)	.07 (.21)
Comp./hr	GDP Def.	Dem adj. UR	4	2	4	1	−.38 (.19) [.13]	1.86	.101*	−.67 (1.22)	.35 (.46)	−1.40 (.55)	.07 (.21)
Comp./hr	GDP Def.	Cap. util.	4	2	4	1	.12 (.05) [.56]	1.87	.090*	−3.73 (3.59)	.37 (.42)	−1.36 (1.79)	.09 (.21)
Comp./hr	GDP Def.	Bldg. perm.	4	2	4	1	1.79 (.81) [.84]	1.87	.076	.04 (.21)	.23 (.37)	.13 (.12)	.07 (.21)
Comp./hr	GDP Def.	Civ. unemp.	4	2	4	3	−.40 (.19) [.33]	1.80	.056	−1.57 (.73)	.01 (.29)	−1.61 (.53)	−.00 (.21)

(Table continues on p. 32.)

TABLE 1.5 / *Continued*

Wage	Price	Activity	Nw	Na	Np	Pr	PC Slope	SER	TVPSE	Δ NAITV: Median UB	Δ Intercept: Median UB	Δ NAITV: 5 percent	Δ Intercept: 5 percent
Comp./hr	GDP Def.	Dem adj. UR	4	2	4	3	−.36 (.18) [.32]	1.80	.056	−1.56 (.79)	.01 (.29)	−1.60 (.58)	−.00 (.21)
Comp./hr	GDP Def.	Cap. util.	4	2	4	3	.11 (.05) [.21]	1.81	.046	−.81 (2.21)	.03 (.24)	−.72 (1.94)	.02 (.21)
Comp./hr	GDP Def.	Bldg. perm.	4	2	4	3	1.84 (.78) [.75]	1.81	.058	.17 (.16)	−.00 (.30)	.18 (.11)	−.01 (.21)
C. Alternative price indices													
Comp./hr	NFB Def.	Civ. unemp.	4	2	4	2	−.36 (.19) [.24]	1.87	.025	−1.58 (.38)	.01 (.14)	−1.52 (.59)	.03 (.21)
Comp./hr	NFB Def.	Dem adj. UR	4	2	4	2	−.32 (.18) [.24]	1.87	.015	−1.58 (.27)	.00 (.09)	−1.50 (.66)	.03 (.21)
Comp./hr	NFB Def.	Cap. util	4	2	4	2	.11 (.05) [.43]	1.88	.000	−.57 (.00)	.00 (.00)	−1.08 (2.00)	.05 (.21)
Comp./hr	NFB Def.	Bldg. perm.	4	2	4	2	2.94 (.84) [.78]	1.84	.017	.17 (.03)	.00 (.09)	.17 (.07)	.02 (.21)
Comp./hr	PCE Def.	Civ. unemp.	4	2	4	2	−.29 (.19) [.10]	1.84	.088*	−.78 (1.42)	.24 (.42)	−1.43 (.72)	.05 (.21)
Comp./hr	PCE Def.	Dem adj. UR	4	2	4	2	−.26 (.18) [.10]	1.84	.086	−.71 (1.56)	.23 (.41)	−1.40 (.81)	.05 (.21)
Comp./hr	PCE Def.	Cap. util.	4	2	4	2	.08 (.05) [.50]	1.84	.074	−3.61 (4.72)	.23 (.36)	−1.45 (2.73)	.07 (.21)

Wage	Deflator	Unemployment	Lags										
Comp./hr	PCE Def.	Bldg. perm.	4	2	4	2	1.73 (.83) [.89]	1.83	.087	.05 (.24)	.22 (.41)	.15 (.12)	.05 (.21)
Comp./hr	CPI	Civ. unemp.	4	2	4	2	−.17 (.20) [.13]	1.85	.098*	−.86 (2.59)	.13 (.45)	−1.53 (1.21)	.01 (.21)
Comp./hr	CPI	Dem adj. UR	4	2	4	2	−.15 (.19) [.12]	1.85	.095*	−.78 (2.97)	.12 (.44)	−1.51 (1.41)	.01 (.21)
Comp./hr	CPI	Cap. util.	4	2	4	2	.06 (.06) [.71]	1.86	.085	−3.27 (6.83)	.16 (.41)	−1.09 (3.54)	.03 (.21)
Comp./hr	CPI	Bldg. perm.	4	2	4	2	2.04 (.87) [.78]	1.83	.109*	.13 (.24)	.08 (.49)	.17 (.10)	−.00 (.21)
D. Alternative wage indices													
AHE PW	GDP Def.	Civ. unemp.	4	2	4	5	−.15 (.12) [.55]	1.12	.077*	−1.33 (2.18)	.04 (.33)	−1.46 (1.32)	.02 (.20)
AHE PW	GDP Def.	Dem adj. UR	4	2	4	5	−.14 (.12) [.48]	1.13	.077*	−1.29 (2.31)	.04 (.33)	−1.44 (1.39)	.02 (.20)
AHE PW	GDP Def.	Cap. util.	4	2	4	5	.04 (.03) [.35]	1.11	.061*	−1.89 (6.85)	.05 (.28)	−1.33 (4.86)	.03 (.20)
AHE PW	GDP Def.	Bldg. perm.	4	2	4	5	1.08 (.55) [.70]	1.11	.086*	.17 (.33)	.00 (.35)	.17 (.18)	.00 (.20)
Comp./hr man.	GDP Def.	Civ. unemp.	4	2	4	5	−.50 (.21) [.45]	2.01	.141*	−1.69 (1.20)	−.05 (.60)	−1.71 (.43)	−.05 (.21)
Comp./hr man.	GDP Def.	Dem adj. UR	4	2	4	5	−.47 (.21) [.45]	2.02	.140*	−1.69 (1.27)	−.05 (.60)	−1.70 (.45)	−.05 (.21)

(Table continues on p. 34.)

TABLE 1.5 / Continued

Wage	Price	Activity	Nw	Na	Np	Pr	PC Slope	SER	TVPSE	Δ NAITV: Median UB	Δ Intercept: Median UB	Δ NAITV: 5 percent	Δ Intercept: 5 percent
Comp./hr man.	GDP Def.	Cap. util.	4	2	4	5	.13 (.06) [.44]	2.04	.137*	-1.19 (4.57)	.08 (.59)	-.29 (1.65)	-.04 (.21)
Comp./hr man.	GDP Def.	Bldg. perm.	4	2	4	5	.98 (.92) [.92]	2.06	.146*	.14 (.62)	.03 (.62)	.22 (.22)	-.04 (.21)
ECC-C	GDP Def.	Civ. unemp.	4	2	4	2	-.14 (.11) [.33]	.58	.000	-1.60 (.00)	.00 (.00)	-1.27 (1.22)	.05 (.17)
ECC-C	GDP Def.	Dem adj. UR	4	2	4	2	-.12 (.10) [.37]	.58	.000	-1.59 (.00)	.00 (.00)	-1.24 (1.37)	.04 (.17)
ECC-C	GDP Def.	Cap. util.	4	2	4	2	.03 (.04) [.01]	.59	.000	-.57 (.00)	.00 (.00)	-4.38 (6.30)	.10 (.17)
ECC-C	GDP Def.	Bldg. perm.	4	2	4	2	.99 (.55) [.66]	.58	.000	.17 (.00)	.00 (.00)	.14 (.17)	.04 (.17)
ECC-WS	GDP Def.	Civ. unemp.	4	2	4	2	-.06 (.12) [.10]	.76	.106*	5.16 (5.83)	.39 (.34)	1.52 (3.17)	.18 (.18)
ECC-WS	GDP Def.	Dem adj. UR	4	2	4	2	-.07 (.12) [.15]	.76	.104*	4.35 (5.06)	.39 (.33)	1.18 (2.78)	.18 (.18)
ECC-WS	GDP Def.	Cap. util.	4	2	4	2	.03 (.05) [.82]	.77	.088*	-10.64 (9.08)	.34 (.31)	-5.62 (5.43)	.17 (.18)
ECC-WS	GDP Def.	Bldg. perm.	4	2	4	2	2.02 (.72) [.10]	.73	.130*	-.06 (.18)	.47 (.36)	.06 (.09)	.22 (.18)

E. Increasing lag length

Comp./hr	GDP Def.	Civ. unemp.	8	4	8	2	−.49 (.25) [.05]	1.79	.055	−1.37 (.57)	.11 (.28)	−1.48 (.43)	.06 (.21)
Comp./hr	GDP Def.	Dem adj. UR	8	4	8	2	−.45 (.24) [.06]	1.81	.053	−1.35 (.62)	.10 (.28)	−1.46 (.47)	.06 (.21)
Comp./hr	GDP Def.	Cap. util.	8	4	8	2	.12 (.07) [.33]	1.81	.029	−.91 (1.29)	.04 (.16)	−1.19 (1.70)	.08 (.21)
Comp./hr	GDP Def.	Bldg. perm.	8	4	8	2	2.47 (.92) [.79]	1.82	.027	.16 (.06)	.02 (.15)	.15 (.09)	.05 (.21)

F. Eliminating lags of price inflation

Comp./hr	GDP Def.	Civ. unemp.	4	2	0	2	−.12 (.17) [.01]	1.93	.000	−1.60 (.00)	.00 (.00)	−1.16 (1.72)	.05 (.21)
Comp./hr	GDP Def.	Dem adj. UR	4	2	0	2	−.09 (.17) [.01]	1.93	.000	−1.59 (.00)	.00 (.00)	−.97 (2.46)	.05 (.21)
Comp./hr	GDP Def.	Cap. util.	4	2	0	2	.01 (.05) [.22]	1.93	.000	−.57 (.00)	.00 (.00)	−6.79 (23.06)	.06 (.21)
Comp./hr	GDP Def.	Bldg. perm.	4	2	0	2	1.07 (.78) [.85]	1.91	.000	.17 (.00)	.00 (.00)	.13 (.20)	.04 (.21)

Notes: This table contains alternative estimates of the wage Phillips curve (PC) equation and the TV-NAIRU. The stub column shows the wage series used to construct ω, the next column shows the price series used to construct π, and the second column shows the activity variable used for *u*. The next columns show a set of parameters that described the specification: Nw = number of lags of real wages; Np = number of lags of inflation; Na = number of lags of activity variable; Pr = trend estimate of productivity growth (1 = average value of nonfarm-business productivity growth, 1960 to 2000; 2 = low-pass filter of nonfarm-business productivity growth using I[0] AR extrapolation; 3 = low-pass filter of nonfarm-business productivity growth using I[1] AR extrapolation; 5 = low-pass filter of manufacturing productivity growth using I[0] AR extrapolation). The remaining columns are described in the notes to table 1.2. The sample period is 1960:1 to 2000:1 for all estimated equations except those including ECC-C and ECC-WS, which used the sample period 1982:1 to 2000:1. For descriptions of AHE PW, ECC-C, and ECC-WS, see the appendix. NFB = nonfarm business; PCE = personal consumption expenditure.

mark estimate, in which the unemployment-rate TV-NAIRU is estimated to have fallen by 1.52 percentage points from 1992 to 2000, the specification using average productivity growth shows a decline of only 0.76 percentage points in the estimated TV-NAIRU. Said differently, when the recent increase in trend productivity is excluded from the specification, the intercept in the Phillips curve adjusts to track the increase in real wages. The amount of the required adjustment is large: the change in the intercept implies an increase in the long-run mean change in the growth rate of wages of 0.84 percentage points.

Summary of Main Findings

These regressions point to a stable Phillips relation between trend unit labor costs and the various activity measures over this period, although the macro wage specifications are more delicate than are the macro price specifications examined in the third section. When the slope coefficient is precisely estimated, these specifications produce estimates of the 1992 to 2000 change in the TV-NAIRU that are strikingly similar to those produced by the price Phillips curves. In contrast, if the dependent variable is future wage inflation less current price inflation and the role of productivity growth is therefore ignored, then the behavior of the wage and price regressions is inconsistent, with real-wage inflation appearing in the second half of the 1990s. Specifications of the wage Phillips curve that ignore productivity growth appear unstable in the 1990s, while those that incorporate productivity growth are stable.

SPECIFICATION AND ESTIMATION OF STATE WAGE PHILLIPS CURVES

Specification of State-Level Wage Phillips Curves

The state regression specifications have the same basic form as the macro regressions, but data limitations lead to several modifications. For example, because the state data are annual, the timing conventions of the quarterly and annual specifications differ. Temporal aggregation—averaging both sides of equation 1.4 over the four quarters in the year—results in a relation between time series with dates that overlap by three quarters. We approximate this by using as the dependent variable $\omega_{t+1} - \theta_{t+1} - \pi_{t+1}$ (robustness to different timing conventions is investigated in the seventh section). Also, we use the unemployment rate as the activity variable in all the state Phillips curves.

These considerations lead to the state-level variant of equation 1.4,

$$\omega_{it+1} - \theta_{it+1} - \pi_{t+1} = \beta(u_{it} - u_{it}^N) + \zeta_t + v_{it+1}, \tag{1.14}$$

where ω_{it+1} is the percentage growth in the nominal wage in state i from year t to year $t + 1$, θ_{it+1} is the annual percentage growth in labor productivity, u_{it} is the unemployment rate, u_{it}^N is the NAIRU for state i in year t (that is, the state TV-NAIRU), ζ_t are macro shocks (the sum of $\gamma_\omega Z_t$ and v_{t+1} in equation 1.4), and v_{it} is an error term that has mean 0 and that is uncorrelated with the macro shocks ζ_t. The subscript t runs over all the years in the sample, which differ slightly across specifications depending on data availability. As is discussed in the next section, in our data set, state nominal-wage growth ω_{it+1} and the unemployment rate u_{it} are computed from the Current Population Survey (CPS). State productivity θ_{it} is constructed in two different ways: either as the annual percentage growth of gross state product, less the growth of state employment, or from national industry-level productivity data weighted by the output share of each industry in the state.

The state TV-NAIRU can usefully be thought of as consisting of several components: the national TV-NAIRU (u_t^N); features that are unique to each state and constant over the sample, such as climate (ϕ_i); and institutional considerations that affect search and matching in the labor market, some of which are measured (X_{it}) and some of which are not (ε_{it}). That is, the state TV-NAIRU can be expressed as,

$$u_{it}^N = u_t^N + \phi_i + \gamma X_{it} + \varepsilon_{it}. \tag{1.15}$$

Substituting equation 1.15 into 1.14 and rearranging yields our base state-regression specification:

$$\omega_{it+1} - \theta_{it+1} - \pi_{t+1} = \alpha_i + \delta_t + \beta u_{it} + \gamma X_{it} + v_{it+1}, \tag{1.16}$$

where $\alpha_i = -\beta\phi_i$ are state effects, and $\delta_t = \zeta_t - \beta u_t^N$ are time effects.

It is worth making three remarks about the specification equation 1.16. First, unlike the macro regressions, this benchmark specification for the state panel regressions does not include lags of either the unemployment rate or the labor share. The reason for this is practical: with only twenty annual observations, it is unlikely that we will estimate lag dynamics with any precision, and, in any event, the lag dynamics will be less pronounced at the annual level than at the quarterly level used in the macro data. In sensitivity checks, however, we report the results of specifications that include lags.

Second, as we have already discussed, there is some debate over whether the correct specification of this model should include a lagged wage level on the right-hand side—that is, should the model be specified in terms of wage levels (the "wage curve") or real-wage growth less productivity (the Phillips curve)? Specifications using wage growth have the implication that states' productivity-adjusted real wages can drift arbitrarily far apart over long periods, and this is implausible since capital and labor can flow across state boundaries. However, the empirical evidence suggests that capital and labor migrate slowly enough that the Phillips curve specification fits that data better than wage-curve specifications with substantial mean reversion (see Blanchard and Katz 1992, 1997; Card and Hyslop 1997; and Autor and Staiger 2001). This leads us to use the Phillips curve as our benchmark specification, although, in our sensitivity analysis, we consider specifications that include the levels of productivity-adjusted real wages.

Third, π_t is not indexed by state in equation 1.16. This is because data on prices by state are not available; thus, the deflation process uses the national price level (the Consumer Price Index for All Urban Consumers [CPI-U]). Because equation 1.16 includes year effects, the estimates of the slope coefficients β and γ are invariant to which inflation variable is used (the CPI, the GDP deflator, and so on), whether the inflation variable used is dated $t + 1$ or t, or, indeed, whether the dependent variable is deflated at all (that is, is $\omega_{it+1} - \theta_{it+1}$). The deflator is used only to identify the time effects $\{\delta_t\}$ and, thereby, to identify the macro TV-NAIRU from this state specification.

Estimation of a National TV-NAIRU from the State Regressions

Estimates of the annual national TV-NAIRU can be obtained from the year effects in the state regressions. The year fixed effects contain movements in the national TV-NAIRU, macro shocks, and estimation error. Thus, these year fixed effects must be filtered to obtain estimates of the national TV-NAIRU.

The filtering strategy used here parallels that used in the macro analysis. That is, the filter is applied so that it estimates the difference between the TV-NAIRU and the univariate trend in unemployment; this univariate trend is then added back in to obtain an estimate of the national TV-NAIRU. Specifically, as noted following equation 1.16, $\delta_t = \zeta_t - \beta u_t^N$. To maintain consistency with the treatment of the NAIRU in the macro regressions, rewrite this as $\delta_t + \beta u_t^* = \zeta_t - \beta(u_t^N - u_t^*)$, where u_t^* is the univariate trend in unemployment. Thus,

$$\delta_t + \beta u_t^* = \mu_t + \zeta_{t}, \tag{1.17}$$

where $\mu_t = -\beta(u_t^N - u_t^*)$.

Equation 1.17 has the same form as equation 1.9, in the sense that the intercept drift term μ_t arises from the difference between the NAIRU and the univariate trend in unemployment, except that equation 1.17 has no regressors (the observable and unobservable macro shocks are combined and contained in ζ_t). Accordingly, the national TV-NAIRU is estimated as $u_{t|T}^N = u_t^* + \mu_{t|T}/\hat{\beta}$ (see equation 1.12), where $\hat{\beta}$ is the estimate of β from the state regressions, $\mu_{t|T}$ is the Kalman smoother estimate of μ_t, and μ_t is modeled as following a random walk (as in equation 1.10), ζ_t is modeled as serially uncorrelated, and the dependent variable in equation 1.17 is $\hat{\delta}_t + \hat{\beta} u_t^*$, where $\hat{\delta}_t$ are the estimated time effects.

Instrumental-Variables Estimation Strategy

As is discussed in the next section, the state data on unemployment are obtained from the merged outgoing rotation groups (MORGs) of the CPS. Because many states have a small number of CPS respondents, these estimates are quite noisy, which leads to errors-in-variables bias. To avoid this bias, we use an IV approach. The MORG sample can be split into two independent samples, depending on whether the month is odd or even (although households appear twice in the MORG, the odd and even months have no households in common). Estimates from both the odd- and the even-month samples will be measured with error, but, because the samples are randomly drawn, the estimation error is independent in these two samples. Thus, one set of estimates can be used as an instrument for the other set of estimates. In particular, we use unemployment rates estimated from the even months as an instrument for unemployment rates estimated in the odd months, and vice versa. In some of our specifications (for example, those with lags of the dependent variable), the measurement error will be correlated between the independent and the dependent variables as well. Therefore, we replace all variables in the equation (both dependent and independent) with estimates from odd months and instrument with corresponding estimates from even months.[6]

Weighting the Observations

There is some ambiguity about whether the state regressions are best estimated by weighting the observations. The sampling error in the dependent variable will be smaller for larger states, but it is only one component of the error term, so the actual form of heteroskedasticity is unknown. Simple IV (two-stage least squares) has the virtue of taking no stand on the form of this heteroskedasticity and treats each state as an independent, equally useful experiment. On the other hand, weighting the observations can provide an approximate adjustment for this heteroskedasticity and, if implemented using employment weights, also produces estimates more directly related to aggregate coefficients; in particular, the aggregate NAIRU estimates constructed from the state data will reflect population weights. Because of this ambiguity, we report results using both weighted and unweighted observations, where the weights are given the values of state employment.

THE STATE DATA SET

Our state-level analysis relies on a data set containing annual observations on each of forty-eight states (excluding Alaska and Hawaii as well as the District of

Columbia) from 1979 to 1999. The annual data on each state were derived from a variety of sources, described in this section.

Data Derived from the Current Population Survey

We derive most of our variables, including annual estimates of wages, unemployment, and labor-force characteristics for each state, from the CPS MORGs. The MORG data are available from 1979 through 1999. Each month, one-quarter of the CPS sample (the outgoing rotation groups) is asked a variety of labor-force questions, for a total sample of over 300,000 individuals each year. For each individual who reports being in the labor force, the survey provides labor-force status (unemployed or not in the reference week), gender, race (white, black, other), marital status (married or not), and age. Education is reported in each year, but, because the format of the question changed in 1992, we have recoded the education variable into a set of ten consistent categories. Most recent industry of employment is reported by all individuals who have worked in the last five years, and we collapsed this information into eleven major industries.

For individuals who are currently working, we calculated hourly wage as usual weekly earnings divided by usual weekly hours. Earnings at the top code were multiplied by 1.5, and wages below the 1st percentile were set equal to the wage at the 1st percentile. We also calculated whether these persons were self-employed, were union members or covered by a union contract (available only since 1983), or worked as temporary help. To be considered a temporary-help worker, one had to report working in the personnel-supply-services industry and being paid by the hour. This definition is the same as that used by David Autor (forthcoming) and Lewis Segal and Daniel Sullivan (1997), but it is believed that at least 50 percent of temporary workers misreport their industry in the CPS. Finally, we calculated potential experience as age minus years of education minus 6, where, after 1991, years of education were imputed on the basis of the respondent's reported education category, race, and gender.

Using the individual-level data from the MORGs for all individuals who were in the labor force, we constructed state-level estimates for each year that were based on three samples: the full MORG sample, the respondents from even-numbered months, and the respondents from odd-numbered months. Households that appear in the MORG sample in even-numbered months do not appear in the odd-numbered months, so, as already noted, the estimation error in these two samples will be independent. In each sample, we constructed weighted estimates for each state and year (using weights provided by the CPS) of the unemployment rate and the fraction of the labor force in each age, education, race, and gender category. In addition, for employed individuals, we calculated the fraction of the workforce in each major industry, working in the temporary-help industry, self-employed, and covered by a union contract (or a union member). Finally, we calculated average and median log hourly wages for all workers, for hourly workers, and for full-time workers.

To construct state-level estimates of wages and unemployment that adjusted for changes over time in characteristics of the workforce, we estimated separate cross-sectional regressions for each year. In particular, for each year, we estimated a regression of either unemployment status or the log hourly wage on state fixed effects and controlled for ten education categories, three race categories, a quartic in experience, and an interaction between gender and all other regressors. In addition, controls for eleven major industries were included in the wage equation (but not in the unemployment equation). On the basis of this regression, each state's adjusted mean wage was predicted using that state's intercept and the average value of the covariates in the United States over the period 1979 to 1998 (calculated from the MORG sample).

Supplemental State-Level Data

In addition to the MORG data, we use a variety of labor-market measures that are available by state and year over most of our time period.[7] Data for each state on the unemployment-insurance replacement ratio are available through 1998 from the Information Technology Support Center unemployment-insurance website *(www.itsc.state.md.us)*. Data on the minimum wage have been derived from various issues of the *Monthly Labor Relations Review.* Data on the proportion of employment in the temporary-services sector come from county business patterns (these data are available only through 1996, so our specifications use them with a one-year lag to avoid losing observations). Finally, the proportion of the population age twenty-five to sixty-four on disability insurance and supplemental security income has been estimated from administrative data and provided to us by David Autor and Mark Duggan.

The Bureau of Economic Analysis website *(www.bea.doc)* was used to obtain data (available by state and major industry from 1978 to 1998) on gross state product (GSP) and total full-time and part-time employment (from table SA25), from which estimates of labor-productivity growth were derived. For each state, we constructed estimates of labor-productivity growth in two ways. Our primary method uses state-level estimates of GSP and employment and calculates labor-productivity growth in each year as $100[\ln(\text{GSP}_t/\text{GSP}_{t-1}) - \ln(\text{employment}_t/\text{employment}_{t-1})]$. Our secondary method is to estimate productivity growth in each state as a weighted average of the national-level estimates of labor-productivity growth in eleven major industries. National-level estimates of labor-productivity growth in each industry were derived from national estimates of GSP and employment as previously outlined. Each industry's productivity growth was weighted by the employment share in that industry (as estimated from the MORG data) in a given state and year to derive state-level estimates of labor-productivity growth.

EMPIRICAL STATE WAGE PHILLIPS CURVES

Benchmark Estimated Phillips Curves

Benchmark wage Phillips curve regressions of the form 1.16 are reported in table 1.6. These benchmark regressions do not include any structural variables (X_{it}) that might explain the movements in the NAIRU; these variables will be added in the eighth section.

Four features of table 1.6 are noteworthy. First, including state effects substantially changes the value of the coefficient on the unemployment rate. Although the state effects are usually jointly insignificant at the 5 percent level in these and subsequent regressions, excluding them evidently introduces omitted-variables bias into the estimated slope, so, henceforth, the state effects will be retained.

Second, using IV estimation to mitigate errors-in-variables bias leads to coefficients on the unemployment rate that are approximately one-third larger than the OLS estimates. This is consistent with the implication of the standard measurement-error model that the OLS estimator is biased toward 0. An important issue in IV regression is whether the instruments are correlated with the variable that they are instrumenting, that is, whether they are "weak." When there is a single variable being instrumented, this can be checked by seeing whether the F-statistic on the instruments in the first-stage regression is at least 10 (Staiger and Stock 1997). For the regressions in table 1.6, this first-stage F-statistic is always at least 100, which gives us confidence in applying standard asymptotic distribution theory to these IV regressions.

Third, the time effects are jointly significant in all specifications.

Fourth, the estimated slope of the state Phillips curve is large and statistically significant. In our preferred specification (IV with state and time effects), the estimated slope is -0.59, with a standard error of 0.11. This estimate is twice what we obtained using the quarterly macro data (-0.28 in column 1 of table 1.2), although it is comparable to the macro estimates in Gordon (1998). Because the state regressions control for both time and state effects, these results suggest

TABLE 1.6 / Phillips Curve Estimates from State Data

$$\omega_{it+1} - \theta_{it+1} - \pi_{t+1} = \alpha_i + \delta_t + \beta u_{it} + v_{it+1}$$

	OLS		IV	
Phillips curve slope (SE)	−.165	−.409	−.208	−.586
	(.045)	(.070)	(.061)	(.113)
Year effects p-value	.00	.00	.00	.00
State effects p-value	Excluded	.81	Excluded	.94
R^2	.26	.29	N.A.	N.A.

Notes: $N = 912$ (1979 to 1997). IV estimates use even months of MORG data as the instrument for odd months. N.A. = not applicable.

that idiosyncratic movements in a state's unemployment rate portend large idiosyncratic changes in the rate of growth of real wages.

Sensitivity Analysis

Tables 1.7 and 1.8 summarize results from several modifications to the benchmark specification. Table 1.7 shows results from changes in the estimation procedure (weighting the observations and alternative IV estimators), changes in the wage and unemployment variables (adjustments for changing demographics, industry mix, and so on), changes in the measurement and treatment of productivity, and changes in the assumed timing of the variables. Table 1.8 summarizes results from specifications with more general dynamics. We discuss each of these in turn.

The first two rows of table 1.7 consider different estimators. The benchmark specification (IV with time and state effects, shown in the last column of table 1.6 and repeated at the top of table 1.7) used unweighted observations, with observations for even months of the MORG sample used as instruments for observations corresponding to odd months. Specification 1 in table 1.7 reverses this and uses odd months as instruments for the even months. Specification 2 weights the state obervations by state employment. In both specifications, there is little change from the benchmark model.

Specifications 3 to 9 use different measures of wages and the unemployment rate. Specifications 3 to 6 use adjusted wage and employment data. The adjusted measures were computed by controlling for education, experience, race, gender, and industry (depending on the variable and the specification), as detailed in the table notes, using the adjustment method described in the sixth section. The benchmark specification uses the sample average wages of all workers (as described in the sixth section), and specifications 7 to 9 consider alternative wage series (median wage of all workers, mean wage of full-time workers, mean wage of hourly employees). The slope coefficient on the unemployment rate is essentially unaffected by these modifications to the benchmark specification.

Specifications 10 to 12 modify the way in which productivity enters the model. Specification 10 omits productivity from the analysis, with the result that the dependent variable in the regression is the log of real-wage growth. Specification 11 adds productivity as a regressor, relaxing the constraint of a unit elasticity implicit in the benchmark model. Both these changes to the benchmark specification lead to slightly larger estimates of the slope coefficient. The estimated productivity elasticity from specification 11 (not shown) is small (0.17, with a standard error of 0.13). There are several possible explanations for this. This result is consistent with substantial measurement error in the state productivity data. Additionally, even state productivity, precisely measured, contains short-term fluctuations, and, if it is trend productivity rather than annual productivity that is reflected in wages (as we have assumed in the macro specifications), then these estimates would be further biased toward 0. Finally, it might

TABLE 1.7 / Alternative Phillips Curve Estimates

$$\omega_{it+1} - \theta_{it+1} - \pi_{t+1} = \alpha_i + \delta_t + \beta u_{it} + v_{it+1}$$

Deviation of Specification from Benchmark	PC Slope (SE)
(0) None	−.586
	(.113)
(1) Odd month IV for even months	−.447
	(.113)
(2) Weighting by size of state workforce	−.542
	(.089)
(3) Adjusted Wages[2] and Unemployment Rate[1]	−.506
	(.097)
(4) Adjusted Unemployment Rate[1]	−.535
	(.111)
(5) Adjusted Unemployment Rate[2]	−.534
	(.129)
(6) Adjusted Wages[2]	−.552
	(.098)
(7) Wages–Median/All	−.625
	(.151)
(8) Wages–Mean/Full-Time	−.526
	(.128)
(9) Wages–Mean/Hourly	−.660
	(.119)
(10) Productivity growth omitted	−.637
	(.092)
(11) Productivity growth used as a regressor	−.654
	(.094)
(12) Weighted industry productivity growth	−.718
	(.095)
(13) Productivity growth dated t	−.418
	(.114)
(14) Unemployment dated $t + 1$	−.385
	(.112)

Notes: The table shows estimates of the Phillips curve slope and the associated standard errors for alternative specifications. The stub column describes the deviation from the benchmark model (given in the last column of table 1.6 and labeled [0] in this table). Specification (1) reverses the role of instruments and regressors in the baseline specification. Specification (2) uses weighted IV, where the weights are the size of the state workforce. Specifications (3) to (6) use adjusted values for wages and/or the unemployment rate. Variables with a "1" superscript were adjusted using cross-sectional regressions each year that controlled for ten education categories, three race categories, a quartic in potential experience, and an interaction between gender and all other regressors. Variables with a "2" superscript used these regressors together with eleven major-industry indicator variables. Specifications (7) to (9) use alternative wage measures: median hourly wage for all workers; mean hourly wage for full-time workers; and mean hourly wage for workers paid on an hourly basis. Specification (10) uses the dependent variables $\omega_{it+1} - \pi_{t+1}$, (11) adds θ_{it+1} as a regressor (relaxing the unit elasticity constraint), and (12) uses a weighted industry measure of state productivity growth. Specification (13) used the dependent variable $\omega_{it+1} - \theta_{it} - \pi_{t+1}$, and specification (14) uses u_{it+1} as the regressor. (The results are invariant to the timing of π_t because of the inclusion of time effects.) The sample period was 1979 to 1998 ($N = 960$) for specification 10 and 1979 to 1997 ($N = 912$) for all other specifications.

be that productivity affects wage growth only with a lag, an explanation that we investigate subsequently.

Specification 12 uses an alternative measure of state productivity, the weighted average industry productivity growth that was described in the sixth section. This change produces a further steepening of the estimated Phillips curve.

The final two specifications in table 1.7 change the dating of productivity growth and the unemployment rate. Specification 13 replaces θ_{it+1} with θ_{it}, and specification 14 replaces u_{it} with u_{it+1}. Both changes result in a somewhat smaller estimated slope, suggesting that the timing convention in the benchmark specification is appropriate.

CHANGES IN THE DYNAMIC SPECIFICATION   Table 1.8 considers changes in the dynamic specification of the model. Panel A allows the lagged level of productivity-adjusted real wages to enter the regression, relaxing the unit root constraint implied by the Phillips curve specification. We show results for both OLS and IV, specifications that include and exclude the productivity adjustments to real wages, and specifications that include the demographic and industry-mix adjustments to wages. The OLS estimates show some evidence supporting mean reversion in real wages: the coefficients on lagged real wages range from -0.09 to -0.15 (implying AR roots of 0.85 to 0.91 for annual real wages) and appear to be statistically significant. However, measurement error in the MORG wage series implies that the OLS estimators have a negative bias. When IV is used to eliminate this bias, the estimated coefficients on lagged wages are much closer to 0 and are statistically insignificant in the specifications that include productivity adjustments. (For similar estimates, see Blanchard and Katz 1997.)

Panel B of table 1.8 summarizes results for two specifications that allow distributed lags of wage growth and the unemployment rate in the model. These changes have little effect on the estimated slope of the Phillips curve, and the additional lagged variables are jointly insignificant in the regression.

SUMMARY OF THE SENSITIVITY ANALYSIS   The benchmark specification relates annual observations of productivity-adjusted real-wage growth to unemployment rates one year earlier together with time and state effects. The estimated slope is approximately -0.6, and there are no additional dynamics. The results presented in tables 1.7 and 1.8 are broadly consistent with this specification.

National TV-NAIRUs Estimated Using the State Data

Estimates of the national TV-NAIRU derived from the estimated time effects in the benchmark model are plotted in figure 1.8. Also shown are results from the specification that omits productivity and uses the real wage instead of unit labor cost as the dependent variables (specification 10 in table 1.7). These estimates were computed by the method described in the fifth section. The figure also plots the national unemployment rate and its univariate trend. The means of the

TABLE 1.8 / Alternative Specification of Phillips Curve Dynamics

A. Relaxing the Unit Root Constraint on Real Wages

$$\omega_{it+1} - \theta_{it+1} - \pi_{t+1} = \alpha_i + \delta_t + \beta u_{it} + \gamma[\ln(W_{it}/P_t) - \ln(\text{productivity}_{it})] + v_{it+1}$$

Variable	OLS			IV		
Unemployment rate	−.401	−.375	−.480	−.581	−.548	−.612
	(.065)	(.062)	(.049)	(.113)	(.097)	(.089)
Real wage	−.103	−.090	−.146	−.010	−.028	−.057
	(.021)	(.022)	(.015)	(.034)	(.030)	(.026)
Productivity adjustment	Yes	Yes	No	Yes	Yes	No
Adjusted Wages²	No	Yes	No	No	Yes	No

B. Allowing Distributed Lags

$$\omega_{it+1} - \theta_{it+1} - \pi_{t+1} = \alpha_i + \delta_t + \beta u_{it} + \alpha_\omega(L)[\omega_{it} - \theta_{it} - \pi_t] + \alpha_u(L)\Delta u_t + v_{it+1}$$

Variable	Coefficient (SE)	
u_{it}	−.486	−.549
	(.131)	(.161)
$\omega_{it} - \theta_{it} - \pi_t$	.051	.031
	(.103)	(.107)
$\omega_{it-1} - \theta_{it-1} - \pi_{t-1}$		−.210
		(.094)
Δu_t	−.404	−.141
	(.345)	(.411)
Δu_{t-1}		−.020
		(.520)
p-value for $\alpha_\omega(L) = 0$	.62	.08
p-value for $\alpha_u(L) = 0$	.24	.86

Notes: For panel A, specifications with "no" productivity adjustment omit the terms θ_{it+1} from the dependent variable and $\ln(\text{productivity}_{it})$ from the regressor. For the definition of Adjusted Wages², see the notes to table 1.7. For panel B, the sample period is 1981 to 1997 ($N = 816$).

dependent variables in the two state regressions differ, so, for comparison purposes, the state estimates of the national TV-NAIRUs have been shifted so that they have the same mean as the national unemployment rate over the period 1979 to 1997.

The estimated national TV-NAIRU based on the state unit labor-cost regression is similar to the univariate trend in national unemployment and, thus, is similar to the TV-NAIRUs estimated using the macro data. In contrast, the estimated national TV-NAIRU based on the state real-wage regression falls only slightly in the 1990s. Mechanically, this arises because the real-wage regressions implicitly introduce drift in the mean productivity-growth rate into the NAIRU: the sharp increase in real wages in the late 1990s implies that the unemployment

FIGURE 1.8 / State Estimates of the TV-NAIRU

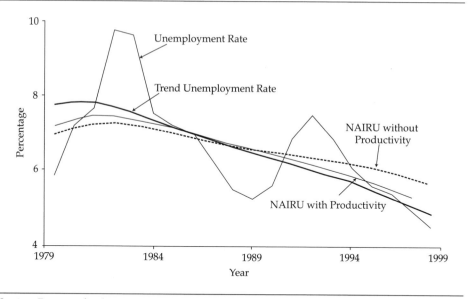

Sources: Bureau of Labor Statistics and authors' calculations.

rate must have been well below the NAIRU during this period, if one neglects increases in the growth rate of productivity. On incorporating productivity into the dependent variable in the state panel regressions, the NAIRU falls substantially. This, then, is consistent with the conclusion from the analysis of the macro data that incorporating productivity reconciles the strong real-wage growth of the 1990s with an estimate of a declining unemployment TV-NAIRU estimated in price regressions.

We conclude from these estimates that, despite substantial differences in the data sets, span, and periodicity, the state evidence and the macro evidence are mutually consistent. This sanguine conclusion must be tempered by a recognition that both state estimates of the TV-NAIRUs are quite imprecise: the Kalman smoother estimate of the standard error on the decline in the state estimate of the TV-NAIRU from 1992 to 1997 using unit labor costs is 0.7 percentage points, and this standard error ignores estimation error. This imprecision should not be too surprising because the national estimates are based on smoothing the time series of estimated time effects, which has only twenty annual observations.

STATE EVIDENCE ON STRUCTURAL SOURCES OF SHIFTS IN THE NAIRU

This section reports the results of state panel regressions that examine the stability of the Phillips curve over time and across regions and that include variables that represent possible structural factors that determine the NAIRU. Our conclusions from the state regressions are summarized at the end of this section.

Stability

The stability of the wage Phillips curves over time and across regions is investigated in table 1.9. There is no evidence that the slope of the Phillips curve has changed over time. This is shown in table 1.9 using productivity-adjusted real-wage growth; similar results, not reported in the table, were obtained using real-wage growth without a productivity adjustment. This confirms Katz and Krueger's (1999) finding (obtained using OLS) that the state Phillips curve has been stable over time.

Interestingly, there is some evidence that the coefficient on the unemployment rate differs depending on region of the country (where regions are defined to be the four census regions). The Northeast and the West are estimated to have flatter Phillips curves than other regions do. These regional interactions are marginally significant (the p-value is .07). Understanding whether there actually is regional variation in this slope, and, if so, why, is an interesting topic for future research.

TABLE 1.9 / Stability of the Phillips Curve Through Time and Space

$$\omega_{it+1} - \theta_{it+1} - \pi_{t+1} = \alpha_i + \delta_t + \beta_{it}u_{it} + v_{it+1}$$

Variable	Coefficient (SE)		
u_{it}	$-.586$	$-.623$	$-.736$
	$(.113)$	$(.142)$	$(.139)$
$u_{it} \times 1(t \leq 1984)$		$.066$	
		$(.143)$	
$u_{it} \times 1(t \geq 1992)$		$.014$	
		$(.204)$	
$u_{it} \times 1(i$ in Northeast$)$			$.509$
			$(.198)$
$u_{it} \times 1(i$ in North Central$)$			$.065$
			$(.159)$
$u_{it} \times 1(i$ in West$)$			$.214$
			$(.203)$
Temporal stability p-value		$.895$	
Spatial stability p-value			$.065$

Notes: The sample period is 1979 to 1997 ($N = 912$). The temporal stability p-value is associated with the Wald test for the hypothesis that the coefficients on u_{it} interacted with the time indicators are zero. The spatial stability p-value is associated with the Wald test for the hypothesis that the coefficients on u_{it} interacted with the region indicators are 0.

Demographics and Education

We now turn to regressions that investigate possible structural reasons that the NAIRU might change over time. The first such regressions examine the role of demographics and education, a theme recently emphasized by Robert Shimer (1998).

Table 1.10 reports the results of regressions that include, either individually or together, the percentage of high school dropouts, the percentage of college graduates, the percentage white in the work force, the percentage female in the workforce, and the percentage of the workforce between twenty-five and fifty-four years of age. These variables and the unemployment rate are measured in percentage points. The estimated coefficients are large, but so are their standard errors, and none of the demographic or education variables are statistically significant at the 5 percent level, either individually or jointly. For example, the coefficient on the percentage of high school dropouts in the second column is -0.099, which implies that a 1 percentage point increase in the fraction of high school dropouts is associated with a decrease in the NAIRU of 0.15 percentage points ($-0.099/0.642$). However, the standard error of this estimated effect is very large (0.23 percentage points), with the result that this specification produces a 95 percent confidence interval for the effect of a 1 percentage point increase in high school dropouts on the NAIRU that ranges from a decline of 0.6

TABLE 1.10 / Demographic Variables and the Phillips Curve

$$\omega_{it+1} - \theta_{it+1} - \pi_{t+1} = \alpha_i + \delta_t + \beta u_{it} + \gamma X_{it} + v_{it+1}$$

Variable	Coefficient (SE)					
Unemployment rate	$-.586$	$-.642$	$-.550$	$-.604$	$-.542$	$-.526$
	(.113)	(.147)	(.134)	(.120)	(.159)	(.320)
Percent high school		$-.099$				$-.081$
dropout		(.140)				(.189)
Percent college		.299				.577
graduate		(.345)				(.918)
Percent white			.233			.164
			(.543)			(2.000)
Percent female				$-.328$		.030
				(.621)		(1.378)
Percent age twenty-					$-.113$	$-.381$
five to fifty-four					(.285)	(.981)
Education variables		.339				.704
p-value						
All demographics						.712
p-value						

Note: The sample period is 1979 to 1997 ($N = 912$).

percentage points to an increase of 0.3 percentage points. The large standard errors reflect the fact that, once state and time effects have been removed, there is only limited within-state variation in these slowly moving demographic variables.

Robert Lerman and Stefanie Schmidt (1999) have claimed that the recent rise (and impending decline) in the share of prime-age workers and the continuing rise in the share of college-educated workers are key factors in understanding recent (and future) changes in the labor market.[8] However, the timing of these demographic shifts does not coincide well with the downturn in the estimated NAIRU since 1992. In particular, the share of the workforce with a college degree increased steadily in both the 1980s and the 1990s, which would suggest a steady decline in the NAIRU over the entire period. Similarly, the share of the workforce between the ages of twenty-five and fifty-four increased dramatically between 1979 and 1992 but has been flat or has even declined since then. Thus, neither of these factors increased at a higher rate in the 1990s, which is what would be needed to explain the sudden decline in the NAIRU after 1992. Despite the inability of these demographic shifts to explain recent changes in the NAIRU, it is worth noting that the point estimates imply that the impending decline in the share of prime-age workers over the next twenty years (as the baby boomers retire) would exert upward pressure on the NAIRU. Thus, reconciling the state-level estimates of demographic effects on the NAIRU with the macro-level evidence of changes in the NAIRU is an important topic for future research.

Industry Characteristics and Temporary Help

Table 1.11 reports results for regressions including industry characteristics and the relative size of the temporary-help industry in the state. The results suggest that increases in the share of retail trade and services are associated with increases in the NAIRU, relative to manufacturing, but these effects are not statistically significant. Similarly, the point estimates suggest that increases in temporary help and self-employment lead to declines in the NAIRU, but, again, these estimated effects are not statistically significant.[9]

Government Policies

Table 1.12 examines the effect of state labor-market policies on the NAIRU. These policies include the percent of the prime-age workforce on disability insurance and supplemental security income, the minimum wage, the growth of the minimum wage, and the unemployment insurance replacement ratio. None of the coefficients on these regressors are statistically significant at the 5 percent level in any of the specifications.

TABLE 1.11 / Industry Characteristics and the Phillips Curve

$$\omega_{it+1} - \theta_{it+1} - \pi_{t+1} = \alpha_i + \delta_t + \beta u_{it} + \gamma X_{it} + v_{it+1}$$

Variable	Coefficient (SE)					
Unemployment rate	−.586	−.823	−1.084	−.599	−.575	−.854
	(.113)	(.170)	(.397)	(.115)	(.115)	(.179)
Percent durable mfg.		.333				.196
		(.227)				(.283)
Percent nondurable mfg.		−.166				−.247
		(.303)				(.312)
Percent retail trade		.275				.161
		(.708)				(.715)
Percent services		1.045				1.113
		(.501)				(.526)
Percent temp. help (CPS)			−19.239			
			(13.567)			
Percent temp. help (CBP)				−.290		−.159
				(.324)		(.383)
Percent self-employed					−.196	−.437
					(.272)	(.487)
Major industry p-value		.153				.164
All industry variables p-value						.312

Note: The sample period is 1979 to 1997 ($N = 912$).

TABLE 1.12 / Government Policy Variables and the Phillips Curve

$$\omega_{it+1} - \theta_{it+1} - \pi_{t+1} = \alpha_i + \delta_t + \beta u_{it} + \gamma X_{it} + v_{it+1}$$

Variable	Coefficient (SE)				
Unemployment rate	−.586	−.576	−.603	−.591	−.600
	(.113)	(.120)	(.114)	(.114)	(.122)
Percent of twenty-five to sixty-four on DI		.360			.376
		(.606)			(.611)
Percent of twenty-five to sixty-four on SSI		.046			.025
		(.577)			(.578)
Minimum wage (1999 dollars)			−.414		−.354
			(.864)		(.879)
Percent growth in minimum wage			−.085		−.084
			(.049)		(.049)
UI replacement rate				.015	.017
				(.043)	(.043)
DI/SSI variables p-value		.746			.749
Min. wage variables p-value			.207		.210
All policy variables p-value					.566

Notes: The sample period is 1979 to 1997 ($N = 912$). DI = disability insurance. SSI = supplemental security income. UI = unemployment insurance.

Summary of State Results

The finding that the unemployment rate significantly enters equations for either the change in labor share or change in real-wage equations is highly robust to changes in specification, including using different lags, using different measures of wages, using demographically adjusted data, and controlling for a large number of possible structural determinants of the NAIRU. The coefficient is estimated to be approximately -0.6. This coefficient is stable over time, although there seem to be some intriguing but uninvestigated variations in this coefficient over different regions of the country.

In contrast, the state evidence on the determinants of the NAIRU is generally negative. None of the state labor-market-policy variables are statistically significant. Neither industry composition nor the size of the temporary-help sector is a statistically significant determinant of the NAIRU in the IV regressions. Of the demographic and education variables, there is some evidence that the presence of relatively more workers in the prime-age work group contributes to reductions in the NAIRU, but this effect is estimated very imprecisely.

Despite the lack of statistical significance of these effects, it is worth checking whether the point estimates of the coefficients are consistent with these variables potentially having an economically substantial effect on the NAIRU and, in particular, on the evolution of the NAIRU through the 1990s. The point estimates associated with the demographic variables are, in fact, consistent with these variables having economically large effects, but the timing of these effects is inconsistent with their playing an important role in the fall in the NAIRU since 1992; rather, they contribute to a decline in the NAIRU prior to 1992, but their contribution is estimated to have increased the national NAIRU since 1992.

The point estimates associated with the industry-mix variables, including temporary help (the last column of table 1.11), do point to a contribution that would lower the NAIRU by approximately 0.5 percentage points from 1992 to 1997, but this effect is not statistically significant.

Overall, these state panel regressions fail to pinpoint any economic determinants of the TV-NAIRU. This accords with the macro evidence presented in Stock (forthcoming) that education and demographic variables are inconsistent at the macro level with the trends in the NAIRU. Our finding contrasts somewhat with that of Katz and Krueger (1999), who find some evidence that the rise of the temporary-help industry has contributed to the fall in the national NAIRU (they estimate that temporary help has reduced the national TV-NAIRU by approximately 0.4 percentage points since 1990). Our specifications differ somewhat from theirs, however, and we find that the effect of temporary help is not robust.

CONCLUSIONS

We assess these results by returning to the three questions of the introduction. First, did the Phillips curve break down in the 1990s, or did it simply shift, with a new and evolving NAIRU? In both our macro and our state analyses, we found abundant evidence of a stable relation both between the change in price inflation and economic activity gaps and between unit labor costs and these activity gaps. These two pieces of evidence are confirmatory and are particularly striking because the state panel estimates included time effects, thereby eliminating the variation in the data that drives the macro estimates. Moreover, in the macro analysis, we found evidence that there was little intercept drift when the regressions were estimated as gaps; that is, when specified in terms of gaps, neither the price nor the wage Phillips curve has shifted in the 1990s. Thus, this evidence falls squarely on the side of "the Phillips curve is alive and well but . . ." theories.

Second, given this finding, why has the price Phillips curve shifted in? The macro analysis suggests that the answer is *not* that we have had a particularly fortunate string of supply shocks; we did in the mid-1990s, but they were subsequently reversed. In addition, both the macro evidence and the state evidence suggest that an autonomous shift in wage- or price-setting behavior by firms is also not an important part of the inflation-unemployment story of the 1990s: had changes in price- or wage-setting behavior been the reason for the apparent decline in the NAIRU, the NAIRU and the univariate trend in unemployment would differ, but they do not. This finding is reinforced by the limited role that we found for industry-mix variables in the state-panel-data analysis. This suggests that labor-market factors, such as demographics, the rise of the temporary-help industry, or labor-market policies, must be the source of the changes in the NAIRU. Curiously, however, our results do not point in this direction. The macro estimates of the change in the NAIRU from 1992 to 2000 derived using the demographically adjusted unemployment rate are virtually the same as those derived using the total unemployment rate. Similarly, our attempts to identify structural determinants of the NAIRU using the state data were disappointing. Several effects pointed in the right direction, but the state data did not provide precise estimates of these effects.

Third, can the labor-productivity gains of the 1990s explain the apparently aberrant recent behavior of real wages as displayed in figure 1.2? Yes. The TV-NAIRUs estimated both on the macro and on the state data are the same whether the change in inflation or the changes in real wages less productivity is the dependent variable and differ sharply during the 1990s only when the productivity component is omitted from wages.

The simplest summary of these results is that, once one accounts for the univariate trends in the unemployment rate and in productivity, the 1990s present no price or wage puzzles. Thus, the task is to explain trend movements in productivity and in unemployment. In our framework, trend unemployment and the NAIRU are identified separately, but, as it happens, these two series track each other very closely. Because the long-run trend components of the rates of inflation and unemployment are essentially unrelated in the postwar U.S. data (Stock and Watson 1999a), we are skeptical of explanations that link the two, such as those of Akerlof, Dickens, and Perry (1996) or Taylor (2000).

It is potentially more promising to consider explanations that directly link the trend components of productivity growth and the unemployment rate. These univariate trends, which are plotted in figure 1.9, show a striking and intriguing negative correlation. The recent coincident increase in productivity growth and decrease in the unemployment rate recall a similar pattern in the early 1960s. This pattern reversed itself in the 1970s, when trend productivity growth fell and the trend unemployment rate increased. The close relation between the series can also be seen in the scatterplot of the series shown in figure 1.10. Of course, the figure must be viewed with caution since unrelated trends can spuriously appear to be correlated. Indeed, it seems reasonable to think of figure 1.10 as four data observations—1960 to 1967, 1967 to 1980, 1980 to 1993, and 1993 to 2000—and it is difficult to be sure of a correlation with only four observations. Yet we find the empirical results strong enough, and the question important enough, to warrant further attention by both macro and labor economists.

FIGURE 1.9 / Trend Unemployment and Productivity Growth

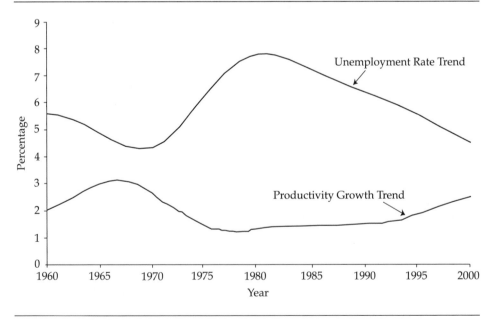

Source: Authors' calculations.

FIGURE 1.10 / Unemployment Rate and Productivity-Growth Trends

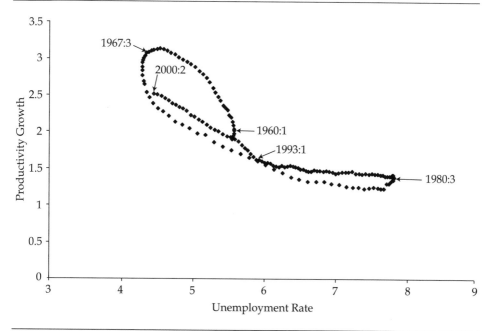

Source: Authors' calculations.

DATA APPENDIX

This appendix documents some features of the macroeconomic data used in the first four sections of this paper. All series are from the DRI Basic Economics Database (formerly Citibase). Quarterly averages were used for variables that were available monthly. Table 1A.1 lists the database mnemonic, a brief series description, and the series abbreviation used in tables 1.2 to 1.4.

We thank David Autor for helpful discussions and William Dickens and Robert Solow for detailed comments on an earlier version of this paper.

TABLE 1A.1 / Definitions of the Macroeconomic Data

Price series

GDPD   Gross domestic product: implicit price deflator (GDP Def.).

GMDC   PCE, implicit price deflator (PCE Def.).

PUNEW   CPI-U all items CPI (CPI).

LBGDPU   Nonfarm business: implicit price deflator (NFB Def.).

Wage series

LBPUR   Compensation per hour, employees: nonfarm business (Comp./Hr).

LEH   Average hourly earnings of production workers: total private nonagricultural (AHE PW).

LCP   Employment cost index (compensation): private industrial weeks (ECC-C).

LWI   Employment cost index (wage and salary): private industrial weeks (ECC-WS).

Real activity variables

LHUR   Unemployment rate: all workers, sixteen years and over (Civ. Unemp.).

HSBR   Housing authorized: total new private housing units (Bldg. Perm.).

IPXMCA   Capacity-utilization rate: manufacturing (Cap. Util.).

Productivity

LBOUTU   Output per hour of all persons: nonfarm business.

LOUTM   Output per hour of all persons, index—manufacturing.

Other variables

PUXX   CPI-U: all items less food and energy.

EXVUS   Foreign exchange value of the U.S. dollar.

Constructed variables

Exchange rate   EXVUS from 1973:1 through 2000:6. From 1959:1 to 1972:12 this is a trade-weighted average of the dollar exchange rates for France, Germany, Italy, Japan, and the United Kingdom, described in Stock and Watson (1989). The two series were linked in 1973:1.

Relative price of food and energy $\ln(punew_t/punew_{t-1}) - \ln(puxx_t/puxx_{t-1})$.

TABLE 1A.1 / *Continued*

Wage- and price-control variable	This variable takes on the values .8 from 1971:3 to 1972:3, − .4 from 1974:2 to 1974:2, −1.6 from 1974:3 to 1974:4, − .4 from 1975:1 to 1975:1, and 0 for all other dates. It is taken from Gordon (1982).
Supply shocks	The specifications that included supply shocks included four lags of the relative price of food and energy, four lags of the log difference of the exchange rate, and the wage- and price-control variable.
Demographically adjusted unemployment rate	See the text.
Bias corrections for the inflation series	(CPI) inflation was adjusted for the improvements in measurement implemented by the Bureau of Labor Statistics, as suggested in Gordon (1998). The adjustments were taken from Council of Economic Advisers (1998, table 2.4, p. 80). The values used are − .12 from 1995:1 to 1995:4, − .22 from 1996:1 to 1996:4, − .28 from 1997:1 to 1997:4, − .49 from 1998:1 to 1998:4, and − .69 from 1999:1 to 2000:2.

Source: Authors' compilation.

NOTES

1. Application of the Horvath-Watson (1995) test rejects the null hypothesis of the non-cointegration of these two series in favor of the alternative, that they are cointegrated with the cointegrating vector of (1, −1) at the 1 percent significance level (the test statistic was computed with four lags).

2. Gordon's (1998) derivation differs from ours, and he does not discuss cointegration explicitly. However, by imposing sums of coefficients in his lag polynomials to equal 1 (which he does in his empirical work), the resulting system is equivalent to equations 1.2 and 1.4, which in turn implies that the system is cointegrated.

3. Garner (1994) pointed out the stability of Phillips curves specified with capacity utilization and estimated with data through the early 1990s. Gordon (1998) and Stock (1998) estimated TV-NAIRUs for capacity utilization and found that they were quite stable compared with TV-NAIRUs for the unemployment rate. Our results confirm these findings and extend them through the end of the 1990s.

4. W. C. Brainard and George Perry (2000) estimate wage and price Phillips curves allowing for time variation in the coefficients and also find little change in the estimated slope. Their specification differs from ours in several respects; most notably, their equations are estimated using the levels of price and wage inflation, while we use the

change in price inflation and the change in productivity-adjusted real wage. Although their estimates suggest that the coefficients on lagged inflation have changed over time, they do not provide standard errors or any evidence of whether these changes are statistically significant. Doing so in their specification would require handling the persistence of their regressors in addition to the usual issues arising in time-varying coefficients.

5. The difference between the levels of the NAIRUs in price and wage Phillips curves reflects the decline in labor's share over the sample period computed using nonfarm-business wages, nonfarm-business productivity, and the GDP price deflator. The magnitude of this decline is evident from the tenth row of table 1.1. However, as the last row of table 1.1 shows, there is a much smaller decline when the nonfarm-business price deflator is used. Consequently, the levels of the NAIRU for the wage Phillips curves obtained using the nonfarm-business deflator are closer to those for the price Phillips curves.

6. This instrumenting strategy is simple but statistically inefficient. For an alternative, more efficient method, see Autor and Staiger (2001).

7. We thank David Autor for providing us with many of these data.

8. Lerman and Schmidt (1999) also present some limited evidence suggesting that there is no relation between the unemployment rate and wage growth in the late 1990s, which is at odds with the evidence that we present in table 1.6. In particular, they report, on the basis of 3 months of CPS data from 1995 and 1998, no relation between growth in wages at the state level from 1995:1 to 1998:1 and a state's unemployment-rate quartile in 1998:1. A number of aspects of the Lerman and Schmidt evidence are likely to bias their estimate toward finding no relation. In particular, the small sample sizes that result from using only three months of data exacerbate the measurement-error issues in the unemployment rate. More important, their focus on a single three-year difference with unemployment measured at the end of the difference is at odds with the usual Phillips curve specification, which focuses on short differences and lagged unemployment.

9. Katz and Krueger (1999) find a statistically significant effect of temporary help on the NAIRU in Phillips curves estimated from state data. Their result appears to depend in an important way on the particulars of their specification and estimator (OLS).

REFERENCES

Akerlof, George A., William T. Dickens, and George L. Perry. 1996. "The Macroeconomics of Low Inflation." *Brookings Papers on Economic Activity* (1): 1–76.

———. 2000. "Near-Rational Wage and Price Setting and the Optimal Rates of Inflation and Unemployment." *Brookings Papers on Economic Activity* (1): 1–60.

Andrews, Donald W. K. 1993. "Tests for Parameter Instability and Structural Change with Unknown Change Point." *Econometrica* 61(4): 821–56.

Autor, David A. Forthcoming. "Why Do Temporary Help Firms Provide Free General Skills Training?" *Quarterly Journal of Economics.*

Autor, David A., and Max G. Duggan. 2000. "Disability Recipiency and the Decline in Unemployment: Assessing the Contribution of the 1984 Disability Reforms." Unpublished manuscript. MIT.

Autor, David A., and Douglas Staiger. 2001. "Is There a Phillips Curve in Regional Wage Data?" Manuscript in progress. MIT.

Barlow, D., and G. W. Stadler. N.d. "The Dynamics of Wages and Prices in the United States." Unpublished manuscript. University of Newcastle upon Tyne.

Blanchard, Olivier J., and Lawrence F. Katz. 1992. "Regional Evolutions." *Brookings Papers on Economic Activity* (1): 1–61.

———. 1997. "What We Know and Do Not Know about the Natural Rate of Unemployment." *Journal of Economic Perspectives* 11(1): 51–72.

Blanchflower, David G., and Andrew J. Oswald. 1994. *The Wage Curve.* Cambridge, Mass.: MIT Press.

Brainard, W. C., and George L. Perry. 2000. "Making Policy in a Changing World." In *Economic Events, Ideas, and Policies: The 1960s and After,* edited by George L. Perry and James Tobin. Washington, D.C.: Brookings Institution Press.

Brayton, F., J. Roberts, and J. Williams. 1999. "What's Happened to the Phillips Curve?" Unpublished manuscript. Washington, D.C.: U.S. Federal Reserve Board, Division of Research and Statistics.

Card, David, and D. Hyslop. 1997. "Does Inflation 'Grease the Wheels of the Labor Market'?" In *Reducing Inflation: Motivation and Strategy,* edited by Christina D. Romer and David H. Romer, 71–122. Chicago: University of Chicago Press.

Cogley, T., and T. Sargent. In press. "Evolving Post–World War II U.S. Inflation Dynamics." *NBER Macroeconomics Annual.*

Council of Economic Advisers. 1998. *Economic Report of the President.* Washington: U.S. Government Printing Office.

Fuhrer, Jeffrey C. 1995. "The Phillips Curve Is Alive and Well." *New England Economic Review of the Federal Reserve Bank of Boston* (March/April): 41–56.

Galbraith, James K. 1997. "Time to Ditch the NAIRU." *Journal of Economic Perspectives* 11(1): 93–108.

Garner, C. Alan. 1994. "Capacity Utilization and U.S. Inflation." *Economic Review of the Federal Reserve Bank of Kansas City* 79(4): 5–23.

Gordon, Robert J. 1982. "Inflation, Flexible Exchange Rates, and the Natural Rate of Unemployment" In *Workers, Jobs, and Inflation,* edited by Martin N. Baily. Washington, D.C.: Brookings Institution Press.

———. 1990. "U.S. Inflation, Labor's Share, and the Natural Rate of Unemployment." In *Economics of Wage Determination,* edited by Heinz Konig. Berlin: Springer.

———. 1997. "The Time-Varying NAIRU and Its Implications for Economic Policy." *Journal of Economic Perspectives* 11(1): 11–32.

———. 1998. "Foundations of the Goldilocks Economy: Supply Shocks and the Time-Varying NAIRU." *Brookings Papers on Economic Activity* (2): 297–333.

Hall, Robert. 1999. "Comment on Rethinking the Role of the NAIRU in Monetary Policy: Implications of Model Formulation and Uncertainty." In *Monetary Policy Rules,* edited by John B. Taylor. Chicago: University of Chicago Press.

Holden, S., and R. Nymoen. 1999. "Measuring Structural Unemployment: NAWRU-Estimates in the Nordic Countries." Unpublished manuscript. University of Oslo.

Horvath, Michael T. K., and Mark W. Watson. 1995. "Testing for Cointegration When Some of the Cointegrating Vectors Are Prespecified." *Econometric Theory* 11(5): 952–84

Katz, Lawrence F., and Alan B. Krueger. 1999. "The High-Pressure U.S. Labor Market of the 1990s." *Brookings Papers on Economic Activity* (1): 1–87.

King, Robert G., James H. Stock, and Mark W. Watson. 1995. "Temporal Instability of the

Unemployment-Inflation Relationship." *Economic Perspectives of the Federal Reserve Bank of Chicago* (May/June): 2–12.

Lerman, Robert I., and Stefanie R. Schmidt. 1999. "An Overview of Economic, Social, and Demographic Trends Affecting the U.S. Labor Market." Unpublished manuscript. Washington, D.C.: Urban Institute.

Quandt, R. E. 1960. "Tests of the Hypothesis That a Linear Regression System Obeys Two Separate Regimes." *Journal of the American Statistical Association* 55(290): 324–30.

Sargan, J. D. 1964. "Wages and Prices in the United Kingdom: A Study in Econometric Methodology." In *Econometric Analysis for National Planning*, edited by P. E. Hart, G. Mills, and J. K. Whitaker. London: Butterworths. Reprinted in *Econometrics and Quantitative Economics*, edited by David F. Hendry and Kenneth F. Wallis (Oxford: Blackwell).

Segal, Lewis M., and Daniel G. Sullivan. 1997. "The Growth of Temporary Services Work." *Journal of Economic Perspectives* 11(2): 117–36.

Shimer, Robert. 1998. "Why Is the U.S. Unemployment Rate So Much Lower?" *NBER Macroeconomics Annual*, 11–60.

Staiger, Douglas, and James H. Stock. 1997. "Instrumental Variables Regression with Weak Instruments." *Econometrica* 65(3): 557–86.

Staiger, Douglas, James H. Stock, and Mark W. Watson. 1997a. "How Precise Are Estimates of the Natural Rate of Unemployment?" In *Reducing Inflation: Motivation and Strategy*, edited by Christina D. Romer and David H. Romer, 195–242. Chicago: University of Chicago Press.

———. 1997b. "The NAIRU, Unemployment, and Monetary Policy." *Journal of Economic Perspectives* 11(winter): 33–51.

Stock, James H. 1991. "Confidence Intervals for the Largest Autoregressive Root in U.S. Macroeconomic Time Series." *Journal of Monetary Economics* 28(3): 435–60.

———. 1998. "Discussion of Gordon's 'Foundations of the Goldilocks Economy.'" *Brookings Papers on Economic Activity* (2): 334–41.

———. In press. "Monetary Policy in a Changing Economy: Indicators, Rules, and the Shift towards Intangible Output." In *Eighth International Conference on Monetary Policy, Bank of Japan*. Tokyo: Bank of Japan.

Stock, James H., and Mark W. Watson. 1989. "New Indexes of Coincident and Leading Economic Indicators." In *Macroeconomics Annual*, vol. 4. Cambridge, Mass.: MIT Press.

———. 1998. "Median Unbiased Estimation of Coefficient Variance in a Time Varying Parameter Model." *Journal of the American Statistical Association* 93(441): 349–58.

———. 1999a. "Business Cycle Fluctuations in U.S. Macroeconomic Time Series." In *Handbook of Macroeconomics*, edited by John B. Taylor and Michael Woodford, 1: 3–64. Amsterdam: North Holland.

———. 1999b. "Forecasting Inflation." *Journal of Monetary Economics* 44(2): 293–335.

Taylor, John B. 2000. "Low Inflation, Pass-Through, and the Pricing Power of Firms." *European Economic Review* 44(7): 1389–1408.

Chapter 2

Productivity Growth and the Phillips Curve

Laurence Ball and Robert Moffitt

T
he "new economy" in the United States has since the mid-1990s featured surprisingly benign inflation and unemployment behavior. Before this experience, most estimates of the NAIRU—the nonaccelerating inflation rate of unemployment—were in the neighborhood of 6 percent. Yet unemployment has fallen far below this level, reaching 4.2 percent in 2000, and inflation has not risen substantially. This paper presents an explanation for the apparent improvement in the unemployment-inflation trade-off. We argue that it is caused by another feature of the new economy: the rise in the growth rate of labor productivity.

Our argument builds on an old idea: that workers' wage aspirations adjust slowly to shifts in productivity growth. As a result, such shifts produce periods when aspirations and productivity are out of line, causing the Phillips curve to shift. Dennis Grubb, Richard Jackman, and Richard Layard (1982), for example, use this idea to argue that the productivity slowdown of the 1970s caused an unfavorable Phillips curve shift. Alan Blinder (2000) and Council of Economic Advisers (2000) suggest that this process worked in reverse in the late 1990s, with a productivity speedup causing a favorable Phillips curve shift. This paper presents new evidence that changes in productivity growth do, indeed, affect the Phillips curve. In addition to documenting this idea in general, we show that it explains most of the Phillips curve puzzle since 1995.

Our argument proceeds in several steps. In the first section of this paper, we discuss the ideas about wage determination that underlie our story. We draw on previous research suggesting that concepts of fairness affect wage setting and that perceptions of fair wage increases are tied to past wage increases.

The second section embeds these ideas in an otherwise standard model of the Phillips curve. In the model, an increase in productivity growth feeds one-for-one into lower price inflation for given wage inflation. It has less effect on wage inflation, which is determined largely by past wage increases. Wage inflation also depends negatively on unemployment. Combining these assumptions yields a Phillips curve in which the change in inflation depends on unemployment *and* the difference between current productivity growth and past real-wage growth. Shifts in productivity growth cause shifts in the unemployment-inflation relation for a period while wage aspirations are adjusting.

The third section discusses the measurement of key variables in our model, and the fourth section presents our central empirical results. We estimate alternative Phillips curves with annual U.S. data from 1962 to 1995 and then use these equations to forecast inflation over the period 1996 to 2000. We first confirm previous findings that a conventional Phillips curve overpredicts inflation after 1995. We then estimate the Phillips curve from our model and find that the new variable—the gap between productivity growth and past real-wage growth—has the effect predicted by our theory. When this variable is included, the overprediction of inflation since 1995 disappears. The fifth section discusses extensions of the analysis, such as the addition of traditional "supply-shock" variables to the Phillips curve.

The next two sections leave aggregate U.S. data to look for other evidence for our theory. The sixth section is a case study of Chile in the 1990s—another episode in which a productivity acceleration appears to have caused a favorable Phillips curve shift. The seventh section examines micro data from the U.S. Current Population Survey. Here, we show that our model helps explain differences in wage growth across workers as well as movements in aggregate variables.

The eighth section concludes the paper.

WAGE ASPIRATIONS

It is clear that, in the long run, real wages are closely tied to labor productivity. Consequently, our model will have the feature that productivity, real wages, and real-wage aspirations all grow at the same rate in a steady state. We consider the possibility, however, that a shift in productivity growth is not matched immediately by a shift in wage aspirations because these are tied partly to past wage increases. Many authors have suggested ideas along these lines; recent examples include Olivier Blanchard and Lawrence Katz (1997), Joseph Stiglitz (1997), Alan Blinder (2000), and J. Bradford DeLong (2000). However, these authors seldom justify their ideas about wage aspirations in much detail. We will not attempt a full theory of aspirations, but we will briefly review some relevant literature.

By *wage aspirations* we mean the real wages that workers consider fair. Our model rests on two assumptions about aspirations: that they affect the actual wages that workers receive and that they are tied to past wage increases. We discuss these points in turn.

The assumption that wages depend on what workers consider fair represents a departure from neoclassical microeconomics, but one with strong empirical support. George Akerlof and Janet Yellen (1990) discuss a likely channel: workers reduce their effort if they perceive wages as unfair, making it in firms' interests to pay fair wages. An experimental literature in psychology (surveyed by Akerlof and Yellen) shows that workers' performance deteriorates when they believe that wages are unfair. Management textbooks such as George Milkovich and Jerry Newman's (1996) stress the importance of paying fair wages to elicit effort. Truman Bewley's (2000) field research suggests the similar idea that firms pay fair wages to maintain worker morale.

What wages do workers consider "fair"? The psychology literature suggests that workers judge the fairness of their wages by comparing them to *reference transactions*—certain wages that they have observed in the past (see Kahneman, Knetsch, and Thaler 1986; Oswald 1986; and Elliot 1991). Researchers disagree about which wage payments are the reference transactions for a given worker. One possibility is wages paid to the same worker in the past, and another is wages paid to other workers of the same type. When we examine micro-economic data in our seventh section, we will ask whether a worker's wage is more closely tied to his own past wage or to others' wages. However, this distinction is not crucial at an aggregate level. If wage setters base their actions on past wages, aggregating across the economy yields a relation between current and past wage increases regardless of *whose* past increases are relevant to individuals.[1]

THE PHILLIPS CURVE AND THE NAIRU

This section embeds our ideas about wage aspirations in a canonical model of wage and price setting and derives a Phillips curve. Specifically, the model follows Olivier Blanchard and Lawrence Katz (1997) and Lawrence Katz and Alan Krueger (1999) except for our treatment of productivity and aspirations.

Deriving the Phillips Curve

We denote inflation by π and wage inflation by ω, so real wage growth is $\omega - \pi$. We assume that wage setters have a target for real-wage growth given by

$$(\omega - \pi)^* = \alpha - \gamma U + \delta\theta + (1 - \delta)A + \eta, \quad \alpha, \gamma > 0, 0 \leq \delta \leq 1, \quad (2.1)$$

where U is unemployment, θ is labor-productivity growth, A is an aspiration-wage increase, and η is an error term. This equation makes the conventional assumption that higher unemployment reduces target real-wage growth. The target also depends on an average of productivity growth and the aspiration-wage increase, which is given by

$$A = \frac{1 - \beta}{\beta} \sum_{i=1}^{\infty} \beta^i (\omega - \pi)_{-i}. \quad (2.2)$$

To interpret equations 2.1 and 2.2, consider first the special case of $\delta = 1$. This is a neoclassical benchmark in which productivity growth feeds one-for-one into wages and aspirations are irrelevant. At the other extreme of $\delta = 0$, productivity is irrelevant, and wage increases are based on aspirations. This period's aspiration for a real-wage increase is a weighted average of past increases, with exponentially declining weights. The aspiration real-wage increase can also be written recursively as $A = \beta A_{-1} + (1 - \beta)(\omega - \pi)_{-1}$. As this shows, aspirations adjust over time in response to the most recent wage increase. The adjustment is fast if β is small and slow if β is close to 1.[2]

Our model nests the two special cases, allowing both productivity growth and past real-wage growth to influence wage setting. Note that we assume that these two variables have coefficients that sum to 1. This implies that the target depends one-for-one on productivity growth in a steady state with real-wage growth equal to productivity growth.

Wage setters must choose nominal wages one period in advance. They choose a nominal increase ω equal to their target real-wage increase, $(\omega - \pi)^*$, plus expected inflation. Expected inflation equals last period's inflation, π_{-1}. Combining these assumptions with equation 2.1 yields a *wage Phillips curve*:

$$\omega = \alpha + \pi_{-1} - \gamma U + \delta\theta + (1 - \delta)A + \eta. \qquad (2.3)$$

Wage inflation depends on past price inflation, unemployment, and an average of θ and A.

We complete the model with a standard equation for price inflation:

$$\pi = \omega - \theta + v, \qquad (2.4)$$

where v is another error. Price inflation depends one-for-one on the increase in unit labor costs, which is wage inflation minus productivity growth. Substituting the wage Phillips curve into 2.4 yields a *price Phillips curve*:

$$\pi = \alpha + \pi_{-1} - \gamma U - (1 - \delta)(\theta - A) + \varepsilon, \qquad (2.5)$$

where $\varepsilon = \eta + v$. This Phillips curve will be the centerpiece of our empirical analysis.

Discussion

To interpret our Phillips curve, we again start with the case of $\delta = 1$: target real-wage increases depend on productivity growth but not on aspirations. In this case, the $\theta - A$ term drops out of equation 2.5, and the equation reduces to a conventional Phillips curve. For $\delta = 1$, productivity growth has a negative effect on price inflation given wage inflation, but it has a fully offsetting positive effect on wage inflation. Thus, productivity growth has no role in the Phillips curve. Since $\delta = 1$ is a natural neoclassical baseline, this result explains why research on the Phillips curve does not usually emphasize productivity growth.

Productivity growth does matter if wage growth is partly tied to past wage growth, that is, $\delta < 1$. Productivity growth is still irrelevant in a steady state with $\theta = A$. But, if productivity growth accelerates or decelerates, A does not adjust immediately, and $\theta - A$ moves in the direction of θ. A productivity acceleration causes a favorable shift in the unemployment-inflation relation, and a slowdown causes an unfavorable shift. The shift can last a long time if wage aspirations adjust slowly—if β is close to 1.

While the aspiration variable A can differ from productivity growth, the *actual* growth of real wages cannot. Inverting the price equation 2.4 gives a formula for actual real-wage growth: it equals $\theta + v$. In equilibrium, this fact is reconciled with the behavior of wage setters by movements in unemployment or inflation. During a productivity slowdown, target wage growth rises relative to productivity growth *for given unemployment,* but higher unemployment offsets this effect, or accelerating inflation reduces actual real-wage growth below the target. Thus, the model captures the stylized fact that U.S. wages are closely tied to labor productivity, as shown by the near constancy of labor's share of income.

We define the NAIRU in our model as the level of unemployment consistent with stable inflation *and* $\theta - A = 0$, which must hold in steady state. The NAIRU equals α/γ, the ratio of the constant in the Phillips curve to the unemployment coefficient. If a productivity acceleration raises $\theta - A$ above 0, we will say that unemployment can fall below the NAIRU temporarily without accelerating inflation, not that the NAIRU itself has fallen. In other words, we treat movements in $\theta - A$ as "supply shocks" that shift the unemployment-inflation trade-off for a given NAIRU.

DATA AND MEASUREMENT

Our measurement of inflation and unemployment follows previous work, especially Blanchard and Katz (1997) and Katz and Krueger (1999). The data are annual. The inflation rate π is the change in the log of the consumer price index, and the wage-inflation rate ω is the change in the log of compensation per hour in the business sector. Unemployment is the unemployment rate for all civilian workers. All these series are produced by the Bureau of Labor Statistics (BLS).

The rest of this section describes the construction of the two key variables in our theory: the growth rate of labor productivity and aspirations for real-wage growth.

Measuring Productivity Growth

Our starting point for measuring productivity growth is the change in the log of output per hour in the business sector, obtained from the BLS. As we will show, this series captures both the productivity slowdown of the 1970s and the speedup since 1995. For our present purposes, the reasons for these productivity shifts are not important. For example, we need not take a stand on whether the recent acceleration in productivity reflects rapid total-factor-productivity growth or capital deepening.

A practical issue in measuring productivity is cyclic adjustment. Output per hour is an imperfect measure of labor productivity because labor input varies through shifts in worker effort as well as measured hours. In particular, productivity growth is overstated in expansions because effort rises. In our underlying theory, price and wage setting depend on true rather than measured productivity, so we need to adjust our productivity variable to eliminate the effects of cyclic movements in effort.

Our approach to measuring true productivity follows Susanto Basu and Miles Kimball (1997), who build on Mark Bils and Jang-Ok Cho (1994). Basu and Kimball assume that, over the business cycle, effort moves proportionately with average weekly hours of employed workers. This relation follows from a model in which firms costlessly adjust both effort and weekly hours when they need more labor input (but adjusting employment may be costly). Empirically, a close link between effort and weekly hours is supported by time-motion studies that directly measure effort (Schor 1987). Given this link, we can use variation in weekly hours as a proxy for variation in effort. To purge productivity fluctuations of the part of these fluctuations caused by changes in effort, we regress measured productivity growth on the change in the log of weekly hours. We use the residuals from this regression to measure true productivity growth θ, adding a constant to make the mean of θ equal the mean of measured productivity growth.

For 1962 to 2000, regressing measured productivity growth on the change in log hours yields a coefficient of 0.66. The $\bar{R}^2$ is only 0.06, however, which means that our cyclic adjustment removes a small fraction of productivity fluctuations. As a result, the adjusted and unadjusted series for θ, shown in figure 2.1, are not very different. Our results confirm previous findings that measured labor productivity is only mildly cyclic (unlike total factor productivity).[3]

The series in figure 2.1 capture the broad phenomena of the productivity slowdown and the recent acceleration. With cyclically adjusted data, θ averages 3.3 percent over the period 1962 to 1973, 1.4 percent over 1974 to 1995, and 2.7 percent over 1996 to 2000. However, these broad trends do not fully explain the data. There is considerable year-to-year variation in productivity growth, even after our cyclic adjustment.

Wage Aspirations

The most novel variable in our analysis is A, which determines workers' aspirations for real-wage increases. In each period, A is an exponentially weighted average of past real-wage increases (equation 2.2). Two issues arise in constructing A: the choice of the weighting parameter β and the need to approximate the infinite sum in the definition of A. We begin with the second issue.

FIGURE 2.1 / Productivity Growth (θ)

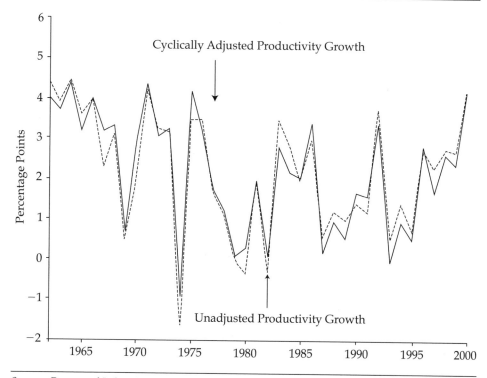

Sources: Bureau of Labor Statistics and authors' calculations.

In principle, A depends on real-wage increases back to the infinite past. In practice, our data on real-wage growth start in 1948. To address this problem, we make a reasonable guess of the value of A in 1948. Given this value, we can derive A for 1949, 1950, . . . using the recursive definition $A = \beta A_{-1} + (1 - \beta)(\omega - \pi)_{-1}$. That is, we assume an A in 1948 and update A in each year on the basis of the evolution of real wages.

Specifically, we set A for 1948 equal to trend real-wage growth in that year, as measured by the Hodrick-Prescott (HP) filter over the period 1948 to 2000 with smoothing parameter 1,000. This yields $A = 4.2$ percent. The implicit assumption is that wage aspirations in 1948 were close to the actual trend in real wages: 1948 was *not* a time like the 1970s or late 1990s when aspirations and actual wage growth diverged. Fortunately, our results are not very sensitive to the choice of A for 1948 because our regressions use data starting in 1962. The 1948 value of A has a weight of only β^{14} in the A for 1962 and smaller weights in later A's.[4]

The exponential parameter β can in principle be estimated from the data. Our estimates are imprecise, however, so we end up imposing values that are plausible a priori and not rejected by the data. Figure 2.2 shows the series for actual

FIGURE 2.2 / Real-Wage Growth and Aspirations

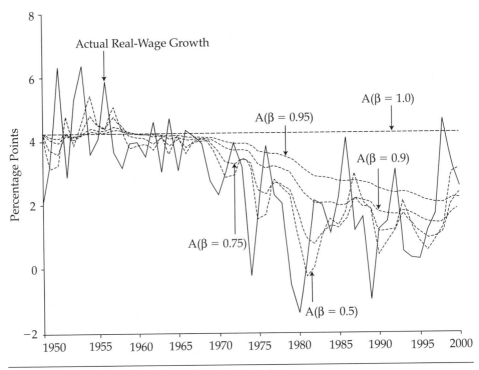

Sources: Bureau of Labor Statistics and authors' calculations.

real-wage growth from 1948 through 2000 and for A with various values of β. Real-wage growth fluctuates around a trend that is stable until the late 1960s and then declines as a result of the productivity slowdown. For most values of β, A follows the downward trend in real-wage growth with a lag. Real-wage growth rises sharply and aspirations modestly at the end of the sample.

Much of our analysis will focus on the case of $\beta = 0.95$. A fairly high β captures Stiglitz's (1997) suggestion that the adjustment of aspirations to the 1970s productivity slowdown continued into the 1990s. Moreover, values of β that are much smaller than 0.95 or very close to 1 are unappealing. As illustrated in figure 2.2, values of 0.8 or below imply that aspirations fluctuate substantially in response to year-to-year movements in real-wage growth. It seems unlikely that concepts of fair wages fluctuate so much. At the other extreme, a β of 1 implies that workers still want the wage increases that they received in the 1950s. In this case, the real-wage growth of the last five years falls short of aspirations, even though it is high compared to the previous twenty-five years.

For $\beta = 0.95$, figure 2.3 shows the difference $\theta - A$, the new term that appears in our Phillips curve, for the period 1962 to 2000. To isolate long-run

FIGURE 2.3 / The Gap Between Productivity Growth and Aspirations (β = 0.95)

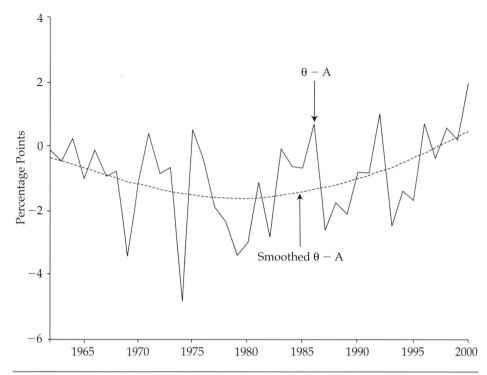

Source: Authors' calculations.

trends, the figure also presents a smoothed version of the series based on the HP filter with a parameter of 1,000. The recent new economy can be seen in the high values of θ − A for 1996 to 2000: the average value for this period is the highest for any five-year period since 1948. θ − A was high after 1995 because θ rose sharply *and* A reached low levels after finally adjusting to the productivity slow-down. θ was higher in the 1950s and 1960s, but then it was balanced by high wage aspirations.

ESTIMATES OF THE PHILLIPS CURVE

This section estimates the Phillips curve from our model, equation 2.5, with an-nual U.S. data. We examine the general performance of the equation by estimat-ing it with data from 1962 through 1995. We then perform out-of-sample fore-casts to see whether the equation explains inflation in the post-1995 new economy.

A Conventional Phillips Curve

As a benchmark, we first examine a Phillips curve that lacks our new variable $\theta - A$. This is a simple textbook equation: the change in inflation depends on a constant and unemployment. As discussed earlier, this equation follows from our model if wage growth depends one-for-one on productivity growth and aspirations have no effect.

For 1962 to 1995—the old-economy period—OLS estimation of the Phillips curve yields

$$\Delta\pi = 4.41 - 0.710U, \quad \bar{R}^2 = 0.34, \tag{2.6}$$
$$\quad\quad (1.14) \quad (0.161)$$

where standard errors are given in parentheses. These results look reasonable. One point-year of unemployment reduces inflation by 0.7 percentage points. The NAIRU—the ratio of the constant to minus the unemployment coefficient—is 6.2 percent.

Using these estimates, we next compute forecasts of inflation over the period 1996 to 2000, given the actual evolution of unemployment. Figure 2.4 plots the forecasts along with two-standard-error bands and compares them to actual inflation. This figure shows why many authors have suggested that a new economy has arrived. Since unemployment falls far below the NAIRU estimate of 6.2 percent, predicted inflation rises rapidly and reaches 8.3 percent in 2000. In contrast, actual inflation fluctuates mildly and ends at 3.3 percent. The overprediction of inflation with a 6.2 percent NAIRU suggests that the NAIRU has fallen for some reason.

The Phillips Curve with $\theta - A$

We now estimate the Phillips curve from our model, equation 2.5. This is the conventional Phillips curve estimated earlier with the addition of the term $\theta - A$.

Our modification of the Phillips curve introduces the parameter β, the weighting factor in the formula for A. Table 2.1 presents Phillips curve estimates for the period 1962 to 1995 with different values of β imposed. The table also reports joint estimates of β and the Phillips curve coefficients obtained by nonlinear least squares. The nonlinear-least-squares estimate of β is imprecise: a two-standard-error confidence interval runs from 0.01 to 1.03. This reflects the fact that a wide range of β's fit the data equally well: the $\bar{R}^2$'s are close when different values of β are imposed. The point estimate of β is 0.52, which is far from the value of 0.95 that we suggested a priori. However, there is little evidence against $\beta = 0.95$: an F-test of this hypothesis yields $F = 2.24$ ($p = .15$).[5]

Fortunately, we can draw conclusions from the data without knowing the

FIGURE 2.4 / Dynamic Inflation Forecasts—Conventional Phillips Curve

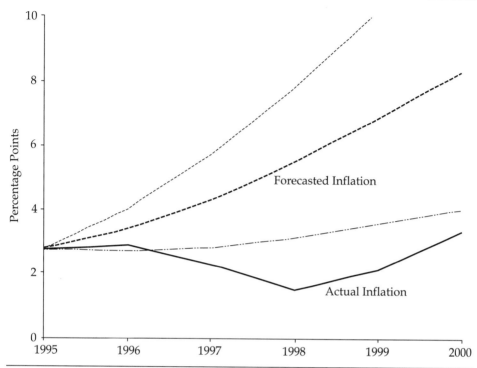

Source: Authors' calculations.

value of β. As illustrated in table 2.1, the coefficient on $\theta - A$ is significantly negative for all β's from 0 to 1. Thus, as implied by our model, a rise in productivity growth relative to wage aspirations has a negative effect on inflation. The coefficient on $\theta - A$ is usually near -0.6. In terms of underlying parameters, this means that the aspiration term A has a weight of 0.6 in the formula for target wage growth (equation 2.1) and that productivity growth has a weight of 0.4. The $\bar{R}^2$'s for the various β's lie between 0.5 and 0.6, compared to 0.34 for the equation without $\theta - A$. Thus, our new variable explains a significant part of inflation variation over the period 1962 to 1995.

Figure 2.5 shows forecasts of inflation over the period 1996 to 2000 for various values of β. In most cases, adding $\theta - A$ to the Phillips curve greatly improves the accuracy of forecasts. For β's ranging from 0.5 to 0.95, predicted inflation stays close to actual inflation throughout the period and ends up *lower* by statistically insignificant amounts. For $\beta = 0.95$, predicted inflation in 2000 is 2.1 percent. Thus, our model eliminates the overprediction of inflation that arises with the usual Phillips curve. Our equation predicts that inflation stays low despite low unemployment because the productivity acceleration produces high values of $\theta - A$.

TABLE 2.1 / Phillips Curve Estimates, 1962 to 1995 (Dependent Variable = $\Delta\pi$)

	β Estimated		β Imposed			
Value of β	.515	.500	.750	.900	.950	1.000
	(.255)					
Constant	.0244	.0245	.0258	.0303	.0328	.0377
	(.0107)	(.0099)	(.0108)	(.0115)	(.0111)	(.0096)
Coefficient	−.409	−.410	−.449	−.565	−.649	−.777
on U	(.166)	(.157)	(.171)	(.180)	(.175)	(.154)
Coefficient	−.613	−.609	−.640	−.623	−.619	−.498
on $\theta - A$	(.205)	(.160)	(.192)	(.200)	(.187)	(.152)
$\overline{R}^2$	.552	.566	.547	.534	.539	.508

Source: Authors' calculations.

FIGURE 2.5 / Dynamic Inflation Forecasts—Phillips Curve with $\theta - A$

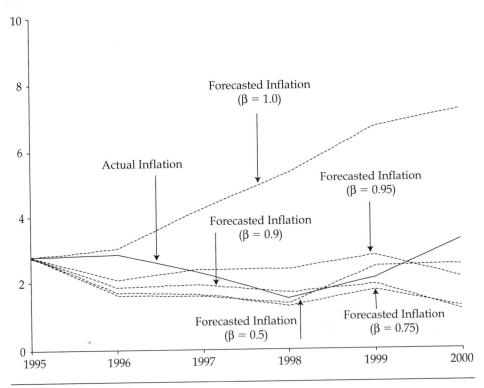

Source: Authors' calculations.

The only qualification is that our equation overpredicts inflation if β is very close to 1. As discussed earlier, $\beta = 1$ means that wage aspirations over the period 1996 to 2000 are still tied to the rapid wage growth of the 1950s. In this case, $\theta - A$ is negative for most of 1996 to 2000, so adding it to the model does not reduce inflation forecasts. Our story about the new economy depends on the assumption that $\beta < 1$: there must be *some* adjustment of aspirations over time.

Short-Run and Long-Run Variation in $\theta - A$

Our results partly reflect broad trends in the data. In the early 1970s, the productivity slowdown reduced $\theta - A$, and the unemployment-inflation trade-off worsened; these facts help produce the negative coefficient on $\theta - A$ in the pre-1996 Phillips curve. Similarly, the success of our model over the period 1996 to 2000 reflects the fact that $\theta - A$ rose while the output-inflation trade-off improved. However, these broad trends are not the *only* reason for our model's success. As shown in figure 2.3, there is considerable year-to-year variation in $\theta - A$ because of fluctuations in θ. These movements also help explain shifts in the U/π relation.

To make this point, we decompose the variable $\theta - A$ (for $\beta = 0.95$) into two components: a trend, given by the HP filter in figure 2.3, and deviations from the trend. For the period 1962 to 1995, entering these components separately in the Phillips curve yields the regression

$$\Delta\pi = \underset{(1.15)}{3.19} - \underset{(0.210)}{0.719U} - \underset{(0.412)}{1.080(\theta - A)^T} - \underset{(0.174)}{0.568(\theta - A)^D}, \tag{2.7}$$

where $(\theta - A)^T$ is the trend component of $\theta - A$, and $(\theta - A)^D$ is the deviation from trend. Both components have statistically significant effects. The point estimate is higher for the trend component, but one cannot reject the hypothesis that the two coefficients are equal ($p = .17$). Thus, both long-term and short-term movements in $\theta - A$ have the effects predicted by our theory.

Researchers often give different interpretations of long-term and year-to-year shifts in the U/π relation. The former are interpreted as shifts in the NAIRU, the latter as "supply" or "inflation" shocks. This is the case, for example, in the Kalman filter approach to estimating time-varying NAIRUs (for example, Gordon 1998). In contrast, our results suggest that parts of the short-term and long-term shifts in the U/π relation have a common explanation.

Is Low Unemployment Sustainable?

This paper was originally written for a conference on the "sustainability" of today's low unemployment. At first glance, our analysis appears to have pessimistic implications for sustainability. The Phillips curve has shifted favorably because a productivity acceleration has produced positive values of $\theta - A$. But, when productivity growth stabilizes, aspirations for real-wage growth will eventually adjust to the new trend. In the long run, we must see values of $\theta - A$ that average to 0, implying a worse U/π trade-off than in the recent period of positive $\theta - A$'s.

On the other hand, it will *not* be necessary for future unemployment to rise back to the level thought to be the NAIRU in the mid-1990s. The apparent NAIRU has fallen in the period 1996 to 2000 relative to the period 1962 to 1995 both because $\theta - A$ has been positive in the recent period and because it was negative on average in the earlier period. The average $\theta - A$ was negative before 1996 because, as shown in figures 2.1 to 2.3, A lagged behind the falling θ during the productivity slowdown. In steady state, the economy must give up the gains from today's positive $\theta - A$'s but not the gains from eliminating negative $\theta - A$'s. In other words, the true NAIRU is higher than the apparent NAIRU of today but lower than the apparent NAIRU before 1996, when unemployment was raised by the slow adjustment of aspirations to the productivity slowdown.

Specifically, recall that a Phillips curve for the period 1962 to 1995 without the $\theta - A$ term yields a NAIRU estimate of 6.2 percent. In contrast, the equation with $\theta - A$ implies a NAIRU of 5.1 percent (for $\beta = 0.95$). The figure 5.1 percent is our estimate of the unemployment rate consistent with stable inflation when $\theta - A$ equals 0. If the true Phillips curve has not shifted since 1995, our equation implies that unemployment must eventually rise to 5.1 percent from its 2000 level of 4.2 percent. But it need not rise to the 6.2 percent level suggested by a conventional Phillips curve.[6]

EXTENSIONS

This section considers various extensions of our time-series analysis.

The Wage Phillips Curve

So far we have focused on our model's implications for price inflation. To further test the model, we now turn to the wage Phillips curve, equation 2.3. Recall that wage inflation depends on lagged price inflation, unemployment, and a weighted average of θ and A. We also consider the neoclassical special case in which the weight on θ is fixed at 1.

Table 2.2 presents estimates of wage Phillips curves for the period 1962 to 1995 ($\beta = 0.95$). These estimates support the model. The estimated weights on θ and A are 0.16 and 0.84, respectively; the weight on θ is smaller than the weight implied by the price Phillips curve, but the difference is not statistically significant. The hypothesis of a unit weight on θ is strongly rejected. When we relax the restriction that the θ and A coefficients sum to 1, it is not rejected ($p = .76$).

TABLE 2.2 / Wage Phillips Curves, 1962 to 1995 (Dependent Variable = $\omega - \pi_{-1}$)

	Our Model	Coefficient on θ Set at 1.0
Constant	.0388	.0541
	(.0068)	(.0103)
Coefficient on U	−.789	−.871
	(.121)	(.145)
Coefficient on θ	.163	1.000
	(.170)	
Coefficient on A	.837	
Forecast errors (percentage points):		
1996	.50	2.20
1997	.84	1.64
1998	−1.43	.22
1999	−1.19	.14
2000	−.61	2.25
Sum for 1996 to 2000	−1.89	6.44
(SE for sum)	(1.53)	(2.00)

Source: Authors' calculations.

Using the estimates for the period 1962 to 1995, table 2.2 also reports forecast errors for $\omega - \pi_{-1}$ after 1995. The results parallel those for price Phillips curves. The neoclassical equation overpredicts wage inflation relative to π_{-1} by a total of 6.4 percentage points. This equation assumes that wage growth rises one-for-one with the productivity acceleration, when in fact the effect was much smaller. Our wage Phillips curve is more accurate: it underpredicts wage growth by an insignificant amount.

Additional Phillips Curve Variables

Most authors who estimate Phillips curves include additional variables, in particular lags of unemployment and inflation changes and measures of supply shocks (for example, Gordon 1998; Staiger, Stock, and Watson 1997). Here, we check the robustness of our conclusions to adding such variables. We experiment with two lags of the change in inflation; unemployment lags are never significant, so we omit results with these variables. We measure supply shocks with three standard variables: the change in the relative price of food and energy, the change in the trade-weighted real exchange rate, and Gordon's dummy for the Nixon price controls.[7]

Table 2.3 presents estimates of our generalized Phillips curves for the period 1962 to 1995. We estimate equations with and without the three supply shocks, with and without the 2 $\Delta\pi$ lags, and with and without $\theta - A$, in all possible

TABLE 2.3 / Generalized Phillips Curves, 1962 to 1995 (Dependent Variable = $\Delta\pi$)

	(1)	(2)	(3)	(4)	(5)	(6)	(7)	(8)
Constant	.0441	.0328	.0367	.0299	.0274	.0215	.0319	.0271
	(.0114)	(.0111)	(.0079)	(.0077)	(.0055)	(.0038)	(.0083)	(.0066)
U	−.710	−.649	−.585	−.575	−.437	−.422	−.505	−.494
	(.161)	(.175)	(.121)	(.122)	(.096)	(.064)	(.136)	(.096)
$\theta - A$		−.619		−.501		−.379		−.316
		(.187)		(.155)		(.107)		(.096)
$\Delta\pi_{-1}$			.281	.184			−.061	−.083
			(.150)	(.121)			(.117)	(.099)
$\Delta\pi_{-2}$			−.448	−.362			−.295	−.253
			(.115)	(.111)			(.069)	(.100)
Δfood/energy price					1.234	.976	1.192	1.000
					(.191)	(.139)	(.186)	(.150)
Δexchange rate					−.065	−.080	−.045	−.061
					(.035)	(.033)	(.033)	(.028)
Nixon					−.010	−.006	−.020	−.018
					(.011)	(.007)	(.010)	(.008)
$\overline{R}^2$	.343	.539	.513	.636	.684	.781	.770	.812

Source: Authors' calculations.

combinations. In all cases, we set $\beta = 0.95$ in calculating A. There are two robust conclusions to be drawn.

First, the three supply shocks are jointly significant, as are the two $\Delta\pi$ lags, regardless of whether $\theta - A$ is included. The various coefficients have reasonable signs and magnitudes. Including all the variables (column 8) yields an $\bar{R}^2$ of 0.81.

Second, the term $\theta - A$ remains significant in all the specifications. However, the magnitude of the coefficient falls when additional variables are included. In the most general specification, the coefficient is -0.32 ($t = 3.3$), compared to -0.62 when the supply shocks and $\Delta\pi$ lags are excluded.[8]

Figure 2.6 shows forecasts of inflation for the period 1996 to 2000 based on the 1962 to 1995 estimates. The four panels give results with and without the supply shocks and with and without inflation lags. In each case, we show actual inflation and forecasts that arise when $\theta - A$ is included and when it is excluded. The forecasts vary across specifications, but, again, broad conclusions can be drawn.

First, if one leaves $\theta - A$ out of the Phillips curve, accounting for supply shocks reduces the overprediction of inflation by only a moderate amount. When supply shocks are included, predicted inflation stays low through 1998 because the dollar appreciates and energy prices fall in that year. But predicted inflation rises sharply in the period 1999 to 2000 as the appreciation of the dollar slows and energy prices rise. In the most general specification without $\theta - A$, predicted inflation reaches 6.4 percent in 2000, compared to 8.3 percent in the simplest Phillips curve.

Second, including $\theta - A$ always reduces predicted inflation by a large amount. In most cases in figure 2.6, adding $\theta - A$ turns an overprediction of inflation into a fairly accurate prediction. In one case, it turns a moderate overprediction into a moderate underprediction.

Finally, our most general specification—the one including $\theta - A$, supply shocks, and $\Delta\pi$ lags—produces remarkably accurate forecasts throughout the period 1996 to 2000. In the first three years, the combination of the productivity acceleration and favorable supply shocks more than offsets the effect of falling unemployment, and inflation is predicted to fall modestly. In 1999 and 2000, when productivity growth stays high but the supply shocks reverse, inflation is predicted to rise modestly. Actual inflation follows a path very close to this predicted one.

Time-Varying NAIRUs

The recent behavior of unemployment and inflation has suggested to many observers that the NAIRU has fallen. This idea has increased interest in estimating Phillips curves with time-varying NAIRUs (for example, Staiger, Stock, and Watson 1997; and Gordon 1998). So far this paper has estimated constant-NAIRU models. However, our idea that such a model forecasts inflation better when

FIGURE 2.6. / Dynamic Inflation Forecasts—Generalized Phillips Curves

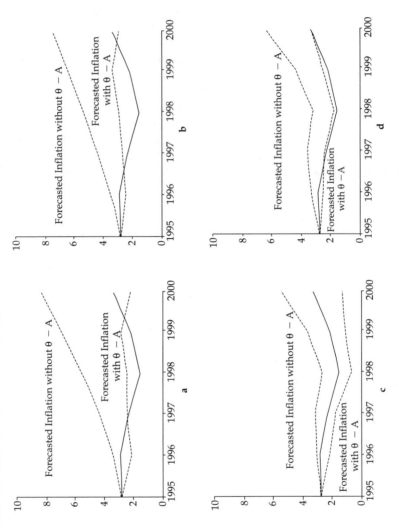

Source: Authors' calculations.

Notes: a: Simple Phillips curves; *b:* Phillips curves with Δπ lags; *c:* Phillips curves with supply shocks; *d:* Phillips curves with supply shocks and Δπ lags.

$\theta - A$ is included can be turned around to say that there is less time variation in the NAIRU once $\theta - A$ is included. In particular, the NAIRU falls less since 1995 if we account for the anti-inflationary role of the productivity acceleration. Here, we explore this version of our story.

We estimate time-varying NAIRUs in the following way. We start with the simple Phillips curves that we have already estimated. Shocks to these equations cause fluctuations in the level of unemployment consistent with stable inflation. For example, in 1974, it would have taken very high unemployment to offset the OPEC shock and keep inflation stable. As discussed earlier, economists generally do not interpret such shocks as year-to-year fluctuations in the NAIRU. Instead, they assume that the NAIRU changes gradually and interpret shifts in the U/π relation as NAIRU shifts only if they appear persistent. In this spirit, we define the time-varying NAIRU as the long-term component of movements in the U/π relation.

Specifically, consider two Phillips curves:

$$\Delta\pi = -\gamma (U - U^N), \tag{2.8}$$

$$\Delta\pi = -\gamma (U - U^N) + (1 - \delta)(\theta - A). \tag{2.9}$$

If U^N is a constant, these reduce to the Phillips curves with and without $\theta - A$ that we estimated earlier. We impose values of γ and of $1 - \delta$ obtained by estimating constant-U^N equations over the period 1962 to 2000: $\gamma = 0.636$ in (2.8); $\gamma = 0.668$ and $1 - \delta = 0.550$ in (2.9). Given these coefficients and the data on $\Delta\pi$, U, and $\theta - A$, each equation defines a series for U^N over the period 1962 to 2000. In (2.8), U^N is the unemployment rate that would produce stable inflation; in (2.9), it is the unemployment rate that would produce stable inflation if $\theta - A = 0$. Finally, we extract a long-term trend from each U^N series using the HP filter with parameter 1,000. These smoothed series are our measures of time-varying NAIRUs.

Figure 2.7 presents the U^N and smoothed-U^N series for each equation. Note first that the average U^N is 6.0 percent when $\theta - A$ is excluded from the Phillips curve and 5.2 percent when it is included. This result confirms our earlier finding that including $\theta - A$ reduces the NAIRU when it is assumed to be fixed. The new result is that adding $\theta - A$ also reduces the time variation in the NAIRU. When $\theta - A$ is excluded, the smoothed U^N rises by 1.7 percentage points from 1962 to 1979, then falls by 1.9 points from 1979 to 2000. This hump-shaped path is similar to the NAIRU behavior estimated by previous authors. When $\theta - A$ is included, by contrast, the NAIRU rises only 0.7 points from 1962 to 1980 and remains almost constant thereafter. The NAIRU fall from 1990 to 2000—a rough measure of the new-economy effect—is 1.2 points without $\theta - A$ but less than 0.1 points with $\theta - A$. Once our new variable is included, there is no need to search for explanations for a falling NAIRU.

The choice of a smoothing parameter for the HP filter is arbitrary. Reducing the parameter increases the time variation in both NAIRU series but does not change the result that the NAIRU is more stable when $\theta - A$ is included.

FIGURE 2.7   /   A Time-Varying NAIRU?

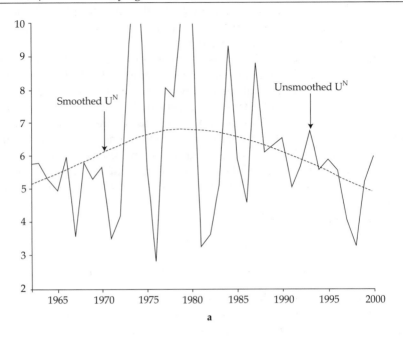

a

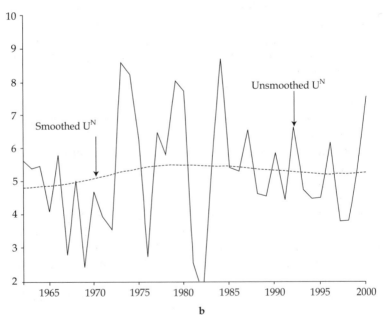

b

Source: Authors' calculations.

Notes: a: conventional Phillips curve; *b:* Phillips curve with $\theta - A$.

THE CHILEAN MIRACLE

So far we have focused on the United States. It is natural to ask whether our theory also explains apparent Phillips curve shifts in other countries. The experience of the 1970s suggests that it does. Productivity growth slowed throughout the OECD during the 1970s, and the NAIRU appeared to rise in most countries. Grubb, Jackman, and Layard (1982) and many others discuss this experience.

Unfortunately, it is difficult to produce international evidence for our theory beyond a broad observation about the 1970s. One might hope to find a cross-country relation between the size of productivity slowdowns or speedups and the size of NAIRU shifts. A look at OECD data suggests, however, that no clear relation exists. The problem is that the NAIRU has moved sharply in many countries for reasons unrelated to our model, involving labor-market institutions and long-run effects of monetary policy (see Blanchard and Wolfers 1999; and Ball 1999). These NAIRU movements usually swamp the effects of productivity shifts that we would like to detect.

The good news is that the cross-country data yield one useful case study: Chile in the 1990s. Chile experienced a major productivity acceleration during this period, one that is usually attributed to economic liberalization. Figure 2.8 plots the growth rate of labor productivity in Chile for the period 1976 to 1997 (measured as the change in log output per worker, from World Development Indicators). Average productivity growth was 0.85 percent over the 10 years from 1977 to 1987 and 4.96 percent over 1987 to 1997. The increase of 4.11 percent is much larger than the recent productivity acceleration in the United States.

Indeed, the Chilean episode is an outlier in international data. There are forty countries for which twenty or more years of data on productivity growth are available from either the World Development Indicators or the OECD. (The starting dates range from 1961 to 1977 and the ending dates from 1992 to 2000.) For each of these countries, we compute the largest productivity acceleration, defined as the largest difference between average productivity growth in a ten-year period and that in the previous ten years. For Chile, the largest acceleration is the 4.11 percent increase between 1977 to 1987 and 1987 to 1997. This is the largest acceleration for any country in the sample. The country with the next largest acceleration is Jamaica, with 3.27 percent, but this reflects an increase from −4.39 percent to −1.12 percent. After that comes Thailand, with an acceleration of 2.96 percent between 1976 to 1986 and 1986 to 1996. Only three other countries have accelerations above 2 percent starting from positive initial growth rates. Thus, Chile's productivity acceleration is more than twice the largest one experienced by most countries and more than a full point above the second best in the sample (ignoring Jamaica).

If productivity shifts affect the Phillips curve, there should have been a favorable Phillips curve shift in Chile. And there was. The shift took a different form than did the recent shift in the United States: it showed up mainly as falling inflation with stable unemployment rather than vice versa. That is, Chile had the

FIGURE 2.8 / Productivity Growth in Chile

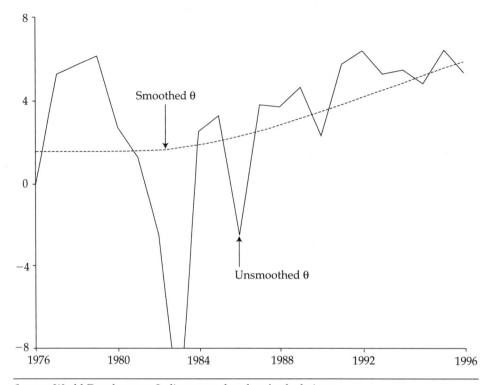

Sources: World Development Indicators and authors' calculations.

rare experience of a costless disinflation. Research has shown that a substantial reduction in inflation almost always reduces output and raises unemployment in the short run. For example, Laurence Ball (1994) examines twenty-eight disinflations in OECD countries and finds output losses in twenty-seven of them. Rudiger Dornbusch and Stanley Fischer (1993) find that disinflations from moderate levels reduce output in middle-income countries as well.

Chile is a stark exception to this stylized fact. Figure 2.9 plots inflation, unemployment, and output growth from 1985 through 1997 (after which the miracle was interrupted by the world financial crisis). As shown in the figure, inflation peaked at 26 percent in 1990 and then fell steadily, reaching 3 percent in 1997. But one can see no adverse effects on the real economy. Unemployment fell from 9.6 percent in 1990 to 6.6 percent in 1997. Output growth was 3.7 percent in 1990 and exceeded 5 percent in every year from 1991 through 1997.[9]

Thus, the Chilean episode combined an unusual productivity acceleration with an unusual shift in the Phillips curve. It stands out from the cross-country data on both counts. Of course, the Phillips curve might have shifted for some other reason, but we doubt it. A leading view within Chile is that inflation ex-

FIGURE 2.9 / Chile's Phillips Curve Shift

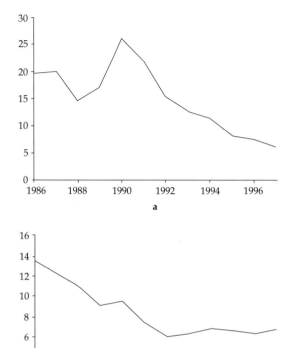

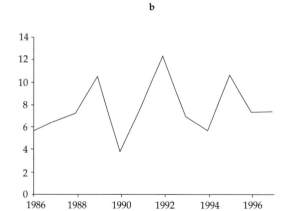

Sources: Bank of Chile and University of Chile.

Notes: *a:* inflation; *b:* unemployment (Santiago); *c:* output growth.

pectations shifted because the central bank introduced a credible inflation target (for example, Corbo 1998). However, other countries have adopted inflation targets, and research has not detected a favorable effect on the Phillips curve. Disinflations usually cause recessions even under inflation targeting (Bernanke et al. 2001).

MICRO EVIDENCE

So far we have examined aggregate relations among productivity growth, unemployment, and wage and price inflation. We now turn to micro evidence on wage changes for individual workers to corroborate our aggregate findings and to explore the formation of wage aspirations in more detail. Our model assumes that workers use lagged wage increases to form their wage aspirations, but, at an individual level, we must be more specific about which lagged wages are relevant. In the language of Daniel Kahneman, Jack Knetsch, and Richard Thaler (1986), we are interested in who forms the *reference group* with which workers compare themselves in judging the fairness of their wages.

We consider two alternative assumptions about reference groups. The first is that workers form aspirations on the basis of the lagged wages of workers who have the same level of skill and belong to the same birth cohort. This idea generalizes the concept that workers use their own, individual lagged wages to form aspirations. (The idea that workers examine only their own past wages seems overly narrow and also requires panel data that are not available.)[10] Our second hypothesis is that workers form aspirations on the basis of the lagged wages of other cohorts of the same age and skill level; that is, a worker of age a in year t bases his or her aspirations on the wages of workers of age a in years $t - 1$, $t - 2$, and so on. The difference in these two hypotheses relates to the familiar demographic distinction between *cohort* and *period* effects.

Following Katz and Krueger (1999), we use individual data from the Current Population Survey (CPS). The May CPS is available from 1973 to 1978, and data for the outgoing rotation group are available from 1979 to 1999. We use both hourly wage and weekly wage measures, for the latter are measured more reliably. Like Katz and Krueger, we measure skill by education level and consider four education groups: less than high school, high school, some college, and college degree or more. We use data on workers aged twenty-five to sixty-four over the period 1973 to 1999 and group workers by five-year birth cohorts ranging from the period 1916 to 1920 to the period 1971 to 1975. Our data cover a total of 888 year-education-cohort cells.

The equation that we estimate is a micro version of the wage Phillips curve presented earlier:

$$\omega(e, c, t) - \pi(t - 1) = a(e) + b(t) + \tau_1(\text{age}) + \tau_2(\text{age})^2 \\ - \gamma U(e, t) + (1 - \delta)A(e, c, t), \tag{2.10}$$

where $\omega(e, c, t)$ is wage inflation for education group e and cohort c in year t, $\pi(t - 1)$ is price inflation at $t - 1$, $U(e, t)$ are BLS-published unemployment rates by education group, and $A(e, c, t)$ is an average of past wage growth. A is constructed in the same way as before, using a β of 0.95 and an HP-filtered value for the start of the process in 1974—but using, in one case, a cohort's own lagged-wage-growth profiles and, in the other, the wage growth of workers of the cohort's current age in past years. We include a quadratic in age to capture life-cycle patterns in wage growth and dummies for education groups and for years. Including these variables means that the coefficient on A is determined by the cross-sectional relation between year-to-year changes in A for different education and birth-year groups and changes in real-wage growth.

The major difference between equation 2.10 and the aggregate equations estimated earlier is the absence of a productivity variable. Unfortunately, productivity data are not available for education groups and other disaggregate portions of the labor force, and, hence, the productivity variable must be omitted. The education and year dummies and the age variables capture productivity growth that is common to all groups in each year (that is, aggregate) as well as productivity growth that is common to each education and age group in all years. They omit the portion of productivity growth that is specific to different education groups in different years. However, productivity shocks of this kind should be orthogonal to lagged wages and hence to A and thus should not bias the coefficients.

The top panel of table 2.4 shows our initial estimation results. We denote the aspirations variable by AC when it is constructed from a cohort's own lagged wages and by AA when it is based on wages of workers of the same age. The unemployment coefficients in the regressions are significantly negative, as expected, albeit smaller than in the aggregate results. Most important, the aspirations variables are all positive and significant. Thus, the micro data corroborate our aggregate finding that wage growth is tied to lagged wages. The effect is significant when aspirations are measured by either AC or AA.

While significant, the coefficients on aspirations are smaller in our initial micro regressions than in our aggregate regressions. However, a common problem with micro data is that regressors based on lagged dependent variables are noisy and contain large random fluctuations. It is unlikely that individuals change their aspirations in response to these fluctuations, and, indeed, a certain fraction of the fluctuations represents sheer measurement error. The consequence of this problem, which is formally equivalent to an errors-in-variables problem, is downward bias in the coefficients. To remedy the problem, we replace the raw aspirations variables with variables that are smoothed over year, education, and age. The results are shown in the lower panel of table 2.4. The coefficients on A rise substantially and reach magnitudes close to those obtained with aggregate data. This result strongly suggests the presence of errors-in-variables bias in the raw data.[11]

Table 2.5 shows the results of including both aspirations variables, AC and AA, in the model at the same time. The two coefficients are both smaller than

TABLE 2.4 / Wage Phillips Curves Estimated on Micro Data

Dependent Variable	Hourly Wage Growth		Weekly Wage Growth	
Results with raw aspirations variables				
Coefficient on $U(e, t)$	−.16	−.17	−.25	−.27
	(.07)	(.07)	(.08)	(.08)
Coefficient on $AC(e, c, t)$	.31		.25	
	(.14)		(.14)	
Coefficient on $AA(e, c, t)$		.38		.38
		(.07)		(.07)
Results with smoothed aspirations variables				
Coefficient on $U(e, t)$	−.34	−.31	−.40	−.37
	(.08)	(.08)	(.09)	(.09)
Coefficient on $AC(e, c, t)$	.87		.72	
	(.20)		(.19)	
Coefficient on $AA(e, c, t)$		.53		.49
		(.08)		(.08)

Source: Authors' calculations.

Notes: N = 888. AC: aspirations variable based on cohort experience; AA: aspirations variable based on period trends. All equations include a quadratic in age, education dummies and year dummies. The smoothed-A specifications smooth the A variable with education-year polynomial interactions and education-age polynomial interactions, as well as a quadratic in age, education dummies, and year dummies.

they are in table 2.4, but they are both significant, and they are close to each other in size. This result suggests that, in forming ideas about fair wage increases, workers put roughly equal weight on their own past experience and on the wage growth of similar workers in the past.

Tests reveal no significant differences across the four education groups in the

TABLE 2.5 / Wage Phillips Curves with Both Aspirations Variables (Smoothed)

Dependent Variable	Hourly Wage Growth	Weekly Wage Growth
Coefficient on $U(e, t)$	−.30	−.35
	(.08)	(.09)
Coefficient on $AC(e, c, t)$	.46	.40
	(.21)	(.20)
Coefficient on $AA(e, c, t)$	.46	.44
	(.09)	(.08)

Source: Authors' calculations.

Notes: N = 792. AC: aspirations variable based on cohort experience; AA: aspirations variable based on period trends. All equations include a quadratic in age, education dummies, and year dummies. Only smoothed-A specifications shown.

coefficients on unemployment and aspirations. That is, while unemployment and lagged wages move in different ways for different groups, the effects of given movements on wage growth are the same.

Further inspection of the data reveals that A has been drifting upward for the more-educated groups and downward for the less-educated groups, thus producing very different patterns of wage growth. Note that A represents real-wage growth in the past, not the level of the wage, so this is not necessarily to be expected from the well-known increasing dispersion of wages by education level. Instead, it implies that the spreading out accelerated over most of the period that we examine. Because A has declined so severely for the less-educated group, the average A has also fallen, consistent with the aggregate data. However, the less-educated groups experienced above-average real-wage growth in the second half of the 1990s, which slowed the decline in A for those groups.

CONCLUSION

This paper proposes a new variable for the Phillips curve: the difference between productivity growth and an average of past real-wage growth. Theoretically, this variable appears if workers' aspirations for real-wage increases adjust slowly to shifts in productivity growth. Empirically, our new variable shows up strongly in the U.S. Phillips curve. Including it explains the otherwise-puzzling shift in the unemployment-inflation relation since 1995.

Our theory contributes to a parsimonious interpretation of macroeconomic history. It yields a unified explanation of why unemployment rose during the productivity slowdown of the 1970s and why it fell after 1995. The theory also explains part of the year-to-year fluctuations in the unemployment-inflation trade-off as arising from fluctuations in productivity growth. Finally, our story links two features of the post-1995 new economy. The Phillips curve shift was caused by the productivity acceleration rather than happening to occur at the same time for some other reason.

In the mid-1990s, the consensus estimate of the NAIRU was 6 percent. Since then, unemployment has fallen near 4 percent, and inflation has not risen substantially. Our results suggest that the noninflationary fall in unemployment is partly but not entirely sustainable. The economy has moved from a regime in which wage aspirations exceed productivity growth, raising unemployment, to one in which aspirations are below productivity growth. Eventually, the economy must move toward a steady state in between. We estimate the NAIRU in this steady state to be around 5.1 percent.

We are grateful for research assistance from Cristian de Ritis, Daniel Leigh, Kevin Moore, Yelena Takhtamanova, Robert Tchaidze, Gergana Trainor, and Huiyan Zhang. We received helpful suggestions from Martin Baily, Susanto Basu, Hasan Bakhshi, Francisco Gallego, N. Gregory Mankiw, Stephen Nickell, Robert Solow, David Weiman, and many seminar participants.

NOTES

1. Note that we assume that ideas about fairness concern wage *increases* rather than wage *levels*. This seems natural because, with productivity increases and life-cycle wage growth, workers are accustomed to fairly steady increases rather than steady levels. We have, however, explored a version of our model in which workers care about levels as well as about growth rates. In this case, the Phillips curve includes an "error-correction" term, the lagged difference between the levels of productivity and real wages. This variable is never significant in our regressions.

2. In our empirical work, we have experimented with alternatives to the exponentially declining weights in equation 2.2. For example, we have defined A as a simple moving average of past real-wage changes. These variations have little effect on our results.

3. As this fact suggests, our results do not change much if we use the unadjusted productivity-growth series. Similarly, changing the coefficient of 0.66 in our procedure does not make much difference.

4. We add a constant to the series on real-wage growth to make its mean equal to the mean of productivity growth. That is, we impose the restriction that there is no trend in labor's share of income. The means of real-wage growth and productivity growth differ in the raw data, mainly because these variables are constructed from price indices with different trends.

5. This F-test compares the sum of squared residuals with and without the restriction that $\beta = 0.95$. Following Douglas Staiger, James Stock, and Mark Watson (1997), we use this test because it appears more accurate than a test based on the asymptotic standard error.

6. Following Staiger, Stock, and Watson (1997), we can construct confidence intervals for the NAIRU by performing a series of F-tests for whether the NAIRU equals various values. A 95 percent confidence interval is (3.5, 5.9). This confidence interval becomes (3.8, 6.1) when lagged inflation changes are added to the Phillips curve to eliminate serial correlation in the errors (see the subsequent discussion).

7. The change in the relative price of food and energy is the log change in the food-energy component of the CPI minus the log change in the CPI. The exchange-rate variable is the change in the log of the trade-weighted real exchange rate from Data Resources, Inc. Following Robert Gordon (1998), we add constants to these variables to make their means equal 0. The Nixon dummy equals 0.5 in 1972 and 1973, -0.3 in 1974, and -0.7 in 1975.

8. The proper interpretation of the lower coefficient is not clear. According to our model, it implies a lower coefficient on A in the target-wage equation and a higher coefficient on θ. However, estimating these coefficients from wage rather than price Phillips curves yields an A coefficient above 0.7 regardless of whether supply shocks and inflation lags are included.

9. The data on inflation and output are from the Bank of Chile. The data on unemployment (in Santiago) are from the University of Chile.

10. One might use the Michigan Panel Study of Income Dynamics, but its sample is too small to allow disaggregation by skill group.

11. The smoothed series for A are fitted values from regressions of A on education-year polynomial interactions, education-age polynomial interactions, a quadratic in age, and year and education dummies.

REFERENCES

Akerlof, George A., and Janet Yellen. 1990. "The Fair Wage–Effort Hypothesis and Unemployment." *Quarterly Journal of Economics* 105(May): 255–83.

Ball, Laurence. 1994. "What Determines the Sacrifice Ratio?" In *Monetary Policy,* edited by N. Gregory Mankiw. Chicago: University of Chicago Press.

———. 1999. "Aggregate Demand and Long-Run Unemployment." *Brookings Papers on Economic Activity* (2): 189–251.

Basu, Susanto, and Miles S. Kimball. 1997. "Cyclical Productivity with Unobserved Input Variation." *NBER* working paper no. 5915. Cambridge, Mass.: National Bureau of Economic Research, February.

Bernanke, Ben S., Thomas Laubach, Frederic S. Mishkin, and Adam S. Posen. 2001. *Inflation Targeting: Lessons from the International Experience.* Princeton, N.J.: Princeton University Press.

Bewley, Truman. 2000. *Why Wages Don't Fall during a Recession.* Cambridge, Mass.: Harvard University Press.

Bils, Mark, and Jang-Ok Cho. 1994. "Cyclical Factor Utilization." *Journal of Monetary Economics* 33(April): 319–54.

Blanchard, Olivier, and Lawrence F. Katz. 1997. "What We Know and Do Not Know about the Natural Rate of Unemployment." *Journal of Economic Perspectives* 11(winter): 51–72.

Blanchard, Olivier, and Justin Wolfers. 1999. "The Role of Shocks and Institutions in the Rise of European Unemployment: The Aggregate Evidence." *NBER* working paper no. 7282. Cambridge, Mass.: National Bureau of Economic Research, August.

Blinder, Alan. 2000. "The Internet and the New Economy." *Brookings Institution* policy brief no. 60. Washington, D.C.: Brookings Institution, June.

Corbo, Vitorio. 1998. "Reaching One-Digit Inflation: The Chilean Experience." *Journal of Applied Economics* 1(November): 123–63.

Council of Economic Advisers. 2000. *Economic Report of the President.* Washington: U.S. Government Printing Office.

DeLong, J. Bradford. 2000. "What Went Right in the 1990s? Sources of American and Prospects for World Economic Growth." In *The Australian Economy in the 1990s,* edited by David Gruen and Sona Shrestha. Sydney: Reserve Bank of Australia.

Dornbusch, Rudiger, and Stanley Fischer. 1993. "Moderate Inflation." *World Bank Economic Review* 7(March): 1–44.

Elliot, Robert F. 1991. *Labor Economics: A Comparative Text.* New York: McGraw-Hill.

Gordon, Robert J. 1998. "Foundations of the Goldilocks Economy: Supply Shocks and the Time-Varying NAIRU." *Brookings Papers on Economic Activity* (2): 297–333.

Grubb, Dennis, Richard Jackman, and Richard Layard. 1982. "Causes of the Current Stagflation." *Review of Economic Studies* 49(special issue): 707–30.

Kahneman, Daniel, Jack L. Knetsch, and Richard Thaler. 1986. "Fairness as a Constraint on Profit-Seeking." *American Economic Review* 76(4): 728–41.

Katz, Lawrence F., and Alan B. Krueger. 1999. "The High-Pressure US Labor Market of the 1990s." *Brookings Papers on Economic Activity* (1): 1–65.

Milkovich, George T., and Jerry M. Newman. 1996. *Compensation.* 5th ed. New York: McGraw-Hill.

Oswald, Andrew. 1986. "Is Wage Rigidity Caused by 'Lay-Offs by Seniority'?" In *Wage Rigidity and Unemployment,* edited by Wilfred Beckerman. Newburyport, Mass.: Duckworth.

Schor, Juliette B. 1987. "Does Work Intensity Respond to Macroeconomic Variables? Evidence from British Manufacturing, 1970–86." Unpublished manuscript. Harvard University.

Staiger, Douglas, James H. Stock, and Mark W. Watson. 1997. "How Precise Are Estimates of the Natural Rate of Unemployment?" In *Reducing Inflation: Motivation and Strategy,* edited by Christina D. Romer and David H. Romer. Chicago: University of Chicago Press.

Stiglitz, Joseph. 1997. "Reflections on the Natural Rate Hypothesis." *Journal of Economic Perspectives* 11(winter): 3–10.

Chapter 3

The Fabulous Decade: Macroeconomic Lessons from the 1990s

Alan S. Blinder and Janet L. Yellen

Macroeconomically speaking, the 1990s, and especially the second half of the decade, was a remarkably successful period for the United States (see table 3.1). Early in the decade, no one would have bet that the 1990s would prove to be the most fabulous decade since the 1960s. Inflation had flared up in 1989–1990, the economy suffered a recession in 1990–1991, and, at the time of the 1992 election, Americans told pollsters that they were quite pessimistic about the economic outlook. But all that was to change dramatically in the ensuing years.

The unemployment rate, which reached a decade high of 7.8 percent in June 1992, fell steadily thereafter and ended the 1990s at 4.1 percent—the lowest level since the late 1960s. Despite this extraordinary employment performance, the inflation rate (measured by the twelve-month trailing CPI), which hit a decade high of 6.3 percent in October and November 1990, declined to 2.7 percent by December 1999. By the decade's end, there was even a developing consensus that America's productivity-growth rate, which had languished near 1.4 percent for more than twenty years, was perking up—perhaps substantially.[1]

How and why did all these wonderful things happen to the U.S. economy? What constellation of good policies, good luck, and related historical developments provided the underpinnings for all this good news? And can we expect it to last? Most important, what lessons should we take away from this period? These are the questions to be explored in the pages that follow.

THE SETTING

The calendar does not always align with historical events. In terms of economic history, the marvelous "sixties" probably began around 1962 and ended around 1973. Similarly, the unhappy "seventies" probably stretched from late 1973 until 1983 or so. True to form, in terms of macroeconomic events, the "nineties" can be said to have started in 1992 or 1993 and now look like they may have ended in 2000. (But, at this writing, it is too early to tell for sure.)

TABLE 3.1 / Economic Performance by Decade

	1990s (Second Half)	1980s	1970s	1960s
Real GDP growth (percent)[a]	3.2 (4.0)	3.0	3.3	4.4
Unemployment rate (percent)[b]	5.8 (5.0)	7.3	6.2	4.8
Inflation rate (percent)[c]	2.9 (2.4)	5.1	7.4	2.5

Sources: GDP growth figures are from the U.S. Department of Commerce, Bureau of Economic Analysis; unemployment rate and inflation rate are from the U.S. Department of Labor, Bureau of Labor Statistics.

[a]Average compound growth rate from last quarter of previous decade to last quarter of stated decade, seasonally adjusted at annual rates.

[b]Average civilian unemployment rate for the 120 months of each decade.

[c]Average compound rate of increase of the CPI from December of the previous decade to December of the stated decade, annualized.

During the 1992 presidential campaign, no one could have imagined what a wonderful position the U.S. economy would be in by the end of the decade. Then-Governor Bill Clinton's famous campaign motto, "It's the economy, stupid," graphically pointed out the terrific political opportunity—for the challenger—that had been created by the widespread voter discontent with the state of the economy. Consider the following:

- The recovery from the 1990–1991 recession was both weak by historical standards and remarkably "jobless" in its early stages. Nonfarm-payroll employment rose by just 611,000 jobs between the March 1991 recession trough and October 1992, a mere 36,000 per month (compared with the 250,000 or so monthly gains that would become the norm later). Furthermore, more than half these meager employment gains were in government jobs. Not only were payrolls barely expanding, but many employed Americans plainly were worried about retaining their jobs.

- Real wages had been doing miserably for years. Misleading but widely cited numbers suggested at the time (and after) that the average real wage had not advanced in over twenty-five years.[2] While that was certainly incorrect, the truth was bad enough: productivity and real wages had stagnated since about 1973. And, during the decade ending in 1992, real wages failed to keep up with even the sluggish growth of labor productivity.[3]

- Median real wages had done even worse than mean real wages because wage inequality had been rising since around 1980.[4] Thus, the "typical" worker had done worse than the average numbers suggested.

- The large and growing federal-budget deficit was the source of a great deal of angst—not only in financial circles, where the "bond-market vigilantes" were in high dudgeon, but also among the general public. It came to be seen as a symbol of government incompetence.

In fact, the U.S. economy was not in nearly as bad shape as the citizenry thought at the time. Economic growth during the 4 quarters of 1992 averaged a hefty 4 percent. Inflation, which had briefly spiked above 6 percent in 1989 and 1990, had been pushed back down to about 3 percent. But all this was little solace to incumbent president George Bush as Bill Clinton hammered away on the economic issue. It was voter perceptions that mattered. A *Wall Street Journal/* NBC News poll as late as mid-September found that an astonishing 86 percent of Americans believed that the country was still in a recession. That was a full 18 months after the recession trough. Fully two-thirds thought that the country was "on the wrong track," whatever that means (Carlson 1992). Just a few days before the election, *USA Today* reported that 60 percent of voters thought that economic conditions were getting worse, while only 28 percent believed that they were improving (Lee and Minzesheimer 1992). The public was wrong; the economy was definitely on the mend. But this misconception surely hurt President Bush at the polls. Such lags of public perceptions behind economic realities are not unusual; in this case, they may have been helped along by the fact that job growth was unusually weak early in the recovery.

More important for our story, three of the foundation stones for what was to become the Fabulous Decade had already been put in place: tighter fiscal policy, looser monetary policy, and industrial restructuring that made American business "leaner and meaner." We begin the story with fiscal policy.

The Budget Agreement of 1990

The 1990 budget agreement was much maligned at the time and proved to be a political albatross around the neck of President Bush. As a candidate in 1988, he had famously pledged "no new taxes." But, as president in 1990, he acceded to Democratic demands for higher taxes to reduce the deficit. Despite its bad press, the agreement marked the first giant step down a path that would eventually lead the federal government to sizable budget surpluses. Unfortunately, contemporary observers did not see it that way. What they saw, instead, was that the budget deficit was on the rise despite the so-called deficit-reduction package. That made the 1990 budget agreement look bad, and it was prematurely and unfairly pronounced a failure.

In fact, the two main reasons why the budget deficit rose rather than fell after 1990 were not failures of the agreement at all. Instead, they were (1) the 1990–1991 recession, which raised the annual deficits by about $160 billion between fiscal years 1991 and 1993 (according to Congressional Budget Office [CBO] estimates), and (2) the huge costs of mopping up after the savings-and-loan debacle—which averaged over $60 billion a year in fiscal years 1990 and 1991. But never mind. The seemingly inexorable rise of the deficit, coupled with the remnants of Reaganite hostility to tax hikes, conspired to give the 1990 agreement a bad name.

The budget agreement also included a real sleeper: the Budget Enforcement Act (BEA) of 1990. This seemingly boring procedural innovation was barely noticed at the time, but it would assume great importance in the coming years. Prior to 1990, Congress had tried to use the Gramm-Rudman-Hollings (GRH) approach to tie itself to the mast of deficit reduction. Under GRH, a five-year program that was first enacted in 1985 and then modified (after failing) in 1987, Congress set legally binding targets for each year's budget deficit. If Congress failed to enact legislation to comply with that year's deficit target, an automatic "sequester" was supposed to enforce the target via equiproportionate reductions in most categories of spending.

The central problem with GRH was clear to economists at the outset and eventually became clear to members of Congress as well: the law set a target for an endogenous variable that Congress cannot control—the budget deficit. What Congress can and does control are (1) tax rates and other provisions of the tax code, (2) the rules governing the generosity of and eligibility for entitlement programs, and (3) the volume of discretionary spending on the programs that receive annual appropriations (which constitute a minority of the budget). Wisely, these were precisely the three items on which the BEA focused congressional attention.

Discretionary spending was limited by annual "caps," much as in the GRH approach—but with an important difference: the caps applied to something that Congress actually could control. Taxes and entitlements were grouped together in a separate pay-as-you-go, or PAYGO, pool. Under the BEA rules, any member of Congress who proposed a tax cut or an increase in entitlement spending was obligated to propose offsetting revenue increases or cuts in other entitlements to "pay for" it. In other words, within the portion of the budget covered by the PAYGO requirement—the clear majority—the new rule was budget balance *at the margin*. But endogenous changes in the budget due to, say, changes in the economy were not to elicit any policy response.

The new approach worked. Unlike GRH, under which Congress repeatedly changed its deficit targets but violated them anyway, the BEA established rules by which Congress could and did live. Indeed, the enforcement mechanisms established in 1990 played pivotal roles in keeping spending in check in several subsequent budget battles. Furthermore, they endured and remain on the books through fiscal year 2002.

Business Restructuring

Industrial restructuring was probably even more important than the 1990 budget agreement.[5] By 1992, the nation had already proceeded pretty far down the difficult path that was popularly (although somewhat misleadingly) referred to as *downsizing*—something it accomplished well ahead of the rest of the world.[6]

Why did restructuring come first to, and go furthest in, America? That is an issue that merits thorough exploration—but not here. We will just briefly mention two reasons. One is that the United States has always practiced a more hard-edged brand of capitalism than either Europe or Japan. Legal barriers to layoffs are negligible in this country, and the government does not make them difficult by regulatory means. There is not even much social disapprobation. The European and Japanese traditions are starkly different in all these respects, although they have been changing of late.

The second reason is the behavior of the exchange rate, which rarely receives even a mention in this context. The pruning of American industry began in the severe recession of 1981–1983, but it gained further momentum in the mid-1980s under the pressure of a grotesquely overvalued dollar. The superdollar rendered U.S.-made products uncompetitive in world markets, thereby showing American firms the hangman's noose. Just as Dr. Johnson had anticipated, that concentrated their minds. In the ensuing struggle to survive, the fittest reduced slack, slimmed down, and became more efficient. The weaker firms perished. Both developments increased the efficiency of U.S. businesses, especially in the heavily exposed manufacturing sector.

The U.S. financial system was also brusquely restructured at the time. The bad-loan problems that had decimated the savings-and-loan industry spread in the 1980s to the commercial banks (which added a few mistakes of their own), and bank failures rose to levels not seen in America since the advent of federal deposit insurance. The banking system was, thus, in a vulnerable position when the recession of 1990 to 1991 hit it with a further body blow, leaving our financial system in its weakest condition in decades. This financial fragility, in turn, created some of the major "headwinds" that were cited at the time as serious impediments to recovery. (We will have more to say on this in a subsequent section.)

The difficult period of industrial and financial restructuring certainly had its dark side: job losses were rampant, and American workers felt insecure and powerless. But our harsh brand of industrial Darwinism probably left American businesses "leaner and meaner" in the end. As we will discuss in a later section, it may also have left the U.S. economy with a more favorable Phillips curve, as traumatized workers pushed less aggressively for wage increases.

Starting around 1992 or 1993, and helped by the lagged effects of a cheaper dollar, American businesses began to reap the rewards of their earlier investments in restructuring. The process began to move into a new phase that placed more emphasis on "leaner" and less on "meaner." As this process progressed, the harsh climate that labor faced as late as 1992 began to give way to a new, more productive industrial environment in which capitalists enjoyed higher profits and workers enjoyed greater employment. With economic activity picking up, American businesses were well positioned to capitalize on the new opportunities.

One simple numerical indication of this transition comes from the annual survey of downsizing conducted by the American Management Association

TABLE 3.2 / American Management Association Downsizing Surveys

Twelve Months Ending	(1) Percentage Reporting Eliminating Jobs	(2) Average Percentage Reduction among These	(3) (1) × (2)
June 1991	43.8	11.4	5.0
June 1992	36.0	10.5	3.8
June 1993	32.6	13.9	4.5
June 1994	30.3	N.A.	. . .
June 1995	27.3	10.2	2.8
June 1996	27.9	10.4	2.9
June 1997	19.0	10.7	2.0

Source: American Management Association, private communication.

Note: N.A. = not available.

(AMA). Each year, the AMA asks its members whether they eliminated jobs (both gross and net) in the previous year and, if so, how many. Table 3.2 shows a sample of the results.[7] Multiplying the fraction of firms reporting net job elimination (column 1) by the average percentage job reduction among such firms (column 2) produces a handy summary measure of the extent of downsizing in the American job market as a whole (column 3). Clearly, the picture for labor improved markedly between the 1992–1993 and the 1994–1995 surveys. The typical firm in the survey—which is, unfortunately, not a random sample of all U.S. firms—shed almost 4.5 percent of its labor annually in the three-year period from mid-1990 to mid-1993 but only about 2.5 percent in the three years from mid-1994 to mid-1997.

The data from the government's Displaced Workers Survey, which is a random sample (but of workers, not of businesses), tell a similar story but with somewhat different timing. Tabulations of these data, summarized in table 3.3, show a notable drop-off in the rate of job displacement between the periods 1993 through 1995 and 1995 through 1997 (see Farber 2001).[8] (Since these are three-year displacement rates, the year 1995 belongs to both periods.) In either case, our basic point is the same: the jobs famine of the early 1990s helped set the stage for the feast that was to come.

TABLE 3.3 / Displaced Worker Surveys

Three-Year Period	Rate of Job Loss (percent)
1989 through 1991	11.8
1991 through 1993	10.9
1993 through 1995	11.5
1995 through 1997	9.1
1997 through 1999	8.6

Source: Farber (2001).

Monetary Policy

The Federal Reserve was severely criticized in 1991 and 1992 for not providing more support to what was, at first, a very weak recovery from recession. Indeed, President George Bush blamed Federal Reserve Chairman Alan Greenspan for costing him the election—which may well have been true. But the Fed finally brought the federal funds rate down to about 3 percent—roughly equal to the rate of inflation—by the middle of 1992. That was too late for George Bush, but not too late to contribute to the subsequent economic expansion. Most important for our story, the Fed then held the real federal funds rate at about 0 for over eighteen months—thereby providing a hefty and sustained dose of monetary stimulus.

Thus, as President Bill Clinton took the oath of office in January 1993, three key ingredients for macroeconomic success were at least partly in place:

- Although it was not recognized at the time, the alarming path toward ever-rising federal-budget deficits (as a share of GDP) had been deflected downward by the 1990 budget agreement.

- Many U.S. businesses had slimmed down and become more efficient. In addition, the dollar had tumbled from its 1985 highs. Both these factors made American industry once again competitive on world markets.

- The Fed had lowered the real federal funds rate to 0 and had its foot pressed firmly on the monetary accelerator.

Notice the beginnings here of what were to become the two major themes of the 1990s: a shift in the policy mix toward tighter budgets and easier monetary policy and improvements in the efficiency of American industry. However, the pre-1993 developments only set the stage. Decisive monetary and fiscal actions were required to unleash the potential, and productivity was as yet showing no signs of accelerating. (In fact, productivity performance was weak during the first half of the 1990s.) What made the Fabulous Decade so fabulous is that all this did happen in the ensuing years.

LAGS AND THE FED'S SUSTAINED EASY-MONEY POLICY

As just mentioned, the Federal Reserve was accused of being insufficiently aggressive in cutting interest rates during and after the 1990–1991 recession. Figure 3.1 shows the basis for this accusation by plotting both the Fed's target for the federal funds rate—its main monetary-policy instrument—and the inflation rate (measured by the twelve-month trailing CPI) during the years 1990 through 1993. The difference between the two lines is, thus, the real federal funds rate, a reasonable measure of the tightness or ease of monetary policy.[9]

When the recession began in July 1990, the federal funds rate was at a high

FIGURE 3.1 / The Federal Funds Rate and CPI Inflation

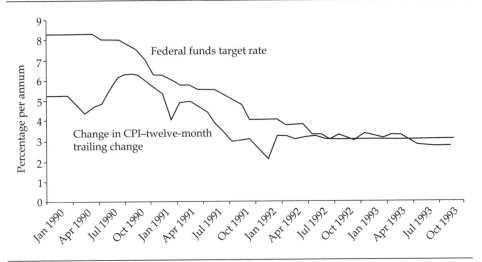

Sources: The federal funds target rate was obtained from the Board of Governors of the Federal Reserve System; CPI inflation was obtained from the U.S. Department of Labor, Bureau of Labor Statistics.

8.25 percent—a rate that the Fed had maintained since December 1989. The initial policy easing on July 13 turned out to be the first in a series of nine rate cuts over 10 months that brought the federal funds rate down to 5.75 percent on the last day of April 1991—just a month after the recession trough. As the figure shows, the real federal funds rate over this period narrowed from over 3 percent to below 1 percent. After pausing for a few months but seeing few signs of vigorous growth, the Fed resumed cutting rates on August 6—taking the federal funds rate down to 4 percent by the end of the year. However, with inflation falling sharply during 1991, the real federal funds rate declined much less (and, indeed, actually rose for part of that period). By year-end, the real federal funds rate was still around 1 percent. The Fed then paused once again—for more than 3 months this time—to take the economy's pulse and to puzzle over why the recovery from recession was so weak. A final round of rate cuts brought the real federal funds rate down to roughly 0 by July 1992.

In searching for explanations for why the economy was not responding to its medicine, the Fed eventually embraced the view that the U.S. economy was being restrained by a variety of stiff "head winds," most of them financial. These included, most prominently, the weakened banking system and the decimated savings-and-loan industry but also extended to overleveraged corporate balance sheets and heavily indebted consumers. Many critics at the time also suggested that bank supervisors—having been burned by the savings-and-loan debacle and castigated by Congress for being too lax—were forcing bankers to be excessively conservative by casting a jaundiced eye on all but the safest loans.[10]

The Fed's extreme caution about lowering rates in 1991 and early 1992 probably delayed a vigorous recovery and may well have tipped the election to Bill
Clinton; President George Bush certainly thought so. But what happened next is
far more important to understanding what made the 1990s roar. The Fed held
the federal funds rate at the extremely low level of 3 percent until February 1994.
Since inflation was quite steady at roughly 3 percent during this period, the real
federal funds rate was kept around 0 for about a year and a half—providing an
extraordinary dose of easy money. As Chairman Greenspan reflected at the September 1993 Federal Open Market Committee (FOMC) meeting, "We finally got
it right and decided to sit with it" (FOMC Transcript, September 23, 1993, 36).
Notice the adverb: *finally*.

How much stimulative effect did this medicine have? To answer this question
quantitatively, we utilized two large macroeconometric models of the U.S. economy, the Fed's own FRB-US model and the proprietary WUMM model of Macroeconomic Advisers in St. Louis.[11] Both are fundamentally Keynesian models in
which aggregate demand drives real output in the short run because prices and
wages are sticky and a Phillips curve mechanism drives wage and price inflation. The long-run properties of both models are basically classical, however, so
real output is influenced by fiscal and monetary policy only temporarily. The
two models differ greatly in their details (for example, in their treatments of
expectations), including especially their respective dynamics.[12] While large-scale
macroeconometric models like these can be (and are) used in forecasting, we
believe that they are best suited for simulation exercises—which is what we use
them for here.

We used each model to compare actual history with a counterfactual simulation in which the federal funds rate never fell below 4 percent. Since the actual
federal funds rate dipped below 4 percent in 1992:2 and remained there through
1994:2, this simulation amounted to holding the federal funds rate higher (by
amounts ranging between 6 and 100 basis points) for nine quarters (1992:2
through 1994:2) and then matching history thereafter. Table 3.4 shows the results.

This table, like others to follow, displays the marginal effects of the change
indicated in the title of the table (in this case, a tighter monetary policy) on three

TABLE 3.4 / Effects of Tighter Monetary Policy from 1992 to 1994

Deviation from Baseline	Model	1993:4	1994:4	1995:4	1996:4
Real GDP growth (fourth quarter	WUMM	−.7	.0	.3	−.2
over fourth quarter)	FRB-US	−.7	−.6	−.2	−.3
CPI inflation rate (fourth quarter	WUMM	.0	−.5	−.5	−.3
over fourth quarter)	FRB-US	−.3	−.6	−.8	−1.0
Unemployment rate (difference)	WUMM	.4	.4	.2	.2
	FRB-US	.4	.7	.7	.9
Federal funds rate (difference)	Both	1.0	.0	.0	.0

Source: Authors' calculations.

variables: the growth rate of real GDP, the inflation rate (measured by the CPI), and the level of the unemployment rate. Thus, for example, the upper-left-hand number in the table means that, according to the WUMM model, real GDP would have grown 0.7 percentage point less during 1993 under the tighter monetary policy.

In appraising this and subsequent tables, it may be useful for the reader to know that, while monetary-policy effects are larger in the FRB-US model, they take longer to build. The top two rows of table 3.4 are an example of a pattern that we will see over and over again. While the two models agree that, had the Fed not driven the federal funds rate all the way down to 3 percent, real GDP growth would have been about 0.7 percentage point lower in 1993 (that is, 1.8 percent growth instead of 2.5 percent), they differ thereafter. Depending on which model you believe, GDP growth during 1994 would have been either the same or 0.6 percent lower. Because of the slower growth (and consequently higher unemployment), inflation would have been reduced. If you cumulate the inflation reductions shown in the table, the price level winds up lower by 1.3 or 2.7 percent by 1996:4. The tighter monetary policy, thus, would have made a substantial difference, especially in the FRB-US model, which implies that the unemployment rate would have been 6.3 percent instead of 5.6 percent by late 1994.

THE FISCAL TURNING POINT: THE 1993 BUDGET AGREEMENT

On the fiscal front, the turning point came in 1993. During his successful campaign for the presidency in 1992, Bill Clinton seemed no more eager to tackle the nagging deficit problem than George Bush was. Neither campaign paid much more than lip service to the need for either significant tax increases or large cuts in expenditures—both of which were viewed as political losers. Bush, of course, was further burdened both by having reneged on his famous pledge, "Read my lips, no new taxes," and by the perceived failure of the 1990 budget agreement. Clinton, for his part, proposed spending cuts and tax increases on upper-income taxpayers. But he also promised both a variety of new spending initiatives and a tax cut for the middle class.

But, during the November 1992 to January 1993 transition period, the president-elect became convinced that reducing the budget deficit by cutting spending and raising taxes should be his overriding priority. Why? Economists at the time enunciated two main reasons to seek a smaller budget deficit.

The first was the traditional "crowding-out" argument: that high budget deficits lead to high real interest rates and therefore damage private investment spending. By reducing its deficit, economists argued, the government could boost investment, which would raise productivity and therefore real wages and living standards. Late in the decade, this argument would assume great prominence in the context of the interlocked debates over social security and paying down the national debt. But, in 1992 and 1993, it did not resonate much with politicians—and, in particular, not with Bill Clinton, who correctly perceived that voters cared about only three things: jobs, jobs, and jobs.

Instead, a second, quite different argument likely persuaded Clinton to opt for a major deficit-reduction program: the fear that some sort of financial calamity—perhaps imperiling the banking system as well as the stock and bond markets—might occur if the deficit was not brought under control quickly. This collapse scenario had more adherents on Wall Street than among academic economists—which, of course, did not handicap it politically. In addition, and significantly, Alan Greenspan was sympathetic. Since a financial cataclysm would surely bring a recession in its wake, this scare story rationalized portraying deficit reduction as a way to "save jobs." Notice, however, that viewing deficit reduction as a net job creator embodies a decidedly anti-Keynesian fiscal theory: that raising taxes and/or reducing government spending *increases* output and employment. We will have much more to say about that later in this section.

Whatever his reasons, Clinton decided to take a big gamble—both politically and economically—by making significant deficit reduction his first major initiative.

The political risk was that Congress might reject his budget package, thereby hobbling the fledgling administration in its first months. After all, Congress had demonstrated little appetite for either tax increases or expenditure cuts over the preceding years. Despite much subsequent criticism of President Clinton as a political opportunist, it is hard to resist the conclusion that he chose major deficit reduction in 1993 because he thought that it was the right thing to do—and he was willing to take the political heat. Either that, or he perceived that the political tides were about to turn. For example, some observers claim that the insurgent candidacy of Ross Perot in 1992 presaged such a turn. In any event, the feared political-disaster scenario very nearly came to pass. The budget squeaked through Congress by one vote in each chamber, without a single Republican supporter. Vice President Al Gore's vote was needed to break a 50–50 tie in the Senate.

The economic risk was that the spending cuts and tax increases would slow the economy unless either the Fed or the bond market bailed the economy out with lower interest rates. Clinton was keenly aware of both risks but went ahead anyway (see Woodward 1994, especially chapters 11 and 12).

The economic plan that the new president presented with great fanfare on February 17, 1993, followed a tortuous path through Congress and was changed in hundreds of ways in the process.[13] Nonetheless, although the budget package that eventually emerged from the legislative meat grinder in August 1993 was slightly bigger than Clinton's original proposal in terms of total deficit reduction, it followed the original proposal's broad contours.

The 1993 budget agreement galvanized the bond market, and the thirty-year bond rate plummeted by more than 160 basis points from Election Day 1992 to October 1993. While no one can ever be sure why markets react the way they do, the view that the bond-market rally should be attributed to the markets' approval of the Clinton plan is buttressed by several facts.

First, contemporary observers saw it that way. Market commentary at the time focused on the deficit-reduction plan as the principal—if not, indeed, the only—reason for the rally. At the July 1993 meeting of the FOMC (a month before the budget bill passed), Chairman Greenspan told his committee, "I don't know how much of the long-term interest rate reduction is attributable to the expectation that there will be a credible reduction in the deficit somewhere out there. I suspect most of it is, rightly or wrongly" (FOMC Transcript, July 6–7, 1993, 66).

Second, figure 3.2, which is based on a diagram that appeared in the February 1994 *Economic Report of the President* (Council of Economic Advisers 1994), offers a persuasive "event study" suggesting that news about the content and legislative progress of the president's proposal moved long-term bond rates sharply downward from January 1993 through August 1993. Notice that the bond rate started falling about a month after the election, as reports on what the new president was planning began to leak to the media. The decline in rates accelerated noticeably when the Clinton plan was introduced, when the House passed it (with many changes), and then again when the Senate and House approved the conference report.

Third, it is *not* true—as some have claimed—that the bond-market rally in 1993 simply continued the trend toward lower long-term rates that had already been in progress for several years. In fact, the preceding multiyear decline in bond rates had come to a halt in January 1992, and, as figure 3.2 shows, long rates moved up and down during the following year with no obvious trend. In fact, yields on long-term bonds were almost exactly the same in January 1993 as

FIGURE 3.2 / Yield on Ten-Year Constant-Maturity Treasury Securities, September 1992 to December 1993

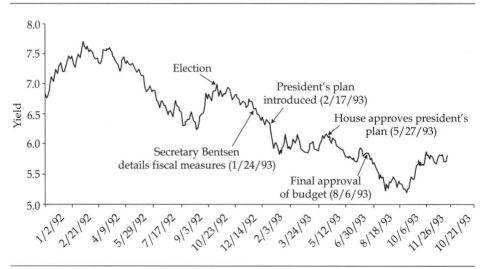

Source: Board of Governors of the Federal Reserve System.

they had been a year earlier. The bond market did not begin rallying again until it started to hear leaks about the content of the Clinton budget proposal in December 1992.

So suppose that the 1993 budget agreement did indeed ignite the bond-market rally. That raises at least two questions. First, did the observed declines in *nominal* interest rates constitute declines in *real* interest rates, or was it expected inflation that fell? While no one can ever be sure, we are inclined to attribute most of the lower nominal interest rates to falling real interest rates. In support of this view, the Blue Chip panel of professional economists' consensus forecasts of inflation—both the CPI and the GDP deflator—barely changed between January and August 1993. But these are only short-run inflation forecasts, not the long-run inflationary expectations that are presumably relevant to bond rates.

The second, and much deeper, question is, How did the agreement so successfully win over the bond-market vigilantes, a hard-bitten bunch who had grown quite cynical after years of "smoke-and-mirrors" budgets—and who were certainly not predisposed to trust a new Democratic government? We believe that five factors contributed to the proposal's unusual and virtually instant credibility in the financial markets.

First, the Clinton budget package, which was originally advertised as $473 billion over five years (although the CBO scored it lower), took a far bolder line on deficit reduction than the market had been anticipating. As noted earlier, Clinton had not emphasized deficit reduction very much in his campaign. The proposal that he submitted to Congress in February 1993, not only surprised markets by its large size, but somehow also seemed to change the tenor of the political debate. Prior to February 17, 1993, raising taxes and cutting spending were viewed as sure political losers; deficit reduction had been dubbed *root-canal economics.* But most of the rancorous battle from that day forward was over how to reduce the deficit even more than Clinton had proposed. How Bill Clinton transformed deficit reduction from a political sow's ear into a silk purse is something of a mystery. But he did it.[14]

Second, the new administration proved its seriousness of purpose by calling for significant tax increases—mainly higher personal-income-tax rates for upper-bracket taxpayers and a new tax on energy use (the ill-fated BTU tax). These decisions, made after George Bush had paid such a heavy political price for agreeing to a smaller tax hike, impressed the bond market. Notice in figure 3.2 the sharp reaction the day after Treasury Secretary Lloyd Bentsen "leaked" the administration's plan to propose an energy tax.

Third, the new administration pointedly rounded up some budgetary sacred cows for slaughter. Prominent among these was a modest reduction in social security benefits (accomplished by making more benefits taxable), thereby touching the alleged third rail of American politics. This, too, helped establish Clinton's bona fides as a serious deficit cutter.

Fourth, the administration's first budget was remarkably free of the gimmicks and accounting subterfuges that the markets had come to expect but grown to detest. Even Clinton's severest critics rarely, if ever, claimed that the package relied on smoke and mirrors to reduce the deficit. By common consent, the proposed cuts and tax hikes were real.[15] That earned the proposal some much-needed credibility.

Fifth, the one gimmick that Clinton did adopt actually cut in the opposite direction: amazingly, the administration "cooked the books" against itself. Specifically, after a short but heated internal debate, the Clinton economic team decided to base its budget projections on the CBO's forecast even though that forecast was more pessimistic than its own.[16] The president made this decision personally, knowing full well that, by so doing, he would not only raise the level of projected future deficits but also reduce the amount of deficit reduction that he could claim for his program.

Together, these five aspects of the package seemed to imbue the Clinton program with a remarkable degree of credibility, especially considering the fact that the new administration had no track record. Interest rates tumbled immediately and sharply (again, see figure 3.2). The extent of the eventual bond-market rally—more than 150 basis points from January to October 1993—surprised virtually everyone. It probably also gave the economy a big lift, although no one would claim it was the only factor behind the investment boom.

How big a lift? We used the two econometric models mentioned earlier to simulate the effects of the bond-market rally, but, unfortunately, they give rather different answers—although mainly on timing (see table 3.5). In each counterfactual simulation, we removed the rally by assuming that the yield on ten-year government bonds remained at its 1992:4 value (6.74 percent) right through 1994:1—whereas, in fact, it fell as low as 5.61 percent. In the WUMM model, long bond rates have a strong, quick effect on GDP, but one that soon dissipates. The bond-market rally, therefore, is estimated to have lowered the unemployment rate by a large 0.6 percentage point by 1994:4, but nothing is left by 1996:4. The effects of lower bond yields build more slowly in the FRB-US model, but they last much longer. According to that model, rising bond prices reduced the 1994:4 unemployment rate by only 0.4 percentage point, but they cut the 1996:4 unemployment rate by 0.6 percentage point. The maximum effect on the *level* of real GDP is almost 1.5 percent in each model, but it comes about a year earlier in the WUMM—according to which the bond-market rally added a full percentage point to the 1993 growth rate. These are not trivial impacts. In a word, the economy received a significant, although transitory, boost from the bond market.[17]

This episode raises a fascinating intellectual question: How, and under what circumstances, can what we normally think of as contractionary fiscal policy really be expansionary? One view common among macroeconomists these days holds that monetary policy can and does offset the effects of any fiscal action on aggregate demand, thereby rendering fiscal changes neither expansionary nor contractionary. On that view, the Clinton deficit-reduction program should not have been expected to cause a slump. But neither should it have precipitated a boom.

TABLE 3.5 / Estimated Effects of 1993 Bond-Market Rally

Deviation from Baseline	Model	1993:4	1994:4	1995:4	1996:4
Real GDP growth (fourth quarter	WUMM	1.0	.2	− .5	− .6
over fourth quarter)	FRB-US	.6	.7	.0	− .1
CPI inflation rate (fourth quarter	WUMM	.3	.3	.4	.3
over fourth quarter)	FRB-US	.1	.1	.1	.5
Unemployment rate (difference)	WUMM	− .3	− .6	− .3	.0
	FRB-US	− .1	− .4	− .6	− .6
Yield on ten-year Treasury bonds	Both	− 1.13	.00	.00	.00
(difference)					

Source: Authors' calculations.

So consider a hybrid theory that, while admittedly impure, may be more empirically relevant to the events of 1993.[18] Specifically, suppose that:

1. Long-term interest rates are the appropriate weighted average of expected
   future short-term rates—the so-called expectations theory of the term structure.

2. The short rate in each period is jointly determined by the Fed's monetary
   policy (which fixes the supply schedule of bank reserves) and the level of
   nominal demand (which determines the position of the demand schedule).

3. The announced fiscal change pertains to the future, not to the present. So it
   has no immediate effect on spending.

4. Market participants expect the central bank to offset the effects of future fiscal
   policy on aggregate demand.

Under these assumptions, a credibly promised future tax increase or expenditure cut could, ceteris paribus, lead markets to expect a different policy mix in
the future—easier money and tighter fiscal policy—with no net effect on aggregate demand. That should mean lower expected future short rates but no slump.
The expectations theory of the term structure will then telescope these lower
expected future short rates into lower long-term interest rates today, which will
stimulate the economy.

While this story is coherent, it is not entirely consistent with the events of
1993. For example, it assumes that the Fed was prepared to offset the effects of
fiscal policy on future demand but for some reason was not prepared to offset
the effects on current demand. After all, at least some of the negative impact of
the Clinton deficit-reduction plan on spending came immediately, as did the
bond-market rally. Why would the Fed not offset this? One possible answer is
that the Fed was having trouble stimulating the economy and therefore welcomed any assistance that it could get from the bond market. That is probably
true. But it throws a bit of cold water on the facile notion that the Fed controls
aggregate demand on a period-by-period basis. And, besides, as we will see

shortly, there are repeated references in the 1993 FOMC minutes to the possible depressing effects of the deficit-reduction program on aggregate demand—plus a few to the stimulative effects of the lower bond rates that the deficit-reduction program may have engendered.

Furthermore, at least some contemporary observers, especially Republicans who opposed the Clinton plan, predicted that the tax hikes would lead to recession. That, the critics argued, is why long-term interest rates went down. Not only were these naysayers quite wrong, but they were also a tiny minority group: the Blue Chip consensus forecast for real growth in 1994 stood at 2.8 percent in August 1993 (when the budget agreement passed), which at that time was a forecast for above-trend growth.

Another theory that is carelessly tossed about holds that lowering the expected future path of the national debt reduces the "risk premium" on government-bond rates. This notion probably makes sense for many countries, especially those that finance their public debt in foreign currencies. But, when we think about applying it to the United States, what, precisely, is the risk that deficit reduction reduces? Default on the national debt? That hardly seems plausible for the United States. Future inflation? That depends on the Fed's propensity to monetize deficits, which appears to be very low. And, in any case, a rise in inflationary expectations might raise *nominal* interest rates but lower *real* interest rates.

One possible answer to this question harks back to the financial-collapse scenario discussed earlier. Suppose that the risk that markets fear is that a rising national debt (especially one that is rising faster than GDP) might eventually lead to a financial cataclysm. Then deflecting the path of the debt downward may alleviate such concerns and, therefore, lower the risk premiums built into real interest rates.

Finally, there is a decidedly nonrational-expectations possibility. Suppose that the markets expected the Clinton program to cause a slump later on but the Fed surprised everyone by preventing the slump from occurring. Then expectations of a future recession could have stimulated the economy in 1993 by provoking a bond-market rally even though no actual slump ever arrived. However, anyone who uses this theory to explain the events that followed August 1993 must answer the following difficult question: When, exactly, did the Fed ease monetary policy by enough to avert a recession? Remember, the Fed held rates steady throughout 1993 and then raised them aggressively between February 1994 and February 1995.

Our own favorite explanation is that an unusual coincidence of timing and policy conspired to change market psychology fundamentally. The time was right: Clinton's election marked the end of the twelve-year Reagan-Bush presidency, and change was expected. So both the public and the markets were receptive. And the policy was right: the budget package had the market-pleasing features that we outlined earlier. So the bond market rallied strongly. Needless to say, this is not a formula that can be repeated at will. Lower bond rates, in turn, ignited the economy. The Fed watched all this happen for a while, somewhat surprised by the large reaction, and then decided to rein in demand.

In this regard, another interesting counterfactual question arises: Did the Clinton deficit-reduction program induce an easier monetary policy by pushing back the date when the Fed would finally remove its foot from the monetary accelerator and start raising interest rates? Such a delay could have happened for either economic or political reasons. The political reason is clear: central bankers who abhor large budget deficits may want to reward politicians for good behavior. In some sense, both Greenspan and Paul Volcker before him had been "offering" the politicians this deal for years. The economic reason is also straightforward: a fiscal contraction will naturally lead a stabilizing central bank to pursue an easier monetary policy. However, in this case, the bond-market rally gave the economy a strong push forward, which the Fed may have felt obliged to counter.

Did this happen in the United States in 1993–1994? Implicitly, it may have. But a close reading of the verbatim FOMC transcripts for 1993 uncovers only scattered mentions of the thought that a tighter fiscal policy ought to call forth a looser monetary policy. For example, in the March 1993 meeting, Robert Parry, president of the Federal Reserve Bank of San Francisco, observed, "Most of the people who have looked at the Clinton program contend that it's going to produce weakness over the next several years" (FOMC Transcript, March 23, 1993, 6). Making the link more explicit at the May meeting, Governor John LaWare asserted, "It can't have escaped any reasonably intelligent observer that the [budget] proposals . . . are essentially contractive. A premature move to tighten policy against that background could be disastrous to economic growth and could run the risk of [reducing] enthusiasm for . . . budget discipline" (FOMC Transcript, May 18, 1993, 28).

But other FOMC members were either thinking about the implications of the bond-market rally or wary of tying monetary-policy decisions too closely to fiscal policy. At the February 1993 meeting, when substantial deficit reduction was expected but had not yet been proposed by the White House (and the bond market was rallying on the rumors), Vice Chairman David Mullins cautioned that, "even if we had this credible deficit reduction package and long rates fell, it's not clear that we should respond by lowering short rates because we could have a . . . stimulative impact of a fall in long rates" (FOMC Transcript, February 2–3, 1993, 27). In September, after the package had been enacted into law, President Jerry Jordan of the Cleveland Federal Reserve Bank warned against adopting "a monetary policy in the future that is different than it would have been in absence of the fiscal package" because, in that case, "monetary policy is being adjusted because of the fiscal regime" (FOMC Transcript, September 23, 1993, 5).

On balance, the FOMC transcripts do not provide much support for the view that fiscal discipline prolonged the period of easy money. Nonetheless, Greenspan allegedly told President Clinton some years later, "If you had not turned the fiscal situation around, we couldn't have had the kind of monetary policy we've had" (Woodward 2000, 221). In any case, the facts remain: the Fed's period of extraordinarily easy money lasted into early 1994, and the first Clinton budget represented a substantial tightening of fiscal policy. The sharp swing in the fiscal-monetary-policy mix was under way.

THE FED ENGINEERS A SOFT LANDING, 1994 TO 1996

By the winter of 1993–1994, the economy had been growing strongly for two years or more,[19] the unemployment rate was down to about 6.5 percent and falling, and the Fed decided that it was time to raise the real federal funds rate above 0. While its first rate hike did not come until early February, a consensus that rates would be going up had developed in the FOMC a few months earlier. By the time of the December 1993 FOMC meeting, six of the nineteen committee members already thought that the Fed should start raising rates immediately—and two of those six dissented when Chairman Alan Greenspan recommended that they wait a bit longer.[20] This hawkish attitude marked a big change from the November meeting, when virtually no one had objected to Greenspan's recommendation to stay put. The Fed was plainly chomping at the bit.

And not without reason. The economy was growing well above what was then believed to be the trend growth rate, and contemporary estimates of the output gap suggested that there was not much slack left.[21] Yet the real federal funds rate was still fixed at 0—indicative of an extremely loose monetary-policy stance. Overshooting seemed a real possibility in such an environment—even though inflation was not rising—and the Fed decided to make what it called a "preemptive strike" against incipient inflation.

In fact, it was a foregone conclusion that rates would go up at the February 1994 FOMC meeting, and Greenspan had to press unusually hard to restrain the committee from raising the federal funds rate even more. Transcripts of FOMC meetings are normally deadly dull—just try reading one—but this meeting had real drama. Greenspan opened the normal policy roundtable by proposing a 25-basis-point increase in the federal funds rate coupled with a symmetric directive. But, by the time ten of the other sixteen members had spoken,[22] only four had registered support for Greenspan's recommendation; six wanted to go up by 50 basis points instead. Alarmed, the Fed chairman interrupted the roundtable to try to stem the tide: "I will tell you that if we do 50 basis points today, we have a very high probability of cracking these markets. I think that would be a very unwise procedure" (FOMC Transcript, February 3–4, 1994, 53). This was a highly unusual intervention on Greenspan's part in the midst of the go-round. Yet only two of the remaining six FOMC members were persuaded to side with him—leaving the final "straw poll" at ten votes for 50 basis points and only seven (including the chairman's) for 25 basis points.

At this point, Greenspan really cracked the whip, virtually insisting on a unanimous vote in favor of his proposal. He declared: "I would be very concerned if this committee went 50 basis points now because I don't think the markets expect it. . . . I am telling you—and I've seen these markets—this is not the time to do this. . . . I really request that we not do this. . . . I would also be concerned if this Committee were not in concert because at this stage we . . . are going to have to do things which the rest of the world is not going to like. . . . If we are perceived to be split . . . , I think we're risking some very serious problems for this organization" (FOMC Transcript, February 3–4, 1994, 55). Then, in one of the most misleading "unanimous" votes in FOMC history, every member of the FOMC voted to support its chairman's recommendation.

At the White House, President Clinton was livid that Greenspan and his colleagues would have the temerity to raise interest rates just six months after his painful deficit-reduction program had passed. But administration economists saw rate hikes as both inevitable and appropriate; the only questions were when the hikes would start and how high rates would go. Clinton was counseled not to browbeat the Fed publicly, and he scrupulously heeded the advice—beginning a hands-off-the-Fed policy that was to continue, virtually without exception, throughout the Clinton presidency. Few, if any, previous presidents have cut the Fed such slack.

In this context, it is important to note that the Fed's goal in 1994 was not to push the economy below full employment in an aggressive attempt to pull inflation down. In fact, FOMC hawks complained repeatedly that the committee was contenting itself with stabilizing, rather than lowering, the inflation rate—a policy that they thought inappropriate.[23] But Greenspan and the FOMC majority were seeking to achieve a so-called soft landing at about full employment (say, an unemployment rate of 6 percent), as depicted in figure 3.3. If successful, the Fed would stabilize inflation more or less where it was—about 3 percent.

FIGURE 3.3 / A Soft Landing

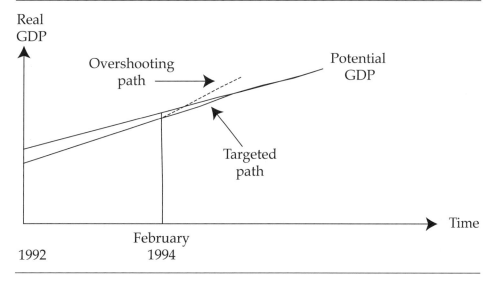

In other words, the Fed sought to move the real federal funds rate up to its "neutral" value.[24] But what rate was neutral? Greenspan kicked off a considerable public debate over precisely that question when he explicitly mentioned the concept—without offering a number, of course—in his explanation of the Fed's initial rate hike. The Fed itself wondered at first whether the neutral real rate might be as low as 1 percent, which would mean a 4 percent nominal federal funds rate.[25] But one thing was clear: when it started raising rates, the FOMC had no clear notion of what the neutral rate might be. At the March 1994 FOMC meeting, Greenspan suggested a 4 to 4.5 percent nominal rate (FOMC Transcript, March 22, 1994, 44). By July, the staff estimate of the neutral (nominal) federal funds rate was up to about 5.25 percent (FOMC Transcript, July 5–6, 1994, 15). But, at the September meeting, President William McDonough of the New York Federal Reserve suggested that a 4.75 percent rate (the rate at the time) was neutral (FOMC Transcript, September 27, 1994, 39). Such estimates, which placed the neutral nominal rate in the 4.25 to 5.25 percent range (hence about 1.25 to 2.25 percent in real terms), seem to reflect an appropriate range of uncertainty. This important parameter is simply not known.

There are two apparent ways to estimate the neutral real federal funds rate. The first method applies the definition directly, by solving an econometric model explicitly for the real short rate that will stabilize inflation, given the level of other relevant variables. Such a calculation, of course, is sensitive to the details of the model, and different models will give different answers. It also implies that a variety of other variables, such as government spending and exports, affect the neutral interest rate. So the neutral rate moves around a great deal. A study by a Fed staff economist using the Federal Reserve Board's own model estimated that the federal funds rate was only slightly below neutral before the Fed started tightening monetary policy in 1994 and then rose to neutral early in 1994—more or less what Greenspan believed early in the tightening cycle (but disbelieved later) (see Bomfim 1997).

The second method uses historical data to calculate the long-run average ex post real rate. On the assumption that monetary policy must have been neutral on average over periods as long as thirty to forty years, that should approximate the long-run average neutral rate (although not the neutral rate of any particular time period).[26] This method tends to produce estimates of the neutral real rate around 2 percent, depending on the exact time period used. For example, the real federal funds rate, defined as the nominal federal funds rate less the four-quarter trailing-CPI inflation rate, averaged 2.3 percent between the first quarter of 1960 and the fourth quarter of 1993. The range of plausible estimates left by these two methods led one of us (Blinder), while vice chairman of the Fed in 1994, to enunciate a likely range for the neutral real federal funds rate between 1.75 and 2.75 percent, implying a nominal federal funds rate around 4.75 to 5.75 percent. If neutrality was the FOMCs target, the 100-basis-point range left it with plenty of room for disagreements over monetary policy.

During 1994 and 1995, various Federal Reserve officials repeatedly warned the markets and the public of the difficulty of achieving a perfect soft landing.

FIGURE 3.4 / The Federal Funds Target Rate, 1994 to 2000

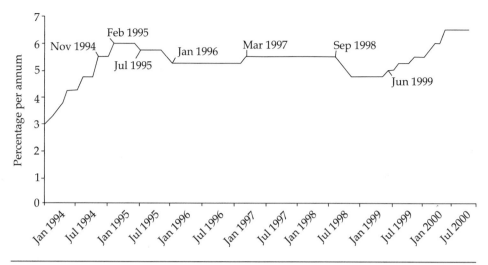

Source: Board of Governors of the Federal Reserve System.

Doing so would require the Fed not only to guesstimate the neutral interest rate fairly accurately, but also to arrive at that rate with just about the right timing (given the long lags in monetary policy). To do this, the Fed would have to be lucky as well as skillful. If a major shock to aggregate demand or supply occurred during the Fed's fine-tuning operation, even the best-laid plans would go awry. In the event, the Fed ultimately raised interest rates seven times over the course of a year, by a total of 300 basis points—bringing the federal funds rate to 6 percent on February 1, 1995, when the tightening cycle stopped. (Figure 3.4 shows the path of the federal funds rate during this tightening phase and its subsequent evolution.) This seemed to do the job, although the final rate hikes in this series, 75 basis points in November 1994 and 50 basis points in February 1995, were highly contentious.

At the time of the November 1994 meeting, the federal funds rate was at 4.75 percent, and the financial markets were clamoring for much higher rates to stave off inflation. However, several FOMC members (including the authors of this paper) began to voice concerns that the Fed might engage in "overkill" by underestimating the lags in monetary policy. The committee voted unanimously to raise the federal funds rate by 75 basis points—the only move of that magnitude in the entire Greenspan era. But several members expressed a preference for going up by only 50 basis points, and others made it clear that they disagreed with the staff's view that 150 basis points of additional tightening—which would have taken the federal funds rate to a peak of 6.25 percent—would eventually be needed.

The Fed's final rate hike of 50 basis points came at the January 31–February 1, 1995, meeting, even though several FOMC members (especially the authors of this paper) voiced concerns that the Fed might be raising rates too precipitously. Around that time, the economy was just starting to show indications of slowing down. As Greenspan put it, "There are now tentative signs, not necessarily persuasive but definitely beginning to appear, of slight cracks along the road" (FOMC Transcript, January 31–February 1, 1995, 104). In addition, U.S. exports were clearly poised to decline in the aftermath of the Mexican financial crisis. Since the traditional inventory accelerator mechanism could be expected to exacerbate any slowdown in spending, the danger of a hard landing was rising.[27] Although financial markets were still clamoring for more tightening, Greenspan noted, "It is by no means evident that, if this cracking that we have seen continues, . . . there will be another tightening of policy" (FOMC Transcript, January 31–February 1, 1995, 108).

As the year progressed, the danger of monetary overkill became a concern of the FOMC. Fortunately, long-term interest rates played a stabilizing role during this episode, as they did later in the expansion (see Meyer 1997a). Even before the Fed's final rate hike in February 1995, the yield on the thirty-year Treasury bond had declined about 40 basis points from its November 1994 high. This drop in long-term rates probably reflected the market's perception that signs of a slowdown were emerging—prompting a reevaluation of the amount of tightening that the Fed would have to do. In the following months, long-term rates fell further as evidence of a slowdown accumulated, dropping from 7.75 percent on February 1, 1995, to 6.61 percent on July 5, the day before the FOMC's first rate cut.

Statements by Fed officials reinforced the market's reassessment of the likely future stance of policy. Three weeks after the Fed raised rates on February 1, 1995, Greenspan hinted at the possibility of a preemptive strike against a downturn when he noted in congressional testimony that "there may come a time when we hold our policy stance unchanged, or even ease, despite adverse price data, should we see signs that underlying forces are acting ultimately to reduce inflation pressures" (Greenspan 1995). Between July 1995 and January 1996, the FOMC finally validated market expectations by reducing the federal funds rate from 6 to 5.25 percent in three steps. In the view of some observers, this shifted monetary policy from mildly restrictive to approximately neutral, although an alternative interpretation of the rate cuts is that they merely kept the real federal funds rate from rising in the face of declining inflationary expectations.

The prospective impact of more contractionary fiscal policy also affected monetary-policy decisions, at least in the eyes of some FOMC members (including the authors), reinforcing the desirability of bringing the federal funds rate down. An agreement between the administration and the new Republican-led Congress to balance the budget via another round of budget cuts was widely anticipated and was discussed in the FOMC (see, for example, FOMC Minutes, March 26, 1996). Macroeconometric-model simulations at the time suggested that the ensuing fiscal restraint might lower the equilibrium real federal funds rate by 150 basis points, a very large amount.

By the end of 1995, it appeared that the Fed had defied the odds and achieved the elusive soft landing at full employment. The unemployment rate was 5.6 percent, which was considered an optimistic estimate of the nonaccelerating inflation rate of unemployment (NAIRU) at the time; the GDP growth rate in the second half of 1995 was 3.2 percent;[28] and the core inflation rate (twelve-month trailing-core CPI) was still 3 percent. It was this stunningly successful episode, we believe, that elevated Greenspan's already lofty reputation to that of macroeconomic magician. From that point until recently, it seemed that the Fed could do no wrong in the market's eyes.

But how, precisely, did the Fed's fine-tuning exercise affect GDP growth? To answer that question, we again utilized the WUMM and FRB-US models to simulate the path of the U.S. economy under alternative monetary policies. This time we considered two. The first alternative embodies a looser monetary policy: it asks what would have happened if the Fed had held the federal funds rate at 3 percent right through the first half of 1995. While this is not a serious policy option that anyone would have entertained, it does provide a gross measure of the Fed's (negative) impact on GDP and other variables.[29] The second assumes a tighter monetary policy: it asks how different things would have been if the Fed had listened to the more-hawkish market sentiment that prevailed in late 1994 and kept pushing rates higher, reaching a 7.5 percent federal funds rate by the May 1995 meeting.

Table 3.6 presents the three different paths for the federal funds rate. Tables 3.7 and 3.8 summarize the simulation results for the looser and tighter alternatives.

Under the easier monetary policy, the economy grows substantially faster in 1994 (in both models) and 1995 (sharply faster in 1995 in the FRB-US model). By the end of 1995, real GDP is 2.6 or 3.9 percent above baseline in the two models. In both models, unemployment falls further and faster (reaching 4.0 or 4.3 percent by the end of 1995) and inflation rises by about 1 percent above its historical level (to a bit above 4 percent in 1996) (see table 3.7). In the WUMM model, the delayed monetary tightening produces a pretty hard landing: the numbers in the table imply that real growth would have slowed to barely above 0 during 1996 and unemployment would have reached 6.3 percent by 1997:3.

The tighter monetary-policy scenario (see table 3.8) naturally produces effects that go in the opposite direction. Growth is about 0.5 percent slower during

TABLE 3.6 / Federal Funds Rate under Three Different Monetary Policies (by Quarter)

	1994				1995				1996:1
	1	2	3	4	1	2	3	4	
Looser	3.00	3.00	3.00	3.00	3.00	3.00	3.75	4.50	5.25
Actual	3.21	3.94	4.49	5.17	5.81	6.02	5.80	5.72	5.36
Tighter	3.21	3.94	4.49	5.23	6.50	7.35	6.68	6.02	5.36

Source: Authors' calculations.

TABLE 3.7 / Estimated Effects of Easier Monetary Policy during 1994–1995

Deviation from Baseline	Model	1994:4	1995:4	1996:4	1997:4
Real GDP growth (fourth	WUMM	2.0	.6	−3.8	−1.4
quarter over fourth quarter)	FRB-US	1.2	2.7	−1.3	−1.2
CPI inflation rate (fourth	WUMM	.1	.1	.9	.2
quarter over fourth quarter)	FRB-US	.2	.9	1.2	2.1
Unemployment rate (difference)	WUMM	−.6	−1.3	.3	1.5
	FRB-US	−.4	−1.6	−1.7	−1.1
Yield on ten-year Treasury	WUMM	−1.84	1.21	2.06	−.58
bonds (difference)	FRB-US	−1.84	1.21	2.06	.00

Source: Authors' calculations.

1995, unemployment is 0.2 or 0.4 percentage point higher during 1995–1997, and inflation is roughly 0.3 percentage point lower during 1996 and 1997. Together, these two simulations agree with the market's view that the Fed threaded the needle pretty well in the 1994–1996 episode. The tightening in 1994–1995 certainly should not have been delayed, and it does not appear to have been excessive. The easing in 1995–1996 might have been judged a bit too permissive at the time, but the wisdom of hindsight belies that view.

THE FED FORBEARS, AND THE PHILLIPS CURVE COOPERATES

The state of the U.S. economy looked superb at the start of 1996, and it just kept getting better over the ensuing years. The unemployment rate belied the popular view that the NAIRU was between 5.5 and 6 percent by falling steadily right through 1999. By December 1999, unemployment stood at 4.1 percent, its lowest level in twenty-nine years.[30] Real GDP growth averaged 4.5 percent during these four years—well in excess of contemporaneous estimates of potential output growth. Yet, as figure 3.4 shows, aside from one minor upward adjustment of 25

TABLE 3.8 / Estimated Effects of Tighter Monetary Policy during 1994–1995

Deviation from Baseline	Model	1994:4	1995:4	1996:4	1997:4
Real GDP growth (fourth quarter	WUMM	.0	−.6	.0	.1
over fourth quarter)	FRB-US	.0	−.5	−.3	−.1
CPI inflation rate (fourth quarter	WUMM	.0	.1	−.3	−.3
over fourth quarter)	FRB-US	.0	−.2	−.3	−.4
Unemployment rate (difference)	WUMM	.0	.2	.3	.2
	FRB-US	.0	.2	.4	.4
Yield on ten-year Treasury bonds	WUMM	.02	.37	.02	.14
(difference)	FRB-US	.01	.20	.06	.02

Source: Authors' calculations.

basis points in March 1997, the federal funds rate was not raised again until June 1999.

Thus, apart from the Fed's reaction to the 1998 financial crisis, the best one-word description of its monetary policy from early 1996 to the summer of 1999 is *forbearance*. The FOMC watched, scratched its collective head in a struggle to understand the forces restraining inflation, worried that the good luck would soon end and inflation would again rear its ugly head, but largely held its fire. In fact, the Fed actually cut the federal funds rate by 75 basis points to combat growing international turmoil during the worldwide financial crisis in the fall of 1998.

One important question for macroeconomic historians is why the Fed chose to forbear even as the unemployment rate drifted down to levels that previously had been associated with accelerating inflation. Part of the answer is simply that, despite the inflation fears of FOMC hawks and many outside forecasters, the worst never came to pass. As table 3.9 illustrates, inflation did not rise; on the contrary, it fell.

The table displays the behavior of three broad-based measures of consumer prices from 1994 to 1999: the CPI for all urban consumers (CPI-U), the chain-weighted price index for personal consumption expenditure (PCE),[31] and a new research series—the CPI-U-RS, which is an estimate of the (hypothetical) rate of inflation in the CPI-U under the methodology in place as of 1999. The core versions of each index, which exclude food and energy prices, were mostly declining during this period. The fact that core inflation was falling while unemployment was so extraordinarily low surprised both the FOMC and outside observers. The Blue Chip forecasters, for example, regularly overestimated inflation in 1996, 1997, and 1998. Similarly, official inflation forecasts from the White House, the CBO, and the Fed were routinely too pessimistic about both inflation and real growth.

A major puzzle—perhaps *the* major puzzle—about this entire period is why

TABLE 3.9 / Measures of Consumer-Price Inflation (Twelve-Month or Fourth-Quarter Trailing Change)

	Last Month or Quarter of:					
	1994	1995	1996	1997	1998	1999
CPI-U	2.7	2.5	3.3	1.7	1.6	2.7
PCE, chain weighted	2.1	2.1	2.3	1.5	1.1	2.0
CPI-U-RS	2.3	2.4	3.0	1.6	1.4	2.7
Core CPI-U	2.6	3.0	2.6	2.2	2.4	1.9
Core PCE, chain weighted	2.3	2.3	1.8	1.7	1.6	1.5
Core CPI-U-RS	2.2	2.8	2.4	2.1	2.2	2.0

Sources: All CPI-U and CPI-U-RS data are from the U.S. Department of Labor, Bureau of Labor Statistics; PCE data are from the U.S. Department of Commerce, Bureau of Economic Analysis.

inflation remained so low after 1995. The leading candidate (or candidates) is a series of disinflationary "supply shocks." FOMC discussions dating back to 1995 focused on the moderation in employee benefits due to health-care restructuring and the possible role of worker insecurity as factors restraining compensation increases. Productivity developments also attracted some attention, especially from Alan Greenspan, even though the evidence for productivity improvement was mainly anecdotal or indirect at the time.[32] During 1997, the behavior of oil and nonoil import prices was added to the FOMC's list of pertinent supply shocks.

The following simple wage-price model provides a useful framework for organizing our discussion of these favorable shocks:

$$\omega = \theta^w + \pi^e + f(u - u^N) + Z_1 + \text{error} \tag{3.1}$$

$$\pi = \omega - \theta^f + Z_2 + \text{error} \tag{3.2}$$

Equation 3.1 is a standard Phillips curve: the rate of increase of nominal labor compensation (ω) depends on the growth rate of productivity (θ), expected inflation π^e, the deviation of unemployment (u) from its natural rate (u^N), and "shocks" to the wage equation (z_1). (The stochastic error terms in the two equations are inessential here and will be ignored.) Equation 3.2 is a conventional markup equation: prices rise at the same rate as unit labor costs ($\omega - \theta$), except when shocks to the price equation (z_2)—such as food or energy prices—perturb this relation. The superscripts on the productivity-growth rates in each equation—w for worker and f for firm—are important and will be explained presently.

Solving 3.1 and 3.2 together, and using lagged inflation as a crude proxy for expected inflation, yields what is often called *the price-price Phillips curve:*

$$\pi - \pi_{-1} = \theta^w - \theta^f + f(u - u^N) + Z_1 + Z_2 + \text{errors} \tag{3.3}$$

Equation 3.3 says that the normal relation between unemployment and *changes* in inflation (or, if you reject the proxy, *unexpected* inflation) can be perturbed by wage shocks (z_1), price shocks (z_2), and any deviation between the productivity-growth rates perceived by workers and firms ($\theta^w - \theta^f$). In addition, the NAIRU (u^N) might change. In what follows, we will pay some attention to each of these four possible explanations for why inflation remained so low during the period 1995 through 1999.[33]

But, first, it is worth looking at figure 3.5, which uses data for the period 1960 through 1999 to illustrate the gross relation between unemployment and changes in inflation—without controlling for any of the other factors in equation 3.3.[34] The figure embodies an extremely simple theory of changes in inflation—after all, it allows for no other variables. Nonetheless, it fits the data better than might be expected. It also shows, perhaps surprisingly, that inflation performance was not very exceptional during the 1994–1996 period but that it was unusually

FIGURE 3.5 / Unemployment and the Change in CPI Inflation, 1960–1999

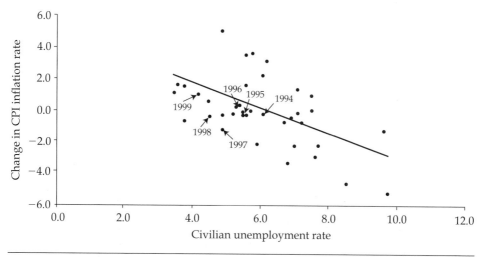

Source: U.S. Department of Labor, Bureau of Labor Statistics.
Note: The regression line is based on 1960 to 1995 data.

low during 1998 and, especially, 1997. Bearing this in mind, we proceed now to some explanations.

Surprisingly Moderate Wage Inflation

We begin with wage shocks (z_1). Equations like 3.3 tracked the data quite well while the Fed was piloting the economy to a soft landing in 1994–1995. Indeed, at the time, one of us (Blinder) dubbed the excellent fit of the (price-price) Phillips curve "the clean little secret of macroeconometrics."[35] But, if you peered below the surface, trouble was brewing: wages were coming in lower than expected and markups higher. Although the errors were not huge, they were notably one-sided. The econometric puzzle was twofold: Why was compensation growing so slowly given the apparent tightness of the labor market? And why, given the slow growth of labor costs, wasn't inflation falling more?

We can think of two plausible—and related—explanations, both of which were much discussed at the time. According to what might be called the *traumatized-worker hypothesis,* after being terrorized by corporate restructuring, suffering through a recession, and then struggling through an initially "jobless" recovery, American workers became more concerned with job security than with real-wage increases.[36] Think of the traumatized-worker hypothesis as either a decrease in u^N or a negative z_1 shock, possibly accompanied by a positive z_2 shock, as bargaining power shifts from labor to management. Greenspan himself called attention to this idea in numerous speeches, adding the further point that more rapid technological progress also increased insecurity by quickening the pace at which job skills become obsolete (Greenspan 1996b, 9). An even stronger version of the theory would suggest that American labor did not suffer just a temporary trauma but actually saw its bargaining position eroded on a permanent (or at least long-lasting) basis.

Evidence supporting this hypothesis was mixed. Some survey results indicated that levels of job insecurity were unusually high given the unemployment rate, but some did not.[37] Again controlling for the state of the labor market, the data seemed to show low levels of voluntary quits and high levels of job loss—both indicators of insecurity (on job loss, see Farber 2001). And work stoppages were also at forty-five-year lows.[38]

A second hypothesis starts with the observation that fringe benefits, which had been rising faster than wages and salaries for years, decelerated sharply in 1993 and 1994—and actually grew more slowly than wages starting in 1995 (see figure 3.6). One can think of this event as a negative *benefit shock*, although by that label we do not necessarily mean to imply that it was some sort of an exogenous event. It could be that the downward deflection of benefit costs was the way the market happened to register some deeper phenomenon—such as a decline in labor's bargaining power.

Decelerating health-insurance costs were the best-known part of the benefits story and were certainly of substantial importance. Medical-care-cost inflation, which had skyrocketed into double digits in the late 1980s, began to deescalate early in the 1990s. Cost increases for group health insurance began to abate in 1993 and 1994 and actually turned negative during 1995–1998. Substantial restructuring took place in the health-care sector in the aftermath of the failed

FIGURE 3.6 / Changes in Wages and Salaries and Benefits in the Employment
Cost Index

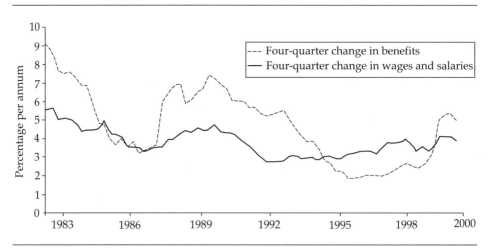

Source: U.S. Department of Labor, Bureau of Labor Statistics.

Clinton initiative, and employers shifted workers out of fee-for-service and into managed-care plans. Part of the decline reflected decreases in coverage, increases in copayments and deductibles, and the like (see, for example, Krueger and Levy 1997). Figure 3.7 shows the behavior of employers' costs for private group health insurance per hour of work in the nonfarm-business sector. These costs grew by 7.4 percent per year between 1990 and 1994, then *declined* at an average 2.3 percent per year during 1995–1998. That was a stunning turnaround.

But health insurance was not the whole story. Figure 3.7 also shows that employer contributions for pensions and retirement benefits plummeted, as the soaring stock market allowed firms to pay much less into their defined-benefit retirement plans. The costs of worker's compensation also fell.[39] In other words, workers "took their hit" mainly in the benefits component of total compensation rather than in the wage component.

A simple calculation suggests that this containment of employee-benefit costs could have translated into a substantial decline in the inflation rate of overall compensation. During 1992–1994, employee-benefit costs (excluding employers' contributions for social insurance) per hour of work rose 1.4 percent per annum more rapidly than an index of nonfarm-business prices. During 1995–1998, these benefit costs actually *declined* by 4.4 percent per year relative to this same price index. Although these fringe benefits account for only about 10 percent of total compensation, the 5.8 percentage point reduction in the growth rate of real hourly benefit costs, other things equal, should have reduced the pace of compensation growth by about 0.5 percentage point.

FIGURE 3.7 / Growth in Employers' Hourly Cost for Selected Private Benefits

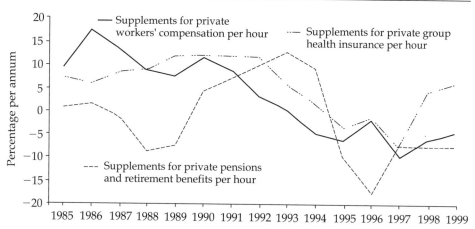

Sources: Supplements from U.S. Department of Commerce, Bureau of Economic Analysis; hours from U.S. Department of Labor, Bureau of Labor Statistics.

Note: Benefits are defined as supplements divided by hours of work in the nonfarm-business sector.

But wait. Doesn't economic theory suggest that market forces determine the growth rate of total compensation, not just wages? The answer is yes. So, in the long run, wages and salaries should accelerate to offset any slowdown in benefits.[40] However, this one-to-one offset need not appear in the short run. When workers are not pressing very hard for higher compensation, or when firms are successfully resisting labor's demands, companies that manage to economize on benefit costs may be able to pocket the gains for a while. In fact, labor's share of nonfarm-business output fell by a remarkable 4 percentage points between 1992 and 1997, reaching its lowest level in the postwar period, which is consistent with the view that workers lost out. Profit margins and the return to capital naturally increased.[41]

To assess the effect of lower benefit costs on the economy, we again used the WUMM and FRB-US macroeconometric models. Specifically, we asked how different economic performance would have been if hourly employer costs for fringe benefits had continued to increase at a rate 1.4 percentage points faster than the index of nonfarm-business prices in 1995–1999—just as they had in 1992–1994.[42] Since faster growth of fringe benefits would raise inflation, it is hardly plausible that the Federal Reserve would have held the nominal federal funds rate constant in such an environment. So our simulations assumed that the Fed would have kept the *real* federal funds rate constant, adjusting the nominal federal funds rate point for point with inflation. The results, which are reported in table 3.10, suggest that slower growth of benefit costs had a large economic impact. In both models, the "benefits shock" lowers price inflation by an average of almost 1 percentage point during 1995–1998, even though unemployment is reduced substantially.[43] These are sizable effects, bigger than the simple back-of-the-envelope calculation suggests. Why?

In the FRB-US model, nominal-wage bargains depend on expected inflation. The benefits shock kicks off a virtuous circle in which lower inflation in one year

TABLE 3.10 / The Effects of Slower Growth in Real Employee-Benefit Costs after 1994 (Real Federal Funds Rate Held at Baseline Level)

Deviation from Baseline	Model	1995:4	1996:4	1997:4	1998:4	1999:4
Real GDP growth (fourth quarter over fourth quarter)	WUMM	.2	1.0	1.0	.1	−.4
	FRB-US	.0	.2	.3	.4	.1
CPI inflation rate (fourth quarter over fourth quarter)	WUMM	−.8	−1.3	−1.5	−.7	−.3
	FRB-US	−.2	−.7	−1.2	−1.4	−1.0
Unemployment rate (difference)	WUMM	−.0	−.4	−.9	−.9	−.7
	FRB-US	−.0	−.1	−.4	−.7	−.7
Hourly nominal-compensation growth (fourth quarter over fourth quarter)	WUMM	−1.1	−.8	−1.2	−.1	−.1
	FRB-US	−1.4	−1.3	−2.0	−.4	−.2

Source: Authors' calculations.

reduces expected future inflation, nominal-wage increases, and therefore actual inflation in subsequent years. As a result, inflation remains about a percentage point below its baseline level in 1999, even though the benefits shock is gone. In the WUMM, nominal-wage growth depends on anticipated nominal-wage inflation instead of on anticipated *price* inflation, but the virtuous-circle mechanism is similar.

Regardless of whether the z_1 shock came from traumatized workers or from decelerating benefit costs, there remains the question of how long it continued to pull inflation down. As job prospects brightened in the tight labor markets of 1998 and 1999 and permanent layoffs declined to more normal levels, Americans workers should have overcome their trauma.[44] And benefit-cost increases began to rise again in 1998. Moreover, any downward deflection of the path of benefits should ultimately have led to an upward deflection of the path of straight wages, as we have already noted. However, the expected effects of these wage-reducing events would have been more durable if labor's bargaining power had been permanently eroded. Furthermore, there were other factors holding price inflation down, factors to which we now turn.

Price Shocks During the Good-Luck Period, 1996–1998

Between 1996 and 1998, a series of favorable price shocks—negative z_2's—were reducing inflation below the rates that would have been predicted from the prevailing unemployment rate and past inflation history. In this section, we discuss three such shocks, leaving the surprising acceleration of productivity—surely the most important shock of the period—for separate treatment in a later section. Simulations with the WUMM and FRB-US macroeconometric models described subsequently suggest that these shocks are more than enough to explain why inflation was so well contained between 1996 and 1998.

THE DOLLAR AND IMPORT PRICES   A first favorable—albeit transitory—influence on inflation between 1995 and 1999 came from import prices. From the narrow standpoint of U.S. inflation, the sharp appreciation of the dollar from the spring of 1995 to the summer of 1998, coupled with a weak world economy, constituted a stroke of good fortune. As figure 3.8 illustrates, the dollar rose sharply in real terms over these three years—at roughly a 4 percent average annual rate. With a short lag, the prices of nonoil imports mirrored this behavior, declining at a 4 percent annual rate during 1996–1998 after rising at just under 1 percent per year during 1993–1995. Because prices of imported goods are included in all indices of consumer prices, falling import prices lowered these measures of inflation directly. They probably also constrained the pricing power of American businesses.

With imports accounting for roughly 10 to 12 percent of the consumption basket, a simple back-of-the-envelope calculation suggests that the 18 percent appreciation of the dollar (on a trade-weighted basis) between 1995:2 and the

FIGURE 3.8 / Non-Oil Import Prices and the Dollar

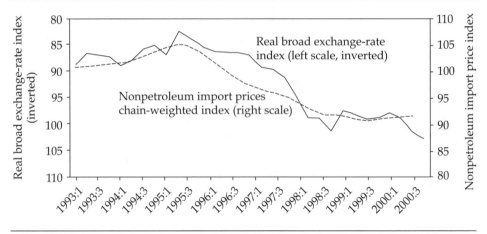

Sources: Import prices from U.S. Department of Commerce, Bureau of Economic Analysis; exchange rate from Board of Governors of the Federal Reserve System.

end of 1998 should have lowered the level of consumer prices by about 2 percent. But this computation ignores all feedback and secondary effects. For a more serious assessment of the impact of the rising dollar on the U.S. economy during the good-luck period, we again simulated both the WUMM and the FRB-US macro models—asking what would have happened if the dollar had remained fixed in real terms after 1995:2.[45] The simulation again maintains the real federal funds rate at its actual baseline level. Table 3.11 shows the results, and, unfortunately, the two models once again disagree—this time sharply.

In the WUMM model, the appreciation of the dollar has an extremely large negative effect on inflation, lowering CPI inflation by 0.6 percent during 1996, 1

TABLE 3.11 / Effect of the Real Appreciation of the Dollar after 1995:2 (Real Federal Funds Rate Held at Baseline Level)

Deviation from Baseline	Model	1995:4	1996:4	1997:4	1998:4	1999:4
Real GDP growth	WUMM	−.0	−.2	−.8	−2.2	−2.5
(fourth quarter over	FRB-US	−.0	−.2	−.5	−1.0	−1.2
fourth quarter)						
CPI inflation rate (fourth	WUMM	−.1	−.6	−1.0	−2.2	−2.0
quarter over fourth	FRB-US	−.0	−.2	−.3	−.5	−.3
quarter)						
Unemployment rate	WUMM	.0	.1	.4	1.4	2.5
(difference)	FRB-US	.0	.0	.1	.5	1.0
Real broad exchange-rate	Both	3.3	5.3	14.6	17.9	18.5
index (percent)						

Source: Authors' calculations.

percent during 1997, and a whopping 2.2 percent during 1998. In the absence of the appreciation, inflation during 1998 would have reached 3.7 percent (versus 1.5 percent in actuality), according to this model. The stunningly large effect, roughly triple what the elementary calculation suggests, comes largely from the sharp drop in real GDP (the growth-rate effects shown in the table cumulate to a 5.5 percent level effect by the end of the simulation) and the accompanying rise in unemployment (2.5 percentage points). The FRB-US model produces inflation effects that are similar qualitatively but much smaller quantitatively—owing largely to more-muted effects on GDP and unemployment. According to this model, the biggest effect of the dollar appreciation on inflation reaches only −0.5 percent in 1998. Both models agree, however, that the dollar's appreciation spared the Federal Reserve the need to raise the real federal funds rate to contain aggregate demand. Simulations of the two models (not shown) suggest that an increase in the real federal funds rate of 250 to 350 basis points would have been needed to hold unemployment to its historical path if the dollar had not appreciated.

FALLING OIL PRICES The effect of the strong dollar on inflation subsequently was reinforced by falling oil prices. Figure 3.9 shows that, after rising during 1996, the price of petroleum fell roughly in half between the fourth quarter of 1996 and the first quarter of 1999. The decline in oil prices reduced energy costs, which directly lowered headline inflation relative to core measures. Lower energy costs may also have fed through into lower core inflation by holding down production costs.

FIGURE 3.9 / Daily Price of West Texas Intermediate Oil

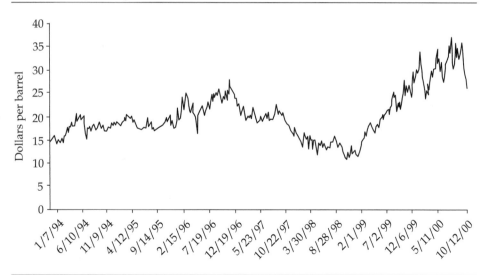

Source: Data taken from price quoted daily in the *Wall Street Journal.*

In addition, the declining prices of both imports and energy may have led to more modest nominal-wage increases, thereby reducing pressure on business costs and prices. Standard Phillips curve logic—embodied in equation 3.2—holds that tighter labor markets lead workers to demand (and businesses to provide) higher real-wage increases. But falling import and energy prices may satisfy some of those demands without costing domestic producers anything. Consistent with this idea, the real consumption wage—defined as hourly compensation deflated by the CPI-U-RS—was essentially unchanged over the three years 1994 to 1996 but then rose 2.7 percent per year during 1997 and 1998 as oil and import prices fell.

To study the consequences of the plunge in oil prices, we used the WUMM and FRB-US models to simulate what would have happened if the price of oil had remained at its 1996:1 level through the end of 1999 instead of fluctuating as it did—rising during 1996, falling during 1997 and 1998, and then rebounding during 1999.[46] (We again held the real federal funds rate constant.) Table 3.12 reports the results. In both models, the oil shock lowers inflation slightly in 1997 and substantially (0.6 or 0.8 percent) in 1998. But note that the effects of the oil-price shock are estimated to have been substantially smaller than those of the other two shocks, even though it probably garnered the most public attention. Why? The bottom rows of table 3.12 show the simple answer: the oil shock in 1996–1999 was small compared to the OPEC shocks in the 1970s and early 1980s.

METHODOLOGICAL REVISIONS TO THE CPI   Measurement changes are not genuine economic shocks; they merely recalibrate the economy's thermometer. However, they did make macroeconomic performance look even better than it was between 1995 and 1999. Beginning in 1995, the Bureau of Labor Statistics introduced a series of technical adjustments to the CPI that lowered measured inflation.[47] Although each individual change was small, the cumulative effect of these methodological changes was substantial: in total, they reduced measured CPI inflation by about 0.6 percent per annum by 1999.[48] Without these measurement

TABLE 3.12   /   Impact of Oil-Price Fluctuations after 1996:1 (Real Federal-Funds Rate Held at Baseline Level)

Deviation from Baseline	Model	1996:4	1997:4	1998:4	1999:4
Real GDP growth (fourth	WUMM	−.2	.1	.6	.4
quarter over fourth quarter)	FRB-US	.0	.1	.0	−.1
CPI inflation rate (fourth	WUMM	.2	−.1	−.6	.0
quarter over fourth quarter)	FRB-US	.3	−.1	−.8	.0
Unemployment rate	WUMM	.1	.1	−.1	−.4
(difference)	FRB-US	.0	.0	−.1	−.2
Price of oil (percent difference)	WUMM	20.2	−4.9	−69.7	20.2
	FRB-US	21.4	1.5	−53.2	20.9

Source: Authors' calculations.

changes, the reported CPI inflation rate would have been about 2.5 percent (rather than 1.9 percent) during 1999, and there would have been much less talk about the "miraculous" decline of inflation.

In adjusting the measurement system, the administration was not rigging the deck. Researchers had long believed that the CPI and other price indices suffered from a variety of upward biases. Although bias in a price index is an esoteric subject, it began to captivate lawmakers when budget cutters (led by Senator Daniel Patrick Moynihan) focused on reducing the CPI as a source of budgetary savings. Since the CPI is used to compute cost-of-living adjustments in social security, other federal retirement programs, and the tax system, lower measured inflation would reduce federal outlays and boost tax receipts. In 1996, the Senate Finance Committee published the Boskin Commission report (named for its chairman, economist Michael Boskin), which estimated that the CPI inflation rate was biased upward by about 1.1 percentage points. The commission estimated that fixing this bias in 1997 would lower the federal deficit by $148 billion in 2006 and reduce the outstanding federal debt by $691 billion by that time (see Boskin et al. 1996, figures A1, A2).

It is difficult to know whether the lower announced inflation rates affected economic behavior in any way. Homo economicus should not be deluded by bad data. But much of the observed decline in core CPI inflation from 1995 to 1999 was due to measurement changes rather than to genuine disinflation, and we doubt that many members of the public understood this.[49] Hence, we do not rule out the possibility that lower reported inflation was mistaken by at least some wage and price setters as lower true inflation, thereby leading to more modest wage settlements.

ASSESSING THE IMPACT OF WAGE-PRICE SHOCKS   Are the wage-price shocks discussed thus far sufficient to account for the favorable inflation-unemployment performance during the good-luck period? We summarize the results of this section in tables 3.13 and 3.14. These tables show, for the FRB-US and WUMM models, respectively, the combined impact of the wage-price shocks on the paths of unemployment and inflation between 1994 and 1999. The underlying simulations all assume that the Federal Reserve would have held the real federal funds rate at its actual historical level in the absence of the shocks.

According to the FRB-US model, the joint impact of the benefits, exchange-rate, oil, and measurement shocks was to lower unemployment slightly and inflation substantially during 1997 through 1999. Remember, it was the low inflation rates of the years 1997 and 1998 that stood out in figure 3.5. Absent the shocks, the model says that inflation would have accelerated by 2 percentage points between 1994 and 1998, reaching 4.6 percent in 1998. According to the WUMM model, the shocks had little net effect on the *average* unemployment rate in 1997 and 1998 but lowered inflation substantially in every year from 1995 through 1999. Absent the shocks, inflation would have accelerated from 2.6 percent in 1994 to 5.4 percent in 1998, rather than falling to 1.5 percent.

So do the four supply shocks listed in tables 3.13 and 3.14 explain what actu-

TABLE 3.13 / Estimated Impact of Wage-Price Shocks on Inflation and
Unemployment, FRB-US Model (Real Federal Funds Rate Held at
Baseline Level)

	1994	1995	1996	1997	1998	1999
Actual CPI inflation—fourth quarter over fourth quarter	2.6	2.7	3.1	1.9	1.5	2.6
Difference without:						
Benefits shock	.0	.2	.7	1.2	1.4	1.0
Real-exchange-rate appreciation	.0	.0	.2	.3	.5	.3
Oil-price fluctuations after 1996:1	.0	.0	−.3	.1	.8	.0
Measurement changes	.0	.1	.2	.2	.4	.6
CPI inflation without "wage-price shocks"	2.6	3.0	3.9	3.7	4.6	4.5
Actual unemployment (fourth quarter)	5.6	5.6	5.3	4.7	4.4	4.1
Difference without:						
Benefits shock	.0	.0	.1	.4	.7	.7
Real-exchange-rate appreciation	.0	.0	.0	−.1	−.5	−1.0
Oil-price fluctuations after 1996:1	.0	.0	.0	.0	.1	.2
Unemployment without "wage-price shocks"	5.6	5.6	5.4	5.0	4.7	4.0

Source: Authors' calculations.

ally happened to inflation and unemployment between, say, late 1994 and late 1998? Both models say yes. Each estimates that, with the real federal funds rate held constant, the supply shocks barely changed the average unemployment rate over the four-year period but reduced the 1998 inflation rate by 3.1 percentage points (in the FRB-US model) or 3.9 percentage points (in the WUMM). These are very sizable effects. By comparison, the differences across the two models seem small.

To put these estimates into perspective, suppose you believed that the NAIRU was about 6 percent, as many economists (and the Fed) did in 1994. Then, from the end of 1994 through the end of 1998, the economy enjoyed 3.6 "point years" of unemployment below NAIRU. According to a popular Phillips curve rule of thumb, that should have pushed inflation up by about 1.8 percentage points. Instead, inflation actually fell by 1.1 percentage points. The discrepancy—an inflation "surprise" of 2.9 percentage points—is very close to the FRB-US estimate of the disinflationary impact of the supply shocks (but less than the WUMM's). In brief, according to the models, the four supply shocks either explain (FRB-US) or overexplain (WUMM) the drop in inflation. Without those shocks, inflation would have risen to about 5 percent by the end of 1998, according to the models.

TABLE 3.14   /   Estimated Impacts of Wage-Price Shocks on Inflation and
Unemployment, WUMM Model (Real Federal Funds Rate Held at
Baseline Level)

	1994	1995	1996	1997	1998	1999
Actual CPI inflation—fourth quarter over fourth quarter	2.6	2.7	3.1	1.9	1.5	2.6
Difference without:						
Benefits shock	.0	.8	1.3	1.5	.7	.3
Real-exchange-rate appreciation	.0	.1	.6	1.0	2.2	2.0
Oil-price fluctuations after 1996:1	.0	.0	−.2	.1	.6	.0
Measurement changes	.0	.1	.2	.2	.4	.6
CPI inflation without "wage-price shocks"	2.6	3.7	5.0	4.7	5.4	5.5
Actual unemployment (fourth quarter level)	5.6	5.6	5.3	4.7	4.4	4.1
Difference without:						
Benefits shock	.0	.0	.4	.9	.9	.7
Real-exchange-rate appreciation	.0	.0	−.1	−.4	−1.4	−2.5
Oil-price fluctuations after 1996:1	.0	.0	−.1	−.1	.1	.4
Unemployment without "wage-price shocks"	5.6	5.6	5.5	5.1	4.0	2.7

Source: Authors' calculations.

The Fed Ponders the Supply Shocks

As these favorable price developments nudged inflation downward, the Fed was pleased, if somewhat surprised. Although aware that favorable supply shocks could permit very low unemployment to coexist with stable or even falling inflation for a time, the FOMC retained a nagging fear: maybe the lucky streak was about to end, and inflation would rise again. Members were justifiably concerned that the disinflationary benefits of the strong dollar and lower oil prices were only temporary, and they worried that employee benefits would rise more rapidly once workers had been shifted into managed care and the "trauma" of a weak labor market had disappeared from memories. Federal Reserve Governor Laurence Meyer began calling the period one of "temporary bliss" (see Meyer 1998).

But what about the possibility that the superior inflation performance reflected permanent, or at least very long-lasting, "bliss"? It was during this good-luck period (1996–1998) that Greenspan, the alleged inflation hawk, revealed himself to be the committee's most ardent advocate of new-economy thinking: that productivity gains and worker insecurity were holding down both compensation and inflation and might do so for a significant period of time. This view rationalized a strategy of continued forbearance in the face of extraordinarily low unemployment, and Greenspan led his sometimes-balky committee to do precisely that. The Fed raised interest rates only once—and then by a mere 25 basis points (in March 1997).

Many outside observers, and some within the FOMC, thought that the dovish Greenspan was "pushing the envelope." During 1996 and 1997, one or two members occasionally dissented in favor of tightening, and the minutes indicate pretty clearly that others held similar views but did not oppose the chairman. However, given increased uncertainty about structural shifts—and the fact that inflation was falling, not rising—Greenspan was able to persuade his committee not to attack inflation "preemptively" but rather to wait to shoot until they could see the whites of rising inflation's eyes. And that, of course, never happened.

In a series of speeches, Meyer articulated an intellectual justification for the Fed's change in strategy—which amounted to abandoning the former policy of preemption in favor of forbearance (see Meyer 1997b, 2000). The essence of the case was pretty simple. The preemptive strategy relied on some (albeit imperfect) ability to forecast inflation. With extreme uncertainty over the NAIRU and other aspects of the Phillips curve, one could argue that it no longer made sense to act on the basis of forecasts, for the risks of making a major policy error were simply too great. Instead, Meyer suggested, the Fed should wait until it saw clear evidence of rising inflation. But then, he added, since the Fed would be "behind the curve" when it finally acted, it should raise rates aggressively.

Regardless of this intellectual debate and of disagreements within the FOMC, no one should think that the FOMC's "experiment" of allowing unemployment to drift down to thirty-year lows was a deliberate policy decision. It was largely inadvertent. For most of the period 1996 to 1998, the Fed was consistently surprised by the strength of aggregate demand and the drop in the unemployment rate, just like most forecasters. We find it impossible to believe that the committee would have deliberately chosen to push unemployment below 5 percent, much less all the way down to 4 percent. Indeed, a substantial number of FOMC members shared the typical staff forecasts that higher inflation was likely if unemployment remained at prevailing rates. Like the Blue Chip consensus, the Fed's staff forecasts typically saw a growth slowdown just around the corner. But the slowdown never materialized. On the other hand, as growth constantly outstripped forecasts and unemployment fell, the Fed made no effort to push unemployment back toward any preconceived notion of the NAIRU. That was its real experiment.

The Role of Demand Shocks in the Good-Luck Period

The unexpected strength of demand during the period 1996–1998 arguably derived from the gravity-defying stock market, which stoked demand and drove the personal-saving rate down.[50] The stock market was, thus, a topic that preoccupied the Fed. At a consultants' meeting in November 1996, the Board of Governors heard opinions about the stock market from a group of academic economists and Wall Street analysts—including stock-market bears Robert Shiller and John Campbell. In a speech the next month, Greenspan added a phrase to the English language when he famously ruminated: "But how do we know when irrational exuberance has unduly escalated asset values, which then become subject to unexpected and prolonged contractions. . . ? And how do we factor that assessment into monetary policy?" (Greenspan 1996a). Such "thinking out loud"—said to be the first time a Fed chairman had discussed stock-market valuations in thirty years—touched off a short but furious flurry of selling.

The (consistently incorrect) belief that stock-market gains would cease or be reversed was one justification for forecasting a slowdown. But the stock market was not the only phenomenon that consistently surprised forecasters on the upside; so did business investment. The behavior of both stock prices and capital formation was consistent with the argument that an unrecognized productivity shock was driving both aggregate supply and aggregate demand during the second half of the 1990s.

Nonetheless, the Fed seemed poised to tighten further in the summer of 1997 when a series of events in Asia cast doubt on the durability of the U.S. expansion. In July, the Thai baht succumbed to speculative attack and was devalued. The minutes of the August FOMC meeting contain no reference to the Thai situation, which may seem surprising. But few observers initially imagined that this episode would mark the beginning of a global financial crisis that would, in some sense, continue to rumble around the world for more than a year.

By September, however, the crisis had spread to Indonesia, Malaysia, and the Philippines; Singapore and Taiwan had floated their currencies; and contagion was also affecting Hong Kong. The deteriorating international situation altered the FOMC's calculus profoundly. The Fed recognized that the Asian shock would both reduce inflationary pressures and cut U.S. exports. Furthermore, there was a danger that the financial crisis might spread—thereby creating more downside risk. The crisis thus created a rationale to continue the policy of forbearance despite rapid growth in already-tight labor markets (FOMC Minutes, September 30, 1997).

Continued forbearance may also have been motivated by a concern that further tightening would intensify financial pressures on the crisis countries and their major trading partners, thereby exacerbating a rapidly deteriorating international financial situation. Treasury Secretary Robert Rubin repeatedly urged all G-7 countries to pursue expansionary policies, including monetary policy, to mitigate the growing downside risks to the global economy. A tightening of U.S. monetary policy, regardless of its domestic logic, would have undermined this broader economic agenda. The May 1998 FOMC minutes justify the committee's inaction as due, in part, to "the possibility that even a modest tightening action could have outsized effects on the already very sensitive financial markets in Asia." Since the Fed's statutory mandate provides no authority for policy actions undertaken mainly to foster improved economic conditions abroad, the committee rationalized its decision by stating that, "The resulting unsettlement could have substantial adverse repercussions on U.S. financial markets and, over time, on the U.S. economy" (FOMC Minutes, May 19, 1998).

By the spring of 1998, the Fed again had its finger on the interest-rate trigger. But, once again, it did not fire. Just a few months later, Russia's devaluation and default in August 1998 dramatically changed the outlook, the risks, and the Fed's policy. Between September and November 1998, the Fed actually eased the federal funds rate by 75 basis points in response to the worsening international financial crisis. The first cut came in the wake of the Russian default, amid evidence of sharply higher risk spreads, more cautious lending by U.S. banks, a decline in equity prices, and a distinct downgrading of prospects for global growth. The second cut came as a rare intrameeting move following the collapse of the huge (and poorly hedged) hedge fund Long Term Capital Management, a shock that resulted in a temporary but frightening drying up of liquidity in most financial markets and an alarming spike in risk spreads.[51]

Thus, the Fed might well have tightened monetary policy in 1997 and again in 1998 were it not for surprising, and somewhat ominous, events originating abroad. The period of forbearance was, thus, extended unnaturally.

THE END OF FORBEARANCE

By the start of 1999, most of the supply shocks that had held inflation down during the good-luck period had dissipated or even reversed. Nonetheless, both unemployment and core inflation continued to inch downward. By June, however, the policy of forbearance had finally taxed the Fed's patience, and the FOMC embarked on a tightening cycle (depicted earlier in figure 3.4) that would take the federal funds rate from 4.75 percent in June 1999 to 6.5 percent by May 2000. For the second time during the 1990s, the Fed would attempt a soft landing.

Given the inherently temporary nature of at least some of the favorable supply shocks, economists were hardly surprised when these factors began to ebb or reverse:

- The dollar peaked against a broad basket of currencies in August 1998, then fluctuated in a relatively narrow band near that level through 1999. This brought the inflation bonus from falling import prices first to a crawl and then to a halt.

- Energy prices reversed course during 1999. With OPEC production cuts and recovery in the global economy, the price of oil soared 93 percent during 1999, fully retracing its downward steps and then rising even further in 2000. Table 3.9 shows that surging energy prices pushed headline inflation measures up by more than a full percentage point during 1999, even though core inflation was stable or falling.

- Forecasters had long feared that employer costs for health benefits would escalate again once the onetime gains from switching workers from fee-for-service to managed care were exhausted. And they did. By the end of 1999, benefit costs were increasing sharply.

- The pace of price declines for computers and semiconductors, which had soared to near 30 percent per annum during the good-luck period, slowed to a "mere" 21 percent on a quality-adjusted basis during 1999 (see the next section).

Despite all this, core consumer inflation dropped in 1999. Why did inflation remain low during 1999 despite such reversals of good fortune? Perhaps the most plausible answer credits accelerating productivity growth with keeping unit labor costs in check. Between 1996 and 1999, productivity growth averaged 2.5 percent per year—almost a percentage point higher than its average from 1991 to 1995. But, importantly, productivity was actually accelerating during this period, reaching a stunning 4.1 percent annual rate during 1999. The consequence was that unit labor costs rose at only a paltry 0.7 percent pace that year.[52] At the end of the day, the acceleration in productivity proved to be a more important influence on inflation than the disappearance of the favorable supply shocks. Although still too new to be fully understood, this phenomenon merits detailed consideration.

PRODUCTIVITY GROWTH AND COMPUTER PRICES

As late as 1998, advocates of the new-economy view—that computers and information technology (IT) were transforming American businesses and boosting productivity growth—could point to little in the way of hard data to make their case. Productivity growth had risen somewhat, but normal statistical tests attributed this rise to the cyclic upturn; there was no real evidence of any change in the underlying trend.[53] Yet stories about how the computer and the Internet were "changing everything" proliferated. In brief, "Solow's paradox" was in full flower: the computer could be seen everywhere except in the productivity statistics (see Solow 1987).

Still, a number of people entertained a tantalizing thought: suppose that, despite the official data, productivity really was surging. That could explain why investment was so strong, why corporate earnings were growing so rapidly, and why stock-market valuations were skyrocketing. A rising statistical discrepancy in the national accounts, showing that incomes were growing notably faster than production (which is impossible), also suggested that productivity growth might be higher than recognized by the official (product-side) measure. Alan Greenspan was a leading advocate of this more optimistic view.

With the benefit of hindsight, and after several data revisions, it now appears that the anecdotes were running well ahead of the data: productivity growth was about a full percentage point higher in the years 1996–1999 than during the earlier period 1991–1995. Statistical tests for a change in trend-productivity growth clearly point to a break in late 1995 or early 1996, and figure 3.10 indi-

FIGURE 3.10   /   Four-Year Average Growth of Productivity in Nonfarm Business, 1963 to 2000

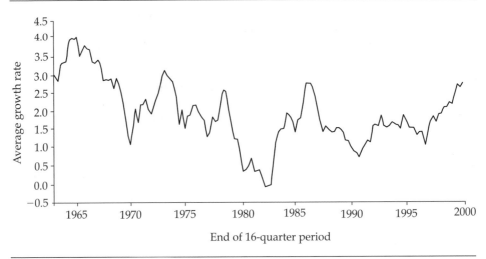

Source: U.S. Department of Labor, Bureau of Labor Statistics.

cates why. It gives a distinct visual impression of an acceleration in productivity beginning sometime around the end of 1995. But this was less obvious in real time.

A series of simple regressions illustrates just how quickly the statistical story changed. Using quarterly data on hours and output in the nonfarm-business sector, we estimated the following simple model to separate the trend and cyclical components of productivity growth:

$$h_t = \text{constant} + a_1 y_t + a_2 y_{t-1} + b_1 h_{t-1} + b_2 h_{t-2} + \text{time trends} + \text{error}, \quad (3.4)$$

where h is the log of hours of work, and y is the log of output. Productivity is therefore $y - h$. The constraint (imposed in estimation) that $a_1 + a_2 + b_1 + b_2 = 1$ makes hours proportional to output in the long run, thus guaranteeing that any output effect on productivity is transitory. That is how we distinguish cycle from trend. Dummy variables for different time periods then pick up any breaks in the underlying trend, and the regressions that we ran estimate three distinct time trends in order to test for two such structural breaks: one beginning in 1973:3 (the slowdown) and another beginning in 1995:4 (the speedup).

Table 3.15 summarizes the results of a series of regressions, each starting in 1959:3 but ending at different points. Since none of the other coefficients change much as we extend the sample, the table reports only the estimated break in the productivity trend at 1995:4 and its t-ratio.

It is clear that, through early 1998, there was no substantial statistical evidence that the productivity trend had increased—even though the point estimate suggested roughly a 1 percentage point rise relative to the trend that prevailed from

TABLE 3.15 / Regression Estimates of Equation (3.4) with Different End Points

End Point	Estimated Change in Trend (%)	t-Ratio
1996:4	+ .82	.52
1997:1	+ .58	.46
1997:2	+ .71	.70
1997:3	+ 1.06	1.24
1997:4	+ .96	1.30
1998:1	+ .98	1.52
1998:2	+ 1.11	1.95
1998:3	+ 1.10	2.14
1998:4	+ .99	2.12
1999:1	+ 1.11	2.62
1999:2	+ 1.02	2.60
1999:3	+ 1.07	2.94
1999:4	+ 1.18	3.44
2000:1	+ 1.22	3.75
2000:2	+ 1.39	4.40
2000:3	+ 1.51	4.87
2000:4	+ 1.61	5.26

Source: Authors' calculations.

1973 to 1995. (The highest *t*-ratio registered through 1998:1 is only 1.52, corresponding to a *p*-value of .13.) But the picture begins to change rapidly after that. By the time the third quarter of 1998 is added to the sample, the point estimate of the increase in trend productivity starting in 1995:4 is still around 1 percentage point, but its *t*-ratio has jumped to 2.14 (*p*-value = .03). By the time 1999:4 is included, the *t*-ratio reaches 3.44 (*p* = .0007), and the point estimate of the trend break is about 1.2 percentage points. In sum, it was not until mid- to late 1998 that the data finally caught up with the anecdotes and verified that productivity had indeed accelerated.

What caused the surge in productivity growth? Technological improvements in the production of computers and semiconductors probably account for the lion's share, both directly and indirectly. First, impressive gains in computer-industry productivity were a direct and major contributor to overall, economy-wide productivity growth. Second, the falling prices of computers and software led to increased investment in and use of computers throughout the economy—so-called capital deepening. Third, and perhaps most controversially, improvements in IT boosted productivity in the sectors of the economy that use computers intensively.

Figure 3.11 depicts the truly remarkable behavior of computer prices. After falling at an average annual rate of around 14 percent in nominal terms over the fifteen-year period from 1980 to 1995, computer deflation soared into the 25 to 30 percent range during the following three years. These sharp price declines reflected the stunning pickup in total-factor-productivity (TFP) growth in this sec-

FIGURE 3.11 / Changes in Computer Prices

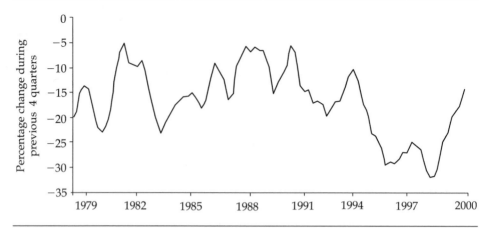

Source: U.S. Department of Commerce, Bureau of Economic Analysis.

Note: Prices change is the four-quarter trailing change in the chain-type price index for final computer sales.

tor, as Moore's law was violated.[54] Although computers and semiconductors account for a mere 1.5 percent of nonfarm-business output, estimates by Fed economists Stephen Oliner and Daniel Sichel suggest that the speedup in TFP growth in computers was sufficient to raise aggregate TFP by about 0.35 percentage point during the second half of the 1990s (see Oliner and Sichel 2000). Oliner and Sichel estimate about an equal contribution from TFP in the rest of the nonfarm-business sector. Robert Gordon estimates about the same effect in the computer industry but no speedup in TFP growth in the rest of the economy (see Gordon 2000). The key reason for the difference is that Gordon makes a cyclical adjustment while Oliner and Sichel do not.

Beyond this direct effect, rapid price reductions for computers and IT equipment raised productivity growth via an important indirect channel that is often ignored: lower equipment prices helped trigger an investment boom.[55] By 1999, real investment as a share of GDP stood at its highest level in the postwar period, and this flood of new investment was concentrated in high-tech equipment and software. Stephen Oliner and Daniel Sichel (2000) estimate that capital deepening raised the productivity-growth rate during 1996–1999 by 0.5 percent, with almost the entire increase concentrated in computers and IT equipment. In retrospect, some of this high-tech investment may have been part of the great speculative bubble of 1998 to 2000, but few observers were saying so at the time.

A pickup in productivity growth is, of course, extremely good news for long-run living standards, especially following decades of disappointingly slow real-wage growth. From the standpoint of unemployment and inflation, however, the key question is whether and how such productivity improvement affected the Phillips curve.

One plausible story is that the productivity shock reduced the "short-run NAIRU," the unemployment rate consistent with stable inflation, at least for a time, by holding down increases in unit labor costs despite gains in nominal wages. But wait. Shouldn't faster productivity growth translate one-to-one into faster wage settlements, as in equation 3.1, leaving no net change in the path of unit labor costs? After all, economists normally assume that this is so—that is, that $\theta^w = \theta^f$. However, the speedup in productivity growth may have gone *un-recognized*, at least for a time. Alternatively, the real-wage aspirations of workers, embodied in the norms that condition wage bargaining (θ^w), might have been depressed after two decades of real-wage stagnation and therefore slow to react to the new reality of faster productivity growth (see Ball and Moffitt, chapter 2 in this volume). These two hypotheses sound, and in some sense are, different. But they carry almost identical implications for observable variables. In either case, wage settlements should come in "too low" relative to the now-faster productivity gains.

The failure of wage settlements to increase in tandem with productivity would, in turn, have two principal effects. First, with labor now suddenly cheaper relative to its productivity, firms would naturally want to do more hiring. So unemployment would fall. Second, the path of unit labor costs would be deflected downward, easing any pressures on firms to raise prices. So inflation would also fall. In brief, a surprise increase in the productivity-growth rate should reduce unemployment and inflation at the same time, which is precisely what happened in the late 1990s.[56] Indeed, this story simply takes a widely accepted explanation for the stagflation of the 1970s and runs it in reverse. In the 1970s, an unrecognized productivity *slowdown* led to "excessive" wage settlements, more inflation, and less employment. In the 1990s, an unrecognized productivity *speedup* had precisely the opposite effects.

To quantify the effects of the productivity improvement, we again employed our two macroeconometric models with the real federal funds rate held at baseline levels. But, since the two models treat trend productivity differently, the two simulations had to be done in rather different ways. We began with a simulation using the FRB-US model, which zeroed out the entire speedup in productivity growth in the nonfarm-business sector that began in 1994.[57]

The results, displayed in table 3.16, show that productivity growth raises aggregate demand by even more than it raises aggregate supply in the FRB-US model. Wealth effects boost consumption, and faster GDP growth produces notable accelerator effects on housing, consumer durables, and business investment. As a result, while the level of trend labor productivity in the nonfarm-business sector is up 5.4 percent, raising *potential* real GDP about 4.3 percent by the end of the simulation, the growth rate of *actual* real GDP rises enough (about 1.15 percentage points per annum for six years) to leave the level of GDP 6.8 percent higher. So the unemployment rate actually winds up 1.3 percentage points lower by the end of 1999. Although inflation is initially depressed a bit by the productivity surge, the lower unemployment causes it to creep up over time—ending up slightly above the baseline level in 1999.[58]

TABLE 3.16 / Impact of Faster Trend Productivity after 1993 (Real Federal Funds Rate Held at Baseline Level)

Deviation from Baseline	Model	1996:4	1997:4	1998:4	1999:4
Real GDP growth (fourth quarter over fourth quarter)	WUMM	.9	1.2	.9	1.1
	FRB-US	1.1	1.3	1.7	1.6
CPI inflation rate (fourth quarter over fourth quarter)	WUMM	−.9	−1.1	−1.4	−1.7
	FRB-US	−.3	−.2	−.0	.3
Unemployment rate (difference)	WUMM	.1	.0	.1	.0
	FRB-US	−.4	−.7	−1.0	−1.3
Trend labor productivity in nonfarm business (percent difference)	Both	1.5	2.5	3.9	5.4
Growth rate of trend labor productivity in nonfarm business, fourth quarter over fourth quarter (difference)	Both	.7	1.0	1.3	1.5

Source: Authors' calculations.

To create a comparable simulation with the WUMM model, we began by asking what would have happened in the absence of more rapid TFP growth in computers. So we started by holding the relative price decline for computers to its 1993 pace (which was −7.5 percent per annum in the model), thus disallowing the apparent acceleration in technological change after 1994.[59] But that canceled out only part of the post-1994 surge in productivity, so we also reduced TFP outside the computer sector by just enough to replicate the productivity decline in the nonfarm-business sector simulated in the FRB-US model.

In the WUMM simulation, the aggregate-supply and aggregate-demand effects of the productivity shock roughly cancel one another out, leaving the unemployment rate essentially unchanged under a monetary policy that holds the real federal funds rate constant. According to the WUMM, the productivity shock added roughly a percentage point a year to the growth rate of real GDP while reducing the inflation rate a remarkable 1.7 percent by 1999. Both models agree that accelerating productivity lowered inflation after 1995, but the WUMM model estimates a far larger impact.

A natural question to ask is why the two models yield such different estimates of the disinflationary impact of the productivity surge. One reason is that the dividend resulting from the productivity shock is disproportionately devoted to lower *unemployment* in the FRB-US model but to lower *inflation* in the WUMM. In addition, the two models differ in their treatment of wage-price dynamics. The FRB-US model incorporates differential lags in the responses of wages and prices to productivity shocks, which is reminiscent of our canonical Phillips curve model—equations 3.1, 3.2, and 3.3—with $\theta^w < \theta^f$. Following a one-time jump in productivity growth, price expectations take about a year to adjust, but wage expectations take longer—about three years. So it is as if $\theta^f > \theta^w$ for about two years.

In the WUMM model, this asymmetry is far more pronounced and lasts substantially longer. The response of nominal-wage growth to productivity shocks is especially sluggish because, in contrast to equation 3.1, the WUMM model assumes that past nominal-wage growth, not expected inflation or perceived productivity growth, influences wage bargains. Thus, the two models agree that the productivity shock had a profound impact on economic performance during the second half of the 1990s, but they disagree about the magnitude and duration of the "disinflation" resulting from the shock.[60]

Does the hypothesis that productivity growth influenced the Phillips curve trade-off really explain what happened? Absent hard data on either perceived productivity gains or wage aspirations, it is impossible to know for sure. But notice one critical implication of the misperception view: The extraordinary combination of low inflation and low unemployment that we have enjoyed in recent years should be mostly transitory. As workers come to realize that productivity is rising faster, they will demand more generous real-wage increases. As firms begin to grant these wage increases, their costs will rise. On this view, the short-run Phillips curve trade-off should return to normal as perceptions catch up to reality. In theory, and in both simulation models, the "bliss" is only temporary.

More or less the same story holds if lagging real-wage aspirations lie behind the shifting Phillips curve. However, the effect would be expected to last longer if the underlying phenomenon was a durable weakening of labor's bargaining position. In that case, the favorable shift in the Phillips curve might be expected to endure.

The Impact of Supply Shocks: A Summary

The United States enjoyed a large dose of good luck during the second half of the 1990s: a productivity surge, slower growth in fringe benefits, a rising dollar, falling oil prices, and a series of measurement changes that lowered inflation. How different would the U.S. experience after 1994 have been if none of these favorable shocks had occurred (but the Federal Reserve had nevertheless held the real federal funds rate to its actual historical path)? Table 3.17 summarizes the answers given by our two macroeconometric models; it essentially adds the impacts of the productivity shock to the results shown earlier in tables 3.13 and 3.14.

According to the FRB-US model, unemployment would have stayed in the 5 to 6 percent range—essentially remaining near 1994 levels. Yet inflation would have drifted up from just above 2.5 percent to over 4 percent. In a word, there would have been no macroeconomic miracle. The WUMM's answer is different. According to this simulation, the Fed's actual monetary policy would have been so easy under the circumstances that unemployment would eventually have fallen below 3 percent. Not surprisingly, that would have driven inflation much

TABLE 3.17 / The Effect of Supply Shocks on Inflation and Unemployment after 1994 (Real Federal Funds Rate Held at Baseline Level)

	Model	1993	1994	1995	1996	1997	1998	1999
Actual CPI inflation (fourth quarter over fourth quarter)		2.7	2.6	2.7	3.1	1.9	1.5	2.6
CPI inflation without any shocks	WUMM	2.7	2.8	4.4	5.9	5.8	6.8	7.2
	FRB-US	2.7	2.6	3.3	4.2	3.9	4.6	4.2
Actual unemployment (fourth quarter)		6.6	5.6	5.6	5.3	4.7	4.4	4.1
Unemployment without any shocks	WUMM	6.6	5.4	5.4	5.4	5.1	3.9	2.7
	FRB-US	6.6	5.6	5.8	5.8	5.9	5.7	5.3

Source: Authors' calculations.

higher—to above 7 percent by the end of the decade. These calculations suggest that, once the improvement in trend productivity is taken into account, all the supply shocks together overexplain the excellent inflation performance slightly after 1994. The favorable effect of the shocks on the Phillips curve is so large, according to the two models, that we are left wondering why inflation was not even lower.

MONETARY POLICY IN 1999 AND AFTER

About midway through 1999, the Fed abandoned its policy of watchful waiting and embarked on a campaign to slow the growth of aggregate demand down to that of aggregate supply, thereby preventing labor markets from tightening even further. By the time this decision was taken, the unemployment rate had fallen to 4.2 percent, the favorable supply shocks had ended or were reversing, and the global economy was clearly on the mend. That might seem like sufficient reason to justify rate hikes. But the FOMC still saw no evidence of rising inflation. Productivity was rising sharply, and the Fed believed that the prolonged period of low inflation had reduced inflationary expectations and therefore compensation growth. In view of all this, why tighten?

What finally motivated the switch to a tightening stance was the recognition that aggregate-demand growth was unlikely to diminish toward the (now faster) estimated trend in potential output unless interest rates were raised. The FOMC had expected and waited for such a slowdown for a long time. The committee's minutes suggest that members had, in effect, agreed to disagree over whether structural changes had reduced the NAIRU permanently. Some were obviously skeptical that an unemployment rate as low as 4.2 percent could be maintained for long without rising inflation—even if productivity growth was still on the rise. Others, presumably including Alan Greenspan, were less enamored of the NAIRU approach, more willing to believe that wage-setting behavior had changed, and more open to the possibility that productivity might accelerate even more. But even the Fed's doves agreed that inflation risks would rise if the labor market were allowed to tighten further. The strategy of raising the federal funds rate by enough to slow aggregate-demand growth to trend—thus holding the unemployment rate constant—was a kind of middle ground that reduced, but did not eliminate, the risk of rising inflation.

Another factor pushing the federal funds rate up was the Fed's belief that the economy's demand for both consumer and investment goods had increased, raising the equilibrium real federal funds rate. In explaining the FOMC's decisions, Greenspan argued that the acceleration in productivity had boosted the equilibrium real federal funds rate. Faster productivity growth not only raised the growth rate of potential GDP, he said, but also raised the growth rate of actual GDP—as was the case in the FRB-US simulation in table 3.16. One channel works through investment: when falling computer prices and technological innovation raise the anticipated real rate of return, the investment function shifts out. The other channel works through consumption: wealth effects from the soaring stock market spur consumption growth in excess of income growth.[61]

The surge in stock prices, in turn, arguably reflected higher anticipated future earnings, another presumed result of the productivity boom. In addition, many economists argued that there were good reasons to think that the equity premium might have declined.[62] However, many observers—both economists and non-economists—continued to wonder whether the behavior of stock prices could really be justified by the improved "fundamentals," favorable as they were. If soaring equity prices reflected "irrational exuberance" as much as (or more than) any rational assessment of likely future earnings streams, the economy was riding in part on an artificial high. This possibility—which by late 2000 certainly looked like a strong probability—clearly worried the Fed in 1998 and 1999.

Of course, one way in which a higher federal funds rate works to contain aggregate demand is by reining in the stock market. The Fed, thus, had a difficult public-relations task on its hands: explaining that monetary policy was not targeting the stock market but that it nonetheless had to take the effect of stock prices on the economy into account.

The notion that the productivity shock contributed to robust domestic-demand growth is interesting and empirically plausible. But it was not the only rationale for tighter monetary policy. Broader measures of financial conditions, which accounted inter alia for the booming stock market, suggested that financial markets were not feeling much of a pinch. And, most important, there was simply too little evidence that demand was slowing down—suggesting to the Fed that a higher real federal funds rate was warranted. So rates headed up.

THE AMAZING, VANISHING BUDGET DEFICIT

While the Federal Reserve was first practicing forbearance and then tightening, the government's fiscal position was changing at breathtaking speed. We argued earlier that the 1993 budget agreement was a turning point for fiscal policy. But it did not complete the job of deficit reduction, and it certainly did not end the partisan rancor. The years 1995 and 1996 were marked by particularly contentious budget battles between the White House and the Republican-controlled Congress—leading to two government shutdowns, a threat by Congress to force the Treasury to default on the national debt, and the frequent operation of the U.S. government under a series of stopgap spending bills (so-called continuing resolutions). In 1995, the House passed and the Senate nearly passed a balanced-budget amendment to the Constitution, a centerpiece of Speaker Newt Gingrich's "Contract with America."

The budget deficit fared far better than the politics, however, declining much faster than the administration had claimed in 1993: from $290 billion in 1992 to just $108 billion in 1996. Nonetheless, as Bill Clinton began his second term, the CBO was projecting that the deficit would again rise to $188 billion by 2002. Furthermore, some critics attributed the falling deficit to the strong economy. That was mostly incorrect. While a portion (about 25 percent) of the improvement in the budget was indeed cyclical, the lion's share reflected a better structural balance.[63]

The 1993 agreement had set strict caps on discretionary spending through 1998, and those caps effectively constrained appropriations. But the caps were about to expire, and Congress was once again threatening to pass a balanced-budget amendment. Eager to finish the job and to claim fiscal victory, the president made negotiating a new agreement to achieve a balanced budget by 2002 his highest postelection priority.

As political negotiations opened in early 1997, it appeared that, although the task of balancing the budget by 2002 was feasible, it was going to be painful. Tax hikes were off the table; indeed, both parties were now on record as favoring a variety of tax cuts. And discretionary spending had already declined roughly 11 percent in real terms between 1992 and 1997. Further progress would be difficult because the entire cut had, to that point, come from the defense budget. Because the scope for additional cuts in defense was deemed limited, contentious cuts in civilian spending or in entitlements such as Medicare, Medicaid, and social security would be needed—not to mention battles over the size and nature of any tax cuts. But, despite these formidable obstacles, the White House and Congress did manage to reach an agreement to balance the budget, enabling the president to declare victory in the war against deficits.

As politics, the 1997 budget agreement was a notable achievement. It included significant cuts in entitlements, particularly in Medicare—a sign of its "seriousness"—and it extended the budget-enforcement mechanisms that had effectively restrained discretionary spending since 1990. Newly negotiated spending caps promised (if implausibly) to hold discretionary spending approximately constant in nominal terms between 1998 and 2002. However, the agreement conveniently postponed the difficult decision as to how the corresponding real cuts—roughly 10 percent over four years—would be achieved. In the event, Congress and the president found it impossible to live within the caps and busted them with emergency appropriations and other budgetary devices in fiscal years 1999, 2000, and 2001. Nonetheless, the caps set in the 1997 agreement continued to shape budget debates by determining the baseline for discussion.

From a macroeconomic perspective, however, the 1997 budget agreement did not amount to much. In fact, with its small tax cuts and more generous cap on discretionary spending for 1998, the 1997 agreement actually increased the deficit by about $21 billion in its first year.[64] Naturally, it did not provoke any noticeable reaction either in the financial markets or from the Federal Reserve.

But a minor budget miracle happened. By the beginning of 1998, the fiscal outlook had improved so dramatically that President Clinton could propose using the emerging surpluses to tackle the massive fiscal problems implied by an aging population—as he put it, to "save social security first." A year and a half later, the administration projected that the entire publicly held federal debt would be paid off by 2015 (see White House 1999), a time frame that was subsequently shortened. Either of these ideas would have been greeted with howls of incredulity only a few years earlier. A program that was advertised to produce budget balance by 2002 had somehow produced a surplus by 1998.

The emergence of budget surpluses raises several interesting questions. The first is simply how they materialized. Figure 3.12 depicts the CBO's projections of the federal budget for fiscal years 1997 to 2002, made at roughly six-month intervals from January 1997 to July 2000.[65] It shows a dramatic sequence of upward revisions. For example, between January 1997 and August 2000, the CBO's forecast of the fiscal-year-2000 balance rose from a $171 billion deficit to a $232 billion surplus—a swing of $403 billion. The CBO's forecast of the fiscal-year-2002 surplus rose even more: by $593 billion. These are staggering revisions.

FIGURE 3.12 / The Evolution of CBO Surplus Projections for Fiscal Years 1997 to 2002

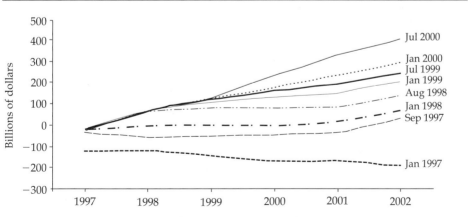

Source: Congressional Budget Office.

FIGURE 3.13 / Accounting for the Change in the CBO's Surplus Projections Between
January 1997 and July 2000

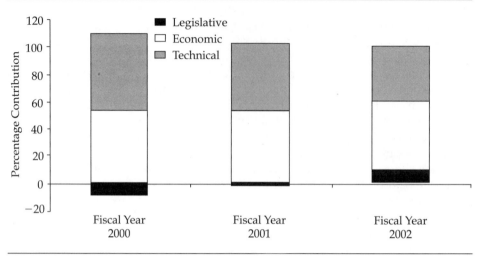

Source: Congressional Budget Office.

Figure 3.13 breaks these upward revisions into three sources: legislative or
policy changes; changes in economic forecasts; and "technical revisions." The
figure clearly shows that the policy changes, including those in the 1997 budget
agreement, were not the source of the improved outlook. In fact, for fiscal years
2000 and 2001, policy changes added slightly to the deficit.

Roughly half the budget surprise reflected improvements in the CBO's forecast for U.S. economic performance. For example:

- the estimated growth rate of potential output rose from roughly 2.1 to roughly
  3.0 percent;

- the baseline level of potential GDP was revised up several times on the assumption that previous output surprises reflected permanent increases in potential output, not just transitory influences;

- the assumed NAIRU was lowered from 5.8 percent in 1997 to 5.1 percent in
  July 2000; and

- the estimated share of taxable income in GDP was raised, partly because of an
  unanticipated reduction in (untaxed) benefits as a share of compensation.

In effect, many of the good-luck factors that we discussed earlier were also responsible for the improved budget outlook.

The remaining half of the budget surprise is attributed to "technical
changes"—mainly upward shifts in the functions relating tax collections to key
economic variables. Why did the tax function relating revenues to GDP shift up
so markedly? Subsequent analysis by the CBO using Internal Revenue Service
data shows that several factors were at work. Taxable income rose faster than

GDP because of strong capital gains, rising distributions from 401(k) plans, and the slow growth of untaxed benefits that we discussed earlier. The ratio of total taxes paid to adjusted gross income also rose substantially—because of bracket creep and disproportionately strong income growth among high-income tax-payers, particularly in the forms of bonuses, stock options, and partnership income. For example, the share of adjusted gross income earned by those whose adjusted gross income exceeded $200,000 rose from 14.5 percent in 1993 to 20.6 percent in 1998, and these individuals' share of tax liabilities increased from 29.8 to 39.8 percent. The consequence of all this was an increase in the ratio of federal revenues to GDP of about 2.5 percentage points between 1994 and 2000—despite the 1997 tax cuts (see Congressional Budget Office, *The Budget and Economic Outlook*, January 2000, 52–58). During the 2000 presidential campaign and after, this increase in effective tax rates would become a major political issue.

A final macroeconomic question relating to fiscal policy concerns the likely effect of the budget rules adopted in 1999 on future surpluses and trends in national saving. In the budget law passed in November 1999, Congress and the administration shifted the norm for fiscal policy fundamentally by declaring the social security surplus (then roughly $125 billion) off budget and forever untouchable.[66] With surprisingly little fanfare or debate, the fiscal bar was thus raised enormously. When Bill Clinton took office in 1993, *balancing the budget* meant eliminating the deficit in the unified budget, including the social security surplus. The far more stringent goal of balancing the budget excluding social security was unthinkable. Now, however, *balancing the budget* means precisely that.[67]

With an off-budget surplus of $150 billion in fiscal year 2000, projected to rise to $331 billion by 2011, this "definitional" change actually implies a giant step toward boosting public saving (see Congressional Budget Office, *The Budget and Economic Outlook*, January 2001, table 1.1, 2).[68] If future Congresses succeed in avoiding on-budget deficits, the new fiscal benchmark will result in unified budget surpluses that range between 1.5 and 2 percent of GDP for over a decade—until the baby boomers begin to retire.[69]

However, the 1997 to 2001 budget surprise was so large that, in January 2001, the CBO projected, not only off-budget surpluses, but also on-budget surpluses. Prior to the enactment of tax-cut legislation this May, the on-budget surplus was projected to rise from $86 billion in 2000 to a mind-boggling $558 billion in 2011—$3.1 trillion in total over the next decade. How best to use these large on-budget surpluses became, of course, a central part of the political debate under the new rules of the fiscal game. Should they be used for tax cuts, for new spending initiatives, to shore up the finances of social security and Medicare, and/or to pay down more debt?[70] President George W. Bush made a big tax cut his top priority and succeeded in enacting a tax-cut package that uses the lion's share (or more) of the surplus. He argued that the looming surpluses make it that much more affordable.

One cynical, but perhaps accurate, interpretation of the bipartisan agreement reached in 2000 to put the social security (and Medicare) surpluses in a tamper-proof "lockbox" might see it as the product of deadlock over competing policy priorities. Republicans favored tax cuts; Democrats were more inclined toward "new" spending; and, absent an agreement to do either, the surpluses were left to pile up and go to paying down the debt. Placing the surpluses in a lockbox had the further political advantage of making them unavailable to the opposing party in the event that it could muster a sufficient congressional majority. Perhaps most surprising of all, polls during the 2000 election campaign and after suggested that voters were attracted to the strategy of reducing the national debt—preferring it even over tax cuts.

Whatever the political motivation, the emergence of sizable budget surpluses in the decade before the baby boomers retire is probably desirable on long-run, public-finance grounds. These surpluses boost national saving and promote capital formation, which should help sustain more rapid productivity growth. Using the surpluses to pay down the national debt also means that the interest burden in the federal budget will be substantially lower when the baby boomers retire, leaving more room in the budget for higher projected outlays on social security and Medicare. Already, economists and others are debating how financial markets will function without Treasury debt for benchmarking, how the Federal Reserve will conduct monetary policy once the debt is gone, and whether and how the federal government should acquire private assets.[71] We leave an analysis of these fascinating issues to the chroniclers of the next decade of macroeconomic history.

CONCLUSIONS: LESSONS FOR POLICY

Readers with sufficient patience have now followed us through a long historical discourse—replete with much data and factual detail plus a number of econometric-model simulations. Our justification for telling the tale at such length is the importance of understanding this episode. It is, after all, one of the great shining moments of American economic history, and we would like to be able to replicate it. But how did we do it? And what lessons should policy makers carry away from the story? These are the questions that we address in this section.

A Brief Summary

First, a brief recapitulation of the story is in order so that we can see the proverbial forest for the numerous and leafy trees of earlier chapters.

The Fabulous Decade began around 1992 or 1993 under a set of propitious circumstances: the process of restoring fiscal probity was in train thanks to the 1990 budget agreement, monetary policy was pressing firmly on the gas pedal, many American industries had been profoundly restructured, and the economy was growing nicely. Fortunately, U.S. policy makers, led by Bill Clinton and Alan Greenspan, were wise enough to capitalize on this opportunity by continuing the fiscal consolidation and by maintaining extremely loose monetary policy until early 1994. Operating in tandem, this combination of promised fiscal tightening and loose money, not only gave GDP a boost, but also shifted its composition strongly toward investment.

Once the economy had built up enough forward momentum, the Federal Reserve expertly removed its foot from the accelerator and applied it to the brake—but lightly enough to achieve the proverbial soft landing in 1995. This successful bit of fine-tuning marked a departure from historical norms: most previous episodes of monetary tightening had ushered in recessions. While undoubtedly skillful, the Fed was also lucky that no major shock came along in 1994–1995 to spoil its attempted soft landing. Folk wisdom holds that "I'd rather be lucky than good." The Fed was both.

Starting in 1995–1996, the U.S. economy was blessed by a series of favorable supply shocks that no one could have anticipated. Foremost among these was the acceleration of productivity—the arrival of the much-heralded new economy. By conventional definitions, labor productivity stems from two sources: technological advance and capital deepening. Both were in overdrive in the late 1990s. Part of the capital deepening can be attributed to the change in the policy mix—after all, higher investment was the basic goal of the tight budget–easy money mix. But the boom in IT probably contributed much more to both TFP growth and capital deepening (by lowering the cost of capital). It also undoubtedly helped power the soaring stock market—which rose to heights in 1999 to 2000 that proved to be unwarranted.

However, the technology spurt was not the only favorable supply shock. The costs of fringe benefits, especially health insurance, decelerated sharply in 1994 and 1995, moderating wage settlements and perhaps shifting the Phillips curve. The dollar soared from 1995 to 1998, driving down import prices. Oil prices declined steadily throughout 1997 and 1998. And, on top of all this good news, data revisions raised the real-growth rate and reduced the measured inflation rate, making appearances even better than reality—which was good enough.

Favorable supply shocks like these allow a nation to enjoy some combination of lower inflation and faster real growth. Importantly, the Federal Reserve—whether by design or by accident—took a good deal of the largesse in the form of faster growth and lower unemployment. This it did mainly by forbearance rather than by easing monetary policy. In fact, the FOMC held the federal funds rate virtually constant from January 1996 until September 1998.

Many of these positive developments—especially the faster growth and the booming stock market—also contributed to the remarkable turnaround in the federal-budget position: from a unified deficit of $164 billion in fiscal year 1995 to a surplus of $236 billion by fiscal year 2000.

At this writing, the Fed is attempting to achieve the second soft landing in five years. If that can be accomplished, it would be truly remarkable. But the Fed is having its troubles. The stock market has tumbled, and economic growth in the first half of 2001 looks extremely weak.[72]

Five Lessons for Policy Makers

Perhaps the most obvious lesson from this period is that it is smart to be president of the United States or chairman of the Federal Reserve Board when large, favorable supply shocks come along. But that is not a very useful piece of advice. What other lessons can future policy makers glean from the Fabulous Decade? We would like to call attention, somewhat tentatively, to five.

Lesson 1 is the well-known point about the monetary-fiscal policy mix that we have made several times: *tight government budgets and (relatively) easy monetary policy can create a proinvestment macroeconomic climate by holding down real interest rates.* The resulting high rates of investment should then push up productivity and real wages. Economists have been preaching this gospel for decades. And it all seemed to work out according to Hoyle (actually, quite a bit better) in the United States in the 1990s, when the 1980s mix of tax cuts and tight money was finally and decisively reversed.

But did the policy mix really drive the investment boom of the 1990s? Our two macroeconomic models are doubtful. One major reason is a channel that textbook presentations often leave out: while lower interest rates stimulate investment spending, they also boost stock-market values—which in turn spur consumption (via the wealth effect) more than investment.[73] Specifically, when we simulated the effects of tighter budgets—balanced by easier money to hold the time path of unemployment constant—most of the rise in government saving was canceled out by lower personal saving, leaving the investment share of GDP up only slightly. The main impetus to investment, it appears, came from the surge in productivity.

The underlying reality, however, is probably messier than the models recognize. For example, while faster productivity growth undoubtedly spurs both more investment and faster GDP growth, just as the models say, a rapidly growing, high-investment economy probably also speeds up (embodied) technical progress. Why else did the explosion in IT—which was, after all, a worldwide phenomenon—yield such rich productivity dividends in the United States but not in Europe or Japan?

Lesson 2 is related: *what we normally think of as "contractionary" fiscal policy need not harm economic growth.* One reason is implicit in what we just said: expansionary monetary policy can offset any demand-reducing effects of budget cuts and tax hikes. But the 1993 budget agreement appears to have done more than that; it seems actually to have spurred the growth of aggregate demand even with no easing of monetary policy. The bond market, it appears, did the work for the Fed, as declining expected future deficits pulled down current long-term interest rates.

But *need not* is not synonymous with *will not.* We argued earlier that a particularly fortuitous set of circumstances, market psychology, and design features of the budget agreement combined to ignite the 1993 bond-market rally. We would not bet that this constellation can be replicated regularly, and, hence, we would not bet that all (or even most) fiscal contractions will be expansionary.[74] Still, under the right circumstances, the trick can be pulled off. And this appears to have been done in 1993.

Lesson 3 is also one that we advance only tentatively. In considering the experience of the 1990s, we are impressed by the fact that *well-designed fiscal policy rules can effectively constrain spending*—and apparently did so in the United States. The 1990 BEA, with its spending caps and PAYGO procedures, is the most important example in this history. When it replaced the ill-conceived GRH rules, things started to fall into place. But the recent decision to take social security "off budget," thereby redefining what it means to balance the budget, is another example that will, we believe, be important in years to come.[75] Nonetheless, it must be admitted that even well-designed rules can outlive their usefulness.

Having briefly extolled (good) rules, we hasten to add that the Fabulous Decade seems also to have resurrected an idea that most economists thought had died in the 1970s. *Lesson 4* is that it now appears that *fine-tuning is at least possible.* If not, we would like to know what Alan Greenspan has been up to since 1992. Indeed, we nominate Greenspan as the greatest fine-tuner in history. Once again, however, a caution is in order: to declare that something is possible is not to assert that it can be done easily or regularly. Successful fine-tuning requires a blend of skill and luck that may well be rare.[76] Alan Greenspan has had both, in abundance; others have had neither. And some people feel that even Greenspan's luck may have run out in the Fed's 1999 to 2000 tightening cycle, which went too far, according to some critics.

Furthermore, nothing in the history of the 1990s makes us at all optimistic about the feasibility of fiscal fine-tuning—the sort of thing that Walter Heller (1966) preached and tried to practice back in the 1960s. At least in the United States, the federal-budget-making process looks extremely cumbersome, highly politicized, and not terribly responsive to economic logic. It is not for naught that Congress has shackled itself with rules. Among economists, there is an evolving tacit consensus that demand management should be left to monetary policy while fiscal policy is used as a long-run allocative tool—although the Bush administration fought this consensus by selling a large income-tax cut on stabilization-policy grounds.[77] Without elevating this principle to the status of a commandment, for we must allow for exceptions, we agree that monetary, not fiscal, policy should carry most of the stabilization burden—at least in countries that have independent and capable central banks.

And that leads us to *lesson 5: to achieve good macroeconomic outcomes, the central bank should have sensible objectives that include aversion to both inflation and unemployment.* During the Fabulous Decade, the Greenspan Fed revealed itself to be much enamored of economic growth—much more so than, say, the old Bundesbank or the current European Central Bank, with its mandate to pursue price stability only. It is true that the favorable supply shocks of the later 1990s cut the FOMC a lot of slack: even though they allowed aggregate demand to soar, inflation fell. But think about what the Fed did both before and after the good-luck period (1996–1998). By the fall of 1995, Greenspan had already been chairman of the Fed for eight years, and, during that time, the inflation rate had been beaten down from about 4 percent to about 3 percent. Does that suggest a single-minded devotion to the goal of price stability? And, after core CPI inflation bottomed out at just below 2 percent at the end of 1999, it crept up more than 0.5 percentage point (as of this writing) without any noticeable effort by the Fed to push it back down.[78] Headline inflation has roughly doubled, largely because of rising energy prices, and the Fed has essentially swallowed this increase with barely a whimper.

The Federal Reserve's attitudes toward inflation and unemployment—and especially the way it "split" the gains offered by the supply shocks—go a long way, we believe, toward explaining why the Fabulous Decade was so fabulous.

NOTES

1. Here, and throughout the chapter (except where noted), we use the latest revised data rather than the contemporaneous data that people were seeing at the time. According to contemporaneous data, the productivity trend was closer to 1 percent.

2. Real average hourly earnings, as measured by the Department of Labor, *declined* almost 14 percent between 1973 and 1993. But those numbers were misleading for two main reasons: they overdeflated by using the "old" CPI, and they excluded fringe benefits, which grew faster than straight wages. During that same twenty-year period, real compensation per hour, which includes fringes and is deflated by the "new" CPI, *rose* 17 percent.

3. With the numbers in use at the time, output per hour in nonfarm business grew at a 1.3 percent average compound annual rate, while real compensation advanced less than 0.6 percent per annum. With current numbers, these two figures are both higher—1.9 and 0.9 percent, respectively—but the gap is even larger. Why is there such a large gap between productivity and compensation? One reason is that the prices of nonconsumer goods and services (for example, investment goods) rose less than consumer prices. This factor alone accounts for more than half the gap: nominal compensation deflated by the implicit deflator for nonfarm-business product rose at 1.5 percent per annum. The rest was accounted for by rising markups.

4. Calculations made by the Economic Policy Institute show that median real wages (not total compensation, but properly deflated) fell by 5 percent between 1973 and 1993. At the 20th percentile, they fell even more (−9.4 percent); at the 80th percentile, they rose (3.6 percent) (see Mishel, Bernstein, and Schmitt 2001, table 2.6, 124).

5. However, the productivity-enhancing effects of what was called *downsizing* were frequently exaggerated and may not even have existed (see, for example, Baily, Bartelsman, and Haltiwanger 1995).

6. The term is misleading because average establishment size did not fall in the late 1980s and early 1990s, except in manufacturing. Layoff announcements captured a great deal of public attention, but gross layoffs always greatly exceed net reductions in employment. However, there was plenty of labor-market churning during this period.

7. These numbers come from various issues of the AMA's annual publication, which has changed names several times over the years but is now called the *American Management Association Survey of Staffing and Structure*. The name changes are themselves revealing: in 1991, the report was called the *American Management Association Survey of Downsizing and Assistance to Displaced Workers*.

8. While the sample is random, there are other drawbacks. First, the data come only in three-year increments, so it is hard to isolate timing. Second, a worker is considered "displaced" if the firm terminates her job but moves her to another job in the same company—which we would not consider to be job loss. Third, Farber's tabulations cover only people between the ages of twenty and sixty-four.

9. We are tacitly using the twelve-month moving average as an admittedly imperfect proxy for expected inflation. The real federal funds rate is, of course, not the only possible measure of monetary policy. It ignores, among other things, the exchange rate, the levels of longer-term interest rates, and equity prices—variables that are included in some broader indices of financial conditions.

10. For recent evidence in favor of this hypothesis, see Berger, Kyle, and Scalise (2000).

11. The acronym stands for Washington University Macro Model; it was originally developed by Laurence Meyer, now a Fed governor. We are extremely grateful to David Reifschneider of the Federal Reserve Board and his staff and to Joel Prakken and Chris Varvares of Macroeconomic Advisers for running simulations on their respective models for us.

12. Large econometric models are essentially very high-order difference equations. So seemingly subtle differences in specification can lead to very different dynamics.

13. Two major examples: a small "stimulus package" that Clinton had included as a kind of insurance policy against a relapse into recession was rejected by Congress, as was a proposed broad-based energy tax (the BTU tax).

14. As noted earlier, some people would say that this process began with Ross Perot.

15. However, critics did argue that raising the top income-tax rate would not raise much revenue (see, for example, Feldstein 1993).

16. Cumulative economic growth over the period 1992 to 1998 (which was relevant to the budget numbers) was about 1.4 percent less in the CBO's forecast than in the administration's forecast (see White House 1993, table 3.2, 25).

17. Note that the GDP gains in the WUMM model are given back in 1995 and 1996.

18. See Stephen Turnovsky and Marcus Miller 1984; and Olivier Blanchard 1984.

19. The real-growth rate averaged 3.2 percent from 1991:4 to 1993:4.

20. Of the other four dissidents, two did not have a vote at that meeting, and the other two voted along with the chairman after verbalizing their disagreements. (This and other such information about FOMC meetings comes from the published transcripts.)

21. Common estimates of the NAIRU (nonaccelerating inflation rate of unemployment) then placed it around 6 percent. The Fed's staff estimate was a little higher. The actual unemployment rate in February 1994 was 6.6 percent.

22. Two positions on the Board of Governors were vacant at the time. They would subsequently be filled by the authors.

23. This idea was subsequently codified as the "opportunistic-disinflation" strategy: prevent inflation from drifting higher, and seize opportunities (such as favorable supply shocks or accidental recessions) to push inflation down (see Orphanides and Wilcox 1996).

24. We use the definition of *neutrality* suggested by Blinder (1998): the federal funds rate that, once all the lags have worked themselves out, is consistent with neither rising nor falling inflation.

25. See statements by Governor Wayne Angell and Chief Monetary Economist Donald Kohn in the FOMC meeting transcript, December 21, 1993, 21, and Appendix, Kohn statement, 1.

26. A very long time period is needed to apply this method because there is no reason to think that shocks average to 0 over short periods.

27. With a lower growth rate of final sales, a lower level of inventory investment suffices to keep inventory-sales ratios at constant levels. This did indeed happen in 1995. After averaging about $67 billion (1996 chained dollars) in 1994, inventory investment declined to just $30 billion in 1995.

28. The (current) data reported here have seen substantial revision since 1996. GDP data available at the end of 1996 recorded real GDP growth of just 2.0 percent in the second half of 1995.

29. The first alternative assumes in addition that long-term-bond yields spike sharply following the beginning of Fed tightening in 1995:3 (see table 3.6), analogous to their actual behavior in 1994 following the Fed's shift to tighter policy.

30. The cyclical low of the unemployment rate, 3.9 percent, was reached in September and October 2000.

31. In 2000, the FOMC adopted this index for its official inflation forecasts. As the table shows, inflation since 1993 is substantially lower when gauged by the PCE index instead of by the CPI-U. The average gap is about 0.6 percentage point. The two series differ mainly in their treatment of medical care and housing.

32. For example, profit margins were widening despite allegedly intense competitive pressures and rising wages.

33. Equations 3.1, 3.2, and 3.3 generate a long-run Phillips curve that is vertical at the NAIRU, $u = u^N$. Some argue, however, that, owing to the reluctance of workers to accept nominal-wage cuts and/or their failure to incorporate inflation expectations into wage bargains on a point-for-point basis, the long-run Phillips curve is probably not vertical at low inflation rates (see Akerlof, Dickens, and Perry 1996, 2000). This criticism notwithstanding, equations 3.1 to 3.3 suffice as a simplified organizational framework for our discussion of supply shocks.

34. A similar graph using the PCE measure of inflation (not shown) looks substantially identical.

35. Alas, this excellent fit would not last long, as we discuss below.

36. In efficiency-wage models, any shock that leads workers to view their outside opportunities less favorably will lower equilibrium unemployment, u^N, reduce the efficiency-wage premium, and raise firms' markups. An unusually low level of quits

(into unemployment), given the duration of unemployment, suggested an increase in job insecurity.

37. On this and several other matters discussed in this paragraph, see Schmidt and Thompson (1997) and Schmidt (1999).

38. The percentage of estimated working time lost to work stoppages involving one thousand or more workers hit a postwar low of 0.01 in 1992 and remained at or below 0.02 through 1999 (see U.S. Department of Labor 2001).

39. These three benefits constitute about 96 percent of what is called *other labor income* (supplements to wages and salaries other than employer contributions to social insurance).

40. For evidence, see Lawrence Summers (1989), Jonathan Gruber (1997), and Jonathan Gruber and Alan Krueger (1991). Gruber and Krueger found that changes in employers' costs for workers' compensation are largely shifted to workers in the form of lower wages.

41. A price-price Phillips curve augmented to include the markup of price over trend unit labor costs is stable and fits the data well throughout the 1990s, whereas standard specifications show evidence of a substantial NAIRU shift beginning in 1994:4. According to estimates in Flint Brayton, John Roberts, and John Williams (1999), the markup swelled between 1993 and 1995 and declined to its mean between 1996 and 1998, holding down inflation during the later period.

42. We simulate the benefit shock by adjusting each model's counterpart of equation 3.1. The direct impact of the benefit shock on compensation growth in the simulations averages -1.0, -0.7, and -1.1 percent in 1995, 1996, and 1997, respectively, and -0.1 percent in both 1998 and 1999.

43. The simulations reported in table 3.9 ignore any direct effect of slower medical-care-cost inflation on consumer-price inflation. WUMM simulations that also include a direct effect of slower escalation of medical-care prices in the PCE price index produce CPI inflation rates that are 0.1 to 0.2 percent lower than those reported in table 3.9.

44. Henry Farber found that, conditioning on the unemployment rate, permanent layoffs were unusually high between 1993 and 1997. Permanent layoffs subsequently declined to more normal levels (see Farber 1998).

45. Our simulation holds the Federal Reserve Board's broad (thirty-five-country) price-level-adjusted exchange rate at its 1995:2 level.

46. In the WUMM model, we held the refiners' acquisition cost of imported oil at its 1996:1 level of $18.38 per barrel. In the FRB-US model, we held the unit value oil import price at its 1996:1 level of $17.46 per barrel.

47. A convenient table of these changes can be found in Council of Economic Advisers (1999, 94). For more details, see Kenneth Stewart and Stephen Reed (1999) and Council of Economic Advisers (2000, 61).

48. Between 1992 and 1994, a period in which no significant methodological changes were implemented, the CPI-U rose 0.39 percent more rapidly, on average, than did the CPI-U-RS. The introduction of a new market basket with revised expenditure weights in 1998 lowered inflation rates in both series by an estimated further 0.17 percent per

annum. Thus, methodological changes likely lowered inflation in the CPI-U by about 0.6 percent per annum between 1995 and 1999.

49. The CPI revisions also reduced the inflation measures in the national income and product accounts (GDP deflator, PCE deflator, and so on), although by smaller amounts. But these measures garner much less public attention.

50. Models explaining the falling saving rate by the rising stock market are quite successful during this period—and beyond.

51. This was the time, for example, that a stunning gap opened up between the yields on thirty- and twenty-nine-year Treasury bonds.

52. The growth in nominal compensation, as measured by the employment cost index (ECI), accelerated only slightly between 1995 and 1999, rising, on a fourth-quarter over fourth-quarter basis, from 2.7 percent in 1995 to 3.4 percent in 1999. During the first three quarters of 2000, however, ECI compensation rose at a 4.5 percent annual pace. A second measure of compensation in the nonfarm-business sector shows greater overall acceleration through 1999. This alternative measure of compensation rose 2.6 percent in 1995 and 4.7 percent in 1999. This measure of compensation growth, however, declined from mid-1998 through the first quarter of 2000.

53. It has long been known that productivity tends to rise when output grows rapidly.

54. Named for Intel's Gordon Moore, Moore's law predicted that the number of transistors integrated on circuits would double every eighteen months.

55. According to the basic theory of investment, it is important to distinguish between the effects of *lower* prices and those of *falling* prices on the cost of capital and, hence, on investment. A lower price of capital goods spurs investment spending. But a more rapid pace of (expected) price decline deters spending because it represents (expected) capital losses. In practice, the price-level effect was the dominant one.

56. U.S. Phillips curve equations that include a productivity-growth term typically find a significant (temporary) adverse effect of slower productivity growth on inflation (see Braun 1984; and Braun and Chen 1996; see also Council of Economic Advisers 2000, 90–91).

57. The simulation assumes that, after 1993, trend labor productivity in the nonfarm-business sector continued to grow at its 1974 to 1993 average of about 1.5 percent per year rather than accelerating sharply. The assumed deviation of the level and growth rates of nonfarm-business trend productivity from baseline are shown in the last two rows of table 3.16.

58. In FRB-US-model simulations that adjust the real federal funds rate to hold unemployment at baseline levels, the identical productivity shock lowers inflation by 0.7 percent relative to baseline in 1999.

59. In the WUMM model, this relative price is measured by the ratio of the computer price index for producers durable equipment to an index of nonfarm prices.

60. An alternative way to summarize the effect of the productivity shock on the Phillips curve trade-off is in terms of its effect on the model's short-run NAIRU, which falls by about 0.4 percentage points in the FRB-US model and about 0.8 percentage points in the WUMM model during the second half of the 1990s.

61. The personal-saving rate declined from 8.7 percent in 1992 to 2.2 percent in 1999 (and then turned slightly negative).

62. For an extreme example, see James Glassman and Kevin Hassett (1999), which essentially argues for a zero risk premium for equities. Less-extreme versions simply hold that the equity premium fell.

63. On a standardized basis—that is, adjusting for cyclical effects and for extraneous factors such as asset sales and meaningless shifts in the timing of receipts between one fiscal year and the next—the deficit as a share of potential GDP fell by 1.8 percentage points between 1992 and 1996 (see Congressional Budget Office, *The Budget and Economic Outlook,* January 2001, table F-3, 141).

64. One reason that the 1997 agreement contained so little fiscal restraint is that, at the last minute, the CBO announced that it had underestimated future federal tax receipts by $45 billion per year between 1998 and 2002 (see Chandler 1997). This eleventh-hour news led the budget negotiators to scrap some of the most painful cuts contained in their draft agreement (see *Washington Post* 1997).

65. The data underlying figures 3.12 and 3.13 come from various issues of the CBO publication *The Budget and Economic Outlook.* For each date, we chose CBO surplus projections that assume (counterfactually, as it later turned out) adherence to the discretionary-spending caps in the 1997 budget agreement.

66. In addition to social security, the off-budget surplus also includes revenues and spending of the Postal Service. At this writing, there is some debate over whether President George W. Bush's budget request (including his large tax cuts) can be accommodated without "invading" the social security surplus.

67. In its mid-session review of the budget in 2000, the Clinton administration proposed placing the surpluses of Medicare's hospital insurance fund off budget as well. (At present, Medicare is "on budget.") Then-candidate Al Gore and both parties in Congress rushed to embrace this proposal. But then-candidate George W. Bush did not.

68. These estimates assume that discretionary spending grows at the rate of inflation.

69. A sufficiently large recession could cause current on-budget surpluses to shrink or turn to deficits. In this event, Congress might decide to abandon the new budget rule.

70. Under the CBO's capped baseline, any proposal to raise appropriations above the 1997 caps is treated as "new spending" even if it does no more than keep discretionary spending from declining in real terms.

71. On the first two issues, see, for example, Vincent Reinhart and Brian Sack (2000). On the last, Alan Greenspan created a stir in January 2001 when he opined that the federal government should not acquire private assets. A tax cut would be better, he said.

72. As of this writing (the numbers will subsequently be revised), the annualized growth rate of real GDP has averaged just 1.3 percent over the last two quarters of 2000 and the first half of 2001.

73. This is only partially offset by the fact that higher stock prices lower the cost of capital to firms.

74. As Robert Solow reminds us, those who promote the idea that, say, cutting government spending can be expansionary never suggest raising government spending to calm an overheating economy.

75. Douglas Elmendorf and Jeffrey Liebman (2000) argue that the new political-economy rule will substantially change the effect of entitlement reforms and other budget policies on national saving.

76. We would also argue, perhaps controversially, that greater transparency helps make fine-tuning work. Since 1996, the markets have developed a better and better understanding of what the Fed was up to. In consequence, it was often said that long-term interest rates were "doing the Fed's work for it."

77. This is slightly odd since the Bush tax proposal long predated the economic slowdown and was not designed to alleviate it. For example, the amount of tax cutting originally proposed for fiscal years 2001 and 2002 is small.

78. The Fed has been pretty clear that the 1999 to 2000 tightening cycle was intended to slow the growth rate of aggregate demand to that of aggregate supply, thereby capping inflation—not bringing inflation back to 2 percent.

REFERENCES

Akerlof, George A., William T. Dickens, and George L. Perry. 1996. "The Macroeconomics of Low Inflation." *Brookings Papers on Economic Activity* (1): 1–76.

———. 2000. "Near-Rational Wage and Price Setting and the Long-Run Phillips Curve." *Brookings Papers on Economic Activity* (1): 1–60.

Baily, Martin, Eric Bartelsman, and John Haltiwanger. 1995. "Downsizing and Productivity Growth: Myth or Reality?" In *Sources of Productivity Growth in the 1980s*, edited by D. G. Mayes. Cambridge: Cambridge University Press.

Berger, Allen, Margaret Kyle, and Joseph Scalise. 2000. "Did U.S. Bank Supervisors Get Tougher during the Credit Crunch? Did They Get Easier during the Banking Boom? Did It Matter to Bank Lending?" *NBER* working paper no. 7689. Cambridge, Mass.: National Bureau of Economic Research, May.

Blanchard, Olivier. 1984. "Current and Anticipated Deficits, Interest Rates, and Economic Activity." *European Economic Review* 25(May/June): 7–27.

Blinder, Alan. 1998. *Central Banking in Theory and Practice.* Cambridge, Mass.: MIT Press.

Bomfim, Antulio. 1997. "The Equilibrium Federal Funds Rate and the Indicator Properties of Term-Structure Spreads." *Economic Inquiry* 35(4): 830–46.

Boskin, Michael J., et al. 1996. *Toward a More Accurate Measure of the Cost of Living: Final Report to the Senate Finance Committee from the Advisory Commission to Study the Consumer Price Index*, December 4.

Braun, Steven N. 1984. "Productivity and the NIIRU (and Other Phillips' Curve Issues)." *Economic Activity Section* working paper no. 34. Washington: Federal Reserve Board.

Braun, Steven N., and Ron Chen. 1996. "The NAIRU as a Policy Target: Refinements, Problems, and Challenges." Unpublished manuscript. Council of Economic Advisers.

Brayton, Flint, John Roberts, and John Williams. 1999. "What's Happened to the Phillips Curve?" *Federal Reserve Board* discussion paper. Washington: Federal Reserve Board, September.

Carlson, Eugene. 1992. "Campaign '92: While Voters Still Sing the Blues about the Economy, Hints of Optimism Emerge." *Wall Street Journal*, September 18, p. A6.

Chandler, Clay. 1997. "CBO Gives Negotiators a Windfall of $225 Billion in Tax Revenue." *Washington Post*, May 3, p. A15.

Congressional Budget Office. Various dates. *The Budget and Economic Outlook*. Washington: Congressional Budget Office, Congress of the United States.

Council of Economic Advisers. 1994. *Economic Report of the President*. Washington: U.S. Government Printing Office, February.

———. 1999. *Economic Report of the President*. Washington: U.S. Government Printing Office, February.

———. 2000. *Economic Report of the President*. Washington: U.S. Government Printing Office, February.

Elmendorf, Douglas, and Jeffrey Liebman. 2000. "Social Security Reform and National Saving in an Era of Budget Surpluses." *Brookings Papers on Economic Activity* (2): 1–71.

Farber, Henry S. 1998. "Has the Rate of Job Loss Increased in the Nineties?" *Industrial Relations Section* working paper no. 394. Princeton University, January.

———. 2001. "Job Loss in the United States, 1981–1999." *Industrial Relations Section* working paper no. 452. Princeton University, April.

Federal Open Market Committee, (FOMC Minutes). Various dates. Meeting minutes.

———. (FOMC Transcripts). Various dates. Meeting transcripts.

Feldstein, Martin. 1993. "Clinton's Path to Wider Deficits." *Wall Street Journal,* February 23, p. A20.

Glassman, James, and Kevin Hassett. 1999. *Dow 36,000.* New York: Times Books.

Gordon, Robert J. 2000. "Does the 'New Economy' Measure Up to the Great Inventions of the Past?" *Journal of Economic Perspectives* 14(4): 49–74.

Greenspan, Alan. 1995. Testimony before the Committee on Banking, Housing, and Urban Affairs. February 22.

———. 1996a. "The Challenge of Central Banking in a Democratic Society." Francis Boyer Lecture. Presented to the American Enterprise Institute for Public Policy Research, Washington, D.C., December 5.

———. 1996b. Testimony before the Committee on Banking, Housing, and Urban Affairs. February 20.

———. 2001. Testimony before the Committee on the U.S. Budget. U.S. Senate, January 25.

Gruber, Jonathan. 1997. "The Incidence of Payroll Taxation: Evidence from Chile." *Journal of Labor Economics* 15(3, pt. 2): S72–S101.

Gruber, Jonathan, and Alan Krueger. 1991. "The Incidence of Mandated Employer Provided Insurance: Lessons from Workers' Compensation Insurance." In *Tax Policy and the Economy,* edited by David Bradford, 111–43. Cambridge, Mass.: MIT Press.

Heller, Walter. 1966. *New Dimensions of Political Economy.* Harvard University Press.

Krueger, Alan, and Helen Levy. 1997. "Accounting for the Slowdown in Employer Health Care Costs." In *1996 Proceedings of the 89th Annual Conference on Taxation, National Tax Association.* Washington, D.C.: Tax Institute of America.

Lee, Jessica, and Bob Minzesheimer. 1992. "Statistics Do Support What Bush Is Saying." *USA Today,* October 27, p. 6A.

Meyer, Laurence. 1997a. "Monetary policy and the Bond Market: Complements or Substitutes?" Speech presented to the Fixed Income Summit of PSA, the Bond Market Trade Association. Washington, D.C., September 12.

———. 1997b. Speech presented to the Charlotte Economics Club. Charlotte, N.C., January 16.

———. 1998. Speech presented to the 40th annual meeting of the National Association for Business Economics, Washington, D.C., October 5.

———. 2000. "Structural Change and Monetary Policy." Remarks presented to a joint conference of the Federal Reserve Bank of San Francisco and the Stanford Institute for Economic Policy Research. San Francisco, March 3.

Mishel, Lawrence, Jared Bernstein, and John Schmitt. 2001. *The State of Working America, 2000–2001.* Ithaca, N.Y.: Cornell University Press.

Oliner, Stephen, and Daniel Sichel. 2000. "The Resurgence of Growth in the Late 1990s: Is Information Technology the Story?" *Finance and Economics* discussion paper no. 20. Washington: Board of Governors of the Federal Reserve System, March.

Orphanides, Athanasios, and David Wilcox. 1996. "The Opportunistic Approach to Disinflation." *Finance and Economics* discussion paper no. 24. Washington: Board of Governors of the Federal Reserve System.

Reinhart, Vincent, and Brian Sack. 2000. "The Economic Consequences of Disappearing Government Debt." *Brookings Papers on Economic Activity* (2): 163–209.

Schmidt, Stephanie. 1999. "Long-Run Trends in Workers' Beliefs about Their Own Job Security: Evidence from the General Social Survey." *Journal of Labor Economics* 17(October): S127–S141.

Schmidt, Stephanie, and Christopher Thompson. 1997. "Have Workers' Beliefs about Job Security Been Keeping Wage Inflation Low? Evidence from Public Opinion Data." Milken Institute working paper no. 97–4. Santa Monica, Calif.: Milken Institute, October.

Solow, Robert M. 1987. "We'd Better Watch Out." *New York Times Book Review,* July 12, p. 36.

Stewart, Kenneth J., and Stephen B. Reed. 1999. "CPI Research Series Using Current Methods, 1978–98." *Monthly Labor Review* 122(6): 29–38.

Summers, Lawrence. 1989. "Some Simple Economics of Mandated Benefits." *American Economic Review* 79(2): 177–83.

Turnovsky, Stephen J., and Marcus H. Miller. 1984. "The Effects of Government Expenditures on the Term Structure of Interest Rates." *Journal of Money, Credit, and Banking* 16(1): 16–33.

U.S. Department of Labor. Bureau of Labor Statistics. 2001. "Major Work Stoppages in 2000." Washington: U.S. Department of Labor Release 01–44, February 9.

Washington Post. 1997. "Ducking the Hard Ones." May 6, p. A18.

White House. 1993. *A Vision of Change for America.* Washington: Executive Office of the President, Office of Management and Budget, February 17.

———. 1999. "Mid-Session Review, Fiscal Year 2000." Washington: Executive Office of the President, Office of Management and Budget, June.

Woodward, Bob. 1994. *The Agenda: Inside the Clinton White House.* New York: Simon & Schuster.

———. 2000. *Maestro: Greenspan's Fed and the American Boom.* New York: Simon & Schuster.

Part II

Flexible, Open Labor Markets

Chapter 4

Comparative Analysis of Labor-Market Outcomes: Lessons for the United States from International Long-Run Evidence

Giuseppe Bertola, Francine D. Blau, and Lawrence M. Kahn

T he contrast between the labor-market performance of the United States and that of most other advanced economies over the last thirty years has been striking. During the period 1970 to 1975, the unemployment rate was 5.4 percent in the United States but under 3 percent in Australia, Austria, Belgium, France, West Germany, Japan, the Netherlands, Norway, New Zealand, Spain, Sweden, and the United Kingdom.[1] Among major Western countries, Italy's unemployment rate of 4.3 percent was the only one close to the U.S. unemployment level. American observers pondered the explanation for the persistently higher U.S. unemployment levels. This concern was well captured in the title of an influential paper about the U.S. experience that appeared at this time—"Why Is the Unemployment Rate So High at Full Employment?" (Hall 1970). High turnover rates of U.S. workers, which resulted in high quit rates accompanied by spells of unemployment, were seen as an important part of the story (Flanagan 1973).[2]

Indeed, one does not need to spend much time in a library to find statements of fact and theory extolling Europe and Japan as examples for American labor markets during that period. For example, Lester Thurow (1985) noted that unemployment corresponding to "full employment in the United States is far above what is considered full employment in any other industrial country, and since World War II American unemployment has been far above that in Japan" (9–10). Robert Heilbroner and Lester Thurow (1981) pointed to a number of features of European economies that, in their view, contributed to this difference: "European nations have generally gone much further than we have in providing labor exchanges or in seeking to remedy structural unemployment, and they have been willing to accept a higher level of inflation as a lesser evil than a high level of unemployment. This superior performance has worsened considerably in the last few years, but Europe is still ahead of the United States in its anti-unemployment programs" (50). And Roger Kaufman (1979) argued that "the generosity of unemployment insurance systems abroad may not significantly increase foreign unemployment rates in the 'open' sector because layoffs and discharges are greatly inhibited. In the United States, however, these benefits do increase the unemployment rate significantly" (168).

Since the early 1970s, after two oil crises, vastly increased globalization, and rapid technological change, the unemployment position of the United States and the other Western countries has dramatically reversed. By 1999, the U.S. unemployment rate had fallen to 4.2 percent and was as low as 3.9 percent as of September 2000 (according to the U.S. Bureau of Labor Statistics website). In contrast, unemployment had risen sharply in virtually every other Western country. By 1999, unemployment averaged 9.2 percent in the European Union and had been at such levels there for nearly 20 years (OECD 1999, 2000), with particularly high rates in Finland (10.3 percent), France (11.3 percent), Italy (11.4 percent), and Spain (15.9 percent).

By the 1980s and 1990s, it was European observers who were searching for explanations for persistently high unemployment rates. Increasing labor-market flexibility—freeing up the forces of supply and demand to determine pay and employment and diminishing the role of union contracts or government regulations—was seen by some as the key to lowering European unemployment (OECD 1994b). Interestingly, this reasoning implies that the type of high worker mobility that had been a concern in the United States in the earlier period could now be viewed as one component of the more flexible U.S. labor market, which, taken as a package, was associated with lower unemployment rates. Others, however, doubt that greater flexibility would in fact achieve lower unemployment, pointing instead to low levels of demand for labor as the culprit behind Europe's higher unemployment rates (Glyn and Salverda 2000).

Following Olivier Blanchard and Justin Wolfers (2000) and other recent contributions, this paper examines the role of labor-market flexibility and labor-demand factors in determining the divergent employment experience of the United States and other industrial countries. There is, however, another side to this comparison. While the United States has fared well in recent years in creating jobs and maintaining low unemployment, its wage levels have deteriorated relative to those overseas. And wage inequality, always higher in the United States than in other advanced countries, has increased more sharply in the United States than it has elsewhere. Between 1979 to 1981 and 1994 to 1998, median real weekly earnings of male full-time workers in the United States fell by 5.5 percent, while, across six major OECD countries (Australia, Austria, Canada, West Germany, Sweden, and the United Kingdom), they rose by 22.6 percent.[3] Similar trends of falling real earnings of U.S. workers compared to those in other Western countries prevailed among women. However, in contrast to men, U.S. women experienced absolutely rising, rather than stagnating, real earnings, and the other countries did not gain on the United States as rapidly: women's wages rose by 15.3 percent in the United States and by 31.6 percent in the other countries.

To some degree, these trends in relative real wages may reflect the other Western countries catching up to U.S. levels, a process that started long before 1979.

For example, OECD indices of real compensation per employee rose by 29.2 percent from 1970 to 1980 in the six countries just mentioned, compared to a rise of only 8.0 percent in the United States.[4] While, as noted, this convergence continued into the late 1990s, U.S. median real (purchasing-power-parity-corrected) wages in the period 1994 to 1998 were still 12 percent higher for men and 14 percent higher for women than were median real wages in these six other OECD countries. Thus, some further catch-up may still occur. Moreover, regardless of the reasons for these trends, the slower growth of real wages in the United States over at least the last thirty years may or may not be a cause of its falling relative-unemployment rate. In what follows, we seek to shed light on this question.

At the same time that the real wages of the median worker in the United States deteriorated relative to those of the median worker in other Western nations, Americans at the bottom fared even worse. U.S. men at the 10th percentile experienced a 16.3 percent decline in their real wages between 1979 to 1981 and 1994 to 1998, while male workers at the 10th percentile in the six OECD countries listed previously saw an increase in real wages of 18.8 percent. Among women, the real wages of workers at the 10th percentile fell by 2.8 percent in the United States but rose by 28.8 percent in the other countries. Moreover, by the period 1994 to 1998, workers at the 10th percentile in these other countries had surpassed Americans in real earnings levels, with men having a 21 percent advantage and women a 9 percent advantage over their U.S. counterparts. At the bottom of the wage distribution, the United States has some catching up of its own to do.[5]

Thus, while the U.S. economy may have been an impressive job-creation machine since the 1970s, real wages in the United States have risen more slowly than have those in other countries, and workers at the bottom have fared particularly poorly. If unemployment is Europe's signature problem at the turn of the century, low and declining real and relative wages for those at the bottom of the wage hierarchy are America's.

This chapter seeks to examine the unemployment experience of the United States in an international context. We analyze the dynamics of aggregate unemployment, building on the framework proposed by Blanchard (1999) and Blanchard and Wolfers (2000). In addition, we track international differences in the composition of employment and wage outcomes across demographic groups. These disaggregated outcomes are of interest in their own right, and evidence on them can also help us understand the fundamental causes of differing aggregate unemployment outcomes. We aim at characterizing possible labor-market configurations with respect to a variety of performance indicators, on the one hand, and the relation of those labor-market configurations to various institutional features of the labor markets of industrialized countries, on the other.

The first section discusses the basic theoretical approach that we adopt in our attempt to understand international differences in unemployment. Like Blanchard and Wolfers (2000) and other recent contributions, we argue that institutions and economic shocks interact to produce differing outcomes. This framework offers a "unified theory" of labor-market outcomes (Blank 1997) and suggests that the same macroeconomic forces will produce differing unemployment and wage outcomes depending on a country's institutional makeup.

The second section offers a preliminary descriptive analysis of long-run labor-market developments across a broad panel of industrialized countries. We initially focus on two headline indicators of labor-market performance, aggregate unemployment and overall wage inequality. The dynamics of these two variables have been sources of concern in the past twenty years—the latter increasing in the United States and other Anglo-Saxon countries, the former increasing in Continental European and other heavily regulated countries. We find that country and period fixed effects account for a large proportion of labor-market-performance variation. However, the available data do appear to evince a trade-off between wage inequality and unemployment, albeit one that is far from being stable over time and across countries.[6] We also find evidence of a weaker trade-off between unemployment and real-wage levels.

We proceed to analyze the role that country-specific macro shocks play in policy trade-offs (in the third section) and the role of microeconomic structural features such as the demographic composition of the population (in the fourth section). The fifth section reviews theoretical perspectives on the relevance of institutions (such as the extent and character of collective-bargaining arrangements and employment-protection systems) and assesses their empirical explanatory power in our data set. In this section, we also discuss recent changes in labor-market institutions in the OECD countries and estimate the effects of these changes on unemployment in the United States compared to unemployment in other countries. In the sixth section, we discuss the demographic composition and character of employment and unemployment.

Our empirical specifications allow macro shocks and microeconomic structural factors to interact with country-specific institutional features in their effects on aggregate and disaggregated labor-market-performance indicators. We use our econometric estimates to explicitly account for U.S.–other country differences in employment outcomes. For each empirical specification, we apply the parameter estimates to U.S.–other country differences in institutional, demographic, and macro-shock variables. This comparative approach brings information beyond U.S. time trends to bear on our understanding of the sources of U.S. success in achieving low unemployment. It also makes it possible to simulate what would have happened to the U.S. unemployment rate under different labor-market institutions given the macro shocks experienced. The seventh section updates our empirical analysis to check its robustness and explore its implications for current U.S. developments. The final section concludes.

LABOR-MARKET INSTITUTIONS AND OUTCOMES: A UNIFIED THEORY?

The U.S. labor market has long been much less subject to collective intervention by unions or the government than have the labor markets of other Western countries. It is commonly argued that this difference is the key to understanding the differences in unemployment, wage levels, and wage inequality discussed previously (for example, Siebert 1997). While some controversy surrounds the effort to link the institutional differences to labor-market outcomes, the broad outlines of these disparities are clear.

First, collective bargaining plays a much smaller role in determining workers' wages in the United States, with its low rate of collective-bargaining coverage and predominantly single-firm bargaining units in the union sector, than in many of these other countries, particularly those in Central and Northern Europe, where wage agreements are made at the industry or even the economy level. And legislated minimum-wage levels are also higher relative to average wages in these other countries than they are in the United States (OECD 1998a). There is abundant evidence that these more interventionist labor-market institutions, which are prevalent in the other OECD countries, lead to compressed wage differentials along several dimensions, such as industry, age, and gender. However, the evidence that this wage compression generates employment problems for those with high relative wages is mixed (Blau and Kahn 1999). Second, unemployment-insurance (UI) benefits are much more generous in other OECD countries than they are in the United States, and, while in the United States UI benefits usually run out after six months, unemployed workers can collect for much longer periods in other countries. Third, it is much more expensive and administratively cumbersome for firms in other OECD countries to lay off workers or employ temporary workers than it is for firms in the United States to do so (OECD 1999). Moreover, the government is typically a much more important employer in other OECD countries than it is in the United States. While the public-sector share of employment has been falling steadily in the United States since the 1970s, largely as the result of strong growth in private employment, the opposite is true in most other OECD countries (Gregory and Borland 1999, 3575). Finally, mandated benefits such as parental leave and sick leave are much more generous in these other countries than they are in the United States (Nickell and Layard 1999).

As previously noted, some have pointed to several of these major differences in the degree of intervention in the labor market as important causes of the relatively high unemployment in other Western nations compared to that in the United States, although it should be acknowledged that some of these differences (for example, the high incidence of government employment or the generosity of unemployment benefits) may be in part a *response* to high unemployment in these other countries. One difficulty with such an argument, taken at face value, is that, in the 1960s and early 1970s, with largely the same differences in labor-market institutions between the United States and other Western nations, it was the United States that was the high-unemployment country. Thus, it cannot be true that interventionist institutions produce high unemployment all the time. However, consideration of the vast differences between the United States and other Western countries in wage setting and other labor-market institutions has suggested a plausible interpretation of the relation between these institutions and the unemployment disparities that have prevailed since the early 1970s. This view essentially posits an interaction between labor-market institutions and labor-market shocks.

This interaction can be understood by first noting that, since the early 1970s, there have been a variety of shocks to which labor markets in all countries have been exposed, including the slowdown in productivity growth dating from the early 1970s, the oil-price increases of the 1970s and early 1980s, the fall in the relative demand for unskilled labor since 1980, and disinflation in the 1980s and 1990s (Layard, Nickell, and Jackman 1991; Freeman and Katz 1995; Blanchard and Wolfers 2000; Ball 1997, 1999). It has been hypothesized that the flexible U.S. labor market was able to accommodate these shocks by letting absolute and relative real-wage levels adjust, allowing the U.S. unemployment rate to stay low. In contrast, in most other OECD countries, labor-market institutions kept overall real wages rising and prevented unskilled workers' relative wages from falling as fast as they did in the less restricted U.S. market (in some cases preventing any fall in low-skilled workers' relative pay), thus producing sharp increases in unemployment in these countries (Blanchard and Wolfers 2000; Freeman 1994). As discussed further subsequently, some of these macroeconomic factors, particularly disinflation policies or shifts in the demand for unskilled workers, can be affected by institutions or by unemployment itself. However, the logic of the argument is still compelling: keeping wages rigid in the face of shifting supplies and demands is likely to have effects on employment.

From the perspective of such a unified theory (Blank 1997), Europe's experience of rising unemployment, rising real wages, and comparatively stable relative-wage levels is the other side of the coin to the U.S. experience of falling unemployment, falling to steady real wages, and rapidly rising wage inequality. Up to the early 1970s, the relatively low unemployment rates of European countries may have reflected the slow catch-up of real wages in the presence of relatively fast productivity growth or the small amount of frictional unemployment noted previously. Thereafter, the United States allowed real and relative wages to adjust, while, in Europe and other Western nations, employment took the brunt of the shocks.

To illustrate the basic argument, consider the effect of productivity trends. From the 1960s to the 1990s, annual growth in total factor productivity (TFP) in the OECD fell from 5 to 6 percent to 1 to 2 percent (Blanchard and Wolfers 2000). TFP growth is the growth in output per worker beyond that which can be explained by changes in the amounts of labor and capital used. It is thus a measure of technological progress. In the relatively flexible U.S. labor market, real wages were allowed to grow more slowly and even to decline, thus mitigating the adverse effect of the fall in productivity growth on unemployment.[7] As shown by Laurence Ball and Robert Moffitt (2001), even in the United States, real wages adjust with a lag to changes in productivity growth. But, in many other OECD nations, unions and other labor-market institutions kept real wages growing at their customary pace instead; this led to higher unemployment. In Ball and Moffitt's terms, this argument suggests that wages in these other countries adjusted to productivity with considerably longer lags than they did in the United States. Conversely, when productivity growth is unusually rapid, real wages may adjust more quickly in flexible labor markets like those in the United States than they do in rigid labor markets, implying that employment should actually grow by more in the countries with interventionist institutions. This kind of interaction may indeed play a role in explaining the low unemployment observed in the 1960s in much of Europe. It could also, at least in principle, be relevant to U.S. labor-market dynamics in the aftermath of the recent high labor-productivity growth documented and analyzed by Stephen Oliner and Daniel Sichel (2000).

In addition to explaining why a flexible labor market should be better able to generate higher aggregate employment rates under certain conditions, the unified theory has implications for disaggregated employment indicators: to the extent that high wage floors prevent low-wage employment opportunities, employment problems in the interventionist countries should be especially severe for individuals who would command relatively low wage rates in laissez-faire labor markets. Available evidence on these employment problems is mixed, with some studies finding that intervention does reduce the relative employment of the less skilled and others finding that it does not (Blau and Kahn 1999). This question is difficult to answer conclusively because wage and employment opportunities depend on demographic and other less readily observable worker characteristics as well as on measured skills, and earnings inequality also reflects heterogeneity across jobs when worker mobility is not perfect (Bertola and Ichino 1995). We next examine available data from the theory's perspective and proceed to evaluate the theory's aggregate and compositional predictive power.

WHAT IS TO BE EXPLAINED?

To analyze recent trends in labor-market outcomes across countries, we have assembled a cross-country time-series data set building on that constructed and analyzed by Blanchard and Wolfers (2000). We draw variables pertaining to unemployment, macro shocks, and labor-market institutions from the Blanchard-Wolfers data set. We have added data on wage distributions, labor force by age groups, population by age groups, and unemployment rates by age groups for male and female workers separately. We have also included additional labor-market institution indicators. (For additional details, see the appendix.) The countries included are Australia, Austria, Belgium, Canada, Denmark, Finland, France, Germany, Ireland, Italy, Japan, the Netherlands, New Zealand, Norway, Portugal, Spain, Sweden, Switzerland, the United Kingdom, and the United States. Along the time dimension, observations are arranged in five-year intervals from 1960 to 1964 until 1990 to 1994, so as to smooth out short-term fluctuations. The final observation of the Blanchard-Wolfers data set refers to 1995 to 1996 time-averaged data. To preserve comparability with those authors' results, the data set analyzed in this and the next few sections also uses only 1995 to 1996 information in constructing the "1995" period average. In the last section of the paper, we present some updated information for the period 1995 to 1999 for a limited sample of countries and discuss how the proposed long-run, cross-country perspective may illuminate the recent striking developments in the U.S. labor market.

To begin with, we review time-series and cross-country variation in a few key variables of interest. Table 4.1 contains data on unemployment rates for the subset of countries for which data are available for both 1970 to 1974 and 1995 to 1996 in the Blanchard and Wolfers data set. The table shows that unemployment is highly variable along both time-series and cross-sectional dimensions, ranging from less than 1 percent in 1970 to 1974 for New Zealand to 23 percent in 1995 to 1996 for Spain. From the perspective of this paper, it is of course most interesting to focus on the U.S. unemployment rate vis-à-vis that of other industrialized countries. For the purpose of such comparisons, throughout the paper we contrast the U.S. unemployment rate with the unweighted average of unemployment rates in the non-U.S. countries represented in the sample.

In 1970 to 1974, unemployment averaged 2.54 percent in the non-U.S. countries of the Blanchard-Wolfers sample, while it was 5.41 percent in the United States. By 1995, the non-U.S. countries had experienced a well-publicized increase in unemployment to 10.66 percent, while the U.S. rate was 5.50 percent, roughly its 1970 level. It is this reversal of unemployment fortunes that we are most interested in documenting and interpreting, focusing in particular on its association with other labor-market-performance indicators. (Of course, the U.S.

TABLE 4.1 / Overall Unemployment Rate (Common Definition), Selected Countries (percent)

| | Period | |
Country	1970 to 1974	1995 to 1996
Australia	2.21	8.54
Belgium	2.21	14.23
Canada	5.83	9.61
Finland	2.15	16.74
France	2.71	11.54
Italy	4.27	12.04
Japan	1.30	3.24
Netherlands	1.79	7.11
New Zealand	.23	6.20
Spain	2.97	22.96
Sweden	2.24	7.87
United Kingdom	2.53	7.88
Non-U.S. average (unweighted)	2.54	10.66
United States	5.41	5.50

Source: Blanchard and Wolfers (2000).

unemployment rate eventually came down to a September 2000 level of 3.9 percent. In the concluding section of the paper, we discuss how our long-run, cross-country empirical perspective may shed light on such recent developments.)[8]

Our data include comparable wage-distribution statistics for a subset of countries and periods. Not surprisingly, heterogeneous levels and dynamics are observable in the United States and other countries as regards such indicators. First, table 4.2 shows log median real wages (using the personal consumption expenditures deflator) in purchasing-power-parity-corrected 1998 U.S. dollars for full-time male workers. We focus on men's wages as an indicator of wage trends because men are a more homogeneous group than women, although our database and other work have shown similar trends for women's wages and wage inequality in the United States and other countries (Blau and Kahn 2000a). Median real wages have grown more slowly in the United States than in the

TABLE 4.2 / Log Median Male Weekly Earnings, Full-Time Workers, Purchasing-Power-Corrected Constant 1998 U.S. Dollars (GDP Personal-Consumption-Expenditures Deflator)

	Level				Change
Country	1975 to 1979	1980 to 1984	1990 to 1994	1995 to 1996	1975 to 1979 until 1995 to 1996
Australia	6.01	6.01	6.06	6.14	.14
Austria	. . .	5.77	6.04	. . .	. . .
Belgium	. . .	. . .	6.13	6.17	. . .
Canada	. . .	6.25	6.40	. . .	. . .
Finland	5.85	5.89	6.08	6.17	.33
France	5.64	5.71	5.75	5.75	.11
Germany	. . .	6.26	6.29	6.36	. . .
Italy	. . .	. . .	6.03	6.02	. . .
Japan	5.66	5.76	5.94	6.04	.38
Netherlands	. . .	. . .	6.21	6.28	. . .
New Zealand	. . .	6.11	6.05	6.10	. . .
Spain	. . .	. . .	. . .	5.98	. . .
Sweden	5.96	5.98	6.06	6.08	.11
Switzerland	. . .	. . .	6.49	6.53	. . .
United Kingdom	5.92	5.99	6.21	6.23	.31
Non-U.S. average (current-year sample)	5.84	5.97	6.13	6.14	. . .
Non-U.S. average (1975 to 1979 sample)	5.84	5.89	6.02	6.07	.23
United States	6.37	6.37	6.34	6.33	−.04

Source: Unpublished OECD data.

other OECD countries shown in table 4.2. For example, between 1975 to 1979 and 1995 to 1996, real wages fell by 4 percent in the United States, while they rose by 23 percent in the other six countries for which data were available (Australia, Finland, France, Japan, Sweden, and the United Kingdom),[9] although, as discussed earlier, in the 1990s real wages were still higher in the United States than they were elsewhere, suggesting room for further convergence.

Table 4.3 shows data on wage inequality (measured by the 50–10 percentile log difference over the distribution of wages). We focus on the 50–10 wage gap in view of the importance of wage floors in economies with extensive collective-bargaining coverage and centralized wage-setting institutions in which these floors are negotiated (Blau and Kahn 1999). The data are sparse, especially in the early periods. Their message, however, is similar regardless of whether the U.S.– other countries unweighted average comparison is done on all available data in each year or only on the subset of countries for which wage information was already available in 1975 to 1979 (that is, Australia, Finland, France, Japan, Sweden, and the United Kingdom). The data indicate that wage inequality has

TABLE 4.3 / 50-10 Differential in Male Log Weekly Earnings, Full-Time Workers

Country	1975 to 1979	1980 to 1984	1990 to 1994	1995 to 1996	1975 to 1979 until 1995 to 1996
Australia	.45	.49	.50	.52	.07
Austria	. . .	.49	.51	. . .	. . .
Belgium	. . .	. . .	.33	.32	. . .
Canada	. . .	.73	.80	. . .	. . .
Finland	.48	.44	.38	.38	−.10
France	.52	.49	.48	.47	−.05
Germany	. . .	.42	.38	.38	. . .
Italy	. . .	. . .	.35	.34	. . .
Japan	.46	.48	.48	.47	.02
Netherlands	. . .	. . .	.41	.45	. . .
New Zealand	. . .	.49	.57	.58	. . .
Spain	. . .	. . .	. . .	.67	. . .
Sweden	.28	.27	.30	.34	.06
Switzerland	. . .	. . .	.40	.41	. . .
United Kingdom	.46	.50	.58	.59	.13
Non-U.S. average (current-year sample)	.44	.48	.46	.45	.01
Non-U.S. average (1975 to 1979 sample)	.44	.45	.45	.46	.02
United States	.66	.71	.77	.79	.13

Source: Unpublished OECD data.

always been higher in the United States than in other industrialized countries and that it has increased more rapidly there as well.

How are wage and unemployment performance related to each other? Raw data are not revealing: univariate regression coefficients of unemployment on wage levels or on wage inequality are insignificant. Patterns are much more readily apparent, however, if the variability of key labor-market indicators is decomposed into its country-specific, period-specific, and residual components. To pursue this decomposition, we first regress unemployment rates, wage levels, and wage-inequality indicators on country and period dummies:

$$y_{it} = a_i + b_t + c_{it}, \tag{4.1}$$

where for country i and period t, y is one of the three outcomes (unemployment rate, wage level, or wage inequality), a is a country fixed effect, b is a common period effect, and c is a country-period residual. To understand the meaning of the residual c_{it}, consider the unemployment-rate version of 4.1 and the U.S. observation for 1990 to 1994. From estimating equation 4.1, we find that the U.S. country effect is 4.97 percent, while the period 1990 to 1994 effect is 3.23 percent. This implies that the expected U.S. unemployment rate in 1990 to 1994 assuming normal U.S. behavior in the world economy would have been 8.20 percent (4.97 + 3.23). The actual U.S. unemployment rate in 1990 to 1994 was 6.58 percent, implying a residual of -1.62 percent; in other words, unemployment in the United States was unexpectedly low in 1990 to 1994.

Having estimated equation 4.1 for unemployment, wage levels, and wage inequality, we next analyze statistically and graphically relationships between the residuals and the role of time effects. This procedure allows us to remain agnostic as to the direction of causality between labor-market-performance indicators and offers useful insights into possible structural relationships among them.

In pairwise regressions of unemployment residuals on wage-level residuals or wage-inequality residuals, the coefficients are significant, subject to some interesting qualifications. After controlling for country and time effects, a positive wage level unemployment residual relation is apparent (see figure 4.1). One interpretation of this relation is that the period effects remove the effect of common increases in productivity from wage-level determination. If a country's real wage is especially high relative to this trend and to its normal real-wage level, then unemployment is also on average unexpectedly high. The statistical significance of the unemployment residual-wage-level residual relation, however, is largely driven by U.S.-specific time-series developments, possibly reflecting the role played by convergence phenomena in shaping U.S. relative-average-wage dynamics. When the United States is in the sample, the partial correlation coefficient is 0.305, but it is only 0.087 when the United States is excluded, and its statistical significance drops to 15 percent if the panel structure of the residuals is taken into account when computing the variance-covariance matrix (even with the United States in).

The relationship between unemployment and wage inequality (as measured

FIGURE 4.1 / Unemployment Rate and Median Log Male Real Wage (Purchasing-Power-Parity Corrected in 1998 U.S. Dollars) for Full-Time Workers, After Removing Country and Period Effects

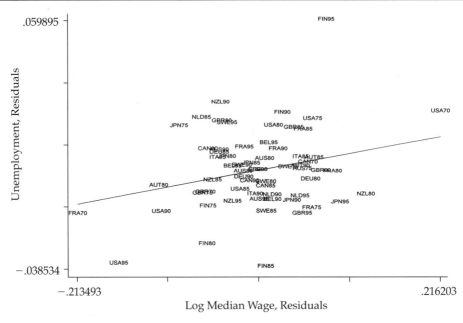

Notes: The slope *t* coefficient, 2.416, is significant at better than 2 percent.

by the 50–10 log wage differential and illustrated in figure 4.2 after controlling for country and period effects) is very strong and much more robust. When unemployment residuals are regressed on wage-inequality residuals (to yield the regression line plotted in the figure), and also when the reverse regression is run, the statistical significance of the negative slope coefficient is robust to the exclusion of U.S. observations and to correction for residual variance clustering. The slope of the unemployment–wage inequality trade-off is significant, not only from the statistical, but also from the economic point of view. Controlling for country and period effects, the coefficient on the 50–10 log wage differential in a regression where unemployment is the dependent variable is −0.241, with a *t*-statistic of −4.68 (the coefficient on unemployment in the reverse regression is −0.944, with a *t*-statistic of −4.07). The inequality-unemployment trade-off illustrated by such regressions indicates that an increase of 0.1 in the wage inequality measure "buys" up to 2.41 percentage points of unemployment reduction. To put this trade-off in perspective, consider that, between 1970 and 1995, U.S. wage inequality as measured by 50–10 log wage differentials increased by 0.18 and French inequality decreased by 0.11. If these movements had happened along a stable trade-off, relative-wage-inequality developments should have been associated with a divergence of 6.96 percentage points in the unemployment rates

FIGURE 4.2 / Unemployment and 50–10 Differential, Male Log Weekly Earnings for Full-Time Workers, After Removing Country and Period Effects

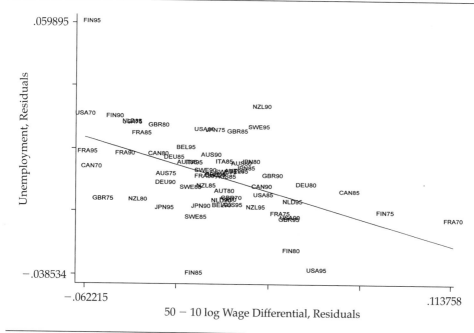

Note: Slope $t = -4.820$.

of the two countries. As table 4.1 shows, French unemployment rose by 8.83 percentage points, while the U.S. rate rose by only 0.09 percentage points. Thus, the trade-off illustrated in figure 4.2 could account for almost 80 percent of the diverging unemployment patterns for these two countries over this period.

Importantly, a trade-off between unemployment and wage inequality is apparent only after removing country and period effects. We do not report country effects, which presumably reflect institutions as well as the demographic features (on which more subsequently) and structural features of each economy. Spain's large fixed unemployment effect over the period, for example, may well be a reflection of the transition of its labor force out of the agricultural sector, a convergence phenomenon. Treating such features as time invariant is only an approximation, of course. To the extent that unemployment and wage inequality both depend endogenously on a host of country- and time-dependent variables, the evolution of unemployment and wage inequality should be explained in terms of the evolution over time of each country's specific characteristics, some of which we will be able to include in more structural empirical specifications in what follows.

The scope of empirical exercises is, however, obviously constrained by the fact that potentially relevant country-specific characteristics are not always observable and certainly more numerous than the countries on which we have information. Accordingly, the proposed organization of information in terms of fixed and period effects does offer a useful summary perspective on labor-market developments. Most interestingly, we find that period effects increase over time in both the unemployment and the wage-inequality regressions whose residuals are plotted in figure 4.2. If we treat unemployment as the dependent variable and regress deviations from country means for unemployment on wage-inequality deviations from country means and period dummies, we find that the coefficients on the latter increase significantly over time. For example, this period effect is found to be 1.47 percentage points higher in 1975 to 1980 than in 1970 to 1975, to increase further (by 1.49, 0.23, and 1.17 percentage points) in the following five-year periods, and to be 0.78 points higher in 1995 to 1996 than in 1990 to 1994. This means that, within countries, the unemployment–wage inequality relation is getting worse over time.

In summary, the evidence does point to a trade-off between unemployment and wage inequality, but it also indicates that the trade-off—not unlike an expectations-adjusted Phillips curve—is not stable. Its slope is negative and statistically constant over time: only the period 1995 to 1996—inequality interaction is significant (p-value = 0.07), while allowing all other slopes to change over time receives no statistical support (p-value = 0.67). The trade-off's intercept, however, is different across countries and appears to deteriorate steadily over time, moving to higher unemployment for a given level of wage inequality.

This evidence is descriptive rather than causal, of course, but structural mechanisms may easily imply a negative association between wage inequality and unemployment across different institutional arrangements. As we discuss in the fifth section, collective bargaining and other labor-market institutions tend to reduce wage inequality, effectively truncating the underlying distribution of wages across different individuals and jobs and eliminating employment opportunities for low-wage workers. This will contribute to overall unemployment and affect the observed levels of median wages and wage inequality.

While structural interpretations are plausible, it must be acknowledged that, if unemployment primarily affects those at the bottom of the skill distribution, there will be a mechanical positive relationship between unemployment and the observed wage median. Moreover, if the wage distribution realistically has more mass near the median than at the 10th percentile, then truncation from below will also narrow the observed 50–10 gap, producing a negative relation between unemployment and observed wage inequality. Since anything else that raises unemployment will very likely also affect the observed wage distribution, this discussion of truncation raises the possibility that the causality runs from unemployment to median wages and wage inequality rather than the reverse. However, Francine Blau and Lawrence Kahn (1996 and 2000a) control for this truncation and still find higher levels of wage inequality in the United States than in other countries. Their evidence suggests that laissez-faire labor-market institutions, the supply of literacy skills, and population heterogeneity could play important roles in shaping the extent of wage inequality. Of course, the shape of wage distributions across those observed to be employed is likely not independent of the fact that their low-wage portion is truncated. For example, workers may be induced to upgrade their skills when they do not succeed in obtaining a job, especially if education and training are subsidized. Thus, labor-market institutions may affect wage inequality indirectly through their effect on the supply of skills.

THE ROLE OF MACROECONOMIC SHOCKS

In this and the following two sections, we examine possible explanations for the reversal of unemployment fortunes characterizing the United States and the other OECD countries. Can we understand why the United States went from being a high-unemployment to a low-unemployment country between the 1970s and the 1990s? An obvious possible explanation for such a reversal is that macroeconomic shocks may have been less favorable for the United States than for other countries in the 1970s but more favorable in the 1990s. To investigate this possibility, we turn to Blanchard and Wolfers's (2000) data and use their analysis as a base from which to proceed. Blanchard and Wolfers summarize the macroeconomic shocks affecting each country by measures of the following:

1. *Changes in productivity growth, measured on a TFP basis as the growth in output per work hour after controlling for changes in the quantities of other factor inputs.* This measure of technological progress has substantially slowed across the OECD since the 1960s. Reduced TFP growth can result in higher unemployment for several years if labor-market institutions keep real wages rising at their customary pace.[10] In the long run, there is no reason for unemployment to be affected by the particular level of TFP growth on which a country has settled, but it may take a long time for real-wage growth to decelerate to its new equilibrium level. Thus, higher unemployment in the face of slower TFP growth can persist over the five-year periods used in the analysis.

2. *Changes in the ex post real interest rate, a summary measure of the cost of capital, which fell across the OECD from 1965 to 1975 but then rose steadily.* Higher real interest rates restrain economic activity and therefore contribute to higher unemployment. As was the case for the productivity-growth slowdown, rising real interest rates are expected to cause larger increases in unemployment the more rigid are real wages. The fact that real interest rates were higher overall in the 1990s than they were in the 1960s and 1970s can therefore help explain the rise in OECD unemployment rates.

3. *Shifts in labor demand over time, measured in terms of changes in labor's share of total business-sector income.* By this measure, labor demand shifted upward in Europe between 1960 and 1975 but fell steadily through the 1990s to well below its 1960 level. Labor's share fell steadily in the United States over the same period. As Blanchard and Wolfers note, this reduction in labor's share could have been due to downsizing and leaner production methods. The lower level of labor demand can be associated with lower employment if, again, real wages fail to adjust to the decline.

4. *Changes in inflation that, to the extent that they are not fully anticipated and nominal wages are preset, can cause deviations of observed unemployment from its equilibrium level.*[11] Across the OECD, inflation was increasing in the 1970s but was decreasing in the 1980s and 1990s, so unemployment may have been below its equilibrium level in the 1970s and above it in the 1980s and 1990s, at least on average.

Table 4.4 shows mean values for unemployment, these four shocks, and time-invariant measures of institutions (discussed subsequently) in 1970 to 1974 and 1995 to 1996. Data are displayed for the United States and for the unweighted average of other countries for which data are available for both periods: Australia, Belgium, Canada, Finland, France, Italy, Japan, the Netherlands, New Zealand, Spain, Sweden, and the United Kingdom. Each variable is signed so that an increase is expected to raise unemployment. Thus, labor demand, TFP growth, and the change in inflation have all been multiplied by −1. Table 4.4 indicates that the unemployment rate rose in the non-U.S. countries relative to the United States by 8.04 percentage points over this period, and it is this change that we wish to explain.

The data presented in table 4.4 indicate that the labor-demand variable—which, as explained by Blanchard and Wolfers (2000) in their data appendix, is based on the log of labor's share of income—shows an increase for both the United States and the non-U.S. countries over the period 1970 to 1995. This means that labor's share fell. The last column of table 4.1 shows that labor's share actually fell by more in the United States than elsewhere and thus should have contributed to a rising U.S. unemployment rate relative to the other countries. This means that, in order to explain the reversal of relative-unemployment rates between the United States and the other countries, other factors must outweigh the effects of labor demand.

Real interest rates rose both in the United States and in the other countries, with a larger rise in the other countries. The difference in real-interest-rate behavior is thus a contender for explaining the U.S.–other country unemployment divergence. The TFP-growth variable is less negative in 1995 than in 1970 for both the United States and the other countries. This means that TFP growth slowed, and the last column of table 4.1 shows that it decreased more outside the United States. This, then, is another factor that could help explain the divergence in unemployment experience between the United States and other countries.

Finally, the change in inflation is also signed in the perverse way. The negative signs in 1970 mean that inflation increased over the period 1970 to 1974. The inflation figures for 1995 are positive, implying that inflation decreased during 1995 and 1996. The last column of table 4.1 shows that inflation decreased by more in the other OECD countries than in the United States, a further potential factor contributing to the rising unemployment rates in the non-U.S. countries.[12]

We now examine the extent to which the shock measures proposed and exhaustively discussed by Blanchard and Wolfers (2000) can explain the declining unemployment rate in the United States relative to the other OECD countries.

TABLE 4.4 / Mean Values of Key Variables: Blanchard-Wolfers Sample, Countries with Complete Observations in 1970 to 1974 and 1995 to 1996

| | 1970 | | 1995 | | Change: 1970 to 1995 | | Difference in Change: |
	Non-U.S.	U.S.	Non-U.S.	U.S.	Non-U.S.	U.S.	Non-U.S. vs. U.S.
Unem Rate	.0254	.0541	.1066	.0550	.0813	.0009	.0804
Labor Demand	.0013	.0046	.0501	.0697	.0488	.0651	−.0163
Real Interest Rate	.0152	.0196	.0529	.0389	.0378	.0192	.0185
TFP	−.0370	−.0087	−.0082	−.0015	.0289	.0072	.0216
Change in Inflation	−.0043	−.0037	.0027	.0009	.0070	.0046	.0023
UI Rep. Rate	54.1667	50.0000	54.1667	50.0000	.0000	.0000	.0000
UI Duration	2.6521	.5000	2.6521	.5000	.0000	.0000	.0000
Cbcov90	69.7500	18.0000	69.7500	18.0000	.0000	.0000	.0000
Emp. Protection	10.5000	1.0000	10.5000	1.0000	.0000	.0000	.0000
Almphat	−12.2783	−2.5900	−12.2783	−2.5900	.0000	.0000	.0000
Union Density	41.3458	17.3000	41.3458	17.3000	.0000	.0000	.0000
Labor Tax Rate	49.7583	43.2000	49.7583	43.2000	.0000	.0000	.0000
Coord.	−3.6667	−2.0000	−3.6667	−2.0000	.0000	.0000	.0000

Notes: All variables are signed so that they are expected to have a positive effect on unemployment (Labor Demand, TFP, Change in Inflation, Almphat, and Coord. all have been multiplied by −1). Non-U.S. countries include Australia, Belgium, Canada, Finland, France, Italy, Japan, the Netherlands, New Zealand, Spain, Sweden, and the United Kingdom.

We first present and discuss our regression results and then use the parameters to see how much of the U.S.–other country difference the regression models can explain. We augment Blanchard and Wolfers's models by adding the change in inflation as an explanatory variable, by controlling for period effects in some of our models, by examining the extent of autocorrelation, and by controlling for demographic developments (the fourth section). These modifications are discussed in the context of our consideration of the results of estimating the models.

The first two columns of table 4.5 show OLS unemployment-rate results for the Blanchard and Wolfers (2000) sample where we include only macroeconomic shocks and country dummies as explanatory variables.[13] Rather than computing equilibrium-unemployment rates by making a priori assumptions about the effect of inflation changes on unemployment, as do Blanchard and Wolfers (2000), we have simply included the change in the inflation rate as a regressor determining the actual unemployment rate. This allows the data to resolve the essentially empirical question of the extent to which unemployment can deviate from its medium-run equilibrium level over the five-year periods considered. It also gives macro shocks their best shot at explaining the evolution of relative-unemployment rates over time before we appeal to institutions as an additional explanatory factor. As we shall see in the fifth section, the effect of the change in inflation on unemployment is empirically much smaller in the United States than elsewhere, suggesting a more flexible nominal-wage response to changing inflation there. Our decomposition results, however, were not substantially different in specifications where equilibrium unemployment was imputed as in Blanchard and Wolfers (2000).

The first model reported in table 4.5 shows that each of the shocks is associated with unemployment in the expected direction. We must be aware, however, that each of these macro variables can itself be affected by unemployment. For example, one would expect the government to attempt to lower real interest rates in response to high unemployment. Or, to take another example, higher unemployment is likely to lead to declining inflation, as demand falls. Such reasoning, thus, implies a simultaneous-equations bias on policy-affected macro variables, such as real interest rates or disinflation, which makes it harder than otherwise to find the expected effect of these variables on unemployment. Moreover, while labor's share may be influenced by downsizing, as argued by Blanchard and Wolfers (2000), it can also be influenced by the technical elasticity of substitution between labor and capital. Thus, the long-term decline in labor's share shown in table 4.4 may not reflect shifts in the demand for labor. Finally, it may be artificial to assume that each country is affected only by its own macroeconomic shocks. We are all part of a world economy, and there may be many common effects across countries.

Lacking suitable instruments for macro policy, we must acknowledge that our estimates for these variables may be biased downward in absolute value. And the previous comments about labor's share and common shocks across countries suggest that these variables may at best measure macroeconomic effects with

TABLE 4.5 / OLS Regression Results: Original Blanchard-Wolfers Sample, 1960 to 1995 (Dependent Variable = Unemployment Rate)

	Coeff.	SE	Coeff.	SE
Explanatory variables				
Labor Demand	.169	.070	.143	.061
Real Interest Rate	.610	.113	.235	.152
TFP	.309	.147	−.230	.146
Change in Inflation	2.331	.626	1.049	.577
Country Dummies (including post–Portugal Revolution)	Yes		Yes	
Year Dummies	No		Yes	$p < .001$
R^2	.6971		.8092	
Sample Size	131		131	
Rho-AR1 (SE)	.317	.085	.577	.083
Actual unemployment-rate change, 1970 to 1995				
United States	.0009		.0009	
Common non-U.S. sample	.0813		.0813	
Predicted unemployment-rate change, 1970 to 1995				
United States	.0358		.0758	
Common non-U.S. sample	.0564		.0753	
Percent of U.S.–other country difference in 1970 to 1995 unemployment-rate change explained	25.62		− .62	

Notes: All variables are signed so that they are expected to have a positive effect on unemployment (Labor Demand, Change in Inflation, and TFP have been multiplied by −1). Common non-U.S. countries include Australia, Belgium, Canada, Finland, France, Italy, Japan, the Netherlands, New Zealand, Spain, Sweden, and the United Kingdom. Rho is the auto-correlation coefficient.

errors. However, the OLS model does yield the credible results that decreased labor demand, higher real interest rates, slower growth in TFP, and disinflation are all associated with relatively high unemployment across countries and over time. Examination of the residuals shows a significantly positive autocorrelation coefficient of 0.317. The presence of autocorrelation does not bias the coefficient estimates, but the estimated standard errors are potentially biased. Since we are primarily interested in whether the coefficients can explain the U.S.–other country unemployment gap over time, and since we would lose 20 of 131 observations in correcting for autocorrelation, we use the OLS coefficients. Table 4.5 shows that, using this model, changes in macro shocks predict a rise of 3.58 percent in U.S. unemployment, compared to an increase of 5.64 percent in the other countries. Macro shocks have evidently been more favorable in the United States. However, they can on the basis of these estimates explain only 26 percent of the divergence in relative-unemployment rates.

The second model reported in table 4.5 adds period dummies, which were not included in Blanchard and Wolfers's (2000) specification. This accounts for the possibility mentioned earlier that worldwide events, such as oil crises, affected all countries similarly. The advantage of including period effects rather than measures of specific worldwide factors such as changing oil prices is that period effects pick up the net effect of all these events. Of course, such events should in principle work through the shock variables. To the extent that the significant period effects that we typically find (even when, in results not shown here, we take account of autocorrelation) absorb the common disinflation or real-interest-rate trends across OECD countries, the model including period effects under-states the full effect of these macro shocks.[14] Conversely, if unemployment is partly driven by omitted worldwide forces that are positively correlated with the included macro-shock measures, then the models without period effects over-state the effect of macro shocks. While we cannot be certain of the underlying explanation, we note that, when we add period effects, the coefficient of TFP becomes perversely signed, and the coefficients for the real interest rate and the change in inflation become much smaller (the labor-demand coefficient rises moderately). After accounting for period effects, macro shocks explain none of the U.S.–other country divergence in unemployment (accounting for -0.6 percent of the change).

On the basis of the results obtained in these two OLS specifications, we conclude that, by themselves, macroeconomic shocks can explain at most 26 percent of the reversal of the unemployment fortunes of the United States compared to the other OECD countries. The possible simultaneous-equations and measurement-error biases discussed previously imply that the estimated effects of the macroeconomic shocks in these simulations using the estimated coefficients may be biased downward. However, these estimates suggest that it would be fruitful to consider other possible explanatory variables, which we do in the following sections.

DEMOGRAPHIC DEVELOPMENTS

One of the ways in which we extend the analysis of Blanchard and Wolfers (2000), in addition to focusing explicitly on U.S.–other country comparisons, is to bring in demographic changes as a factor that may help explain international unemployment patterns. In particular, we focus on the youth share of the population (that is, the number of people between the ages of fifteen and twenty-four as a fraction of the number of people fifteen years old and over) as a potentially important factor influencing the overall unemployment rate. We use youth population share rather than youth labor-force share since labor-force decisions are directly affected by unemployment (youth population share is also potentially so affected, and we deal with this possibility subsequently). While institutions such as schooling policies can affect the pressure that a given youth population puts on the labor market, the inclusion of country dummies may control for these. There are several, possibly opposing routes through which the youth share can affect the overall unemployment rate.

First, in an accounting sense, a larger youth share can raise unemployment since youths as a group experience high unemployment. Lawrence Katz and Alan Krueger (1999) have attributed a portion of the decrease in the U.S. unemployment rate in the 1990s to a falling youth share of the population. Second, in contrast to this accounting mechanism, Robert Shimer (1999) argues that a greater youth share may actually lower unemployment by reducing employer search costs. In this framework, business formation and business expansion depend on employers' ability to find workers willing to relocate. A larger youth share of the population implies a larger number of such mobile workers and may thus contribute to higher employment for both youths and complementary adults. Shimer (1999) finds evidence in favor of this hypothesis within the United States: states with larger increases in the youth share of the population had larger reductions in unemployment, even taking into account the endogeneity of the youth share (more on this subsequently). However, across countries, there was no effect of youth share on unemployment. Shimer suggests that the different within-U.S. and cross-country findings reflect the far greater mobility of capital across states in the United States than across countries in the OECD. Sanders Korenman and David Neumark (2000), however, do find cross-country evidence that a higher youth share is associated with higher *relative* unemployment of young people, suggesting imperfect labor-market substitution effects on the demand side.

As we noted above, the youth share may be endogenous with respect to unemployment. Specifically, we expect young people, who tend to be more mobile than older people, to be attracted to expanding labor markets. There may thus be a spurious negative correlation between youth share and unemployment. To take account of this possibility, both Shimer (1999) and Korenman and Neumark (2000), in their analyses of the effect of youth share on overall unemployment and youth unemployment, use as an instrument for youth share the incidence of births fifteen to twenty-four years ago. This variable is clearly expected to affect the current youth share and is related to current economic activity only if the latter is serially correlated with at least a fifteen-year lag. Thus, to address the endogeneity problem, in some of our specifications we replace youth share with births fifteen to twenty-four years ago/population fifteen to twenty-four years ago, in effect running reduced-form models.[15]

We were able to obtain youth-share and prior-births data for a subset of the original Blanchard-Wolfers database, as shown in table 4.6.[16] We lost 28 of the original 131 observations, and table 4.6 shows mean values for key variables among the common countries that had 1970 to 1974 and 1995 to 1996 data for all variables. In addition to the United States, these countries include Australia, Canada, Finland, France, Italy, Japan, Spain, Sweden, and the United Kingdom.

TABLE 4.6 / Mean Values of Key Variables: Youth Sample, Countries with Complete Observations in 1970 to 1974 and 1995 to 1996

	1970		1995		Change: 1970 to 1995		Difference in Change: Non-U.S. vs. U.S.
	Non-U.S.	U.S.	Non-U.S.	U.S.	Non-U.S.	U.S.	
Unem. Rate	.0291	.0541	.1116	.0550	.0825	.0009	.0816
Labor Demand	.0110	.0046	.0567	.0697	.0457	.0651	−.0194
Real Interest Rate	.0181	.0196	.0539	.0389	.0358	.0192	.0166
TFP	−.0305	−.0087	−.0147	−.0015	.0158	.0072	.0086
Change in Inflation	−.0046	−.0037	.0022	.0009	.0068	.0046	.0021
Youth Pop. Share	.2246	.2426	.1702	.1713	−.0544	−.0713	.0169
Births/Pop. Fifteen to Twenty-Four Years Ago	.0209	.0248	.0155	.0154	−.0054	−.0093	.0040
UI Rep. Rate	54.0000	50.0000	54.0000	50.0000	.0000	.0000	.0000
UI Duration	2.3139	.5000	2.3139	.5000	.0000	.0000	.0000
Cbcov90	67.6667	18.0000	67.6667	18.0000	.0000	.0000	.0000
Emp. Protection	10.8889	1.0000	10.8889	1.0000	.0000	.0000	.0000
Almphat	−13.7578	−2.5900	−13.7578	−2.5900	.0000	.0000	.0000
Union Density	40.9111	17.3000	40.9111	17.3000	.0000	.0000	.0000
Labor Tax Rate	50.6056	43.2000	50.6056	43.2000	.0000	.0000	.0000
Coord.	−3.6667	−2.0000	−3.6667	−2.0000	.0000	.0000	.0000

Notes: All variables are signed so that they are expected to have a positive effect on unemployment (Labor Demand, TFP, Change in Inflation, Almphat, and Coord. all have been multiplied by −1). Non-U.S. countries include Australia, Canada, Finland, France, Italy, Japan, Spain, Sweden, and the United Kingdom.

Data on Belgium, the Netherlands, and New Zealand were not available for at least one of these two periods; hence, these countries are dropped. Table 4.6 shows that unemployment in the subsample of remaining countries behaved similarly to unemployment in the larger sample shown in table 4.4, rising 8.25 percentage points, very close to the increase of 8.13 percentage points shown in table 4.4. The macro shocks also changed similarly in the subsample as in the larger Blanchard-Wolfers sample.

Results presented in table 4.6 indicate that, indexed either by the current share of youths in the population or by the incidence of births fifteen to twenty-four years ago, youth share fell both in the United States and elsewhere, reflecting the aging of the baby-boom generation. However, the decrease in both measures was larger in the United States than in the other countries. Therefore, if a larger youth share raises the unemployment rate, demographic trends are a potential explanation for the relative fall in U.S. unemployment. On the other hand, if Shimer's (1999) model is valid, then a falling share of youths in the population will actually raise unemployment, and these demographic trends would run counter to the observed unemployment trends.

Table 4.7 shows results from the unemployment model, including only macro shocks, but estimated on the subsample of 103 country-period observations with demographic information. The results are quite similar to those for the full Blanchard-Wolfers sample shown in table 4.5. In particular, macro shocks can explain at most only 10.66 percent of the divergence between U.S. unemployment rates and those in other countries over the period 1970 to 1974 until 1995 to 1996.

Table 4.8 illustrates what happens when we add youth population share or the more exogenous prior-birth incidence to the macroeconomic shocks. The results are qualitatively similar for both variables. When we exclude period effects, the macro shocks all have positive effects, and the effect of youth population share and that of prior births are inconsistent in sign and small in absolute value relative to their standard errors in both cases. When we add period effects, macro shocks again appear less important, but the effect of youth population share and that of birth incidence, now positive in both cases, become much stronger and are large relative to their (albeit uncorrected) standard errors. In our data, unemployment is trending upward, and youth share (or prior births) is trending downward. If, as noted earlier, the period effects represent unmeasured factors affecting unemployment, then these are negatively correlated with youth share and prior births. Excluding period effects in this case will impart a negative bias to the estimated effect of youth share or prior births on unemployment.

The results presented in table 4.8 suggest that differences in demographic trends between the United States and the other countries can help explain their divergent unemployment experiences. Nonetheless, the full set of macro shocks and demographic trends can explain only between 9 and 26 percent of the divergence in unemployment changes. Multiplying the largest estimates for the effect of the demographic variables (that is, with period effects included) by the U.S.–other country difference in the change in these variables (the last column of table

TABLE 4.7 / OLS Regression Results: Youth Sample (Dependent Variable = Unemployment Rate)

	Coeff.	SE	Coeff.	SE
Explanatory variables				
Labor Demand	.299	.088	.197	.091
Real Interest Rate	.519	.122	.295	.187
TFP	.102	.183	−.308	.187
Change in Inflation	2.356	.652	1.455	.633
Youth Pop. Share	. . .	. . .	. . .	. . .
Country Dummies (including post–Portugal Revolution)	Yes		Yes	
Year Dummies	No		Yes	$p < .001$
R^2	.7274		.811	
Sample Size	103		103	
Rho-AR1 (SE)	.218	.096	.471	.102
Actual unemployment-rate change, 1970 to 1995				
United States	.0009		.0009	
Common non-U.S. sample	.0825		.0825	
Predicted unemployment-rate change, 1970 to 1995				
United States	.0411		.0745	
Common non-U.S. sample	.0498		.0760	
Percent of U.S.–other country difference in 1970 to 1995 unemployment-rate change explained	10.66		1.84	

Notes: All variables have been signed so that they are expected to raise unemployment (Labor Demand, Change in Inflation, and TFP have been multiplied by −1). Common non-U.S. sample includes Australia, Canada, Finland, France, Italy, Japan, Spain, Sweden, and the United Kingdom. Rho is the residual autocorrelation coefficient.

4.6), we can account for 11.4 percent (youth-share specification) to 23.7 percent (prior-birth-incidence specification) of the diverging unemployment rates. These effects constitute the bulk of the U.S.–other country difference in the change in unemployment rates explained by the regression in this specification (13.1 and 26.3 percent, respectively) and suggest that differential demographic trends are more important than differential macro shocks, which are partly absorbed by period effects. When period effects are omitted, however, the effect of demographics is very small.

The results presented so far suggest that we have part of the answer to the puzzle of declining unemployment rates in the United States compared to the other OECD countries. Macro shocks and demographic developments have been

TABLE 4.8 / OLS Regression Results: Youth Sample (Dependent Variable = Unemployment Rate)

Explanatory variables	Coeff.	SE	Coeff.	SE	Coeff.	SE	Coeff.	SE
Labor Demand	.302	.090	.141	.088	.291	.094	.194	.085
Real Interest Rate	.529	.134	.308	.176	.508	.130	.294	.175
TFP	.110	.189	−.200	.179	.085	.196	−.190	.178
Change in Inflation	2.359	.656	1.212	.600	2.354	.656	1.249	.594
Youth Pop. Share	.028	.152	.550	.169	...	...	...	...
Births/Pop. Fifteen to Twenty-Four Years Ago	...	...	...	...	−.347	1.340	4.843	1.408
Country Dummies (including post–Portugal Revolution)	Yes		Yes		Yes		Yes	
Year Dummies	No		Yes	$p < .001$	No		Yes	$p < .001$
R^2	.7276		.8349		.7277		.8373	
Sample Size	103		103		103		103	
Rho-AR1 (SE)	.210	.096	.421	.110	.230	.095	.419	.110

(Table continues on p. 184.)

TABLE 4.8 / Continued

	Coeff.	SE	Coeff.	SE	Coeff.	SE	Coeff.	SE
Actual unemployment-rate change, 1970 to 1995								
United States	.0009		.0009		.0009		.0009	
Common non-U.S. sample	.0825		.0825		.0825		.0825	
Predicted unemployment-rate change, 1970 to 1995								
United States	.0396		.0625		.0435		.0550	
Common non-U.S. sample	.0489		.0732		.0506		.0765	
Percent of U.S.–other country difference in 1970 to 1995 unemployment-rate change explained	11.40		13.11		8.75		26.33	

Notes: All variables have been signed so that they are expected to raise unemployment (Labor Demand, Change in Inflation, and TFP have been multiplied by −1). Non-U.S. sample with information on 1970 to 1974 and 1995 to 1996 includes Australia, Canada, Finland, France, Italy, Japan, Spain, Sweden, and the United Kingdom. Rho is the residual autocorrelation coefficient.

relatively favorable in the United States. However, our estimates indicate that these factors can explain only a modest portion of the observed fall in the U.S. relative-unemployment rate. This suggests that the full explanation must be more complicated than a simple comparison of macro shocks and demographic trends for the United States and the other countries. In the next section, we undertake an analysis designed to illuminate this relationship.

THE ROLE OF INSTITUTIONS

While macro shocks and other structural features may each have independent effects on employment, wages, and their composition, the unified theory discussed previously suggests that labor-market institutions should interact with these shocks to influence unemployment. In this section, we attempt to evaluate the explanatory power of this approach, following and extending Blanchard and Wolfers's (2000) work and focusing on the contrast between the experience of the United States and that of the other OECD countries.

Following Blanchard and Wolfers (2000), we initially consider eight measures of institutional intervention in the labor market originally compiled by Stephen Nickell (1997): (1) replacement-rate indicators for the UI system; (2) duration indicators for the UI system; (3) a measure of collective-bargaining coverage;[17] (4) a summary indicator of the stringency of employment-protection legislation (EPL); (5) an instrumented indicator of expenditure on active labor-market policies; (6) a measure of union density;[18] (7) a summary indicator of labor taxation;[19] and (8) an OECD indicator of wage-bargaining coordination.

Values of these indicators for the United States and for the average of the other countries are summarized in table 4.4 (for the original Blanchard-Wolfers sample) and table 4.6 (for the youth subsample). Note that these institutional variables are treated as invariant over time. As discussed further subsequently, there has been institutional change along several dimensions, often concentrated in particular countries. The assumption of time-invariant institutions may, however, be a reasonable approximation for the purposes of comparing the extreme case of the United States with other OECD countries, particularly since it has been found that international differences in institutions are much greater than are changes in institutions over time within countries (Kahn 2000; Blau and Kahn 2000c). Moreover, Blanchard and Wolfers (2000) obtained stronger findings when they used time-invariant institutional measures than when they attempted to allow for time variation. This may reflect the poor quality of available information on such time variation (on EPL indicators, see Addison, Teixeira, and Grosso 2000) and the fact that many forward-looking decisions in the labor market are based on expectations, rather than actual values, of future institutions. Nonetheless, in this section, we also report on some results that allow institutions to vary over time, using several data sources that were often incomplete.[20]

Institutions and Worker Protection

Like the macro and demographic shocks analyzed above, institutional indicators are imperfect measures of the complex real-life phenomena that they are meant to summarize. The definitions of the institutional characteristics that we include in our analysis conform to those used in earlier analyses of similar issues and need not be discussed in detail. Before proceeding to the empirical analysis, however, it is useful to discuss briefly possible rationales for collective institutional interference with the workings of the labor market and, in particular, the role of the specific institutions that we considered in the context of the simple theoretical framework outlined in the first section.

Most of the labor-market institutions listed earlier (unemployment-insurance, collective-bargaining, and unionization indicators) play a straightforward role in limiting wage competition and eliminating low-wage employment relationships. From a static perspective, their association with high-wage and low-employment labor-market configurations follows straightforwardly from the simple reasoning outlined in the first section. To understand the rationale of such institutional configurations and clarify the role of employment-protection provisions, however, it is helpful to adopt a dynamic perspective. When labor-market outcomes are not only different for different individuals at a point in time, but also variable for a given individual over time, then labor-market institutions can be seen as providing income insurance—insurance that, owing to the usual adverse-selection and moral-hazard problems, would not be provided by (or would be severely limited in) an unregulated private-market economy (Hepple 1986; Agell and Lommerud 1992). Labor-market rigidity may in fact be part of an income-insuring mechanism whereby workers' incomes are shielded in a variety of ways from market forces. As in other insurance markets, insurance in the labor market may have adverse allocative effects, on both the labor-demand and the labor-supply sides of the market. It is possible that, in the face of the macroeconomic shocks mentioned earlier, the "fairness" and insurance provided by institutions in much of Continental Europe and Australia in the 1980s and 1990s have had especially large allocative effects leading to higher unemployment.[21]

From this perspective, one may wonder why the United States has many fewer income-insuring institutions than do other countries. Supply-side effects may well be important since better-developed financial markets and easier geographic mobility can make collective insurance mechanisms less necessary for American workers. On the demand side, insurance is likely to be a normal good, and U.S. wage levels (at least in purchasing-power-parity terms) are at least as high as those elsewhere (table 4.2). So, if there is a lesser demand for insurance in the United States, it is not likely to be because of income effects. Rather, labor-market flexibility may reflect the same factors that have resulted in such a low rate of unionization in the United States.

The origins of this difference date back to the nineteenth century, when, it has been argued, individuals perceived much greater opportunity for upward social mobility and wealth accumulation in the United States than in Europe (Pelling 1960). If these perceptions were in fact held, then it is easy to see why collectivist policies of social-democratic trade unionism and welfare capitalism took hold to a lesser extent in the United States than in Europe. It is possible that American workers perceive greater opportunity for upward mobility and that there is, thus, at any given wealth level, a lesser demand for insurance in the United States than elsewhere. Ultimately, however, the sources of institutional differences are immaterial to our analysis if, as is likely, they are deeply rooted in history. In most of our work, we view U.S.–other country differences in labor-market institutions during the period 1970 to 1995 as having been predetermined and discuss institutional changes and reform tensions only briefly.

If institutions are meant to smooth out labor-income shocks, they can do so in a variety of ways. Most obviously, unemployment insurance makes job loss less painful for workers, shifting the burden of labor reallocation in the face of shocks to a central pool of funds, and tends to reduce search effort and increase reservation wages. The implications of EPL for wage and employment outcomes are less obvious, but such institutions can also be viewed as being meant to provide insurance (Bertola 2000). The EPL provisions summarized in our data have a similar character but a very different intensity across countries (for a recent review, see Bertola, Boeri, and Cazes 2000). As regards the termination of individual employees, workers must be given reasonable notice, or financial compensation in lieu of notice, and are granted rights to appeal against termination, sometimes stipulating reinstatement with back pay when the appeal is successful. As regards collective dismissals, legislation often mandates administrative procedures, involving formal negotiations with workers' organizations and with local or national authorities. Such EPL provisions reduce the likelihood of job loss and shift reallocation costs from workers to employers. Theory suggests that employers should refrain from shedding labor in downturns, when firing is costly, and also refrain from hiring in upturns. Hence, more stringent EPL should be associated with smoother dynamic employment patterns, but the contrasting effects on employers' propensity to hire and fire yield an a priori ambiguous effect on average employment and wages. When employment is averaged across aggregate cycles, theory suggests that, at given wages, EPL should not significantly bias it away from what would be implied by standard static labor-demand models.

Empirically, however, wage outcomes are not unrelated to the stringency of EPL. The same countries featuring strong EPL (and stable aggregate employment) also tend to display compressed wage distributions and relatively stable wage dynamics for individual workers. In our data set, the simple correlation between the EPL indicator and the 50–10 log wage differential is negative and has an absolute value of about 0.75 in both the period 1985 to 1990 and the period 1990 to 1995, when wage information is available for most countries. The negative correlation between wage inequality and the active labor-market-policy indicator in our data set is similarly strong. From a theoretical point of view, it is not surprising that relative-wage variation should be heavily constrained in the same markets where EPL is most stringent. Quantitative firing restrictions, in fact, could hardly be binding if wages were completely unrestrained over time for a given individual: in response to the labor-demand shocks from which EPL is meant to protect workers, wages could fall, thereby making stable employment profitable or inducing voluntary quits. Hence, limiting the freedom given to employers and workers in setting wages gives force to quantity constraints.

Like EPL, minimum wages and other forms of wage compression need not reduce aggregate employment, which is ultimately determined by average wages and may be favorably affected by government-labor-management coordination of aggregate wage setting. Moreover, active labor-market policies may serve to counter the positive effect that high wage floors would otherwise have on unemployment rates. However, high-wage floors should tend to reduce relative-employment rates for low-productivity workers, at least assuming that firms are on their marginal revenue product of labor schedules (Blau and Kahn 1999; Kahn 2000). Even here, there are policies or behavioral responses that may to some degree undo the disemployment effects of institutional interventions like minimum wages or collectively negotiated wage floors. These include not only active labor-market policies, which, as we noted earlier, are inversely correlated with wage inequality, but also public employment, which may be an especially strong factor in Scandinavia (Björklund and Freeman 1997; Edin and Topel 1997; Kahn 1998) and in Germany as well (Blau and Kahn 2000b). In addition, school enrollment among young adults is more prevalent in more heavily unionized countries, while young adults' relative wages are high and relative employment low in such settings (Kahn 2000). In an economy with scarce jobs, the opportunity cost of schooling may be low.[22]

Institutions and Shocks: Time-Invariant Institutional Measures

Labor-market institutions may be generally meant to protect individual workers (or labor as a group) against market forces, but they also have important implications for dynamics at the macroeconomic level. Similar shocks can have very different effects in countries with different institutions. In the aftermath of the productivity-growth slowdown of the 1970s and 1980s, for example, extensive collective bargaining may have kept real wages rising in many European countries, while in the United States, with its lack of unionization, real wages fell. Similarly, high wage floors or greater employment protection of incumbents in Europe may have made the labor-market accommodation of the baby-boom generation more difficult there than in the United States.[23] Conversely, the same institutions may have different effects in different environments, as we sometimes observe important trends in labor-market performance (for example, wage dispersion increases in some countries, or employment decreases in other countries) without significant changes in institutions (Bertola and Ichino 1995; Ljungqvist and Sargent 1998). This reasoning provided the basis for Blanchard and Wolfers's (2000) models, where shocks and institutions were interacted in explaining the evolution of unemployment over the period 1960 to 1995. In this section, we further explore these relations using the institutional data summarized in tables 4.4 and 4.6.

UI replacement rates, UI duration, collective-bargaining coverage, union density, employment protection, and labor taxes are expected to interact positively with macro shocks that raise unemployment. For example, if there is disinflation, anything that makes nominal wages rigid will amplify its effect on unemployment. Conversely, if there is an increase in inflation, anything that keeps nominal wages rigid will amplify its unemployment-reducing effects.[24] The variables are signed so that a positive value is expected to raise unemployment. Therefore, active labor-market policies[25] and coordination have been multiplied by −1 (active labor-market policies help reduce unemployment, and coordination of wage setting is believed to result in wage restraint as unions take into account the effects of their wage bargains on all workers).

Looking at table 4.6, which contains the data for the youth sample (table 4.4 for the whole sample is quite similar), we see that the United States has less generous UI benefits, shorter UI duration, lower collective-bargaining coverage, lower union density, lower labor taxes, and less employment protection than do the other countries. These differences would all imply that similar adverse macro shocks would raise the U.S. unemployment rate by less than in the other countries. However, the United States also has less coordinated wage setting and less generous active labor-market policies, which would imply a larger effect of macro shocks for the U.S. unemployment rate than for those in other countries. Therefore, the ultimate effect of interactions between shocks and institutions on the U.S. unemployment rate in relation to that in other countries is an empirical question.

Table 4.9 reports results obtained when shocks and institutions are allowed to interact, that is, when the functional relation

$$\text{unemployment} = f(\text{shocks, countries}) \qquad (4.2)$$

is not separable and features "shocks × institutions" terms.

In order to conserve degrees of freedom, we estimate—following Blanchard and Wolfers (2000)—the following specific form of equation 4.2:

$$U = (\Sigma_i a_i S_i)(1 + \Sigma_j b_j I_j) + \Sigma_k d_k C_k + e, \qquad (4.3)$$

where U is the unemployment rate, S_i is the ith shock (the list includes a Portuguese Revolution dummy), I_j is the jth institution (in terms of deviations from the sample mean), C_k is the kth country dummy, and e is an error term. Each institution is allowed to interact separately with the same linear combination of the shocks. This model is estimated using nonlinear least squares.

The first set of results reported in table 4.9 shows the basic interaction model without time dummies and with the youth-population share as one of the shocks. Overall, the results are quite credible. Each shock is found to have a

TABLE 4.9 / NLS Regression Results, Shocks and Institutions (Dependent Variable = Unemployment Rate)

Explanatory variables	Coeff.	SE	Coeff.	SE	Coeff.	SE	Coeff.	SE
Labor Demand	.123	.083	.046	.051	.110	.080	.031	.037
Real Interest Rate	.626	.112	.294	.098	.554	.106	.234	.082
TFP	.260	.194	.089	.144	.124	.196	.203	.131
Change in Inflation	3.061	.623	1.443	.530	3.043	.597	1.061	.419
Youth Pop. Share	−.003	.149	.648	.145	. . .	. . .	. . .	. . .
Births/Pop. Fifteen to Twenty-Four Years Ago	. . .	. . .	. . .	. . .	−2.407	1.516	4.582	1.330
XRRATE	.005	.008	.019	.016	.003	.007	.050	.026
XBENEFIT	.398	.108	.533	.168	.434	.100	.588	.213
XCB	−.013	.011	−.035	.022	−.013	.010	−.065	.031
XEMPRO	.056	.030	.111	.067	.069	.029	.248	.111
XALMPHAT	.008	.011	−.028	.021	.004	.010	.004	.027
XUDEN	.011	.010	−.023	.017	.011	.010	.002	.023
XT	.027	.013	.015	.022	.021	.012	.062	.035
XCOORD	.307	.176	.341	.245	.286	.153	.743	.375

Country Dummies (including post–Portugal Revolution)	Yes	Yes	Yes	Yes
Year Dummies	No	Yes	No	Yes
		p < .001		p < .001
Sample Size	103	103	103	103
Rho-AR1 (SE)	−.044	−.024	−.001	.184
	.102	.120	.103	.124
Actual unemployment-rate change, 1970 to 1995				
United States	.0009	.0009	.0009	.0009
Common non-U.S. sample	.0825	.0825	.0825	.0825
Predicted unemployment-rate change, 1970 to 1995				
United States	.0193	.0373	.0189	.0287
Common non-U.S. sample	.0601	.0765	.0644	.0798
Percent of U.S.–other country difference in 1970 to 1995 unemployment-rate change explained	50.00	48.04	55.72	62.67

Note: All variables have been signed so that they are expected to raise unemployment (Labor Demand, TFP, Change in Inflation, COORD and ALMPHAT have been multiplied by −1). Institutional variables are defined as follows: RRATE = UI replacement rate; BENE-FIT = UI benefit duration (4 = indefinite); CB = continuous measure of collective-bargaining coverage; EMPRO = employment protection rank; ALMPHAT = instrumented active labor market policy measure; UDEN = union density; T = labor tax rate; COORD = coordination rank. NLS = nonlinear-least-squares model (linear combination of shocks) × (each institution). Rho = autocorrelation coefficient.

positive effect on unemployment, with the exception of youth share, which has a small and insignificant negative effect. Seven of the eight institutional variables have the expected positive interaction effects; the exception is the collective-bargaining interaction, where the estimated coefficient is negative and insignificant.[26] Moreover, the model shows small and insignificant autocorrelation.

To illustrate the interaction between shocks and institutions, consider the average effect on unemployment of a 1 percentage point increase in disinflation. This effect is 3.22 percentage points in the non-U.S. countries shown in table 4.1 but only 1.62 percentage points in the United States. This suggests much more nominal-wage responsiveness to changes in inflation in the United States than in the other countries.

Finally, and most important, the model explains 50 percent of the divergence between the unemployment rates in the United States and those in the other countries over the period 1970 to 1996.[27] Recall from table 4.8 that the corresponding model without institutions explained only 11 percent of the divergence. Thus, a large portion of the reversal of unemployment fortunes between the United States and the other OECD countries appears to be due to the interaction between the laissez-faire labor-market institutions in the United States and the macroeconomic shocks of the 1980s and 1990s.

The other models reported in table 4.9 show what happens when we add period dummies and/or replace the youth-share variable with the more exogenous previous-births measure. With time effects included, the effect of youth share or previous births becomes significantly positive (as in the models in table 4.8), and the effects of the macro shocks become smaller. There continues to be no evidence of autocorrelation in the interaction models. Most important, the interaction models continue to explain a high portion (48 to 63 percent) of the U.S.–other country divergence in unemployment rates.

Table 4.9 shows that the shocks-institutions interaction framework can account for a large portion of the 1970 to 1995 change in the U.S. unemployment rate relative to that in the other OECD countries. As in Blanchard and Wolfers (2000), macroeconomic shocks alone can explain only a relatively small portion of the cross-country developments. Moreover, the demographic indicators, which we have added to the Blanchard and Wolfers model, are found to play a significant role, especially when period effects are included.

As we noted earlier, reasonable objections can be raised to the assumption that these macroeconomic and demographic shocks are exogenous factors affecting unemployment. As a further check on the basic shocks-institutions framework, we reestimated our basic model, shown in equation 4.3, replacing the shocks with period dummies. We included interactions of a linear combination of the period effects with each of the institutions as well as period main effects. This specification allows all countries to be affected by the same worldwide shocks and requires no assumptions about the exogeneity of country-specific shocks or even about which shocks are important enough to include in the regression. However, the inclusion of the period-institution interaction terms does permit each country's institutions to filter common shocks in potentially different ways. Using this model, we predict that unemployment should have risen by 6.26 percentage points more in the non-U.S. countries included in table 4.9 than in the United States over the period 1970 to 1996. This is 77 percent of the actual divergence between the non-U.S. and the U.S. unemployment rates over this period.

Again, the shocks-institutions model is strongly supported. However, in this case, part of each country's response to the worldwide shocks may involve different macroeconomic policies as well as different wage responses implied by the labor-market institutions, and the model allows for the possibility that institutions can affect policy responses. For example, highly unionized economies may have a different monetary-policy response to global events from that of less unionized countries (for theoretical and empirical models of monetary policy in the presence of centralized unions, see Cukierman and Lippi [1999] and the references therein). The higher share of the unemployment divergence between the United States and the other OECD countries explained by the period effects–institutions model (77 percent) than by the measurable shocks–institutions models presented in table 4.9 (48 to 63 percent) lends support to the idea that institutions may affect macroeconomic policies themselves in addition to influencing the labor-market effects of given policies.[28]

Institutions and Shocks: Time-Varying Institutional Measures

As we noted above, institutions have changed in several countries. In this subsection, we attempt to take into account the effects of these changes in explaining U.S. relative-unemployment levels over time. We were able to construct time-varying measures of five of the eight institutions considered earlier. First, we use the one-year UI replacement rate employed by Blanchard and Wolfers (2000). This is a time-varying measure that was constructed from OECD annual data from the period 1961 to 1995 and thus covers virtually the entire period under consideration here. Second, we use Blanchard and Wolfers's (2000) time-varying employment-protection index, which the authors constructed from a variety of sources (for a careful discussion of these and other relevant data sources, see Addison, Teixeira, and Grosso 2000). If there was no information on a given period, Blanchard and Wolfers either interpolated or assumed no change. Third, we added three time-varying measures not used by Blanchard and Wolfers. These included union density, taken primarily from Jelle Visser (1996), and collective-bargaining coverage and coordination, taken from OECD (1997).[29] Visser's (1996) union-density measures were usually available annually from 1970 to 1993. When there were missing data, we interpolated, where possible, and assigned the 1970 value to periods before 1970 and the latest value to 1995. The collective-bargaining coverage and coordination variables were generally available for 1980, 1990, and 1994. Again, we used interpolation and assigned the

1980 values to periods before 1980 and the 1994 values to 1995. These instances of imputation illustrate some of the difficulties in accounting for institutional change in a regression context.

Appendix table 4A.1 illustrates the changes in these institutions for the United States and for the nine other countries included in table 4.9. In each case, since 1970 institutions have changed, on average, in ways that one might reasonably expect to lower the U.S. relative-unemployment rate.[30] First, UI replacement rates rose both in the United States and elsewhere, but they increased by far more outside the United States (16.89 versus 3.18 percentage points). Second, despite recent reductions in the strength of employment protection in several non-U.S. countries (OECD 1999), the employment-protection index was constant in the United States but rose slightly on average from 1970 to 1995 outside the United States. Third, collective-bargaining coverage decreased in the United States and elsewhere, with a larger decrease in the United States. Fourth, union density was roughly constant outside the United States (a fall of 0.07 percentage points) but fell by 11.17 percentage points in the United States. Finally, coordination fell slightly outside the United States (recall that the variable has been multiplied by -1 to reflect the idea that more coordination is expected to lower unemployment) and stayed the same in the United States.[31]

Appendix table 4A.2 contains selected regression results from unemployment-rate equations that allow time-varying institutions. Country dummies are included, so the effect of institutions reflects only the effect of changes within countries. We do not include time effects in order to give shocks their best chance of explaining the results, although the findings were not greatly affected by the inclusion of period dummies. The main effects of the institutions are typically positive, as one would expect (recall that the effects of employment protection are theoretically ambiguous), although the interaction effects are mixed. After estimating the models in table 4A.2, we used them to examine the degree to which they can account for the divergence between unemployment in the United States and that in other countries over the period 1970 to 1995. First, the model without interactions accounts for 29.8 percent of the rise in relative unemployment in the other countries, a figure that is more than double the amount explained in the corresponding model in table 4.8, which assumed time-invariant institutions. Of this 29.8 percent, 12.4 percentage points were associated with the less favorable macro shocks and demographics in the other countries, and the remaining 17.4 percentage points were due to the less employment-favorable institutional changes in these countries. Second, and similar to the results reported in table 4.9 that assumed time-invariant institutions, when we allow shocks and institutions to interact and include institutional main effects as well, the model explains 63.0 percent of the unemployment divergence.[32]

The implications of the models that use constructed, time-varying measures of institutions are twofold. First, institutional changes have raised unemployment outside the United States relative to that in the United States by a modest amount, one that is slightly larger than the effects of macro shocks and demographics. Second, as was the case in models that assumed time-invariant institutions, the interaction between labor-market institutions and macro and demographic shocks remains very important in accounting for the divergence in unemployment between the U.S. and the other countries since 1970.

Wages and Wage Inequality

Recall that we have interpreted our interaction models as reflecting the greater flexibility of U.S. real and relative wages in the face of macro and demographic developments compared to those of other OECD countries. From the simple theoretical perspective of the first section, the negative employment effect of shocks should be particularly strong when they would tend to increase the dispersion of earnings in an unregulated labor market, and this outcome is forestalled by labor-market institutions. Structural changes such as increasing international competition and skill-biased technological progress are potentially important in this respect and may not be captured appropriately by the macro shocks considered earlier.

To obtain some more evidence on this notion, we have estimated linear unemployment models with shocks augmented by including median male log real-wage levels and the male 50–10 log wage gap for the subsample considered in tables 4.2 and 4.3. Like all our models, this specification is not fully structural. Yet the effect of adding wages and wage inequality directly can provide further evidence on the basic perspective that we adopt in interpreting the data. We have regressed unemployment on macro shocks, youth share or prior births–prior population, median male log wages, male 50–10 log wage gap, country dummies, and year dummies. In each case, median male wages has a positive (insignificant) coefficient, while male wage inequality has a negative, significant effect on unemployment. Among the shock variables, only the change in inflation and the real interest rate are significant—and much less strongly so than the wage-inequality indicator.[33]

In the wage sample, there were seven countries with data for 1975 and 1995: Australia, Finland, France, Japan, Sweden, the United Kingdom, and the United States. Unemployment in the United States fell from 7.02 percent in 1975 to 1979 to 5.50 percent in 1995 to 1996, while in the other countries it rose from 3.96 percent in 1975 to 1979 to 9.30 percent in 1995 to 1996. Thus, unemployment increased by 6.86 percentage points in the other countries relative to the United States. A model without wage variables explains 33 percent of the divergence, while one with wage variables explains 79 percent of the decrease in the unemployment rate in the United States relative to that in the other countries. These accounting results are quite similar to those in tables 4.8 and 4.9 and give us some further confidence that wage behavior, mediated by institutions, is an important part of the explanation of the U.S. unemployment experience.[34]

Replacing the youth-share variable with previous births left the wage and wage-inequality effects the same but improved the explanatory power of the model without wages. Specifically, shocks and births explain 52 percent of the divergence, while adding wage data increases the explanatory power to 75 percent. Either way, macro shocks and wage behavior together account for most of the decrease in unemployment in the United States relative to other countries. Of course, the wage variables are clearly endogenous, as previously argued, and this analysis should be seen as simply suggestive evidence supporting the idea that wage behavior may be an important part of the U.S. unemployment story.[35]

Persistence and Hysteresis

We consider next the possibility that changes in inflation, or, more generally, in aggregate demand, may affect unemployment persistently through mechanisms of hysteresis. One such mechanism, emphasized by Ball (1997, 1999), results from the notion that the long-term unemployed may not search very hard for jobs. In this view, when unemployment becomes long term, it takes more and more overall unemployment to establish the downward real-wage pressure needed to induce firms to hire more labor. If this is true, then not only will falling inflation raise the actual unemployment rate. A decrease in inflation, if severe and long-lived, can also lead to a higher eventual unemployment rate, and the effects of aggregate demand on unemployment will be understated by a model that considers only the effect on current unemployment.

Ball (1997, 1999) uses this reasoning to suggest that the favorable performance of the U.S. natural unemployment rate over the 1980s and 1990s is tied to the shorter deflationary period in the United States in the 1980s and the more expansionary monetary policy in the 1990s. Since the unemployment effects of disinflation become more severe the longer the potential duration of UI benefits, U.S. unemployment outcomes should also be more favorable because of U.S. labor-market structure. Specifically, Ball (1997) constructed a measure of the natural unemployment rate and then examined how inflation and UI duration affected the 1980 to 1990 change in the natural-unemployment-rate measures across twenty countries.[36] He did not perform an explicit accounting of U.S.–other country differences in the changes in the natural unemployment rate, but his paper did include all the data used, allowing us to implement this accounting now.

According to Ball's (1997) data, the natural unemployment rate in the United States fell by 1.4 percentage points over the period 1980 to 1990. In contrast, across the other nineteen countries, the natural unemployment rate rose by an average of 2.32 percentage points. Thus, the natural unemployment rate rose by 3.72 percentage points more in the other countries than it did in the United States. Somewhat surprisingly, the United States had a larger fall in inflation than did the other countries (8.1 percentage points for the United States, 6.41 percentage points for the other countries), suggesting that the depth of the disinflation cannot explain the U.S.–other country unemployment comparison. However, the longest period of disinflation in the United States was only 3 years, in comparison to an average of 4.32 years elsewhere. Thus, in Ball's (1997) framework, the U.S. disinflation allowed less time for hysteresis to set in. And, of course, the United States has a shorter duration of UI benefits (0.5 years, compared to an average of 2.71 years elsewhere), again suggesting a smaller hysteresis response to disinflation in the United States.

Using Ball's (1997) regression model for the 1980 to 1990 change in the natural unemployment rate as a function of two inflation variables only (the 1980 to 1990 fall in the inflation rate and the square of the length of the longest period of disinflation), we predict a rise of 1.30 percentage points in the natural unemployment rate in the United States and an increase of 2.19 percentage points elsewhere.[37] Thus, the model with inflation shocks predicts that the natural rate should have risen by only 0.89 percentage points more in the other countries than in the United States, or roughly 24 percent of the U.S.–other country difference in the change in the natural unemployment rate (3.72 percentage points). However, when we add UI duration and its interactions with the two inflation variables, we predict a fall of 1.20 percentage points in the natural unemployment rate for the United States and a rise of 2.35 for the other countries. These predictions are remarkably close to the actual changes of −1.4 for the United States and 2.32 for the other countries. The shocks-institutions model in this case explains fully 95 percent of the U.S.–other country difference. This reflects the facts that the United States had a less disinflationary environment in the 1980s than the other countries, shorter UI duration, and also that a given disinflation produces less unemployment in the United States than elsewhere. Thus, this exercise, using an alternative concept of unemployment and a different specification, confirms our earlier results, presented in tables 4.8 and 4.9. Namely, macroeconomic shocks explain part of the U.S.–other country experience, but the real story is how they interact with the more laissez-faire institutions in the United States.[38]

DISAGGREGATED LABOR-MARKET PERFORMANCE

Theory has stronger predictions for the effects of labor-market institutions on the dynamics and composition of (un)employment than for their effects on aggregate or average levels. For example, as discussed earlier, job-security provisions reduce both hiring and firing and, hence, have small and ambiguous effects on average (un)employment at given wages and productivity. But high job security should unambiguously stabilize employment dynamics and lengthen both tenures and unemployment spells (Bertola 1999b).

Composition effects also have important normative or interpretive implications: while the unemployment rate or the average-real-wage level may be an adequate performance indicator from a macro perspective, the welfare and distribution implications of short- or long-term unemployment and differences in employment and wage rates across groups are clearly also very important in evaluating the success of labor-market policies. Hence, a positive theory of institutional effects on labor-market performance should take composition effects into account. Our work is intended to extend and corroborate existing work in this area, which has been surveyed in Giuseppe Bertola (1999b) and Blau and Kahn (1999).

As noted earlier, poor wage outcomes for the less skilled are America's signature labor-market problem. But high employment levels may be one benefit of downwardly flexible real wages in the United States. In this section, we document the extent to which high employment levels covary with the demographic composition of the labor force.

We have been able to assemble long-run population and employment information for demographic subgroups in a number of countries (these data are from country-specific sources, hence not fully comparable [see the appendix]). For our sample of ten countries with data for 1970 to 1974 and 1995 to 1996, table 4.10 shows what happened to unemployment and employment-to-population ratios by age and gender over this period. As can be seen, not only did the overall unemployment rate fall in the United States relative to other countries, but so too did the unemployment rate of every age-gender group. And the employment-to-population ratios of each group also rose in the United States relative to those in other countries. Of particular interest, the last five rows of table 4.10 indicate that employment-to-population ratios of young people and older people (relative to prime aged), and prime-age women (relative to prime-age men) also rose in the United States compared to other countries. That is, over the period 1970 to 1996, the relative-employment propensity of low-wage workers (women and youths) and/or workers with below-average labor-force attachment (women, youths, and older workers) rose in the United States compared to the other countries. This outcome is exactly what the unified theory would predict in the light of the more laissez-faire institutions prevailing in the United States. Of course, the large increases in unemployment in the non-U.S. countries could by themselves have produced such changes in relative (un)employment if these low-wage and less than fully attached workers are last hired in a queue of job seekers. Our evidence might be consistent with this last conjecture since the relative employment-to-population ratios of both younger (age fifteen to twenty-four) and older (age fifty-five and over) individuals, compared to those age twenty-five to fifty-four, are countercyclic for both men and women.

To shed light on the causes of these changes in relative employment in the United States, we have estimated two kinds of regression model. First, using the male prime-age/youth employment differential as an example, we have estimated models such as the following:

$$\ln(\text{epopmen } 2554/\text{epopmen } 1524) = f(\text{overall unemployment, youth share, country dummies, period dummies, post–Portuguese Revolution dummy}). \quad (4.4)$$

By estimating equation 4.4, we can determine whether overall economic and demographic conditions can explain the U.S.–other country differences in the changes in relative employment.[39] Second, we augment equation 4.4 by interacting the Blanchard-Wolfers (2000) time-invariant institutions with unemployment and youth share.[40]

TABLE 4.10 / Group-Specific Employment-to-Population Ratios and Unemployment Rates: Youth Sample

	1970		1995		Change: 1970 to 1995		Difference in Change: Non-U.S. vs. U.S.
	Non-U.S.	U.S.	Non-U.S.	U.S.	Non-U.S.	U.S.	
Overall Unem. Rate	.029	.054	.112	.055	.082	.001	.082
Unem. Rate: men 15 to 24	.057	.100	.209	.122	.152	.022	.131
Unem. Rate: men 25 to 54	.019	.029	.087	.041	.068	.012	.056
Unem. Rate: men 55+	.025	.029	.082	.034	.058	.005	.053
Unem. Rate: women 15 to 24	.052	.118	.239	.111	.188	-.007	.195
Unem. Rate: women 25 to 54	.018	.048	.107	.044	.089	-.005	.094
Unem. Rate: women 55+	.014	.033	.069	.033	.055	.000	.055
Epop: men 15 to 24	.673	.585	.463	.536	-.210	-.049	-.161
Epop: men 25 to 54	.943	.931	.860	.883	-.083	-.048	-.035
Epop: men 55+	.510	.530	.302	.355	-.208	-.175	-.034
Epop: women 15 to 24	.492	.400	.412	.496	-.080	.096	-.176
Epop: women 25 to 54	.461	.474	.652	.734	.191	.260	-.069
Epop: women 55+	.181	.236	.144	.208	-.037	-.028	-.009
Ln(epop men 2554/epop women 2554)	.755	.675	.299	.184	-.456	-.491	.035
Ln(epop 2554/epop 1524) men	.342	.464	.642	.499	.301	.035	.266
Ln(epop 2554/epop 55+) men	.628	.564	1.097	.910	.469	.346	.122
Ln(epop 2554/epop 1524) women	-.093	.171	.498	.393	.591	.222	.368
Ln(epop 2554/epop 55+) women	.966	.696	1.586	1.261	.620	.565	.054

Notes: Non-U.S. countries include Australia, Canada, Finland, France, Italy, Japan, Spain, Sweden, and the United Kingdom. Epop is the employment to population ratio. These data are computed from country-specific labor market indicators and interpolated International Labor Organization population series (for details, see the appendix).

We now briefly summarize the decomposition results. The strongest results are for youths and older men. Taking first the example of the employment gap between prime-age (twenty-five to fifty-four) and young (fifteen to twenty-four) men, a model that includes only unemployment and youth share (plus the country, post–Portugal Revolution dummy, and period effects) explains 58.2 percent of the divergence between other countries and the United States in this gap. Replacing youth share with the previous-birth incidence raises the fraction explained to 66.8 percent. The United States has better overall unemployment performance and a more rapidly falling youth-population share and previous-birth incidence, both of which contribute to the more slowly rising prime-age male–youth employment gap in the United States. However, when we allow the effects of overall unemployment and youth share or birth incidence to interact with our eight time-invariant institutional measures, we are able to explain 94.1 to 111.5 percent of the diverging employment gap. While these interactions do not have consistent sign patterns, the decomposition results indicate that excluding these interactions (that is, forcing unemployment and demographic developments to have the same effect for all the countries) causes us to underpredict the rising employment gap in non-U.S. countries relative to the United States. Other countries' interventionist institutions interact with their unemployment rate and youth share to accentuate employment differences between young and prime-age men, relative to the United States.

We obtain largely similar results for the female employment gap between twenty-five- to fifty-four-year-olds and fifteen- to twenty-four-year-olds as well as for the gap between prime-age men and older men. In each case, the model without interactions is able to explain 47 to 60 percent of the rising U.S.–other country difference in employment gaps, but allowing interactions with institutions greatly increases our explanatory power to 91 to 138 percent. However, when comparing prime-age and older women, the model does at least as well with no interactions as it does with interactions. And, when comparing prime-age men and prime-age women, the model does much better without interactions than it does with them. Clearly, we have not accounted for all possible institutions, most notably, the characteristics of the retirement system (Gruber and Wise 1997). And male-female employment differentials are especially likely to be affected by differential changes in female labor supply that may not be well captured by our institutional measures. However, overall youth employment appears to behave in ways that conform with the unified theory, and our results suggest that any attempt by the United States to imitate European institutions could have an especially large negative effect on American youth employment.

The broad and quite sensible message conveyed by our analysis of the data is that, in interventionist countries, the employment and unemployment rates of youths and older age groups bear the brunt of aggregate fluctuations and trends, while prime-age males are protected as "breadwinners" by labor-market institutions. Our results for youths are similar to those obtained by Kahn (2000), who found that, during the period 1985 to 1994, all else equal, greater union coverage was negatively associated with youth relative employment, where the latter was defined in a regression-adjusted context on the basis of micro data.[41] Moreover, Kahn found that greater union coverage was positively associated with school attendance of those age eighteen to twenty-nine, a possible outlet for those encountering difficulties finding a job.

RECENT U.S. LABOR-MARKET DYNAMICS AND ROBUSTNESS CHECKS

In this final substantive section of the paper, we outline the lessons of our theoretical perspective and empirical results for current developments, especially as regards the remarkably good recent performance of the U.S. labor market. Then we explore the robustness of our empirical results with more recent and different data and discuss the implications of our findings for the interpretation of current U.S. experience.

Implications for Recent U.S. Developments

Much of our work has focused on reinterpretations and extensions of Blanchard and Wolfers's (2000) results, with particular attention to the contrast between the long-run experiences of the United States and that of other countries. This contrast, which is quite sharp in terms of broad trends over the past few decades, may in some respects be even more dramatic at the turn of the millennium. In the year 2000, the American labor market was enjoying unemployment rates as low as 3.9 percent. At the same time, Japan's unemployment rate edged toward the unprecedented (for that country) 5 percent level, and some European countries, such as France, Italy, Belgium, and Spain, found it difficult to decrease their unemployment rates substantially below two-digit levels (OECD 2000). While overall European unemployment levels remain stubbornly high, there have been some reductions (albeit from very high levels) in France (2.8 percentage points from 1996 to August 2000), Italy (1.4 percentage points from 1998 to July 2000), Sweden (4.3 percentage points from 1997 to August 2000), Spain (7 percentage points from 1995 to 1999), and the Netherlands (3.6 percentage points from 1995 to 1999).[42] These reductions may represent the effects of policy changes (on the United Kingdom and the Netherlands, see, for example, Nickell and van Ours 2000), or they may represent moves back to a more "normal" unemployment level for a given country. However, the overall unemployment rate in the European Union came down only modestly—from 10.7 percent in 1995 to 9.2 percent in 1999. At the same time, the U.S. rate fell from 5.6 to 4.2 percent during the same period, a comparable decline.[43]

Can the recent developments in the United States be understood in the context of the framework put forward in this paper? As shown in the second section, broad long-run labor-market trends (after removing country- and period-specific effects) display a trade-off between unemployment and wage inequality. Consistent with this, the United States could be viewed as trading relatively low levels of unemployment for relatively high levels of wage inequality. Slow U.S. real-wage growth is consistent with the milder trade-off that we detected between unemployment and wage levels. Over the 1990s, however, real-wage growth has been strong for all American workers and somewhat stronger for those at the bottom of the earnings distribution than for others. For example, Kenneth Deavers, Max Lyons, and Anita Hattiangadi (1999) report that median real hourly wages (CPI corrected) rose about 7 to 8 percent between 1989 and 1999, with virtually all the increase coming after 1996. Moreover, wages at the 20th percentile rose by 11 to 12 percent during this period, again with most of the increase coming after 1996, while wages at the 80th percentile increased by 9 percent from 1989 to 1999.

These data indicate that, in the 1990s, the United States has had falling unemployment, rising overall wages, and, by some indications, falling wage inequality. The theoretical and empirical perspective developed in this paper would then point to unusually favorable period-specific shocks, rather than to movements along a stable trade-off, as the source of favorable employment developments during this time for the United States. And it would point to relatively favorable country-specific developments as the reason why the U.S. unemployment rate has been declining further in relation to those of many other OECD countries.

To flesh out this implication, and to test the robustness of our empirical strategy, we have recalculated the Blanchard-Wolfers (2000) shock variables using recent data from the OECD Business Sector Database.[44] The data extend to 1998 and 1999 for most countries but are not available for earlier periods in some countries, presumably because of data revisions at the OECD.[45] Table 4.11 reports updated summary statistics for the United States and the available sample of non-U.S. countries with information both for the period 1990 to 1994 and for the period 1995 to the present, in the same format as tables 4.4 and 4.6. In the more recent period, the U.S. labor market does appear to feature lower unemployment and faster TFP growth than it does in samples that stop in 1996. Specifically, favorable shocks come to the U.S. labor market in the form of faster TFP growth: the TFP measure computed from the available OECD data grows at roughly 2 percent over the second half of the 1990s, as opposed to 0.15 percent in the Blanchard-Wolfers data set. This feature of the OECD updated data reflects both newly available 1997 observation, and revisions of the 1995 to 1996 data used by Blanchard and Wolfers. It is quite consistent with recent detailed discussions of the determinants of rapid labor-productivity growth in the current U.S. experience (see Oliner and Sichel 2000 and the references therein). In the table, we also report yearly information on unemployment and shocks for the United States over the period 1995 to 1999, which we subsequently discuss in the context of our model.[46]

Table 4.11 reports differences between the unemployment and shock variables for the United States and the average of the available comparison group of fif-

TABLE 4.11 / Mean Values of Key Variables: Updated Blanchard-Wolfers Sample, Countries with Complete Observations in 1990 to 1994 and 1995 to 1998 or 1999 and the United States in 1995 to 1999

	1990 to 1994		1995 to 1998 or 1999		Change: 1990 to 1994 to 1995 to 1998 or 1999		Difference in Change: Non-U.S. vs. U.S.
	Non-U.S.	U.S.	Non-U.S.	U.S.	Non-U.S.	U.S.	
Unem. Rate	.0939	.0659	.0934	.0494	-.0005	-.0165	.0160
Labor Demand	.0398	.0693	.0488	.0682	.0090	-.0011	.0101
Real Interest Rate	.0524	.0401	.0393	.0398	-.0131	-.0003	-.0128
TFP	-.0179	-.0172	-.0197	-.0210	-.0018	-.0038	.0020
Change in Inflation	.0019	.0006	-.0001	.0005	-.0020	-.0001	-.0019
Youth Pop. Share	.1875	.1844	.1715	.1713	-.0160	-.0131	-.0029
Births/Pop. Fifteen to Twenty-Four Years Ago	.0160	.0160	.0153	.0154	-.0007	-.0006	-.0001
Predicted Unem. Rate[a]	.0963	.0687	.0879	.0688	-.0084	.0001	-.0085

Recent Developments in the United States

	1995	1996	1997	1998	1999
Unem. Rate	.0560	.0540	.0494	.0451	.0425
Labor Demand	.0667	.0690	.0690	.0695	.0705
Real Interest Rate	.0409	.0425	.0427	.0348	.0380
TFP	-.0040	-.0298	-.0292	-.0357	-.0206
Change in Inflation	.0001	-.0012	-.0006	-.0004	-.0003
Predicted Unem. Rate[b]	.0695	.0670	.0678	.0659	.0676

Notes: All variables are signed so that they are expected to have a positive effect on unemployment (Labor Demand, TFP, Change in Inflation, Almphat, and Coord. all have been multiplied by −1). Non-U.S. countries include Belgium, Canada, Denmark, Finland, France, Germany, Ireland, Italy, Japan, the Netherlands, New Zealand, Norway, Spain, Sweden, and the United Kingdom.

Model includes shocks, country dummies, Portugal Revolution dummy, births/population, and institutions; original Blanchard-Wolfers augmented data used to estimate the model.

[a]This prediction is based on the same regression model used earlier in this table and assuming no demographic change.

teen countries over both the early 1990s and the late 1990s. The table shows that the unemployment rate fell by 1.65 percentage points in the United States but by only 0.05 percentage points elsewhere. Changes in labor demand and productivity growth favored the United States, while changes in real interest rates and inflation favored the comparison group. Finally, youth share and prior births fell everywhere, with larger declines in the comparison countries. Thus, the overall shocks moved in potentially offsetting ways.

In an attempt to explain the U.S. experience in the late 1990s both absolutely and relative to the other countries, we use the shocks-institutions model from table 4.9 that excludes year dummies and uses the prior-births demographic variable (which is arguably more exogenous than the youth-share variable). We exclude period dummies in light of our discussion that they may partially include the effects of the shocks, although the basic results were similar when we included period effects. As discussed subsequently, we have also estimated models on the updated OECD data, obtaining similar results, but we use the original Blanchard-Wolfers regression sample from table 4.9 to compute regression coefficients because this is a larger sample than is available in the corrected data.

Table 4.11 shows how far the model can go in explaining the remarkable U.S. performance in the late 1990s. Stated simply, the answer is not very far. Specifically, the model predicts that unemployment should have fallen by 0.84 percentage points in the other countries and stayed virtually the same in the United States. Further, using annual data from 1995 to 1999 in the United States to form predicted unemployment rates, table 4.11 shows that the model overpredicts U.S. unemployment in each case and underpredicts the decline between 1995 and 1999. While our earlier discussion indicates that the basic regression framework does a good job of explaining developments in the United States relative to those in other countries between the 1970s and the 1990s, the post-1995 decline in U.S. unemployment appears to be due to U.S.-specific events not captured by our shock variables. Of course, if the true effect of productivity growth is larger than we have estimated, then the apparent acceleration in productivity growth in the United States could help explain the late-1990s fall in U.S. unemployment. As discussed by Ball and Moffitt (2001), if wage expectations in the United States have lagged the recent rise in productivity growth, then we would expect falling unemployment. However, our wage-setting framework suggests that the same rise in productivity in much of Europe would produce an even greater fall in unemployment there to the extent that wages are more rigid. Thus, it would have to be the case that productivity growth increased substantially in the United States relative to other countries for this to be the explanation for the especially low unemployment in the United States after 1995.

Table 4.12 provides more evidence on the model's ability to explain the superior U.S. unemployment performance in the period 1995 to 1999, showing unemployment residuals for the United States from various specifications of the basic shocks–institutions interaction model. While U.S. residuals in the pre-1995 years are sensitive to alternative specifications, the residual for 1995 to 1999 is always

TABLE 4.12 / U.S. Unemployment Residuals from Equations with Shocks and Institutions

	Specification			
	Youth Share		Prior Births/Prior Population	
Period	Without Period Effects	With Period Effects	Without Period Effects	With Period Effects
1965 to 1969	−.0154	.0079	−.0144	.0019
1970 to 1974	.0033	.0122	.0049	.0081
1975 to 1979	.0139	.0003	.0158	.0018
1980 to 1984	.0093	−.0148	.0155	.0025
1985 to 1989	−.0064	−.0191	−.0052	−.0098
1990 to 1994	−.0005	.0011	−.0028	.0018
1995 to 1999	−.0161	−.0238	−.0194	−.0212

Notes: Country dummies and Portuguese Revolution dummy also included. Equations are estimated using the original augmented Blanchard-Wolfers data, and residuals are constructed using the corrected OECD data.

negative and large in absolute value (ranging from −0.0161 to −0.0238) relative to the actual unemployment rate of 0.0494. Again, we conclude that the most recent five years in the United States have, indeed, been a period of remarkably low unemployment, with unemployment at rates that are substantially lower than one would have expected given the shocks and institutions that the United States has experienced.

Robustness of the Basic Model to Alternative Data Sources

As noted, we have constructed an updated version of the Blanchard and Wolfers (2000) database on a subset of their countries. We have reestimated our models on this subset with results that are close to those presented in tables 4.8 and 4.9. The regression coefficients are similar, as are our conclusions about explaining unemployment developments between the 1970s and the 1990s. Specifically, using the prior-births specification, shocks alone can explain 8 to 21 percent of the divergence between the average unemployment rate in the United States and those in the eight other countries for which data for 1970 to 1974 and 1995 to 1999 were available (Canada, Finland, France, Germany, Italy, Japan, Spain, and Sweden). When we add institutions, we explain 25 to 34 percent of the divergence. While the model with institutions does better than the shocks-only model, we have seen that the model with the larger sample (table 4.9) does even better than this. However, the corrected OECD data allow for a larger number of countries to be compared for 1975 to 1995 than for 1970 to 1995, permitting us to add the Netherlands and Norway. For this larger sample of countries, the interaction model explains up to 60.2 percent of the divergence between the United States and the other countries' unemployment rates over the period 1975 to 1995. On the original Blanchard and Wolfers (2000) data and sample, our table 4.9 models explain up to 72 percent of the divergence over the period 1975 to 1995.

We have also checked the robustness of our qualitative results to use of different definitions of the unemployment rate. The OECD Statistical Compendium CD-ROM includes a series of "standardized unemployment rates," which are available only for a subset of countries and periods. Aggregated over five-year periods, this unemployment series is available for a total of seventy-six observations merged with the OECD-corrected macro and demographic information. When this unemployment measure is regressed on macro shocks, lagged birthrate, country dummies, and period dummies, the model explains 21.1 percent of the decrease in the U.S. unemployment rate between 1980 to 1985 and 1995 to 1996 relative to the available comparison group (Belgium, Canada, Denmark, Finland, France, Germany, Italy, Japan, the Netherlands, Norway, Spain, and Sweden). Including institutional interactions increases the portion explained to 58.3 percent. These results are qualitatively similar to those obtained, on the same sample and with the same specification, for the unemployment measure used by Blanchard and Wolfers (2000). Thus, even though measured unemployment differs depending on which definition one uses (Sorrentino 2000), our results are robust to different definitions and, implicitly, to different sets of countries for which data are available.

CONCLUSIONS

The comparative information collected and discussed in this paper can be brought to bear on two important issues:

- First, can the United States sustain its current low unemployment rates, despite the relatively high rates that it experienced in the 1960s and 1970s?

- Second, has the United States achieved low unemployment at the expense of wage inequality, or can it improve labor-market outcomes for those at the bottom without threatening its high employment levels?

To the first question, we answer that the improvement in the U.S. unemployment rate relative to those in other countries since the 1970s is explained partly by more favorable macroeconomic shocks and partly by institutional changes that were more favorable to employment in the United States than elsewhere. The macro shocks may or may not continue in the future, although they did accelerate positively in the late 1990s. With its largely laissez-faire labor market, there is seemingly little room for further major institutional change toward even more flexibility in the United States. To the contrary, recent concerns in the United States about low pay for the less skilled have spurred proposals for raising the minimum wage from $5.15 per hour to $6.15. More important, however, we find that the superior overall unemployment performance in the United

States since the 1970s is due largely to the interaction between macro shocks and our laissez-faire labor-market institutions. Shocks that produced 10 to 12 percent unemployment levels in Europe, with its rigid wage-setting institutions and interventionist benefit systems, led to much smaller increases in unemployment in the United States, increases that were eventually reversed.

Our analysis of the post-1995 years has revealed some important insights that are relevant to the question of sustainability. The shocks-and-institutions model appears successfully to characterize the United States in international perspective until 1995. After that, the model overpredicts U.S. unemployment. An empirical model fitted on a broad range of cross-sectional and time-series data could hardly be expected to fit a single country-period observation perfectly (in fact, the prediction error for the United States in the period 1995 to 1999 is well within the model's prediction-confidence bands). The result, however, is in line with those of many other papers in this volume, which also find it hard to explain the exceptionally favorable character of recent U.S. labor-market performance. From the perspective of our model, something changed in the United States after 1995 that evidently did not affect the other countries to the same extent. While the technological progress associated with the Internet is available worldwide, it is possible that the more flexible labor-market and product-market institutions in the United States (Krueger and Pischke 1997) have permitted a more rapid implementation of this technology through, for example, business formation. If this is the case, then, eventually, other countries may catch up here as well, as they appear to have been doing with respect to real-wage levels.

To the second question, we answer that, not surprisingly, high wage inequality and low wage levels are associated with low unemployment. To document this well-rehearsed claim in a structured way, our empirical analysis of a long-run panel-data set offers an interpretation of recent U.S. experience in terms of policy choices along a given technological "menu" and shifts in policy menus. The relevant shifts are partly common across industrial countries, and, while essentially unobservable, they may correspond to the popular notion that globalization and new technologies make it increasingly difficult for OECD countries to deliver favorable employment and wage opportunities to some of their workers. Thus, the same flexibility that allows the U.S. labor market to absorb macroeconomic shocks with smaller changes in unemployment than occur in other countries also makes for more flexible real wages and relative wages.

DATA APPENDIX

This paper's data set is based on that constructed by Blanchard and Wolfers (2000), documented at *http://econ-wp.mit.edu/RePEc/2000/blanchar/harry_data/*. The data set contains macroeconomic and institutional data on twenty-six OECD countries for eight mostly five-year periods covering the time span 1960 to 1996.

We have added data on wage distributions, labor force by age groups, labor force by sector, population by age groups, and unemployment rates by age groups for male and female workers separately. We have also included additional labor-market institution indicators.

Wage-level and inequality data were constructed from data found in the OECD database (the data are those published in *OECD Employment Outlook*, but the file that we have is more comprehensive). We calculated the upper bound of the 10th, 50th, and 90th percentiles of the wage distribution for each country and year available and used the arithmetic mean of each five-year period as the indicator for wage inequality. The name format of the inequality variables is *pxxg* for the upper bound of *xx*th wage distribution for gender *g* (*m* = male, *f* = female).

The labor-force and population data are taken directly from the International Labor Organization database Economically Active Population 1950–2010. The name format of the labor-force and population data is *vv(v)gcccc*, where

vvv = *lf* (for labor force),
vvv = *pop* (for population),
g = *m* (for male) or *f* (for female),
cccc = *xxyy* (for age group from *xx* to *yy* years of age [65_ refers to 65 and over]),
cccc = *total* (for aggregate of all age groups and sectors),
cccc = *ser* (for service employment),
cccc = *agr* (for agricultural employment),
cccc = *ind* (for industrial employment), and
cccc = *man* (for manufacturing employment).

The data on unemployment rates by age group have been constructed from data found in the OECD publication *Labour Force Statistics* (various issues). These are country-source data, and we did not attempt to harmonize their definitions. To compute the average unemployment rate for each five-year period, we calculate the arithmetic mean of the yearly unemployment rates within the period. To obtain similar data on as many countries as possible, we also aggregate the data to broad age groups by computing the labor-force weighted average of the time-averaged unemployment rate of the relevant age groups. The labor-force weights themselves are constructed as linearly interpolated weights from the labor-force data used earlier. The name format of the unemployment data is *urgxxyy*, where *g* = *m* (male) or *f* (female), and *xxyy* = age group from *xx* to *yy* years of age (55_ refers to 55 and over).

The measures for the labor-market institutions are taken from the publication *OECD Employment Outlook, July 1996* (OECD 1996) and Nickell (1997), with the exception of the collective-bargaining coverage (*cbcov90*) variable. Nickell's (1997) variable, which was used by Blanchard and Wolfers (2000), took on only three values. We have replaced it with the more accurate continuous variable reported in OECD (1994a).

Portions of this paper were written while Francine Blau and Lawrence Kahn were visiting scholars at the Russell Sage Foundation. We are grateful to Olivier Blanchard and Justin Wolfers for making their macroeconomic data set available and to Justin Wolfers for his help in assembling and using the data; to David Neumark for providing us with demographic data; and to Jonas Pontusson and David Rueda for their help in obtaining union-density and unpublished OECD-earnings data. We are indebted to Julian Messina, Abhijay Prakash, Andre Souza, and especially Thomas Steinberger for excellent research assistance. For helpful comments and suggestions, we thank Alan Krueger, Lisa Lynch, David Weiman, other participants in the Russell Sage/Century Foundation Conference on Sustainable Employment, Olivier Blanchard, Pierre Cahuc, and especially Robert Solow.

TABLE 4A.1   /   Mean Values for Time-Varying Institutions

	Non-U.S.			U.S.		
	1970	1995	Difference: 1995 to 1970	1970	1995	Difference: 1995 to 1970
UI Replacement Rate (1 year)	32.41	49.30	16.89	23.74	26.92	3.18
Employment-Protection Index	2.06	2.13	.07	.20	.20	.00
Collective-Bargaining Coverage	72.22	69.22	−3.00	26.00	18.00	−8.00
Union Density	40.65	40.58	−.07	26.45	15.28	−11.17
Coordination	−1.97	−1.92	.06	−1.00	−1.00	.00

Sources: UI Replacement Rate and Employment-Protection Index: Blanchard and Wolfers (2000). Collective-Bargaining Coverage and Coordination: OECD (1997). (Original data included only 1980, 1990, and 1994. 1980 values [or earliest available] assigned to 1970, and 1994 values assigned to 1995.) Union Density: Visser (1996). (Original data spanned 1970 to 1993, and the earliest values were assigned to 1970, while the latest values were assigned to 1995.)

Note: Non-U.S. countries include Australia, Canada, Finland, France, Italy, Japan, Spain, Sweden, and the United Kingdom.

TABLE 4A.2 / Selected Results for Unemployment Regression Models with Time-Varying Institutions

	OLS Model		NLS Model	
	Coeff.	SE	Coeff.	SE
Main effects				
Labor Demand	.3093	.0978	.1763	.0612
Real Interest Rate	.4242	.1408	.3828	.1179
TFP	.1735	.2087	.0529	.1317
Change in Inflation	1.9540	.6721	2.3455	.6871
Births/Pop. Fifteen to Twenty-Four Years Ago	.8599	1.3967	1.9944	1.1261
UI Replacement Rate (1 year)	.0007	.0003	.0014	.0003
Collective-Bargaining Coverage	− .0007	.0007	− .0012	.0006
Employment-Protection Index	− .0067	.0079	− .0184	.0071
Union Density	.0006	.0005	.0002	.0005
Coordination	.0164	.0196	.0164	.0197
Shock-institution interaction effects				
XRRATE	. . .	. . .	.0134	.0098
XBENEFIT	. . .	. . .	.2108	.1893
XCB	. . .	. . .	.0333	.0196
XEMPRO	. . .	. . .	− .0714	.2155
XALMPHAT	. . .	. . .	− .0065	.0195
XUDEN	. . .	. . .	− .0319	.0155
XT	. . .	. . .	− .0070	.0234
XCOORD	. . .	. . .	.8268	.5139
Rho-AR1 (SE)	.2501	.0962	.0439	.1033

Notes: Youth sample of 103 observations is used. Equations include country dummies and post–Portuguese Revolution dummy but not period effects. NLS = nonlinear least squares.

NOTES

1. These figures are computed from the data set prepared and generously made available by Blanchard and Wolfers (2000), which we further analyze and extend in what follows.

2. While in what follows we do not emphasize views of unemployment as a frictional phenomenon, that component of overall unemployment is indeed likely to be strongly affected by labor-market institutions. Union coverage has been found to lower workers' turnover propensities greatly (Freeman 1980), employment-protection mandates are positively associated with worker job tenure (Bertola 1998), and regional wage differentials and labor mobility are much more important in the United States, likely reflecting at least in part its decentralized wage-setting processes (Bertola 1999a).

3. We take these earnings data from an OECD electronic data set, portions of which are published in OECD (1996). We are grateful to Jonas Pontusson for his help in obtaining that file. All figures are expressed in 1998 U.S. dollars using the personal consumption expenditures deflator; foreign earnings figures are purchasing-power-parity-corrected using OECD (1998b).

4. Data are from the OECD Statistical Compendium CD-ROM, deflated by own-country prices.

5. In 1979 to 1981, these positions were reversed, with U.S. men at the 10th percentile outearning their foreign counterparts by 18 percent and U.S. women at the 10th percentile having a 21 percent wage advantage.

6. There is a large literature investigating the degree to which wage inequality is associated with relative unemployment or employment of particular skill groups. Some studies find that, in countries where a specific group, for example, young people, has high relative wages, members of that group experience low relative employment, while other studies do not find evidence of such a relationship between relative wages and relative employment. For a review, see Blau and Kahn (1999).

7. The theory sketched here views employment as demand determined. Thus, anything that restrains real-wage growth raises employment. In other models of employment determination at the micro level, including efficient bargaining or employer-monopsony models, wage increases may instead be positively associated with employment changes. For further discussion, see Henry Farber (1986) or David Card and Alan Krueger (1995).

8. The unemployment rates discussed here are not standardized. However, in a later section, we analyze a subset of countries and periods for which OECD-standardized data are available and reach largely the same conclusions.

9. These statements about percentages are approximations since the data are expressed in logs.

10. While one might also consider the oil shocks as worthy of inclusion, their effect may be subsumed by the change in TFP. Moreover, Blanchard and Wolfers (2000) show that the magnitude of the effect of the TFP slowdown on labor markets dwarfs that of the oil shocks.

11. This equilibrium unemployment rate is best thought of as a kind of medium-term equilibrium that corresponds to a particular set of macroeconomic shocks and a constant inflation rate (Blanchard 1997; Blanchard and Wolfers 2000). How long it takes the economy to adjust to changes in TFP growth, real interest rates, and labor-demand shifts (the major shocks considered here) is an empirical question. In the fifth section, we consider the possibility that disinflation can have more permanent effects on unemployment, as argued by Ball (1997, 1999).

12. Ball (1997, 1999) emphasizes disinflation as a key factor explaining the rise in natural unemployment rates in Europe. Subsequently, we evaluate his models to see how well they explain U.S.–other country differences in the natural unemployment rate.

13. In addition, in all our models, we include a pre–Portuguese Revolution dummy variable (a variable that equals 1 for Portugal before 1975 and 0 otherwise) in light of Blanchard and Wolfers's (2000) arguments that such a control is warranted. Our basic results were not affected by excluding this variable.

14. We note that the macro shocks are highly correlated with period effects. For example, when we regressed each shock on country dummies and period dummies, the latter were significant as a group in each case at better than the .0001 level.

15. We also tried instrumental variables (IV) models with similar results. However, the IV version of the nonlinear-least-squares models that we use in the fifth section to analyze institution-shock interactions failed to converge. We did, however, obtain convergence when we replaced youth share with the lagged-birthrate variable.

16. Much of the population data came from the International Labor Organization, and in many cases were available only in ten-year intervals. We interpolated where possible to produce five-year intervals that matched the five-year intervals in Blanchard and Wolfers (2000).

17. In the original Nickell (1997) database, this variable was essentially defined in three categories. We have defined it as the actual fraction of workers covered by collective-bargaining agreements in 1990, a more accurate, continuous measure. This variable was obtained from OECD (1994a).

18. We include both union density and collective-bargaining coverage because it is reasonable to assume that, for a given level of collective-bargaining coverage, unions will be stronger the higher the fraction of the workers who are actually union members.

19. Labor taxation includes income and payroll taxes as well as mandated benefits. It is, thus, a measure of the wedge between the cost of labor to the employer and the after-tax value of working from the employee's point of view (Nickell and Layard 1999).

20. Our results were unchanged when we included a "Thatcher Revolution" dummy variable.

21. It is also possible that equalizing wages across industries, which is a goal of encompassing collective-bargaining agreements, may raise economic welfare by equalizing the marginal revenue product of labor across different sectors (Freeman 1994).

22. This relation is predicted in a theoretical paper by Jonas Agell and Kjell Erik Lommerud (1997).

23. Of course, those involved in setting wage floors may well take the youth population into account and adjust their wage policies to limit the number of people priced out of the labor market. This can be accomplished by not aggressively raising the floor underneath wages. But, if insiders dominate wage determination, as has been emphasized in many analyses of unemployment in Continental Europe, they may be relatively unconcerned about how many young people are without jobs. Moreover, the young have better alternative time uses (school) than adults, making it optimal for employment reductions to be concentrated on the former.

24. It is easy to think of mechanisms linking real-wage rigidity to collective-bargaining coverage, union density, employment protection, and UI systems. Labor taxes may influence unemployment rates through their effect on wage-setting practices (Daveri and Tabellini 2000). More important for our purposes, labor-income taxation can affect the after-tax effect of unemployment benefits and therefore interacts with shocks in a way that is similar to that in which the UI replacement-rate variable does (Blanchard and Wolfers 2000).

25. Nickell (1997) instrumented active labor-market policy because it is likely to increase in response to unemployment, and we use the instrumented value here, as did Blanchard and Wolfers (2000) as well. Active labor-market policy is defined as spending per unemployed worker as a fraction of output per employed worker.

26. We tested and accepted the hypothesis that youth share had the same interaction effects as the other shocks.

27. The non-U.S. figure is the average of the individual countries' predicted unemployment rates rather than the predicted unemployment rate at the average of the countries' explanatory-variable values. This procedure is followed because of the nonlinearity of the interaction models.

28. The fact that the period-institutions model explains a larger share of the U.S.–other country unemployment divergence than the corresponding models in table 4.9 with measurable shocks might suggest that the former model fits the data better than the latter. However, we must bear in mind that this decomposition refers to ten countries and two periods, while the regression has 103 data points. The overall goodness of fit of the period-institutions model and the fourth specification of the measurable shocks-institutions model shown in table 4.9 (that is, including country and year dummies and the incidence of births fifteen to twenty-four years previously) is quite similar, with residual standard deviations of 0.0143 for the period-institutions model and 0.0141 for the measurable shocks-institutions model.

29. We thank Jonas Pontusson and David Rueda for providing additional union-density data beyond what is available in Visser (1996).

30. Benefit systems became less generous in the 1980s and 1990s in certain countries, such as the United Kingdom and the Netherlands (Nickell and van Ours 2000), and collective-bargaining coverage decreased dramatically after 1991 in New Zealand (Maloney 1994) and after 1980 in the United Kingdom (OECD 1997). However, on average across the nine non-U.S. countries, institutions have changed since 1970 in ways that should have raised their unemployment rates relative to that of the United States.

31. The coordination measure clearly does not take into account the fact that, even in the United States, bargaining became less coordinated in the 1980s and 1990s (Katz 1993).

32. We obtained very similar results when we used youth share instead of prior births. And, as noted, adding period effects led to qualitatively similar decomposition results as well. Note that the interaction model in table 4A.2 includes institutional main effects as well as country dummies. In the models reported by Blanchard and Wolfers (2000) that allowed employment protection and the UI replacement rate to vary over time, the authors did not include main effects for these variables. However, in a personal communication (June 9, 2001) with us, Olivier Blanchard stated that, when main effects were included, they had little effect on unemployment.

33. An interesting paper by Matthew Higgins and Jeffrey Williamson (1999) shows that income inequality and earnings inequality are tightly related to demographic-growth variables in a World Bank panel-data set including observations from less developed countries. Such a link would be readily implied by a data-generating process where wage distributions are generated by similar wage-age curves and different cohort sizes. In our data, the correlation between wage inequality and the age fifteen-to-twenty-four share of the population (or the lagged birthrate) is indeed positive (about

0.5). The coefficient on wage inequality, after controlling for demographic characteristics (which are not significant), gives an indication of the effect of wage-compressing labor-market institutions on unemployment.

34. Using the second specification in table 4.9 (that is, including youth share and time effects), we explain 71 percent of the 1975 to 1995 divergence between the unemployment rate in United States and that in these six other countries. This is a very similar effect to the one, reported here, based on a model with wage behavior replacing the institution-shock interactions.

35. It would interesting to estimate the determinants of wage inequality in the same shocks-institutions framework that we used for unemployment. However, the small number of observations for wages (58, as opposed to 103 for the unemployment analysis) precludes estimating such a model.

36. These are the same twenty countries that were used in Stephen Nickell and Richard Layard (1999).

37. Questions of endogeneity arise here, as they did in Blanchard and Wolfers's (2000) framework. Specifically, increases in the natural unemployment rate may affect macro policy. As N. Gregory Mankiw (1999) argues in his comments on Ball (1999), a falling natural unemployment rate may enable the government to pursue a more expansionary monetary policy. Regression results showing a negative effect of inflation on the natural unemployment rate may thus reflect the effect of the natural unemployment rate on inflation. Note that Blanchard and Wolfers's (2000) analysis of the actual unemployment rate implies the opposite reverse-causality bias from the one that Mankiw (1999) emphasizes. When the actual unemployment rate falls relative to the natural unemployment rate, we expect compensating monetary policy.

38. Ball (1997) found that using other institutions added no additional explanatory power. We note that a model with disinflation, UI duration, but no interactions explained 57 percent of the U.S.-other difference in the change in the natural rate.

39. We recognize that the overall unemployment rate is endogenous; however, one should view the results of equation 4.4 in an accounting sense—is the fall in total unemployment in the United States relative to other countries over the period 1970 to 1995 sufficient to account for the rise in youth relative employment? We tried models like our original equation 4.1 for relative employment (with the underlying macro shocks replacing the overall unemployment rate), but, unfortunately, we were not able to achieve convergence of the nonlinear-least-squares estimator.

40. We obtained decomposition results that were qualitatively similar to the ones that we report subsequently when we used time-varying institutions, as described in the fifth section.

41. Specifically, education and marital status were controlled for.

42. This information is taken from the U.S. Bureau of Labor Statistics website and OECD (2000).

43. Richard Freeman and Ronald Schettkat (2000) argue that percentage point differences or changes in the unemployment-rate level (as opposed to relative changes, where, for example, a change from 5 percentage points to 4 percentage points would be a 20 percent reduction) are the proper measure of changes in the demand for labor. To see this, note that

$$E/P = (LF/P)(1 - UR),$$

where LF is the labor force, and UR is the fraction of the labor force that is unemployed. Then, if the labor-force-participation rate is constant, and if UR is relatively small,

$$\ln(E/P) = k + \ln(1 - UR) \approx k - UR,$$

where $k = \ln(LF/P)$. Therefore changes or differences in $\ln(E/P)$ are approximately the same magnitude and opposite in sign to changes or differences in the unemployment rate (Freeman and Schettkat 2000, 15). This argument implies that the reduction in unemployment corresponds to similar increases in the demand for labor in Europe and in the United States.

44. The data are those available in the 2000:1 edition of the OECD Statistical Compendium CD-ROM. We are grateful to Justin Wolfers, who sent us the original program for computing the macro shock indicators, and to Julian Messina and Thomas Steinberger, who organized the updated data and prepared the data set.

45. The version of the OECD Business Sector Database available to us does not contain a capital-stock series for Australia. GDP business-sector data are missing before 1987 for the United Kingdom and before 1970 for Finland, and the long-term interest rate is missing before 1985 for Ireland. Pre-1978 unemployment-rate data for Australia were also not available from the CD-ROM.

46. The business-sector capital-stock data were missing in the OECD source for 1998 and 1999. The shock variables that need such information are computed for these two years extrapolating the series on the basis of the average 0.79 percent quarterly growth rate of the capital stock over the whole sample, which is close to the capital-growth rate in the last available period (in 1997:4, the capital stock increased by 0.84 percent).

REFERENCES

Addison, John T., Paulino Teixeira, and Jean-Luc Grosso. 2000. "The Effect of Dismissals Protection on Employment: More on a Vexed Theme." *Southern Economic Journal* 67(1): 105–22.

Agell, Jonas, and Kjell Erik Lommerud. 1992. "Union Egalitarianism as Income Insurance." *Economica* 59(235): 295–310.

———. 1997. "Minimum Wages and the Incentives for Skill Formation." *Journal of Public Economics* 64(1): 25–40.

Ball, Laurence. 1997. "Disinflation and the NAIRU." In *Reducing Inflation: Motivation and Strategy*, edited by Christina Romer and David Romer, 167–185. Chicago: University of Chicago Press.

———. 1999. "Aggregate Demand and Long-Term Unemployment." *Brookings Papers on Economic Activity* (2): 189–236.

Ball, Laurence, and Robert Moffitt. 2001. "Productivity Growth and the Phillips Curve." Paper presented to the Russell Sage/Century Foundation Conference on Sustainable Employment. Amelia Island, Fla. (January 26–28).

Bertola, Giuseppe. 1998. "Labor Demand, Institutions, and Tenure Lengths." Unpublished manuscript. European University Institute, November.

———. 1999a. "Labor Markets in the European Union." Working paper RSC 99/24. European University Institute. Reprinted in *Ifo Studien* 1 (2000): 99–122.

———. 1999b. "Microeconomic Perspectives on Aggregate Labor Markets." In *Handbook of Labor Economics,* edited by Orley Ashenfelter and David Card, 3C: 2985–3028. Amsterdam: North-Holland.

———. 2000. "A Pure Theory of Job Security and Labor Income Risk." Unpublished manuscript. European University Institute, January.

Bertola, Giuseppe, Tito Boeri, and Sandrine Cazes. 2000. "Employment Protection in Industrialized Countries: The Case for New Indicators." *International Labour Review* 139(1): 57–72.

Bertola, Giuseppe, and Andrea Ichino. 1995. "Wage Inequality and Unemployment: U.S. versus Europe." *NBER Macroeconomics Annual,* 13–54.

Björklund, Anders, and Richard B. Freeman. 1997. "Generating Equality and Eliminating Poverty, the Swedish Way." In *The Welfare State in Transition: Reforming the Swedish Model,* edited by Richard B. Freeman, Robert Topel, and Birgitta Swedenborg, 33–78. Chicago: University of Chicago Press.

Blanchard, Olivier Jean. 1997. "The Medium Run." *Brookings Papers on Economic Activity* (2): 89–141.

———. 1999. "European Unemployment: The Role of Shocks and Institutions." Baffi Lecture. Presented to the Banca d'Italia. Rome (January).

Blanchard, Olivier J., and Justin Wolfers. 2000. "The Role of Shocks and Institutions in the Rise of European Unemployment: The Aggregate Evidence." *Economic Journal* 110(462): C1–C33.

Blank, Rebecca M. 1997. "Is There a Trade-Off between Unemployment and Inequality? No Easy Answers: Labor Market Problems in the United States versus Europe." Public Policy Brief no. 33. Levy Economics Institute.

Blau, Francine D., and Lawrence M. Kahn. 1996. "International Differences in Male Wage Inequality: Institutions versus Market Forces." *Journal of Political Economy* 104(4): 791–837.

———. 1999. "Institutions and Laws in the Labor Market." In *Handbook of Labor Economics,* edited by Orley Ashenfelter and David Card, 3A: 1399–1461. Amsterdam: North-Holland.

———. 2000a. "Do Cognitive Test Scores Explain Higher U.S. Wage Inequality?" Unpublished manuscript. Cornell University, June.

———. 2000b. "Gender and Youth Employment Outcomes: The U.S. and West Germany, 1984–91." In *Youth Employment and Joblessness in Advanced Countries,* edited by David G. Blanchflower and Richard B. Freeman, 107–67. Chicago: University of Chicago Press.

———. 2000c. "Understanding International Differences in the Gender Pay Gap." Manuscript. Cornell University, August. To appear in *Journal of Labor Economics.*

Card, David, and Alan Krueger. 1995. *Myth and Measurement: The New Economics of the Minimum Wage.* Princeton, N.J.: Princeton University Press.

Cukierman, Alex, and Francesco Lippi. 1999. "Central Bank Independence, Centralization of Wage Bargaining, Inflation, and Unemployment: Theory and Some Evidence." *European Economic Review* 43(7): 1395–1434.

Daveri, Francesco, and Guido Tabellini. 2000. "Unemployment, Growth, and Taxation in Industrial Countries." *Economic Policy* 15(1): 49–104.

Deavers, Kenneth L., Max R. Lyons, and Anita U. Hattiangadi. 1999. *A Century of Progress—a Century of Change: The American Workplace, 1999.* Washington, D.C.: Employment Policy Foundation.

Edin, Per-Anders, and Robert Topel. 1997. "Wage Policy and Restructuring: The Swedish Labor Market since 1960." In *The Welfare State in Transition: Reforming the Swedish Model,* edited by Richard B. Freeman, Robert Topel, and Birgitta Swedenborg, 155–201. Chicago: University of Chicago Press.

Farber, Henry S. 1986. "The Analysis of Union Behavior." In *Handbook of Labor Economics,* edited by Orley Ashenfelter and Richard Layard, 2: 1039–89. Amsterdam: North-Holland.

Flanagan, Robert J. 1973. "The U.S. Phillips Curve and International Unemployment Rate Differentials." *American Economic Review* 63(1): 114–31.

Freeman, Richard B. 1980. "The Exit-Voice Tradeoff in the Labor Market: Unionism, Job Tenure, Quits, and Separations." *Quarterly Journal of Economics* 94(4): 643–73.

———. 1994. "How Labor Fares in Advanced Economies." In *Working under Different Rules,* edited by Richard B. Freeman, 1–28. New York: Russell Sage Foundation.

Freeman, Richard B., and Lawrence F. Katz, eds. 1995. *Differences and Changes in Wage Structures.* Chicago: University of Chicago Press.

Freeman, Richard B., and Ronald Schettkat. 2000. "The Role of Wage and Skill Differences in U.S.-German Employment Differences." *NBER* working paper no. 7474. Cambridge, Mass.: National Bureau of Economic Research, January.

Glyn, Andrew, and Wiemer Salverda. 2000. "Does Wage Flexibility Really Create Jobs?" *Challenge* 43(1): 32–43.

Gregory, Robert G., and Jeff Borland. 1999. "Recent Developments in Public Sector Labor Markets." In *Handbook of Labor Economics,* edited by Orley Ashenfelter and David Card, 3C: 3573–3630. Amsterdam: North-Holland.

Gruber, Jonathan, and David Wise. 1997. "Social Security Programs and Retirement around the World." *NBER* working paper no. 6134. Cambridge, Mass.: National Bureau of Economic Research, August.

Hall, Robert. 1970. "Why Is the Unemployment Rate So High at Full Employment?" *Brookings Papers on Economic Activity* (3): 369–410.

Heilbroner, Robert L., and Lester C. Thurow. 1981. *Five Economic Challenges.* Englewood Cliffs, N.J.: Prentice-Hall.

Hepple, Bob Alexander, ed. 1986. *The Making of Labour Law in Europe: A Comparative Study of Nine Countries up to 1945.* London: Mansell.

Higgins, Matthew, and Jeffrey G. Williamson. 1999. "Explaining Inequality the World Round: Cohort Size, Kuznets Curves, and Openness." *NBER* working paper no. W7224. Cambridge, Mass.: National Bureau of Economic Research.

Kahn, Lawrence M. 1998. "Against the Wind: Bargaining Recentralisation and Wage Inequality in Norway, 1987–1991." *Economic Journal* 108(448): 603–45.

———. 2000. "Wage Inequality, Collective Bargaining, and Relative Employment, 1985–94: Evidence from 15 OECD Countries." *Review of Economics and Statistics* 82(4): 564–79.

Katz, Harry C. 1993. "The Decentralization of Collective Bargaining: A Literature Review and Comparative Analysis." *Industrial and Labor Relations Review* 47(1): 3–22.

Katz, Lawrence F., and Alan B. Krueger. 1999. "The High-Pressure U.S. Labor Market of the 1990s." *Brookings Papers on Economic Activity* (1): 1–65.

Kaufman, Roger. 1979. "Why the U.S. Unemployment Rate Is So High." In *Unemployment and Inflation: Institutionalist and Structuralist Views,* edited by Michael J. Piore, 155–69. White Plains, N.Y.: M. E. Sharpe.

Korenman, Sanders, and David Neumark. 2000. "Cohort Crowding and Youth Labor Markets: A Cross-National Analysis." In *Youth Employment and Joblessness in Advanced Countries,* edited by David G. Blanchflower and Richard B. Freeman, 57–105. Chicago: University of Chicago Press.

Krueger, Alan B., and Jörn-Steffen Pischke. 1997. "Observations and Conjectures on the U.S. Employment Miracle." Working paper no. 390. Princeton University Industrial Relations Section, August.

Layard, Richard, Stephen Nickell, and Richard Jackman. 1991. *Unemployment.* Oxford: Oxford University Press.

Ljungqvist, Lars, and Thomas J. Sargent. 1998. "The European Unemployment Dilemma." *Journal of Political Economy* 106(3): 514–50.

Maloney, Tim. 1994. "Estimating the Effects of the Employment Contracts Act on Employment and Wages in New Zealand." *Australian Bulletin of Labour* 20(4): 320–43.

Mankiw, N. Gregory. 1999. "Comments and Discussion [on Ball 1999]." *Brookings Papers on Economic Activity* (2): 237–41.

Nickell, Stephen. 1997. "Unemployment and Labor Market Rigidities: Europe versus North America." *Journal of Economic Perspectives* 11(3): 55–74.

Nickell, Stephen and Richard Layard. 1999. "Labor Market Institutions and Economic Performance." In *Handbook of Labor Economics,* edited by Orley Ashenfelter and David Card, 3C: 3029–84. Amsterdam: North-Holland.

Nickell, Steve, and Jan van Ours. 2000. "The Netherlands and the United Kingdom: A European Unemployment Miracle?" *Economic Policy*(30): 137–80.

OECD. 1994a. *Employment Outlook, July 1994.* Paris.

———. 1994b. *The OECD Jobs Study: Evidence and Explanations.* Paris.

———. 1996. *Employment Outlook, July 1996.* Paris.

———. 1997. *Employment Outlook, July 1997.* Paris.

———. 1998a. *Employment Outlook, June 1998.* Paris.

———. 1998b. *Purchasing Power Parities and Real Expenditures.* Paris.

———. 1999. *Employment Outlook, June 1999.* Paris.

———. 2000. *Employment Outlook, June 2000.* Paris.

———. Various issues. *Labour Force Statistics.* Paris.

Oliner, Stephen D., and Daniel E. Sichel. 2000. "The Resurgence of Growth in the Late 1990s: Is Information Technology the Story?" Unpublished manuscript. Washington: Federal Reserve Board of Governors.

Pelling, Henry. 1960. *American Labor.* Chicago: University of Chicago Press.

Shimer, Robert. 1999. "The Impact of Young Workers on the Aggregate Labor Market." *NBER* working paper no. 7306. Cambridge, Mass.: National Bureau of Economic Research, August.

Siebert, Horst. 1997. "Labor Market Rigidities: At the Root of Unemployment in Europe." *Journal of Economic Perspectives* 11(3): 37–54.

Sorrentino, Constance. 2000. "International Unemployment Rates: How Comparable Are They?" *Monthly Labor Review* 123(6): 3–20.

Thurow, Lester C. 1985. Introduction to *The Management Challenge: Japanese Views,* edited by Lester C. Thurow, 9–10. Cambridge, Mass.: MIT Press.

Visser, Jelle. 1996. "Unionisation Trends Revisited." Research paper no. 1996/2. Amsterdam: Centre for Research of European Societies and Industrial Relations, February.

Chapter 5

Have New Human-Resource Management Practices Lowered the Sustainable Unemployment Rate?

Jessica Cohen, William T. Dickens, and Adam Posen

The way in which work is organized in the United States has undergone a radical change in the last twenty years. Job stability has declined for long-tenured workers, there has been a large increase in the use of contract and temporary workers, especially on the manufacturing shop floor, and there has been widespread adoption of new forms of workplace organization.[1] The business press and industrial-relations experts who have traced and documented these trends often associate them with an increasingly competitive environment for U.S. business, driven by international trade and technological change.

The effects of these transformations on income distribution and productivity have been studied, but almost no attention has been paid to the effect that they may be having on the ability of the economy to maintain low unemployment. This is surprising considering the coincidence of these changes with an extended decline in unemployment that seems to have produced little inflation and with evidence of a striking improvement in the efficiency with which workers are matched with jobs. The combination of low unemployment and inflation suggests a decline in the nonaccelerating inflation rate of unemployment (NAIRU).[2] Several authors have argued that such a change has taken place over the last five to fifteen years. The most popular explanations suggested for such a decline ignore the changes in the organization of work and focus instead on developments on the supply side of the labor market. The possibility that there is a link between the decline in the NAIRU and the adoption of these new practices has not been developed.

In this paper, we discuss recent changes in how U.S. firms hire, train, fire, compensate, and manage workers. We then develop explanations for the motivations behind these changes using interviews with human-resource executives from U.S. manufacturing.[3] Finally, we use these components to suggest how the major changes in American corporations' human-resource management (HRM) practices could have led to a drop in the NAIRU.[4] A decline in labor rents that has made queuing for high-wage jobs less attractive is an important part of our story. This decline in rents occurred even as returns to skill (and, therefore, wages) rose for some workers. In fact, we show that interindustry wage differences, a measure of rents, declined in a two-step sequence with a pattern and timing similar to movements in the Beveridge curve—a measure of matching efficiency. These comovements also match in some important ways the spotty data on the adoption of innovative work practices.

This last point—parallel timing—is a key criterion of explanatory success. Any full account of the decline in the U.S. NAIRU should explain the timing and cause of the discrete inward shifts in the Beveridge curve that took place in the period 1985 to 1989 and in the period since 1994.[5] Explanations for the decline in the NAIRU that rely on unbroken long-term trends (for example, the decline in the fraction of the workforce organized by unions, the aging of the workforce) or on factors evident only in the 1990s (for example, the explosion of the Internet) must be viewed as partial at best. Our explanation, emphasizing how changes in the practices of firms have affected labor demand and matching efficiency not only takes into account important facts overlooked in most studies of matching, but also allows us to generate such a time path for changes in the NAIRU.

It is possible that some slow-moving long-term forces, such as demographics, could build over time but have only abrupt observable effects once some threshold is reached. Such effects, however, usually require an observable institutional shift and/or a centralized (policy) decision following the threshold being reached, which is difficult to reconcile with recent developments. It is also hard to reconcile a threshold explanation with the two discrete periods of improvement that the data show. This is not to say that we believe that the decline in the NAIRU has a single cause—there are a few strong candidate explanations for developments in the 1990s that may be complementary to ours. The idea that workers' perceptions of productivity gains and, therefore, their real-wage demands, lagged behind actual gains seems plausible to us (Ball and Moffitt, chapter 2 in this volume). The positive supply shocks of declining health-care costs, lower import and oil prices, and the productivity effects of information and communications technology each had a turn in the 1990s.[6] Nevertheless, the evidence that the improvements in the Beveridge and Phillips curves predate the 1990s suggests that these are only partial explanations for the changes.

Our story links the radical restructuring in firms' management and hiring of labor and the two-step decline in the NAIRU. Starting in the early to mid-1980s, the wave of international competition and technical change resulted in greater competitive pressures for customer specialization, cost reduction, and quality improvement. One effect of this change in product-market structure was a move by firms to more frequent switching between and turnover of products—the so-called flexible specialization. Responding to the demands of their product markets, many companies began experimenting with a wide range of practices known collectively as *high-performance work organization* (HPWO). Examples of these practices include job rotation, pay for knowledge, autonomous teams, total-quality management (TQM), and quality circles. A key characteristic of nearly all these HPWO systems is that core production workers' jobs are broadened and that those workers are more interchangeable among tasks. This increasing ability to move workers between jobs or production lines within firms and the easier matching of hires that accompanies such substitutability may be part of the explanation for improved labor-market efficiency.

At the same time, a more flexible production process means that workers must learn new task-specific skills more frequently. If workers with greater endowments of general human capital (or learning skills) can learn new skills more quickly and cheaply, the increased depreciation rate of task-specific human capital associated with the more rapid turnover of skills should increase the demand for general human capital. With implicit or explicit wage bargaining, increasing the level of general human capital may increase the firm's relative wage. But increasing demand for general skills and the falling value of specific skills reduces worker rents since bargaining leads firms and workers to share the returns on capital that either bring to the job. As these changes take place, the return on the capital that workers bring to the table becomes a larger fraction of the wage, and the return to the firm's capital becomes a smaller portion. When rents are reduced, workers become less willing to wait unemployed for these jobs and instead apply to lower-wage jobs, where the vacancy rate is higher. This reduces both the unemployment rate and the vacancy rate, shifting the Beveridge curve in.

The process just described affects mainly the more-skilled blue-collar workers—the firm's "core" workforce. However, firms also employ a large number of less-skilled workers who do not invest as extensively in specific human capital and whose jobs are not affected as much by the demands for flexibility. An equity constraint links the pay of these workers to the pay of the more-skilled core workers. As the firm demands more general skills from its core workforce but not from these other workers, the equity constraint becomes more costly. Eventually, the cost of maintaining pay parity between these different types of workers exceeds the costs of reorganizing and coordinating with outside contractors, and the less-skilled workers are moved outside the firm through contracting and the use of workers provided by temporary-help firms. A wave of consolidation and downsizing in U.S. business in the early 1990s left in its wake a greatly revised view of what tasks should be done inside the firm and what should be contracted out.[7] Although the use of outsourcing, contracting, and temporary workers has been increasing over the entire period in which we are interested, there appears to have been a concentration of restructuring activity during the "mean leaning" of the early 1990s. During this time in particular, an increasing number of firms pursuing such practices created economies of scale in contracting and temporary services, increased the acceptability of the practices, and increased the competitive pressures on those who had not adopted the practices. Thus, growing use of these practices produced pressure for them to spread further and faster.

Several factors are probably responsible for the apparent halt in the progress toward increasing labor-market efficiency between 1990 and 1994. The poor performance of the Japanese economy during this period may have taken away some of the motivation to copy Japanese practices, while the U.S. recession left firms with fewer resources to experiment with new ways of organizing. Data presented in the next section suggest a slowdown, and possibly even a reduction, in the use of HPWO during this period. The recession of the early 1990s probably also gave firms both the motive and the opportunity to pursue restructuring of their workforce. The transitory rise in turnover and churning associated with the restructuring process and the slow adjustment of some workers' wage expectations to their reduced opportunities may help explain the relative stability of the Beveridge curve during this period.

By the mid-1990s, however, the transition to what we will term *confident deployment* of the new high-performance work techniques began. No longer were these practices viewed as experimental. HPWO, utilizing worker flexibility, and jobs requiring a broader set of tasks had become widespread in manufacturing. Firms that had not adopted them viewed themselves as having fallen behind the norm. During this period, firms continued to upgrade general human capital for their core workforces and to outsource for lower-skilled labor. Temporary-help workers have grown from less than ½ percent of employment in the early 1980s to over 2 ½ percent today, with a large share of this increase coming in manufacturing temps. Since most temporary workers are looking for permanent employment while temping, and since they seldom count as unemployed, the growth in their numbers reduces measured vacancies and unemployment.

Recapping, we see three important routes by which the changes in the way firms use labor have improved the efficiency of the labor market. First, the increasing demand for general skills has made workers more interchangeable, and this may have improved matching efficiency. Second, the falling number of good high-wage jobs (caused by restructuring), and the increasing extent to which the wages in the remaining good jobs reflect workers' skills instead of job-specific rents, means that fewer people are willing to wait unemployed to get one of these jobs. Instead, people apply for lower-wage jobs, for which the vacancy rates are higher. The slight increase in the vacancy rate for the remaining high-wage jobs is more than outweighed by the decline in the vacancy rate for low-wage jobs. Similarly, the large decline in the number of people waiting unemployed for good jobs is considerably greater than the small increase in the number of people waiting unemployed for the low-wage jobs. Thus, the Beveridge curve shifts in. Third, the increased use of temporary workers, who search for jobs just like the unemployed while not counting as unemployed, also leads to a decline in vacancies and unemployment.

The chapter proceeds in five parts. The first section surveys the literature, drawing together facts that our story will synthesize. The second section describes the results of our interviews with human-resource managers at several manufacturing firms and executives at a contracting and temporary-help firm. The third section presents our analysis of interindustry wage differences, showing that, despite increasing wage inequality in general, interindustry wage differences have fallen at the same time that the new work practices have been adopted and the Beveridge curve has been inwardly shifting. This combination of stylized facts, interviews, and data analysis motivates the model described in the fourth section. The fifth section recaps our argument, with a look at areas for future research and some policy implications.

WHAT HAS BEEN CHANGING IN AMERICAN LABOR MARKETS?

Since 1980, facing increasing competitive pressure from abroad, pressure from financial markets to cut costs, and significant technological change, American firms have done a great deal to adapt their human-resource practices.[8] Most notably, firms have changed how they hire and pay workers of different skill levels and how they use firm-specific and general skills. These adaptations have arguably had a marked effect on the nature of both labor demand and compensation, which could have caused shifts in the Phillips curve. This section reviews the literature on these changes. It first establishes that an inward shift in the Beveridge curve occurred in two distinct periods, separated by intervening years of corporate restructuring. It is much harder to discern the timing of changes in the Phillips curve, but it appears to have begun to shift about the same time as the Beveridge curve did (see Staiger, Stock, and Watson, chapter 1 in this volume).

This coincidence of the changing Phillips and Beveridge curves with the introduction of the new HRM practices points us toward demand-side explanations for the change in the NAIRU. The remaining subsections discuss the changes in various aspects of employers'—particularly manufacturing employers'—hiring, compensation, and management of workers. These include the changes in job turnover, layoffs, and insecurity; the rising reliance on temporary workers and contracting of business services; the development of compensation flexibility and wage decompression; and the adoption of HPWO practices. These stylized facts are then summarized as the basis for a story that can explain the drop in the NAIRU.

The Beveridge Curve's Inward Shifts

In the past, unemployment rates below 5 to 6 percent have been associated with increasing rates of inflation. In the last several years, however, we have seen unemployment rates consistently below those rates with almost no increase in core inflation. Adding to the phenomenon to be explained, a measure of job vacancies computed from the index of help-wanted advertising was near its all-time low in 1998—even before Internet job search and advertising became widespread—despite the low unemployment. That we have maintained a low level of unemployment while keeping a large fraction of jobs filled and inflationary pressures in check suggests a vast improvement in the efficiency of the labor market.[9]

It is useful to think of the Beveridge curve—a convex relation between vacancies and unemployment—as representing the efficiency of the labor market in pairing workers and jobs. The closer the curve to the origin, the more efficiently workers and jobs are being matched.[10] For the United States, where no official government vacancy data exist, the vacancy rate has been proxied by the ratio of the Conference Board's help-wanted index of classified newspaper advertising to nonfarm-payroll employment. The ratio is adjusted using a method developed by Katherine Abraham (1987) to account for shifts in newspaper circulation and for the influence of affirmative action and anti-discrimination laws on job advertising.[11] This measure has done rather well at matching up with fluctuations seen in micro (for example, state-level) data on actual vacancies.

Figure 5.1 shows the U.S. Beveridge curve for 1960 to 1998.[12] Abraham (1987) documents an outward shift of the U.S. Beveridge curve in the 1970s, attributing it largely to the growing disparity of regional economic conditions. Olivier Blanchard and Peter Diamond (1989, 1990) focus on incidence of unemployment when a recession occurs, arguing that the shift in the United States happened because workers, including women and nonwhites, experienced long-term unemployment, which made them less likely to be rehired. But it is clear from examination of the scatterplot that, while there was a stable Beveridge curve from 1975 to 1985, the curve shifted inward markedly from 1986 to 1989, then drew a new stable curve from 1990 to 1994, and has shifted significantly inward

FIGURE 5.1 / Annual Vacancy and Unemployment Rates, 1960 to 1998

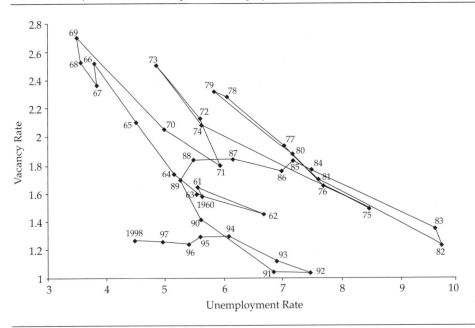

Sources: Vacancy data from Katz and Krueger (personal communication); unemployment from BLS CPS.

again since 1995. In short, there were two distinct episodes of considerable improvement in labor-market efficiency.[13]

The gaps in research to date on the employers' role in the labor market become even more important as we tackle the question of why the U.S. Beveridge
curve has now shifted in. In line with the standard explanations of the Beveridge
curve's outward shift in the 1970s, if there was a wholesale sectoral shift of
worker demand by firms in the U.S. "new economy," say because of the expansion of an information-technology (IT) sector requiring new skills and/or new
locations, this should have increased churning and turnover. Given even a positive technological shock, we would expect the Beveridge curve to have shifted
out again by the mid-1990s, but there is no evidence of that. A straightforward IT
explanation would also have difficulty with the first shift occurring in the period
1986 to 1989, given the vanishingly small ratios of IT per worker or IT as a share
of total business equipment at the time. As Daniel Sichel (1997) and, more recently, Jacob Mincer and Stephan Danninger (2000) document, the most important increases in IT investment did not begin until 1993—and then from a very
low base.[14]

Other prominent explanations suggest that the Beveridge curve changes
should have been considerably more gradual than what we observe. Demographic changes, emphasized by Robert Shimer (1998) and Lawrence Katz and
Alan Krueger (1999), seem too gradual to account for the Beveridge curve shift.
Furthermore, as Gary Burtless (1999) points out, most of the aging of the American workforce took place between 1979 and 1989, beginning before the first shift
that we identify here and preceding several years the other. The fraction of the
workforce that is unionized has been declining since about 1950. The rate of
decline accelerated in the 1970s and again after the PATCO strike, but most of
the decline in unionization rates was complete before the beginning of the period in which the Beveridge curve is shifting.

Rising Job Turnover, Layoffs, and Insecurity

Even without taking the precise timing of the shifts in the Beveridge curve into
account, making sense of the apparent increasing efficiency of the U.S. labor
market is all the more difficult because of one of the most-discussed recent developments in American labor markets: the slight but clear downward shift in
job stability for at least some workers in the 1980s and 1990s. Greater job turnover would normally be expected to lead to higher frictional unemployment,
especially if much of the turnover was involuntary. Although it is clear that
press reports from the early 1990s bemoaning downsizing and the end of lifetime employment were exaggerated, extensive subsequent research on trends in
job stability has finally converged on a broad picture.[15] The main finding in this
literature of interest here is the decreasing job stability and security in the 1990s
for men who are older and have longer job tenures. This fits with case evidence
of a long period from the mid-1980s to the mid-1990s of corporate downsizing,

especially in the manufacturing sector. For example, David Neumark (2000) comes to the conclusion that four- and eight-year retention rates fell for longer-tenured older men in the 1990s and that there has been some general "weakening of worker-firm bonds" in the decade. His findings are significant given his earlier skeptical views on these changes.

Accompanying this general decline in job stability for longer-tenured workers in the 1990s have been some adjustments in the experience and use of layoffs in manufacturing. As shown by Lawrence Katz and Bruce Meyer (1990), the number of unemployed workers expecting recall was always higher than the number who actually were recalled. The perceived likelihood of recall had a significant effect on the unemployed workers' search behavior. On the occasion of redesigning the Current Population Survey (CPS), Anne Polivka and Stephen Miller (1995) pointed out that perceived likelihood of recall had dropped across the board following the periods of restructuring in the 1980s and early 1990s. Survey questions had to be changed because the word *layoff* was now associated in the public's mind with permanent job loss. This change in perception was coincident with an increase in actual layoffs found by the survey (even after accounting for a change in the counting of reentrants). Todd Idson and Robert Valletta (1996) document that, through the early 1990s, the positive influence of job tenure on recall probability from layoff was declining.

The Explosive Growth of Contracting Out and Blue-Collar Temporary Employment

At the time that these shifts in job stability and security occurred in the 1980s and 1990s, American firms also changed their hiring behavior in another way. They massively increased their hiring of temporary workers and expanded their use of outside contractors to replace in-house staff. Outsourcing of business support services, and the accompanying changes in employment and firm compensation, is an understudied phenomenon. Our interviews with human-resource and strategic-planning managers in large corporations indicate that the move to outsourcing is an important part of their workplace reorganization (see the next section), and we will argue that it plays a critical role in the chain of events linking changes in the firms' management and compensation of labor to the decline in the NAIRU.

One study directly discussing firms' use of outside contractors is Katherine Abraham and Susan Taylor (1993). Using industry wage surveys from 1986 and 1987, these authors document that the share of establishments contracting out services in their sample rose in several areas after 1979.[16] The motivations for contracting out appear to have been a combination of savings on wages and benefits for lower-skilled workers, accommodating fluctuations in demand, and taking advantage of economies of scale or specialized management techniques (for example, food-service inventory management). One effect has been to reduce the access of lower-skilled workers to employment with industrial (as opposed to business-service) companies. As Burtless (1999) conjectures, "Unskilled workers become less numerous on big company payrolls, but they still find jobs. The jobs are in smaller companies and offer worse pay and fewer fringe bene-fits" (72). As one would expect, this also applies to temporary workers.

Figures 5.2 to 5.5 show the growth of employment in sectors, and a few spe-cific industries, that we have identified with the contracting of business services. The pattern of growth in the fraction of contractor employees in total business employment shows significant accelerations in the mid- to late 1980s and again in the 1990s after the recession. The rapid growth in the 1990s precedes the second shift in the Beveridge curve but coincides with the wave of downsizing that may have temporarily increased equilibrium unemployment. On our rough accounting, the gains in employment over the relevant period are considerable, amounting to several million workers.

The similar expansion of temporary employment has recently received a great deal of academic attention. Maria Ward Otoo (1999) calculates that temporary employment tripled from around 0.7 percent of total nonfarm-payroll employ-ment in the mid-1980s to 2.3 percent of total employment by the end of 1998 (see fig. 5.5). In theory, businesses using temporary-help service companies to find permanent employees could directly improve the matching process if these tem-porary agencies help overcome information difficulties or achieve economies of scale in job search and/or hiring. Otoo (1999) attributes 0.25 percent of the de-cline in the NAIRU to improvements in matching efficiency due to the growth of the temporary-help industry. Katz and Krueger (1999), offering similar intuition for benefits to matching from temporary-help services through provision of screening and training as well as lowering hiring costs and alleviating bottle-

FIGURE 5.2 / Total Employment in Business Services as a Fraction of Total Nonfarm Employment

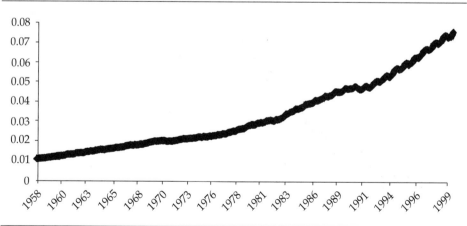

Source: BLS Current Employment Survey.

FIGURE 5.3 / Employment in Computer and Data-Processing Services as a Fraction of Total Nonfarm Employment

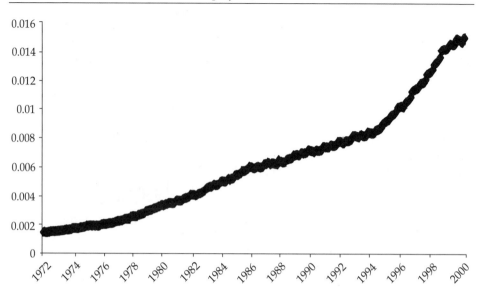

Source: BLS Current Employment Survey.

FIGURE 5.4 / Employment in Services to Buildings as a Fraction of Total Nonfarm Employment

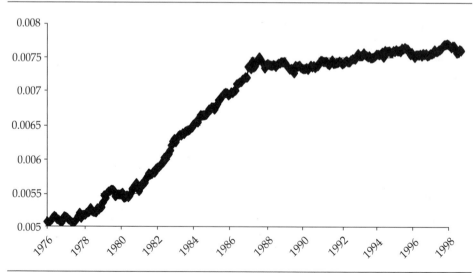

Source: BLS Current Employment Survey.

FIGURE 5.5 / Employment in Temporary-Help Services as a Fraction of Total Nonfarm Employment

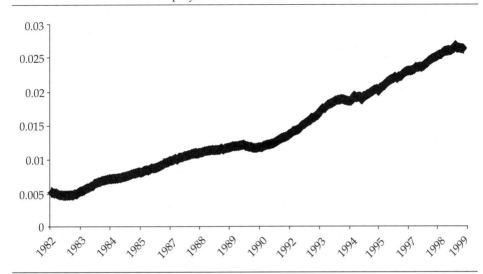

Source: BLS Current Employment Survey.

necks, estimate that the growth of temporary-help services has taken 0.39 percent off the NAIRU in the 1990s.

We believe that the increasing use of temporary-help services has improved labor-market efficiency, but not primarily because firms are using them to screen new hires. Permanent hiring of temps is rare except for clerical workers, and even then it is not all that frequent (Houseman and Polivka 1999). The hiring firms seem to benefit less from screening than from the flexibility that temps offer both staffing levels and compensation programs.[17] Lewis Segal and Daniel Sullivan (1995, 1997) establish that these workers experience very high cyclical variability of employment, as one might expect if part of firms' motivation is to deal with excess demand without hiring permanent staff. Otherwise, why would temporary employment fluctuate so much, and why would temporary employees be more likely than permanent employees to change employment, become unemployed, and even leave the labor force, as Susan Houseman and Anne Polivka (1999) demonstrate they do?[18] As with the decline in job stability discussed earlier, under normal conditions the direct effect of a greater number of workers in temporary jobs, moving in and out of active employment, should be to *raise* the NAIRU. Houseman and Polivka (1999), for example, estimate that the rise in flexible staffing arrangements from 1986 to 1996 raised the average rate of unemployment by 0.3 percent through increasing turnover and friction, an effect equal and opposite to those hypothesized earlier.

Of most interest to us in explaining the inward shifts of both the Beveridge and the Phillips curves is that the growth in temporary employment in the 1990s was concentrated in blue-collar manufacturing jobs. While every nonagricultural sector showed a rise in the use of temporary workers from 1977 to 1997, Marcello Estevao and Saul Lach (1999b) estimate that, up to 1997, growth in the use of temps in the manufacturing and service sectors made up 85 percent of the growth in total temps in U.S. employment in the 1990s. In fact, the manufacturing-sector use of temps rose from 1 percent of sectoral employment in 1992 to 4 percent in 1997, catching up with the level in services. Blue-collar employees went from 6 percent of temporary-help services in 1985 to 25 percent in 1995, according to Estevao and Lach (1999b). Similarly, in Autor's (2000b) 1994 survey of a large sample of temporary-help-services firms, blue-collar workers made up 45 percent of the temp population. Segal and Sullivan (1997) date the increase in the proportion of male and blue-collar temporary workers to the end of the 1980s and the beginning of the 1990s.

That dating puts the sharp increase in manufacturing reliance on temporary employees coincident with the decline in direct hiring by manufacturing from peak employment in 1989.[19] Estevao and Lach (1999a) go so far as to put bounds on their estimates of the increase in temporary-labor outsourcing in U.S. manufacturing 1992 to 1997 at 340,000 minimum and 510,000 maximum; in other words, the entire decline in manufacturing employment over the period is essentially matched by their estimate of the rise in temporary-help-services blue-collar employment. This is consistent with the popular view that not all the hires into temporary services came out of unemployment, or even short-tenure employment, but that some came out of "good" jobs. A similar replacement phenomenon came up during our interview with an executive from a contracting firm who volunteered that, in many cases, the contracting firm will hire the workers let go by a company when they sign a contract to replace an in-house service.

It is worth emphasizing how different these manufacturing temporaries are from the lingering stereotypical image of the temp as a "Kelly Girl" or some other young pink-collared female clerical worker. In Estevao and Lach's (1999a) assessment, the typical manufacturing temp is male, thirty-five to fifty years old, with some college, working full-time in the Midwest. This happens also to be the type of worker who traditionally has the largest within-occupation wage differentials, meaning in all likelihood rents from a "good job" in a high-wage firm and/or firm-specific skills. In David Autor's (2000a) sample, 62 percent of blue-collar temps were classified as "handlers/equipment cleaners/labor," and 24 percent were "operators/assemblers/inspectors."

Autor (2000b) explores the phenomenon of "free general skills training" by temporary-help firms, but, in his sample from a 1994 survey, the 45 percent of temp workers classified as blue collar were markedly less likely to get that training: while 81 percent of clerical temps received some training, only 59 percent of blue-collar temps did; 74 percent of clerical temps, but only 14 percent of blue-collar temps, were given computer training. Only on the soft skill of "business conduct" did a comparable proportion of clerical (68 percent) and manufacturing (60 percent) temps receive training. It is not a surprise, therefore, that, in Autor's (2000a) wage regressions showing the positive effects of training for white- and pink-collar temps, the blue-collar category shows no significant positive effects of training. In fact, the wage equations have a notably poor fit for those workers.

While it may be unusual for temporary workers to be hired permanently by the firms that employ them, most temporary workers are looking for permanent work and are temping only because it is the best opportunity available to them. Katz and Krueger (1999) note that 70 percent of temporary-help-service employees in the February 1997 CPS supplement said that they were temping for "economic" reasons rather than by choice.

To get to a story where these major shifts in corporate personnel practices could be associated with the declining NAIRU, we have to take seriously the motivations for the rise in temporary hiring and in contracting—and, as we have seen, these are not primarily screening workers for permanent employment or benefiting from someone else's worker training. The efficiency gains pursued by firms must be those that arise for the other widely recognized reasons: the possibility of decompressing wages between higher- and lower-skilled workers; the advantages of scale economies and specialized skills in outsourcing some noncore tasks; and the flexible adjustment of company labor forces to swings in demand.[20] Secular growth in temporary-help-services employment could thus account for some of the shifts in the Beveridge curve, if hiring temps substitutes for what would previously have been listed as vacancies, and in the Phillips curve, if some of those who became temps previously would have been unemployed.

The Efforts to Decompress Wages Within Firms

Unionization and internal equity constraints have generally led to the compression of wages within firms. This is inefficient for firms, which have little choice but to pay the going rate for needed highly skilled workers and then find themselves constrained to reward other employees in relation to that wage rather than to the individual worker's productivity. In recent years, there have been a number of developments in compensation practices that have the potential to increase within-firm wage dispersion (see Lebow et al. 1999, which is based on surveys done for the Federal Reserve "Beige Books"): increased use of lump-sum payments; profit sharing and stock options extending below top management; merit-pay raises (outside seniority); wider bands within wage levels for large corporations; pay for skills and outsourcing. Of course, the broader shift to temporary and contract workers, to whom the establishment need not pay usual wages and benefits, increases the wage dispersion of the firm's effective labor force even as the internal payroll gets more concentrated.[21]

Widespread Adoption of HPWO

Workplace organization—that is, the definition, organization, and supervision of workers' tasks—has also undergone considerable change in the last twenty years. Worker involvement in quality control, the design of products and production processes, job rotation, and team production have become widespread in manufacturing and beyond.[22] Eileen Appelbaum and Rosemary Batt (1994) set out a view of an American economy beset by international competition and deregulation as well as worker frustration and fear, a situation that compelled businesses to produce higher-value-added, higher-quality, more-customized products on a faster product cycle. These non- or less-standardized goods erode the benefits of mass production and standardized (or Taylorite) job descriptions. Instead, the workplace is shifted to HPWO, seen in American forms of lean production and team production.[23] In the early 1980s, such practices were essentially nonexistent in U.S. firms. As of 1992, however, when Appelbaum and Batt completed their research, HPWO practices had already been adopted by a growing minority of American manufacturers.

Paul Osterman (1994) presents the results of a 1992 survey for the spread of four such practices sampled from nonagricultural establishments with more than fifty employees. He finds that there is team production for half or more of core workers at 40.5 percent of firms surveyed, job rotation at 26.6 percent, TQM at 24.5 percent, and quality circles at 27.4 percent.[24] Reprising the survey in 1997, Osterman (2000) finds that the share of establishments with 50 percent penetration of self-managed teams has largely stagnated (38.4 percent) but that the incidence of the other three practices has risen: 55.5 percent have job rotation; 57.2 percent have TQM; and 57.7 percent have quality circles. Table 5.1 presents the results of several surveys of such practices, including Osterman's. In longitudinal data on firms in both of Osterman's surveys, 81.5 percent of those establish-

TABLE 5.1 / Percentage of Firms Adopting New Methods of Labor Organization

	Teams	TQM	Quality Circles	Job Rotation	Source
1987			28	15	Lawler et al. (1992)[a]
1990			32	16	Lawler et al. (1992)
1992	40.5	24.5	27.4	26.6	Osterman (1994)[b]
1993	32	46	15.8	24.2	BLS[c]
1994	29			21	Census[d]
1997	38.4	57.2	57.7	55.5	Osterman (2000)

[a]Companies reporting some use or more (excludes those reporting no or almost no use). Job-rotation numbers are fraction of companies reporting that they use pay-for-skill compensation systems for at least "some" of their workers.
[b]Greater than 50 percent of core employees involved.
[c]Presence measure only—no cutoff for percentage of employees involved. From BLS Survey of Employer Provided Training as cited in Osterman (2000).
[d]Approximation to Osterman's definition from census, National Employer Survey as cited in Osterman (2000).

ments that had at least two HPWO practices in 1992 still had two or more in 1997, while 53.5 percent of those establishments with one or none of the HPWO practices in 1992 had two or more in 1997.

Figure 5.6 plots the change over time in the percentage of firms using job rotation (the practice for which we have the most observations) and an index of the position of the Beveridge curve.[25] As can be seen in the admittedly spotty data, the adoption of job rotation in Osterman's surveys and others displays the same two-step shift as the Beveridge curve, increasing in the late 1980s, plateauing or going back slightly from 1990 to 1994, and rising again in the late 1990s.[26] This coincidence in the development of HPWO and the shifts in the Beveridge curve is of great interest because none of the other explanatory variables for changes in matching efficiency show this rise-flat-rise sequence.

These practices, particularly those involving teamwork and job rotation, usually require some stability of the relevant workforce—a fact that would seem to be at odds with the evidence on job instability. What appears to have happened is that employers have identified "core employees" who are retained and are expected to be the ongoing participants in these practices. This does not deny that some of the firms adopting HPWO are also the same firms laying off workers and restructuring in the last two decades. In fact, Osterman (1994, 2000) finds that firms facing international competition that engaged in layoffs are more likely to have adopted HPWO.

In short, despite layoffs, employers have retained their core employees, who are presumably those who embody the most-firm-specific human capital and who, in the new structure, are required to have the most-general skills as well. This would be consistent with the desire for increased within-enterprise wage dispersion and for the employment of temps and outside contractors. In a recent study, Simon Burgess, Julia Lane, and David Stevens (2000) establish that churn-

FIGURE 5.6 / The Fraction of Firms Using Job Rotation and Beveridge Curve Index

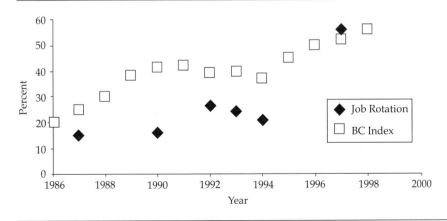

Source: See text.

ing (firms hiring and firing workers at the same time) takes place in all phases of demand-driven cycles, consistent with the empirical literature on job flows documenting that even shrinking firms hire and growing firms fire. Using firm-level data from Maryland, they show that, for most firms, there exists a stable core of workers that does not change, even when churning takes place. Interestingly, they find evidence of a declining churn rate overall and a steady decline in the churn rate of the highest quintile of churn establishments over their 1985 to 1994 sample—which would be consistent with firms shedding without replacing non-core workers over this period.

Finally, it is in the adoption of HPWO that IT makes an appearance in our discussion of changes in how U.S. firms have hired, fired, and compensated employees in the last two decades.[27] In a thought-provoking case study of a bank adopting the image processing of deposited checks in 1994, David Autor, Frank Levy, and Richard Murnane (2000) describe how the adoption of the particular IT advancement of optical character recognition led to substitution for the (low-skilled) check-clearing labor but increasing demands for integrated and/or flexible work and self-management from the (higher-skilled) "Exceptions Department." While this is consistent with the usually invoked trend toward skill-biased technological change, there is more to the story: as IT investment occurs, lower-skill jobs are moved out of the firm, while higher-skill jobs are switched to HPWO and, presumably, greater stability.

Assar Lindbeck and Dennis Snower (1996, 2000) assert that such an interaction between what they perceive as advances in technology, worker preferences for jobs with variety requiring versatility (meaning HPWO), and a steady rise in human capital and training constitutes a general OECD-wide shift from "Taylorite" to "holistic" organization of production. In such a world, workers' initially unobservable abilities to work flexibly and in teams are revealed in tandem with wage decompression to reward those increasingly valuable general skills. Lindbeck and Snower (1996, 2000) suggest that this shift explains the increasing dispersion of wages within worker types in the United States and of job opportunities (given nominal-wage rigidities) in Europe. This dynamic is supported by evidence from firm-level panel-data studies, including Timothy Bresnahan, Erik Brynjolfsson, and Lorin Hitt (1999), Sandra Black and Lisa Lynch (2000), Timothy Dunne et al. (2000), and Paul Osterman (2000), that find a positive correlation between IT, HPWO practices across firms, and human capital.

Yet, for all the appeal of this explanation, and particularly its potential as a description for a force likely to increase as adoption of IT moves forward, the empirical evidence for its being central in American, or even European, wage developments to date cannot be deemed entirely convincing. Bresnahan, Brynjolfsson, and Hitt's (1999) model and data emphasize white-collar industries, not manufacturing, where the shifts in employment practices have been greatest, and where IT adoption was not yet widespread by the time of their survey (1995 to 1996); Dunne et al. (2000) find only weak statistical support for the direct link between IT investment and wage dispersion across firms, given the very small quantities of and variation in IT investment by the time of their sample (the mid-1990s).

Many of Lindbeck and Snower's (1996, 2000) claims do not fit well with the facts more broadly. Their claim that production capital, like machine tools, has become more flexible is, while plausible, at odds with the ongoing occurrence of layoffs when firms change production lines.[28] The claim that IT induces HPWO is difficult to reconcile with, albeit not strictly contradicted by, the fact that many of the countries that preceded the United States in such practices, such as Germany and Japan, have remained behind the United States in IT investment. The claim that workers' previously imperfectly observed ability to work flexibly and in teams has become a source of widening pay differentials would seem to imply that churning and mismatch should have gone *up* for the firm's core workforce until the firm learns to screen and train for those skills, but the opposite has been observed. On this last point linking IT and matching, Mincer and Danninger (2000) provide a useful caution that usually turnover and unemployment duration rise for several years after a technological shift, as workers with the skills required to use the new technology are rewarded with higher wages, while others have to train and catch up. In Mincer and Danniger's estimation, this cycle is likely to be just beginning in the United States, where computer equipment per worker started rising markedly (from a very low base) only in 1992 or 1993 and computer equipment as a share of total equipment accelerates (again from a very low base) only after after 1994 (see also Oliner and Sichel 1994, 2000).

So, although we share some objects of concern with Lindbeck and Snower (1996, 2000), we have a different view of the role that technology plays in leading to the widespread use of HPWO. In our view, the effect has been much less direct as only one of several factors—along with international competition, financial-market pressures, and growing customer sophistication—leading to an increased turnover of products and, as a result, both a faster depreciation rate of specific human capital and a higher value placed on general skills. We believe that this change in the structure of product markets may have led firms to organize their production so that core workers invest less deeply and more broadly in task- or firm-specific skills. We see this as being the primary salient characteristic of the new modes of work organization for our approach to explaining the decline in the NAIRU.

Summary of the Changing American Workplace, 1980 to 1998

The significant changes in American business's HRM practices in the 1980s and 1990s are promising candidates to explain the decline in the NAIRU, although the macroeconomic implications of these developments have remained largely unexamined as yet. The remainder of this paper builds on these changes to tell a story synthesizing the major developments in U.S. firms' hiring, firing, and compensation of workers of different skills and the aggregate trends in labor-market efficiency and wage dispersion. This effort is much in the spirit of Lindbeck and Snower's attempt, but it fits the sequence of developments better, including the aspects of firms' contracting out and increasing use of temps as well as the accumulation of IT investment to meaningful levels. As set out in this review, the elements of such a story should be the following:

- an explanation for why the changes should have taken place at the same time as the two abrupt changes in the Beveridge curve and the adoption of HPWO;[29]
- the decline in job stability and security for older and long-tenured male workers in the 1990s;
- a relatively constant use of layoffs by manufacturing employers, controlling for cyclical conditions, but a greater perception on the part of workers that layoffs, when used, constitute permanent dismissals;
- increased insecurity in the early 1990s, which declines but remains abnormally high even as employment increases in the middle of the decade;
- a mounting use of temporary workers and outside contractors by employers, who generally do not bring these temporary workers into permanent employment, with an explosive growth in blue-collar-temp employment in manufacturing in the 1990s;
- significant changes in corporate compensation practices designed to increase wage dispersion and flexibility within firms' workforces (not just firms' employees alone, once temps and contractors are included) and some evidence of such an increase;
- the spread of HPWO, especially of job rotation and TQM, for core employees in the mid-1980s and mid-1990s; and
- the expectation that, owing to the eroding value of firm-specific investments and internal equity constraints as well as lower-skilled workers' diminished access to "good" jobs, worker rents will shrink.

We believe that greater product-market competition—due to increasing trade, deregulation, and technology—has led to a speeding up of the product cycle and to an increase in the demand for customization. In our view, these changes drove changing employer behavior.[30] Analyzing the often-overlooked effect of changes in employer behavior on the demand side of the labor market should contribute to an understanding of the decline in the U.S. NAIRU.

INTERVIEWS WITH HUMAN-RESOURCE MANAGERS

We undertook nine interviews with senior executives in private corporations in order to get additional insight into trends in the way in which firms have organized labor in the 1980s and 1990s. All but two of our interviews were conducted with executives in either human resources or strategic planning. Seven of the interviews were with representatives of multinational manufacturing firms, ranging from low- to relatively high-tech, although none in the IT sector—our focus on "old-economy" manufacturing firms was in line with our hypotheses. If the labor market gained in matching efficiency in the 1990s sufficiently to explain part of the drop in the NAIRU, that gain must have taken place in those sectors most subject to worker separations and delays in rehiring. The other two interviews were with executives from a multinational contracting firm and from a small temporary-employment agency. We undertook these interviews to gain some insight into whether the developments in the demand for their firms' services matched up with our understanding of the changes that have been taking place in their client establishments.[31]

Some clear patterns emerged across the interviews with manufacturing executives about the general trends in how their companies have used labor. Five of the seven stressed a shift to team production and the use of HPWOs as well as a trend toward increased contracting out of tasks not considered core competencies:[32] "The most significant change in the way that the company uses manufacturing labor has been in the transition to team production"; "the manufacturing that is left in the United States does take a team approach"; "many of the tasks which are not core competencies of the company are outsourced"; "the company now outsources or has sold off many areas that are not core to the business." One of the remaining two interview subjects is with a firm that has been a trendsetter in teamwork practices since the early 1980s, but he/she did not volunteer any discussion of contracting out. The lowest-tech and most-unionized firm of the seven was an exception to both trends—"the company is about ten years behind in innovative work-organization practices such as team production"—although even this company had begun experimenting with new production practices in its newer plants and expressed an intent to "catch up."

Increases in worker flexibility, including the broadening of tasks that were previously quite narrow, were mentioned by five of the seven executives often, but not always, as part of the move toward worker teams:[33] "The highly specialized-segregated individual is gone; team production and job broadening happened after several rounds of layoffs"; "the idea is to be as flexible as possible in what jobs are done, in moving people from one product line to another." Significantly, none of the executives attributed the increase in flexibility to improvements in technology (neither technology generally nor IT specifically) that made workers more substitutable. Instead, those who commented on the reason for the change attributed it to demand factors, such as the need to keep up with just-in-time inventory and customer expectations.

While only four of the executives interviewed mentioned that their firms now screened for "broader" or "more-general" skills—and two explicitly denied that their firms' screening processes had changed at all—there was certainly a general thrust toward demanding more from the workers already employed by the firms. Only one of the seven manufacturing-company executives interviewed said that his/her firm gives its workers greater training opportunities now, and another volunteered that his/her firm offers fewer. Discussion of IT skills or of machines that relied on a more common set of controls and processes did not arise.

Most of the executives indicated that there had been a significant, single wave of workforce reductions within the last fifteen to twenty years: "Automation and technological changes have reduced the number of manufacturing jobs overall"; "first, the company employs far fewer employees than in the past because of layoffs, technology, and downsizing." All but one (again the executive with the lowest-tech, most-unionized firm) did indicate that their firms rely less—sometimes significantly less—on temporary layoffs among their remaining core workforce than they did in the past: "The permanent employees are left with much more employment stability"; "the company still uses temporary layoffs when dealing with low demand (although they [plant managers] try to avoid them)"; "they no longer lay off manufacturing workers as frequently as they used to." But only one of the seven manufacturing executives indicated that his/her firm had not used layoffs at all in recent years and did not expect to do so when demand slowed again.

The reduction in (but not the elimination of) layoffs was, according to our interviewees, accompanied by an increase in the use of temporary workers. Many temps are production workers, hired on during times of high demand, and let go during slack periods. These are lower-skilled workers whom the company can pay less than it does its permanent employees: "The use of temps has increased dramatically in the last fifteen years . . . ; temporary workers are useful during periods of rapid growth because they fill in and the company does not have to pay them benefits"; "the company has become more disciplined in using temporary help when it is needed and then letting the workers go"; "much more use of contingent workers than in the past, less rehiring of those laid off." According to the temporary-employment-agency executive interviewed, demand has been increasing for the last twenty years, but the answer to the question, "Why now and not twenty years ago?" is, "Nobody thought of it. There are no obvious changes in the ways that temp firms organize themselves to explain the increase in demand for their services."

These temporary workers constitute from 5 to 20 percent of the high-demand workforce at the companies whose executives we interviewed. Even the contracting-services firm relies on temps for 20 percent of its workforce, laying them off during slow seasons (the summer for university jobs, winter for groundskeeping jobs). None of the executives indicated that more than a tiny fraction of temps are considered for permanent hiring. In fact, none of the executives interviewed mentioned their companies' use of temporary workers as a screening device for hiring, except for a couple of instances of clerical hires.

Contracting out has become the norm. Almost all the executives we interviewed mentioned outsourcing cafeteria and janitorial services, but four mentioned IT services as well, while three mentioned each of medical and child care, real estate (both selling buildings and maintaining them), and some administrative tasks. The now-familiar phrases about "competitive pressures" and the need to narrow production to "core competencies" were invoked repeatedly as explanations for the shedding of labor: "All of the tasks which are not core competencies of the company are outsourced—if it is not a task which it is desirable to be good at, it is not worth investing in the task;" "so, if they cannot make a particular area of their business more productive and it is not a core competency, they contract out." The contracting-firm executive with whom we spoke stated that the trend toward outsourcing has shown particularly strong growth in the last three years in the United States; while his/her firm has expanded hiring to meet rising corporate demand, none of the factors influencing its costs or production structure have changed recently.

The contracting-firm executive lists three main benefits that, in his/her own estimation, the firm provides to client firms: expertise in managing specific services; willingness to invest in upgraded facilities (in return for a long-term contract); and cost savings from economies of scale (materials purchasing and, more important, investment in systems of administration). While our corporate interviewees generally attributed the trend in contracting out to reductions in labor costs, two went further and articulated a more complicated motivation:

"Part of the reason is that benefits no longer have to be spread across occupations. Instead, certain occupation areas can be contracted out or outsourced so that lower-skilled workers will no longer reap the benefits of being in the 'right industry.'"

"When cost reductions are required and labor is a fixed cost, there has been a shift to contracting out (not just in this industry). The primary factor has been that internal equity constraints made the company pay some low-skill jobs more than they are worth, and it was difficult to cut compensation because of those constraints, which leads to contracting out the positions."

This process did not result in wage increases (beyond the secular trend) for the remaining higher-skilled workers employed by these companies. Three of the executives interviewed specifically stated that their companies' pay remained roughly at the industry median. However, since the comparisons being made are between high-wage firms, it is difficult to tell whether these companies' pay has remained unchanged relative to the pay of comparable workers in the economy as a whole. In fact, over the period during which the firms in question were restructuring, the real wages of male workers with high school degrees were declining.

Unions would normally be expected to play a role in decisions regarding the breadth of job descriptions and work rules, the use of temps and layoffs, and the effect of contracting out on wage differentials in American manufacturing industries. Of all the topics covered in our interviews, however, the role of unions elicited the widest range of views. Three executives did not mention them at all, having little unionization in their plants, while the remainder split over whether

unions supported or opposed tight job descriptions: "The company was responsible for the proliferation of job titles in union plants . . . because laying off by
seniority was within job class . . . ; then the union would respond by insisting on
people doing only what their job description said they should do"; "the unions
and the company had always agreed to broad job descriptions, so rotating workers within plants was never a problem." Only one executive, in the most unionized industry in our sample, made a direct connection between contracting out
and union disapproval. Clearly, much of what went on in the 1980s and 1990s
could not have taken place without these firms being only partially or completely nonunionized. Equally clear, however, was that the executives we interviewed considered the role of unions, and even their decline, as having already
been established by the time these trends began, not as causing the trends.

The causal factors behind the joint movement toward HPWO, contracting out,
the reduced use of layoffs, and the increased use of temporary workers in production that our interviewees did cite were threefold: First, as already discussed,
the cost pressures on these manufacturing firms—felt in just-in-time inventory
and the pressure to respond to customer demands for immediate shipping—
forced changes in work practices (cited in one form or another in five of the
seven interviews with manufacturing executives). Second, four of the interviewees mentioned a "speeding up of the product cycle," usually attributed to
increased competition (including that due to globalization) and/or the demands
of customers. Third, it was clear that, especially with regard to the adoption of
HPWO and the contracting out of noncore services, there was a tendency to
follow the intellectual fashion: "The change was due to an effort to follow the
Japanese model, with increased flexibility and team production."

Strikingly, two interviewees explicitly denied that advances in IT were an
independent motivating force, and all but one of the others either did not mention IT or downplayed its effect, characterizing it as limited to administrative
matters: "The transition to team production was not significantly driven by technological changes . . . ; technology could be more productive even in a more
traditional work environment." The one remaining subject did draw the connection that "E-commerce has been important in speeding up the business cycle."
None of the executives interviewed mentioned direct links between the adoption
of IT and the increase in the flexibility of workers and/or the use of temps and
contracting out. Both the temporary-agency executive and the contracting-firm
executive also denied that IT had played a major role in the past changes in their
operations, instead attributing their (and their industries') success to their cost
advantages from economies of scale and their expertise in relevant practices.

HAVE LABOR RENTS ERODED?

The erosion of labor rents in high-wage jobs and the disappearance of worker
rents in low-wage jobs played a key role in the connection made in the previous
two sections between changes in the organization of work and improved labor-

market efficiency. If our story is correct, we would expect changes in rents to parallel shifts in the Beveridge curve and in the adoption of HPWO. Moreover, if the motivations for adopting HPWO and increasing the use of contractors and temps do, indeed, include the desire to loosen the equity constraint, as our interviewees indicated, then rents should have eroded in step with these developments.

The identification of labor rents is less than straightforward. For one thing, their very existence is controversial among some economists. While few would question that unions are able to obtain a share of company rents for themselves through bargaining, the notion that nonunion workers should be able to secure higher wages for themselves, either through bargaining or through the implicit threat of collective action, has not been fully accepted. William Dickens (1986) argues that even nonunion workers with the potential to bargain collectively should benefit from that threat, but Alan Krueger and Lawrence Summers (1987) question whether this in fact happens.

If rents do differ among workers, one might consider using the extent of wage dispersion to measure rents. However, the growth in overall wage inequality in the United States during this period—widely attributed to growing returns to human capital—would confound this method. Given that residual inequality has been growing along with overall inequality, even using the dispersion of wages net of observable human capital to measure rents would not work.[34] A feasible indicator of the magnitude worker rents is the dispersion of interindustry wage differences. Dickens and Katz (1987a, 1987b) and Katz and Summers (1989) have proposed that interindustry wage differences primarily measure worker rents.[35] Subsequently, we examine changes in the dispersion of interindustry wage differences for evidence that changing rents may be driving the observed changes in the efficiency of the economy.

To measure interindustry wage dispersion, we analyze the outgoing rotation groups of the monthly CPS from 1982 through 1999. We group together all workers surveyed in each calendar year. We use as our measure of wages the hourly wage, if workers are paid hourly, or normal weekly earnings divided by normal weekly hours, if they are not. We include in our analysis all workers for whom wage data are available. Figure 5.7 presents the time series of the standard deviation of the natural log of wages. It shows the familiar pattern of rising inequality, conforming with prior work.

Figure 5.8 presents our first measure of interindustry wage differences along with our index of the shifting Beveridge curve.[36] Interindustry wage differences are measured as the standard deviation of the average log wage within three-digit industries. Given the extent of increasing inequality, the significant decline in raw interindustry wage differences is remarkable.[37] Even more remarkable is the timing of these changes. Like the movements in the Beveridge curve, the declines in the raw interindustry wage differences are concentrated in the same two periods—the late 1980s and the late 1990s—with a flat period in between. The correlation of the levels of the two series is 0.93 (statistically significant at the .01 level). Figure 5.9 shows that nearly the same pattern can be seen in the

FIGURE 5.7 / Standard Deviation of ln (wages)

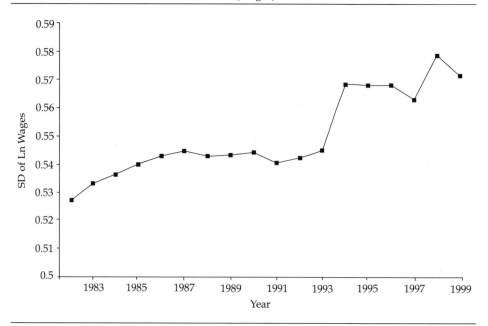

Source: Authors' calculations from CPS.

FIGURE 5.8 / Standard Deviation of Average Log Wages in Three Digit Industries

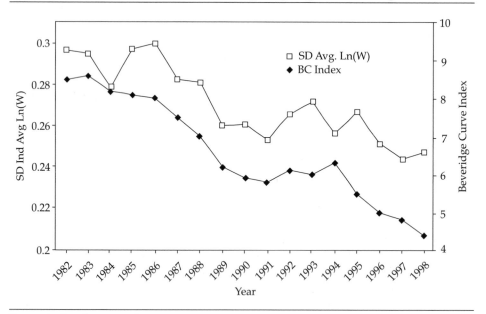

Source: Authors' computation, see text.

FIGURE 5.9 / Beveridge Curve Index and Standard Deviation of Industry Fixed-Effects

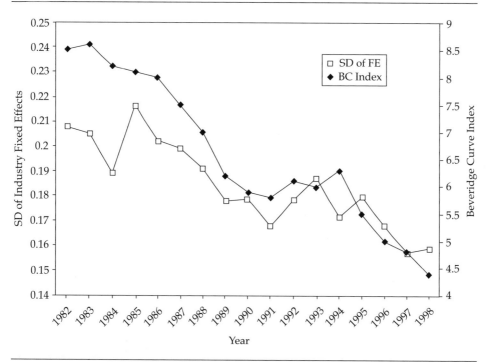

Source: Authors' computation, see text.

dispersion of what is usually considered the preferred measure of rents—the industry fixed effects from an elaborate human-capital regression including controls for a wide range of personal characteristics and workers' occupations. The pattern is nearly identical to that of the raw interindustry wage differences seen in figure 5.8. The correlation with the index of the Beveridge curve is 0.91 (statistically significant at the .01 level).[38]

These results tell us two things, which provide surprisingly strong support of the story presented so far. First, there is a near-perfect coincidence of the two periods of decline in both interindustry wage difference series with the shifts in the Beveridge curve and in HPWO adoption. This lockstep motion is not easily attributed to artifacts such as coincidence with the business cycle. The 1990 recession was officially over by 1992, and a robust recovery was under way by the end of 1993—the first year that unemployment fell. Yet the changes in the Beveridge curve and in the dispersion of interindustry wage differences did not commence again until 1995 and 1996, respectively. Second, as described previously, this hiatus corresponds as well to the period of retrenchment in the deployment of HPWO apparent in figure 5.6.

CONNECTING THE COINCIDENT CHANGES INTO A COHERENT STORY

This section first summarizes our theory of the changes that have been taking place within high-wage manufacturing firms. We describe how a speeding up of the rate of introduction of new products can lead to an increase in demand for general skills, to an erosion of worker rents, and, ultimately, to the decision to hire contracted and temporary workers for a substantial fraction of jobs within the firm. Second, we present our explanation of how these changes have led to improved labor-market efficiency and provide some illustrative calculations of potential gains. The firm and market models discussed are described in greater detail in Jessica Cohen and William Dickens (2001). At this point, the purpose of the model is simply to demonstrate our ability to tell a consistent story about how changes in the way in which firms use labor have affected the NAIRU. In future work, we hope to develop a model we can estimate that will allow us to test our hypotheses directly.

Inside the Firm

In order to analyze the effect of shortened product cycles and greater flexibility on the increased demand for general skills and the use of contracted and temporary workers, we consider a representative primary-sector firm's behavior when the possibility of contracting out some of its workforce exists. The firm earns a fixed revenue for a fixed output, so profit maximization requires the minimization of the present value of expected total costs. This minimization problem involves two decisions: the firm must choose the level of general skills that it requires of its workforce, and it must decide whether to operate with all tasks performed in-house or to contract out and use temporary workers for some of those tasks. As illustrated in what follows, the firm's decision to outsource some fraction of its jobs rather than to have all jobs performed in-house is a discrete choice by the following logic. We assume that there are a fraction of workers in whom specific human-capital investments are profitable and that the firm will not replace these workers with contracted or temporary labor. The firm must then, however, decide whether to keep the jobs of the remaining workers in-house or to outsource them and/or fill them with temporary workers. The firm's choice is discrete rather than continuous because the difference between the marginal cost of a noncontracted, unskilled worker and the marginal cost of a contracted worker is unaffected by the total number of these types of workers employed. Thus, the firm either uses contracted and temporary workers for all the jobs that must be filled by unskilled workers, or it operates these jobs in-house.

The firm faces two expected-total-cost functions, one for the no-contracting state ("nc") and another for the state ("c") in which the firm contracts out and/ or uses temporary workers for some fraction of its jobs:

$$E(\text{PVTC})_{nc} = \frac{w_{nc}}{\delta} + \frac{\phi c(g)(d + \delta)}{\delta}, \tag{5.1}$$

$$E(\text{PVTC})_c = \frac{\phi w_c}{\delta} + \frac{\phi c(g)(d + \delta)}{\delta} + \frac{(1 - \phi)}{\delta}[\mu w_s + (1 - \mu)w_T] + Q. \tag{5.2}$$

In equation 5.1—the expectation of the present value of the firm's total costs if it does no contracting—the firm incurs costs from the wage bill (w_{nc}) and from training its workers. The function c represents the cost per unit of labor of investing in firm-specific human capital and is assumed to be declining in g, the level of general training possessed by the worker. The d parameter is the rate of depreciation of task-specific human capital, which can also be thought of as the speed of the product cycle. The parameter ϕ is the fraction of required efficiency units of labor in which the firm can profitably invest in specific human capital. We assume that the firm discounts future earnings over an infinite future at the rate δ.

We assume that w_{nc} is a collectively bargained wage that satisfies the Nash bargaining solution with bargaining power. The wage satisfying the Nash bargaining solution is a weighted average of the reservation wage and the rents due to the firm's investment in specific human capital (with weights determined by relative bargaining power). Note that the firm pays the wage w_{nc} to each of its workers. There is strong evidence of wage compression within firms, due both to unionization and to equity constraints. This latter source of wage compression was commonly cited in our interviews as a motivating factor in firms' decisions to outsource. We simplify the representation of this phenomena by assuming that all workers receive w_{nc}.

Equation 5.2 represents the expectation of the present value of total costs when the firm contracts out. The bargained wage w_c (derived in a manner similar to that in which w_{nc} is derived) is paid to the core workforce in the firm—that is, to ϕ workers. Of the remaining jobs (performed by the $1 - \phi$ workers), μ of them are contracted out and $1 - \mu$ filled with temporary workers, to whom the firm must pay w_T. The distinction between temporary and contract workers is not important for our analysis of the firm's decisions, but it will become important when we examine the causes of the declining unemployment in our market-equilibrium model. The contracted workers are compensated with wage w_s, the wage paid in the secondary sector, which the firm takes as given. We assume that, when the firm decides to contract out some of its jobs, it must pay a fixed, one-time coordination and restructuring cost, Q. The fixed cost of contracting can result from, for instance, the potentially substantial cost of reorganizing production so that some jobs can be kept in-house and others contracted and the cost of negotiating the complex contracts required to specify job requirements to the contracting firm.

Assuming a functional form for $c(g)$—the cost function for investing in specific human capital—which is declining at an increasing rate in g, and assuming a functional form for the reservation wage, which is increasing in the flow cost of g, we can derive the optimal level of general human capital that the firm will desire of its workforce (g^*). As demonstrated in Cohen and Dickens (2001), the optimal value of g for both regimes is increasing in the depreciation rate of specific skills (d). As the length of time over which the firm can amortize its investment in specific skills decreases (that is, as the firm is required to invest in specific skills more frequently), the firm is induced to reduce the cost of this investment by increasing g.

For sufficiently large values of the coordination cost Q, at low levels of d a firm will prefer to operate all its jobs in-house (that is, $E[PVTC]_{nc} < E[PVTC]_c$). When the product cycle is relatively lengthy, the firm's investment in the specific skills of its ϕ core workers depreciates less quickly. Less-general human capital is needed by core workers, and the equity constraint is less costly. Thus, the firm will prefer the cost of the equity constraint (paying the less-productive workers the same wage as the skilled workers) to the cost of coordination and restructuring.

Figure 5.10 plots the present value of expected total costs for the contracting and noncontracting regimes (equations 5.1 and 5.2) for a particular set of parameter values with the depreciation rate of specific human capital (d) ranging from 0.3 to 0.6.[39] We assume the following: (1) the firm invests in specific human capital for 75 percent of its workforce and divides the remaining 25 percent evenly between contractors and temps; (2) only half as many workers with specific training are required as workers without specific training to produce the same output; (3) workers and firms have equal bargaining power; (4) w_T and w_s are both 3 percent higher than the reservation wage (which is normalized to 1);

FIGURE 5.10 / Expected Total Costs for Contracting and Noncontracting Regimes

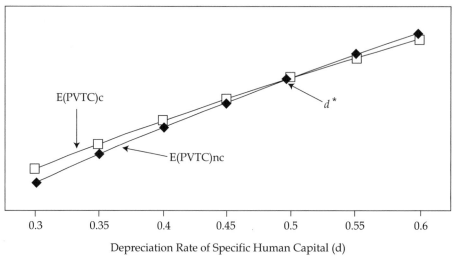

Depreciation Rate of Specific Human Capital (d)

Source: Authors' computations.

(5) the coordination cost is 15 percent of annual earnings; and (6) the discount rate is 5 percent.

At very low levels of d, the expected total costs of contracting and using temps for the noncore jobs are higher than the costs of operating the noncore jobs in-house. As d increases, the equity constraint becomes more costly. This is because, as the product cycle quickens, the firm demands a more generally skilled core workforce that will learn new tasks quickly as it is moved between production activities. This increase in the demand for g leads to an increase in the bargained wage paid to all workers (both skilled and unskilled). Note, however, that, although wages are increasing with g, since the wage is bargained, both the firm and the worker share the return on the increased value of the worker's general skills. Thus, workers' wages rise less than their reservation wages, and rents decline.[40] Figure 5.11 plots the increase in g^* and the decrease in rents per worker as the depreciation rate of specific human capital (d) increases. Note that there is a discrete jump up in g^* and a jump down in rents per worker when the firm shifts from the no-contracting to the contracting regime at d^*. When the firm begins to contract and use temporary workers for the tasks that do not require specific skills, the level of general skills required of its remaining core workers will increase sharply, and, thus, the portion of core workers' wages that can be attributed to their general training increases, decreasing rents.

From Firm to Market

Cohen and Dickens (2001) describes the market-equilibrium model in which the firm model is embedded in order to calibrate the potential effects of the changes

FIGURE 5.11 / Rents per Worker and General Human Capital (g^*)

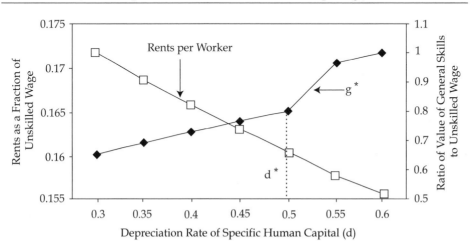

Source: Authors' computations.

that we describe on the efficiency of the labor market. Here, we describe the essence of how the firm-level changes translate into changes in overall labor-market efficiency.

Think of the American economy as starting out in the early 1980s with a high-wage primary sector where decisions about demand for general human capital and whether to contract are made as described earlier. We imagine at this time that there is little use of temporary help or contracting. There is also a low-wage secondary sector that pays a fixed minimum or an efficiency wage.

Unemployed workers choose to apply for jobs in either the primary or the secondary sector and allocate themselves between search in the two sectors so as to equate the expected income from searching in both sectors with the reservation wage. Secondary-sector workers can search for primary-sector employment while employed, but with a reduced efficiency compared to unemployed workers.

Once primary-sector firms make the move to contracting out on a large scale, a temporary-help sector is added to the economy. We can assume that all workers—including the unemployed—who want to temp can and that they will never count as unemployed while in that sector. Nonetheless, we assume that temps will search for primary-sector employment with efficiency between that of a secondary-sector worker and that of an unemployed worker.

Our model describes the improved efficiency of the labor market as deriving mainly from the decline in rents in the primary sector and the increased use of temporary workers. Prior to the rise of contracting out and temporary-help services, an increase in the depreciation rate of human capital increases the demand for general human capital in the primary sector and causes the rents in primary-sector jobs to fall (see the earlier discussion), making them less attractive. Unless primary-sector job vacancies are filled only by workers searching for jobs while employed in the secondary sector, this decline in the attractiveness of the primary sector will lead some unemployed workers to shift their search efforts from the primary to the secondary sector. In that sector, the vacancy rate is higher and equilibrium unemployment lower, with the result that these workers will spend a larger fraction of their time employed. They will also contribute to lowering the vacancy rate in the secondary sector, with the result that both the overall unemployment rate and the vacancy rate will decline.

When the depreciation rate of specific human capital rises high enough, primary-sector firms switch to outsourcing noncore jobs, as described earlier. When they do, there is a further abrupt decline in rents as well as a decline in the number of jobs available in the primary sector. These factors combine to make primary-sector jobs relatively less attractive, even if their wages remain high relative to the secondary sector. This causes the unemployment rate in the primary sector to drop further and more workers to search for the relatively easier to find jobs in the secondary sector. Further, the increased number of secondary-sector workers searching for a smaller number of primary-sector jobs—combined with the even more effective search of the temporary workers—displaces still more unemployed workers from the queue for primary-sector jobs. This further lowers unemployment and vacancies. Any ongoing increase in the speed of the product cycle and/or the value of flexibility in the primary sector will also increase the rate of depreciation of specific human capital and will continue to cause a decline in rents—translating into a decline in the NAIRU.

The parameters chosen yielded an unemployment rate of 6.9 percent when the vacancy rate was 1.5 percent. Unemployment resulted mainly from workers queuing for primary-sector jobs, which were assumed to make up about two-thirds of the jobs in the economy. The unemployment in the primary sector is created by rents equal to about 15 percent of the reservation wage of an unskilled worker. The job-destruction rate in both the primary and the secondary sectors is assumed to be 10 percent a year and the rate of depreciation of task-specific skills three times that.

Starting from this point, a 50 percent increase in the rate of depreciation of task-specific skills in primary-sector jobs investing heavily in such skills results in a reduction of labor rents in the primary-sector wage of about 30 percent. At a vacancy rate of 1.5 percent, it also leads to a reduction in the rate of unemployment to 4.7 percent, if no temporary workers are added to the labor force, or to 4.0 percent, if there is an increased use of temps amounting to 2.5 percent of the workforce. Thus, in this scenario, the reduction in rents reduces the unemployment rate associated with 1.5 percent vacancies by over 2 percentage points, while the increased use of temporary workers accounts for another 0.7 percentage points of decline.

An increase of 50 percent in the rate of depreciation of specific skills may seem large, but it may not be, given the dimension of the changes in work practices described in the literature and evident at the firms whose executives we interviewed. Further, it is the decline in labor rents that is the crucial intermediate variable between the increased depreciation rate and the decline in unemployment, and the change produced by the model is commensurate with the changes in interindustry wage differences documented in the previous section.

There seems to be considerable sensitivity of the results to parameters that are not known with precision. Thus, the actual effects could easily be much larger or much smaller. However, the results do show that we are able to tell a story that is consistent with the facts.

CONCLUSION

There is considerable agreement that the lowest sustainable rate of unemployment has declined in the United States in the last fifteen years. Examination of data on unemployment and vacancies suggests that the improvements in market efficiency were concentrated in two discrete periods. The first runs from 1985 to 1989. The second, which began in 1995, may still be continuing. These abrupt changes in the vacancy-unemployment relation, or the Beveridge curve, contrast starkly with the time path of changes that have been proposed by past researchers to explain the improvement in the inflation-unemployment relation, but they seem to mirror the time pattern of adoption of a host of new HRM methods—particularly in manufacturing, where a disproportionate share of unemployment is concentrated. The changes in efficiency also parallel declines in workers' rents as measured by interindustry wage differences.

We propose an explanation for improved overall efficiency of matching in the U.S. labor market since 1985 that links these synchronized changes in a sensible fashion. This approach has six steps, drawing on important developments in HRM by U.S. manufacturing firms that altered the demand side of the labor-matching function:

1. Technological innovation and increased competitive pressures (including those coming from abroad) have led to a speeding up of the rate at which product lines are switched and production (levels and lines) adjusted in primary-sector firms.

2. This speeding up of the product cycle causes investments in firm-specific human capital to have a higher rate of depreciation. We view this as the main cause of the adoption of the new HRM policies. These policies emphasize generality of skills and the ability to move between jobs over deep investment in a narrow set of skills. These policies also make more demands on workers' general skills and flexibility since they require more substituting between tasks by workers.

3. Higher demand for general skills means higher wages for those core workers who remain, but, because bargained wages do not increase one-for-one with reservation wages, the increased demand for general skills also lowers rents to workers. Internal equity constraints force firms to pay higher wages, not just to core employees utilizing flexibility, but also to those lower-skilled workers who have narrowly defined jobs. This creates a tension that mounts as demands for general human capital rise along with cost pressures.

4. Eventually the tensions between the rising demand for skills and the equity constraint lead primary-sector firms to adopt new forms of organization in which they contract out all jobs for which investments in specific human capital are not important (that is, jobs that are not part of the firm's core competency). This relaxing of the equity constraint leads to a further decline in rents for all workers, both those who now seek employment outside the primary sector and those in good jobs.

5. Falling rents make high-wage jobs relatively less desirable and reduce worker willingness to wait unemployed to get such jobs. Vacancies in the primary sector decline as well. More workers then apply for jobs in lower-wage sectors, where jobs are easier to find owing to the presence of more vacancies. This lowers both the unemployment rate and the vacancy rate.

6. The growth in the market for temporary-help services leads to the development of a large temporary-help sector in which workers have considerable freedom to search for jobs while still being employed most of the time (and almost never counting as being unemployed). These workers displace still more unemployed workers from the queue for high-wage jobs, the displaced workers again

switching their search to lower-wage jobs. This too reduces both the unemployment and the vacancy rates.

Our story is, admittedly, at present more an intriguing linkage of hypotheses with stylized facts than a directly tested model. Our two-step alignment of shifts in interindustry wage differentials, the Beveridge curve, and the adoption of HPWO, combined with complementary developments in American labor markets, requires supplementation with additional empirical analysis to be fully convincing. And, while we offer our story in opposition to certain classes of explanations for the decline in the NAIRU, such as those relying on gradual forces without clear institutional-transmission mechanisms, we do not claim that this breakdown of firms' internal equity constraints is the only cause of that decline.

Nevertheless, we believe that our approach to explaining the decline in the NAIRU offers promising aspects, in addition to being able to match with the specific time-series sequence of relevant shifts in the 1980s and 1990s:

First, we are able to synthesize several of the most notable developments in firms' use of workers into a coherent story—the widening use of HPWO and the increasing demand for more *generally* skilled employees in firms' core workforces; the rise in the share of temporary workers in blue-collar manufacturing employment; the sudden expansion of contracting out of noncore activities despite no apparent change in the supply curve of those services; the "mean leaning" downsizing movement of the early 1990s; the growing sense of the permanency of layoffs among workers in good jobs; the increased competitive pressures on American firms, starting in the 1980s, for production to be flexible and high quality; the increasing flexibility of compensation; and the decline in interindustry wage differentials. To date, all these developments have been largely ignored in considerations of the NAIRU.

Second, we are relying on what we believe to be a more realistic view of the importance of technological improvement, and IT specifically, than some of the more vague new-economy hypotheses do. In our view, technological change, international competition, financial pressure to cut costs, and increased customer demands result in a speeding up of the rate at which firms switch between products and a general increase in the demand for workforce flexibility. Workers must now make shallower investments in specific human capital more frequently, and this can be accomplished more quickly and at less cost if the workers possess more general skills. Thus, it is the change in work organization, and not the need to operate IT equipment, that drives the increased demand for general human capital.

Finally, we should note that, although we believe that the process of restructuring and the increase in temporary and contract workers may have facilitated today's low unemployment and low inflation, we do not claim that these changes have been without cost. There is no doubt that at least part of the widening of the income distribution can be attributed to the changes that we describe and that many individuals have had their lives severely disrupted by displacement from good-paying jobs at which they had worked for many years. But our work does suggest that there may have been some overlooked benefits, accruing both in the aggregate and to individual workers, from these changes beyond the improvements in productivity (and profitability) that others have already argued occurred.

A full cost-benefit analysis is well beyond the scope of this paper, but, if one were conducted, it would at a minimum have to balance the falling wages of less-skilled workers and the lost rents of workers displaced from good jobs with the gains of increased employment. If our story is right, the United States did get something beyond a redistribution of income for the changes that have occurred.

We are grateful to Janet Yellen, our discussant at the Sustainable Employment Conference, as well as to Gary Burtless, Robert Solow, David Weiman, and conference participants for their helpful comments. We thank Daniel Puskin and Yi Quan for dedicated research assistance and the Russell Sage, Century, and National Science Foundations (grant SBR-970925) for generous research support. Posen's work on this paper is part of the Institute for International Economics (IIE) project on globalization, the NAIRU, and monetary policy. The views expressed here, and any remaining errors, are solely those of the authors and not necessarily those of the Brookings Institution, of the IIE, or of any funding organization.

NOTES

1. The adoption of these methods of production has been remarkably widespread within U.S. firms. For instance, Osterman (2000) finds that, by 1997, 57.2 percent of the firms in his survey had adopted total-quality-management practices involving more than 50 percent of their core workforce.

2. We use the term *NAIRU* in this paper for conformity with the rest of the papers in this volume and common usage. As we use that term here we mean it to be synonymous with the term *LSRU*, or lowest sustainable rate of unemployment, which encompasses the NAIRU/natural-unemployment-rate concept of a unique unemployment rate consistent with constant inflation as well as the concepts described by George Akerlof, William Dickens, and George Perry (1996, 2000), concepts that allow a range of unemployment rates to be consistent with constant inflation.

3. Although we have interviewed only human-resource management executives from manufacturing, we believe that our theory of the restructuring that has taken place within these firms is applicable to other sectors as well. Manufacturing was the trendsetter, although the changes have spread widely. In future work, we plan to interview executives from service industries as well.

4. The formal model, which is only described here, is presented and analyzed in Cohen and Dickens (2001).

5. Dickens's (1999) comments on Katz and Krueger (1999) first raise this challenge.

6. Allowing for all these positive shocks and the effects for which we argue here would seem to explain all the change in the NAIRU and then some. However, we will also argue that some causes that have been cited by others are not likely to have made important contributions to reducing the NAIRU.

7. Where companies may have run their own cafeterias in the past, today over 90 percent of corporate food service is provided by contractors (with half that 90 percent provided by the three biggest contracting companies). And food service is only the tip of the iceberg. While it is very common for firms to outsource such services as security, groundskeeping, and payroll, some firms have outsourced everything from their computer services to their mail rooms. See the more detailed discussions that follow.

8. This sense of greater competitive pressure is commonly expressed by American business managers and the financial press. We note that this sense is difficult to reconcile with the rapid growth in corporate profits in the 1990s and the rise in consensual mergers without antitrust intervention since 1980. Looking for the sources of both this sensibility and the actual HRM changes is a primary topic for future research.

9. Katz and Krueger (1999) also suggest that the auspiciously timed movements in the U.S. Beveridge curve point toward a matching efficiency explanation for these improvements.

10. Blanchard and Diamond (1989) develop a theoretical model to support such a link.

11. For a discussion of the validity of this proxy, see also Zagorsky (1998). Note that the development of Internet advertising, search, and placement services may presently be transforming this process as well as decreasing the reliability of newspaper ads as a measure, as argued by Autor (2000c).

12. We do not attempt to plot the Beveridge curve after 1998 because of the widespread use of the Internet after this date, which makes us suspicious of the help-wanted index as a measure of vacancies. Were we to do so, the plot would show *both* unemployment and vacancies declining in 1999 and 2000.

13. Note that it is unlikely that any measurement problems with the help-wanted index could have caused such a pattern.

14. This does not rule out productivity-enhancing effects of IT in the last few years or even going forward. It simply points out that the labor-market developments that we believe are the main motivating force behind the decline in the NAIRU predate the growth in IT investment.

15. Including the Current Population Survey Displaced Worker Surveys (Farber 1997, 1998) and tenure supplements (Neumark, Polsky, and Hansen 1997; Neumark 2000), the Panel Study of Income Dynamics (Jaeger and Stevens 1999), the National Longitudinal Survey of Youth (Monks and Pizer 1998; Bernhardt et al. 1998), and the Survey of Income and Program Participation (Bansak and Raphael 1998).

16. The number of companies in their survey contracting out janitorial services increased by 18 percent between 1979 and 1987, and contracting out of machine maintenance increased by 6 percent, drafting services by 12 percent, accounting by 11 percent, and computers and technical support by 12 percent.

17. As another source for rising temp demand, Autor (2000a) argues that the new "unjust dismissal doctrine" adopted in the majority of American states has induced part (20

percent) of the growth in temps because firms wish to retain their discretion to fire workers with the fewest firm specific skills.

18. Houseman and Polivka (1999) explicitly downplay the role of screening for permanent hires as a major motivation for the move to flexible staffing arrangements. In their words, "Only a small minority of employers stated that they often move workers in flexible arrangements into regular positions" (8).

19. As Estevao and Lach (1999b) point out, this implies that the growth in temporary-help services was due to a change in the hiring behavior of firms, not to a rise in employment in those sectors that were disproportionate users of temps at the start of the 1990s. The finance, insurance, and real estate and the transportation, communications, and utilities sectors have shown a slow, although steady, rise in temporary-help services use since the early 1980s, and, in construction, the use of temporary-help services has been stable since 1987.

20. Abraham and Taylor (1993), Estevao and Lach (1999a), and Houseman and Polivka (1999) all come up with essentially this same list of three reasons, plus training and/or screening, as potential motivations. As will be seen in the next section, those of our corporate interviewees who discussed the motivations for moving to flexible staffing volunteer the same three reasons (but not training), while the one (clerical) temporary-agency executive interviewed largely denies there being migration from his agency to permanent employment by client firms.

21. While, to an economist, compensation is compensation, be it wages or benefits, there is reason to think that, in practice, the divide between wages and benefits and the absence of benefits in many temp jobs are significant in workers' minds. On the one hand, from an internal moral or equity point of view it is even harder to justify giving different workers different health coverage than it is to justify different wage premiums for seniority. There are also important tax considerations mandating that benefits being offered to some workers be widely shared within the firm for them to qualify as deductions from pretax earnings.

22. Whether these practices significantly increase worker productivity and production efficiency net of labor costs is subject to dispute (although no responsible observer appears to claim to have evidence that they harm productivity). See Casey Ichniowsky, Kathryn Snow, and Giovanna Prennushi (1997), Lynch and Black (1997), Cappelli and Neumark (1999), and Black and Lynch (2000).

23. American forms because, as Appelbaum and Batt (1994), along with others, note, many of these other practices were already implemented in different forms or combinations in Germany, Japan, Sweden, and elsewhere and the American firms and workers were very conscious of the international examples.

24. Osterman (1994) distinguishes between those establishments that have had these practices penetrate at least 50 percent of their core workforces and those at which these practices were merely adopted somewhere within the (sometimes large) organization. The figures for those merely adopting somewhere within the organization were 54.5 percent for teams, 43.4 percent for job rotation, 33.5 percent for TQM, and 40.8 percent for quality circles.

25. The Beveridge curve index is computed as the unemployment rate at a 1.5 percent vacancy rate in a given year (assuming that the Beveridge curve had a constant

slope), subtracted from 10, and then multiplied by 10 to put it on the same scale as the fraction of firms using job rotation.

26. We have reasonable confidence in the 1992 and 1997 data points since, as noted, Osterman (2000) used a genuine panel, resurveying previous respondents, to get the results, which were consistent with his new full survey.

27. In the future, there is likely to be a direct effect of IT on employers' and employees' job-search efficiency and perhaps even on outsourcing via telecommuting, as described in Autor (2000c), but these effects were felt in 1997 to 1998 at earliest, about the time the apparent new level of the NAIRU was reached (when employment pushed up wage inflation), and long after the Beveridge curve shifted. Thus, to repeat an earlier point, IT cannot be held responsible for the improvement in matching already evident by 1995.

28. A practice attested to by many whom we interviewed (see the next section).

29. We have empirical work under way to test whether the changes that appear obvious from visual inspection of the Beveridge curve can also account for the shifts in the Phillips curve. We are estimating a multiple-indicator model of the error processes in the two curves in a way that will allow us to test whether a common error component shares the time pattern evident in the Beveridge curve shifts and completely accounts for the movement of both curves. Developments in HPWO and interindustry wage differentials (discussed in the third section) also feed into this multiple-indicator model.

30. Eileen Appelbaum and Rosemary Batt (1994), John Duca (1998), and Assar Lindbeck and Dennis Snower (1996, 2000), along with many others, point to these forces of competition and pressures for high-value-added production as one of the major factors behind the shift to HPWO and to contracting out and/or wage decompression. A strict interpretation of these changes as being driven by a shortening of the narrowly defined product cycle is not supported by the one source of data that we could find. Brent Moulton and Karin Moses (1997) do not find any significant change in the fraction of items leaving the CPI product survey between 1983 to 1984 and 1995. However, these are the only dates for which data are available, and the years are not at comparable points in the business cycle.

31. These interviews were conducted with a guarantee of complete anonymity, and all quotations given here have been cleared with the interview subjects.

32. Lisa Lynch has pointed out to us that HRM managers are more likely to be excited about HPWO practices than average management is and may overstate their actual implementation. In future research, we intend to interview shop managers to document the extent of HPWO usage.

33. Interestingly, the lower-tech and/or higher-unionization firm was part of the majority here: "The significant increase in the variety of products produced has led to increased demand for workers with a broader skill base. In the older plants, workers always rotated between machines. . . . In the newer plants, workers are reassigned almost on a daily basis."

34. Measured by the dispersion of the residuals of a human-capital wage equation, with controls for individual characteristics such as age, gender, education, location, and occupation.

35. Krueger and Summers (1987) interpret interindustry wage differences as indicating the presence of efficiency wages, while Kevin Murphy and Robert Topel (1987) argue that interindustry wage differences may reflect compensating wage differences or unobservable human capital. For a review of the evidence, see William Dickens and Kevin Lang (1993).

36. The latter being the predicted unemployment rate at a 1.5 percent vacancy rate in a given year, subtracted from 10, then multiplied by 10.

37. Preliminary analysis of annual earnings data from the CPS does not show declining interindustry wage differences. We are investigating this discrepancy.

38. In contrast to these results, very recent work with survey and firm data by David Levine et al. (forthcoming) finds that the variance and persistence of employer wage effects appear to be fairly stable in the 1990s. We have not yet had the opportunity to examine, and perhaps thereby reconcile, these results in light of the clear (and opposing) ones that emerge from our use of a standard methodology on wage data. But we would note that, to the extent that firms are specializing in employing either low- or high-wage workers, there would be a tendency for firm differences to grow at the same time that industry differences might decline.

39. If the time period of analysis is assumed to be one year, one can interpret a value of $d = 0.3$ to mean that workers must be retrained to learn a new task roughly once every three years.

40. Rents are defined as wages minus reservation wages.

REFERENCES

Abraham, Katherine. 1987. "Help-Wanted Advertising, Job Vacancies, and Unemployment." *Brookings Papers on Economic Activity* (1): 207–43.

Abraham, Katherine, and Susan Taylor. 1993. "Firms' Use of Outside Contractors: Theory and Evidence." *NBER* working paper no. 4468. Cambridge, Mass.: National Bureau of Economic Research.

Akerlof, George, William Dickens, and George Perry. 1996. "The Macroeconomics of Low Inflation." *Brookings Papers on Economic Activity* (1): 1–60.

———. 2000. "Near-Rational Wage and Price Setting and the Long-Run Phillips Curve." *Brookings Papers on Economic Activity* (1): 1–45.

Appelbaum, Eileen, and Rosemary Batt. 1994. *The New American Workplace: Transforming Work Systems in the United States.* Ithaca, N.Y.: ILR Press.

Autor, David. 2000a. "Outsourcing at Will: Unjust Dismissal Doctrine and the Growth of Temporary Help Employment." *NBER* working paper no. 7560. Cambridge, Mass.: National Bureau of Economic Research.

———. 2000b. "Why Do Temporary Help Firms Provide Free General Skills Training?" *NBER* working paper no. 7637. Cambridge, Mass.: National Bureau of Economic Research.

———. 2000c. "Wiring the Labor Market." *NBER* working paper no. 7959. Cambridge, Mass.: National Bureau of Economic Research.

Autor, David, Frank Levy, and Richard Murnane. 2000. "Upstairs, Downstairs: Computer-Skill Complementarity and Computer-Labor Substitution on Two Floors of a Large

Bank." *NBER* working paper no. 7870. Cambridge, Mass.: National Bureau of Economic Research.

Bansak, Cynthia, and Steven Raphael. 1998. "Have Employment Relationships in the United States Become Less Stable?" Mimeo. University of California at San Diego, August.

Bernhardt, Annette, Martina Morris, Mark Handcock, and Marc Scott. 1998. "Job Instability and Wage Inequality among Young Men: A Comparison of Two NLS Cohorts." Mimeo. New York: Russell Sage Foundation.

Black, Sandra, and Lisa Lynch. 2000. "What's Driving the New Economy: The Benefits of Workplace Innovation." *NBER* working paper no. 7479. Cambridge, Mass.: National Bureau of Economic Research.

Blanchard, Olivier, and Peter Diamond. 1989. "The Beveridge Curve." *Brookings Papers on Economic Activity* (1): 1–76.

———. 1990. "The Cyclical Behavior of the Gross Flows of U.S. Workers." *Brookings Papers on Economic Activity* (2): 85–155.

Bresnahan, Timothy, Erik Brynjolfsson, and Lorin Hitt. 1999. "Information Technology, Workplace Organization, and the Demand for Skilled Labor: Firm-Level Evidence." *NBER* working paper no. 7136. Cambridge, Mass.: National Bureau of Economic Research.

Burgess, Simon, Julia Lane, and David Stevens. 2000. "Job Flows, Worker Flows, and Churning." *Journal of Labor Economics* 18(3): 473–502.

Burtless, Gary. 1999. "Comment on Katz and Krueger." *Brookings Papers on Economic Activity* (1): 66–72.

Cannon, Sandra, Bruce Fallick, Michael Lettau, and Raven Sals. 2000. "Has Compensation Become More Flexible?" Mimeo. Federal Reserve Board, April.

Cappelli, Peter, and David Neumark. 1999. "Do 'High Performance' Work Practices Improve Establishment Level Outcomes?" *NBER* working paper no. 7374. Cambridge, Mass.: National Bureau of Economic Research.

Cohen, Jessica, and William Dickens. 2001. "The Consequences for Labor Market Efficiency of the New Human Resource Management Practices." Working paper. Washington, D.C.: Brookings Institution.

Dickens, William. 1999. "Comment on Katz and Krueger." *Brookings Papers on Economic Activity* (1): 72–79.

———. 1986. "Wages, Employment, and the Threat of Collective Action by Workers." NBER working paper 1856. Cambridge, Mass.: National Bureau of Economic Research.

Dickens, William, and Lawrence Katz. 1987a. "Inter-Industry Wage Differences and Industry Characteristics." In *Unemployment and the Structure of Labor Markets,* edited by Kevin Lang and Jonathan Leonard. New York: Blackwell.

———. 1987b. "Inter-Industry Wage Differences and Theories of Wage Determination." *NBER* working paper no. 2271. Cambridge, Mass.: National Bureau of Economic Research.

Dickens, William, and Kevin Lang. 1993. "Labor Market Segmentation: Reconsidering the Evidence." In *Labor Economics: Problems Analyzing Labor Markets,* edited by William Darity. Norwell, Mass.: Kluwer Academic.

Duca, John. 1998. "How Increasing Product Market Competition May Be Reshaping America's Labor Markets." *Federal Reserve Bank of Dallas Economic Review.* Fourth Quarter: 2–16.

Dunne, Timothy, Lucia Foster, John Haltiwanger, and Kenneth Troske. 2000. "Wage and Productivity Dispersion in U.S. Manufacturing: The Role of Computer Investment."

NBER working paper no. 7465. Cambridge, Mass.: National Bureau of Economic Research.

Estevao, Marcello, and Saul Lach. 1999a. "The Evolution of the Demand for Temporary Help Supply Employment in the United States." *NBER* working paper no. 7427. Cambridge, Mass.: National Bureau of Economic Research.

———. 1999b. "Measuring Temporary Labor Outsourcing in U.S. Manufacturing." *NBER* working paper no. 7421. Cambridge, Mass.: National Bureau of Economic Research.

Farber, Henry. 1997. "The Changing Face of Job Loss in the United States, 1981–1995." *Brookings Papers on Economic Activity: Microeconomics*: 55–142.

———. 1998. "Has the Rate of Job Loss Increased in the Nineties?" Working paper no. 394. Princeton Industrial Relations Section.

Houseman, Susan, and Anne Polivka. 1999. "The Implications of Flexible Staffing Arrangements for Job Stability." Staff working paper no. 99–56. Kalamazoo: W. E. Upjohn Institute for Employment Research.

Ichniowski, Casey, Kathryn Snow, and Giovanna Prennushi. 1997. "The Effects of Human Resource Management Practices on Productivity: A Study of Steel Finishing Lines." *American Economic Review* 87(3): 291–313.

Idson, Todd, and Robert Valletta. 1996. "Seniority, Sectoral Decline, and Employee Retention: An Analysis of Layoff Unemployment Spells." *Journal of Labor Economics* 14(4): 654–76.

Jaeger, David, and Ann Huff Stevens. 1999. "Is Job Stability in the United States Falling? Reconciling Trends in the Current Population Survey and Panel Study of Income Dynamics." *IZA* discussion paper no. 35. Bonn, Germany: Forschungsinstitut Zur Zukunftder Arbeit (Institute for the Study of Labor), March.

Katz, Lawrence, and Alan Krueger. 1999. "The High Pressure U.S. Labor Market of the 1990s." *Brookings Papers on Economic Activity* (1): 1–65.

Katz, Lawrence, and Bruce Meyer. 1990. "Unemployment Insurance, Recall Expectations, and Unemployment Outcomes." *Quarterly Journal of Economics* 105(4): 973–1002.

Katz, Lawrence, and Lawrence Summers. 1989. "Industry Rents: Evidence and Implications." *Brookings Papers on Economic Activity: Microeconomics*: 209–75.

Krueger, Alan, and Lawrence Summers. 1987. "Reflections on the Inter-Industry Wage Structure." In *Unemployment and the Structure of Labor Markets*, edited by Kevin Lang and Jonathan Leonard. New York: Blackwell.

Lawler, Edward, Susan Mohrman, and Gerald Ledford. 1992. *Employer Involvement and Total Quality Management: Policies, and Results in Fortune 1000 Companies*. San Francisco: Jossey-Bass.

Lebow, David, Louise Sheiner, Larry Slifman, and Martha Starr-McCluer. 1999. "Recent Trends in Compensation Practices." Mimeo. Federal Reserve Board, July.

Levine, David, Dale Belman, Gary Charness, Erica Groshen, and K. C. O'Shaughnessy. Forthcoming. *How New Is the "New Employment Contract": Evidence from North American pay Practices*. Kalamazoo, Mich.: W. E. Upjohn Institute for Employment Research.

Lindbeck, Assar, and Dennis Snower. 1996. "Reorganization of Firms and Labor-Market Inequality." *American Economic Review* 86(2): 315–21.

———. 2000. "Multi-Task Learning and the Reorganization of Work: From Tayloristic to Holistic Organization." *Journal of Labor Economics* 18(3): 353–75.

Lynch, Lisa, and Sandra Black. 1997. "Beyond the Incidence of Training." Discussion paper no. 362. London School of Economics, Centre for Economic Performance.

Manski, Charles, and John Straub. 2000. "Worker Perceptions of Job Insecurity in the

Mid-1990s: Evidence from the Survey of Economic Expectations." *Journal of Human Resources* 35(3): 447–79.

Mincer, Jacob, and Stephan Danninger. 2000. "Technology, Unemployment, and Inflation." *NBER* working paper no. 7817. Cambridge, Mass.: National Bureau of Economic Research.

Monks, James, and Steven Pizer. 1998. "Trends in Voluntary and Involuntary Job Turnover." *Industrial Relations* 37(4): 440–59.

Moulton, Brent, and Karin Moses. 1997. "Addressing the Quality Change Issue in the Consumer Price Index." *Brookings Papers on Economic Activity* (1): 305–49.

Murphy, Kevin, and Robert Topel. 1987. "Unemployment, Risk, and Earnings: Testing for Equalizing Wage Differences in the Labor Market." In *Unemployment and the Structure of Labor Markets,* edited by Kevin Lang and Jonathan Leonard. New York: Blackwell.

Neumark, David. 2000. "Changes in Job Stability and Job Security: A Collective Effort to Untangle, Reconcile, and Interpret the Evidence." *NBER* working paper no. 7600. Cambridge, Mass.: National Bureau of Economic Research.

Neumark, David, Daniel Polsky, and Daniel Hansen. 1997. "Has Job Stability Declined Yet? New Evidence for the 1990s." *NBER* Working Paper no. 6330. Cambridge, Mass.: National Bureau of Economic Research.

Oliner, Stephen, and Daniel Sichel. 1994. "Computers and Output Growth Revisited: How Big Is the Puzzle?" *Brookings Papers on Economic Activity* (2): 273–317.

———. 2000. "The Resurgence of Growth in the Late 1990s: Is Information Technology the Story?" *Journal of Economic Perspectives* 14(4): 3–22.

Osterman, Paul. 1994. "How Common Is Workplace Transformation and Who Adopts It?" *Industrial and Labor Relations Review* 47(2): 173–88.

———. 2000. "Work Reorganization in an Era of Restructuring: Trends in Diffusion and Effects on Employee Welfare." *Industrial and Labor Relations Review* 53(2): 179–96.

Otoo, Maria Ward. 1999. "Temporary Employment and the Natural Rate of Unemployment." Mimeo. Federal Reserve Board, July.

Polivka, Anne, and Stephen Miller. 1995. "The CPS after the Redesign: Refocusing the Economic Lens." Mimeo. Bureau of Labor Statistics, March.

Segal, Lewis, and Daniel Sullivan. 1995. "The Temporary Labor Force." *Federal Reserve Bank of Chicago Economic Perspectives* 19(2): 2–19.

———. 1997. "The Growth of Temporary Services Work." *Journal of Economic Perspectives* 11(spring): 117–36.

Shimer, Robert. 1998. "Why Is the U.S. Unemployment Rate So Much Lower?" *NBER Macroeconomics Annual* 13: 11–16.

Sichel, Daniel. 1997). *The Computer Revolution: An Economic Perspective.* Washington, D.C.: Brookings Institution.

Zagorsky, Jay. 1998. "Job Vacancies in the United States: 1923–1994." *Review of Economics and Statistics* 80(2): 338–45.

Chapter 6

The Effects of Growing International Trade on the U.S. Labor Market

George Johnson and Matthew J. Slaughter

Since the 1960s, the United States has moved from being an essentially closed to being a fairly open economy, and it is likely that this trend will continue into the foreseeable future. The purpose of this paper is to explore the major implications of the increasing openness of the economy for the performance and the potential of the U.S. labor market.

The first section looks briefly at the major trends in recent decades in U.S. wages and in trade and other measures of U.S. economic openness. Trade has been continuing to increase, and only since about 1996 have the real wages of production workers stopped (temporarily?) their long decline both in absolute terms and relative to more-skilled workers.

The major contribution of the paper is to be found in the second section, in which we attempt to explicate and evaluate the open-economy approach to medium- and long-run labor-market analysis. The increasing openness of the U.S. economy means that the distribution of earnings among the labor force is both more susceptible to foreign developments and less responsive to domestic policies that attempt to mitigate unfavorable developments. How far the U.S. economy has progressed toward the textbook case of a small economy facing completely exogenous prices is a matter on which there is some disagreement among economists. Barring major international political catastrophes, however, the trend toward this benchmark situation is likely to continue.

The third section of the paper looks at two shorter-run issues. First, what is the evidence concerning trends in the vulnerability of the U.S. economy to foreign "shocks"? (Our tentative answer is that this vulnerability does not seem to have increased.) Second, what are the potential effects of foreign prices on the natural rate of unemployment in the United States?

THE MAJOR STYLIZED FACTS ABOUT GLOBALIZATION AND U.S. WAGES

The Rising Globalization of the U.S. Economy

In the past few decades, the United States has become much more open to cross-border flows of goods, people, and capital. Figures 6.1 through 6.3 offer three pictures of globalization at work on the U.S. economy. Figure 6.1 plots U.S. exports and imports, each as a share of U.S. GDP. Figure 6.2 plots the share of the total U.S. population that is foreign born, and figure 6.3 plots the market value of total inward and outward foreign-direct-investment (FDI) stocks, each as a share of U.S. GDP. All three figures show rising flows of goods and services, people, and multinational capital across U.S. borders in recent decades.

In figure 6.1, from a 1970 level of about 5 percent for both imports and exports, exports/GDP has risen to 12 percent, and imports/GDP has risen to 15 percent. This is, of course, part of a long-term, worldwide trend. World exports as a fraction of total world production rose steadily from the early nineteenth century until the outbreak of World War I and, after a severe decline through

FIGURE 6.1 / Globalization in Terms of U.S. Imports and Exports

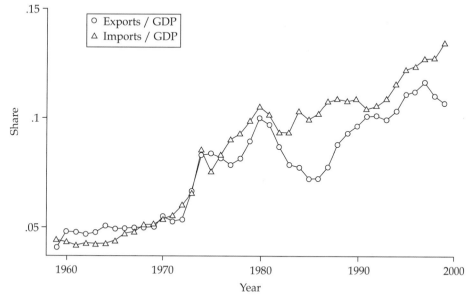

Source: U.S. Bureau of the Census, Bureau of Economic Analysis.

Note: The figure plots the value of total U.S. exports and imports, each as a share of U.S. GDP.

World War II, have been rising since 1950 to the present value of about 15 percent.[1]

Figure 6.2 documents the rising presence of immigrants in the U.S. economy. Since the 1960s, the United States has undergone a surge in immigration. The share of the U.S. population that is foreign born reached 10.4 percent in 2000, up from a 150-year low of 5 percent in 1970 (but still below the 1910 high of 15 percent). During the 1990s, an average of 1 million legal immigrants and 300,000 illegal immigrants entered the United States each year, accounting for 40 percent the decade's population growth.[2] As we will discuss subsequently, relative to that of U.S. natives the skill mix of recent immigrants displays the "twin-peaks" phenomenon: there are higher concentrations of both the very low skilled and the very high skilled among immigrants than among the native born. The high rate of immigration of both very low- and very high-skilled labor is, in principle, a variable that can be controlled by policy. We will discuss the labor-market effects of current and prospective U.S. immigration policy.

Figure 6.3 shows the ongoing rise in cross-border FDI. Both inward and outward FDI flows surged in the second half of the 1980s and then again more dramatically in the second half of the 1990s. It is well-known that the largest share of world FDI flows is those from high-income countries into other high-

FIGURE 6.2 / Globalization in Terms of U.S. Immigrant Inflows

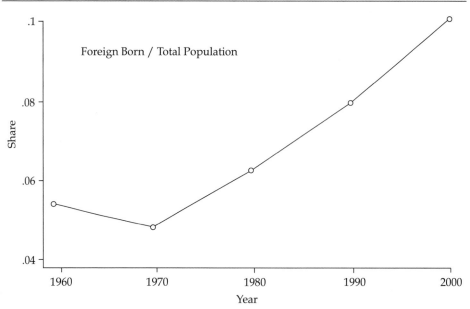

Sources: Borjas, Freeman, and Katz (1997, table 1, 4); U.S. Bureau of the Census (2000).

Note: The vertical axis plots the foreign-born U.S. population as a share of the total U.S. population.

FIGURE 6.3 / Globalization in Terms of U.S. Inward and Outward FDI

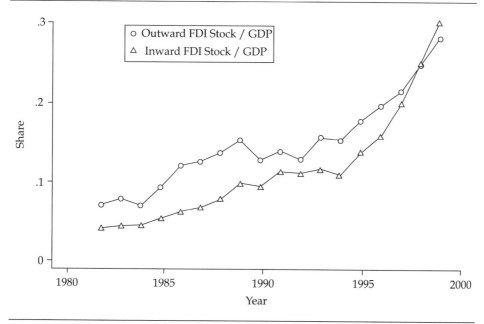

Source: Scholl (2000, table 2).

Note: The vertical axis plots the market value of total inward and outward FDI stocks, each as a share of U.S. GDP.

income countries, and figure 6.3 shows the United States to be an important player on both sides of these flows. Manufacturing has traditionally been a significant sector for FDI flows, but a rising share of FDI activity has been accounted for by service sectors such as finance, insurance, and real estate.

Changes in U.S. Relative and Real Incomes

As cross-border flows of goods, people, and capital have risen, the U.S. labor market has experienced important changes in both relative and real incomes. Less-skilled Americans have experienced poor income performance in both relative and real terms.

FACT 1: RISING INEQUALITY ACROSS SKILLS Figure 6.4 shows the rising U.S. skill premium. For each year since 1958, the figure plots for U.S. manufacturing the average annual earnings of a nonproduction worker divided by the average annual earnings of a production worker, a relation based on research documenting that nonproduction workers tend to have more labor-market skills than do production workers. This ratio of nonproduction/production earnings, one possible measure of the skill premium, generally declined from the late 1950s until the

FIGURE 6.4 / The Rising U.S. Skill Premium

Source: The National Bureau of Economic Research Productivity Database.

Notes: The skill premium is measured as the ratio of the average annual wages of nonproduction workers to the average annual wages of production workers in U.S. manufacturing.

late 1970s. But, since about 1979, this skill premium has been rising sharply. In 1979, the average nonproduction worker earned about 50 percent more than did the average production worker, but, by 1996, this gap had grown to over 70 percent.

This rise in the U.S. skill premium has been going on since the late 1970s *across all skill measures,* for example, education, experience, and job classification. For example, in 1979, male college-educated workers earned on average 30 percent more than male high school–educated workers. By 1995, this premium for college-educated workers had risen to about 70 percent. Perusal of the overall wage distribution reveals a similar picture of rising inequality. Both the 90/50 and the 50/10 earnings ratios for males were flat or declining from 1967 until about 1979, but they then rose steadily from 1979 through 1995. Obviously, the exact timing and magnitude of skill-premium changes vary somewhat with the data series used. But all series show the same dramatic picture of sharply rising returns to skills.[3]

FIGURE 6.5 / Stagnant U.S. Average Real Wages

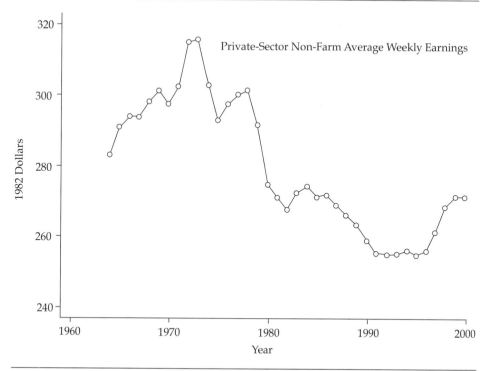

Source: U.S. Department of Labor, Bureau of Labor Statistics, Nonfarm Payroll Statistics from the Current Employment Statistics, Data Series EES00500051, downloaded from *http://www.bls.gov/datahome.htm.*

FACT 2: SLUGGISH GROWTH IN AVERAGE REAL WAGES Turn now from relative to real wages. In addition to relative-wage changes, average real-wage growth in the United States has been very sluggish since the early 1970s. Figure 6.5 documents this real-wage slowdown. For all nonfarm workers in the private sector for each year since 1964, the figure plots U.S. average weekly earnings in real 1982 dollars (that is, nominal dollars deflated by a price index set equal to 1 in 1982). From 1964 through 1973, U.S. average real weekly earnings rose strongly, from just over $280 to nearly $320. But, since 1973, real earnings have slid dramatically, falling below $260 by the mid-1990s. By 2000, real earnings had recovered to just under $280, back to early 1980s levels, but still well below the 1973 peak.

Of course, the exact pattern in U.S. real wages depends on both the measure of nominal wages (for example, just salary or all compensation, including fringes) and the measure of the price index used to translate nominal into real wages (for example, a consumer price index or a producer price index). A good deal of research has examined these measurement issues (see, for example, Council of Economic Advisers 1997; and Abraham, Spletzer, and Stewart 1999).

But, across a wide range of possible real-wage measures, there is a consistent pattern: growth in average real earnings in the United States has been very sluggish since the early 1970s.

FACT 3: ZERO OR EVEN NEGATIVE REAL-WAGE GROWTH FOR MOST U.S. WORKERS
The combination of the sharp rise in income inequality and the sharp slowdown in real-wage growth means that real-wage growth has been flat or even negative for less-skilled U.S. workers in recent decades. Figure 6.6 (reproduced from Katz and Krueger 2000) shows this pattern. This figure plots real-wage patterns from 1973 to 1998 for four different skill groups: more-skilled workers at the 90th percentile of the overall wage distribution; medium-skilled workers at the 50th percentile; less-skilled workers at the 10th percentile; and workers earning the statutory minimum wage. For each group, wages are benchmarked to 1979 levels, so all four lines intersect at 0 that year. Only more-skilled workers at the 90th percentile enjoyed higher real wages in 1998 than in 1979; real wages for all other skill groups were lower in 1998 than in 1979.

FIGURE 6.6   /   Differential Real-Wage Performance Across Skill Groups

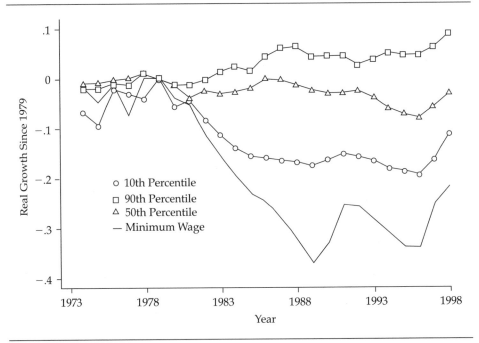

Source: Katz and Krueger (2000, figure 4).

Notes: Average real earnings measured as nominal earnings deflated by the CPI-UX1. Wage growth is shown for four different skill groups: more-skilled workers at the 90th percentile of the overall wage distribution; medium-skilled workers at the 50th percentile; less-skilled workers at the 10th percentile; and workers earning the statutory minimum wage. Each group's real-wage growth is relative to its 1979 level.

Again, exact real-wage movements depend on many measurement issues, but the overall pattern of differing real-wage performance across skill groupings is clear for all measures. For example, the 2000 *Economic Report of the President* (Council of Economic Advisers 2000) shows the dramatically different real-income performance for families across different quintiles of the overall income distribution. From 1973 to 1993, the bottom 40 percent of families suffered real-income declines—the lowest quintile nearly 1 percent per year and the second quintile about 0.3 percent per year. The third quintile experienced basically no real-income growth. Only the fourth and top quintiles enjoyed real-income increases—about 0.4 and 1.3 percent per year, respectively. So, from 1973 through 1993, 60 percent of all U.S. households had flat or declining real incomes. Looking at less-skilled groups, Richard Freeman (1995) reports that the real hourly earnings of male high-school graduates fell by 20 percent from 1979 through 1993, with an even larger 30 percent decline for "entry-level" male high-school graduates.

We make two final points about U.S. wages. First, real-wage growth for all skill groups has been much stronger since about 1996—but these impressive real-wage gains of the past few years have *not* undone the poor performance of the past few decades. Figures 6.5 and 6.6 document this strength for all workers and for different skill groups, respectively. The same strength is evident in other earnings data: for example, the 2000 *Economic Report of the President* (Council of Economic Advisers 2000) reports real-income growth of 2 to 2.5 percent across all five family-income quintiles from 1993 to 1998. This real-wage growth at all levels of the skill distribution is important, and research on its causes and prospects has recently been emerging.[4]

But it is important to put this recent growth in context to see that it has *not* completely undone the poor performance of recent decades. In figure 6.5, we see that, in 2000, average real earnings had returned to early 1980s levels—but this was still well below the pre-1980 levels. Similarly, in figure 6.6, we see that, by 2000, the growth since 1996 had not returned wages to 1979 levels for workers at the 50th and 10th percentiles.

Second, recent U.S. wage changes differ markedly from U.S. wage movements earlier in the twentieth century. Paul Krugman (1992) reports that, from 1900 to 1970, U.S. output per worker rose at an average annual rate of 2.3 percent—with an even higher rate of 2.8 percent during the 1950s and 1960s. From 1970 through the start of the 1990s, however, output per worker grew at only 1.2 percent per year. To the extent that workers earn their marginal product, these productivity measures also indicate the likely pattern of real wages. And, in earlier decades, inequality across skills and households was generally flat or falling, not rising dramatically. For example, from 1948 through 1973, family income grew faster for the lowest quintile than for the highest (Council of Economic Advisers 2000).

Summary

The facts presented in this section outline the juxtaposition of rising U.S. integration with the world economy with adverse wage developments for less-skilled

U.S. workers. The timing of this juxtaposition suggests that the former has contributed to the latter.[5] But do economic theory and empirical evidence bear this out? In our next section, we try to answer this question. Before we do that, however, we comment on the prospects of further integration of the United States into the world economy.

There are many reasons to suppose that this process will continue: falling transportation and communication costs; technological innovations that widen the scope of traded goods and services; growth in developing countries that builds their capacity to produce and trade. But set against these relative certainties related to "natural" trade barriers are the relative uncertainties of political trade barriers. Rosy prognostications made in August 1914 on the basis of recent decades were almost surely off the mark. As Dani Rodrik (2000) cogently discusses, the extent of integration depends heavily on political developments—in particular, changes in legal institutions that allow for the enforcement of contracts. Rodrik believes that these changes—which require a fairly drastic alteration in world political organization—are more likely than not to occur, albeit slowly.

We would agree with a forecast that, over the next thirty years, the degree of openness of the U.S. economy will continue to increase. The standard error of such a forecast, however, is fairly large. That said, we now turn to an analysis of the labor-market effects of this increased openness.

HOW DOES GLOBALIZATION AFFECT THE LONG-RUN PERFORMANCE OF U.S. LABOR MARKETS?

Having demonstrated the ongoing integration of the U.S. economy with the world economy via cross-border flows of goods and services, people, and physical capital, we turn to the labor-market effects of this integration. How are employment, real wages, and income distribution determined in an open economy? What is the implication of increased openness for labor-market behavior? Conversely, how does openness condition labor-market responses to a range of macro- and microeconomic policies?

In this section, we present two different, polar models of labor-market behavior in an open economy. The first model, which is commonly used in labor economics, ignores the possibility of trade between nations in *any* goods; that is, it assumes autarky. The second model is derived from the standard Heckscher-Ohlin (HO) trade model, the key features of which are many distinct output sectors and some goods traded between the relevant national economies. As we will show, the fundamental difference between these "trade" and "labor" perspectives is the shape of the national relative-labor-demand function. The distinction is not merely academic, for the two perspectives make radically different predictions about whether and how globalization matters for labor-market outcomes. After systematically presenting the labor-market side of the HO trade model, we then discuss how empirically relevant this model really is to the U.S. economy of the 1990s and the near future.

Following the usual approach to questions involving the medium and long run of the U.S. economy, in this section we will assume that labor markets are characterized by full employment and, thus, that the relevant labor-market outcomes are real and relative wages. The implications of this section, therefore, are relevant to periods of about three years or more, in which there is sufficient time for prices to adjust to shocks.[6] In our third section, we will relax this assumption and consider linkages between trade and employment levels.

The Overall Framework: Demand, Supply, and Institutions

Applying the basic economist's tool kit, equilibrium wages can change because of one of three shifts: in relative labor demand, in relative labor supply, or in labor-market institutions. The usual suspects believed responsible for shifts in these three ingredients include international trade, technological change, the composition of aggregate demand, demographic trends, immigration, changes in real minimum wages, and changes in the scope and power of unions or other nonmarket forces.

The contrast alluded to above between the labor-economics framework and the multisector trade framework has been an important issue in the scores of academic studies produced over the past decade exploring the causes of the rising U.S. skill premium. Within this research area, sharp disagreements have arisen about the proper methodology for attacking the problem. We will demonstrate that the essence of these disagreements is the shape of the national labor-demand schedule. From the labor economist's perspective, this schedule slopes downward everywhere. From the trade economist's perspective, it has infinitely elastic segments. This difference stems from different assumptions concerning the source of demand for the economy's output of some sectors.

The Labor Perspective

In a closed economy, the relative demand for more-skilled relative to less-skilled labor in each firm depends inversely on the relative wage of more- relative to that of less-skilled workers, conditional on production technology and product prices. To obtain the national labor-demand schedule, simply aggregate this relation across all firms in the country. More formally, let S and U be the quantities of more-skilled and less-skilled labor, respectively. Output in sector k, Y_k, is produced according to a constant-elasticity-of-substitution (CES) production function with an elasticity of substitution σ and technology parameters (to be discussed in what follows) A_k and δ_k; that is,

$$Y_k = A_k \left[\delta_k S_k^{1-1/\sigma} + (1 - \delta_k) U_k^{1-1/\sigma} \right]^{\sigma/(\sigma-1)}. \tag{6.1}$$

All firms choose employment of S and U to maximize profits subject to exogenous factor prices and production technology in equation 6.1. First-order conditions imply that optimal relative labor demand in each firm is

$$\left(\frac{S}{U} \right)_k = \left(\frac{\delta_k}{1 - \delta_k} \right)^{\sigma} \left(\frac{w_s}{w_u} \right)^{-\sigma}. \tag{6.2}$$

In a one-sector economy, equation 6.2 describes economywide relative labor demand. In an economy with many industries, the relative-labor-demand function also depends on the parameters of the industry-product-demand functions (see Bound and Johnson 1992), but, aside from the messiness of its algebra, it is qualitatively similar to equation 6.2.

Figure 6.7 shows the national labor-market equilibrium in the labor framework. The RD curve is national relative labor demand, sloping downward as described above. The RS curve is the national endowment of skilled labor relative to unskilled labor.[7] National labor-market equilibrium is given by point E, where the two curves intersect at the national skill premium (with the level of each factor's real wage, not shown, given from each relevant first-order condition in the optimization leading to equation 6.2).

What forces can change wages? If national relative labor supply is given by $(S/U)^{SUP}$, then the change in the skill premium (where "hats" denote percentage changes in the bracketed quantities) is given by

$$\left(\frac{\hat{w}_s}{w_u} \right) = \left(\frac{\hat{\delta}}{1 - \delta} \right) - \frac{1}{\sigma} \left(\frac{\hat{S}}{U} \right)^{SUP}. \tag{6.3}$$

In equation 6.3, the first term on the right-hand side captures shifts in RD, the second term shifts in RS. Notice that, in this one-sector version, the RD shifts only with shifts in δ_k. This is technological change that has some "factor bias," that is, that alters the relative marginal productivity between skill groups. Skill-biased technological change (SBTC) raises δ_k and thereby shifts RD to the right; technological change that is biased toward less-skilled workers lowers δ_k and thereby shifts RD to the left.[8] Hicks-neutral technological change, represented in equation 6.1 by a shift in A_k, does not shift RD and thus does not affect the skill premium. It does, however, raise real wages for both types of labor proportionately.

What shifts the RS curve? From the labor perspective—despite the fact that the model was developed from the assumption of a closed economy—international trade is one possibility. The reason for this is that internationally traded goods embody the services of factors of production. For example, because the United States is well endowed with skilled labor relative to the rest of the world, it exports lots of skilled-labor services (in products like aircraft and software) and imports lots of unskilled-labor services (in products like textiles and toys).

FIGURE 6.7 / Labor-Market Equilibrium—the Labor Perspective

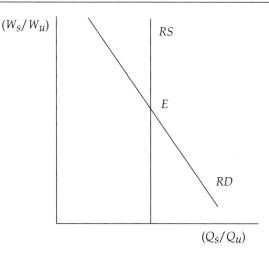

Notes: Skilled labor is subscripted *s* and unskilled labor *u*. The *RS* schedule is relative supply, and the *RD* schedule is relative demand.

This intuition of trade in factor services has led some labor researchers to calculate the effect of trade on wages as follows. First, use input-output tables to translate observed trade flows into the quantity of embodied factor services. Then treat these factor-service quantities as shifts in the "effective" U.S. labor supply (that is, the supply of people plus the supply of factor services embodied in trade flows), which, when interacted with the appropriate labor-demand elasticity, can quantify the effect of international trade on wages. Thus, trade is treated as a force shifting the *RS* schedule. Trade tends to increase U.S. inequality by shifting *RS* leftward thanks to the flow of factor services described earlier. Researchers such as Adrian Wood (1995) and George Borjas, Richard Freeman, and Lawrence Katz (1992, 1996, 1997) have used this "factor-content" approach. Such studies, however, find rather small trade effects, particularly for sample years beyond 1985 when the U.S. trade deficit was declining.

Beyond trade, domestic demographics can obviously shift *RS*. For the U.S. case, many researchers have focused on the baby-boom generation. This swell in the U.S. population increased college enrollments and skilled entrants into the labor force during the 1970s; since then, this swell has slackened somewhat (see, for example, Katz and Murphy 1992). This would suggest *RS* shifting right over time, albeit at different rates in different decades. Following David Ellwood (chapter 9 in this volume) at the end of this section we will conjecture what *RS* shifts lie ahead for the United States.

The Trade Perspective

The key contrast between the labor perspective and the trade perspective is that the latter assumes that international trade is important in some sectors of the economy. Many fundamental ideas in HO trade theory, for example, comparative advantage, require multiple sectors distinguished by their factor intensity, so the convenient assumption of a single sector made by labor (and macro) economists must be replaced. A multisector framework is also suggested by recent empirical work on SBTC, which has documented its pervasiveness across many disaggregated sectors (see, for example, Berman, Bound, and Griliches 1994; and Berman, Bound, and Machin 1998).

To derive the standard HO labor-demand schedule for a country, there are four crucial assumptions above and beyond that of multiple sectors of differing factor intensity. The first is perfect intersectoral factor mobility, which implies a single national wage for each factor. The second is that the country is "small," that is, unable to affect world product prices in perfectly competitive product markets. Third, the country need not be completely "open," that is, without any trade barriers, but trade barriers cannot be prohibitive. Fourth, consumers of traded goods are indifferent between goods produced domestically and those produced abroad. We will say more on these assumptions subsequently.

The HO production equilibrium obtained by the decentralized optimization of all profit-maximizing firms in a country is equivalent to that country choosing the national output mix that maximizes GNP subject to the constraints of world product prices, national factor supplies, national production technology, and, if the country is not completely open to trade, trade barriers (for example, Dixit and Norman 1980). This optimal output mix consists of both the sector chosen in which to concentrate production and production quantities. It also determines the national labor-demand schedule and thus the national wage structure. To derive the national labor-demand schedule, simply vary national factor supplies, and see how the optimization problem is re-solved as supplies vary.

Figure 6.8 does this derivation for the case of two factors (skilled and unskilled labor) and three sectors (an unskilled-labor-intensive good, a "middle"-factor-intensity good, and a skilled-labor-intensive good). Start with the leftmost downward-sloping branch, where the national relative supply of skilled labor is very low. Given this endowment, the country maximizes GNP by producing only one product, the unskilled-labor-intensive good. A relatively high quantity of unskilled labor is demanded, and, since skilled labor is relatively scarce, it earns a high relative wage. Now increase the relative supply of skilled labor, but by a small enough amount that GNP is still maximized by producing only the one product. Since only one product is made, there is no scope for output-mix effects, and the labor framework's one-sector intuition holds: to price themselves into full employment, skilled workers' relative wages must fall.

Now increase the supply of skilled labor until the first perfectly elastic portion is reached. Here, the country maximizes GNP by producing both the un-

FIGURE 6.8 / Labor-Market Equilibrium—The Trade Perspective

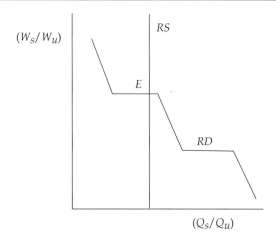

Notes: Skilled labor is subscripted *s* and unskilled labor *u*. The *RS* schedule is relative supply, and the *RD* schedule is relative demand.

skilled-labor-intensive product and the middle-factor-intensity product. With two products, there is now scope for output-mix effects to accommodate shifts in labor supplies. Additional skilled labor can be completely absorbed with no change in wages by increasing the output of the middle-factor-intensity good and reducing the output of the unskilled-labor-intensive good. Thanks to perfect interindustry factor mobility, the new skilled labor can be employed in middle-factor-intensity sector in combination with some skilled and unskilled labor moved from the unskilled-labor-intensive sector. Because its economy is open, the country can export to international markets whatever part of this new output mix it does not consume. And, because the county is small, the change in outputs going to world markets does not affect world product prices and thus does not induce any wage effects. Thus, the *RD* schedule has a flat portion where the *same* relative wage is consistent with a range of quantities of relative labor demanded. This insensitivity of national wages to national factor supplies is what Edward Leamer and James Levinsohn (1995) call the *factor-price-insensitivity* (FPI) theorem. The output-mix response to labor-supply change is commonly formalized in various statements of the Rybczynski (1955) theorem.

The remaining portions of *RD* follow the same intuition as just outlined. Beyond the first perfectly elastic portion, the country switches to producing just the middle-factor-intensity good; on the next perfectly elastic portion, it produces both that good and the skilled-labor-intensive good; and, on the last downward-sloping branch, it produces just the skilled-labor-intensive good. Note that, because a different set of products is made on each elastic part, each has different relative wages.

This derivation of figure 6.8 used an example with three goods and two factors, but it can be reinterpreted for the more general case of M factors and N tradable sectors. With N tradable sectors in the output mix, there are N zero-profit equations with M endogenously determined factor prices. If $N \geq M$, then FPI holds, with output-mix effects fully absorbing changes in national factor supplies. If $M > N$, then changes in factor supplies do trigger wage effects as well. Thus, in figure 6.6, the infinitely elastic parts of RD are where $N \geq M$, while the downward-sloping parts are where $M > N$. In the jargon of trade economists, each infinitely elastic segment of RD corresponds to a different *cone of diversification* in which a different set of diverse products is made in equilibrium.[9]

Closing the HO labor market just requires adding a relative-supply schedule to figure 6.8, such that national labor-market equilibrium is given by point E at the intersection of the two curves. We have drawn figure 6.8 assuming that equilibrium holds for a region with FPI, as HO trade theory usually assumes at least as many traded sectors as primary factors of production.

We can formalize wage-setting behavior in the HO model with reference to the "zero-profit conditions" that describe how domestic firms just cover costs in industries optimally chosen to have positive production. Suppose that an economy produces I different tradable goods, each of which requires some combination of J primary factors and I intermediate inputs. Then, for each sector i, we write the zero-profit condition as

$$p_i{}^G = \sum_{j \in J} a_{ji} w_j + \sum_{i \in I} b_{ii} p_i{}^G, \quad i = 1, \ldots, I, \tag{6.4}$$

where $p_i{}^G$ is the domestic gross-output price in sector i, w_j is the unit cost of the jth input, a_{ji} is the employment of input j per unit of output in sector i, and b_{ii} is the amount of intermediate input required to produce a unit of good i. There are I equations in 6.4, one for each sector where production occurs. There are three points to note about 6.4. First, with perfect factor mobility across sectors, wages w_j in 6.4 are not indexed by sector i. Second, the assumption that different sectors have different factor intensities means that the a_{ji} and b_{ii} coefficients differ across sectors. These a_{ji} and b_{ii} are optimally chosen and so depend on production technology and wages. Third, in the special case of a small open economy, $p_i{}^G$ is also the world price.

Note that which sectors appear in equation 6.4 for a country varies as one moves along the RD schedule in figure 6.8. For example, in the derivation presented earlier, the leftmost portion of RD would correspond to an economy that had only one equation in 6.4. Here, there would be two endogenously determined national wages, w_s and w_u, but only one equation relating these wages to exogenous product prices and production technology. Prices and technology alone could not determine wages, so the quantity of labor supplies would matter as well. But the segments of RD for which FPI holds would correspond to economies for which there would be two (or more) binding zero-profit conditions in equation 6.4. Here, there would still be two endogenously determined national wages, w_s and w_u, but two or more equations relating these wages to exogenous product prices and world technology. Now wages would be fully determined by prices and technology alone. Thus, equation 6.4 formalizes how in the HO framework wages depend on product prices, production technology, and (directly or indirectly) factor supplies.

So what role does globalization play in the structure of real and relative wages for an HO economy? Consider the demand side first. Given the intuition described above for the *shape* of RD, it is important to emphasize that its *position* depends on product prices and production technology. Hence, changes in prices or technology shift the position of the relevant parts of RD, and wages change to restore zero profits in all sectors. At initial factor prices, any change in product prices or technology means that zero profits no longer hold in one or more sectors. Producers respond by trying to expand output in now-profitable sectors and reduce output in now-unprofitable sectors. Relative labor demand increases for the factors employed relatively intensively in expanding sectors; labor demand decreases for the factors employed relatively intensively in the contracting sectors. To restore equilibrium, at fixed labor supply, relative wages must respond to the demand shifts until all profit opportunities are arbitraged away.

The key empirical implication of this intuition is that the wage effects of changes in product prices and/or technology tend to depend on their *sector* bias, that is, on the distribution across sectors of induced profit changes. Any change that initially increases profits in a particular sector tends to raise the economy-wide wage for factors employed relatively intensively in that sector. In terms of figure 6.6, segments of RD tend to shift *up* when price growth and/or technological progress is concentrated in skilled-labor-intensive sectors. Conversely, segments of RD tend to shift *down* when these changes are concentrated in relatively unskilled-labor-intensive sectors.

Algebraically, RD shifts arise by totally differentiating 6.4 with respect to time, to obtain

$$\Delta \log p_{it} + \Delta \log \text{TFP}_{it} = \sum_{j \in J} V_{jit} \Delta \log w_{jt}, \qquad (6.5)$$

where $\Delta \log p_{it} = (\Delta \log p_{it}^G - \sum V_{iit} \Delta \log p_{it}^G)$ is the change in value-added prices, V_{jit} is the share of factor j in total costs in sector i at time t, and $\Delta \log \text{TFP}_{it}$ is the growth in total factor productivity (TFP) for sector i. The final term in equation 6.5, $\Delta \log w_{jt}$, is the change in the wage of factor j, which again is economywide since all factors are mobile across sectors. Equation 6.5 shows how economywide factor prices ($\Delta \log w_{jt}$) adjust to changes in product prices ($\Delta \log p_{it}$) or technology ($\Delta \log \text{TFP}_{it}$) to restore zero profits in all sectors. This equation captures the wage adjustments to shifts up or down in aggregate relative labor demand described earlier.

One of the central messages of the HO framework is that an important shifter of *RD* is international trade working through domestic product prices. Now, as Deardorff and Hakura (1994) and others have correctly emphasized, one needs to be careful to make explicit what one means by the phrase *trade causes wage changes* as both trade flows and wage levels are endogenously determined in the HO framework. One sensible interpretation of this phrase is a reduction in a country's trade barriers, where this trade liberalization reduces the "wedge" between domestic and world prices. Another is developments in the rest of the world—reductions in foreign trade barriers, factor-supply growth, technological change, and so on—that are communicated to the domestic labor market via changes in world product prices and, thus, to some extent, domestic product prices. In either case, "trade" moves domestic product prices and, thus, domestic wages.[10]

It is well-known from the theory of gains from trade that trade liberalization tends to raise a country's average living standards, that is, its average real wage. But, as Wolfgang Stolper and Paul Samuelson (1941) first formalized, trade liberalization need *not* raise the real wage of all factors individually. Indeed, for a setting of two goods and two factors of production, Stolper and Samuelson demonstrated that a change in product prices necessarily reduces the real wage of the factor employed relatively intensively in the sector suffering the relative price decline. Since this seminal paper, the Stolper-Samuelson theorem has been extended and restated in many broader contexts. Alan Deardorff (1994) provides a comprehensive overview of the many different theoretical statements of this theorem. Throughout, this key message of trade imparting very different real-wage effects on different factors persists. Of course, different real-wage movements imply movements in relative wages as well.

In recent years, the Stolper-Samuelson theorem has guided many studies analyzing the rising U.S. skill premium. Following the sector-bias intuition of HO wage setting, these studies—including Baldwin and Cain (1997), Alan Deardorff and Dalia Hakura (1994), Robert Feenstra and Gordon Hanson (1995, 1999), Alan Krueger (1997), Robert Lawrence and Matthew Slaughter (1993), Edward Leamer (1998), and Jeffrey Sachs and Howard Shatz (1994)—have examined whether the United States has experienced falling prices for unskilled-labor-intensive products relative to the prices of skilled-labor-intensive products. Edward Leamer (1998) and Robert Baldwin and Glen Cain (1997) find that U.S. relative product prices fell for unskilled-labor-intensive sectors during the 1970s, but these two studies plus Robert Lawrence and Matthew Slaughter (1993) and Jagdish Bhagwati (1991) find no clear trend in relative prices during the 1980s. The 1990s also show no clear sector bias to price changes (Slaughter 2000).

Thus, changes in U.S. product prices do not obviously match up with changes in the skill premium documented in figure 6.4 (for a survey of these product-price studies, see Slaughter [2000]). This suggests that, if demand shifts have played a role in rising U.S. wage inequality, from the HO perspective these shifts (shifts "up" in the *RD* schedule in figure 6.8) have been driven by technological innovations concentrated in skilled-labor-intensive sectors. We will discuss evidence of this in the next subsection.

The Contrasting Wage Implications of the Labor and Trade Perspectives: Policy Issues Beyond Trade Liberalization

The previous discussion showed how the contrasting views of the national labor market derived from the labor and trade perspectives and then discussed how each perspective treats very differently the wage effects of changes in trade policies. In this subsection, we consider another set of questions: whether the wage implications of other kinds of changes differ between the closed-economy and the trade perspectives. The short answer is that they do differ, quite markedly. To make points of contact with other chapters of this book, we briefly consider three other big-picture changes of interest in the U.S. economy in recent years: the new economy and SBTC; rising immigration rates; and policies like welfare reform aimed at altering the size and skill mix of the U.S. labor force.

THE NEW ECONOMY AND SBTC   First, consider the rise of the new economy. The proliferation of computer use and, more recently, associated communication technologies (for example, the Internet and cellular telephony) is often cited as the main engine of technological change in the U.S. economy in recent decades. Many studies in this volume analyze how these technological innovations have affected aspects of employment and unemployment. But what are the wage-inequality implications of these innovations?

Recall that, in the closed-economy framework, technological change alters the skill premium only according to its factor bias. In the light of the sharply rising U.S. skill premium in recent decades, SBTC has been a major research focus of labor economists because, as equation 6.2 and figure 6.7 show, it is the only possible demand shifter that can raise the skill premium (conditional on labor supply).[11] Thus, for the new economy to matter for relative wages, it must be doing so via SBTC.

There is now a large body of empirical work documenting SBTC in many sectors in the United States and many other countries (see Bound and Johnson 1992; Berman, Bound, and Griliches 1994; Autor, Katz, and Krueger 1998; and Berman, Bound, and Machin 1998). The cornerstone of this evidence is within-industry "skill upgrading," that is, shifts in relative employment toward more-skilled workers that are strongly suggestive of SBTC insofar as the rising skill premium should, all else equal, be inducing firms to hire less skilled labor, not more of it.

In the trade framework, technology works differently. Again, by equation 6.5, it is the sector bias of technological change that tends to drive wage changes, not its factor bias. All the new-economy innovations shift the profitability of lots of sectors (both for the producers of the new-economy products and, via capital and input prices, for their consumers in other sectors). What matters for relative wages is the net shift in profitability: relative wages will tend to rise for factors employed intensively in sectors enjoying relatively large technology gains and, thus, relatively large increases in relative profitability. To the extent that new profit opportunities are mainly in the skilled-labor-intensive sectors, inequality would likely rise. This is unambiguously the case when product prices are fixed; if innovation changes product prices as well, wage effects are harder to determine, but sector bias still matters in many circumstances.

Notice that the term *SBTC* did not appear in the previous paragraph. This was deliberate: as equation 6.5 shows, it is, not just SBTC, but all kinds of technological change, as summarized by TFP changes, that can induce wage changes. Again, it is sector bias, not factor bias, that tends to matter. For example, in the two-good trade model, SBTC in the unskilled-labor-intensive sector unambiguously *lowers* the skill premium, the exact opposite result from what obtains in the one-sector model.[12] Equation 6.5 also emphasizes that what matters for technological innovations are the induced cost changes as summarized by TFP. In principle, SBTC need not reduce unit costs. George Johnson (1997) emphasizes this point, demonstrating, for example, that, for the CES production function used earlier, SBTC need not reduce unit costs. All this carries obvious implications for real wages: SBTC in and of itself need not deliver sharp increases in average real wages.

A number of studies have addressed the theory of technology's wage effects in the HO model: Robert Baldwin and Glen Cain (1997); Eli Berman, John Bound, and Steve Machin (1998); Jagdish Bhagwati and Vivek Dehejia (1994); Donald Davis (1998); Jonathan Haskel and Matthew Slaughter (forthcoming); Paul Krugman (1995); Edward Leamer (1998); J. David Richardson (1995); and Adrian Wood (1995). There is some disagreement among these studies, mainly involving the net wage effects of technological change when product prices are affected as well. There have been a few empirical studies of the sector bias of U.S. technological change. Leamer (1998) estimates that the sector bias of TFP raised skill differentials during the 1970s but slightly lowered them during the 1980s. Focusing on SBTC only, for a sample of ten countries over the 1970s and 1980s Haskel and Slaughter (forthcoming) find a strong correlation between SBTC's sector bias and changes in the skill premium. For example, both the United States and the United Kingdom had SBTC concentrated in unskilled-labor-intensive sectors during the 1970s but then in skilled-labor-intensive sectors during the 1980s—sector biases that match both countries' skill-premium changes. And Feenstra and Hanson (1999) decompose U.S. TFP over the 1980s into parts attributable to computerization and outsourcing. They find that the sector bias of both these underlying forces helped raise the skill premium.

RISING IMMIGRATION RATES Second, consider the labor-market effects of the large increase in immigration into the United States, documented in figure 6.2. In a closed economy, the relative-wage effect of increased immigration would depend on how the skill distribution of the immigrants compared to that of the incumbent labor force. If immigrants were disproportionately less skilled relative to the native born, in figure 6.7 RS would shift to the left and W_s/W_u rise. Again, this simply reflects the idea that, without the possibility of output-mix effects, new immigrants can price themselves into employment only via wage movements.

In the open-economy approach, figure 6.8 shows that, if changes in relative labor supplies are not large enough to change the set of goods produced, then they have no wage effects. Real wages of similarly skilled natives are not pressured, nor is the skill premium. Instead, with FPI, endowment changes are completely absorbed through Rybczynski output-mix effects. This is a central message of the HO framework, in stark contrast to that of the closed-economy labor framework: wages need not be the adjustment mechanism by which factor-supply changes are absorbed.

This is not to say that immigration and/or capital flows can never influence U.S. wages in the HO framework. Figure 6.8 shows that they can—but only if the shift in RS is sufficiently large to induce the country to change the set of tradable sectors produced (that is, to change its cone of diversification). Again, by equation 6.4, change the set of zero-profit conditions governing wage setting, and you change equilibrium wages so that, qualitatively, relative-wage changes behave as they do in the closed-economy approach. Factors with sufficiently large increases in relative supply suffer both real- and relative-wage declines.

Empirically, how important have wage and output-mix effects been in absorbing immigrant (and, by similar reasoning, FDI) flows in the U.S. economy? It has been documented that, on average, the education attainment of immigrant men relative to that of native-born men has been declining in recent decades (Borjas, 1999), so immigrants have been a force tending to shift RS back. Borjas, Freeman, and Katz (1997) quantify immigration's RS shifts, and, by multiplying these shifts by assumed values for the elasticity of RD, they find evidence that U.S. high school dropouts have experienced downward wage pressure from immigration inflows. But, in the light of the fact that immigrants tend to concentrate in specific "gateway" communities, much of the research on immigrant inflows has examined the effect of immigration on native wages across regions of the United States. This literature is vast (recent papers include Borjas, Freeman, and Katz [1997] and Card [1997]; for surveys, see Borjas [1994, 1999] and Friedberg and Hunt [1995]). The standard approach is to regress the change in native wages on the change in the stock of immigrants across U.S. metropolitan areas. Most area-analysis studies find that immigration has, at most, a small negative effect on local native wages. Thus, there is mixed evidence, at best, of any wage effect of immigrant inflows into the United States.

This persistent puzzle of very few or no wage effects can be taken as indirect evidence supporting a possible role for output-mix effects. But there is very little direct evidence here. An exception is Hanson and Slaughter (in press), who do find that labor-demand shifts mandated by output shifts help account for absorption of state changes in relative labor supplies. Suggestive evidence can be found in the recent experience of California. Over the 1980s, California's labor supply relative to the rest of the country grew most for college graduates and high school dropouts, with immigrant inflows accounting for nearly all this relative growth. The six fastest-growing industries in California during this period relative to the rest of the country were either very skilled labor intensive (machinery [which contains computers and office products], legal services, and finance, insurance, and real estate) or very unskilled labor intensive (textiles, apparel, and personal household services).

To make all this concrete, consider the U.S. labor market for Ph.D.s. Table 6.1 reports by age the fraction of foreign-born, U.S.-educated Ph.D.s employed in the United States in the fields of the arts and sciences (not medicine). For persons under the age of forty-six, this proportion increased from 14 percent in 1979 to 25 percent in 1995. This means that, holding the supplies of native-born Ph.D.s under the age of forty-six at their 1979 and 1995 levels, the increase in the fraction of immigrants increased the total supply of younger Ph.D.s by about 14 percent.[13]

How have these immigrant Ph.D.s been absorbed into the U.S. labor market? In a closed-economy setting, the percentage change in the wage rate of younger Ph.D.s relative to that of other skilled labor (say, M.B.A.s) that is due to the supply increase resulting from immigration would be equal to the reciprocal of the absolute wage elasticity of demand times 14 percent.[14] Alternatively, these immigrant Ph.D.s may have triggered output-mix effects across tradable sectors employing them (acknowledging that some may have gained employment in nontraded sectors, for example, government). For example, the business sector employed 18 percent of native-born and 24 percent of immigrant Ph.D.'s in 1979, shares that rose to 30 and 40 percent, respectively, in 1995. Data like these can, it is hoped, shed more light on the roles of wages and output-mix effects in absorbing immigrants.

DOMESTIC POLICIES AIMED AT THE SIZE AND SKILL MIX OF THE LABOR FORCE   Finally, consider a wide range of labor-supply-policy reforms like welfare reform and worker training (see Blank and Shapiro, chapter 7 in this volume; Ellwood, chapter 9 in this volume; and Lynch and Nickell, chapter 11 in this volume). From the labor economists' closed-economy perspective, a major problem with these policies is their negative wage effects. For example, a policy of increasing the supply of very low-skilled labor by severely limiting program eligibility would lower the wages of similarly skilled workers already working in similar jobs. Similarly,

TABLE 6.1   /   Proportion of Ph.D.s in the U.S. Who Are Foreign Born

Age	1979	1995
< thirty-five	.139	.296
Thirty-six to forty-five	.149	.225
Forty-six to sixty-five	.179	.156
All	.160	.198

Source: National Science Foundation, Survey of Doctorate Recipients tapes.

training programs that attempt to transform very low-skilled workers into middle-skilled workers would lower the real and relative wages of the incumbent middle-skilled workers. In the light of these presumed wage pressures, it is not surprising that representatives of groups that are now doing what trainees are being prepared for (like construction trade unions) often oppose training programs.

From the perspective of the HO model, concerns about the wage effects of welfare reform and training programs may be ill founded. An increase in the supply of low-skilled workers will—*if* the supply change is small enough not to induce a shift in cones—expand the number of such jobs without any wage changes. A similar conclusion applies to jobs associated with the middle-skilled labor whose supply is increased as a result of the training program.

More generally, a common policy recommendation from the labor-economics literature on increasing inequality is that increases can be mitigated by policies that increase college attendance and completion.[15] By the HO framework, however, these policies will be at least somewhat offset by output-mix effects. How much output-mix effects matter, again, depends on the various assumptions underlying the HO model and, thus, on what portion of the *RD* schedule in figure 6.8 applies to the U.S. economy. If the United States operates on a downward-sloping portion (for example, if there are so few less-skilled workers that the United States has stopped production of unskilled-labor-intensive tradables), then labor-supply shifts do shift wages as predicted by the labor model.

How Empirically Relevant Is the HO Trade Model?

Our discussion has made clear that, in the standard HO framework, economic openness shapes the performance of the U.S. labor market in several important ways. But our discussion has also made clear that the obvious question is, How empirically relevant is the HO framework? Is the best "first-pass" description of the U.S. economy the closed-economy perspective or the multisector, open-economy perspective?

For some research topics, the answer to this question might not seem to matter. It is important to note that empirical work from both perspectives has, on balance, found that international trade has played only a small role in rising inequality. The factor-content studies from the labor perspective generally find that trade's shifts in effective labor supplies explain, at most, about 20 percent of the rise in the skill premium—with this share declining when calculations end in years with relatively small trade deficits. And the Stolper-Samuelson studies have not found clear declines in the relative price of unskilled-labor-intensive products since the onset of the rising skill premium. These price declines occurred during the 1970s, but the skill premium was falling in this decade. Only with some appeal to lags can 1970s price movements be linked to later wage movements.[16]

For many other research and policy topics, however, the presence or absence of FPI and its associated output-mix effects is too important to table this question. Our short answer is that the U.S. economy today is best represented as a blend of the closed economy and HO frameworks—with the relevant weights on both equal to 0.5 (with a standard error of perhaps 0.25) and the weight on the HO framework likely to increase slowly in future years. To elaborate on this short answer, it is instructive to consider each of the central HO assumptions. The more plausible are these assumptions empirically, the greater the weight (and the lower the standard error) we ascribe to the trade framework.

First, consider the assumption that industries display different factor intensities (when faced with the same relative factor prices). This assumption is crucial for generating national demand shifts per the Stolper-Samuelson theorem and for not generating national demand shifts per the Rybczynski theorem. Table 6.2 (from Hanson and Slaughter, in press) shows three measures of industry factor intensity: the ratios of employment of high school dropouts, high school graduates, or those with some college to employment of college graduates. Forty industries are reported, spanning all nonmilitary GDP in the United States. All measures use data for national industry employment as reported in the decennial censuses of 1980 and 1990.

Looking down each column in table 6.2 reveals that factor intensities differ substantially across industries. In 1990, the ratio of high school dropouts to college graduates ranges from 9.3 in household services to 0.05 in legal services. In 1980, the cross-industry spread was even wider: legal services employed twenty-five college graduates for every high school dropout, while, in personal household services, this ratio was almost completely reversed.[17] We read table 6.2 as showing ample evidence of substantial cross-industry differences in factor intensity.

Second, consider the assumption of perfect intersectoral factor mobility. The mechanics of both the Rybczynski and the Stolper-Samuelson theorems hinge entirely on intersectoral resource reallocation. It is worth emphasizing, as a point of contact with other chapters of this book, that simultaneous job destruction and job creation are central to these theorems. Empirically, periods of extensive trade liberalization should trigger a great deal of job churning—indeed, only through the destruction and creation of jobs are the traditional aggregate gains from trade realized. So heightened worker flows in and out of various labor-market states (see, for example, Abraham and Shimer, chapter 8 in this volume) may be partly due to increased globalization.

Intersectoral factor mobility is less unrealistic over longer time horizons. Thus, the HO framework is often characterized as a long-run model that can be contrasted with short-run models in which one or more factors of production are assumed to be completely immobile. These "specific-factors" models, also known as Ricardo-Viner models, are well developed in trade, with each exhibiting very different wage-setting behavior. An important segment of this literature analyzes how various short-run models evolve into the benchmark HO long-run model as intersectoral factor mobility becomes perfect (see Mayer 1974; and Mussa 1974, 1978).[18]

TABLE 6.2 / U.S. Industry Factor Intensity, 1980 and 1990

Industry Name	HSDO/CG, 1980	HSDO/CG, 1990	HSG/CG, 1980	HSG/CG, 1990	SC/CG, 1980	SC/CG, 1990
Agriculture	5.69	4.66	4.56	3.82	1.82	2.15
Agr. services	2.11	1.90	1.41	1.49	1.20	1.58
Mining	1.62	.91	2.21	1.76	1.25	1.31
Construction	3.86	2.47	4.68	3.68	2.29	2.52
Food products	3.71	2.57	3.59	3.12	1.52	2.02
Tobacco	3.29	0.92	3.71	2.62	1.86	1.56
Textiles	9.49	6.41	7.20	8.05	1.76	3.41
Apparel	12.29	5.39	9.29	4.47	2.43	2.12
Lumber	8.69	4.79	8.06	6.28	2.84	3.49
Furniture	5.72	4.41	4.79	4.38	1.74	2.94
Paper	2.72	1.81	3.64	4.13	1.36	1.82
Printing	1.05	.55	2.13	1.32	1.34	1.21
Chemicals	.82	.41	1.67	1.15	.91	1.01
Petro. refining	.71	.28	1.65	1.20	.96	1.49
Rubber	2.59	2.73	4.05	4.40	1.28	2.85
Leather	14.25	4.04	14.25	5.93	2.63	2.03
Stone/clay/glass	4.81	1.75	6.74	3.17	2.63	1.94
Primary metals	3.77	2.03	5.05	3.78	1.90	2.20
Metal products	3.83	2.13	5.36	3.99	2.34	2.60
Machinery	1.76	.80	3.43	1.74	1.78	1.63
Elec. machinery	1.50	.62	2.54	1.23	1.48	1.24
Transport equip.	1.71	.73	3.14	1.70	1.60	1.61
Misc. manuf.	3.12	1.58	3.91	2.02	1.80	1.68
Transport/ utilities	1.79	.82	3.78	2.21	2.28	2.11
Wholesale trade	1.47	.65	2.57	1.49	1.73	1.45
Retail trade	3.88	2.30	4.39	3.16	2.90	2.82
FIRE	.41	.22	1.71	1.02	1.37	1.37
Investment finance	.13	.07	.44	.30	.67	.57
Lodging services	4.67	2.30	4.18	3.07	2.61	2.74
Personal services	5.70	1.70	8.02	3.30	4.32	2.69
Business services	.39	.27	.75	.53	.80	.83
Auto services	7.11	6.96	7.76	8.70	3.24	6.03
Repair services	4.53	3.01	6.12	4.86	3.28	3.62
Entertainment	1.51	1.08	1.57	1.26	1.47	1.59
Health services	.69	.33	1.18	.77	1.20	1.22
Legal services	.04	.05	.37	.24	.43	.43
Educ. services	.18	.11	.30	.26	.34	.35
Social services	.53	.37	.74	.65	.77	.82

(Table continues on p. 284.)

TABLE 6.2 / *Continued*

Industry Name	HSDO/CG, 1980	HSDO/CG, 1990	HSG/CG, 1980	HSG/CG, 1990	SC/CG, 1980	SC/CG, 1990
Household services	22.80	9.26	8.30	5.58	3.90	3.31
Government	.55	.23	1.49	.96	1.18	1.37

Source: Hanson and Slaughter (forthcoming).
Notes: Each cell reports the ratio of national employment of that cell's two factors for the industry and year of that cell. HSDO = high-school dropouts; HSG = high school graduates; SC = some college; and CG = college graduates and beyond. Industry categories combine one- and two-digit SIC industries.

How accurate an assumption is perfect intersectoral labor mobility for the United States, over "reasonable"-enough time horizons? Relative to other countries, very much so—the United States is commonly cited as having the most flexible labor markets in the world. In an absolute sense, increasingly so—labor mobility seems to have increased in the 1990s thanks to sharp corporate restructuring, continued declines in private-sector unionization rates, and information-technology advances (for example, job-matching Internet websites like monster.com) that improve the technology used to match workers with vacancies.

One related issue is interindustry wage differentials. A large literature has documented interindustry wage differentials for observationally equivalent workers, arguing that rent sharing explains these differentials (for example, Katz and Summers 1989). This would suggest a serious flaw in the HO framework, as equation 6.4 does not index wages by industry to allow for these differentials. But, to the extent that *changes* in economywide wages are of central concern here, what matters is whether changes in industry wages are driven mainly by economywide changes common to all sectors or by changes in industry differentials. Equation 6.4 can easily be modified to allow for interindustry wage differentials; the question then becomes the source of wage changes in equation 6.5. Haskel and Slaughter (2000) report for U.S. manufacturing sectors decompositions of decade changes in industry wages into changes in average wages and changes in differentials. They find that changes in differentials account for only about 15 percent of industry wage changes. So differentials clearly exist in levels, but *changes* in industry wages are driven largely by changes in economy-wide wages, not in differentials. This is consistent with evidence (for example, Katz and Summers 1989) that interindustry wage differentials are stable over time.

A third HO assumption to consider is that there are more tradable products than factors of production. For simplicity, we discussed the HO framework with no nontraded sector, but nontraded sectors can easily be incorporated. With nontraded sectors, so long as the number of tradable products at least equals the number of primary factors, national wages are still determined by the zero-profit conditions of the tradable sectors only. Nontraded product prices are endogenously determined by nontraded production technology and by national wages.

Technical progress in nontradables does not affect wages; instead, it lowers non-traded prices.

This is *not* to say that the nontraded sector might not be a much larger employer than the traded sectors. It is well-known that, in recent decades, the share of employment in services—that is, in the nonmanufacturing, nonagricultural sectors that are typically assumed to be nontraded—has been rising in the United States and other advanced economies. But, despite this, wages outside tradables can still be set by the prices and technology in tradables only.

There is also good reason to suppose that the tradability of many goods and services is rising and, thus, by implication, that there are more tradable products than primary factors in the real world. One reason is ongoing declines in political and natural trade barriers. For example, many information services have become tradable at near-zero cost, with well-known cases like firms moving their software programming around the world (say, from Seattle to India to Israel). Another example is how the Internet allows many information-intensive products (software, music) to be traded on-line across borders. Services trade as a share of total trade, admittedly hard to measure, has been rising in recent decades and is very relevant for the United States, whose persistently large trade surplus for services indicates its comparative advantage at these activities.

A fourth critical assumption of the HO framework is that the United States be "small," that is, that its national output supply and demand not be able to affect world prices. In deriving figure 6.8, FPI hinges crucially on Rybczynski output-mix effects not triggering world-price responses and thus domestic-wage responses via the Stolper-Samuelson process. If product prices do change, then infinite elasticity disappears from figure 6.8: sectors with rising relative output see declining relative prices and thus declining relative (and perhaps real) wages for the factors whom they hire most intensively, with the graphic implication that the horizontal demand curves start to slope downward.

How realistic is this small-country assumption, with the resultant property that the absolute price elasticities of product demand are infinite? One piece of country-level evidence that this assumption is increasingly realistic is the declining U.S. share of world GDP. At the end of World War II, the United States accounted for about 50 percent of world output—and, arguably, an even greater share of output in the economically integrated world excluding largely autarkic countries like those behind the Iron Curtain. In 1999, the United States accounted for just under 22 percent of world output (IMF 2000). An increasing share of world production occurs outside U.S. borders, so from this national perspective the United States is moving ever closer to the HO "small" benchmark.

From the perspective of individual industries, the question is obviously more involved. The United States may be a world-price taker in some sectors (for example, crude oil) but a world-price maker in others (for example, operating-system software and commercial aircraft). The question then becomes how imperfect competition affects the structure of the HO framework. Certain kinds of imperfect competition need not be inconsistent with the zero-profits assumption. Elhanan Helpman and Paul Krugman (1985) modify the HO model by having one sector be monopolistically competitive with entry. This sector still earns zero profits, and price changes still generate Stolper-Samuelson wage adjustments. For market structures that generate positive profits, the situation is more involved. Profits that are shared with workers via interindustry wage differentials can still permit the standard HO wage changes, as discussed earlier.[19]

Empirically, there is at least anecdotal evidence of heightened product-market competition throughout the 1990s to today. Many new-economy observers have argued that new information technologies will increase competition in many sectors, thanks to thicker and more-transparent markets. But we are not aware of more-systematic evidence on this issue.

Unfortunately, empirical work in international trade offers very little direct evidence on whether (and over what endowment regions) FPI holds. As discussed earlier, Hanson and Slaughter (in press) find evidence that output-mix effects are part of how U.S. states absorb their labor-supply changes. But they do not directly look for any product-price effects, either at the state or at the national level. Moreover, their analysis tries to condition on labor-demand shifts implied by widespread SBTC.

This highlights a fundamental methodological difficulty of testing for FPI. In deriving figure 6.8, recall that the thought experiment was to shift national labor supplies *holding constant* all other parameters, including world product prices, world technology parameters, and so on. This may be easy to do in theory, but, in reality, it is unclear how to hold constant everything but labor supply—particularly over the long time horizons that seem more reasonable for the HO framework's assumptions like intersectoral factor mobility. In the jargon of natural experiments, *clean treatments* are difficult to come by in general equilibrium. This suggests that, even though many of the assumptions underlying FPI may be increasingly relevant for the U.S. economy, testing directly for FPI is likely always to be a problematic exercise.

Into the Future: Further Liberalization and the U.S. Cone

Without ignoring the discussions of the previous subsection, we now assume that the HO framework is a helpful guide for understanding the U.S. labor market. We close this section of our paper by looking into the future to consider what further trade and/or immigration liberalization may imply for the U.S. economy.

Start with trade. For decades now, the United States has been removing political barriers to trade via ongoing bilateral and multilateral trade negotiations. But the country is still not completely open to trade, which raises the question of what labor-market pressures are likely to be imparted by future trade liberalization.

Haskel and Slaughter (2000) have documented that the U.S. tariffs remaining in 1988 near the end of the Tokyo Round of the General Agreement on Tariffs and Trade were highest in the less-skilled-labor-intensive sectors—in particular, textiles, apparel, and footwear. Figure 6.9 shows this by plotting the level of 1988 industry tariff rates (measured as customs duties collected as a share of imports' customs value) on industry skill intensity measured as the nonproduction/production employment ratio. The clear message of figure 6.9 is that U.S. tariffs were highest in the less-skilled-labor-intensive sectors, particularly in textiles (SIC 22), apparel (SIC 23), and footwear (SIC 31).[20] This suggests that there may be scope for future trade liberalizations—in particular, the now-started Multi-Fiber Agreement (MFA) phaseouts under the Uruguay Round of the World Trade Organization (WTO)—to pressure U.S. less-skilled wages (in both relative and real terms). To the extent that world prices in these unskilled-labor-intensive sectors decline in coming years thanks to these MFA phaseouts and other for-

FIGURE 6.9 / U.S. Tariffs Remain Higher in Less-Skilled-Labor-Intensive Industries

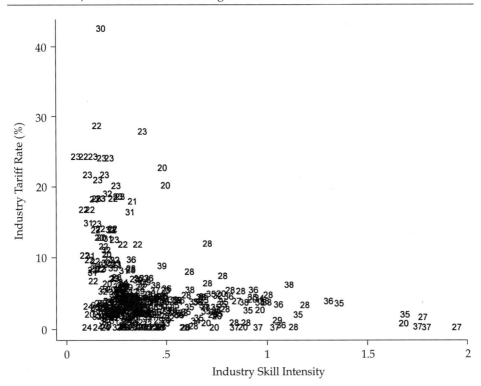

Source: Haskel and Slaughter (2001).

Notes: Each figure reported represents an observation for a four-digit SIC industry from the year 1988; for brevity, only the two-digit SIC code for each observation is reported. Industry skill intensity is the relative employment of nonproduction to production workers. Tariff rates are duties collected as a share of the customs value of imports. For readability, two zero-tariff skilled-labor-intensive industries are omitted: SIC 2721 (skill intensity of 4.83) and SIC 2731 (skill intensity of 3.25).

eign developments (for example, additional liberalization in China as that country accedes to the WTO), there will be even greater wage pressures?

How could the United States avoid these wage pressures? Figure 6.8 suggests the obvious strategy of switching cones of diversification. If the United States relative-supply schedule were somehow to shift rightward enough, then that country would stop producing in such heavily "trade-exposed" industries as textiles and apparel. Less-skilled U.S. workers would transfer out of these industries into employment in nontradables or in other, more-skilled-labor-intensive tradable sectors. Less-skilled real and relative wages would rise (and/or less-skilled employment would increase), with the bonus of insulation from any further declines in world prices of unskilled-labor-intensive products. Once the country no longer produces T-shirts and toys, declines in their prices simply translate into real-wage gains (in consumption terms) for all U.S. workers.

This trade perspective suggests that all the policies aimed at the composition of the U.S. labor force feed at least partially into determining our national output mix and, thus, for trade, our pattern of comparative advantage. It leads directly to the questions, What cone of diversification is the United States in now, and how likely is the country to switch cones in the future? Table 6.3 shows the education distribution of the U.S. adult population since 1940, which is roughly equivalent to the skill mix of the labor force at each point in time.

One can read table 6.3 as an optimist. Looking at how this skill mix has evolved over time, it is clear that the U.S. labor force has been upgrading skills for decades. Thus, in figure 6.8, the RS schedule has been marching rightward for decades, helping boost less-skilled U.S. wages through a virtuous cycle of product upgrading.

One can also read table 6.3 as a pessimist. Looking, not at the trend over time, but at the absolute skill mix at each point in time, even as of 1999, college graduates—the group typically defined as the most skilled—accounted for only about one in four U.S. workers. Adding those with some college still captures only 50

TABLE 6.3 / Education Distribution of the U.S. Population Since 1940

Year	High School Dropouts	High School Graduates	Some College	College Graduates
1940	76	14	5	5
1950	66	21	7	6
1963	52	30	9	9
1970	45	34	10	11
1979	32	37	15	16
1989	23	39	17	21
1999	17	33	25	25

Sources: For all years but 1999, Johnson (1997, table 1). For 1999, U.S. Bureau of the Census (2000).
Note: Each cell reports the share of the total U.S. adult population (aged twenty-five and over) accounted for by that labor group in that year.

percent of the labor force. Even after sixty years of rising education attainment, the median U.S. worker is still a high school graduate—and, as discussed earlier, high school graduates have seen poor wage performance in both real and relative terms for more than a generation. Thus, in figure 6.8, the RS schedule is thought to be not far enough to the right, with little hope of achieving enough of a push to insulate the U.S. labor market from tougher international competition. Ellwood (chapter 9 in this volume) offers another reason to be a pessimist, as his demographic forecasts for the next generation indicate that the skill mix of the U.S. labor force in 2020 will be about what it was in 1999.

So what exactly does research tell us about how to map table 6.3 onto figure 6.8? Almost nothing. For reasons just discussed, there is virtually no empirical research on whether (and over what endowment regions) FPI holds for the U.S. economy. For example, note that all the Stolper-Samuelson studies cited earlier have assumed (either explicitly or implicitly) that any shifts in RS have not been large enough to move the United States to a different flat portion of the RD with a different set of products and thus different links from product prices to wages. But the qualitative issue is clear, nevertheless. A broad range of U.S. labor-supply-policy choices—immigration, education, worker retraining, welfare reform, and so on—will all on net determine what cone the United States produces in and thus what wage structure prevails in U.S. labor markets.

We close this discussion by reporting some simple calculations that we performed to shed light on this product-mix issue. We wanted an intuitive measure of the "trade exposure" of different skill groups in the U.S. economy. Specifically, let j index different skill groups and i different industries. Let e_{ji} be the fraction of group j's total supply employed in industry i. Let x_i be the ratio of exports to output for industry i and m_i the ratio of imports to output in industry i. Then an *index of import sensitivity* for group j, IS_j, can be calculated as

$$IS_j \equiv \Sigma_i \, e_{ji} m_i. \tag{6.6}$$

An analogous *index of export sensitivity* for group j, ES_j, is given by

$$ES_j \equiv \Sigma_i \, e_{ji} x_i. \tag{6.7}$$

These indexes are higher for skill groups employed predominantly in heavily traded sectors; at the extreme, for a group working only in truly nontraded sectors, these indexes equal 0.

We calculated these indexes in equations 6.6 and 6.7 for twenty-four skill groups: two genders; four education groups (high school dropouts, high school graduates, those with some college, and college graduates and beyond); and three age groups (under twenty-five, twenty-five to thirty-nine, and forty and over). Data for the e_{ji} shares came from the merged outgoing rotation files of the Current Population Survey; export and import data for m_i and x_i came from Rob Feenstra via the National Bureau of Economic Research. Corresponding industry classifications across the two data sets left us with twenty-five industries:

twenty-four within manufacturing (at roughly the two-digit SIC level) and one aggregate "nonmanufacturing" sector spanning all other sectors. Trade data were readily available for the twenty-four sectors in manufacturing; for the residual sector, we calculated trade ratios by combining national and manufacturing GDP and trade data (from the Bureau of Economic Analysis). Data limitations restricted us to a span of 1979 as our starting year and 1994 as our ending year.

Table 6.4 reports the values of the indices in 1979 and 1994, respectively. The patterns of the data are summarized in regressions reported in table 6.5 in which each index is regressed on dummy variables for characteristics (with male high school graduates aged twenty-five to thirty-nine being the excluded group). We note two points from these tables.

First, there is some broad stability in trade exposure across groups over time. Women are much less trade exposed than are men, and the less skilled (especially high school graduates as opposed to dropouts) are more trade exposed than are the more skilled.

Second, and more important, there is some suggestive evidence that the United States has been shifting out of a production cone with very unskilled-labor-intensive tradables. Notice that the trade exposure for both male and female young high school dropouts fell considerably relative to other groups between 1979 and 1994. Suppose that, during this period, the ongoing skill upgrading in the United States (per table 6.1) was moving the country out of the cone in which high school dropout labor-intensive products are made domestically. As these sectors shrank, their HSDO employees should have been moving to other sectors, with the sizable nonmanufacturing, largely nontraded sector being the main destination. And if, for various labor-market institutions (for example, unions, seniority hiring and firing), it is the young workers who "grease the wheels" of the labor market, then one would expect to see young high school dropouts moving more into nonmanufacturing.

This is exactly what the tables show. The trade exposure of both male and female young high school dropouts fell considerably relative to that of other groups between 1979 and 1994, which is also consistent with the change in the coefficient on dropouts for IS from 1979 to 1994. Granted, this is only very suggestive evidence, but calculations like these might help shed light on this central issue of the U.S. product mix and implied wage structure.

SOME SHORTER-RUN EFFECTS OF INTERNATIONAL VARIABLES ON THE LABOR MARKET: WHAT ABOUT TRADE AND EMPLOYMENT?

Throughout the previous section, our concern was with the medium- to long-term effects of globalization on relative and real wages. We made the presumption—common to the fields of trade and parts of labor economics—that the U.S. economy tends toward full employment and that recessions are, however bothersome at times, transitory aberrations. We also share the presumption of most

TABLE 6.4 / Indices of Trade Sensitivity by Demographic Characteristics, 1979 and 1994

Gender, Education, and Age	Export ES_j		Imports IS_j	
	1979	1994	1979	1994
Men:				
Dropouts				
< Twenty-five	.064	.065	.077	.064
Twenty-five to thirty-nine	.090	.090	.109	.113
Forty +	.076	.073	.091	.078
High school				
< Twenty-five	.083	.087	.094	.109
Twenty-five to thirty-nine	.096	.099	.107	.119
Forty +	.086	.092	.094	.102
Some college				
< Twenty-five	.075	.075	.084	.079
Twenty-five to thirty-nine	.090	.099	.096	.112
Forty +	.085	.094	.087	.100
College grads				
< Twenty-five	.074	.078	.083	.078
Twenty-five to thirty-nine	.077	.096	.082	.100
Forty +	.079	.086	.081	.088
Women:				
Dropouts				
< Twenty-five	.059	.060	.078	.057
Twenty-five to thirty-nine	.071	.075	.102	.106
Forty +	.058	.065	.077	.072
High school				
< Twenty-five	.065	.070	.083	.081
Twenty-five to thirty-nine	.069	.077	.085	.093
Forty +	.061	.070	.074	.075
Some college				
< Twenty-five	.060	.063	.072	.061
Twenty-five to thirty-nine	.062	.071	.073	.072
Forty +	.057	.067	.068	.064
College grads				
< Twenty-five	.058	.065	.069	.060
Twenty-five to thirty-nine	.055	.070	.065	.066
Forty +	.053	.061	.064	.053

Sources: Current Population Surveys and National Bureau of Economic Research.
Notes: The indices IS_j and ES_j are calculated as reported in the text, eqq. (6) and (7), respectively. The skill groups are also defined in the text, varying by gender, education attainment, and age.

TABLE 6.5 / Determinants of Export- and Import-Sensitivity Indices

Variable	ES_{79}	ES_{94}	IS_{79}	IS_{94}	ΔNX	ΔEX
Women	−.021	−.018	−.015	−.024	.011	−.007
	(.002)	(.002)	(.003)	(.004)	(.002)	(.003)
Dropouts	−.007	−.011	−.001	−.015	.010	−.019
	(.002)	(.003)	(.004)	(.006)	(.003)	(.005)
Some col.	−.005	−.004	−.010	−.015	.007	−.005
	(.003)	(.003)	(.004)	(.006)	(.003)	(.005)
Col. grads	−.011	−.007	−.016	−.022	.011	−.003
	(.003)	(.003)	(.004)	(.006)	(.003)	(.005)
< Twenty-five	−.009	−.014	−.010	−.024	.009	−.019
	(.003)	(.003)	(.003)	(.005)	(.002)	(.004)
Forty +	−.007	−.009	−.010	−.019	.007	−.010
	(.003)	(.003)	(.003)	(.005)	(.002)	(.004)
Constant	.092	.099	.104	.122	−.012	.026
	(.003)	(.003)	(.004)	(.006)	(.003)	(.005)
R^2	.83	.84	.71	.73	.72	.61

Source: Labor Extracts (1979–1999).

macroeconomists that the short-term course of the U.S. economy is not much affected by foreign-trade shocks.[21] There are, however, several interesting and important questions about the effect of trade on the quantity side of the labor market, particularly in a shorter-run context. In this section, we examine three of these questions.

First, how vulnerable is the U.S. economy to foreign shocks? Does the occurrence of a recession in other parts of the world have any effect on the likelihood that unemployment in the United States will rise? Second, is there any effect of changes in foreign prices on equilibrium unemployment (the natural rate, the NAIRU [nonaccelerating inflation rate of unemployment]) in the United States? Third, does globalization somehow make firms' demand for U.S. labor more elastic?

The International Transmission of Unemployment

Suppose that—as was true at the end of 2000—the United States is humming along in an economic expansion with the aggregate unemployment rate approximately equal to its equilibrium rate U_{US*}. In early 2001, however, a severe recession occurs in Europe (because of, say, a drastic reduction in the supply of euros/a sharp interest-rate increase by the European Central Bank). What effect would this event be expected to have on the U.S. economy? Would we observe that the increase in the European unemployment rate, u_{EU}, "causes" u_{US} to rise or fall?

There are several macroeconomic stories about how the rise in u_{EU} could lead to a rise in u_{US} (for a survey of approaches to the question of macroeconomic interdependence, see Cooper 1985). In our example of a rise in u_{EU} due to European monetary policy, the most direct way in which u_{US} could be affected is with fully or partially fixed nominal exchange rates. There are several plausible events, such as common technology shocks, that would be expected to affect u_{EU} and u_{US} in the same direction. There are even some stories involving international competition in which U_{US} and U_{EU} would, with lags, be negatively related (see Johnson and Stafford 1993). For example, what is good for Toulouse is bad for Seattle, and vice versa.

To investigate this general question (in an admittedly preliminary fashion), we relate the current value of the unemployment rate in each of three major economies—the United States, the European Union, and Japan—to the lagged values rates of the unemployment rates in all three economies. This is represented by the VAR model

$$u_j(t) = \alpha_{j,US}u_{US}(t-1) + \alpha_{j,EU}u_{EU}(t-1) + \alpha_{j,JA}u_{JA}(t-1) + c_j(t) + SH_j(t), (6.8)$$

where j = US (the United States), EU (Europe), and JA (Japan). The constant $c_j(t)$ is made a function of time to reflect movements in the underlying equilibrium rate (a problem that is especially acute for Europe). $SH_j(t)$ is a shock term for each country.

The model is estimated on annual data for the period 1956 to 1999. The first coefficient in each set of results constrains the lagged cross-country effects to equal 0, and the second coefficient includes these effects. Each regression includes a cubic in time to pick up movements in equilibrium rates—although this is sufficiently well represented in the United States by a quadratic and in Japan by a linear trend. The results for the determination of the unemployment rate in the United States for the entire period suggest that the lagged unemployment rate in Europe has a marginally significant negative effect on u_{US}. The results for the other two economies suggest that lagged U.S. unemployment has a significant effect on current values of the unemployment rate in both Europe and Japan.

Table 6.6 reports the correlations between the residuals of each of the equations (the calculated values of $SH_j[t]$), and all these are statistically significant for the regressions for the whole period. The positive correlation between the residuals for the United States and those for Europe is consistent with the interpretations of (a) current-year shocks in the United States getting passed on to Europe, (b) current-year shocks in the Europe getting passed on to the United States, and (c) a combination of a and b. One cannot identify the causation of the process without setting out a fully specified structural model.

The statistical significance of $u_{US}(t-1)$ in the equations for Europe and Japan and the lack of significance of $u_{EU}(t-1)$ and $u_{JA}(t-1)$ in the equation for the United States are suggestive of the isolation of the U.S. macroeconomy from those of other industrialized countries. It is interesting to note that the estimated effect of lagged U.S. unemployment on the other economies' rates was stronger

TABLE 6.6 / Vector Autoregressions for Unemployment Rates of the United States (US), the European Union (EU), and Japan (JA), 1956 to 1999

	US		EU		JA	
1956 to 1999						
US(−1)	.61*	.73*		.20*		.07**
	(.13)	(.13)		(.06)		(.03)
EU(−1)		−.46***	.78*	.73*		−.04
		(.24)	(.10)	(.11)		(.05)
JA(−1)		−.03		−.30	.98*	.97*
		(.49)		(.24)	(.10)	(.11)
R^2	.61	.64	.98	.98	.93	.94
1956 to 1977						
US(−1)	.62*	.60*		.03		.02
	(.18)	(.21)		(.07)		(.04)
EU(−1)		−1.05	.88*	.36*		−.09
		(.93)	(.14)	(.30)		(.16)
JA(−1)		1.72		.81***	.88*	.96*
		(1.32)		(.43)	(.10)	(.23)
R^2	.40	.39	.80	.81	.80	.78
1978 to 1999						
US(−1)	.70*	.80*		.44*		.15**
	(.17)	(.22)		(.11)		(.06)
EU(−1)		−.23	.84*	.57*		−.17***
		(.28)	(.13)	(.14)		(.08)
JA(−1)		−.69		−.19	1.09*	1.32*
		(.59)		(.30)	(.15)	(.17)
R^2	.63	.68	.88	.94	.85	.88

Sources: The Economic Report of the President (2000, and various previous issues).

Note: Regressions for 1956 to 1999 include cubic in time; regressions for the two subintervals include time linearly.

* Significant at the 1 percent level.

** Significant at the 5 percent level.

*** Significant at the 10 percent level.

in the second half of the period than in the first. Given that flexible exchange rates roughly coincided with the latter period, one would have hypothesized the opposite result.

The Effect of Foreign Price Changes on Equilibrium Unemployment

A second shorter-run issue concerns the potential for foreign price developments to affect the equilibrium unemployment rate in the United States indirectly through their effect on real-wage growth. One of the more surprising aspects of the performance of the American economy during the past decade is the fact that the overall unemployment rate fell to 4 percent without any apparent inflationary pressure. Most economists had, after the early 1970s, got used to concluding that the natural rate was in the neighborhood of 6 percent.

What was different about the expansion of the 1990s compared to the nearly twenty years before that expansion? For one thing, starting in 1995, real wages began to rise for the first time in almost a quarter of a century (see figure 6.5). Could this have been the cause of the decline in the unemployment rate during the decade?

Assume, in the spirit of Blanchard and Katz (1997), that the rate of wage adjustment in the United States is given by

$$\Delta w_t = a(t) + \Delta P_e - \beta u_t + e_t, \tag{6.9}$$

where ΔP_e is the expected change in the consumer price index, and $a(t)$ is a time-varying constant term. Assume—primarily for the sake of simplicity—that the expected price increase is equal to the actual price increase last year, that is, $\Delta P_e = \Delta P_{t-1}$. In long-run equilibrium, the rate of growth of the real-wage rate, $\Delta W_t - \Delta P_t$, is equal to the rate of productivity growth, θ, and the rate of price inflation is constant. Thus, u^N, the equilibrium unemployment rate (the NAIRU in this story), is given implicitly from equation 6.9 by setting $\Delta w_t - \Delta P_e = \theta$, and its solution value is

$$u^N = \frac{1}{\beta} [a(t) - \theta]. \tag{6.10}$$

By this specification, the equilibrium unemployment rate obviously depends negatively on the rate of growth of the real wage rate, proxied in the long run by θ.

An alternative specification to equation 6.9 is that wage changes depend on a combination of expected price inflation and expected wage inflation, that is,

$$\Delta w_t = a(t) + \lambda \Delta P_e + (1 - \lambda)\Delta w_e - \beta u_t + e_t. \tag{6.11}$$

Assuming that $\Delta w_e = \Delta w_{t-1}$ as well as that $\Delta P_e = \Delta P_{t-1}$, we have a fairly general wage-adjustment function that can be estimated as

$$\Delta w_t - \Delta w_{t-1} = a(t) + \lambda(\Delta P_{t-1} - \Delta w_{t-1}) - \beta u_t + e_t. \tag{6.12}$$

If $\lambda = 0$, this is a pure wage-acceleration equation (of the type originally introduced by Phelps 1968); if $\lambda = 1$, the equation yields the Blanchard-Katz model outlined earlier. The equilibrium unemployment rate in the general case is given by

$$u^N = \frac{1}{\beta}[a(t) - \lambda\theta].$$ (6.13)

Estimates of three versions of the wage equations (using average hourly earnings in manufacturing for w and the Consumer Price Index-Urban (CPI-U) for P) for the sample period 1953 through 1999 are reported in table 6.8. All equations include a quadratic in time to capture movements in u^N that are independent of trend growth in real wages. The regression in column 1 makes the explicit assumption that λ is equal to 1, and that in column 3 is based on the assumption that λ is 0. The regression in column 2 allows for the estimation of λ—under the admittedly questionable assumptions that $\Delta w_e = \Delta w_{-1}$ and $\Delta P_e = \Delta P_{-1}$. This estimate, 0.407 (0.100), is obviously about halfway between the two extremes.

Table 6.8 also reports the estimated values of the equilibrium unemployment rate as of 1999 for alternative average rates of growth of the real-wage rate. The high value, 2.3 percent, is the average value of $\Delta W - \Delta P$ for the period from 1953 through 1973. The low value, -0.7 percent, is the average for the 22-year period from 1974 through 1995. The middle value, 0.6 percent, is the average value in the last four years of the sample. For the assumption that $\lambda = 1$, the difference in the predicted unemployment rate in 1999 between a value of θ of -0.7 percent and one of $+0.6$ percent is 1.7 percentage points.[22] For the intermediate case with the estimated value of λ given by column 2, the increase in average real growth for 1996 to 1999 compared to 1974 to 1995 caused the equilibrium rate to decline by 0.7 percentage points from 5.4 to 4.7 percent. By the model in which λ is assumed to equal 0, of course, u^N is independent of θ.

Real-wage rates in manufacturing had been falling for over twenty years, but their path turned around in 1995 (see figure 6.4). One of the reasons for this is the increase in the strength of the dollar in real terms. The real trade-weighted value of the U.S. dollar (the broad-based version) increased from 84.8 in 1995 to 98.6 in 1999, an annual rate of growth of 3.0 percent. Given the share of imports of 13 to 14 percent during this period, this means that about 0.4 percentage points of the 0.6 percentage point growth in the average real wage in the late 1990s may plausibly be attributed to the increase in terms of trade. In terms of the results with the Blanchard-Katz specification, the model in column 1 of table 6.7, this would have lowered the natural rate by a little more than half a percent-

TABLE 6.7 / Correlations of Contemporaneous Residuals in VARs

	1956 to 1999		1956 to 1977		1978 to 1999	
	US	EU	US	EU	US	EU
EU	.52*		.53*		.52**	
JA	.37**	.41*	.47**	.61*	.06	.14

Sources: The Economic Report of the President (2000, and various previous issues).

Notes: Based on regressions in table 6.6. U.S. = United States. EU = European Union. JA = Japan.

* Significant at the 1 percent level.

** Significant at the 5 percent level.

TABLE 6.8 / Phillips Curves with Price Changes and Wage Changes on the Left-Hand Side and Resultant Estimated Natural Rates

Dependent Variable	$\Delta W - \Delta P_{-1}$ (1)	$\Delta W - \Delta W_{-1}$ (2)	$\Delta W - \Delta W_{-1}$ (3)
U	−.78	−.59	−.45
	(.14)	(.11)	(.12)
$\Delta P_{-1} - \Delta W_{-1}$		.407	
		(.100)	
R^2	.63	.41	.20
$D - W$	1.2	2.1	2.6
$U^*(1999)$:			
$\theta = 2.1$	2.3	3.9	4.5
	(.4)	(.7)	(1.1)
$\theta = .6$	4.2	4.7	
	(.7)	(.8)	
$\theta = -.7$	5.9	5.4	
	(.9)	(.9)	

Sources: The Economic Report of the President (2000, and various previous issues).

age point. In terms of the intermediate model in column 2, the increase in U.S. terms of trade would have lowered U_* by about 0.2 percentage points.

The Effect of Globalization on Labor-Demand Elasticities

Several researchers have argued that the lack of overwhelming evidence that trade has been pressuring U.S. wages is difficult to reconcile with the large amount of anecdotal evidence that trade has been placing substantial pressure on labor markets. This suggests that the pressure may be appearing, not in the prices for labor, but rather in the elasticities of demand for labor.

Labor-demand elasticities measure how sensitive firms are to wage increases: they measure the drop in quantity of labor demanded in response to a rise in wages facing firms. Standard trade theory suggests that increased trade can make labor demands more elastic (that is, make firms more sensitive to wage costs) in two main ways. The first way is by making output markets more competitive: the more competitive product markets are, the more firms must cut back on output and, thus, demand for all factors when faced with rising wage costs. The second way is by making domestic labor more substitutable with foreign factors of production. Higher domestic wages can induce firms to hire more foreign factors, either directly via multinational firms or indirectly via purchases of imported intermediate inputs.

Rodrik (1997) discusses three important implications of more-elastic factor demands. First, higher elasticities shift the wage and/or employment incidence of nonwage-labor costs (for example, payroll taxes) away from employers toward labor. Second, higher elasticities trigger more-volatile responses of wages and/or employment to any exogenous shock to labor demand. Third, higher elasticities shift from labor toward capital bargaining power over rent distribution in firms that enjoy extranormal profits.

Slaughter (in press) looks for empirical evidence of more-elastic U.S. labor demands. Using a panel of several hundred U.S. manufacturing industries from 1961 through 1991, he first estimates time series of labor-demand elasticities for more-skilled and less-skilled labor. He then regresses these estimated elasticities on plausible driving forces, including measures of globalization and technological change. The first-stage estimates indicate that U.S. demand for less-skilled labor has become more elastic over time, with no such trend for more-skilled labor. The stage 2 estimates lend mixed support, at best, to the hypothesis that increased trade has made demands more elastic. For both labor types, time itself is a very strong predictor of elasticity patterns. This result parallels the common finding in studies of wage inequality: for both elasticities and the skill premium, their movements over time remain quite open to interpretation. Still, it does appear that U.S. demand for less-skilled labor has grown more elastic in recent decades.

Effects on Unemployment

The conventional approach to the determination of unemployment for different labor groups in a U.S.-style economy is based on the assumption that—absent short-run demand shocks—relative wage rates tend to adjust such that unemployment rates move toward their equilibrium ("natural") values. The negative trend in the relative labor demand for low-skilled workers, caused by a combination of SBTC and international factors, was met in the United States with an increasing skill differential. This conventional approach goes on to stress that, in Western Europe, on the other hand, the relative wage structure is not free to adjust as it is in the United States, and a decline in the relative demand for less-skilled labor causes an increase in the unemployment rates for low-skilled groups. In other words, by this approach, institutions in the United States are better able to tolerate the wage inequality necessary to sustain full employment.[23]

An alternative approach is to specify that the labor-force-participation rates of some groups of workers depend on their wage rates. Juhn, Murphy, and Topel (1991) claim that the own-wage elasticity of labor supply of persons in the lowest quintile of the wage distribution may be as high as $+0.4$. They argue that, contrary to the conventional view outlined in the preceding paragraph, the diminished relative labor demand of low-skilled workers led to large labor-force withdrawals on the part of high school dropouts. If this is correct, the performance of the labor market in the United States is not as impressive as would be determined on the basis of the behavior of relative unemployment rates.

SUMMARY AND CONCLUSIONS

The major points made in this paper are as follows:

Since World War II, there has been a major increase in the extent to which the U.S. economy is open to international influence. This is manifested by increases in the ratios of both imports and exports to GDP, the fraction of immigrants in the population, and the relative importance of FDI in terms of total investment.

At the same time that the economy became more open, there were two major developments with respect to wage rates in the United States. First, the variance of wages—as represented by the ratio of the wage rates of nonproduction workers to those of production workers, college/high school relative earnings, and the ratios of the earnings of those in the 90th to the earnings of those in the 50th percentile and of the earnings of those in the 50th percentile to the earnings of those in the 10th percentile of the earnings distribution—had been increasing since 1979. Second, from 1973 to 1995, average real wages fell slightly, which means that those with low skills near the bottom of the earnings distribution incurred significant real-wage decreases during this period. Since 1996, the trend of real-wage decreases has turned around, but it is too soon to tell if average real wages will be subject to the pre-1973 trend of positive growth.

These two trends in the openness and in both relative and real wages in the United States suggest that wage trends *may* have been caused by what happened to trade, and some economists and others have made this connection.

Approaching the question of the determination of relative-wage rates from the open-economy perspective has implications for the results obtained that are very different from the implications of approaching the question from the closed-economy perspective. Most important, the two approaches will find different effects of changes in relative supplies on relative wages. The traditional closed-economy approach of labor and macroeconomists implies that relative wages will respond to changes in relative supplies (through, notably, education policy or immigration). The traditional open-economy model, by contrast, implies that changes in the composition of labor supply cause adjustments in the industry mix of the economy rather than in the structure of relative wages.

The relevance of the open-economy model depends on various conditions being satisfied. Among these conditions are that different industries in the tradable-goods sector have different degrees of intensity with respect to labor skill, that there is a fairly rapid rate of interindustry labor mobility, that the U.S. economy is a part of the world economy, and that the demand for goods across countries not be subject to a high degree of home-country bias. To the extent that these assumptions are not satisfied, the relative-labor-demand functions for the economy move from those of the pure version of the open economy (with infinite labor-demand elasticities) to those of the closed economy (with finite labor-demand elasticities depending on elasticities of substitution and product demand). It is possible that the assumptions of the open-economy model will be satisfied for some groups of workers but not for others (in other words, some groups of workers may be outside the cone of diversification).

Determination of just where a particular economy is in the open-closed spectrum is a multistep process. Our judgment about the answer to this question with respect to the U.S. economy is that, over the past thirty years, it has been behaving more and more like the purely open economy of theory. It is tempting to extrapolate this trend into the next few decades, but such an extrapolation requires some strong implicit assumptions about international political stability.

There is some evidence that, between 1979 and 1994, very low-skilled workers in the United States (those who have not finished high school) were forced to transfer out of industries producing tradable goods into industries producing nontradable goods. If this trend continues into the near future, the labor market for very low-skilled workers will be subject to a closed-economy analysis, with very different implications than would apply to more-skilled labor groups whose wage rates are determined (to a large extent) by international rather than domestic considerations.

Our paper reflects the emphasis of the international-trade literature on the medium and long runs rather than on the short run and, therefore, has much more to say about relative wages than about relative employment. It is interesting to note, however, that the short-run behavior of the U.S. economy appears to be less affected by negative shocks in other industrialized countries than the short-run economies of other industrialized countries are affected by negative shocks in the United States.

One interesting feature of labor-market performance in the United States over the past two decades is the fairly large decrease in the labor-force participation rate of very low-skilled workers. Some assert that this reflects a labor-supply response to lower real-wage rates of this type of labor. It is, accordingly, possible that further increases in the degree of openness of the U.S. economy will lead to problems in the sustainability of employment for this segment of the population.

For helpful comments, we thank Bob Solow, David Weiman, and seminar participants at the Sustainable Employment Initiative conference. For financial support, we acknowledge the Century Fund and the Russell Sage Foundation.

NOTES

1. U.S. trade shares are less than those of many European countries, but they are similar to those of the countries of the European Union—whose geographic size is about that of the United States—taken together (see, for example, Krugman 1995).

2. For the period 1990 to 2000, growth in the foreign-born population accounted for 33.7 percent of U.S. population growth. Births to immigrants who arrived in the 1990s accounted for another 6.5 percent of U.S. population growth (Hanson et al. 2001).

3. These basic facts on relative earnings come from Council of Economic Advisers (1997, 2000). Each of these reports devotes substantial space to labor markets and inequality. Inequality has also risen *within* education, experience, and occupation groups.

4. We refer both to the current volume and to "000," a symposium in the *Journal of Economic Perspectives.*

5. The fact that these two trends occurred simultaneously has led many observers—including economists such as George Borjas and Valerie Ramey (1994) and George Johnson and Frank Stafford (1993)—to conclude that there is probably a causal connection between trade and wage developments.

6. We would be reluctant to apply this model to, for example, the current economies of Western Europe, in which the full-employment assumption is at least questionable.

7. The RS curve is vertical under the simplifying assumptions that the numbers of skilled and unskilled workers are fixed and that workers' supply decisions are unaffected by the values of W_s and W_u.

8. In a multisector closed economy, the RD would also be shifted to the right by shifts in the demand for goods that are relatively skill intensive (that is, have large δ_k's in levels).

9. Two additional comments on figure 6.8 are in order. First, note that, when the number of sectors exceeds the number of factors, output mixes are usually indeterminate. That is, there is no unique optimal output mix that can fully employ all factors in a given endowment. Instead, the range of optimal outputs usually lies in an $N - M$–dimensional space. In deriving the RD schedule, for simplicity we focused on output mixes whose relation to the underlying endowments seems most intuitive. For a comprehensive discussion of these "higher-dimensional" issues of HO trade theory, see Wilfred Ethier (1984). Second, the downward-sloping portions of RD assume flexible production technologies that allow substitutability among factors, as in equation 6.1. If technology were Leontief ($\sigma = 0$ in equation 6.1), then these portions would become vertical.

10. It is important to stress that the 1990s entry into the world economy of low-income countries like China and India is communicated to the U.S. labor market via shifts in RD. The entry of these countries increases the world relative supply of less-skilled labor; this, in turn, tends to lower the world relative price of unskilled-labor-intensive products like textiles and toys, and these price changes shift the American RD curve. Recent shifts in bilateral U.S. trade patterns suggest that this process is under way: today, China has overtaken Japan as the country with which the United States runs its largest bilateral trade deficit, the majority of which is accounted for by precisely these unskilled-labor-intensive manufactures.

11. Shifts in the structure of product demand can also influence RD, but, empirically, the correlation between demand shifts and skill intensity during the 1980s was close to 0 (Bound and Johnson 1992).

12. Even though, within the unskilled-labor-intensive sector, relative demand for skilled labor rises, economywide demand for skilled labor falls because firms try to shift resources into this initially more-profitable sector.

13. The total supply of younger Ph.D.s in year t is $L_t = L_{nt} + L_{it} = L_t + b_t L_t$, where L_{nt} and L_{it} are, respectively, the supplies of natives and immigrants, and $b_t = L_{it}/L_t$ is the

immigrants' share of the total supply. Changing b_{95}' to its 1979 value yields L_{95}' (what total supply in 1995 would have been if immigrants still constituted only 14 percent of the total). The value of $\log(L_{95}/L_{95}') = 0.14$.

14. This would, of course, be reduced if, instead of assuming that the domestic supply of younger Ph.D.s through the 1980s was unaffected by the lower wages brought on by the additional immigrants, we assumed that natives who would have finished Ph.D.s followed other pursuits (went into business, law, and the like)—a situation in which the immigrants "crowded out" the natives.

15. Rising college attendance and completion have, somewhat surprisingly, not occurred automatically in recent years (see Card and Lemieux 1999).

16. This conclusion about trade's relatively small role seems widespread. For example, the 1997 *Economic Report of the President* (Council of Economic Advisers 1997) reports results of a poll taken at a Federal Reserve Bank of New York colloquium on inequality attended by many of the important researchers in this area. When asked the cause of the increase in inequality, the average respondent attributed 45 percent of the blame to technological change, about 10 percent to international trade, and less than 10 percent to various other factors.

17. Table 6.3 also shows the well-documented within-industry decline in low-skilled relative employment, discussed earlier in this section. Over the 1980s, there is a large decrease in the employment of high school dropouts and high school graduates relative to that of college graduates and those with some college. Combined with the observed rise in the wage premium to skilled workers, these relative-employment shifts suggest SBTC.

18. If factors cannot move effortlessly, the possibility of equilibrium unemployment is raised as well. Again, as commonly presented, standard trade models (HO and otherwise) assume full employment. That said, there is a literature wedding the HO structure to search models of the labor market in which imperfections in the matching process generates equilibrium unemployment (for example, Davidson, Martin, and Matusz 1999). Our third section addresses these issues.

19. One way to formalize product markets that are less than perfectly competitive is the idea that outputs are subject to Armington-style "home bias": for example, many consumers in the United States would not consider buying a foreign automobile. To the extent that home bias is important, the relative-labor-demand function becomes a blend of figures 6.7 and 6.8 (see Johnson and Stafford 1999), with an absolute relative-wage elasticity between its finite value in the closed-economy case (s with one sector) and infinity. The process of globalization might be interpreted as home bias breaking down, with the result that national labor demand becomes flatter over time.

20. To examine the sector bias of barrier *levels* more formally, Haskel and Slaughter (2000) also regress the levels of tariffs on the shares of more-skilled and less-skilled labor in total industry costs for 1974, 1979, and 1988. In every case, tariffs were significantly concentrated in less-skilled-labor-intensive sectors.

21. Alan Blinder and Janet Yellen (chapter 3 in this volume) offer an interesting twist on the role of the international economy in the economic history of the 1990s. The large tax cuts and enormous budget deficits of the 1980s caused the real exchange rate to rise precipitously, thus causing many inefficient firms in trade-sensitive manufactur-

ing to disappear. This, according to Blinder and Yellen, helped pave the way for the surge of productivity growth in the latter part of the 1990s.

22. All the estimated standard errors of the u^N's are calculated by the delta method. For a discussion of this method and alternatives, see Staiger, Stock, and Watson (1997).

23. This view is consistent with the theme of Giuseppe Bertola, Francine Blau, and Lawrence Kahn (chapter 4 in this volume). For an alternative approach to the problem of European unemployment, see Stephen Nickell and Richard Layard (1999).

REFERENCES

Abraham, Katharine, James Spletzer, and Jay Stewart. 1999. "Why Do Different Wage Series Tell Different Stories?" *American Economic Review* 89(2): 34–39.

Autor, David H., Lawrence F. Katz, and Alan B. Krueger. 1998. "Computing Inequality: Have Computers Changed the Labor Market?" *Quarterly Journal of Economics* 113(4): 1169–1214.

Baldwin, Robert E., and Glen G. Cain. 1997. "Shifts in U.S. Relative Wages: The Role of Trade, Technology, and Factor Endowments." *NBER* working paper no. 5934. Cambridge, Mass.: National Bureau of Economic Research, February.

Berman, Eli, John Bound, and Zvi Griliches. 1994. "Changes in the Demand for Skilled Labor within U.S. Manufacturing: Evidence from the Annual Survey of Manufactures." *Quarterly Journal of Economics* 109(May): 367–97.

Berman, Eli, John Bound, and Steve Machin. 1998. "Implications of Skill-Biased Technological Change: International Evidence." *Quarterly Journal of Economics* 113(4): 1245–80.

Bhagwati, Jagdish. 1991. "Free Traders and Free Immigrationists: Strangers or Friends." Russell Sage Foundation Working Paper.

Bhagwati, Jagdish, and Vivek Dehejia. 1994. "Free Trade and Wages of the Unskilled: Is Marx Striking Again?" In *Trade and Wages,* edited by J. Bhagwati and Marvin Kosters, 36–75. Washington, D.C.: American Enterprise Institute.

Blanchard, Olivier, and Lawrence F. Katz. 1997. "What We Know and What We Do Not Know about the Natural Rate of Unemployment." *Journal of Economic Perspectives* 11(winter): 51–72.

Borjas, George J. 1994. "The Economics of Immigration." *Journal of Economic Literature* 32(3): 1667–1717.

———. 1999. *At Heaven's Gate*. Princeton, N.J.: Princeton University Press.

Borjas, George J., Richard B. Freeman, and Lawrence F. Katz. 1992. "On the Labor-Market Effects of Immigration and Trade." In *Immigration and the Work Force,* edited by George Borjas and Richard Freeman, 213–44. Chicago: University of Chicago Press.

———. 1996. "Searching for the Effect of Immigration on the Labor Market." *American Economic Review* 86(May): 247–51.

———. 1997. "How Much Do Immigration and Trade Affect Labor Market Outcomes?" *Brookings Papers on Economic Activity* (1): 1–90.

Borjas, George J., and Valerie A. Ramey. 1994. "Time-Series Evidence on the Source of Trends in Wage Inequality." *American Economic Review* 84(May): 10–14.

Bound, John, and George Johnson. 1992. "Changes in the Structure of Wages in the 1980s: An Evaluation of Alternative Explanations." *American Economic Review* 82(June): 371–92.

Card, David. 1997. "Immigrant Inflows, Native Outflows, and the Local Labor Market Impacts of Higher Immigration." *NBER* working paper no. 5927. Cambridge, Mass.: National Bureau of Economic Research.

Card, David, and Thomas Lemieux. 1999. "Can Falling Supply Explain the Rising Return to College for Younger Men? A Cohort-Based Analysis." Working paper no. 13. University of California, Berkeley, Center for Labor Economics, March.

Cooper, Richard N. 1985. "Interdependence, Consistency, and Policy Coordination." In *Handbook of International Economics*, Vol. 2, edited by Ronald W. Jones and Peter B. Kenen. Amsterdam: North-Holland.

Council of Economic Advisers. 1997. *Economic Report of the President*. Washington, D.C.: U.S. Government Printing Office.

———. 2000. *Economic Report of the President*. Washington: U.S. Government Printing Office.

Davidson, Carl, Lawrence Martin, and Steven Matusz. 1999. "Trade and Search-Generated Unemployment." *Journal of International Economics* 29(2): 271–99.

Davis, Donald R. 1998. "Technology, Unemployment, and Relative Wages in a Global Economy." *European Economic Review* 42(4): 1613–33.

Deardorff, Alan V. 1994. "Overview of the Stolper-Samuelson Theorem." In *The Stolper-Samuelson Theorem: A Golden Jubilee*, edited by Alan V. Deardorff and Robert M. Stern, 7–34. Ann Arbor: University of Michigan Press.

Deardorff, Alan, and Dalia Hakura. 1994. "Trade and Wages: What Are the Questions?" In *Trade and Wages*, edited by J. Bhagwati and Marvin Kosters, 76–107. Washington, D.C.: American Enterprise Institute.

Dixit, Avinash K., and Victor Norman. 1980. *Theory of International Trade*. Cambridge: Cambridge University Press.

Ethier, Wilfred J. 1984. "Higher Dimensional Issues in Trade Theory." In *Handbook of International Economics*, edited by Ronald W. Jones and Peter B. Kenen, 1:131–84. Amsterdam: North-Holland.

Feenstra, Robert C., and Gordon Hanson. 1995. "Foreign Investment, Outsourcing, and Relative Wages." In *Political Economy of Trade Policy: Essays in Honor of Jagdish Bhagwati*, edited by Robert C. Feenstra and Gene M. Grossman. Cambridge, Mass.: MIT Press.

———. 1999. "Productivity Measurement and the Impact of Trade and High-Technology Capital on Wages: Estimates for the U.S., 1972–1990." *Quarterly Journal of Economics* 114(3): 907–40.

Freeman, Richard. 1995. "Are Your Wages Set in Beijing?" *Journal of Economic Perspectives* 9(summer): 15–32.

Friedberg, Rachel, and Jennifer Hunt. 1995. "The Impact of Immigrants on Host Country Wages, Employment, and Growth." *Journal of Economic Perspectives* 9(1): 23–44.

Hamermesh, Daniel S. 1993. *Labor Demand*. Princeton, N.J.: Princeton University Press.

Hanson, Gordon H., Kenneth F. Scheve, Matthew J. Slaughter, and Antonio Spilimbergo. 2001. "Immigration and the U.S. Economy: Labor-Market Impacts, Illegal Entry, and Policy Choices." Mimeo. Dartmouth College, May.

Hanson, Gordon H., and Matthew J. Slaughter. Forthcoming. "Labor-Market Adjustment in Open Economies: Evidence from U.S. States." *Journal of International Economics*.

Haskel, Jonathan E., and Matthew J. Slaughter. 2000. "Have Falling Tariffs and Transportation Costs Raised U.S. Wage Inequality?" *NBER* working paper no. 7539. Cambridge, Mass.: National Bureau of Economic Research, February.

———. 2001. "Have Falling Tariffs and Transportation Costs Raised U.S. Wage Inequity?" *Review of International Economics*. Forthcoming.

———. Forthcoming. "Does the Sector Bias of Skill-Biased Technological Change Explain Changing Skill Premia?" *European Economic Review.*

Helpman, Elhanan, and Paul R. Krugman. 1985. *Market Structure and Foreign Trade.* Cambridge, Mass.: MIT Press.

International Monetary Fund (IMF). 2000. *World Economic Outlook.* Washington, D.C., October.

Johnson, George. 1997. "Changes in Earnings Inequality: The Role of Demand Shifts." *Journal of Economic Perspectives* 11(spring): 41–55.

Johnson, George, and Frank Stafford. 1993. "International Competition and Real Wages." *American Economic Review* 83(May): 127–30.

———. 1999. "The Labor Market Implications of International Trade." In *Handbook of Labor Economics,* edited by O. Ashenfelter and D. Card. 3B: 2215–88. Amsterdam: North-Holland.

Juhn, Chinhui, Kevin Murphy, and Robert Topel. 1991. "Why Has the Unemployment Rate Increased over Time?" *Brookings Papers on Economic Activity* (2): 75–142.

Katz, Lawrence F., and Alan B. Krueger. 2000. "The High-Pressure U.S. Labor Market." *Brookings Papers on Economic Activity* (2): 1–65.

Katz, Lawrence F., and Kevin M. Murphy. 1992. "Changes in Relative Wages, 1963–1987: Supply and Demand Factors." *Quarterly Journal of Economics* 107(February): 35–78.

Katz, Lawrence F., and Lawrence H. Summers. 1989. "Industry Rents: Evidence and Implications." *Brookings Papers on Economic Activity* (2): 209–75.

Krueger, Alan B. 1997. "Labor Market Shifts and the Price Puzzle Revisited." *NBER* working paper. Cambridge, Mass.: National Bureau of Economic Research, January.

Krugman, Paul R. 1992. *The Age of Diminished Expectations.* Cambridge, Mass.: MIT Press.

———. 1995. "Growing World Trade: Causes and Consequences." *Brookings Papers on Economic Activity* (2): 327–77.

Labor Extracts. 1979–1999. November. Cambridge, Mass.: National Bureau of Economic Research.

Lawrence, Robert Z., and Matthew J. Slaughter. 1993. "International Trade and American Wages in the 1980s: Giant Sucking Sound or Small Hiccup?" *Brookings Papers on Economic Activity* (2): 161–211.

Leamer, Edward E. 1998. "In Search of Stolper-Samuelson Linkages between International Trade and Lower Wages." In *Imports, Exports, and the American Worker,* edited by Susan M. Collins, 141–202. Washington, D.C.: Brookings Institution.

Leamer, Edward E., and James Levinsohn. 1995. "International Trade Theory: The Evidence." In *Handbook on International Economics,* edited by Gene M. Grossman and Kenneth Rogoff, 3: 1339–94. Amsterdam: North-Holland.

Mayer, Wolfgang. 1974. "Short-Run and Long-Run Equilibrium for a Small Open Economy." *Journal of Political Economy* 82(4): 855–967.

Mussa, Michael. 1974. "Tariffs and the Distribution of Income: The Importance of Factor Specificity, Substitutability, and Intensity in the Short Run and Long Run." *Journal of Political Economy* 82(6): 1191–1203.

———. 1978. "Dynamic Adjustment in the Heckscher-Ohlin-Samuelson Model." *Journal of Political Economy* 86(4): 775–91.

Nickell, Stephen, and Richard Layard. 1999. "Labor Market Institutions and Economic Performance." In *Handbook of Labor Economics,* edited by Orley Ashenfelter and David Card, 3C: 3029–80. Amsterdam: North-Holland.

Phelps, Edmund. 1968. "Money-Wage Dynamics and Labor-Market Equilibrium." *Journal of Political Economy* 76(July/August, pt. 2): 678–711.

Richardson, J. David. 1995. "Income Inequality and Trade: How to Think, What to Conclude." *Journal of Economic Perspectives* 9(summer): 33–55.

Rodrik, Dani. 1997. *Has Globalization Gone Too Far?* Washington, D.C.: Institute for International Economics.

———. 2000. "How Far Will International Economic Integration Go?" *Journal of Economic Perspectives* 14(winter): 177–86.

Rybczynski, T. M. 1955. "Factor Endowments and Relative Commodity Prices." *Economica* 22(3): 336–41.

Sachs, Jeffrey D., and Howard Shatz. 1994. "Trade and Jobs in U.S. Manufacturing." *Brookings Papers on Economic Activity* (1): 1–84.

Scholl, Russell B. 2000. "The International Investment Position of the United States at Year End 1999." *Survey of Current Business* 79(July): 46–56.

Slaughter, Matthew J. 2000. "What Are the Results of Product-Price Studies and What Can We Learn from Their Differences?" In *International Trade and Wages,* edited by Robert C. Feenstra, 121–70. Chicago: University of Chicago Press.

———. Forthcoming. "International Trade and Labor-Demand Elasticities." *Journal of International Economics* 51(1): 27–56.

Staiger, Douglas, James H. Stock, and Mark W. Watson. 1997. "The NAIRU, Unemployment, and Monetary Policy." *Journal of Economic Perspectives* 11(winter): 33–50.

Stolper, Wolfgang, and Paul A. Samuelson. 1941. "Protection and Real Wages." *Review of Economics and Statistics* 9(1): 58–73.

U.S. Bureau of the Census. 2000. *Educational Attainment in the United States, March 1999.* Washington: U.S. Government Printing Office.

Wood, Adrian. 1995. "How Trade Hurts Unskilled Workers." *Journal of Economic Perspectives*(summer): 57–80.

Part III

Increasing Labor Supplies and Their Limits

Chapter 7

Labor and the Sustainability of Output and Productivity Growth

Rebecca M. Blank and Matthew D. Shapiro

As the expansion of the 1990s has continued into the first year of the new century, there is ongoing interest in understanding the surge of output and productivity growth that this expansion has brought. The labor market plays a crucial role for both output and productivity. Labor is the most important factor of production in terms of value added. Labor is also substantially more easy to reallocate from old to new activities than is capital, so the dynamics of the labor market should give it a leading role in the economic transition toward new industries and new technologies. On the other hand, the cost of change for labor is not negligible. Workers make investments in specific education and skills and choose to live in specific locations. Firms and workers together make employment matches and undertake match-specific investments. Hence, technological progress that leads to aggregate growth can still have adverse effects on particular individuals or groups.

This paper provides an empirical framework for examining labor inputs and their relation to output and productivity growth. Our basic approach is to decompose the change in the return to labor into its various components, including population growth, employment growth, growth in time worked among the employed, and growth in earnings. We compare the contribution of these components to aggregate earnings over the economic cycles of the 1960s, the 1980s, and the 1990s, all of which included a sustained expansion. The results provide us with insight about how the cycle that started in 1990 is similar to and different from other recent periods of economic growth.

We are particularly concerned with the sustainability of economic growth achieved in the 1990s. Our decomposition of labor input lets us separate components that are likely to be cyclic from those that are likely to be sustainable. We also compare aggregate-earnings growth with growth in output and growth in capital stock to see whether recent earnings increases are moving together with these other measures. Finally, we evaluate the extent to which there is evidence for the "new economy" in the labor market, particularly in terms of the allocation of labor by occupation and industry as well as the differential returns to skilled and unskilled workers.

To preview our main results, the market outcomes for labor in the 1990s are remarkably similar to those of the 1960s and 1980s. The growth in labor input over the cycle comes largely from population growth, with some increase in labor-force participation. In the 1960s and the 1990s, the bulk of annual-earnings growth comes from increased wages (weekly earnings in our calculations), not from the expansion of labor inputs. There is a great deal of heterogeneity in the underlying level and composition of annual-earnings increases among different demographic groups, however. Annual-earnings gains among lower-skill groups are much more reliant on growth in their labor inputs than in their wages.

There is strong evidence that these earnings increases can be sustained by concurrent increases in technology and capital. There are, of course, sources of output expansion in the 1990s, expansion that cannot continue indefinitely. These are largely related to long-run trends in the labor market (for example, deceleration in the growth of female labor-force participation) rather than to short-term unsustainable excesses of an overheated economy. Such factors may limit growth in future expansions, but they do not threaten a reversal of recent gains. Future growth possibilities will also depend on the levels of work and earnings among a growing group of older persons, immigration policy, continued high wage (and productivity) growth among more-skilled workers, and the potential for future wage (and productivity) growth among less-skilled workers.

ANALYTIC FRAMEWORK

A Decomposition of Growth in Labor, Earnings, and Output

We use an identity similar to Okun's law that allows us to decompose total weeks of work into various margins of adjustment.[1] We consider the identity

$$W_t = N_t \cdot \frac{E_t}{N_t} \cdot \frac{W_t}{E_t}, \tag{7.1}$$

where W_t is total weeks of work in year t, N_t denotes population, and E_t denotes employment. This representation of Okun's law is abbreviated: the participation margin and the unemployment margin are not separated but rather treated together in the employment-population ratio (E_t/N_t). Although we use equation 7.1 for many of our results, we will also present separate results on participation and unemployment. This identity can be thought of as applying to the aggregate economy, to specific demographic groups, or, abstracting from population, to an individual.

Equation 7.1 truncates Okun's law at the quantity-of-labor margin. Although this margin is the focus of much of our analysis, we also take the further step of adding earnings or output to this equation. The standard implementation of Okun's law focuses on output or productivity. In steady state with a constant labor share, output and earnings will move proportionally. We focus on the results based on earnings because these data are measured from the same source as our labor-input data. Thus, we complete the Okun's law identity by adding earnings per week (Y_t/W_t) to equation 7.1. We can examine the decomposition of total earnings as

$$Y_t = N_t \cdot \frac{E_t}{N_t} \cdot \frac{W_t}{E_t} \cdot \frac{Y_t}{W_t}. \qquad (7.2)$$

Similarly, we can complete the identity in terms of output (Q_t) by adding productivity (Q_t/W_t) to equation 7.1. The difference between growth in earnings (Y_t) and growth in output (Q_t) is the difference between the growth rates in weekly earnings (Y_t/W_t) and weekly productivity (Q_t/W_t). This leads to the decomposition

$$Q_t = N_t \cdot \frac{E_t}{N_t} \cdot \frac{W_t}{E_t} \cdot \frac{Q_t}{W_t}. \qquad (7.3)$$

Most of our results will be expressed in terms of growth rates. To a first-order approximation, the growth rate in aggregate earnings is the sum of the growth rates of its components. Hence, we will examine the decompositions

$$\Delta Y_t = \Delta N_t + \Delta\left(\frac{E_t}{N_t}\right) + \Delta\left(\frac{W_t}{E_t}\right) + \Delta\left(\frac{Y_t}{W_t}\right) \qquad (7.4)$$

and

$$\Delta Q_t = \Delta N_t + \Delta\left(\frac{E_t}{N_t}\right) + \Delta\left(\frac{W_t}{E_t}\right) + \Delta\left(\frac{Q_t}{W_t}\right), \qquad (7.5)$$

where ΔX_t denotes the growth rate in variable X_t. Because we compute these changes from sequential cross-sectional samples of individuals, the only meaningful results are for groups of individuals or aggregates.

The first step is to decompose the increase in aggregate earnings into its four components during each of the three recent sustained expansions in the 1960s, the 1980s, and the 1990s. We also decompose the growth in aggregate earnings among groups of workers identified by sex, race, age, education, and so on. The aim of these decompositions is to identify from what groups and along what margins labor is adjusting during the expansion.

Sustainable Versus Cyclic Components

The decomposition presented in the previous subsection can be used to tell us something about the question of sustainability. Technological change, population change, and other exogenous changes in labor supply are presumably secular and sustainable sources of long-run growth (Solow 1956). The simple mechanics of a balanced-growth model are as follows:

- Employment grows at rate n.
- Technology grows at rate g.
- Capital accumulation adjusts endogenously to grow at rate $n + g$.
- Consequently, output will grow at rate $n + g$, while labor productivity, per capita income and consumption, and real wages will grow at rate g.

Hence, the rate of expansion of the overall economy is driven by growth in factors of production (labor and capital) plus the growth in technology. The decomposition discussed in the previous subsection aims to quantify these growth rates. Growth in total labor input (measured as total work weeks W in our measurement framework) is decomposed into several sources: growth in population, the employment rate, and weeks worked per worker. Growth in technology is estimated from either the growth in wages (income per week) or the growth in productivity (output per week).

A key insight from the Solow model is that capital accumulation must respond endogenously to exogenous growth in labor and technology to maintain the economy at the steady-state growth rate warranted by growth in labor and technology. Growth in labor input and technology will translate one-for-one into growth in output and earnings only if it is accompanied by the necessary amount of capital accumulation. Hence, capital accumulation is critical to the sustainability of growth from technology and labor input. The boom of the 1990s is distinctive in the high and sustained level of investment that accompanied it. In our sixth section, we present aggregate and industry-level evidence about capital accumulation. Our assessment of whether capital accumulation is keeping up with the pace of growth in labor and technology is an important key to understanding whether growth in income and wages is sustainable.

Cyclic factors can contribute to observed growth rates of labor input, wages, and productivity. Of the four terms in our decomposition, population itself is the only one that is clearly secular (at least at horizons relevant for this analysis). The other components of labor input have both secular and cyclic components. There are important trends in labor-force participation driven by forces beyond the business cycle. Yet the cycle might accelerate and decelerate participation about this trend. Similarly, there have been notable changes in the unemployment rate in the 1990s, some of which might be sustainable (Katz and Krueger 1999). More generally, the employment rate (E/N) and the intensity of employment (W/E) relate to work effort, which is likely to have a substantial cyclic component.

Likewise, real-wage growth (Y/W) and productivity growth (Q/W) are not pure measures of the growth in technology. Starting with Solow's (1957) original work on productivity measurement, economists have recognized that measured productivity has components relating to factor utilization that cause procyclic deviations of measured productivity from technology. Procyclic changes in measured productivity can come from capital utilization or labor effort. Countercyclic changes can come from adjustment costs associated with changes in investment rates.[2] Wage rates have further cyclic complications as measures of productivity because wages are unlikely to reflect marginal products on a period-by-period basis. Over the horizon that we analyze, however, we do not expect this to be a problem.

The cyclic nature of labor input and of deviations in measured productivity from technology confound each other. Cyclic movements in participation, employment, and intensity of work that drive labor input go hand-in-hand with cyclic movements in effort and factor utilization that drive productivity. Indeed, the correlation between labor input and the cyclic component of productivity motivated the formulation of Okun's law that output moves more than one-for-one with unemployment.

One key issue for the sustainability of the current expansion is whether the recent acceleration in the growth in technology is cyclic. There is growing evidence that the increase in the pace of productivity growth during the second half of the 1990s is due to technology rather than cyclic factors (Oliner and Sichel 2000; Jorgenson and Stiroh 2000; Nordhaus 2000). Susanto Basu, John Fernald, and Matthew Shapiro (2001) specifically address the question of cyclic productivity. Using structural econometric techniques, they find that technological change, not cyclic factors, explains the increase in productivity in the second half of the 1990s. Robert Gordon (1999, 2000)—although skeptical that there is in fact a new economy—uses different techniques to conclude that the rebound of productivity in the late 1990s is not mainly a cyclic phenomenon.[3] Finally, there is yet no sign of the typical end-of-expansion slowdown in productivity growth (Gordon 1979).

In this paper, we present peak-to-peak growth rates to abstract from cyclic factors rather than undertaking explicit cyclic adjustments. We also report results showing that the intensive margin of employment does not contribute much to growth over the cycles, which suggests that cyclic factors in productivity are not important over the entire cycle.[4] Nonetheless, there is substantial uncertainty about how much of the growth in the 1990s is cyclic, especially since the business-cycle peak was not in evidence going into 2000. In particular, we can only guess whether the decline in unemployment witnessed in the second half of the 1990s is sustainable.

Industry Reallocation and the New Economy

Employment shifts into industries with relatively high productivity can be a source of aggregate productivity growth. The Industrial Revolutions of the nineteenth century and the early twentieth were accompanied by shifts from agriculture to manufacturing. We can use our industry-specific results to look for evidence of similar shifts to electronics manufacturing and certain business services where the development and use of new technologies are concentrated. We can assess how broadly based any shifts in employment are, that is, the extent to which they are shared across demographic and education groups.

We can also use industrial and occupation detail to look for evidence of the new economy. We will examine whether growth in labor input has been particularly important in industries such as durable-goods manufacturing (that is, computers and telecommunications equipment), telecommunications, and other computer-intensive industries. Similarly, we will examine whether there are distinct patterns in the changing occupation or industry mix that might indicate a departure from trends of past expansions.

DATA

Labor Force and Earnings

Our primary data come from the outgoing rotation groups (ORGs) of the Current Population Survey (CPS), which are available from 1979 through 1999.[5] Our sample includes all noninstitutionalized civilians who are aged sixteen years or older. Because we want to abstract from cyclic changes, we use peak-to-peak data that bracket the cycles of the 1980s and 1990s. We choose the twelve-month periods centered on National Bureau of Economic Research reference peaks as starting and ending points of the cycles. To bracket the peaks in January 1980 and July 1990, our data on the 1980s are measured from July 1979 to June 1980 (referred to as *1979 to 1980*) through calendar year 1990. Our data for the 1990s are measured from calendar year 1990 (which brackets the July 1990 peak of the previous cycle) to calendar year 1999. This end point is mandated by the availability of data at the time this paper was written. It is not yet the peak. Whether the peak occurred in late 2000 or early 2001 remains to be seen. Our resulting samples have between 280,000 and 360,000 observations for the twelve-month periods that serve as beginnings or ends of the cycles.

The CPS ORG data are not available for the 1960s. For this period, we use the CPS data from March 1962 (which include annual-earnings data for 1961 and are the earliest available CPS data) and March 1970 (which include annual-earnings data for 1969).[6] These data are more limited, both in sample size and in variable detail. They also bracket only the expansion and do not adequately describe the entire cycle. Hence, growth rates reported during the 1960s are larger than those that we would see if the entire cycle were included in the data.

In short, we focus on data comparisons between 1961 and 1969, the period from 1979 to 1980 and 1990, and 1990 and 1999. The decade of the 1960s brackets nine years of expansion, that of the 1990s brackets a ten-year cycle, and that of the 1980s brackets an eleven and a half-year cycle. We report aggregate changes over these periods and do not adjust the data for different period lengths. Thus, we are understating the strength of the 1990s cycle relative to that of the 1980s cycle, both because we are truncating it before its peak and because we are reporting aggregate growth rates that are cumulated over a shorter number of years.

The ORG data provide information on employment, hours of work last week, and earnings last week. We deflate nominal earnings to 1999 dollars with the monthly personal-consumption-expenditures price index. To calculate annual earnings, we impute weeks of work to each individual observation, an imputation based on the average weeks of work over the year within the relevant subgroup (defined subsequently). Mean weeks are calculated from the closest March CPS.[7] We can convert these individual data into economywide or group aggregates by adding them up, weighted by the relevant population weights.

While we are interested in the decomposition (introduced in the previous section) of aggregate earnings among all workers, we are also interested in the contributions of specific groups in the population as well. We analyze the contribution to growth in each of the components of earnings discussed in the previous section for the following groups:

- sex (male; female);

- race (Hispanic; non-Hispanic black; non-Hispanic white; non-Hispanic other);

- age (sixteen to twenty-nine; thirty to forty-nine; fifty and older);

- education (no high school degree; high school degree only; more than high school, less than college; college degree or higher);

- marital status (not married, no children; not married with children; married, no children; married with children); and

- region (Northeast; Midwest; South; West).

Productivity and Capital Data

The CPS data, of course, have no information about the output of workers' firms or their capital stock. In order to examine output, productivity, and capital by types of workers, we map industry-level data onto the CPS data. Our basic procedure assigns their industry-level data to individual workers according to their industry and then constructs the relevant aggregates by demographic or occupation group. This procedure clearly glosses over heterogeneity of workers within industries, but it is the best that can be done using readily available, published statistics.

The Bureau of Economic Analysis (BEA) provides data on output, labor input, and capital stocks on a consistent basis at the rough two-digit SIC level. To map these data onto our sample, we have the option of assigning BEA output and dividing by workers in the CPS or directly assigning BEA output per worker (productivity) to individual workers in the CPS. We chose the latter approach because we felt that it was better to measure the numerator and denominator of productivity from a consistent data source. Specifically, we take the ratio of the BEA's real gross product originating (value added) to its measure of persons engaged in production (that is, full-time-equivalent employees plus the self-employed). Each individual observation in our CPS sample is assigned a productivity based on productivity in the industry in the specific year. When we calculate output, these productivities are scaled by individuals' hours of work.[8] For the capital-stock calculations, we assign the BEA's industry estimate of the real net stock of capital per full-time-equivalent worker to each worker in the CPS sample.

THE COMPOSITION OF EARNINGS GROWTH ACROSS THREE CYCLES

In this section, we examine earnings growth and its components across the cycles of the 1960s, the 1980s, and the 1990s using the data from the CPS. We also examine the contribution of different groups to growth in earnings and its components.

Aggregate Changes

Figure 7.1 shows the growth in aggregate annual earnings over the cycles of the 1960s, the 1980s, and the 1990s and its decomposition. As shown in the rightmost set of bars, earnings grew 46 percent in the expansion of the 1960s but less than 30 percent during the 1980s and the 1990s cycles. The other sets of bars in the figure show the four components of earnings growth using the decomposition in equation 7.4. Population growth is very important in all decades and explains 28 percent of the 1960s earnings expansion (13.0/45.6), 45 percent of the 1980s expansion, and 37 percent of the 1990s expansion. Growth in employment explains a relatively small share of the 1960s and 1990s annual-earnings growth but a larger share during the 1980s cycle. Growth in the intensive margin, weeks worked, is minor over all three cycles. Hence, the peak-to-peak growth rate is doing a good job of abstracting from cyclic factors.

Growth in earnings per week is the most important component of annual-earnings growth in the cycles of the 1960s and the 1990s. The 1960s saw particularly high earnings-per-week growth, explaining over 60 percent of the growth in total earnings, and driving the higher annual-earnings growth rates during that decade. Growth in earnings per week constituted just over half the annual-earnings growth in the 1990s but only 32 percent of annual-earnings growth in the 1980s, reflecting much more sluggish wage growth over that decade.

The 1990s cycle produced a sustained decrease in the unemployment rate. Well into the 1990s, most forecasters presumed that an unemployment rate of about 6 percent corresponded to full employment. Since the mid-1990s, the unemployment rate has fallen about 2 percentage points to around 4 percent with only a modest increase in inflation. Assuming that the decline in unemployment was entirely matched by an increase in employment, we can calculate how much

FIGURE 7.1 / Real-Earnings Growth and Its Components—Three Expansions

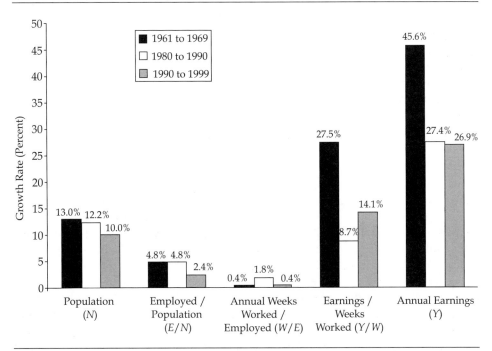

Source: Authors' calculations based on Current Population Survey.

Notes: Based on civilian population, age sixteen and over. Earnings are deflated by the personal-consumption-expenditures price index. 1980 refers to the period July 1979 to June 1980.

additional growth occurred in employment rates. This additional employment growth is a measure of the extent to which non-labor-market participants were drawn into the labor market during these cycles. The results shown in table 7.1 suggest that the decline in unemployment explained over half of employment growth in the 1990s but less than 20 percent of employment growth in the 1980s, reflecting high unemployment rates throughout that decade. Additional labor-force growth was stronger in the 1960s and the 1980s than in the 1990s. Much of this difference reflects higher growth in female labor-force participation in these earlier decades. Other chapters in the volume examine this decline in the unemployment rate. Since our results shed little light on the matching process for workers and jobs, we can say little about whether this decline in unemployment is sustainable.

Changes by Demographic Group

A key question for any expansion is who is most contributing to and benefiting from the growth in earnings and productivity? Some groups may receive a dis-

TABLE 7.1 / Growth in the Employment Rate (Percent)

	1961 to 1969	1980 to 1990	1990 to 1999
Total growth in employment/ population	4.8	4.8	2.4
Growth due to decline in unemployment	1.6	.9	1.4
Additional growth in the employment rate	3.2	3.9	1.0

Source: Current Population Survey, Outgoing Rotation Groups.

proportionate share of the population growth, the employment-share growth, or the earnings-per-week growth. In this subsection, we examine how aggregate-earnings growth is split among different groups in the population. We focus here on a comparison of the 1980s and the 1990s; the patterns in the 1960s are generally similar. A full set of results for each decade is available in the appendix tables.[9] We show summary information in the figures presented here.

Figure 7.2 shows annual-earnings growth and its components and separates the contributions of men and women. As in figure 7.1, the rightmost bar shows the growth in annual earnings, while the first four bars show the decomposition of earnings into its four components. Each of these bars is divided into two shaded areas that show the contribution of men and women to growth in each component. The shares of men's and women's contribution to growth in the component is noted to the right of the bars. The first four bars sum to total earnings growth, shown in the fifth bar. The contributions of each group to each component likewise sum to the total growth for that component. (Figures 7.3 through 7.8 are structured in a similar fashion.)

Not surprisingly, figure 7.2 shows that the contribution from population growth to total earnings is equally split between men and women in both expansions. On the other hand, almost all the growth in employment rate occurred among women. Women contributed about half the growth in earnings per week in the 1980s and only 31 percent in the 1990s. The net result, shown in the rightmost bar, is that women contributed 56 percent of the annual-earnings growth in the 1980s and 42 percent in the 1990s.

Table 7.2 provides further context for these results and shows initial population share and weekly earnings levels as well as growth rates in each of the components of annual earnings. The contribution to aggregate-annual-earnings growth of men and women, shown in the rightmost bar in figure 7.2, is affected by the initial male-female population ratio, differential growth rates in each component, and different starting levels in each component. For instance, although men capture a higher share of weekly earnings growth (69 percent in figure 7.2b) over the cycle of the 1990s, their growth rate in earnings is less than that of women (14 versus 16 percent). Their higher overall share of earnings growth can be attributed to their much higher starting level of weekly earnings ($502 versus

FIGURE 7.2 / Contributions to Real-Earnings Growth and Its Components—Sex

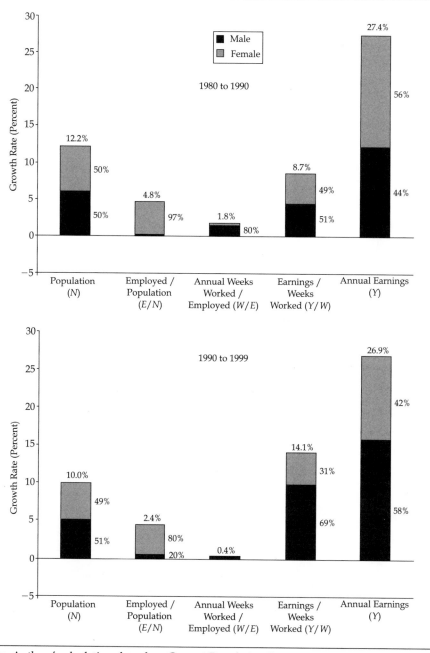

Source: Authors' calculations based on Current Population Survey.

Notes: Based on civilian population, age sixteen and over. Earnings are deflated by the personal-consumption-expenditures price index. 1980 refers to the period July 1979 to June 1980. Each group's share of the contribution to growth is given to the right of the bars.

TABLE 7.2 / Components of Growth in Earnings

	Initial Share of Population	Initial Level of Earnings per Week in 1999 Dollars (Y/W)	Growth Rates (Percent)				
			Population $\Delta(N)$	Employed/ Population $\Delta(E/N)$	Weeks Worked/ Employed $\Delta(W/E)$	Earnings/ Weeks Worked $\Delta(Y/W)$	Annual Earnings $\Delta(Y)$
From 1979–1980 to 1990							
Total	1.00	391	12	5	2	9	27
Male	.47	482	13	−2	3	4	18
Female	.53	275	12	13	1	20	46
White (non-Hispanic)	.82	402	7	5	2	10	24
Black (non-Hispanic)	.10	330	19	5	4	5	33
Hispanic	.05	335	53	6	−1	3	61
Other (non-Hispanic)	.02	381	49	−1	7	11	65
Age under thirty	.34	319	−7	4	3	1	2
Age thirty to forty-nine	.32	469	32	6	1	7	46
Age fifty or over	.34	405	0	2	0	5	6
Northeast	.23	398	4	6	1	18	28
Midwest	.26	396	3	4	2	3	13
South	.32	367	19	5	3	7	33
West	.19	415	22	4	1	8	35
High school or less	.66	334	0	1	3	−2	2
Some college	.19	396	27	5	1	5	38
Bachelor's or more	.14	587	39	2	0	13	54
Married	.61	439	6	5	2	8	21
Not married	.39	315	21	5	3	13	42

From 1990–1999

	1.00	427	10	2	0	14	27
Total							
Male	.48	502	11	0	1	14	25
Female	.52	340	9	5	0	16	31
White (non-Hispanic)	.78	446	4	2	0	16	22
Black (non-Hispanic)	.11	347	14	7	−1	17	37
Hispanic	.08	348	41	3	2	7	53
Other (non-Hispanic)	.03	428	45	3	1	14	63
Age under thirty	.28	323	0	−1	−1	5	3
Age thirty to forty-nine	.39	507	13	2	1	13	28
Age fifty or over	.33	419	14	10	0	20	44
Northeast	.21	475	2	1	2	9	14
Midwest	.24	409	5	5	−1	19	28
South	.34	396	13	3	−1	17	33
West	.21	450	17	1	2	9	29
High school or less	.59	328	−3	1	0	7	6
Some college	.22	417	24	0	1	8	33
Bachelor's or more	.19	672	27	−2	2	15	42
Married with children	.28	491	4	3	1	17	25
Married without children	.29	457	7	3	−1	16	25
Not married with children	.05	370	18	15	−1	13	44
Not married without children	.38	358	15	1	1	12	29

Source: Current Population Survey, Outgoing Rotation Groups. Based on civilian population, age sixteen and over.

Note: 1979–1980 period refers to the period July 1979 to June 1980.

$340). Table 7.2 also demonstrates how very unusual the high female contributions to earnings growth (shown in figure 7.2) were in the 1980s. Women capture almost half the growth in weekly earnings and more than half the overall growth in annual earnings. Women's far lower weekly wage levels are offset by their very high levels of employment growth and weekly earnings growth. In both decades, women's annual-earnings growth was disproportionately due to their relatively larger increases in employment, while men's annual-earnings growth was disproportionately due to their increases in weekly earnings.

Figure 7.3 provides a similar picture for the 1980s and 1990s expansions for non-Hispanic whites, non-Hispanic blacks, Hispanics, and other non-Hispanics (largely persons whose background is Asian or Pacific Islander). In both decades, the growth in annual earnings among the three nonwhite groups (shown in the final column of table 7.2) is larger than their initial population share (shown in the first column of table 7.2).

The vast majority of total earnings growth among Hispanics in both decades is coming from population growth. Around a third of total population growth in both decades is due to growth in the Hispanic population. Blacks and non-Hispanic others also had disproportionately high population growth, indicating the growing diversity in the population as the share of non-Hispanic whites declined. In contrast, whites contribute a vastly disproportionate share of the earnings-per-week growth in both decades relative to their population share. Table 7.2 shows that much higher starting-wage levels, combined with high growth rates in weekly wages, account for the disproportionate share of earnings growth among white workers. In summary, the annual-earnings gains to white workers were disproportionately coming from wage increases; the gains among nonwhite workers were disproportionately coming from population growth and (to a lesser extent) employment-share growth.

Figure 7.4 decomposes the expansions of the 1980s and 1990s by education level. Workers with college degrees or a graduate education account disproportionately for the expansion in annual earnings. Although these workers constitute only 19 percent of the population in 1990 and only 14 percent in the 1979 to 1980 period, they contribute more than two-thirds of the growth in earnings per week during both cycles and almost two-thirds of the growth in annual earnings. Annual-earnings gains among workers with some college result largely from growth in population and the employment rate. Those with a high school degree or less are shrinking as a share of the population in both decades and are responsible for very small shares of the growth in annual earnings. Table 7.2 indicates that this is because those with less education have both much lower starting wages and much slower wage growth over these two decades.

Figure 7.5 provides the results by age. Over these two expansions, the baby boom is moving from ages eighteen to thirty-three (in 1980) to ages thirty-seven to fifty-two (in 1999). The importance of the baby boom is clearly apparent. Figure 7.5 indicates that 92 percent of the population growth over the cycle of the 1980s comes from growth in the population aged thirty to forty-nine. In the 1990s cycle, population growth is split evenly between the thirty- to forty-nine-

FIGURE 7.3 / Contributions to Real-Earnings Growth and Its Components—
Race-Ethnicity

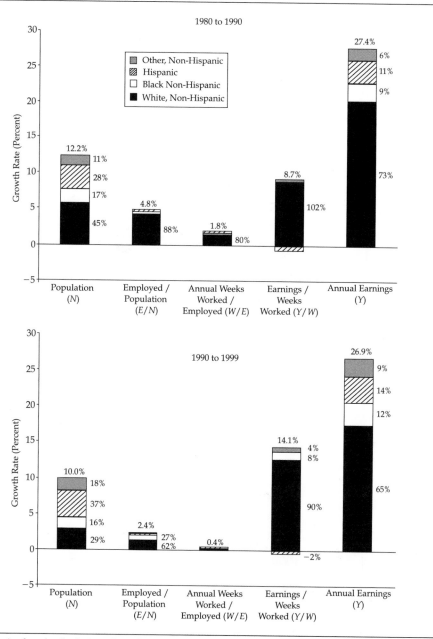

Source: Authors' calculations based on Current Population Survey.

Notes: Based on civilian population, age sixteen and over. Earnings are deflated by the
personal-consumption-expenditures price index. 1980 refers to the period July 1979 to June
1980. Each group's share of the contribution to growth is given to the right of the bars.

FIGURE 7.4 / Contributions to Real-Earnings Growth and Its Components—
Education

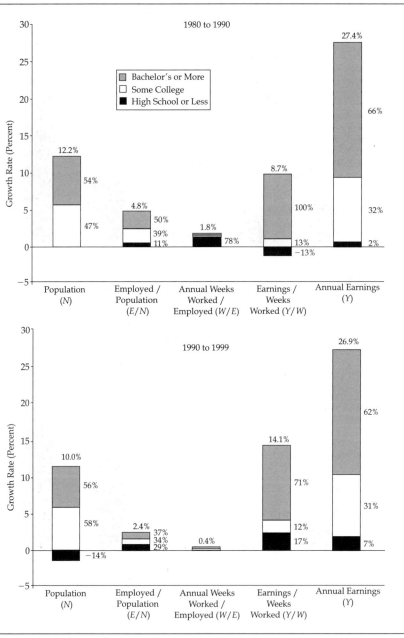

Source: Authors' calculations based on Current Population Survey.

Notes: Based on civilian population, age sixteen and over. Earnings are deflated by the
personal-consumption-expenditures price index. 1980 refers to the period July 1979 to June
1980. Each group's share of the contribution to growth is given to the right of the bars.

FIGURE 7.5   /   Contributions to Real-Earnings Growth and Its Components–Age

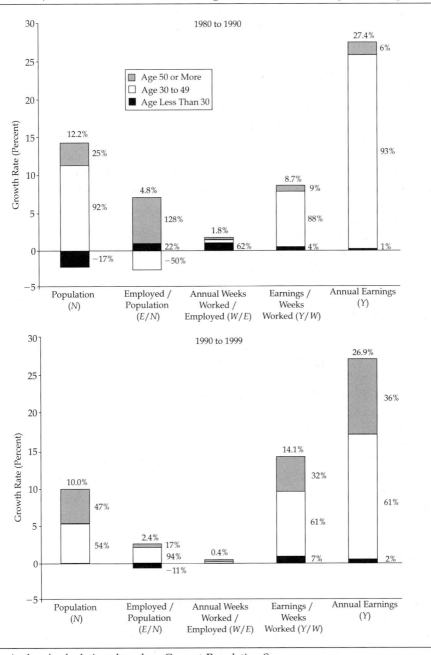

Source: Authors' calculations based on Current Population Survey.

Notes: Based on civilian population, age sixteen and over. Earnings are deflated by the personal-consumption-expenditures price index. *1980* refers to the period July 1979 to June 1980. Each group's share of the contribution to growth is given to the right of the bars.

/   325

year-olds and those older than age fifty. In both decades, the middle age group, which is dominated by the baby-boom cohort, exhibits the largest gains in earnings per week and in annual earnings, although, by the 1990s, the over-fifty group is receiving a growing share of annual-earnings gains.

Figure 7.6 shows the results by family status. (Data on children are not available in the ORG data during the 1980s.) In the 1990s, married persons with and without children are responsible for a disproportionate share of the increase in annual earnings, largely because of their much higher starting-wage levels (see table 7.2). Those who are single with children experienced very large employment and population gains in the 1990s, but their small starting share of the population and their low earnings levels meant that their share of aggregate-earnings growth was small. This finding is consistent with other evidence showing that employment rates among single mothers have increased rapidly over the past decade (Blank and Schmidt 2001).

Finally, figure 7.7 decomposes earnings growth by the four census regions. In the 1980s, the West contributes a high share of annual-earnings growth, largely because of greater population growth. In the 1990s, the West is still exhibiting much higher population growth, but it receives a smaller share of the growth in weekly earnings. These two effects offset each other. The Northeast contributes a relatively small share of annual-earnings gains in the 1990s, while the South gains a great deal.

QUANTITY OF LABOR: A CLOSER LOOK

Figures 7.2 through 7.7 clearly show that both population growth and employment-rate growth within the population have played an important role in increasing total earnings and productivity. This finding appears to be particularly true among less-skilled and lower-wage workers. In the cycles of both the 1980s and the 1990s, a disproportionate share of growth in earnings among more-disadvantaged workers came from population and employment growth rather than from weekly wage growth. In this section, we explore these changes in labor quantity more closely.

Age Distribution

As figure 7.5 makes clear, the age distribution of the population has been an important contributor to the increase in earnings. The baby-boom bulge in both the 1980s and the 1990s was primarily situated in the thirty- to fifty-year age range, an age when many persons work steadily and reap real-wage increases owing to their growing experience. But, even putting wage increases aside, this group experienced disproportionately large population and employment-share growth in both expansions.

As this population ages, we may have stronger offsetting effects as aging

FIGURE 7.6 / Contributions to Real-Earnings Growth and Its Components—Marital Status

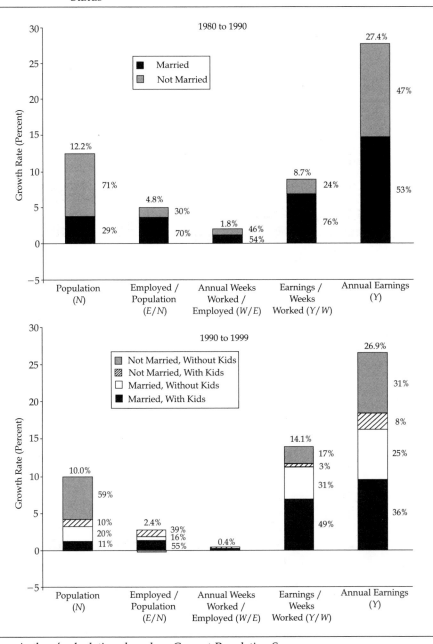

Source: Authors' calculations based on Current Population Survey.

Notes: Based on civilian population, age sixteen and over. Earnings are deflated by the personal-consumption-expenditures price index. 1980 refers to the period July 1979 to June 1980. Each group's share of the contribution to growth is given to the right of the bars.

FIGURE 7.7 / Contributions to Real-Earnings Growth and Its Components—Region

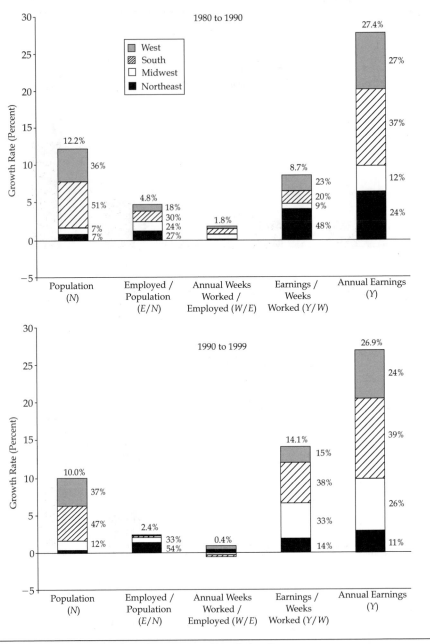

Source: Authors' calculations based on Current Population Survey.

Notes: Based on civilian population, age sixteen and over. Earnings are deflated by the personal-consumption-expenditures price index. 1980 refers to the period July 1979 to June 1980. Each group's share of the contribution to growth is given to the right of the bars.

workers start reducing their employment share and perhaps accept lower real wages. These effects are already visible among the current over-sixty-five population. In both the 1980s and the 1990s, population growth was strong among those over age sixty-five, but their share of employment growth and of weekly earnings growth declined. The net effect is that the over-sixty-five population contributed almost nothing to the growth in annual earnings in either of these cycles.

Offsetting the negative effects of the aging baby-boom generation are several other factors. First, the baby-boom echo is as large a cohort as the baby boom itself was and will be moving into their prime earning years over the next several decades. Second, continued work and earnings among many in the baby-boom generation may be possible. Wage levels among those over sixty-five have actually grown strongly during the past two decades. In addition, employment among older workers has been rising recently. Table 7.3, which shows labor-force-participation rates by sex, education level, and age over the past three decades, indicates that the downward trend in labor-force-participation rates of individuals aged sixty-five years and over ceased in the 1990s and even reversed for women. There has also been a notable increase over the last decade in labor-force participation among individuals aged fifty to sixty-five. This increase in labor-force participation might be sustainable, especially with increases in health and longevity. The very low levels of unemployment surely have facilitated it in recent years.

Labor-Force-Participation Changes Within Demographic Groups

As we have seen, growth in employment rates has been an important component of earnings growth. In this subsection, we ask how much of this change is due to changes in labor-force participation. Table 7.3 indicates that female labor-force-participation rates increased from 49 to 72 percent between 1969 and 1999. The pattern of increase among different groups has varied over time, however. More-skilled women showed strong increases in the 1970s and 1980s, but their participation rate has leveled off at around 82 percent over the 1990s. Less-skilled women, whose labor-force participation was almost flat in earlier decades, have experienced strong labor-force-participation growth in the 1990s. This trend has been correlated with economic growth, with welfare reform, and with expansions in the minimum wage and the earned-income tax credit (see Blank and Schmidt 2001).

In contrast, overall men's labor-force participation has declined slightly over these decades. This decline is most noticeable over the 1970s among less-skilled men. Labor-force participation among more-skilled men has been essentially flat over these decades. With earlier retirement, older men have also shown a marked decline in labor-force participation.

Most of the recent growth in labor-force participation has clearly come from women. If one takes men's labor-force-participation rates as the highest rate po-

TABLE 7.3 / Labor-Force-Participation Rates (Percent) by Sex, Year, Education Level, and Age

	1969	1979	1989	1999
Women				
Total	48.6	59.2	67.7	72.2
By education:				
High school dropout	41.6	43.7	44.5	50.3
High school diploma	51.4	61.2	68.0	70.1
Some college	51.1	65.9	74.3	75.9
College diploma	62.0	73.3	81.1	81.9
By age				
Sixteen to twenty-four	47.7	60.7	61.2	61.9
Twenty-five to forty-nine	48.0	63.1	74.1	77.3
Fifty to sixty-five	45.6	46.2	50.2	59.2
Over sixty-five	9.4	7.7	7.5	9.0
Men				
Total	89.4	87.2	86.3	85.3
By education:				
High school dropout	88.6	79.4	75.4	74.3
High school diploma	93.2	90.7	88.2	85.5
Some college	85.6	87.2	86.9	84.7
College diploma	91.2	92.8	92.3	91.5
By age				
Sixteen to twenty-four	62.1	70.8	69.2	64.7
Twenty-five to forty-nine	94.3	93.6	92.2	90.7
Fifty to sixty-five	85.9	76.7	72.1	74.4
Over sixty-five	24.9	18.3	15.5	14.9

Source: March Current Population Survey data, based on labor-force status in the week of survey.

Note: All persons aged twenty to sixty-five, except in specified age categories.

tentially attainable by women, then there is still some room for labor-force-participation growth among women, but much less than there has been in the past. If one believes that women's labor-force-participation rates are likely to be somewhat below men's because of childbearing as well as social norms and marital sorting, then there may be little room for substantial labor-force-participation increases in the next few decades. The lack of growth in labor-force participation among more-skilled women over the expansion of the 1990s may be an indication that at least these women are not likely to experience further employment-rate increases. In more disaggregated data, the group with the greatest potential to experience large labor-force-participation increases is Hispanic women, who tend to have lower skill levels and participate at a much lower level than other women. Hispanic women constitute only 5 percent of the adult population, however, so that even large increases in their labor-force participation are not likely to increase overall labor-force participation greatly.

In general, we believe that the potential for increased labor-force participation as a significant component in future economic cycles is more limited than it has been in the past, largely because we do not expect women's labor-force-participation rates to expand substantially in future decades. If female labor-force participation had not increased in recent decades, this would have shaved almost 5 points off the growth rates in annual earnings in the 1980s and almost 2 points off the growth rates in annual earnings in the 1990s.

It is an interesting question whether the decline in men's labor-force participation is permanent. To the extent that it is connected to more extended years of schooling and earlier retirement, it is likely to be permanent. To the extent that it reflects deteriorating labor-market conditions among less-skilled men, this group may increase work effort if wages among the less skilled rise in the future. But these effects are likely to be small.

Immigrants

The last two decades have seen high rates of immigration to the United States. We can investigate how much these immigrants have spurred growth in aggregate earnings. The 1999 ORG CPS data explicitly ask respondents whether they immigrated between 1990 and 1999. We take this as a rough measure of immigration over the cycle of the 1990s. Population growth over the expansion was 19.7 million; immigration was 8.5 million, indicating that 43 percent of the population growth was due to immigration. The effects over the 1980s were of a slightly smaller magnitude, with 32 percent of the 12.2 percent growth in population due to immigration.[10]

One might assume that immigration affects not just population growth, but other categories in our decomposition as well, particularly if immigrants are disproportionately employed or experience lower real-wage growth. Table 7.4

TABLE 7.4 / Growth in Earnings (Percent) Including and Excluding Recent Immigrants, 1990 to 1999

	Population $\Delta(N)$	Employed / Population $\Delta(E/N)$	Weeks Worked / Employed $\Delta(W/E)$	Earnings / Weeks Worked $\Delta(Y/W)$	Annual Earnings $\Delta(Y)$
All civilians age sixteen and over	10.0	2.4	.4	14.1	26.9
Excluding recent immigrants	5.8	2.6	.4	14.9	23.8

Source: Current Population Survey, Outgoing Rotation Groups.

presents the decomposition for the 1990s if all those who report immigrating over that decade were removed from the data. This calculation quantifies the direct effect of immigrants. It completely abstracts from changes in employment and wages of nonimmigrants that would result if there were no immigration. Net of immigration, earnings growth in the 1990s would have been 23.8 percent rather than 26.9 percent, all other things equal. This large effect is mainly due to the increased population growth resulting from immigration, which is slightly offset by the fact that immigrants earn substantially lower wages than do nonimmigrants.

Armed Forces

Our calculations are based on the civilian population. Since the last two decades have seen a substantial reduction in the size of the armed forces, it is worth investigating what the effect of this reduction is on civilian earnings. We can produce a rough, upper-bound estimate by calculating how much smaller the military was in 1999 than in 1990 and assuming that this number was added to civilian employment. Between 1990 and 1999, the size of the armed forces fell by over a third. In the absence of this change, civilian population would have grown only 9.5 percent rather than 10.0 percent. The civilian employment-to-population rate would have grown only 2.2 percent rather than 2.4 percent. The net effect is that aggregate earnings would have grown only 26.2 percent rather than 26.9 percent if armed-forces size had stayed constant. Over the 1980s, the effect is slightly smaller. These are not large effects.

Our overall assessment in this section is that several population trends, including increased female labor-force participation, high immigration, and the age distribution of the population, have helped raise growth rates over the past two decades. If these trends shift in upcoming decades, the growth potential of future expansions will be limited.

WAGES AND THEIR DISTRIBUTION: A CLOSER LOOK

In most cycles, one of the largest sources of growth in annual earnings is growth in weekly wages. This section explores changes in wages and annual earnings in more detail. Sustained increases in wages due to increases in technology and capital accumulation unambiguously increase economic well-being, in contrast to increases in annual earnings due to longer hours of work, higher employment rates, or rising population.

Comparing the Early and the Late Expansion in the 1990s

Other evidence indicating that post-1995 wage patterns were different than pre-1995 wage patterns suggests that it might be interesting to compare patterns in the first and second halves of the cycle. Figure 7.8 presents the contributions to earnings growth and its components from the periods 1980 to 1986 and 1986 to 1990 (figure 7.8a) and from the periods 1990 to 1995 and 1995 to 1999 (figure 7.8b). These data indicate very clearly that the expansion in the first half of the 1990s was relatively sluggish. Only 28 percent of the annual-earnings growth between 1990 and 1999 occurred in the first five years of the decade. Furthermore, there was very little growth in real weekly earnings over this time period. It is only after 1995 that the expansion really booms, with strong growth in real weekly wages and in employment-growth rates as well. In contrast, the expansion of the 1980s was more evenly spread over all years. Weekly earnings grow only slightly less between 1980 and 1986 (which includes four years of expansion) than between 1986 and 1990, while annual earnings grew slightly more during these earlier years. We return to this issue later when we discuss other productivity measures and show how the timing of annual-earnings growth diverges from growth in productivity and capital over the 1990s.

Earnings Inequality

During the 1980s, average wage growth was an inadequate descriptor of wage changes. Decreasing wages at the low end of the wage distribution and increasing wages at the high end led to increases in inequality. Evidence suggests that these trends continued through the mid-1990s, but, around 1995, wages started to rise even among the less-skilled population (Council of Economic Advisers 1999). Wages continued to rise among the more skilled as well, however, so wage inequality is not likely to have fallen over the 1990s.

Table 7.5 shows the share of annual earnings by quintile of the earnings distribution at the beginning and the end of the expansions of the 1980s and the 1990s; the last column shows the share of annual-earnings growth within each quintile. If a quintile captures the same fraction of annual-earnings growth as the share it started with at the beginning of the cycle, then its share will not change. As it turns out, quintile shares are shifting in similar ways across both decades in table 7.5, with ongoing widening inequality.

While the shares of earnings by quintile do not change rapidly, the shares of growth in annual earnings experienced by those at the top and the bottom of the distribution are markedly different, with the top 20 percent enjoying around 50 percent of the annual-earnings growth over each of these expansions and the bottom 20 percent capturing only 4 percent. In both decades, the share of annual earnings in the bottom four quintiles falls, while the share of the top quintile rises. The data discussed previously indicate that sources of aggregate-earnings growth were quite different among the top and the bottom of the earnings distribution, with growth at the bottom coming largely from population and employment-rate increases and growth at the top coming from real-wage increases.

These data suggest that earnings inequality widened over the 1980s and over the 1990s by about the same amount. The 1980s may have felt different than the

FIGURE 7.8 / Contributions to Real-Earnings Growth and Its Components—Time Period

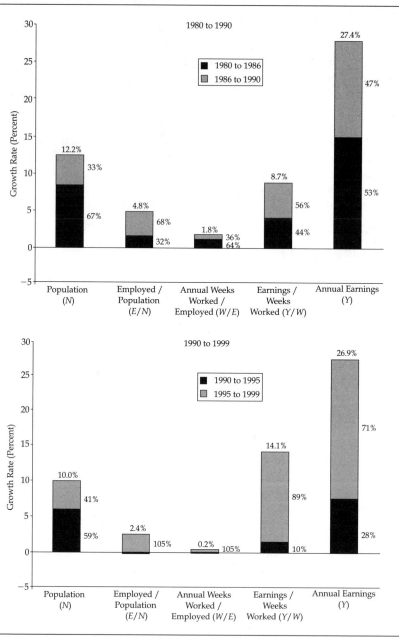

Source: Authors' calculations based on Current Population Survey.

Notes: Based on civilian population, age sixteen and over. Earnings are deflated by the personal-consumption-expenditures price index. 1980 refers to the period July 1979 to June 1980. Each group's share of the contribution to growth is given to the right of the bars.

TABLE 7.5 / Share of Annual Earnings by Quintile and Annual Earnings Growth within Quintiles (Percent)

Quintile	Quintile Share, 1979 to 1980	Quintile Share, 1990	1980 to 1990, Share of Annual Earnings Growth
Bottom 20 percent	5.5	5.1	3.9
20 to 40	11.8	10.9	8.1
40 to 60	17.1	16.4	14.2
60 to 80	24.2	23.8	22.3
Top 20 percent	41.4	43.7	51.6
	Quintile Share, 1990	Quintile Share, 1999	1990 to 1999, Share of Annual Earnings Growth
Bottom 20 percent	5.1	4.9	4.3
20 to 40	10.9	10.5	9.2
40 to 60	16.4	15.8	13.7
60 to 80	23.8	23.2	21.3
Top 20 percent	43.7	45.6	51.5

Source: Current Population Survey, Outgoing Rotation Groups.

1990s for low-wage workers since widening inequality occurred along with falling wages in the 1980s while, in the latter part of the 1990s, wages rose among the less skilled. This stronger wage growth among more disadvantaged workers did not, however, help these workers make gains in their share of earnings.

EARNINGS, PRODUCTIVITY, AND CAPITAL ACCUMULATION

Balanced Growth?

The previous sections document substantial growth in earnings during the sustained expansions of the 1980s and the 1990s. They decompose this growth in earnings into growth in the quantity of labor (population, employment rates, and intensity of employment) and growth in the rewards to labor (the wage rate). This increase in the wage rate is the dual of the increase in labor productivity. Labor productivity, however, will grow at the rate of technological progress only if the growth in technology and labor input is accompanied by the warranted amount of capital accumulation. Specifically, if the economy is close to steady state, we should expect to see capital increasing at the $n + g$ rate of growth to balance increases in labor and technology. Otherwise, diminishing marginal product may attenuate the growth in output and earnings.

The boom of the 1990s is distinguished by the high and sustained level of investment that accompanied it. Unlike the booms of the 1960s and the 1980s, the pace of investment relative to total output remained high late into the expansion (see Basu, Fernald, and Shapiro 2001). If this rapid pace of investment pushed the capital stock ahead of its steady-state value, the return to labor might be temporarily high. On the other hand, as discussed in the first section, the second half of the 1990s did see an increase in the rate of technological progress. This acceleration in technology requires a more rapid growth of the capital stock in steady state, so the acceleration of investment may be the response to the improved prospects for long-run growth.

In this section, we ask whether the economy appears to be approximately in steady state. Figure 7.9 addresses this issue by comparing the growth in real annual earnings from our CPS data and the growth in real value added and real capital from the BEA data (reaggregated as described previously). Although fundamentally an aggregative comparison, matching the BEA industry-specific data with our CPS sample gives us comparable measures in these three categories. Strikingly, for both the 1980s and the 1990s, real aggregate earnings grow at a rate that is very close to the rate of growth in real-value-added output. Both these in turn grow at a rate similar to the rate of growth in capital stock. This result suggests that the earnings increases experienced in both the 1980s and the 1990s were sustainable at the rate of technological progress.[11] In contrast, the 1960s show much greater earnings gains than either the growth of value added or the capital-stock growth would justify. Such an increase might have been

FIGURE 7.9 / Growth in Real Earnings, Production, and Capital—Three Expansions

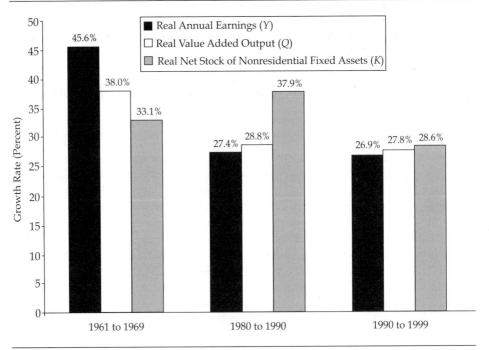

Sources: Authors' calculations based on Current Population Survey and Bureau of Economic Analysis data.

Notes: 1960s growth in Q is calculated as the percentage change in real GDP. 1980 refers to the period July 1979 to June 1980.

caused by an increase in labor's bargaining power or by an increase in wages in anticipation of future gains in productivity. In any case, it did turn out that the 1960s growth rate of earnings was not sustainable. Had technology and capital accumulation in the 1970s caught up with the earnings growth of the 1960s, the earnings growth might have been sustained. But the slowdown in the pace of technological change in the 1970s is a well-known tale. The non-steady-state outcome exhibited in the 1961 to 1969 columns of figure 7.9, taken together with the productivity slowdown of the 1970s, is perhaps part of the explanation of the 1970s stagflation.[12]

Figure 7.8, discussed earlier, shows that earnings accelerated in the second half of the 1990s. Figure 7.10 compares the time path of earnings to those of output and capital over the 1980s and the 1990s. During the earlier, more-sluggish part of the 1990s cycle, real-earnings gains lagged behind gains in real output, and both lagged gains in capital stock. In the second part of the cycle, however, these patterns are reversed. Since 1995, earnings gains have outstripped output gains, and output gains have been larger than capital-stock gains. Figure 7.10 provides a further explanation for the strong boom in earnings

FIGURE 7.10 / Growth in Real Earnings, Production, and Capital—Timing Within Expansions

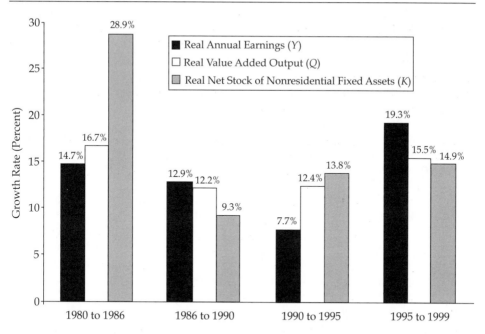

Sources: Authors' calculations based on Current Population Survey and the Bureau of Economic Analysis data.

Notes: Based on civilian population, age sixteen and over. 1980 refers to the period July 1979 to June 1980.

growth of the late 1990s by suggesting that workers were (with a lag) reaping the rewards of growth in the capital stock.

While figures 7.9 and 7.10 show data for the entire economy, we can calculate similar data for any of the demographic subgroups that we examined in figures 7.2 through 7.7. Recall that these attributions of capital are less reliable than are the aggregate or industry-specific figures because they assume that all workers in an industry are equally productive. Hence, we relegate them to the appendix tables, where we show changes in average capital per week worked by subgroup.

Turning first to the industry-specific data, where capital is accurately assigned, the $\Delta(Q/K)$ column of table 7A.6 shows substantial heterogeneity in capital deepening in the 1990s. In most of the services in the 1990s, the capital-output ratio is increasing (that is, there are negative numbers in the last column of the table). There is no reason to expect capital-output ratios to be constant industry by industry. This fact fits new-economy stories based on capital-skilled-labor complementarities (see Hall 2000). There appears to be relatively strong capital deepening in trade, business, and legal and professional services but not in telecommunications and utilities. The 1980s (table 7A.5), however, show similar patterns, so, if these facts are indicative of a change in technology, it has been ongoing since before the late 1990s.

There are some interesting findings by demographic groups. Female employment grew in capital intensity (K/W) at a higher rate than did male employment in the 1990s. The 1980s saw an even larger disparity. This mainly reflects women moving into highly capital-intensive industries traditionally occupied by men, and it also reflects the increased capital intensity of services, where women have a greater employment share. The trend toward equalization of capital-labor ratios by sex is part of the long-term trend toward increasing similarity in women's and men's labor-market activities.

There are also interesting patterns by race. In the 1990s, rates of capital deepening were somewhat greater for whites than for other race groups. In contrast, the 1980s saw greater capital deepening among blacks than among whites but a very low rate for Hispanics. These findings indicate a slow but uneven convergence of labor-market outcomes across the races.

The most striking result among these demographic groups is the rapid growth in the capital intensity of industries that employ highly educated workers relative to that of industries that employ less-educated workers. In the 1990s, the capital per week of work among the highest-educated workers grew by 34 percent; among college graduates, it grew at a rate of 14 percent. For workers with high school degrees and high school dropouts, the increases were 9 or 10 percent. These results parallel those of Hall (2000), who emphasizes the complementarity of highly educated workers and new investments. Moreover, if within-industry heterogeneity is similar to across-industry heterogeneity, these results understate the changes in capital intensity across education groups. Note, however, that the positive correlation between education attainment and capital deepening is a feature not just of the 1990s. The pattern is even stronger in the 1980s, when the capital intensity of jobs worked by high school dropouts actually fell. Hence, the differential capital deepening by education level appears to be not a distinct feature of the 1990s or the new economy, but instead a force concomitant with the increasing skill intensity and increasing wage inequality seen since the 1980s.

Are Workers Moving into High-Productivity Industries?

Reallocation of workers across industries can be an important source of increased productivity. It might be especially important when the economy is undergoing structural changes; for example, these reallocations might be related to the increasing importance of information technology.

In this subsection, we decompose productivity growth into that due to workers shifting among industries with different levels of productivity and that due to different productivity-growth rates within industries. There are a number of ways in which to carry out this decomposition. Table 7.6 presents one such decomposition for the expansions of the 1990s and the 1980s. As with capital, we attribute productivity to individual workers according to the value for their industry. The first row is the actual growth in productivity (output per week). The other two rows consider counterfactuals.

The second row gives the growth in output per week where workers at the end of the expansion are assigned the beginning-of-expansion level of productivity, that is, the effect on the level of productivity coming solely from the reallocation of workers across industries. Hence, the −2.1 percent value for all workers during the 1990s means that workers on average moved into industries that had relatively low productivity at the beginning of the decade.

The third row assigns productivity to workers at the end of the expansion as if their industries' productivities had grown at the average rate rather than at their actual rates. Hence, the fact that this counterfactual growth rate of 11.8 percent for all workers in 1990s is lower than the actual growth rate of 15.0 percent implies that, in the 1990s, workers switched into faster-growing industries.

TABLE 7.6 / Productivity Growth: Effect of Reallocation Across Industries (Percent)

	1979–1980 to 1990	1990 to 1999
Actual	10.0	15.0
No productivity growth[a]	4.0	−2.1
Uniform growth rate[b]	16.5	11.8

Sources: Authors' calculations based on the Current Population Survey and the Bureau of Economic Analysis data.

Note: Productivity is measured as output per full-time-equivalent employee as defined using BEA data reaggregated to match the CPS data as described in text.

[a]Growth in output per worker from shift in industrial composition holding productivity *level* equal to beginning of period levels.

[b]Growth in output per worker from shift in industrial compositon holding productivity *growth* equal to base-period weighted average growth in output per worker.

To summarize, in the 1990s, workers typically moved to industries with slightly lower productivity levels at the beginning of the cycle, but they were more than compensated for this by rapid productivity growth in these industries. This pattern does suggest the importance of industrial reallocation for growth in the 1990s.

Table 7.6 shows the opposite pattern for the 1980s. On average, workers shifted to industries with high initial productivity; overall productivity would have grown 4.0 percent as a result of this reallocation alone. Workers shifted, however, to industries with slower-than-average growth; the actual 10.0 percent productivity growth is less than the 16.5 percent productivity growth that workers would have experienced with uniform growth in all industries. Hence, in the 1980s, industry reallocation did not contribute to productivity growth.

Table 7A.3 makes it clear that both output and productivity growth are particularly strong in durable manufacturing, telecommunications, and finance, insurance, and real estate. These industries are closely linked to the new economy through the production or use of information technology. (Nordhaus [2000] makes the same observation.) Hence, we see, not just high productivity growth in some industries, but a high share of output concentrated in these industries as well. High productivity growth and high output growth need not lead to an increase in employment. Indeed, employment (the sum of the first two columns in table 7A.3) fell in durable manufacturing during the 1990s, although it rose considerably in the telecommunications and service sectors.

SUMMARY AND CONCLUSIONS

The 1990s were a period of remarkable economic expansion. The unemployment rate returned to the low levels of the 1960s, while inflation remained in check. During the second half of the decade, the pace of productivity change increased substantially—equaling the peak rates of productivity change experienced during the whole post–World War II period. This superb economic performance took place in the context of a booming stock market and sustained high levels of fixed investment, especially in information-technology equipment.

The shift in the composition of investment toward information technology, the run-up of stock-market values, especially for companies in technology-creating industries, and the increased rate of technological change together could signal a distinct shift in the structure of production and demand, that is, a new economy. What lessons does our research provide for assessing the claims for a new economy on the basis of the performance of the labor market? We do find substantial evidence of changes in the labor market that suggest a transformation of the economy:

- Workers are shifting to occupations and industries with high output growth, often identified with the new economy.

- The capital intensity of work in these industries and occupations is increasing relative to the average for the economy.

- A disproportionate share of capital accumulation is directed to workers with high levels of education attainment.

- These high-education-attainment workers are also getting disproportionate increases in earnings per week.

While these findings appear consistent with a structural shift toward new-economy employment, that interpretation is not supported by a longer view. With the exception of the first point, the same findings also characterize the expansion of the 1980s. Hence, while changes in the labor market facilitate a shift of production and demand to industries with new technologies, these changes are part of longer-term trends in the labor market rather than a distinctive break in the 1990s.

Other features of the expansion of labor input in the 1990s that affect the sustainability of growth are also related to longer-term developments in the labor market:

- The 1990s continued the convergence of the labor-market outcomes of men and women. Increasing female labor-force participation is likely to be a less-important source of growth in the future. (This accounted for 2 to 5 points in annual-earnings growth over the cycles of the past two decades.) Similarly, women's experience, education outcomes, and occupation choices are becoming more like men's, so closing this gap will become less important for wage growth. Convergence in labor-market outcomes across races could have similar growth-enhancing effects in the future, but this is proceeding slowly and unevenly at present.

- The age distribution of the population placed the baby boom in its prime earning years over the cycles of the 1980s and the 1990s, which contributed to aggregate earning and productivity growth. The negative effects of an aging population on future growth may not be large, however, as the baby-boom echo moves into its prime earning years in the decades head. Ongoing higher labor-force-participation rates and earnings rates of today's baby boomers as they enter their fifties and sixties would also substantially reduce any negative effects.

- Immigration remains an important source of labor supply. Whether this trend continues depends heavily on political support for open-immigration policies in the face of a rising immigrant population share.

- There have been remarkable increases in employment over the 1990s among some groups, especially single mothers. Although these groups are too small to have a substantial effect on the aggregate, the shift in labor-force participation has important implications for members of those groups.

- Skilled workers continue to be increasingly important for aggregate-earnings growth, largely because of their continuing wage increases. Although the bottom of the income and skill distribution did better in the late 1990s than at any time in the last twenty years, there was no decline in inequality because earnings at the top rose even faster. Future growth rates will depend on continued strong wage growth among more-skilled workers and/or the potential for future wage increases among the less skilled.

Our analysis leads us to believe that the U.S. labor force is well poised to sustain the gains in output and productivity seen during the current expansion. In part, these gains reflect population and labor-force changes that represent long-term trends, not cyclic changes. In part, they reflect earnings gains that are well supported by productivity gains and capital deepening.

Whether the U.S. economy can expect to repeat such stellar growth in the decades ahead is a little less clear:

- The increase in female labor-force participation appears to be reaching an end, except for some possible increases at the low end of the skill distribution.

- The baby-boom generation is aging. David Ellwood (chapter 9 in this volume) shows an increasing shortage of labor, especially of skilled workers.

- The drop in the unemployment rate from 6 percent, thought to be the natural rate, to around 4 percent may or may not be sustainable in the long run. If the current rates are temporarily low, some of the gains in employment, output, and earnings of the 1990s will be reversed. In some industries, notably manufacturing, hours of work are high relative to historical norms at the end of expansions. A return to more normal levels would lead to further reversal of some of the gains of the 1990s.

- A high rate of capital accumulation has accompanied the increase in technology and labor in the 1990s. A substantial amount of the saving to sustain this rate of investment has come from abroad. If this pattern were to reverse, either national saving would have to increase, or growth in capital would have to decline.

Finally, we note that distribution issues were as important in the 1990s expansion as in the 1980s expansion. The upper-income quintile disproportionately gained over the 1990s, while the bottom four quintiles lost income share. Less-skilled and low-wage workers experienced substantial aggregate-earnings gains, but these occurred more because of population and employment growth rather than because of wage growth, a more ambiguous signal about increases in well-being. The ongoing growth in productivity, capital intensity, and returns to education among highly skilled workers suggests that it is these workers who will continue to reap disproportionate earnings gains in the years ahead.

Matthew Shapiro acknowledges support from the National Institute on Aging (P01-AG10179) and from the National Science Foundation (SRB-9617437). We are grateful to Robert Shimer, Robert Solow, and Gary Solon for comments on an earlier draft. And we thank Mark Long for outstanding research assistance.

(*Text continues on p. 365.*)

APPENDIX

TABLE 7A.1 / Share-Weighted Growth in Real Earnings and Capital, 1961 to 1969 (Percent)

	Population $\Delta(N)$	Employed / Population $\Delta(E/N)$	Annual Weeks Worked / Employed $\Delta(W/E)$	Annual Earnings / Annual Weeks Worked $\Delta(Y/W)$	Annual Earnings $\Delta(Y)$	Capital / Annual Weeks Worked $\Delta(K/W)$	Capital $\Delta(K)$
Total population	13.0	4.8	.4	27.5	45.6	14.9	33.1
Sex							
Male	5.7	1.7	.5	25.3	33.1	12.6	20.5
Female	7.3	3.1	-.2	2.2	12.5	2.3	12.6
Race							
White (including Hispanic)	11.1	4.4	.5	25.1	41.1	13.4	29.4
Black (including Hispanic)	1.7	.5	-.1	2.1	4.1	1.5	3.5
Other (including Hispanic)	.2	-.1	.0	.2	.4	.1	.2
Age							
Under twenty	3.0	-.2	.0	-1.3	1.4	-1.6	1.2
Twenty to twenty-nine	5.6	2.7	.2	3.2	11.8	2.0	10.5
Thirty to thirty-nine	-1.1	1.5	-.3	7.1	7.2	3.3	3.4
Forty to forty-nine	1.0	1.4	.2	9.0	11.6	4.8	7.4
Fifty to fifty-nine	1.9	1.0	.3	6.8	10.0	5.0	8.2
Sixty to sixty-five	1.0	.0	-.2	2.3	3.1	1.2	2.0
Over sixty-five	1.6	-1.7	.2	.3	.5	.2	.4
Census region							
Northeast	2.7	1.1	.0	6.9	10.6	2.3	6.0
Midwest	3.6	1.8	-.1	8.5	13.7	4.2	9.4
South	5.3	1.7	.4	7.6	15.0	5.1	12.5
West	1.5	.2	.1	4.4	6.3	3.4	5.2

(Table continues on p. 344.)

TABLE 7A.1 / Continued

	Population Δ(N)	Employed / Population Δ(E/N)	Annual Weeks Worked / Employed Δ(W/E)	Annual Earnings / Annual Weeks Worked Δ(Y/W)	Annual Earnings Δ(Y)	Capital / Annual Weeks Worked Δ(K/W)	Capital Δ(K)
Schooling							
No high school diploma	-2.3	-.6	.1	7.8	5.0	.8	-1.9
Just high school diploma	7.8	3.4	.0	8.3	19.5	5.3	16.4
Some college/A.A.	4.7	1.0	.2	4.1	10.0	2.5	8.4
B.A.	1.8	.4	.1	4.8	7.1	4.1	6.5
Beyond college	1.0	.5	.0	2.5	4.0	2.1	3.6
Industry							
Agriculture	-1.2	-.9	.1	1.9	.0	2.1	.2
Forestry and fisheries	.0	.0	.0	.0	.1	.0	.0
Mining	-.1	-.1	-.1	.2	-.1	-.2	-.5
Construction	.3	.6	-.1	2.6	3.5	-.7	.2
Durable-goods manufacturing	2.5	1.9	.2	6.0	10.5	-1.8	2.7
Nondurable-goods manufacturing	.9	.8	.0	2.5	4.2	.6	2.4
Transportation, communication, and public utilities	.8	.7	-.2	2.7	4.0	5.6	6.9
Wholesale trade	.0	.1	-.1	1.4	1.4	.4	.5
Retail trade	1.3	1.1	-.6	2.4	4.2	-1.1	.7
Finance, insurance, and real estate	.7	.5	-.1	1.7	2.8	1.9	2.9
Business services	.4	.3	-.1	.5	1.1	-.3	.3
Repair services	.1	.1	.0	.3	.4	.1	.3
Private households	-.5	-.3	.3	.3	-.1	.4	.0

Hotels, lodging, and personal services other than private household	-.1	.1	-.1	.0	-.1	.9	.8
Entertainment and recreation	.0	.0	.0	.1	.1	-.1	-.1
Hospitals	.7	.6	-.1	.4	1.6	-.9	.2
Medical excluding hospitals	.6	.4	-.2	.0	.8	-.7	.2
Legal, educational, social, religious, and other professional services	2.4	1.8	-.2	2.4	6.3	7.1	11.1
Public administration (excluding postal)	.7	.5	.0	1.7	2.8	3.2	4.4
Marital status							
Never married	5.3	-.2	.3	.3	5.6	-.2	5.1
Married	5.7	5.4	.1	25.3	36.5	14.1	25.3
Widowed, divorced, or separated	2.0	-.4	.0	1.9	3.5	1.0	2.6

Source: March Current Population Survey. Based on civilian population, age sixteen and over.

Note: Within each population subgroup, each cell represents the subgroup's share of variable *x* multiplied by the subgroup's growth rate in variable *x*, where *x* is defined by the column heads. Unweighted growth rates are shown in table 7A.4.

TABLE 7A.2 / Share-Weighted Growth in Real Earnings, Output, and Capital, 1979–1980 to 1990 (Percent)

	Population Δ(N)	Employed / Population Δ(E/N)	Annual Weeks Worked / Employed Δ(W/E)	Annual Earnings / Annual Weeks Worked Δ(Y/W)	Annual Earnings Δ(Y)	Annual Output / Annual Weeks Worked Δ(Q/W)	Annual Output Δ(Q)	Capital / Annual Weeks Worked Δ(K/W)	Capital Δ(K)	Annual Production / Capital Δ(Q/K)
Total population	12.2	4.8	1.8	8.7	27.4	10.0	28.8	19.1	37.9	−9.1
Sex										
Male	6.1	.1	1.5	4.3	12.0	7.8	15.6	11.0	18.7	−3.1
Female	6.1	4.6	.4	4.1	15.1	2.2	13.2	8.1	19.2	−6.0
Race-ethnicity										
White (non-Hispanic)	5.4	4.2	1.4	9.0	20.1	8.8	19.9	16.2	27.3	−7.5
Black (non-Hispanic)	2.0	.3	.3	−.1	2.6	.6	3.2	2.5	5.2	−1.9
Hispanic	3.4	.3	−.1	−.4	3.1	.5	4.1	.2	3.8	.3
Other (non-Hispanic)	1.3	.0	.2	.3	1.7	.2	1.6	.2	1.6	.0
Age										
Under twenty	−1.7	.1	.6	.4	−.7	−.1	−1.1	.2	−.9	−.2
Twenty to twenty-nine	−.4	1.0	.5	.0	1.0	1.3	2.4	1.1	2.2	.2
Thirty to thirty-nine	6.3	3.3	.3	3.0	12.8	3.4	13.3	6.6	16.5	−3.2
Forty to forty-nine	5.0	2.8	.2	4.7	12.6	3.2	11.2	7.3	15.2	−4.0
Fifty to fifty-nine	−.6	.7	.0	.9	1.0	1.8	1.8	2.9	2.9	−1.1
Sixty to sixty-five	.6	−.4	.0	.1	.3	.5	.8	1.0	1.2	−.4
Over sixty-five	3.0	−2.7	.2	−.2	.3	.0	.5	.2	.7	−.2
Census region										
Northeast	.9	1.3	.1	4.2	6.5	2.5	4.8	4.9	7.2	−2.4
Midwest	.8	1.2	.6	.8	3.4	2.3	4.9	3.8	6.4	−1.5
South	6.2	1.4	.8	1.7	10.2	3.3	11.7	7.2	15.6	−3.9
West	4.4	.9	.2	2.0	7.4	1.9	7.3	3.2	8.6	−1.3
Schooling										
No high school diploma	−4.9	.4	.7	−.1	−3.9	1.7	−2.0	.9	−2.9	.9
Just high school diploma	4.8	.1	.7	−1.1	4.5	2.6	8.3	4.6	10.3	−2.0

Some college/A.A.	5.7	1.8	.2	1.2	8.9	2.3	9.9	5.3	13.0	−3.0
B.A.	4.0	1.6	.1	5.0	10.8	2.9	8.7	5.9	11.7	−3.0
Beyond college	2.5	.8	.1	4.4	7.8	.5	3.9	2.5	5.9	−2.0
Occupation										
Executive, administrative, and managerial occupations	1.5	.9	.1	4.1	6.5	3.7	6.1	5.5	7.9	−1.8
Professional specialty occupations	2.0	1.3	.0	4.5	7.8	.1	3.4	3.7	7.0	−3.6
Technicians and related support occupations	.9	.5	.0	.7	2.2	.4	1.9	.1	1.5	.3
Sales occupations	3.5	2.0	.1	−.1	5.5	.8	6.4	.5	6.1	.3
Administrative support occupations, including clerical	1.1	.7	.5	.4	2.7	−.1	2.2	3.8	6.2	−3.9
Private household service occupations	−.2	−.1	.2	.2	.0	.1	.0	.1	.0	.0
Protective service occupations	.3	.2	.0	.3	.8	.1	.6	.9	1.4	−.8
Service occupations (excluding private house and protective)	1.6	.9	.2	−1.1	1.6	−.9	1.8	−.4	2.2	−.05
Farming, forestry, and fishing occupations	−.2	−.1	.0	.3	.1	1.1	.0	.2	−.1	1.0
Precision production, craft, and repair occupations	.8	.4	.2	−.6	.8	2.0	3.4	2.0	3.4	.0
Machine operators, assemblers, and inspectors	−1.7	−.7	.3	.1	−2.0	2.1	.0	2.3	.3	−.3
Transportation and material moving occupations	.3	.2	.0	−.2	.3	.6	1.0	1.2	1.6	−.6
Handlers, equipment cleaners, helpers, and laborers	.6	.3	.1	−.6	.4	.0	1.0	−.7	.3	.6

(Table continues on p. 348.)

TABLE 7A.2 / Continued

Industry	Population Δ(N)	Employed / Population Δ(E/N)	Annual Weeks Worked / Employed Δ(W/E)	Annual Earnings / Annual Weeks Worked Δ(Y/W)	Annual Earnings Δ(Y)	Annual Output / Annual Weeks Worked Δ(Q/W)	Annual Output Δ(Q)	Capital / Annual Weeks Worked Δ(K/W)	Capital Δ(K)	Annual Production / Capital Δ(Q/K)
Agriculture	-.1	-.1	.1	.2	.1	.9	.8	.0	-.1	1.0
Forestry and fisheries	.0	.0	.0	.0	.0	.0	.0	.0	.0	.0
Mining	-.1	.0	.0	-.1	-.3	.6	.5	1.6	1.5	-1.0
Construction	.8	.4	.2	-.2	1.1	-.6	.8	-1.4	-.1	.8
Durable-goods manufacturing	-.7	-.2	.2	.9	.3	3.7	3.0	2.5	1.8	1.2
Nondurable-goods manufacturing	-.3	.0	.2	.5	.4	1.9	1.8	1.2	1.1	.7
Nonspecified manufacturing	.0	.0	.0	.0	.0	.0	.0	.0	.0	.0
Transportation, communication, and public utilities	.5	.3	.1	.7	1.6	2.6	3.5	6.2	7.1	-3.6
Wholesale trade	.5	.3	.1	.4	1.2	1.0	1.9	.5	1.3	.6
Retail trade	2.1	1.1	.3	-.9	2.6	-1.0	2.6	-2.3	1.2	1.3
Finance, insurance, and real estate	1.2	.7	.1	1.9	3.9	4.2	6.2	8.9	11.0	-4.7

Business services	1.8	.9	.0	2.8	-.4	2.3	-2.2	.6	1.7
Repair services	.4	.2	.0	.4	-.2	.4	-.4	.2	.2
Private households	-.2	-.1	.2	.1	.1	.0	.1	.0	.0
Hotels, lodging, and personal services other than private household	.6	.4	.0	.6	-.5	.5	-.3	.7	-.2
Entertainment and recreation	.3	.1	.0	.4	-.1	.3	-.4	.1	.3
Hospitals	.4	.3	.1	2.0	-.6	.1	-.5	.3	-.1
Medical, excluding hospitals	.9	.5	.1	1.8	-.5	1.0	-1.1	.3	.6
Legal, educational, social, religious, and other professional services	2.0	1.3	-.1	5.3	-1.4	1.9	3.2	6.5	-4.6
Public administration (excluding postal)	.5	.4	.1	2.3	.1	1.1	3.3	4.4	-3.3
Family structure									
Never married	4.0	1.2	.9	6.8	1.1	7.3	1.6	7.8	-.5
Married	3.5	3.3	1.0	14.4	7.2	15.0	14.2	21.9	-7.0
Widowed, divorced, separated, or spouse absent	4.7	.2	-.1	6.2	1.8	6.6	3.4	8.1	-1.6

Source: Current Population Survey, Outgoing Rotations Groups. Based on civilian population, age sixteen and over.

Notes: Within each population subgroup, each cell represents the subgroup's share of variable x multiplied by the subgroup's growth rate in variable x, where x is defined by the column heads. Unweighted growth rates are shown in table 7A.5. *1979 to 1980* refers to the period July 1979 to June 1980.

TABLE 7A.3 / Share-Weighted Growth in Real Earnings, Output, and Capital, 1990 to 1999 (Percent)

	Population Δ(N)	Employed / Population Δ(E/N)	Annual Weeks Worked / Employed Δ(W/E)	Annual Earnings / Annual Weeks Worked Δ(Y/W)	Annual Earnings Δ(Y)	Annual Output / Annual Weeks Worked Δ(Q/W)	Annual Output Δ(Q)	Capital / Annual Weeks Worked Δ(K/W)	Capital Δ(K)	Annual Production / Capital Δ(Q/K)
Total population	10.0	2.4	.4	14.1	26.9	15.0	27.8	15.8	28.6	−.8
Sex										
Male	5.1	.5	.4	9.9	15.8	10.8	16.8	9.3	15.2	1.5
Female	4.9	1.9	.1	4.4	11.2	4.2	11.0	6.5	13.3	−2.3
Race-ethnicity										
White (non-Hispanic)	2.9	1.5	.3	12.8	17.6	12.2	17.0	13.2	18.0	−1.0
Black (non-Hispanic)	1.6	.7	−.1	1.1	3.2	1.5	3.6	1.7	3.8	−.2
Hispanic	3.7	.2	.1	−.3	3.7	.9	4.9	.6	4.6	.3
Other (Non-Hispanic)	1.7	.1	.1	.6	2.4	.4	2.3	.2	2.1	.2
Age										
Under twenty	1.1	−.4	−.3	−.2	.2	.3	.7	.1	.5	.2
Twenty to twenty-nine	−1.2	.1	.2	1.3	.4	2.4	1.5	2.4	1.6	−.1
Thirty to thirty-nine	.1	.5	.2	3.8	4.7	3.6	4.5	1.8	2.7	1.8
Forty to forty-nine	5.2	1.8	.2	5.3	12.5	4.4	11.6	5.8	13.0	−1.3
Fifty to fifty-nine	3.5	1.3	.3	4.2	9.3	3.0	8.1	4.7	9.7	−1.6
Sixty to sixty-five	−.4	.3	.1	.4	.5	.6	.7	.5	.6	.1
Over sixty-five	1.6	−1.2	−.1	.0	.4	.4	.7	.3	.6	.1
Census region										
Northeast	.4	.2	.4	2.0	2.9	2.3	3.2	2.3	3.3	−.1
Midwest	1.2	1.3	−.3	4.7	6.9	4.7	6.9	4.4	6.6	.3
South	4.6	.8	−.2	5.4	10.6	5.8	11.0	6.4	11.7	−.6
West	3.7	.2	.5	2.1	6.4	2.2	6.6	2.6	7.0	−.4
Schooling										
No high school diploma	−2.3	1.6	−.4	.5	−.6	2.1	1.0	1.1	.0	1.0
Just high school diploma	.9	−.8	.5	2.0	2.5	4.7	5.2	3.4	3.9	1.3

Some college/A.A.	5.8	.8	.3	1.7	8.6	4.1	11.0	4.0	10.9	.0
B.A.	3.9	.7	.4	5.6	10.5	2.8	7.7	3.7	8.6	-.9
Beyond college	1.7	.3	.1	4.7	6.8	.9	3.0	3.1	5.2	-2.2
Occupation										
Executive, administrative, and managerial occupations	2.4	1.4	.0	5.3	9.1	4.0	7.8	4.1	7.8	-.1
Professional specialty occupations	2.6	1.4	.1	4.8	8.9	.2	4.3	3.5	7.6	-3.3
Technicians and related support occupations	.2	.1	.0	.4	.8	.5	.8	.3	.6	.2
Sales occupations	.9	.5	-.1	1.5	2.9	3.1	4.4	.8	2.2	2.2
Administrative support occupations, including clerical	-.2	.0	-.2	.8	.5	2.2	1.8	3.2	2.8	-1.0
Private household service occupations	.1	.0	.0	.0	.1	.0	.0	-.1	.0	.0
Protective service occupations	.3	.1	.0	.2	.6	.1	.5	1.3	1.7	-1.2
Service occupations (excluding private house and protective)	.9	.5	.0	-.2	1.2	-.1	1.4	-.3	1.1	.3
Farming, forestry, and fishing occupations	.0	.0	.0	.2	.2	.2	.2	-.2	-.1	.4
Precision production, craft, and repair occupations	.3	.4	.1	1.1	1.9	2.5	3.4	1.8	2.6	.8
Machine operators, assemblers, and inspectors	-.4	-.1	.0	.6	.1	1.7	1.2	1.1	.7	.5
Transportation and material moving occupations	.3	.3	.0	.2	.7	.6	1.1	.6	1.1	.0
Handlers, equipment cleaners, helpers, and laborers	.1	.2	-.1	.1	.4	.6	.8	.2	.4	.4

(Table continues on p. 352.)

TABLE 7A.3 / *Continued*

Industry	Population $\Delta(N)$	Employed / Population $\Delta(E/N)$	Annual Weeks Worked / Employed $\Delta(W/E)$	Annual Earnings / Annual Weeks Worked $\Delta(Y/W)$	Annual Earnings $\Delta(Y)$	Annual Output / Annual Weeks Worked $\Delta(Q/W)$	Annual Output $\Delta(Q)$	Capital / Annual Weeks Worked $\Delta(K/W)$	Capital $\Delta(K)$	Annual Production / Capital $\Delta(Q/K)$
Agriculture	.0	.0	−.1	.2	.2	.2	.2	−.2	−.1	.4
Forestry and fisheries	.0	.0	.0	.0	.0	.0	.0	.0	.0	.0
Mining	−.1	.0	.0	.0	−.1	.3	.2	.4	.3	−.1
Construction	.5	.5	.0	.4	1.4	−.1	1.0	−.7	.3	.7
Durable-goods manufacturing	−.4	.0	.0	1.7	1.3	4.7	4.4	1.6	1.3	3.1
Nondurable-goods manufacturing	−.5	−.1	.1	1.1	.6	.8	.3	1.8	1.3	−1.0
Nonspecified manufacturing	.1	.0	.0	.0	.1	.0	.1	.0	.1	.0
Transportation, communication, and public utilities	.7	.4	.0	.9	2.1	3.2	4.4	5.1	6.3	−1.9
Wholesale trade	.2	.2	.0	.7	1.1	2.4	2.8	.7	1.1	1.7
Retail trade	1.3	.8	−.1	1.1	3.1	1.1	3.2	−.8	1.2	2.0
Finance, insurance, and real estate	.4	.2	.1	1.5	2.2	5.0	5.7	3.6	4.3	1.4
Business services	.9	.5	.0	1.3	2.7	−.1	1.3	−.8	.6	.7
Repair services	.0	.0	.0	.1	.1	.0	−.1	.4	.4	−.4
Private households	.0	.0	.0	.0	.0	.0	.0	.0	.0	.0
Hotels, lodging, and personal services other than private household	.0	.0	.0	.4	.3	.0	.0	.0	.0	.0

Entertainment and recreation	.6	.3	-.1	-.1	.8	-.3	.5	-.5	.4	.2
Hospitals	.2	.1	.0	.7	1.1	-.4	-.1	-.2	.2	-.2
Medical, excluding hospitals	.9	.5	.0	.8	2.2	-.7	.7	-1.1	.3	.4
Legal, educational, social, religious, and other professional services	2.4	1.3	-.1	2.9	6.5	-1.2	2.5	3.4	7.1	-4.6
Public administration (excluding postal)	.2	.1	.0	.9	1.2	.3	.6	3.3	3.7	-3.0
Family structure										
Never married, without children	3.6	.1	-.2	1.3	4.8	2.7	6.2	2.4	5.9	.3
Never married, with children	.7	.5	.0	-.3	.9	.0	1.3	-.1	1.1	.1
Married, without children	2.0	.4	-.1	4.5	6.9	4.8	7.1	5.5	7.8	-.7
Married, with children	1.1	1.3	.3	7.1	9.8	5.4	8.1	5.6	8.3	-.2
Widowed, divorced, or separated, without children	2.3	-.4	.5	1.1	3.5	1.5	3.9	1.7	4.1	-.2
Widowed, divorced, or separated, with children	.2	.5	.0	.7	1.3	.5	1.1	.6	1.2	-.1

Source: Current Population Survey, Outgoing Rotations Groups. Based on civilian population, age sixteen and over.

Note: Within each population subgroup, each cell represents the subgroup's share of variable *x* multiplied by the subgroup's growth rate in variable *x*, where *x* is defined by the column heads. Unweighted growth rates are shown in table 7A.6.

TABLE 7A.4 / Growth in Real Earnings and Capital, 1961 to 1969 (percentage)

	Population $\Delta(N)$	Employed / Population $\Delta(E/N)$	Annual Weeks Worked / Employed $\Delta(W/E)$	Annual Earnings / Annual Weeks Worked $\Delta(Y/W)$	Annual Earnings $\Delta(Y)$	Capital / Annual Weeks Worked $\Delta(K/W)$	Capital $\Delta(K)$
Total population	13.0	4.8	.4	27.5	45.6	14.9	33.1
Sex							
Male	12.0	−.6	.7	30.8	43.0	15.4	27.6
Female	13.9	15.0	−.1	25.4	54.1	19.8	48.6
Race							
White (including Hispanic)	12.5	4.9	.5	26.6	44.4	14.7	32.5
Black (including Hispanic)	17.3	4.9	−1.0	41.5	62.7	19.5	40.7
Other (including Hispanic)	20.5	−8.0	−.2	28.8	41.1	4.9	17.2
Age							
Under twenty	30.9	12.3	1.2	27.0	71.4	−7.2	37.2
Twenty to twenty-nine	29.3	10.1	−1.2	21.0	59.3	11.4	49.6
Thirty to thirty-nine	−6.3	8.1	−1.4	29.7	30.0	14.8	15.2
Forty to forty-nine	5.4	5.1	1.1	33.7	45.3	19.4	31.1
Fifty to fifty-nine	12.5	3.2	1.9	32.9	50.4	22.7	40.3
Sixty to sixty-five	13.3	2.1	−2.9	33.5	46.0	17.3	29.8
Over sixty-five	12.7	−14.6	5.8	21.6	25.6	11.2	15.1

Census region							
Northeast	10.6	4.2	-.2	23.7	38.3	10.4	25.0
Midwest	12.6	6.2	-.7	29.1	47.2	16.2	34.3
South	17.8	6.2	1.6	36.0	61.6	15.7	41.3
West	8.9	.9	.8	22.4	33.1	17.5	28.2
Schooling							
No high school diploma	-4.7	-2.3	.3	22.8	16.0	1.2	-5.6
Just high school diploma	26.6	7.6	.0	24.7	58.9	12.7	46.9
Some college/A.A.	34.7	4.8	.6	21.5	61.7	13.3	53.5
B.A.	27.7	-1.6	2.0	24.6	52.7	32.5	60.6
Beyond college	42.4	-.8	1.7	25.7	68.9	44.3	87.6
Industry							
Agriculture	-36.8	-.2	.2	38.0	1.3	41.3	4.6
Forestry and fisheries	18.3	12.1	-1.9	52.3	80.8	4.9	33.4
Mining	-29.7	3.4	-11.8	32.1	-6.0	24.1	-14.0
Construction	9.0	7.8	-2.2	36.5	51.1	1.7	16.3
Durable-goods manufacturing	26.7	1.1	2.4	20.0	50.3	4.6	34.9
Nondurable-goods manufacturing	14.8	1.4	.8	17.3	34.3	17.0	34.1
Transportation, communication, and public utilities	18.1	1.6	-1.7	22.9	40.8	1.3	19.2
Wholesale trade	.4	2.5	-1.4	31.2	32.7	49.8	51.2
Retail trade	14.3	1.0	-2.4	29.9	42.8	7.1	20.0
Finance, insurance, and real estate	23.1	.2	-.2	29.8	53.0	7.6	30.8
Business services	45.3	-1.1	-2.5	19.9	61.6	20.5	62.2

(Table continues on p. 356.)

TABLE 7A.4 / Continued

	Population $\Delta(N)$	Employed / Population $\Delta(E/N)$	Annual Weeks Worked / Employed $\Delta(W/E)$	Annual Earnings / Annual Weeks Worked $\Delta(Y/W)$	Annual Earnings $\Delta(Y)$	Capital / Annual Weeks Worked $\Delta(K/W)$	Capital $\Delta(K)$
Repair services	9.5	.8	-1.1	34.5	43.7	24.4	33.6
Private households	-27.0	.7	5.1	5.0	-16.2	-2.2	-23.3
Hotels, lodging, and personal services other than private household	-2.5	2.5	-3.1	-1.2	-4.2	90.9	87.8
Entertainment and recreation	2.7	1.1	-.8	10.3	13.4	-21.9	-18.8
Hospitals	40.3	1.1	1.6	20.0	63.0	9.4	52.4
Medical excluding hospitals	56.9	.2	-2.4	31.1	85.8	13.8	68.4
Legal, educational, social, religious, and other professional services	41.0	-.4	4.5	19.3	64.4	58.7	103.8
Public administration (excluding postal)	25.5	-.2	.6	19.3	45.2	8.5	34.4
Marital status							
Never married	27.6	-.3	2.3	15.7	45.3	4.9	34.5
Married	8.4	7.0	.1	30.2	45.7	17.2	32.7
Widowed, divorced, or separated	15.3	1.4	-.5	28.8	45.1	17.3	33.5

Source: March Current Population Survey. Based on civilian population, age sixteen and over.

TABLE 7A.5 / Growth in Real Earnings, Output, and Capital, 1979–1980 to 1990

	Population Δ(N)	Employed / Population Δ(E/N)	Annual Weeks Worked / Employed Δ(W/E)	Annual Earnings / Annual Weeks Worked Δ(Y/W)	Annual Earnings Δ(Y)	Annual Output / Annual Weeks Worked Δ(Q/W)	Annual Output Δ(Q)	Capital / Annual Weeks Worked Δ(K/W)	Capital Δ(K)	Annual Production / Capital Δ(Q/K)
Total population	12.2	4.8	1.8	8.7	27.4	10.0	28.8	19.1	37.9	−9.1
Sex										
Male	12.9	−1.7	2.5	4.0	17.7	11.9	25.7	14.3	28.1	−2.4
Female	11.5	12.8	1.0	20.4	45.7	8.2	33.6	32.1	57.5	−23.9
Race-ethnicity										
White (non-Hispanic)	6.8	5.1	1.7	10.2	23.8	10.5	24.1	19.7	33.3	−9.2
Black (non-Hispanic)	18.8	5.2	3.7	4.9	32.6	7.0	34.7	23.3	51.0	−16.3
Hispanic	53.3	5.7	−.9	3.2	61.5	11.7	69.9	10.6	68.8	1.1
Other (non-Hispanic)	48.5	−.9	7.1	10.7	65.3	8.5	63.1	14.7	69.3	−6.2
Age										
Under twenty	−19.4	−5.2	4.4	−17.7	−38.0	−11.8	−32.0	−13.2	−33.5	1.5
Twenty to twenty-nine	−1.8	4.1	1.9	.4	4.6	5.0	9.2	5.2	9.4	−.1
Thirty to thirty-nine	30.8	5.8	.9	4.1	41.6	9.5	47.0	18.7	56.2	−9.2
Forty to forty-nine	32.6	7.2	.0	11.4	51.2	12.0	51.8	26.0	65.7	−13.9
Fifty to fifty-nine	−4.7	5.2	−.2	5.4	5.7	11.8	12.1	18.4	18.7	−6.6
Sixty to sixty-five	8.1	−4.1	.3	2.2	6.3	12.6	16.8	22.5	26.7	−9.9
Over sixty-five	21.8	−6.3	5.9	10.8	32.2	8.6	30.0	25.4	46.7	−16.8
Census region										
Northeast	4.0	6.2	.5	17.6	28.4	12.2	23.0	26.5	37.3	−14.3
Midwest	3.1	4.5	2.4	3.3	13.3	10.0	19.9	16.6	26.6	−6.7

(Table continues on p. 358.)

TABLE 7A.5 / *Continued*

	Population $\Delta(N)$	Employed / Population $\Delta(E/N)$	Annual Weeks Worked / Employed $\Delta(W/E)$	Annual Earnings / Annual Weeks Worked $\Delta(Y/W)$	Annual Earnings $\Delta(Y)$	Annual Output / Annual Weeks Worked $\Delta(Q/W)$	Annual Output $\Delta(Q)$	Capital / Annual Weeks Worked $\Delta(K/W)$	Capital $\Delta(K)$	Annual Production / Capital $\Delta(Q/K)$
South	18.6	4.7	2.6	7.5	33.3	9.0	34.9	17.3	43.2	−8.3
West	22.0	3.7	1.4	8.0	35.0	8.0	35.1	15.3	42.4	−7.2
Schooling										
No high school diploma	−17.1	−6.8	2.7	−13.9	−35.1	6.6	−14.6	−1.7	−22.9	8.3
Just high school diploma	14.3	−.5	1.7	−1.5	13.9	7.8	23.2	12.5	27.9	−4.7
Some college/A.A.	27.2	4.6	.6	5.2	37.5	7.2	39.6	17.8	50.2	−10.6
B.A.	35.2	3.7	.3	11.2	50.4	11.4	50.7	29.1	68.3	−17.6
Beyond college	47.1	−1.1	.7	14.4	61.1	.7	47.4	30.6	77.3	−29.9
Occupation										
Executive, administrative, and managerial occupations	18.8	−.1	.9	14.2	33.8	18.5	38.1	30.5	50.2	−12.1
Professional specialty occupations	24.8	.5	.9	15.5	41.8	2.4	28.6	36.9	63.1	−34.6
Technicians and related support occupations	50.6	−.3	1.8	.7	52.8	7.7	59.7	−3.4	48.7	11.1
Sales occupations	53.0	.4	4.7	5.9	63.9	−6.1	51.9	17.7	75.8	−23.8
Administrative support occupations, including clerical	10.9	.3	3.9	4.0	19.1	−2.6	12.5	16.8	32.0	−19.4

Private household service occupations	−36.1	.0	11.8	36.1	11.8	−2.5	−26.7	−.5	−24.7	−2.0
Protective service occupations	29.3	.7	2.1	7.0	39.1	1.1	33.2	5.4	37.5	−4.3
Service occupations (excluding private house and protective)	22.0	.9	5.7	3.1	31.7	−5.0	23.7	16.9	45.6	−21.9
Farming, forestry, and fishing occupations	−7.4	−.3	.3	15.7	8.4	52.3	44.9	5.9	−1.5	46.4
Precision production, craft, and repair occupations	10.9	−.6	1.6	−6.5	5.5	15.1	27.0	10.0	21.9	5.1
Machine operators, assemblers, and inspectors	−29.7	2.0	3.3	−.8	−25.1	24.9	.6	29.5	5.2	−4.6
Transportation and material moving occupations	9.2	1.0	.9	−5.6	5.5	16.0	27.1	20.3	31.5	−4.4
Handlers, equipment cleaners, helpers, and laborers	21.7	1.6	3.5	−11.5	15.3	1.7	28.6	−17.7	9.2	19.4
Industry										
Agriculture	−5.5	−1.1	1.9	16.0	11.4	58.1	53.4	.6	−4.0	57.5
Forestry and fisheries	−5.6	3.8	.3	−2.8	−4.4	31.3	29.8	−19.7	−21.3	51.1
Mining	−22.5	1.2	.8	−.8	−21.4	50.2	29.7	51.6	31.1	−1.4
Construction	17.6	.5	3.3	−3.3	18.0	−6.6	14.8	−26.7	−5.4	20.2
Durable-goods manufacturing	−8.5	1.0	2.1	6.9	1.5	35.3	29.9	30.2	24.8	5.1
Nondurable-goods manufacturing	−5.3	1.3	2.1	5.9	4.0	21.6	19.7	18.7	16.8	3.0
Nonspecified manufacturing	64.4	−1.3	5.6	−68.3	.5	20.8	89.5	13.3	82.1	7.4
Transportation, communication, and public utilities	10.9	.3	1.4	3.1	15.7	18.2	30.8	10.8	23.4	7.4

(Table continues on p. 360.)

TABLE 7A.5 / Continued

	Population Δ(N)	Employed / Population Δ(E/N)	Annual Weeks Worked / Employed Δ(W/E)	Annual Earnings / Annual Weeks Worked Δ(Y/W)	Annual Earnings Δ(Y)	Annual Output / Annual Weeks Worked Δ(Q/W)	Annual Output Δ(Q)	Capital / Annual Weeks Worked Δ(K/W)	Capital Δ(K)	Annual Production / Capital Δ(Q/K)
Wholesale trade	18.7	-.1	3.1	4.4	26.1	26.0	47.7	48.5	70.2	-22.5
Retail trade	19.2	.2	4.0	3.6	27.0	10.4	33.8	12.6	36.0	-2.2
Finance, insurance, and real estate	29.0	.4	2.6	17.9	49.9	-3.4	28.6	40.3	73.3	-43.7
Business services	80.0	-.5	5.2	5.3	90.0	-3.8	80.9	-8.5	76.2	4.7
Repair services	33.3	.2	2.5	3.9	39.9	-6.2	29.8	-12.2	23.8	6.0
Private households	-24.9	.1	12.0	40.4	27.7	1.9	-10.8	4.0	-8.7	-2.2
Hotels, lodging, and personal services other than private household	33.2	1.1	5.2	9.8	49.4	-4.1	35.4	21.1	60.6	-25.2
Entertainment and recreation	33.0	1.2	5.5	11.7	51.3	5.7	45.3	-25.7	13.9	31.5
Hospitals	15.0	.7	3.6	22.9	42.2	-15.9	3.4	29.4	48.7	-45.3
Medical, excluding hospitals	36.7	.7	4.7	19.6	61.8	-15.7	26.5	27.7	69.8	-43.3
Legal, educational, social, religious, and other professional services	24.7	1.2	1.5	11.3	38.6	-5.8	21.6	49.1	76.5	-54.9
Public administration (excluding postal)	18.4	1.6	2.6	10.6	33.2	1.7	24.3	11.0	33.6	-9.3
Family structure										
Never married	16.5	4.5	5.4	12.8	39.2	7.6	34.1	14.6	41.1	-7.0
Married	5.9	5.2	1.6	7.8	20.5	10.5	23.2	19.7	32.4	-9.3
Widowed, divorced, separated, or spouse absent	27.4	8.7	-1.6	11.4	45.9	11.8	46.3	26.2	60.8	-14.4

Source: Current Population Survey, Outgoing Rotations Groups. Based on civilian population, age sixteen and over.

Note: 1979 to 1980 refers to the period July 1979 to June 1980.

TABLE 7A.6 / Growth in Real Earnings, Output, and Capital, 1990 to 1999 (Percent)

	Population Δ(N)	Employed / Population Δ(E/N)	Annual Weeks Worked / Employed Δ(W/E)	Annual Earnings / Annual Weeks Worked Δ(Y/W)	Annual Earnings Δ(Y)	Annual Output / Annual Weeks Worked Δ(Q/W)	Annual Output Δ(Q)	Capital / Annual Weeks Worked Δ(K/W)	Capital Δ(K)	Annual Production / Capital Δ(Q/K)
Total population	10.0	2.4	.4	14.1	26.9	15.0	27.8	15.8	28.6	−.8
Sex										
Male	10.6	−.3	.6	13.8	24.8	17.0	28.0	13.0	23.9	4.1
Female	9.3	5.5	.3	15.6	30.7	12.4	27.5	21.6	36.7	−9.2
Race-ethnicity										
White (non-Hispanic)	3.9	1.9	.4	15.5	21.7	15.6	21.8	16.9	23.1	−1.4
Black (non-Hispanic)	13.8	7.4	−.9	17.1	37.4	15.9	36.2	14.3	34.6	1.6
Hispanic	40.8	2.6	2.3	7.2	52.9	13.2	58.9	14.1	59.8	−.9
Other (non-Hispanic)	44.9	3.4	.9	13.5	62.7	12.6	61.8	14.8	64.0	−2.2
Age										
Under twenty	15.0	−1.5	−3.1	6.9	17.4	18.4	28.8	17.7	28.2	.7
Twenty to twenty-nine	−6.3	1.7	.7	6.4	2.4	11.2	7.2	12.4	8.5	−1.2
Thirty to thirty-nine	.6	1.8	.8	12.0	15.3	12.5	15.7	6.3	9.5	6.2
Forty to forty-nine	28.2	1.1	.5	12.2	42.0	14.5	44.3	15.9	45.7	−1.5
Fifty to fifty-nine	27.0	5.4	.9	18.4	51.8	17.4	50.7	23.3	56.7	−5.9
Sixty to sixty-five	−5.7	4.7	2.7	11.5	13.3	15.3	17.0	12.3	14.1	3.0
Over sixty-five	10.6	4.9	−3.4	21.5	33.5	25.1	37.1	21.8	33.8	3.3
Census region										
Northeast	1.9	.9	2.2	8.8	13.8	11.9	16.9	13.3	18.3	−1.4
Midwest	5.1	5.2	−1.3	19.5	28.5	20.2	29.2	19.7	28.7	.4
South	13.3	2.6	−.6	17.4	32.7	16.0	31.3	15.8	31.1	.2
West	17.3	.5	2.4	8.8	29.1	10.0	30.3	12.5	32.8	−2.5

(Table continues on p. 362.)

TABLE 7A.6 / Continued

	Population $\Delta(N)$	Employed / Population $\Delta(E/N)$	Annual Weeks Worked / Employed $\Delta(W/E)$	Annual Earnings / Annual Weeks Worked $\Delta(Y/W)$	Annual Earnings $\Delta(Y)$	Annual Output / Annual Weeks Worked $\Delta(Q/W)$	Annual Output $\Delta(Q)$	Capital / Annual Weeks Worked $\Delta(K/W)$	Capital $\Delta(K)$	Annual Production / Capital $\Delta(Q/K)$
Schooling										
No high school diploma	-10.4	5.0	-3.1	-.6	-9.2	18.1	9.5	8.8	.2	9.3
Just high school diploma	2.7	-2.6	1.4	7.6	9.1	14.5	16.1	10.3	11.8	4.2
Some college/A.A.	24.0	.5	1.0	8.0	33.4	13.5	38.9	12.0	37.4	1.5
B.A.	27.6	-1.4	2.0	13.0	41.1	10.3	38.5	14.1	42.3	-3.8
Beyond college	25.2	-2.4	.8	18.6	42.1	8.7	32.2	33.7	57.2	-25.0
Occupation										
Executive, administrative, and managerial occupations	27.1	.4	.1	14.2	41.8	14.6	42.3	15.1	42.8	-.5
Professional specialty occupations	27.6	.0	1.3	12.0	40.9	5.9	34.7	33.0	61.9	-27.1
Technicians and related support occupations	10.1	.9	.3	7.2	18.5	12.8	24.1	8.4	19.7	4.4
Sales occupations	11.4	.4	.1	16.8	28.8	19.8	31.8	11.2	23.2	8.6
Administrative support occupations, including clerical	-1.8	.6	-1.3	6.4	3.8	14.6	12.0	18.8	16.2	-4.2
Private household service occupations	11.7	-2.0	4.2	26.4	40.4	12.6	26.6	14.4	28.3	-1.7
Protective service occupations	22.0	.5	.4	5.5	28.4	5.1	28.0	18.0	40.9	-12.9
Service occupations (excluding private house and protective)	11.9	1.0	1.8	10.1	24.8	4.9	19.6	8.5	23.3	-3.6
Farming, forestry, and fishing occupations	1.1	-.9	.6	22.8	23.7	11.3	12.1	-5.0	-4.2	16.3

Precision production, craft, and repair occupations	8.5	18.3	10.8	26.8	19.3	15.5	8.0	.8	2.3	4.4
Machine operators, assemblers, and inspectors	5.9	13.4	21.3	19.3	27.2	2.8	10.7	.3	2.4	−10.5
Transportation and material moving occupations	7.5	22.1	9.3	29.6	16.8	17.7	4.9	−.6	2.7	10.7
Handlers, equipment cleaners, helpers, and laborers	11.1	14.2	7.0	25.3	18.1	16.4	9.2	−.9	2.9	5.2
Industry										
Agriculture	18.9	−4.6	−5.7	14.2	13.1	29.4	28.3	−1.9	.1	2.9
Forestry and fisheries	−34.1	7.6	16.4	−26.5	−17.7	9.5	18.3	6.6	1.6	−17.0
Mining	6.8	8.4	30.0	15.3	36.8	−13.0	8.5	4.6	−1.0	−25.2
Construction	−10.7	31.6	15.8	20.9	5.1	24.5	8.7	.6	3.9	11.3
Durable-goods manufacturing	21.9	18.0	21.1	39.9	43.0	9.9	13.0	.2	2.4	−5.7
Nondurable-goods manufacturing	−16.2	20.7	28.4	4.5	12.2	7.6	15.3	1.3	1.7	−10.7
Nonspecified manufacturing	4.4	135.0	24.9	139.4	29.3	160.4	50.3	.2	4.7	105.2
Transportation, communication, and public utilities	14.5	22.2	5.8	36.7	20.3	21.3	4.9	−.1	.8	15.7
Wholesale trade	8.6	47.0	36.7	55.6	45.3	24.8	14.6	−.5	1.6	9.1
Retail trade	7.2	31.1	18.0	38.3	25.2	31.6	18.5	.3	1.0	11.8
Finance, insurance, and real estate	2.1	24.2	13.9	26.3	16.0	25.4	15.1	1.1	.4	8.8
Business services	−22.3	57.4	28.5	35.1	6.2	56.5	27.5	1.3	.6	27.0
Repair services	−47.8	42.8	44.4	−5.1	−3.5	9.8	11.4	−.6	1.0	−2.1
Private households	−1.8	10.7	11.5	8.9	9.8	16.7	17.6	5.7	−2.2	−4.4
Hotels, lodging, and personal services other than private household	−1.7	2.9	3.4	1.2	1.7	24.2	24.8	.2	1.1	−1.9

(Table continues on p. 364.)

TABLE 7A.6 / *Continued*

	Population Δ(N)	Employed / Population Δ(E/N)	Annual Weeks Worked / Employed Δ(W/E)	Annual Earnings / Annual Weeks Worked Δ(Y/W)	Annual Earnings Δ(Y)	Annual Output / Annual Weeks Worked Δ(Q/W)	Annual Output Δ(Q)	Capital / Annual Weeks Worked Δ(K/W)	Capital Δ(K)	Annual Production / Capital Δ(Q/K)
Entertainment and recreation	53.9	1.4	.5	12.4	68.2	-1.7	54.1	11.0	66.8	-12.7
Hospitals	7.6	.6	.4	12.6	21.2	-10.9	-2.3	18.1	26.8	-29.0
Medical, excluding hospitals	30.8	.8	.8	23.1	55.4	-11.8	20.5	16.5	48.8	-28.3
Legal, educational, social, religious, and other professional services	25.6	.1	1.0	14.9	41.7	1.6	28.3	60.3	87.1	-58.7
Public administration (excluding postal)	5.6	.7	.3	11.1	17.7	7.9	14.5	20.2	26.8	-12.3
Family structure										
Never married, without children	15.1	.1	-.1	12.5	27.6	27.6	14.5	16.7	31.7	31.7
Never married, with children	45.4	30.1	-1.3	7.4	81.6	81.6	12.9	14.1	88.3	88.3
Married, without children	7.1	2.6	-.6	15.8	24.9	24.9	18.0	20.0	29.1	29.1
Married, with children	4.0	3.2	.7	16.8	24.8	24.8	14.9	14.1	22.0	22.0
Widowed, divorced, or separated, without children	15.2	2.4	3.6	10.4	31.5	31.5	13.2	15.8	36.9	36.9
Widowed, divorced, or separated, with children	5.4	10.2	-.8	18.2	33.0	33.0	12.3	15.0	29.9	29.9

Source: Current Population Survey, Outgoing Rotations Groups. Based on civilian population, age sixteen and over.

NOTES

1. Our use of weeks worked rather than hours worked as the intensive margin for employment is dictated by our judgment that these data are more accurate given our data set and our measurement framework.

2. When factors of production are diverted from production to adjustment, measured output can understate actual output (see Basu, Fernald, and Shapiro 2001).

3. Gordon's view is that, although the increase in technological change witnessed in the late 1990s is genuine, it is not evidence of a technological revolution. Moreover, he argues that the burst in technology is mainly confined to the make, rather than the use, of information technology. Stephen Oliner and Daniel Sichel (2000) and Susanto Basu, John Fernald, and Matthew Shapiro (2001), in contrast, find a substantial acceleration of technology outside the information-technology-producing sector.

4. Susanto Basu and Miles Kimball (1997) argue that there is a correlation between observed intensity of work and potentially unobserved effort or factor utilization and that intensity of work is a sufficient statistic for the unobservables.

5. The ORG data are collected among the ORGs in the CPS in each month and include weekly wage information (which is not available for other persons in the CPS sample). We combine the ORG monthly samples to create annual samples. A data appendix is available on request that describes in detail how all our data are coded.

6. The trough and peak of the 1960s expansion were February 1962 and December 1969. The previous peak was April 1960, before CPS data are available.

7. Since we report earnings only at the subgroup level, imputing mean weeks of work within each subgroup should not induce error. The mismatch of the March and ORG data could potentially create biases in the level of annual earnings. We would expect such biases to have negligible effects on the peak-to-peak changes that are the focus of our analysis.

8. Full-time hours are defined by industry, so a worker who reports thirty hours of work per week in an industry whose average hours per week are forty would be assigned output equal to 0.75 (30/40) of that industry's average output per full-time-equivalent worker.

9. Tables 7A.1 through 7A.3 show share-weighted growth rates by population subgroup (that is, the contribution of each group to aggregate growth, the same data used in figures 7.1 through 7.7). Tables 7A.4 through 7A.6 show growth rates by population subgroup (the data used in table 7.2).

10. These population data refer to persons aged sixteen years or older. The CPS contained no questions about immigration in the 1980s. We use the census data from 1990 on the number of persons who report immigrating between 1980 and 1990. This indicates that immigrant growth accounted for 3.9 percent of the overall 12.2 percent population growth.

11. Recall that our earnings data are wages, not total compensation. In the 1980s, benefits increases ran substantially ahead of wage increases, so the 1980s would look somewhat less sustainable than the 1990s if we were examining total compensation.

12. Another source of deviation between earnings growth and output growth is differential growth rates in GDP prices and consumption prices, that is, a deviation of the product wage from the consumption wage. This will arise because GDP is less service intensive than consumption and the relative price of services is increasing (see Bosworth and Perry 1994; and Shapiro 1994). Note, however, that this phenomenon goes the wrong way as an explanation of the 1960s and that Bosworth and Perry find that it has been a relatively steady factor for the postwar period.

REFERENCES

Basu, Susanto, John G. Fernald, and Matthew D. Shapiro. 2001. "Productivity Growth in the 1990s: Technology, Utilization, or Adjustment?" Carnegie-Rochester Conference Series on Public Policy. Forthcoming.

Basu, Susanto, and Miles S. Kimball. 1997. "Cyclical Productivity with Unobserved Input Variation." *NBER* working paper no. 5915. Cambridge, Mass.: National Bureau of Economic Research.

Blank, Rebecca M., and Lucie Schmidt. 2001. "Work, Wages, and Welfare." In *The New World of Welfare,* edited by Rebecca M. Blank and Ron Haskins. Washington D.C.: Brookings Institution.

Bosworth, Barry, and George Perry. 1994. "Productivity and Real Wages: Is There a Puzzle?" *Brookings Papers on Economic Activity* (1): 317–35.

Council of Economic Advisers. 1999. *Economic Report of the President: 1999.* Washington: U.S. Government Printing Office.

Gordon, Robert J. 1979. "The End-of-Expansion Phenomenon in Short-Run Productivity Behavior." *Brookings Papers on Economic Activity* (2): 447–61.

———. 1999. "U.S. Economic Growth since 1970: One Big Wave?" *American Economic Review Proceedings* 89(2): 123–28.

———. 2000. "Does the 'New Economy' Measure Up to the Great Inventions of the Past?" *Journal of Economic Perspectives* 14(4): 49–74.

Hall, Robert E. 2000. "e-Capital: The Link between the Stock Market and the Labor Market in the 1990s." *Brookings Papers on Economic Activity* (2): 73–118.

Jorgenson, Dale W., and Kevin J. Stiroh. 2000. "Raising the Speed Limit: U.S. Growth in the Information Age." *Brookings Papers on Economic Activity* (1): 125–211.

Katz, Lawrence F., and Alan B. Krueger. 1999. "The High-Pressure U.S. Labor Market of the 1990s." *Brookings Papers on Economic Activity* (1): 1–65.

Nordhaus, William D. 2000. "Productivity and the New Economy." *Cowles Foundation* discussion paper no. 1284. Yale University.

Oliner, Stephen D., and Daniel E. Sichel. 2000. "The Resurgence of Growth in the Late 1990s: Is Information Technology the Story?" *Journal of Economic Perspectives* 14(4): 3–22.

Shapiro, Matthew D. 1994. "Discussion of Bosworth and Perry [1994]." *Brookings Papers on Economic Activity* (1): 336–41.

Solow, Robert M. 1956. "A Contribution to the Theory of Economic Growth." *Quarterly Journal of Economics* 70(1): 65–94.

———. 1957. "Technological Change and the Aggregate Production Function." *Review of Economics and Statistics* 39(3): 312–20.

Chapter 8

Changes in Unemployment Duration and Labor-Force Attachment

Katharine G. Abraham and Robert Shimer

Between the late 1960s and the late 1970s, the U.S. unemployment rate trended consistently upward. The unemployment rate attained at successive cyclic peaks increased from 3.4 percent in September 1968 to 4.6 percent in October 1973, 5.6 percent in May 1979, and 7.2 percent in April 1981 (see figure 8.1). In November 1982, the worst point of the 1981 to 1982 recession, the unemployment rate reached a postwar high of 10.8 percent. Since that time, however, unemployment has fallen back toward the levels of the late 1960s. By March 1989, the unemployment rate had dropped to 5.0 percent, and, from October 1999 through the end of 2000, it hovered near 4.0 percent.

During most business cycles, there is a strong correlation between the unemployment rate and the average length of an unemployment spell, so, not surprisingly, unemployment durations increased steadily during the 1970s. But, subsequently, unemployment durations have not fallen nearly as much as the decline in the unemployment rate might have led one to expect. For example, the first panel of figure 8.2 shows that, historically, the mean duration of in-progress unemployment spells,[1] the solid line, closely tracked the unemployment rate, the dashed line (depicted on a different scale). As the unemployment rate increased from business-cycle peak to business-cycle peak during the 1970s, mean unemployment duration followed suit, rising from eight to eleven weeks during the decade. But, while the unemployment rate has subsequently declined, mean unemployment duration has not fallen commensurately. As a result, the mean duration of an unemployment spell was 50 percent longer at the end of the 1990s than at the end of the 1960s. The remaining panels of figure 8.2 explore how the unemployment-duration distribution has shifted over time. The short-term unemployment rate, defined as the fraction of the labor force that has been unemployed for zero to four weeks, is at its lowest sustained rate since the early 1950s, 40 percent lower than the levels that prevailed from 1975 to 1985 and significantly lower than the levels that one would expect from the historical relation between the short-term and the aggregate unemployment rates. The long-term (fifteen- to twenty-six-week) unemployment rate has also declined steadily during the last two expansions, although it remains slightly high by

FIGURE 8.1 / Aggregate Unemployment Rate, 1948 to 2000

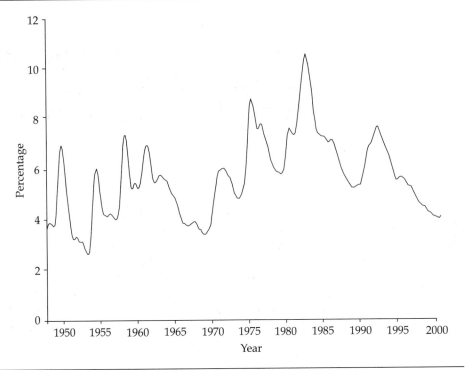

Notes: Monthly fluctuations were smoothed using a Hodrick-Prescott filter with parameter 10. Underlying data are official BLS time series.

historical standards. But most of the action comes from the increase in the very long-term (more than twenty-six-week) unemployment rate. In 1969, persons unemployed half a year or more accounted for just 0.16 percent of the labor force; at the peak of each of the last three expansions, three times as large a share of the labor force had similarly long spells of unemployment.[2]

This chapter seeks to explain the breakdown in the historical relation between the aggregate unemployment rate and measures of unemployment duration. There are several reasons why understanding this change is important. First, if workers are risk averse and labor-income risk cannot be insured, welfare is lower when unemployment duration is longer, holding other things constant. Essentially, longer unemployment durations load more uninsurable risk onto individuals. Lucky workers never lose their jobs, but these workers have a lower marginal utility of income than do their less fortunate peers, who suffer long spells of joblessness. This suggests that ignoring unemployment durations and focusing only on the low unemployment rate at the end of the 1990s may overstate the strength of the U.S. economy. Similarly, the long-term unemployed may lose skills or contact with the labor market, generating hysteresis (Blanchard and

Summers 1987), and blocking the possibility of further reductions in the unemployment rate. This will also limit the downward pressure that the long-term unemployed place on wages, with the result that, in an economy with many long-term unemployed, the Phillips curve may lie to the right of that in an economy with shorter unemployment durations. On the other hand, the existence of long unemployment durations suggests a positive role for government intervention in the labor market. For example, retraining programs might help in reintroducing the long-term unemployed to regular labor-market activity, thereby reducing unemployment duration without increasing the incidence of unemployment. Our first section discusses these issues in more detail.

We then turn to our main task, trying to understand the source of the recent increase in unemployment duration. Each subsequent section focuses on one important factor—the second section on measurement issues, the third section on the aging of the baby boom, and the fourth section on labor-force attachment.

Measurement Issues. In 1994, the Bureau of Labor Statistics (BLS) redesigned the Current Population Survey (CPS), the instrument used to measure the unemployment rate and unemployment duration. There are reasons to suspect that this redesign reduced the measured incidence of short-term unemployment. We conclude that the redesign is likely to explain a decline of about half a percentage point in the short-term (zero- to four-week) unemployment rate and an increase of about a half week in mean unemployment duration, although it does not explain the increase in long-term unemployment.

Aging of the Baby Boom. The mass of the U.S. population has shifted into age groups that report longer unemployment spells. If one assumes that this demographic shift has affected only the share of workers in different age groups, not unemployment duration conditional on age, then the aging of the baby boom can explain another half percentage point decline in the short-term unemployment rate between 1980 and 2000 and another half-week increase in mean unemployment duration over the same time period. It does little, however, to explain the rise in long-term unemployment.

Labor-Force Attachment. Most of the secular increase in unemployment duration is accounted for by women, whose unemployment duration has risen to approach the male level. At the same time, women's unemployment rate has declined toward the men's rate since 1980. This pattern suggests the possibility that increases in women's attachment to the labor force may be responsible for the aggregate trends. Labor-force attachment affects unemployment incidence and unemployment duration in at least two ways. Workers who have a stronger attachment to the labor force tend to stay unemployed when they lose a job, rather than dropping out of the labor force. This raises both the unemployment rate and unemployment duration. On the other hand, because these workers are unlikely to quit their jobs and exit the labor force, they can build up stable employment relations with a minimal incidence of unemployment. This reduces the unemployment rate and may also raise unemployment duration by reducing the pool of workers who chronically transition out of the labor force from unemployment.

FIGURE 8.2 / Aggregate Unemployment Duration and Rates

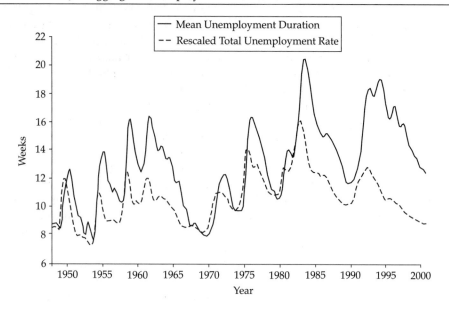

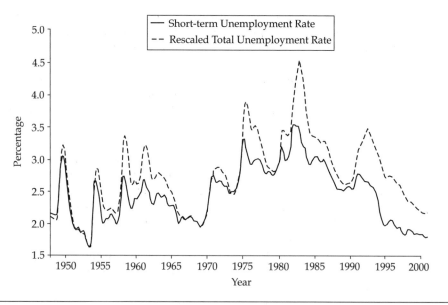

Notes: The first panel shows the mean duration of unemployment spells currently in progress. Subsequent panels show the share of the labor force with zero to four, fifteen to twenty-six, and twenty-seven or more weeks unemployment duration (short-term, long-term, and very-long-term unemployment rates, respectively). The dashed line in each panel shows the

FIGURE 8.2 / *Continued*

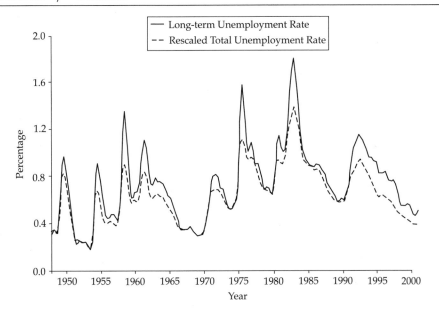

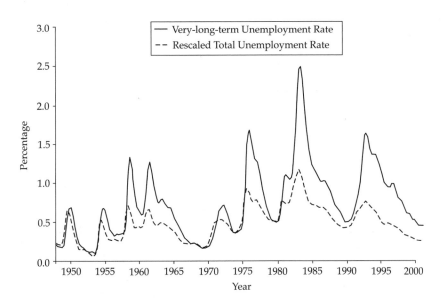

Notes (Continued):

aggregate unemployment rate on a different scale. Monthly fluctuations were smoothed using a Hodrick-Prescott filter with parameter 10. Underlying data are official BLS time series.

We examine evidence on changes in the transition rates of workers across labor-market states (employment, unemployment, and out of the labor force) in order to explore the role that women's increasing labor-force attachment has played in the rise in unemployment duration relative to the unemployment rate. We find that the declining exit rate of employed women from the labor force is quantitatively important for explaining both the decline in women's overall unemployment rate and the increase in their unemployment duration.

To summarize our findings, changes in measurement and changes in demographics each explain part of the increase in unemployment duration relative to the unemployment rate during recent years, especially for men. For women, an important part of the explanation is the increase in their attachment to the labor market, which has reduced their unemployment rate while raising their unemployment duration.

THEORY

Unemployment Duration and Risk

In representative-agent models of the business cycle, labor-market activity is summarized by the number of hours worked. Robert Lucas (1987) has forcefully argued that, in such an economy, there is little value to reducing the variance of output.[3] But representative-agent models may significantly understate the cost of recessions if the burden falls on a small subset of the population. According to this logic, the unemployment rate is an important measure of economic activity in part because it highlights the distributional consequences of recessions. For example, Jonathan Gruber (1997) and Martin Browning and Thomas Crossley (2001) have shown that workers with low asset holdings substantially reduce their consumption following job loss, although the effect is mitigated by unemployment insurance.

Unemployment duration, not just the unemployment rate, is an important determinant of the distributional consequences of recessions. At one extreme, if unemployment spells are very brief, workers can easily use a small stock of savings to smooth consumption across these spells, and hours worked will be a good measure of economic activity. At the other extreme, if unemployment spells never end, no stock of savings will be large enough to allow for consumption smoothing, and average measures will be inadequate for describing individual activity.

To get at this idea more formally, we consider an economy inhabited by rational workers who live for two periods.[4] Workers inelastically supply labor and seek to maximize their expected utility from consumption $U_1(c_1) + U_2(c_2)$, where $c_1 \geq 0$ and $c_2 \geq 0$ are consumption in the first and second periods of life. We assume that the utility function is concave, so workers are risk averse. In each period, a fraction u of them are unemployed and earn an unemployment benefit b, and the remaining $1 - u$ are employed at a fixed wage $w > b$. If a worker is unemployed in the first period of her life, there is a probability λ_{ue} that she will be employed in the second period; and, symmetrically, a worker who is employed in the first period may be unemployed in the second period with probability λ_{eu}. λ_{ue} is inversely related to the mean duration of unemployment (which can vary between one and two periods in this simple model) since it indicates how likely an unemployed worker is to find a job. In order to ensure that the unemployment rate in the second period is u as well, the number of workers who find a job after the first period must equal the number of workers who lose a job, $u \lambda_{ue} = (1 - u)\lambda_{eu}$.

A worker faces a lifetime budget constraint. She is able to borrow and lend at a fixed real interest rate r, so, if she earns y_1 in the first period and y_2 in the second period of her life, consumption must satisfy $(1 + r)c_1 + c_2 = (1 + r)y_1 + y_2$. We assume that c_1 is chosen after y_1 is realized and that c_2 is chosen after y_2 is realized. An optimal consumption plan will depend on the worker's fortune in the labor market as well as on her expectation about future labor-market prospects. For now, think of the unemployment rate (u) and the probability that an unemployed person finds a job in the second period (λ_{ue}) as fixed. A worker who is employed in the first period will choose to consume c_1^e, while an unemployed worker will consume c_1^u. In the second period, consumption will depend on the entire employment history, giving four possible values—c_2^{uu}, c_2^{ue}, c_2^{eu}, and c_2^{ee}—for a worker who is always unemployed, unemployed then employed, and so on. The highest level of consumption in the second period will be that enjoyed by a worker who was employed in both periods, while the lowest level of consumption will be that experienced by a worker who was always unemployed. It is not generally possible to rank c_2^{ue} and c_2^{eu} except to say that they both lie in the interval between c_2^{uu} and c_2^{ee}.

It is important to realize that a worker can set a complete contingent path for consumption, that is, choose the six consumption levels c_1^u, c_1^e, c_2^{uu}, and so on, before realizing any labor-market outcome. Then she simply faces a lottery over the possible consumption levels. When she is young, the chance that she consumes c_1^u is u, and the chance that she consumes c_1^e is $1 - u$, independent of unemployment duration. But, when she is old, the chance that she consumes c_2^{uu} is $u(1 - \lambda_{ue})$, the product of the probability that she is unemployed when young and the conditional probability that she does not move to employment when old. Given the inverse relation between λ_{ue} and mean unemployment duration, this is increasing in mean duration for a fixed unemployment rate. Likewise, the chance that she consumes c_2^{ee} is $(1 - u)(1 - \lambda_{eu}) = 1 - u(1 + \lambda_{ue})$, where we use the fact that $u\lambda_{ue} = (1 - u)\lambda_{eu}$ to simplify the expression. Again, this is increasing in mean unemployment duration for a fixed unemployment rate. The chance of each of the intermediate events—consuming c_2^{ue} or c_2^{eu}—is $u\lambda_{ue}$, decreasing in mean unemployment duration.

But now it is easy to show that shorter average unemployment duration for a fixed unemployment rate must raise the worker's expected utility.[5] She can clearly afford the same consumption in the same states as before, so suppose for now that her consumption plan conditional on employment status does not change. Then a higher level of λ_{ue} is the opposite of a mean-preserving spread. It has no effect on first-period consumption, which remains a lottery placing probability u on c_1^u and otherwise yielding c_1^e. But, in the second period, it shifts probability mass away from the extreme consumption levels c_2^{uu} and c_2^{ee} and toward the intermediate levels. That is, the distribution of consumption in the second period has the same mean, independent of λ_{ue},[6] but the distribution with a higher value of λ_{ue} second-order stochastically dominates the distribution with a lower value. Then it follows immediately from Michael Rothschild and Joseph Stiglitz (1970) that, holding the consumption plan fixed, any risk-averse worker is better off in an economy with shorter mean unemployment duration. Intuitively, the utility gain from consuming c_2^{ue} rather than c_2^{uu} exceeds the utility loss from consuming c_2^{eu} rather than c_2^{ee}. Since the unemployment rate is the same in the first and second periods, the probability of consuming c_2^{ue} must equal that of consuming c_2^{eu}. But having higher transition rates λ_{ue} and λ_{eu} for a fixed unemployment rate raises the probability of each event and, therefore, raises expected utility. All this ignores the fact that, in an economy with shorter mean unemployment duration, the worker can reoptimize her consumption plan. Doing so will trivially yield still higher utility. This establishes that, for a given unemployment rate, workers prefer a shorter mean unemployment duration.

Unemployment Duration and Hysteresis

Unemployment duration is an excellent predictor of whether a worker will find a job. Figure 8.3 shows that the fraction of unemployed workers with a given unemployment duration who find a job in the following month is a decreasing function of duration.[7] From 1976 to 2000, this probability exceeds 50 percent for workers at the short end of the duration distribution and falls to barely 10 percent for workers who have been unemployed for at least ninety weeks.

Broadly speaking, there are two possible explanations for this pattern. First, workers may be heterogeneous. Unemployed workers with low exit probabilities are dynamically sorted into long-term unemployment. According to this theory, changes in mean unemployment duration simply reflect changes in the composition of job losers. But there is some empirical evidence that workers who initially have a high probability of finding a job are less likely to find one if they have been unemployed for a long time (see Abbring, van den Berg, and van Ours, forthcoming). That is, unemployment exhibits hysteresis (Blanchard and Summers 1987). This will be the case if skills atrophy during unemployment (Pissarides 1992), if long-term unemployment stigmatizes workers (Blanchard and Diamond 1994), or if the long-term unemployed lose contact with social networks (Granovetter 1974; Montgomery 1991) and so do not know where to look for good employment opportunities.

To the extent that these models help explain the decreasing hazard rate of finding a job depicted in figure 8.3, then there may also be a role for government

FIGURE 8.3 / Probability of Finding a Job

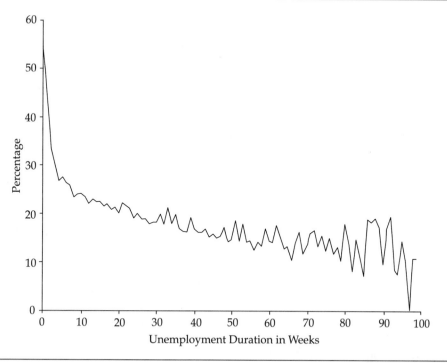

Notes: This figure shows the average probability of an unemployed worker becoming employed in the following month as a function of her unemployment duration, 1976 to 2000. Data are our calculations from the CPS.

intervention in retraining the long-term unemployed. For example, Gary Becker (1964) predicts that workers will bear the costs of general human capital. But, in the presence of credit constraints, this may not be a realistic possibility for the long-term unemployed, creating a role for subsidized training programs. Likewise, a firm with imperfect information about worker quality may use unemployment duration as a screening device. Although it knows that the long-term unemployed would be willing to accept a low wage in return for a job, the firm also realizes that, if it manages to hire a good worker from the long-term unemployed population, the market will quickly perceive the worker's high marginal product and drive up her wage. That is, other firms will free ride, reducing the firm's information acquisition below its efficient level. The government can alleviate this problem by running training programs designed in part to establish participants' ability to partake in environments similar to the workplace. In a similar vein, Andrew Caplin and John Leahy (2000) argue that equilibrium unemployment duration may be excessively long since, in an environment characterized by social networks, unemployed workers do not internalize all the informational benefits of maintaining contact with the labor market. If this is correct, search subsidies for the long-term unemployed may improve welfare by reconnecting groups of discouraged workers with the labor market.

Unemployment Duration and Wage Pressure

The decreasing relation between unemployment duration and job-finding hazard rates depicted in figure 8.3 also suggests the possibility that the long-term unemployed may put less downward pressure on wages than do the short-term unemployed. If this is the case, an increase in unemployment duration will tend to shift the Phillips curve to the right and raise the NAIRU (nonaccelerating inflation rate of unemployment).[8] To assess the quantitative significance of this effect, define an index of unemployment pressure on the labor market equal to the unemployment rate at time t multiplied by the job-finding probability of the average unemployed worker at time t. We calculate the latter term using the average job-finding rate conditional on unemployment duration from 1976 to 2000, weighted by the unemployment-duration distribution prevailing at t. Figure 8.4 depicts the results. The index of unemployment pressure closely tracks the aggregate unemployment rate, although the cyclic variation is slightly muted. It thus seems unlikely that shifts in the unemployment-duration distribution have caused substantive shifts in the Phillips curve.

MEASUREMENT ISSUES

An important issue with respect to analyzing movements in unemployment and unemployment duration over time is whether these data have been affected by the major redesign of the CPS that was introduced in January 1994. This redesign included important improvements in the survey questionnaire as well as the conversion of the survey from a pencil and paper to a computerized instrument. Available evidence suggests that the redesign had no significant effect on the overall unemployment rate or on the unemployment rates for age-sex groups, with the limited exception that it appears to have raised measured unemployment rates for persons aged fifty-five and older (see Polivka and Miller 1998). The proper conclusions to draw with respect to the measurement of unemployment duration, however, are less clear.

Two important changes in the design of the CPS could have affected the measurement of unemployment duration. The first change is the use of dependent interviewing. Households included in the CPS sample are interviewed for four consecutive months, are out of the sample for the next eight months, and then are interviewed for an additional four consecutive months. Prior to the redesign, an individual who was reported as unemployed was always asked the duration of her unemployment spell. Since the redesign, the unemployment duration of a worker who is unemployed in consecutive months is calculated automatically on the basis of the spell length recorded for the earlier month and the number of

FIGURE 8.4 / Index of Unemployment Pressure

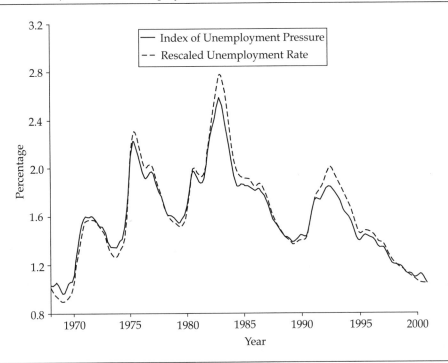

Notes: This figure shows the index of unemployment pressure (the solid line) and the normalized unemployment rate (the dashed line). The definition of the index of unemployment pressure is given in the text. The unemployment rate is normalized so that it has the same average value as the index of unemployment pressure. Monthly fluctuations were smoothed using a Hodrick-Prescott filter with parameter 10. Data are official BLS time series and our calculations from the CPS.

weeks between the two months' survey reference periods. Among other possible effects, this change can be expected to have reduced the number of people recorded as having spells of zero- to four-weeks duration. The second change is to allow individuals to report unemployment duration in months or years rather than only in weeks, although interviewers are instructed to ask for duration in weeks for anyone reporting four or fewer months in their current unemployment spell. It is not a priori obvious what effect this change should have had.

In appendix 8A, we discuss one approach to analyzing the effect of the CPS redesign, the use of a parallel survey that was constructed explicitly for this purpose (Polivka and Miller 1998). For reasons discussed in the appendix, however, we are hesitant to accept the results this approach yields for unemployment duration at face value. Instead, we attempt to assess the likely effect of the CPS redesign on unemployment duration by directly measuring the quantitative significance of the design changes. Consider the effect of dependent interviewing. Before the redesign, there was no difference in the way in which unemployment duration was measured for different rotation groups. But, after the redesign, unemployment duration was measured differently for the "incoming rotation groups" (the first and the fifth months in the sample) than it was for the rest of the sample. Substantial differences between reported unemployment durations have subsequently emerged. According to time series that we constructed from the CPS, since the redesign about 6.5 percent more of the unemployed workers in the incoming rotation groups report that their current unemployment spell has lasted for less than four weeks, compared to the full sample (figure 8.5). There were no meaningful differences across rotation groups before the CPS redesign, so this is almost certainly a redesign effect. More to the point, from 1994 to 2000, the mean unemployment duration averaged 15.20 weeks for the full CPS sample but only 14.83 weeks for the incoming rotation groups. Most of this difference is accounted for by short-duration unemployment (0 to 4 weeks), which averaged 1.97 percent of the labor force for the full sample after the CPS redesign but 2.40 percent for the incoming rotation groups. On the other hand, the rates of long-term unemployment (15 to 26 weeks) and ·very long-term unemployment (27 weeks and longer) were essentially unaffected by the switch to dependent interviewing. They averaged 0.68 and 0.79 percent, respectively, in the full sample and 0.67 and 0.78 percent, respectively, for the incoming rotation groups. Although it is likely that the full sample estimates are more accurate (and certainly are based on a much larger sample), the estimates for the incoming rotation groups are more comparable with the pre-1994 data.[9] Throughout the remainder of our analysis, we use only data for the incoming rotation groups from 1994 forward.

Unfortunately, the absence of an obvious control group means that we cannot perform a similar assessment of the other relevant redesign change, allowing individuals to report their unemployment duration in months or years instead of only in weeks. The redesign resulted in a marked increase in the frequency with which certain unemployment durations were reported.[10] For example, from 1994 to 2000, 98.5 percent of unemployed workers in the incoming rotation groups who reported that their unemployment spell had lasted between forty-nine and fifty-five weeks said that their spell had been in progress for exactly fifty-two weeks (one year). During a roughly comparable period a decade earlier, only 80.7 percent of these unemployment spells were reported as having lasted exactly fifty-two weeks. Similarly, the share of twenty-three- to twenty-nine-week spells that were reported as lasting exactly twenty-six weeks (six months) increased from 34.3 to 91.3 percent, and the share of thirty-six- to forty-two-week spells that were reported as lasting exactly thirty-nine weeks (nine months) increased from 11.0 to 88.6 percent. Other changes were less dramatic.

Obviously, when offered the option to report their unemployment duration in months or years rather than in weeks, many respondents choose a round number. This need not bias the mean unemployment duration if as many workers report fifty-two rather than fifty-one weeks as report fifty-two rather than fifty-three weeks, but, in practice, that may not have occurred. The fact that there are more workers with shorter unemployment durations implies that symmetrical rounding errors like the one just described will result in an increase in measured mean unemployment duration. On the other hand, the rounding errors need not be symmetrical (Baker 1992). For example, it is plausible that a worker is as likely to report a forty-five-week unemployment spell as lasting for nine months as she is to report it lasting for one year. This may further bias the measured unemployment duration, although the direction of the bias is not ex ante obvious.

Fortunately, any effect of the CPS redesign on rounding errors is less likely to alter measured short-term and long-term unemployment rates. Interviewers are instructed to ask for unemployment duration in weeks whenever a respondent reports a duration of less than four months. To the extent that this is in fact done, all individuals should be correctly assigned to two key duration categories, zero to four weeks and five to fourteen weeks (short- and medium-term unemployment). The number of spells that have lasted more than twenty-seven weeks, however, may be underestimated if some respondents report a six-month (twenty-six-week) duration rather than a slightly higher number.[11] We sidestep this by extending the definition of *long-term unemployment* to include durations from fifteen to thirty-two weeks and thus define *very long-term unemployment* to include spells that exceed thirty-two weeks.

To increase our confidence that we are not missing some other important effects of the CPS redesign, we explore whether the relation between the incoming rotation groups' unemployment duration and other cyclic labor-market variables changed in 1994. For this to be a meaningful exercise, the other cyclic indicators must be ones that were not themselves affected by the CPS redesign. We focus on a measure of the employment-population ratio constructed using employment from the monthly BLS establishment survey (the Current Employment Statistics, or CES, survey) and the Census Bureau's projection of the civilian noninstitutional population aged sixteen and older that serves as the CPS control total. The employment-population ratio trends upward over time, so we apply a Hodrick-Prescott (HP) filter to the time series.[12] We similarly detrend the seasonally adjusted mean unemployment duration as well as the short-term unemployment rate (zero to four weeks), the long-term unemployment rate (fifteen to thirty-two weeks), and the very long-term unemployment rate (thirty-three or more weeks).[13] There is a strong negative correlation between the employment-population ratio and measures of longer-duration unemployment: -0.85 with the mean unemployment duration; -0.89 with the long-term unemployment rate; and -0.90 with the very long-term unemployment rate. The correlation with the short-term unemployment rate is weaker but still negative (-0.55).

To test for a break in a CPS-based time series in January 1994, we regress the series on the employment-population ratio using data from 1968 through 1993. We then forecast the series from 1994 through 2000 and plot the residual forecast errors. If there were a break in the time series, we would expect the residuals to look different after the break and, in particular, to jump in January 1994. The results are shown in figure 8.6. The regressions perform remarkably well out of

(Text continues on p. 384.)

FIGURE 8.5 / Unemployment Duration Cumulative Distribution Functions—Incoming Rotation Group Minus Full Sample

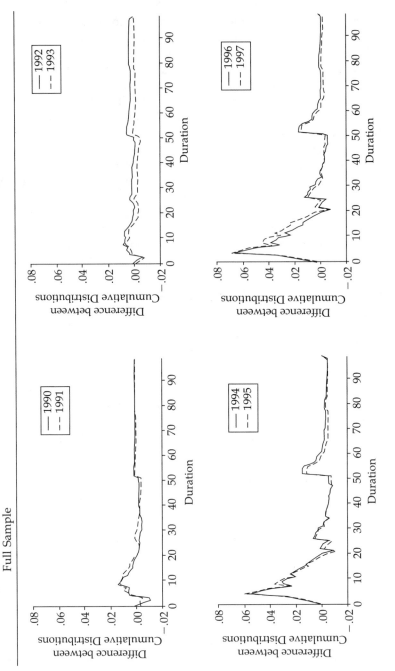

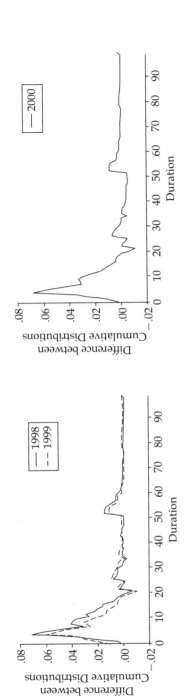

Notes: The difference between the cumulative distribution of unemployment durations for individuals in the first and fifth months in the sample compared to the entire survey sample in the four years before and the seven years since the CPS redesign. Figures are annual averages. The cumulative distribution is the fraction of unemployed workers with unemployment duration less than or equal to *x* weeks. Data are our calculations from the CPS.

FIGURE 8.6 / Residual Unemployment Duration and Rates

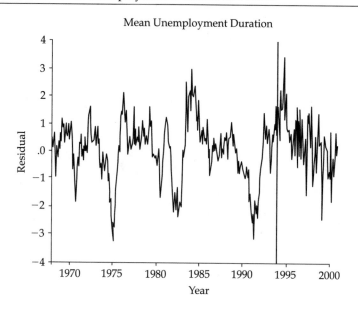

Mean Unemployment Duration

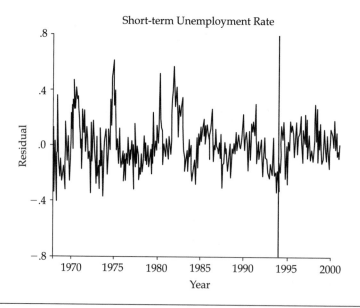

Short-term Unemployment Rate

Notes: Residuals from regressions of the detrended mean unemployment duration, short-term unemployment rate, long-term unemployment rate, and very-long-term unemployment rate on the detrended employment-population ratio. The employment level in the latter ratio comes from the CES survey. The population is the over-sixteen population used by the CPS. We computed the dependent variables from the CPS. They are seasonally adjusted using a

FIGURE 8.6 / *Continued*

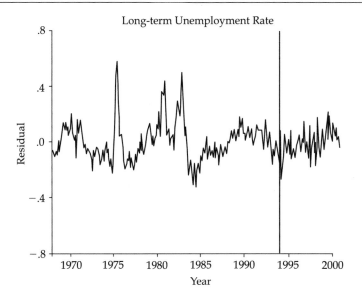

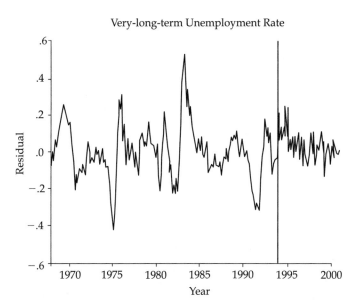

Notes (Continued):

ratio to moving average procedure. For 1994 through 2000, only the incoming rotation groups are included. All series are detrended using a HP filter with smoothing parameter 1,440,000, which eliminates only very-low-frequency fluctuations. Vertical lines indicate the timing of the CPS redesign.

the sample period. In only one case, the very-long-term unemployment rate, is there any indication of a discontinuity in January 1994, and even then the change is not unusual by historical standards. A reasonable measure of the possible effect of the redesign is the mean value of the residuals during the first half of 1994.[14] The unemployment rates show no systematic pattern, with the short-term rate 0.02 percent below, the long-term rate 0.13 percent below, and the very long-term rate 0.13 percent above the expected levels, all small values given the pattern of variation in the residuals. The mean unemployment duration is further from trend, 1.42 weeks above what one would expect in the first half of 1994, but that is not much different than the deviation in the last half of 1993, when it was 0.85 weeks above trend. Because the point estimates are imprecise, we cannot reject the null hypothesis that the CPS redesign had no effect on the measured mean unemployment duration in the incoming rotation groups.

In sum, although it had no significant effect on the unemployment rate, the CPS redesign indisputably affected measured unemployment duration. Only the effects associated with the introduction of dependent interviewing can be identified with confidence, and we control for those in what follows. The results just discussed suggest that the full effect of the redesign on mean unemployment duration could have been somewhat larger, but we have no strong empirical basis for making additional adjustments and so choose not to do so. Figure 8.7 summarizes these findings, depicting our preferred time series for mean unemployment duration and the short-, long-, and very-long-term unemployment rates, with the standard time series depicted as a dashed line.[15] While measurement issues explain much of the recent decline in the short-term unemployment rate, they do not explain the persistently high level of very-long-term unemployment or mean unemployment duration.

THE AGING OF THE BABY BOOM

The youth unemployment rate is much higher than the prime-age unemployment rate. Viewing the aggregate unemployment rate as a weighted average of the unemployment rate of workers in different age cohorts, part of the recent decline in unemployment may be attributed to a simple compositional effect, a consequence of the aging of the baby boom (Shimer 1998). What is true for the aggregate unemployment rate is even more true for the short-term unemployment rate. Young workers rarely suffer long spells of unemployment,[16] so, from 1968 to 2000, the fraction of teenagers unemployed for less than four weeks in a typical month was 6.5 times as high as the comparable fraction of thirty-five- to fifty-four-year-old workers. The short-term unemployment rate for twenty- to twenty-four-year-olds was 3.2 times as high and for twenty-five- to thirty-four-year-olds 1.6 times as high. Since 1980, the share of the labor force accounted for by thirty-five- to fifty-four-year-olds has risen by 13.2 percentage points, mostly at the expense of younger workers. The aging of the baby-boom generation during the last two decades has therefore shifted the population into age groups that suffer fewer short unemployment spells.

Under the assumption that the aging of the baby boom has not affected the unemployment probability or unemployment duration of workers conditional on their age, we can measure the effect of this demographic transition on the overall unemployment rate, the short-, long-, and very-long-term unemployment rates, and the mean duration of unemployment. To illustrate, let u_{it} denote the unemployment rate of age group i in year t and ω_{it} denote the labor-force share of that age group in the same year. Then the unemployment rate is just a weighted average of the unemployment rates of workers of different ages, $\Sigma_{i=1}^{N} \omega_{it} u_{it}$, where N is the number of age groups.[17] Under the assumption described previously, the unemployment rate in year t would have been $u_t^s = \Sigma_{i=1}^{N} \omega_{is} u_{it}$ if the labor-force shares had remained at their year s levels. We refer to this as the *age-adjusted* unemployment rate. Similar calculations can be carried out for the other variables of interest. To apply this procedure, we must select a base year s. To the extent that the differences across age groups in the unemployment rates u_{it} are stable from one year to the next, as is generally the case, the choice of base year is of no real consequence. In what follows, we consistently use 1980 as the base year for our age adjustments, but we have obtained similar results with other base years.

Figure 8.8 shows the effects of age adjustments on the overall unemployment rate. As documented in Robert Shimer (1998), the age-adjusted unemployment rate has been higher relative to rates observed in the past than has the unadjusted rates more commonly the focus of attention. Between 1980 and 1992, 0.67 percentage point of the decline in the aggregate unemployment rate could be attributed to the aging of the baby boom. Some of this trend has been reversed in the last few years, but, comparing across business-cycle peaks, the aging of the baby boom contributed to a 0.21 percentage point increase in the aggregate unemployment rate from 1969 to 1979, a 0.44 percentage point decline over the next decade, and a further 0.14 percentage point decline from 1989 to 2000.[18]

The age-related decline in unemployment has been concentrated at the short end of the unemployment-duration spectrum. Figure 8.9 shows that the age-adjusted short-term unemployment rate was 2.1 percent in 1969 and 2.5 percent in 1973 but that it has not subsequently fallen back to these historic lows. In contrast, age-adjusted mean unemployment duration has increased modestly from expansion to expansion during the last three decades. The age-adjusted long-term unemployment rate has declined somewhat during the 1980s and 1990s, but the age-adjusted very-long-term unemployment rate has not declined at all. Taking the movements in overall unemployment shown in figure 8.8 and the movements in the duration measures shown in figure 8.9 together, neither our measurement adjustments nor our age-structure adjustments alter the qualitative conclusion that long-duration unemployment has been high in recent years compared to the aggregate unemployment rate.

FIGURE 8.7 / Unemployment Duration and Rates Adjusted for Measurement
Changes

Mean Unemployment Duration

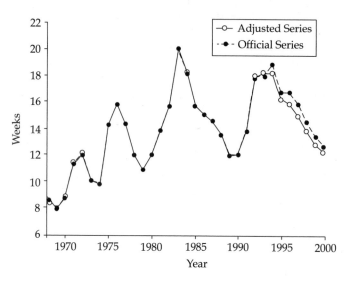

Short-term Unemployment Rate

Notes: The first panel shows the mean duration of unemployment spells currently in progress.
The subsequent panels show the share of the labor force with zero to four, fifteen to thirty-
two, and thirty-three or more weeks unemployment duration (short-term, long-term, and
very-long-term unemployment rates, respectively). We constructed the solid line in each panel

FIGURE 8.7   /   *Continued*

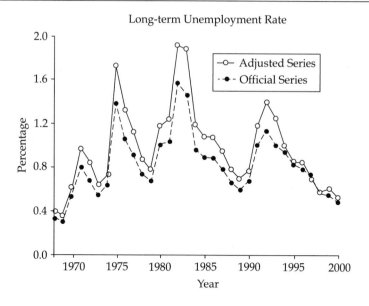

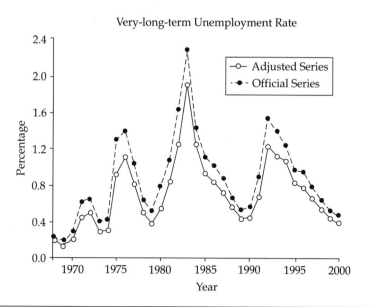

Notes (Continued):

from the CPS, except for values before 1975, which are constructed from BLS weekly unemployment-duration data. From 1994 to 2000, the time series use only the incoming rotation
groups. The dashed line indicates the corresponding official time series, with long-term unemployment defined as fifteen to twenty-six weeks and very-long-term unemployment defined as twenty-seven or more weeks (see figure 8.2).

FIGURE 8.8 / Age-Adjusted Unemployment Rate

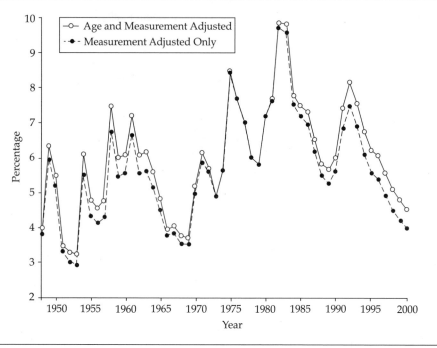

Notes: The figure shows the unemployment rate adjusted for measurement changes and changes in the age composition of the labor force (the solid line) and the unemployment rate adjusted only for measurement changes (the dashed line). Underlying data are official BLS time series and our computations.

LABOR-FORCE ATTACHMENT

Women's and Men's Labor-Market Outcomes

Our analysis so far has ignored an important factor in determining labor-market outcomes, the worker's sex. From 1965 through 1979, women's age-adjusted unemployment rate was on average nearly 2 percentage points higher than men's rate (figure 8.10). Since then, the two rates have converged, with an average difference from 1980 to 2000 of less than 0.1 percentage point, although women's unemployment rate has been somewhat less variable than men's at business-cycle frequencies. Given the close link between the unemployment rate and unemployment duration, one might expect that men's and women's age-adjusted unemployment durations would also have tracked each other quite closely since 1980. Figures 8.11 and 8.12, which graph men's and women's age-adjusted mean unemployment duration and short-, long-, and very-long-term unemployment rates, show that this has not been the case. Men have consistently experienced much less short-term unemployment than have women and hence have had a much longer mean unemployment duration. This observation enables us to refine our understanding of the unemployment-duration puzzle.

Men's unemployment rate and unemployment duration have had a relatively stable relation during the past three decades (figure 8.11). After accounting for age, men's unemployment rate reached 3.0 percent at the end of the 1960s before rising to 5.1 percent in 1979 and 5.6 percent in 1989. By 2000, it had fallen to 4.4 percent, which is by no means an unprecedented level. Likewise, men's mean unemployment duration rose from 8.3 weeks in 1969 to over twelve weeks in 1979, where it has remained during subsequent expansions. Looking at means masks a significant secular increase in men's short-term unemployment rate, which has been offset by an increase in the prevalence of very-long-term unemployment. Given these changes, male unemployment is higher at both extremes of the unemployment-duration distribution than would have been expected given the level of the aggregate unemployment rate, all after adjustment for measurement and age-structure changes. This "bimodality" is consistent with the growing dispersion of labor-market outcomes documented in other contexts, for example, the growth in the dispersion of labor-market earnings (Katz and Murphy 1992). It would be interesting to explore whether the increasing concentration of male unemployment at the short and long ends of the unemployment-duration spectrum can be explained in a similar manner.

In contrast, women's age-adjusted unemployment rate is at the lowest level since the 1950s, having fallen from 6.8 percent during the expansion at the end of the 1970s, to 5.8 percent during the 1980s expansion, to 4.7 percent by the end of the 1990s. Figure 8.12 shows that there has not been any drop in women's age-adjusted unemployment duration during this time period. Instead, women's mean unemployment duration increased from 9.5 weeks in 1979 and 9.4 weeks in 1989 to 11.0 weeks in 1990, primarily a consequence of a sharp drop in women's short-term unemployment rate and a sustained high level in women's very-long-term unemployment rate. The historic link between women's unemployment rate and women's unemployment duration broke down during the 1980s and 1990s, and measurement and demographics do not explain why.

One hint is that, in all cases, men's and women's unemployment durations have converged toward a common level. Our first thought was that this pattern might be linked to changes in the industry and occupation distribution of women's employment, but further investigation showed that unemployment durations do not differ enough across these categories to explain the increase in women's unemployment duration. Instead, we explore another big shift that has occurred during the last two decades, the increase in women's attachment to the labor force.

Labor-Market Transitions

To understand labor-market attachment, we must analyze not only transitions between employment (E) and unemployment (U) but also movements in and

FIGURE 8.9 / Age-Adjusted Unemployment Duration and Rates

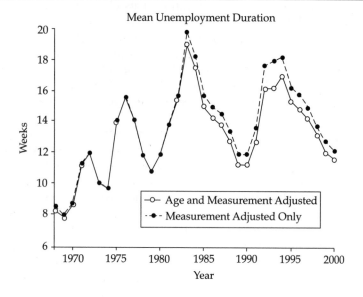

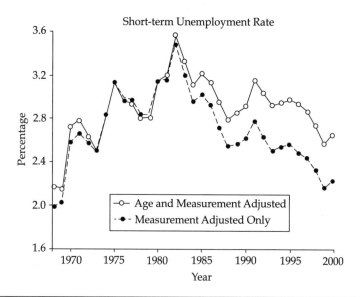

Notes: The first panel shows the mean duration of unemployment spells currently in progress. The subsequent panels show the share of the labor force with zero to four, fifteen to thirty-two, and thirty-three or more weeks unemployment duration (short-term, long-term, and very-long-term unemployment rates, respectively). The solid line in each panel shows

FIGURE 8.9 / *Continued*

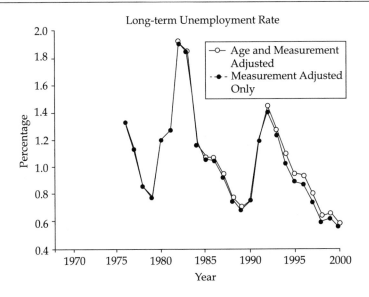

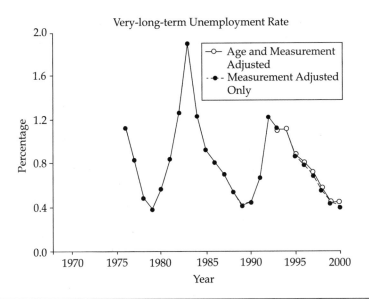

Notes (Continued):

measurement- and age-adjusted time series, while the dashed line indicates the series adjusted only for measurement changes (see figure 8.7). The time series from 1968 through 1975 were constructed using unpublished BLS data; information on the number of people unemployed fifteen to thirty-two and thirty-three or more weeks was not available by age. From 1976 forward, the time series were constructed directly from the CPS. From 1994 forward, the time series use only the incoming rotation groups.

FIGURE 8.10 / Age-Adjusted Unemployment Rate, Women and Men

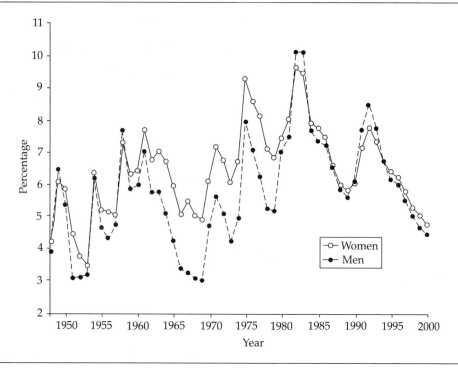

Note: Unemployment data are from the official BLS time series and our calculations.

out of the labor force (N). We construct a time series for women's and men's age-adjusted labor-market-transition rates following the methodology discussed in appendix 8B and display them in figure 8.13. These data are available for the period from 1976 through 2000. The first thing that stands out in this figure is that, for both men and women, the transition probability from E to U (hereafter the EU transition rate λ_{eu}, with similar notation for the other transition rates) and the NU transition rate λ_{nu} are at their lowest levels in twenty-five years, while the UE transition rate λ_{ue} is at its highest level. In an accounting sense, this is a major part of the explanation for the current low level of unemployment. In comparing women's and men's transition rates, there is no evidence of convergence in λ_{eu} or λ_{ue}, but the remaining four transition rates, which all involve the labor-market-participation decision, have steadily converged during the past twenty-five years. Women are now much less likely to exit the labor market directly from employment, a sign of increased attachment, while men have become somewhat more likely to exit the labor market from unemployment and less likely to reenter the labor force once they leave it, two signs of decreased labor-force attachment.

Next, we show how to use the transition data to construct measures of the aggregate unemployment rate and the short-term unemployment rate. Recall that any Markov transition matrix implies a unique steady-state distribution of workers across the three labor-market states E, U, and N, given by the appropriately normalized eigenvector associated with the eigenvalue of 1:

$$e = k(\lambda_{nu}\lambda_{ue} + \lambda_{un}\lambda_{ne} + \lambda_{ue}\lambda_{ne}),$$

$$u = k(\lambda_{ne}\lambda_{eu} + \lambda_{en}\lambda_{nu} + \lambda_{eu}\lambda_{nu}), \tag{8.1}$$

$$n = k(\lambda_{ue}\lambda_{en} + \lambda_{eu}\lambda_{un} + \lambda_{en}\lambda_{un}),$$

where e denotes the fraction of the population that is employed, u the fraction that is unemployed, and n the fraction that is not in the labor force, and k is a proportionality constant that ensures $e + u + n = 1$. From this distribution, we can calculate the "implied steady-state unemployment rate" $u/(e + u)$. Of course, there is no reason to believe that the economy must always be in steady state or, equivalently, that the actual unemployment rate equals the implied unemployment rate. But the first two panels of figure 8.14 document that, in practice, the implied unemployment rate does a remarkable job of tracking the actual age-adjusted unemployment rate both for women and for men. The mean absolute difference between the two time series is 0.14 percentage point for women and 0.17 percentage point for men.

We can also use the labor-market-flow data to construct a measure of the short-term unemployment rate. A fraction $\lambda_{ue} + \lambda_{un}$ of unemployed workers exit unemployment in an average month, and, in steady state this must equal the fraction of unemployed workers who are in their first month of unemployment. The product of this and the unemployment rate implied by the labor-market-transition rates should, therefore, give us an independent measure of the short-term unemployment rate. The last two panels of figure 8.14 show that the implied measure of short-term unemployment is on average about half a percentage point below the standard time series. The most plausible interpretation of this result harks back to our analysis of the effect of the CPS redesign on the measured unemployment rate. Recall that the incoming rotation groups report almost half a percentage point more short-term unemployment than does the full CPS in post-1994 data. This reflects the switch to dependent interviewing, with the result that a worker who is unemployed in consecutive months cannot report less than a five-week unemployment duration in the second month. Our construction of the short-term unemployment rate from labor-market-flow data is analogous to the switch to dependent interviewing, since a worker who is unemployed in consecutive months cannot be counted as short-term unemployed. This suggests that our time series for short-term unemployment is internally consistent but that it does not measure the same quantity as the short-term unemployment rate reported elsewhere in the chapter. Rather, it measures something more like what the redesigned CPS measures for workers who are not in the incoming rotation groups. This view is also quantitatively reasonable. The

(Text continues on p. 402.)

FIGURE 8.11 / Age-Adjusted Unemployment Duration and Rates—Men

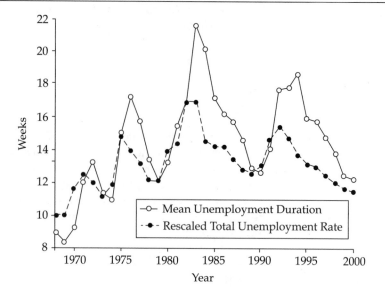

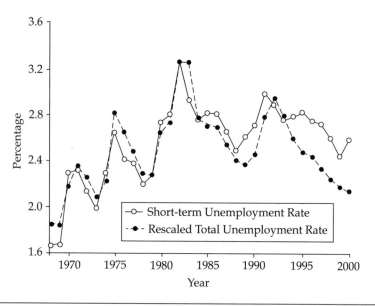

Notes: The first panel shows the measurement- and age-adjusted mean duration of unemployment spells currently in progress for men. The subsequent panels show the similarly adjusted shares of men in the labor force with zero to four, fifteen to thirty-two, and thirty-three or more weeks unemployment duration (short-term, long-term, and very-long-term unemployment rates, respectively). The dashed line in each panel shows men's adjusted unemployment rate on a different scale. Unemployment data are from the official BLS time series and

FIGURE 8.11 / *Continued*

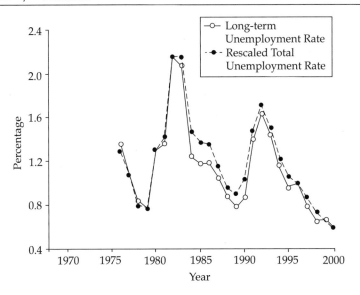

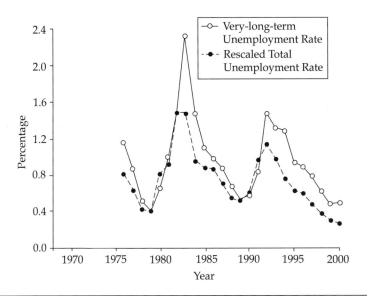

Notes (Continued):

our own calculations. Duration data from 1968 through 1975 were constructed using un-published BLS data; information on the number of people unemployed fifteen to thirty-two and thirty-three or more weeks was not available by age. From 1976 forward, the time series were constructed directly from the CPS. From 1994 forward, the time series use only the in-coming rotation groups.

FIGURE 8.12 / Age-Adjusted Unemployment Duration and Rates—Women

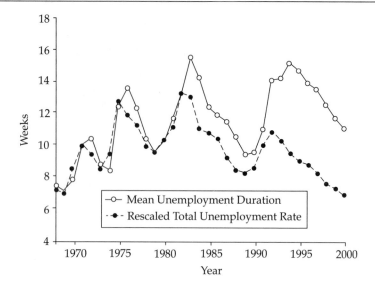

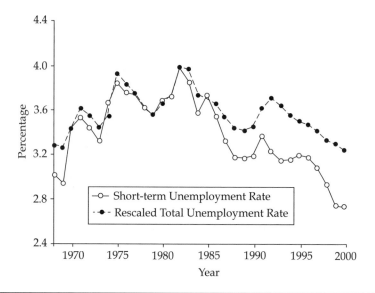

Notes: The first panel shows the measurement- and age-adjusted mean duration of unemployment spells currently in progress for women. The subsequent panels show the similarly adjusted shares of women in the labor force with zero to four, fifteen to thirty-two, and thirty-
three or more weeks unemployment duration (short-term, long-term, and very-long-term
unemployment rates, respectively). The dashed line in each panel shows women's adjusted
unemployment rate on a different scale. Unemployment data are from the official BLS time

FIGURE 8.12 / *Continued*

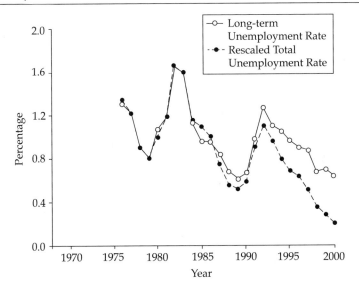

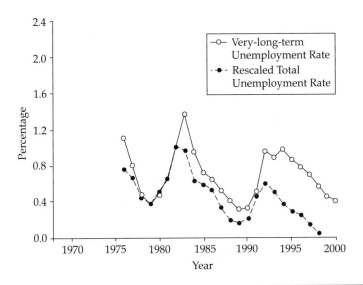

Notes (Continued):

series and our own calculations. Duration data from 1968 through 1975 were constructed using unpublished BLS data; information on the number of people unemployed fifteen to thirty-two and thirty-three or more weeks was not available by age. From 1976 forward, the time series were constructed directly from the CPS. From 1994 forward, the time series use only the incoming rotation groups.

FIGURE 8.13 / Age-Adjusted Monthly Labor-Force-Transition Rates

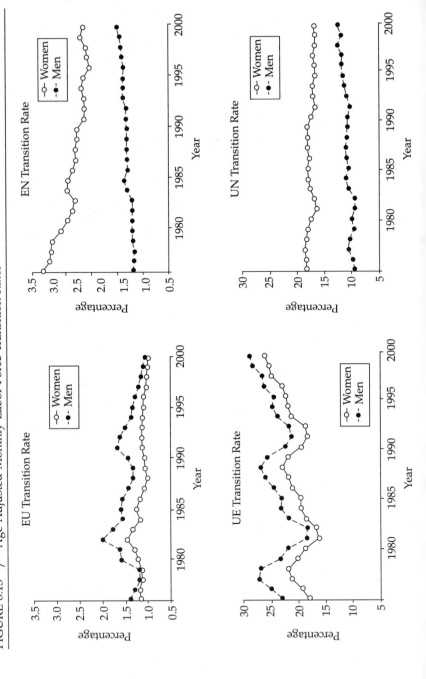

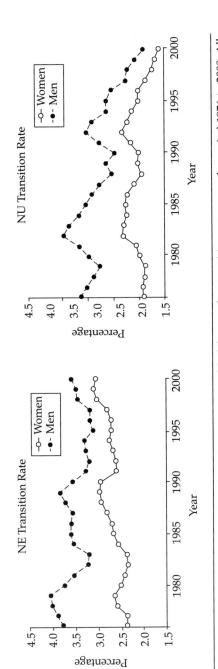

Notes: The figure shows women's and men's average monthly labor-market transition rates over the period 1976 to 2000. All transition rates are adjusted using the Abowd-Zellner correction. λ_{un} and λ_{nu} are adjusted for the effects of the 1994 CPS redesign (for details, see appendix 8B). Data are our calculations from the CPS.

FIGURE 8.14   /   Unemployment Rates Implied by Labor-Market Transitions

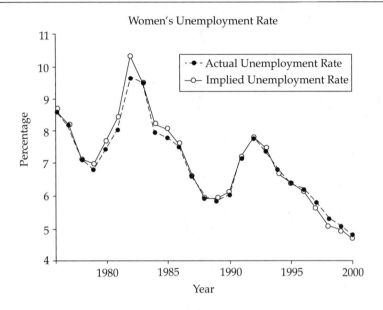

Notes: The first two panels show the steady-state unemployment rate implied by age-adjusted labor-market-transition rates and the actual age-adjusted unemployment rate for women and men, 1976 to 2000. The last two panels show implied and actual short-term unemployment

FIGURE 8.14 / *Continued*

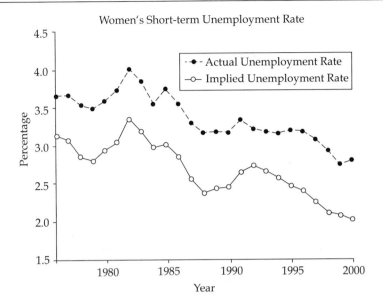

Women's Short-term Unemployment Rate

Men's Short-term Unemployment Rate

Notes (Continued):

rates. All flows are adjusted using the Abowd-Zellner correction. λ_{un} and λ_{nu} are adjusted for the effects of the 1994 CPS redesign (for details, see appendix 8B). Data are our calculations from the CPS.

gap between the short-term unemployment rate constructed using transition data and the actual rate averaged 0.69 percentage point between 1994 and 2000, while the short-term unemployment rate for the incoming rotation group was on average 0.63 percentage point lower than the short-term unemployment rate in the other rotation groups over the same time period.[19]

In any case, the basic puzzle of women's unemployment duration remains in the time series implied by labor-market-transition rates: women's implied unemployment rate fell from 7.0 percent in 1979 to 4.6 percent in 2000, a decline of 33 percent. Under ordinary circumstances, we would expect this to be reflected almost exclusively in declines at longer unemployment durations. But, instead, women's implied short-term unemployment rate fell from 2.8 to 2.0 percent during the same time period, a decline of 29 percent. In contrast, men's implied unemployment rate fell by half as much, 16 percent, over the same time period, while their implied short-term unemployment rate fell by just 7 percent.[20]

To see whether this is related to the increase in women's labor-force attachment (or to the decrease in men's labor-force attachment), we conduct a counterfactual exercise whereby we "shut down" changes in the transitions between various labor-market states in turn. For example, we take women's actual λ_{ue} and λ_{eu} time series but fix the other four transition rates at their 1979 level.[21] Using the constructed sequence of Markov matrices, we calculate the implied aggregate and short-term unemployment rates. We perform similar counterfactual experiments by allowing for time variation only in λ_{un} and λ_{nu} and similarly for time variation only in λ_{en} and λ_{ne}. By plotting the resulting time series, we can see which of the changes in transition rates are important for understanding the secular variation in aggregate and short-term unemployment rates.

Consider first women's aggregate unemployment, depicted in the first panel of figure 8.15. The solid line shows the persistent decline in women's implied age-adjusted unemployment rate. The remaining lines indicate the contribution of the three other pairs of transition rates. Changes in λ_{un} and λ_{nu} are not particularly important for understanding the decline in women's unemployment rate, although they do help explain some of the business cycle fluctuations in the rate. Not surprisingly, the increase in λ_{ue} and the decrease in λ_{eu} reduced the incidence of female unemployment, and their fluctuations are also important contributors to short-run variation in the unemployment rate. But the most surprising finding is the equally important contribution of changes in flows between E and N, with both the decrease in λ_{en} and the increase in λ_{ne} contributing to the secular reduction in women's unemployment.

This finding is even more apparent when we look at the counterfactual time series for women's short-term unemployment rate in the third panel of figure 8.15. Over half the trend decline is explained by changes in λ_{en} and λ_{ne}, much more than changes in the other transition rates can explain. The sharp decline in λ_{en} for women presumably reflects an increase in their attachment to the labor market. It was much less common for a woman to quit her job and exit the labor force in the 1990s than it was two decades earlier. To the extent that this implies that women today are better able to build long-term employment relations, the decline in women's unemployment rate is readily understandable. Worker-flow data give a unique perspective on this fact.

Performing a similar experiment with men's unemployment rates highlights the importance of labor-force attachment (the second and fourth panels of figure 8.15). The increase in λ_{en} for men has *raised* men's unemployment rate by over half a percentage point and men's short-term unemployment rate by over 0.2 percentage point. Variations in the other transition rates are responsible for the observed decline in unemployment. Again, it is not surprising that the decrease in λ_{eu} and the increase in λ_{ue} reduced unemployment, although it is curious that these variables are responsible for virtually all the cyclic fluctuations in men's aggregate and short-term unemployment rate. In contrast, for women, λ_{nu} and λ_{un} also contribute significantly to the cyclic movements in unemployment. More interesting is that the decline in λ_{nu} is equally important for understanding male unemployment. This reflects the well-known decrease in men's labor-market-participation rate over this time period (Juhn, Murphy, and Topel 1991) and provides some justification for the belief that the current low levels of unemployment in the United States are at least partially a consequence of the decline in men's participation rate.

To summarize the importance of labor-force attachment, it is easiest to focus on what would have happened had there been no change in the flows in and out of the labor market, only in λ_{eu} and λ_{ue}. Between 1979 and 2000, women's unemployment rate would have fallen by 16 percent (from 7.0 to 5.8 percent of the labor force), rather than by 33 percent (to 4.6 percent of the labor force), while their short-term unemployment rate would have fallen by only 7 percent, rather than by 29 percent. In contrast, over the same time period, men's unemployment rate would have fallen by 12 percent, rather than by 16 percent with all flow-rate changes taken into account, while their short-term unemployment rate would have fallen by 8 percent, rather than by 7 percent. This suggests that, in the absence of changes in labor-force attachment, men's unemployment duration would have increased relative to women's over this period. Conversely, it suggests that changes in labor-force attachment are responsible for the observed increase in women's unemployment duration relative to their unemployment rate during the last two decades.

CONCLUSION

This chapter started with the observation that there has been a breakdown in the historic relation between the unemployment rate and unemployment duration. We then showed that, for men, much of the relative increase in unemployment duration can be explained by measurement issues related to the 1994 CPS redesign and by the aging of the baby boom. For women, however, these two factors do not have much explanatory power. Instead, we used labor-market transition rates to show that much of the decline in women's unemployment rate since the late 1970s is due to the increase in their attachment to the labor force

FIGURE 8.15 / Effect of Counterfactual Experiments on Unemployment Rates

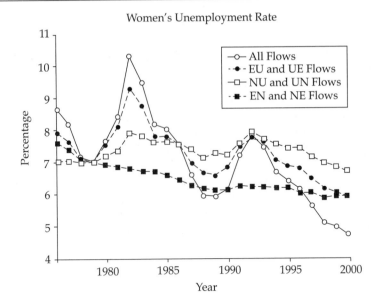

Women's Unemployment Rate

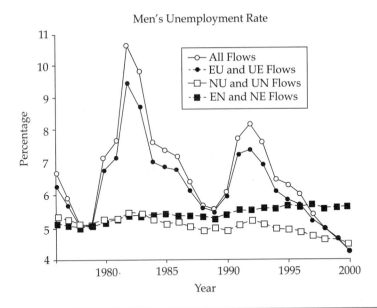

Men's Unemployment Rate

Notes: The figure shows the steady-state unemployment rate and the short-term unemployment rate implied by age-adjusted labor-market flows, men and women, 1976 to 2000, allowing for time variation in all transitions or only in λ_{eu} and λ_{ue}, in λ_{un} and λ_{nu}, or in λ_{en} and λ_{ne}. All flows are adjusted using the Abowd-Zellner correction. λ_{un} and λ_{nu} are adjusted for

FIGURE 8.15 / *Continued*

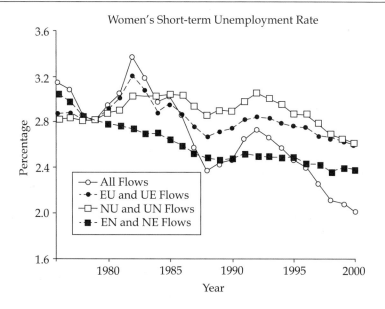

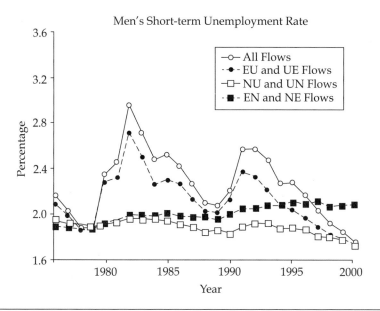

Notes (Continued):

the effects of the 1994 CPS redesign (for details, see appendix 8B). Data are our calculations from the CPS.

and that this likewise explains why the decline has been concentrated at the short end of the unemployment-duration distribution. There are reasons to believe that this process is coming to an end. Women's and men's labor-market experiences have become much more similar, and, in particular, their labor-market-transition rates are converging toward a common level.

The increase in women's labor-force attachment has manifested itself in a variety of other ways. Periodic job-tenure supplements to the CPS indicate that, after accounting for the aging of the labor force, the fraction of employed women who have worked in one job for at least ten years increased from 25 to 27 percent between 1983 and 2000. Over the same time period, the age-adjusted fraction of employed men in the same job actually fell, from 39 to 32 percent (figure 8.16). Many authors have linked the changing occupation distribution of female employment to the increased likelihood that women will be continuously employed, arguing that women who expect to be in the labor market for an extended period are more likely to find it attractive to enter occupations requiring substantial on-the-job training. Similarly, to the extent that employers bear

FIGURE 8.16 / Age-Adjusted Shares of Employed Men and Employed Women Workers with at Least Ten Years' Tenure in Current Job

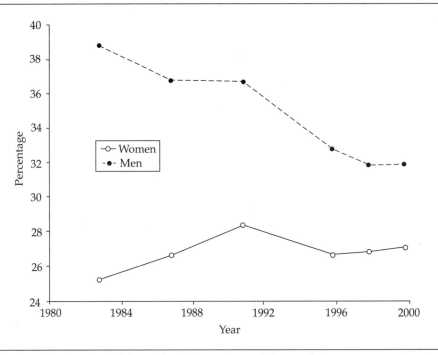

Notes: Age-adjustment weights use the 1983 employment shares of nine age groups: twenty-five to twenty-nine, thirty to thirty-four, . . . , sixty to sixty-four, and sixty-five and over. Data are our calculations from the January 1983, January 1987, January 1991, February 1996, February 1998, and February 2000 job-tenure supplements to the CPS.

the costs of job training, they may be more likely to consider women for such jobs when they believe that their tenure will be longer (Blau and Kahn 2000). Moreover, as shown by Francine Blau and Lawrence Kahn (1997) and June O'Neill and Solomon Polachek (1993), increases in working women's job experience as compared to men's have contributed substantially to the narrowing of the gap between men's and women's earnings. The labor-market transition-rate data that we have examined indicate that the growing stability of women's employment relations is also central to understanding why women's aggregate and short-term unemployment rates have declined while women's unemployment duration has increased. Conversely, men's weakening labor-force attachment appears to be important for understanding the relatively high levels of aggregate and short-term unemployment for men. Although the trend toward declining male labor-force participation has abated in recent years, its resumption would exacerbate these effects.

APPENDIX A: PARALLEL SURVEY ANALYSIS OF THE CPS REDESIGN

Anne Polivka and Stephen Miller (1998) provide a comprehensive and careful analysis of a parallel survey that was designed to assess the effects of the CPS redesign. From July 1992 through December 1993, the parallel survey sample was administered the redesigned CPS instrument. From January 1994 through May 1994, the parallel survey sample was administered the old, pencil-and-paper CPS instrument. With appropriate identifying assumptions, estimates based on the parallel survey can be used in conjunction with those from the official CPS to assess the effect of the CPS redesign on various variables of interest.

Polivka and Miller select the following as their preferred specification for assessing the effects of the CPS redesign:

$$y_{it} = \mu_t + \delta_p p_{it} + \delta_m m_{it} + \varepsilon_{it}, \qquad (8.2)$$

where y_{it} is the variable to be estimated, p_{it} is a dummy variable that equals 1 for parallel survey estimates and 0 for official CPS estimates, m_{it} is a dummy variable that equals 1 for estimates based on data collected using the new CPS methodology and 0 for estimates based on data collected using the old CPS methodology, ε_{it} is the equation error, the μ_t are time period effects, and δ_p and δ_m are parameters to be estimated. We are particularly interested in δ_m, which is intended to capture the magnitude of the effect of the redesign on the measured value of the dependent variable y_{it}. Polivka and Miller fit the model using estimates for the period October 1992 through May 1994 derived from both the parallel survey and the official CPS. Note that this specification allows estimates based on parallel survey data to differ from estimates based on data collected using the same methods as part of the official CPS, but identifies the parallel survey effect by constraining it to be the same before and after January 1994.[22]

Using this methodology, Polivka and Miller conclude that the redesign did not significantly affect the unemployment rate, although they estimate a significant parallel survey effect δ_p. Figure 8A.1 plots seasonally-adjusted versions of the unadjusted series Polivka and Miller use to fit their unemployment rate model.[23] As is true of the unadjusted data, the parallel survey unemployment rate estimates exceed the CPS estimates in all months. Had the higher parallel survey rates observed prior to January 1994 represented a redesign effect, the parallel survey and the CPS lines should have crossed between December 1993 and January 1994, as the parallel survey estimate fell and the CPS estimate rose.

We use similar models to investigate the effect of the redesign on the short-term (zero to four week), long-term (fifteen to twenty-six week) and very-long-term (twenty-seven or more weeks) unemployment rates. The estimated values of δ_m associated with these three dependent variables imply that the redesign reduced the measured short-term unemployment rate by 0.46 percentage point; raised the long-term unemployment rate by 0.17 percentage point; and raised

FIGURE 8A.1 / Unemployment Rate—CPS and Parallel Survey

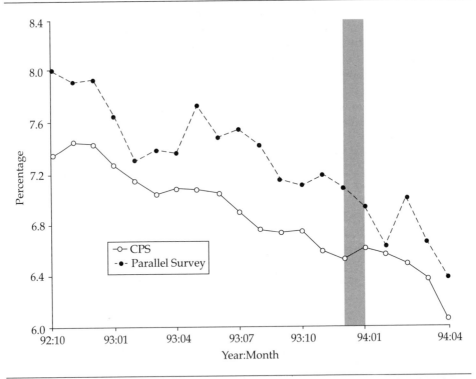

Notes: This figure shows the seasonally adjusted unemployment rate in the CPS and in the parallel survey designed to assess the effect of the CPS redesign implemented in January 1994. The vertical bar indicates the timing of the CPS redesign. Anne Polivka extracted the parallel survey data, and we constructed the time series.

the very long-term unemployment rate by 0.25 percentage point. Application of the model to assess the effect of the redesign on the mean duration of unemployment (in weeks) yields an estimated value for δ_m of 2.37.

An examination of the data underlying these estimates leaves us comfortable with the conclusion regarding the impact of the redesign on the incidence of short-duration unemployment, but raises questions about the implied impact on the other unemployment duration measures. The four panels of figure 8A.2 plot the parallel survey values and the corresponding official CPS values used to estimate each of the four unemployment duration models.[24] The second panel which shows the short-term unemployment rate, looks exactly as one might have expected. The parallel survey short-term unemployment rate jumps upward at the point of transition from the new to the old survey protocol, consistent with the expectation that the new survey protocol should have reduced the number of people reporting unemployment spells of zero-to-four-weeks duration. Presumably because the effects of dependent interviewing in the new protocol are not felt until the second month a person is interviewed, the corresponding drop in the official CPS estimates of the incidence of short-duration unemployment follows with a one month lag. The decrease in the CPS short-term unemployment rate is accompanied by a roughly offsetting increase in the five-to-fourteen-week unemployment rate (not shown in the figure), although there is no offsetting decrease in the corresponding series in the parallel survey.

The third panel displays the long-term (fifteen-to-twenty-six-week) unemployment rate series calculated using data from the two surveys. Consistent with the existence of a redesign effect on these data, the parallel survey and official CPS estimates move in opposite directions between December 1993 and January 1994. On the other hand, the large swings in the gap between the two series during both the pre-transition period and the post-transition period seem inconsistent with the simple model hypothesized by Polivka and Miller, raising questions about its applicability.

We are most troubled by the plot of mean unemployment duration in the first panel and the plot of the very-long-term unemployment rate in the fourth panel. A redesign effect should produce opposing movements in the parallel survey and the official CPS data. Instead, at the point of transition between survey protocols, there is a sharp drop in the two parallel survey series, while the two official CPS series remain essentially unchanged.

In principle, declines in the true level of mean unemployment duration and the true incidence of very-long-term unemployment between December 1993 and January 1994 could be responsible for this pattern. Such declines would have magnified the negative measurement effect of moving to the old methodology in the parallel survey and masked the positive measurement effect of moving to the new methodology in the official CPS. In practice, however, movements of the necessary magnitude are implausibly large. The December 1993–January 1994 drop in (seasonally adjusted) mean unemployment duration implied by our estimates of the Polivka-Miller model is 2.24 weeks.[25] To put this in context, the standard deviation of the month-to-month change in the official seasonally ad-

FIGURE 8A.2 / Unemployment Duration and Rates—CPA and Parallel Survey

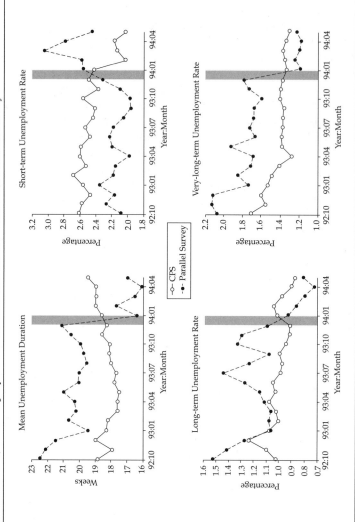

Notes: The first panel shows the mean duration of unemployment spells currently in progress. The subsequent panels show the shares of the labor force with zero to four, fifteen to twenty-six, and twenty-seven or more weeks unemployment duration (short-term, long-term, and very-long-term unemployment rates, respectively). The solid line in each panel shows the seasonally adjusted time series in the CPS, while the dashed line indicates the seasonally adjusted time series in the parallel survey designed to assess the effect of the CPS redesign implemented in January 1994. The vertical bar indicates the timing of the CPS redesign. Anne Polivka extracted the parallel survey data, and we constructed the time series.

justed CPS mean unemployment duration series is just 0.52 weeks and the largest absolute change ever observed over the 1948 to 2000 period is only 1.9 weeks. The corresponding implied drop in the very-long-term unemployment rate is 0.33 percentage point. The month-to-month change in the official CPS very-long-term unemployment rate has a standard deviation of just 0.06 percentage point and the largest post-1948 absolute change in the same series is only 0.26 percentage point. In contrast, the implied December 1993 to January 1994 movements in both the short-term and the long-term unemployment rates are well within those series' one-standard-deviation bounds.

One possible explanation is that the post–January 1994 parallel survey did not yield unemployment duration estimates fully comparable to those that continuation of the old pencil-and-paper CPS would have produced. There are some noteworthy differences in how the two surveys were administered. Fewer than half of the interviewers for the parallel survey from January 1994 forward had any prior experience with the pencil-and-paper instrument. In addition, a substantial share of the post-January 1994 parallel survey interviewers had recent experience with the computerized CPS instrument, which could have contaminated the responses they collected to the questions on the old CPS in unknown ways. This may have been less of an issue with respect to the core CPS questions on which interviewer training presumably concentrated, but could have been a more important issue with the questions on unemployment duration. Although it is difficult to say exactly how these or other differences might have affected the survey estimates, it is well known that seemingly minor differences in survey administration can have a significant effect.[26] A further consideration is that, as compared to many of the other labor market variables for which Polivka and Miller report redesign effects, the sample sizes underlying all of the unemployment duration estimates are very small, and the estimates of mean unemployment duration, in particular, are unusually susceptible to outliers. Because we are not fully comfortable with using the parallel survey data to identify how the redesign affected the unemployment duration estimates, especially the estimates for mean unemployment duration and the incidence of very-long-term unemployment, we pursue a different approach to measuring redesign effects in the text.

APPENDIX B: CONSTRUCTION OF WORKER-TRANSITION DATA

Measures of worker transitions take advantage of the rotating-panel aspect of the CPS by matching workers' labor-market states across months. This requires access to the CPS public-use micro data, which we have only since 1976. Furthermore, there are a few months when we are not able to match workers across months because of survey redesigns or confidentiality suppressions in the available public-use data files.[27] We use the matched worker data to construct the probability that a worker who is in labor-market state X in month $t - 1$ is in state Y in month t, the XY transition rate in month t or, equivalently, λ_{xy}. Although this is the standard measure of worker transitions in the United States, it is important to recognize that it has a number of shortcomings. First, it is relatively noisy. In any month, three-quarters of the CPS households were in the CPS in the previous month and, theoretically, should be matchable. Because of sample attrition, including individuals who move between sample months and therefore are no longer eligible to be interviewed, and mistakes in recording data elements such as age or sex that are essential to the matching algorithm, matched files in practice contain about 70 percent of the observations in the unmatched files.[28] But, since some labor-market transitions (for example, men's UN transitions) are relatively rare, they cannot be estimated very precisely, particularly for small demographic groups. We boost our sample size by working with annual average data.

Perhaps more important, some fraction of measured transitions are spurious. A misreported labor-market status in one month generates two erroneous transitions. In a careful analysis of data from 1977 to 1982, John Abowd and Arnold Zellner (1985) estimate that as many as 40 percent of labor-force transitions are spurious. Unfortunately, Abowd and Zellner's analysis has not been replicated using more recent data, and to do so would go well beyond the scope of our analysis. As a consequence, we do not know whether the spurious transition rate has increased or decreased over time. With no contradictory evidence, we assume that the bias in estimated transitions is unchanged over time, so we adjust our estimated labor-force transition rates using the percentage changes in table 5 of Abowd and Zellner (1985), in particular, the column labeled *Classification and Margin Error to Unadjusted*.

The 1994 CPS redesign may have affected the measured exit rate of unemployed workers from the labor force. There is no obvious reason why this should be so, but an examination of the time series of labor-market transitions indicates an unusually large and persistent increase in λ_{un} between December 1993 and February 1994. To get at this more precisely, we regress each detrended labor-market-transition series on the detrended CES employment-population ratio and look at the residuals for evidence of a break in the normal relation between worker transitions and the state of the business cycle, exactly as in our analysis of the effect of the redesign on measures of unemployment duration. Figure 8B.1 graphically displays the results for the six transition rates. λ_{un} takes a significant jump, with the residual increasing from -0.6 percent in December 1993 to 0.9 percent in February 1994 and then further increasing during the next six months. Comparing the last six months of 1993 to the first six available months of 1994 (February to July), the average value of the residual increases by a full 3.15 percentage points, twice as large as any comparable change in the residual.[29] Although it is conceivable that this represents a structural shift in the relation between λ_{un} and the employment-population ratio, we feel fairly conservative in reducing λ_{un} by 3.15 percentage points after 1994. Since there is no evidence of a change in λ_{ue}, we offset this with an increase in the probability that an unemployed worker remains unemployed.

Figure 8B.1 suggests that λ_{nu} may also have increased with the redesign, although the absolute size of the jump is smaller. The 6-month change in the residual peaks at about 0.34 percent in January 1994, 50 percent larger than any other comparable change, and slightly more than one-tenth of the estimated size of the λ_{un} residual. Although the evidence here is somewhat weaker than it is for λ_{un}, the finding is consistent with Polivka and Miller's (1998) evidence that the CPS redesign did not affect the measured stock of workers in each employment state. To understand why, observe that the worker-transition data imply a unique steady-state distribution of workers across employment states, the solution to a system of three equations:

$$
\begin{bmatrix}
\lambda_{ee} & \lambda_{ue} & \lambda_{ne} \\
\lambda_{eu} & \lambda_{uu} & \lambda_{nu} \\
\lambda_{en} & \lambda_{un} & \lambda_{nn}
\end{bmatrix}
\cdot
\begin{bmatrix}
e \\
u \\
n
\end{bmatrix}
=
\begin{bmatrix}
e \\
u \\
n
\end{bmatrix},
\tag{8.3}
$$

where e denotes the fraction of the population that is employed, u the fraction that is unemployed, and n the fraction that is not in the labor force. The transition matrix is Markov, with columns summing to 1, so has one eigenvalue equal to 1. The solution to these equations is therefore given by the eigenvector associated with that eigenvalue. Moreover, for any change in λ_{un} to $\hat{\lambda}_{un}$ accompanied by a change in λ_{uu} that keeps the matrix Markov, it is possible to find a change in λ_{nu} together with an appropriate change in λ_{nn} that generates the same ergodic distribution of workers across employment states, that is, a change in λ_{nu} to $\hat{\lambda}_{nu}$ that solves $\hat{\lambda}_{eu} \times e + \hat{\lambda}_{uu} \times u + \hat{\lambda}_{nu} \times n = u$, together with a change in λ_{nn} that keeps the transition matrix Markov. Since accounting for the CPS redesign raises our measure of λ_{uu} by 3.15 percentage points but should not have affected the overall unemployment rate, it must reduce our measure of λ_{nu} by $3.15 \times u/n$ percentage points. With the number of unemployed persons averaging approximately one-ninth of the not-in-the-labor-force population during the past several years, this is almost perfectly consistent with our independent finding that the CPS redesign has increased the measured value of λ_{nu} by 0.34 percentage points from 1994 to 2000. A similar analysis finds no evidence of changes in any of the other transitions, so we account for the CPS redesign by reducing λ_{un} by 3.15 percentage points and raising λ_{nu} by 0.34 percentage points throughout our analysis.

We use this methodology to construct separate transition rates for women and men in the usual seven age groups. We then aggregate these into time series for women's and men's age-adjusted transition rates, weighting λ_{xy} for age group i by the share of age group i in the initial labor-market state X in the base year 1980. Finally, we adjust the data according to table 5 in Abowd and Zellner (1985).[30] We then test and do not reject the hypothesis that the CPS redesign had the same effect on age-adjusted values of λ_{un} and λ_{nu} for men and women as it did on the aggregate transition rates, so we subtract 3.15 and 0.34 percentage points, respectively, from these transition rates after 1994.[31]

FIGURE 8B.1 / Residual Worker Flows

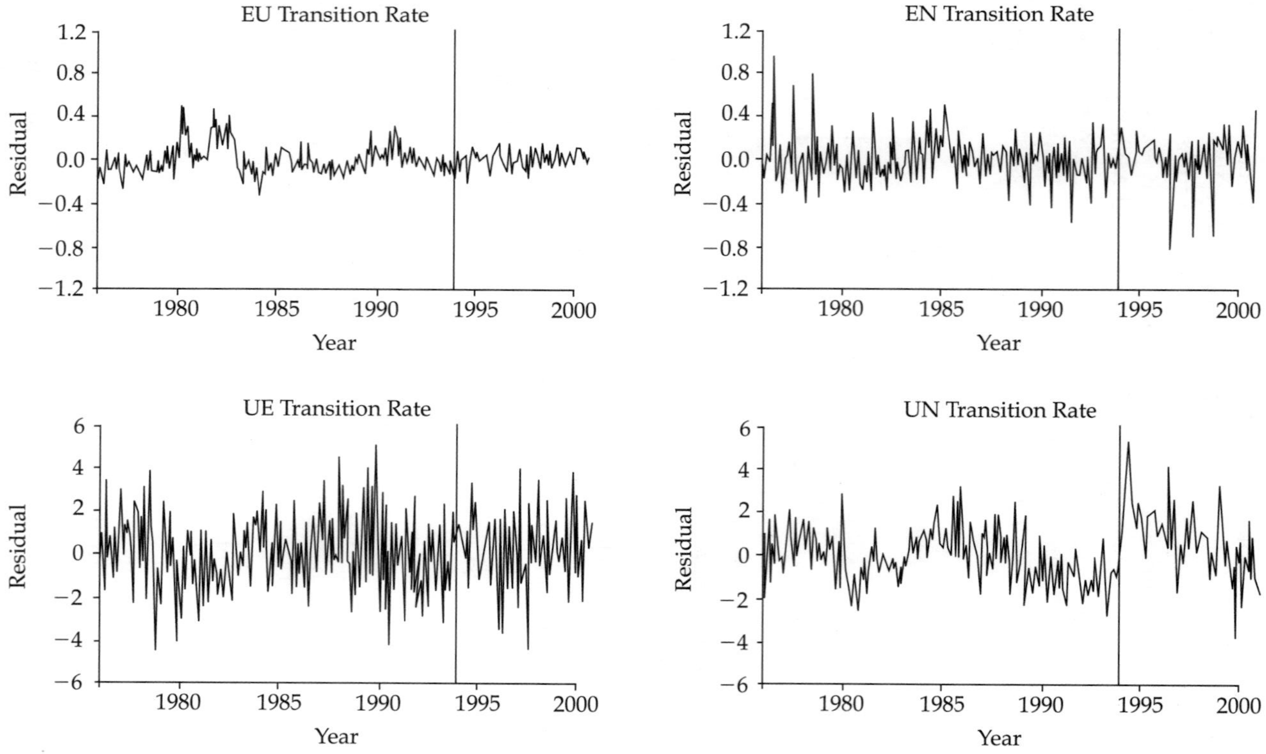

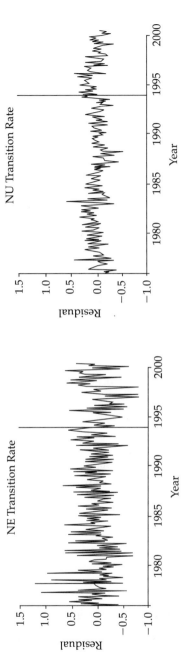

Notes: This figure shows residuals from regressions of detrended worker-flow rates on the detrended employment-population ratio. Worker-flow rates are our calculations from the CPS. The employment level in the latter ratio comes from the CES survey. The population is the over-16 population used for the CPS weights. All series are seasonally adjusted and detrended using a Hodrick-Prescott filter with smoothing parameter 1,440,000, which eliminates only very-low-frequency fluctuations. Vertical lines indicate the timing of the CPS redesign. Breaks in the time series indicate missing observations.

We are grateful to Giuseppe Bertola, Robert Solow, David Weiman, and participants in the Sustainable Employment Initiative conference for their comments and to Fran Horvath, Randy Ilg, Rowena Johnson, Bob McIntire, and Anne Polivka at the Bureau of Labor Statistics (BLS) for their help compiling the data. Ron Tucker of the Census Bureau and Clyde Tucker of the BLS provided useful information concerning the Current Population Survey redesign. Joydeep Roy provided valuable research assistance. Shimer acknowledges financial support from National Science Foundation grant SES-0079345 and the hospitality of the University of Chicago while part of this chapter was written.

NOTES

1. Throughout this chapter, we use data on the duration of in-progress unemployment spells rather than on the duration of completed spells.

2. Lawrence Summers (1986) and Lawrence Katz and Alan Krueger (1999) have also commented on the increase in long-term unemployment as a share of total unemployment.

3. Robert Lucas (1987) asks how much consumption an individual would be willing to give up in order to eliminate any variation of output around its deterministic trend. This presumes, not that recessions are periods when output is below trend and that expansions are periods when output is on trend, but that business-cycle fluctuations are symmetrical deviations around a trend. Lucas's argument is based on assumptions about individual preferences, in particular, about the extent of risk aversion. Fernando Alvarez and Urban Jermann (2000) reach a similar conclusion using evidence from asset prices without having to impose strong restrictions on preferences. They conclude that rational agents would forgo about half a percent of their consumption in order to eliminate business-cycle-frequency fluctuations.

4. The ideas contained here do not depend on the assumption of short-lived workers, although, in a model with a longer time horizon, recurrence of unemployment, not just unemployment duration, would be important for welfare.

5. This argument ignores any general-equilibrium effect on wages or interest rates. We thank Fernando Alvarez for suggesting this method of proof.

6. The expected value of consumption in the second period is given by expected lifetime income minus expected first-period consumption, or $(2 + r)[ub + (1 - u)w] - (1 + r)[uc_1^u + (1 - u)c_1^e]$, which is independent of λ_{ue}.

7. We constructed this figure by matching individual observations in the CPS across months. Appendix 8B discusses the matching process and its limitations. Ideally, one would construct this hazard rate directly from the observed cross-sectional distribution of unemployed workers' unemployment duration, but measurement errors, discussed in more detail in the next section, make this impossible. Crudely put, it would appear that workers who are unemployed for fifty-one weeks have a negative probability of finding a job in the next week since so many more workers report fifty-two weeks of unemployment.

8. A decrease in the number of out-of-the-labor-force workers moving directly into employment could have a similar effect, but we find no evidence that such a shift has occurred.

9. In some cases, an individual observed as unemployed in two successive CPS interviews might in fact briefly have held a job in the intervening period, in which case she would have been properly recorded as having had a very short unemployment duration in the second month. Research conducted as part of the CPS redesign process suggested this to be a relatively rare event (Polivka and Miller 1998), and, in any case, there is a real question as to whether holding a job for only a very short time should be considered as having broken an otherwise continuing unemployment spell.

10. Michael Baker (1992) discusses adjustments to reported unemployment durations to account for "digit preference," but his analysis—conducted before the CPS redesign—does not help with our problem, the effect of the redesign on reported unemployment duration.

11. Note that this bias would tend to reduce the measured very-long-term unemployment rate and so in any case cannot explain the surprisingly high rates at the end of the 1990s noted in the introduction.

12. We set the smoothing parameter to 1,440,000, one hundred times larger than the standard value with monthly data. This does a good job of capturing the low-frequency movements in the various time series without erasing the cyclic variation. Lower values of the smoothing parameter yield similar results. On the other hand, owing to its substantial upward trend during the sample period, the raw time series for the employment-population ratio does a poor job of predicting the unemployment rate.

13. From 1968 to 1993, we calculate the numbers using a monthly time series containing the number of unemployed workers with each week's duration, constructed by the BLS. After 1994, we constructed our own time series from the CPS using only the incoming rotation groups. The data are seasonally adjusted using a ratio-to-moving average procedure. The required data are unavailable before 1968.

14. Filtering the data diminishes our ability to recognize redesign effects many years after the redesign. This should not be a problem during the first year.

15. The standard time series differ from our preferred time series before the CPS redesign as well as after. The large differences in the long- and very-long-term unemployment rates are due to differences in definitions: the solid lines indicate the fifteen-to-thirty-two and thirty-three-or-more weeks unemployment rates, while the dashed lines indicate the fifteen-to-twenty-six and twenty-seven-or-more weeks unemployment rates. The small differences in the mean unemployment duration and the short-term unemployment rate are due to changes in population weights associated with the 1980 and 1990 census. In order to construct the desired time series for the long- and very-long-term unemployment rates, we had to use the original weights based on the 1980 census, while the official time series use adjusted weights based on the 1990 census.

16. This is partly because of how unemployment duration is measured. Young workers who do not have a job often engage in periodic job search, thus moving in and out of the labor force (Clark and Summers 1982).

17. We use the $N = 7$ "standard" age groups—sixteen to nineteen, twenty to twenty-four, twenty-five to thirty-four, thirty-five to forty-four, forty-five to fifty-four, fifty-five to sixty-four, and over sixty-five—for these calculations. In practice, further refinements have little effect on demographic adjustments.

18. Whether this demographic adjustment is quantitatively significant is a matter for debate. Within this volume, Giuseppe Bertola, Francine Blau, and Lawrence Kahn (chapter 4) and Rebecca Blank and Matthew Shapiro (chapter 7) emphasize demographic trends, but Douglas Staiger, James Stock, and Mark Watson (chapter 1) argue that demographics are unimportant for understanding recent shifts in the Phillips curve, and Jessica Cohen, William Dickens, and Adam Posen (chapter 5) claim that demographics cannot explain sudden sharp jumps in the Beveridge curve. Our view is that demographic trends are important for understanding shifts beginning in 1980 but not very important for changes during the last decade.

19. We do not have a good explanation for the widening gap between men's implied and actual short-term unemployment rates after 1994, but we do not believe that this is a redesign effect. The gap has grown slowly over time, while we would expect a redesign effect to have emerged suddenly in 1994.

20. Our choice of base year affects these numbers—particularly for men, who suffered a sharp increase in unemployment in 1980—but not the qualitative result that the decline in women's unemployment has been registered disproportionately at short unemployment durations. From 1980 to 2000, men's unemployment rate fell by 41 percent, and men's short-term unemployment rate fell by 26 percent. The decline in women's unemployment rate was smaller (39 percent), but the decline in their short-term unemployment rate was larger (32 percent) over that time period.

21. Our exercise is similar in spirit to that of Christopher Pissarides (1986), who examines the contribution of increases in λ_{eu} and decreases in λ_{ue} to the increase in British unemployment during the 1970s and early 1980s.

22. The specification shown in the equation in the text treats the CPS redesign effect as additive. Polivka and Miller also estimate models in which the CPS redesign effect is treated as multiplicative. The same general comments would apply to both models and the qualitative conclusions to be drawn from them are similar.

23. Because only twenty months of parallel survey data are available, it was not possible to construct seasonal factors directly from the parallel survey time series. Instead, we apply multiplicative seasonal factors based on official CPS data to adjust the parallel survey data, and then use these seasonally adjusted estimates throughout in what follows. Although the CPS seasonal factors capture the seasonal movements in the parallel survey data imperfectly, the adjustment helps to highlight the nonseasonal movements in which we are interested. None of our conclusions are affected by the use of adjusted rather than unadjusted data.

24. We are grateful to Anne Polivka for making the data that underlie these figures available to us.

25. This is calculated as the difference between the January 1994 and the December 1993 values of μ_t in the specification shown in the text.

26. U.S. Bureau of Labor Statistics and U.S. Census Bureau (1993) discusses a number of differences between the pre–January 1994 CPS and the post–January 1994 parallel

survey that could have produced differences in the resulting estimates. This document also contains information on the projected mix of parallel survey interviewer experience that has been cited by other authors (for example, Polivka and Miller 1998) but turns out not to match the actual mix. The information on interviewer mix that we cite was provided by Ron Tucker of the Census Bureau.

27. We used household ID, line number, race, sex, and age in our matching algorithm. The values for each of these variables were required to be the same in month t and month t − 1, except that we also accepted a value for age in month t equal to one more than the value in month t − 1. The months for which we could not construct matches due to redesigns or suppressions are January 1978, July 1985, October 1985, January 1994, and June to October 1995. In addition, matched data are unavailable for January 1976 since we do not have the required "last-month" file, December 1975.

28. This implies that about 7 percent of the eligible observations (5/75) cannot be matched across months, significantly less than the 15 percent reported by Abowd and Zellner (1985). The source of the difference is unclear, but it seems unlikely that we are matching observations that should not be matched. Our matching algorithm yields transition rates that are almost identical to those computed by the BLS, while one would expect overmatching to yield additional erroneous transitions.

29. The residual gradually reverts to zero over the next three years. This is because we are examining the relation between detrended time series. Eventually, the trend catches up with and erases any effects of the CPS redesign.

30. Abowd and Zellner (1985) report three different adjustments—for "all persons," "male," and "female." The numbers that we report use the "all persons" adjustment because the available evidence suggests a convergence between men's and women's behavior since 1981, the end of the period that Abowd and Zellner (1985) study. In practice, this choice has little effect on our conclusions.

31. These numbers are consistent with the results of Harley Frazis (1996), who, using an entirely different methodology, concluded that the CPS redesign raised λ_{un} by at least 2.8 percentage points and λ_{nu} by about 0.4 percentage points.

REFERENCES

Abbring, Jaap, Gerard van den Berg, and Jan van Ours. Forthcoming. "Business Cycles and Compositional Variation in U.S. Unemployment." *Journal of Business and Economic Statistics.*

Abowd, John, and Arnold Zellner. 1985. "Estimating Gross Labor-Force Flows." *Journal of Business and Economic Statistics* 3(3): 254–83.

Alvarez, Fernando, and Urban Jermann. 2000. "Using Asset Prices to Measure the Cost of Business Cycles." Unpublished manuscript. University of Chicago.

Baker, Michael. 1992. "Digit Preference in CPS Unemployment Data." *Economics Letters* 39(1): 117–21.

Becker, Gary. 1964. *Human Capital.* Chicago: University of Chicago Press.

Blanchard, Olivier, and Peter Diamond. 1994. "Ranking, Unemployment Duration, and Wages." *Review of Economic Studies* 61(3): 417–34.

Blanchard, Olivier, and Lawrence Summers. 1987. "Hysteresis in Unemployment." *European Economic Review* 31(1–2): 288–95.

Blau, Francine, and Lawrence Kahn. 1997. "Swimming Upstream: Trends in the Gender Wage Differential in the 1980s." *Journal of Labor Economics* 15(1): 1–42.

———. 2000. "Gender Differences in Pay." Unpublished manuscript. Cornell University.

Browning, Martin, and Thomas Crossley. 2001. "Unemployment Insurance Benefit Levels and Consumption Changes." *Journal of Public Economics* 80(1): 1–23.

Caplin, Andrew, and John Leahy. 2000. "Mass Layoffs and Unemployment." *Journal of Monetary Economics* 46(1): 121–42.

Clark, Kim, and Lawrence Summers. 1982. "The Dynamics of Youth Unemployment." In *The Youth Labor Market Problem: Its Nature, Causes, and Consequences,* edited by Richard Freeman and David Wise, 199–235. Chicago: University of Chicago Press.

Frazis, Harley. 1996. "Note on CPS Redesign Effects on Gross Flows." Unpublished manuscript. Washington: U.S. Bureau of Labor Statistics.

Granovetter, Mark. 1974. *Getting a Job: A Study of Contacts and Careers.* Cambridge, Mass.: Harvard University Press.

Gruber, Jonathan. 1997. "The Consumption Smoothing Benefit of Unemployment Insurance." *American Economic Review* 87(1): 192–205.

Juhn, Chinhui, Kevin Murphy, and Robert Topel. 1991. "Why Has the Natural Rate of Unemployment Increased over Time?" *Brookings Papers on Economic Activity* (2): 75–142.

Katz, Lawrence, and Alan Krueger. 1999. "The High-Pressure U.S. Labor Market of the 1990s." *Brookings Papers on Economic Activity* (1): 1–87.

Katz, Lawrence, and Kevin Murphy. 1992. "Changes in Relative Wages, 1963–1987: Supply and Demand Factors." *Quarterly Journal of Economics* 107(1): 35–78.

Lucas, Robert. 1987. *Models of Business Cycles.* New York: Blackwell.

Montgomery, James. 1991. "Social Networks and Labor-Market Outcomes: Towards an Economic Analysis." *American Economic Review* 18(5): 1408–18.

O'Neill, June, and Solomon Polachek. 1993. "Why the Gender Gap in Wages Narrowed during the 1980s." *Journal of Labor Economics* 11(1, pt. 1): 205–29.

Pissarides, Christopher. 1986. "Employment and Vacancies in Britain." *Economic Policy* (1): 500–59.

———. 1992. "Loss of Skill during Unemployment and the Persistence of Employment Shocks." *Quarterly Journal of Economics* 107(4): 1371–91.

Polivka, Anne, and Stephen Miller. 1998. "The CPS after the Redesign." In *Labor Statistics Measurement Issues,* edited by John Haltiwanger, Marilyn Manser, and Robert Topel, 249–89. Chicago: University of Chicago Press.

Rothschild, Michael, and Joseph Stiglitz. 1970. "Increasing Risk I: A Definition." *Journal of Economic Theory* 2(3): 225–43.

Shimer, Robert. 1998. "Why Is the U.S. Unemployment Rate So Much Lower?" *NBER Macroeconomics Annual,* 13: 11–61.

Summers, Lawrence. 1986. "Why Is the Unemployment Rate So Very High Near Full Employment?" *Brookings Papers on Economic Activity* (2): 339–83.

U.S. Bureau of Labor Statistics and U.S. Census Bureau (BLS-Census). CPS-Overlap Analysis Steering Committee. 1993. "Implications of Survey Design Differences between the Current CPS and the Proposed New Parallel Survey." Memorandum. Washington: U.S. Bureau of Labor Statistics, December 22.

Chapter 9

The Sputtering Labor Force of the Twenty-First Century: Can Social Policy Help?

David T. Ellwood

T his paper has two distinct parts. The first finds evidence that the growth of the labor force will be very different in the future than it was in the past, a finding that has some very troubling implications about skill levels: First, over the next twenty years, labor-force growth will slow considerably, and the number of prime-age workers will remain essentially unchanged. What growth there is will come from older workers. Second, only a tiny fraction of new workers will be native-born whites. Indeed, the number of prime-age native-born white workers will *decline* significantly over the next twenty years. Third, even under the most optimistic scenario, the education level of the workforce will grow much more slowly in the next twenty years than it has in the past. If the demand for skills continues to grow as in the past, the nation can almost certainly expect a much more severe skill shortage than in the past and, presumably, will see continuing rises in the return to education.

In the second part of the chapter, I examine the potential effect of social policies on the labor force. A number of basic conclusions emerge: Incentives really do matter. There is plentiful evidence that altering benefits or changing administrative procedures can increase work. But, with the exception of social security, virtually all social policies are heavily targeted at less-educated persons. Thus, any success that one may have in increasing work is likely to be among low-skilled workers. The entrance of such workers would do little to alleviate skills shortages and might well exacerbate them. Moreover, altered policies have already pushed up work by single parents considerably, but one has to wonder whether we are nearing the limits. Moreover, single parents constitute a relatively small share of the population. A 20 percent reduction in nonwork by single parents would add to the workforce an additional 540,000 workers, mostly with very little education, some working part-time, and with concurrent childcare costs. The very modest level of means-tested benefits provided to two-parent families and healthy childless adults suggests that additional changes in means-tested aid will do little to increase work.

Among prime-age individuals, the largest group of potential workers classified by family status is married women, particularly married women with children. Since social policies currently provide very little aid to two-parent families, the only hope for encouraging greater work by these persons would be expanded work-related supports such as child care. Ironically, aid that targets low-income working families actually creates disincentives for married women to work as their entrance into the labor market can raise the family income sufficiently to make them eligible for far less aid. If new supports such as child care were to induce 10 percent more married women with children to work, the workforce would increase by 850,000, including some better-educated women.

Recipients of either unemployment insurance (UI) or workers' compensation (WC) seem relatively sensitive to incentives. However, the fact that UI benefits and, to a lesser degree, WC benefits are already time limited and the fact that they reach such a small portion of the populace mean that even fairly radical changes would increase the labor force by at most 300,000 workers.

By contrast, disability benefits clearly have played a significant role in reducing labor-force participation among some groups, particularly older men who have not yet reached retirement age. Radical changes might increase the workforce by 500,000 workers, but doing so could come at a high human cost as all the new workers would face some disabling condition. Programs designed to encourage work by encouraging the employment of disabled persons remain relatively small and untested.

Finally, the social security retirement program has in the past almost certainly played an important role in inducing earlier retirement, but economists have been surprisingly hard-pressed to prove it. In any case, only quite radical changes in benefits such as advancing the early retirement age to sixty-five and moving the normal retirement age to seventy seem likely to have major effects in the next twenty years. If one could effectively shift out the current pattern of retirement by two years (a massive task), one could increase the labor force by nearly 1 million workers. In contrast to the new workers who would be produced by other proposals, many of these would be reasonably well educated.

In the end, it looks like the only really large workforce gains could come from increased work among married women and older workers. But shifting social policy in ways designed to encourage work for both these groups could be expensive and politically difficult.

The labor market of the future looks problematic. Unfortunately, it appears that social-policy changes can improve the situation only to a limited extent. Immigration and education policy are sure to become far more important in the future as alternative ways of coping with the sputtering labor market.

INTRODUCTION

A growing and increasingly better-educated workforce has been a central feature of the prosperity of the past decades. In the last twenty years, the overall labor force grew by 35 percent, and the so-called prime-age workforce—those aged twenty-five to fifty-four—grew by a remarkable 54 percent. The number of college-educated workers more than doubled, increasing from 22 percent of the total labor force to over 30 percent. During this same time period, the racial composition of the workforce was changing gradually, partly because of a sharp rise in immigration. Even so, a sizable majority of the growth in the labor force still came from native-born whites.

Past is not always prologue. The next twenty years of labor-force growth look almost nothing like the past twenty. Rather than growing by 54 percent, the prime-age workforce will grow by only 3 percent. Perhaps even more disturbing is the fact that, even under the most optimistic scenario, barring a major change in immigration policies, the fraction of the labor force that is college educated will grow by only 5 percentage points, as opposed to the nearly 9 percentage point gain on a much larger base in the last two decades. Under more pessimistic assumptions, the fraction that is college educated could hardly change at all. What growth there is in the labor force will not come from native-born whites—they will represent less than 15 percent of new workers. Indeed, the number of prime-age native-born whites in the labor force will likely decline by more than 10 percent.

Social policies by their nature often have incentives built in that tend to reduce work activity. Yet, in recent years, there have been some very visible successes in increasing employment among formerly unemployed aid recipients. Given the radical changes that will be occurring in the labor market, particularly the slowdown in growth, it seems appropriate to ask whether social policies can do anything to expand the labor force.

This chapter has three basic aims. First, I document past changes in the labor force and project changes into the future. Major innovations offered here are the projections of education attainment and the separation of immigrants from natives. Next, I seek to examine what effect current social policies have on employment, paying particular attention to different age and education groups. Finally, I explore whether altered social policies might be expected to influence the size and composition of the employed labor force.

Because I am particularly interested in examining patterns by level of education, this paper focuses almost exclusively on persons over the age of twenty-four, when most education is completed. The under-twenty-five age group is not projected to grow much at all in the next twenty years anyway, and much of this population is still in school. Moreover, these younger workers are often at the lowest section of their productivity profile. For some means-tested benefits, notably public assistance and food stamps, a significant share of recipients are under the age of twenty-five, so I will explore some issues for this younger group. Still, even for these programs, 75 to 80 percent of recipients are over twenty-four.

THE CHANGING FACE OF THE LABOR MARKET, 1980 TO 2000

If one imagines the situation as it looked in 1980, it was easy to project that the following twenty years would be a period of dramatic labor-force expansion with a sizable upgrading of education attainment. Three factors were favorable:

baby boomers were just coming of age, women were entering the labor force in large numbers, and younger cohorts were vastly better educated than older ones.

The coming baby boom as of 1980 can easily be seen in figure 9.1, which shows the population by individual years of age (and by nativity). As the population ages, the mass of the population shifts to the right—the twenty-year-olds become the forty-year-olds, except for mortality. If one focuses on what will happen to the age group between twenty-five and fifty-four, the people represented by the mass of people twenty years to the left of the line drawn at fifty-four will be aging out of the cohort. The group twenty years to the left of the current twenty-five-year-olds will be moving in. It was abundantly obvious in 1980 that the departing cohorts—those between thirty-five and fifty-four—would be vastly smaller than the groups entering (those to the left of the age-twenty-five line). Thus, the prime-age population would grow considerably in the coming twenty years.

The labor-force-participation rate of men and women aged twenty-five to fifty-four and fifty-five to sixty-four from 1962 to 2000 is plotted in figure 9.2. Over the period 1962 to 1980, there was some decline in participation for prime-age men and an even greater decline for older men, but these declines were more than offset by rising participation for women. Slowing rates of marriage and childbirth contributed to the expansion, but it was mostly fueled by a rapid increase in work by married women with children. Thus, there was every reason

FIGURE 9.1 / Resident Population of the United States in 1980 by Years of Age and Nativity

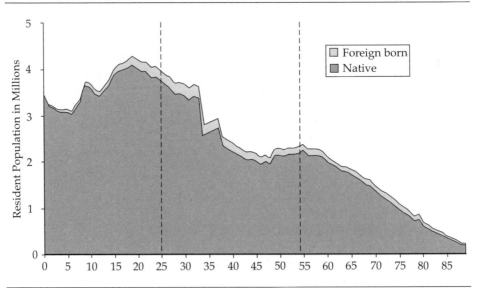

Source: Author's tabulations from 1980 census data.

FIGURE 9.2 / Labor-Force-Participation Rates Among Men and Women Aged
Twenty-Five to Fifty-Four and Fifty-Five to Sixty-Four by Year.

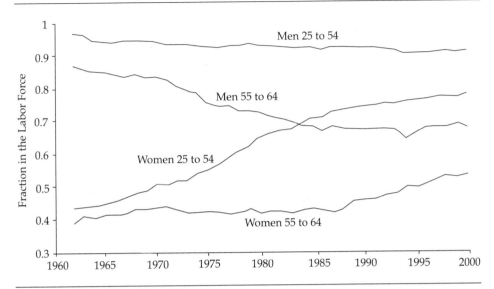

Source: Author's tabulations from March CPS data.

to expect that even more women would be entering the labor force in subsequent decades. And, indeed, the labor force did continue to grow. By the end of
the 1990s, however, participation rates had flattened considerably, suggesting
that the disproportionate growth in the female labor force may now be over.

And, perhaps most important, education trends created a sharp upgrading in
the education mix of the labor force. Figure 9.3 plots the distribution of education among thirty-year-olds from 1955 (the persons who would be just turning
fifty-five in 1980) to 2000. Up to 1980, it is a story of almost continuous growth in
education with each successive cohort. After 1980, however, things flattened out
remarkably. I shall return to this education slowdown later. But, even with this
flattening, the chart still implies dramatic improvements in the level of education
attained by the labor force between 1980 and 2000 as more educated cohorts
replaced less educated ones.

The prime-age (age twenty-five to fifty-four) workforce in 1980 included the
people who turned thirty between 1955 and 1985. Over the subsequent twenty
years, the people who turned thirty in 1955 to 1975 aged out of this population
window, and those who turned thirty after 1985 were brought in. The entering
cohorts (those who turned thirty after 1985) had vastly more education than did
the exiting ones. Moreover, the entering cohorts were part of the baby-boom
generation and so were much larger in absolute number. Thus, during the 1980s
and 1990s, much-larger and more-educated cohorts were replacing smaller, less-
educated ones. The inevitable result was a sharp rise in the overall education
attainment of the labor force.

FIGURE 9.3 / Percentage Distribution of Education Among Thirty-Year-Olds by Year

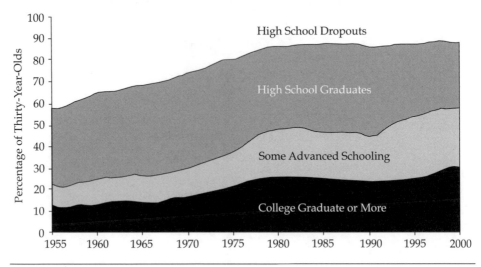

Source: Annual March CPS data (three-year moving averages).

Finally, the workforce grew as a result of a major increase in immigration—one change that probably would not have been predicted in 1980. Figure 9.1 showed that only a relatively small portion of the population was foreign born in 1980. But a variety of policy changes during the subsequent twenty years significantly eased immigration, and the increased immigration that followed added further to the labor force.

In combination, these factors implied a sharply growing and more-educated labor force, especially among twenty-five- to fifty-four-year-olds. Of course, many scholars contend that the level of education demanded of the workforce rose even more quickly than did the level of education actually achieved by the workforce, and this gap between supply and demand is a leading explanation for the rapid rise in inequality over the following twenty years. Still, it is obvious that the workforce was well positioned for sustained economic growth.

Projecting the Workforce to 2020

Economists are properly reluctant to project the future. Many key determinants of future economic health such as labor-force-participation rates and education patterns are unambiguously endogenous. Shortages in one domain drive up prices, reduce demand, and expand supply. Moreover, a major part of the motivation for this paper derives from the premise that social policy can and does affect the labor-supply decisions of potential workers.

Nonetheless, the iron laws of demography (everyone who will be twenty-five or older in 2020 has already been born), the timing of education completion, and the relative stability of labor-force-participation rates imply that one can get a rough sense of the forces shaping the future. And an economist can ask such well-defined questions as: If wages and policies were held constant, what would the future labor force look like? If the picture that emerges is inconsistent with likely changes in demand, one can also begin to forecast how wages might be expected to move in the future and what effect those price changes might have on labor-force participation, education, and policy. For this paper, my goal is not to forecast the future accurately, but rather to explore the range of likely possibilities so as to focus attention on issues that social policy may need to address.

I sought to project the labor force by age, sex, race and ethnicity, nativity, and education over the coming twenty years. I chose to do a somewhat nonconventional racial break by also incorporating nativity. Population assumptions, including racial composition, hinge critically on immigration assumptions. Breaking people into detailed race categories by nativity creates some very small cells. Thus, I created six different race-ethnic-nativity categories: white non-Hispanic native; black non-Hispanic native; Hispanic native; other non-Hispanic native; Hispanic foreign born; and non-Hispanic foreign born. My basic methodology was to age the year-2000 cohort of the March Current Population Survey (CPS) on the basis of assumptions regarding mortality, immigration, labor-force participation, and education.

Sitting in the year 2001 (and looking at data for 2000), the demographic picture is dramatically different than it was in 1980. Figure 9.4 shows the distribution of the population in a way that is comparable to figure 9.1. The baby boom is now right in the middle of the twenty-five- to fifty-four-year-old range. The boom was followed by a baby bust and then a more modest echo. But, for the foreseeable future, the number of people entering this age range each year will be almost exactly the same as the number leaving. Indeed, barring a spurt in immigration, it appears that the population will be level for a while, then perhaps rise slightly in fifteen years as the height of the baby boom reaches their fifties, and then fall off.

The Census Bureau produces far more systematic projections. Given the relative stability of mortality trends and the fact that emigration from the United States is quite low,[1] it is straightforward to predict the native-born population over twenty-five in two decades as all these persons have already been born. The only uncertain factor is immigration.

A detailed discussion of potential trends in immigration and the forces driving them is far outside the scope of this paper. In producing its most recent round of projections, the Census Bureau sought for the first time to model some aspects of immigration and to take account of the longer-term implications of changes in immigration law. Their models and assumptions are documented in detail in Frederick Hollmann, Tammany Mulder, and Jeffrey Kallan (2000). Perhaps the most important assumption is that the large numbers of formerly undocumented immigrants granted permanent residency after the passage of the Immigration Reform and Control Act of 1986 would become "U.S. citizens in increasing numbers. As they became citizens, they could sponsor the legal immi-

FIGURE 9.4 / Resident Population of the United States in 2000 by Years of Age and Nativity

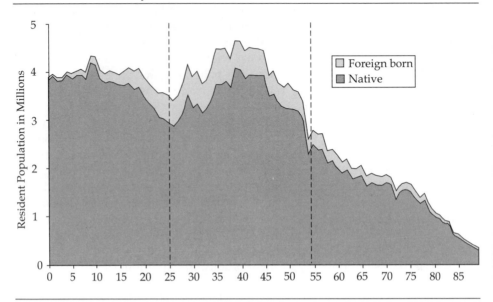

Source: Author's tabulations from March CPS data.

gration of immediate relatives without being subject to numerical limits." This additional flow—composed largely of people from Latin America—was "projected to reach a peak early in the decade of 2000 to 2010, then gradually decline to zero as the supply of potential reunifications is exhausted" (Hollmann, Mulder, and Kallan 2000, 17). Hollmann, Mulder, and Kallan also assumed that other aspects of immigration law, including the current numerical quotas, would remain unchanged.

Whether these assumptions will prove to be accurate depends primarily on political processes. Recently, Congress enacted a temporary increase in the number of H1B skilled-worker temporary visas.[2] If labor shortages appear, there will surely be strong pressures to expand immigration further. At the same time, as immigrants constitute an increasingly larger share of the population, some will push for increased immigration restrictions.

Professing no expertise in either mortality patterns or immigration, I elected to use the Census Bureau's middle-series population projections through 2020. These have the advantage of including projections for each year by individual years of age, race and ethnicity, sex, and nativity. Thus, as I aged the CPS data, I adjusted weights to ensure that the population equaled the fully detailed census projections.

Projecting labor-force-participation rates is a much less scientific business. Howard Fullerton (1999) provides the estimates that the Bureau of Labor Statistics currently uses to make its projections. Generally, Fullerton projects no change in labor-force participation among men within narrow age groups. But he projects some continued growth in labor-force participation among women under fifty-four and relatively significant growth among women over fifty-five. This latter estimate is easy to understand since younger cohorts entered the labor force in larger numbers than they did in previous generations. As these women age, their higher participation patterns seem likely to persist.

The projected growth in the labor-force participation of younger women is harder to understand. The labor-force-participation rates of women aged thirty-five to forty-four have not changed for a decade. Women aged forty-five to fifty-four today work almost exactly as much as they did when they were thirty-five to forty-four. Especially given the later timing of births and marriage, I think that a more plausible assumption is that the participation of women aged forty-five to fifty-four will also remain flat into the future. There has been some growth in work by women aged twenty-five to thirty-four in the past five years, but this has been concentrated almost entirely among single parents. This is almost certainly the result of policy changes such as welfare reform and expansions in the earned income tax credit (EITC) and the unusually strong economy. It seems unreasonable to project that this growth will continue long into the future, barring further policy changes.

I wanted labor-force-participation rates separately by age, sex, and race-ethnicity-nativity. Given the relative stability of rates for most persons in the last four years, I used the average labor-force-participation rate by individual years of age, sex, and race-ethnicity-nativity from the March CPS over the four-year period 1997 to 2000 for men and for women under fifty-five. Using individual years of age clearly creates some noisy estimates, but, since I always aggregate the data in tables, the errors should tend to average out.[3] For women aged fifty-five to sixty-four, I assumed that participation would rise by 1 percentage point per year for the next five years and then level out. For women over sixty-four, I assumed a 3 percentage point rise over the next few years.

Figure 9.5 shows the labor-force-participation rates that result when these projections are applied and the population adjustments made. Mostly, these are flat projections.[4] It is entirely possible that women will work still more or that men will continue to work somewhat less. Moreover, if shortages of workers persist, employers may adjust wages, benefits, or working conditions to entice people to work more. These figures simply give a rough sense of what will happen if current patterns persist.

The story for education is perhaps the most disheartening. As emphasized by David Card and Thomas Lemieux (2000) and many others, there was a dramatic slowdown in education attainment in the 1970s, 1980s, and early 1990s. This slowdown shows up vividly in the patterns of education attainment of thirty-year-olds reported in figure 9.3. In the period after 1980, there was very little change in levels of education attainment until the late 1990s, when there was some rise in four-year college completion and a noticeable jump in education activities beyond high school.

Projecting the future of educational enrollments is notoriously difficult. Econ-

FIGURE 9.5 / Actual and Projected Labor-Force-Participation Rates Among Men and
Women Aged Twenty-Five to Fifty-Four and Fifty-Five to Sixty-Four

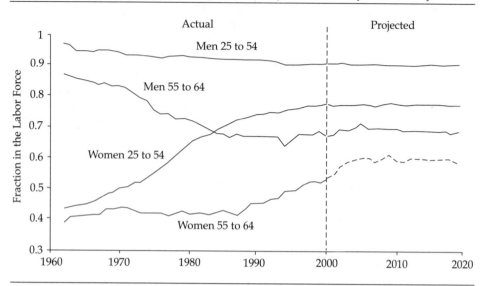

Source: Author's tabulations of March CPS data and author's projections.

omists naturally emphasize factors such as the rate of return to schooling and
tuition costs, along with factors such as parents' income and education, to explain cross-sectional and time-series variation in schooling. In particular, if returns to schooling were to change dramatically, one would expect the school
attainment of entering cohorts to change.

Interestingly, although the rough correlation or the lack thereof in returns to
education and schooling patterns is frequently commented on (see, for example,
Cameron and Heckman 1999; Ellwood and Kane 2000; and Kane 1994), until
recently few authors have actually sought to measure just how responsive
schooling is. Card and Lemieux (2000) find that all the traditional economic factors matter but that, for men, the "decline in enrollment rates in the 1970s and
the slow recovery in the 1980s point to a permanent shift in the intercohort trend
in educational attainment that will affect U.S. economic growth and trends in
inequality for many decades to come" (abstract). They report that the effect of
rising returns on enrollment differs by gender. A rise in the return to education
comparable to that experienced between 1978 and 1988 (when returns to college
almost doubled) is predicted to push up college-entry rates roughly 10 percentage points for men (on a base of 60 percent) but only 3 percentage points for
women. On the other hand, Card and Lemieux find a strong, unexplained positive underlying trend for women and a somewhat weaker negative one for men.
Others, such as Daron Acemoglu and Jorn-Steffen Pischke (2000), find a relatively limited response to college returns in their models. In many ways, the real
puzzle is why there has not been more of an increase in college attendance. Part

of the explanation may have to do with sharply rising tuition (see, for example, Kane 1999). Card and Lemieux (2000) find sizable cohort-size effects as well, although these effects played little role in the most recent years.

Without a closed model projecting both supply and demand factors along with tuition, it is impossible to predict enrollment patterns accurately. Thus, it is perhaps not surprising that there are only a few attempts to do so and that these are often carried out by government agencies charged with making projections. These works make no attempt to examine the role of supply and demand or returns to college. Debra Gerald and William Hussar (2000) use a methodology whereby enrollments are based on projections of real income per capita and unemployment rates. Jennifer Day and Kurt Bauman (2000) use a trend analysis to create high and low projections.

After considerable experimentation, I chose to begin by assigning a level of education to each entering cohort of twenty-five-year-olds. To account for additional education beyond age twenty-five, I created—on the basis of the most recent Survey of Income and Program Participation (SIPP)—an age by education level transition matrix for each sex and for race-ethnicity-nativity that shows the odds that a person of a given age and a given level of education will move to a new level of education. This transition matrix was applied each year as the cohorts aged.

The only question is how to assign levels of education to successive cohorts of twenty-five-year-olds. I chose to use two methods: a level-projection method and a high-growth method. The level-projection method assumes that the education attainment of each group remains at the same level it was at on average over the period 1997 to 2000. The high-growth method assumes that, for all groups, graduation rates from high school rise 0.25 percentage points per year over the next twenty years, that the entry rate from high school into some college rises by 1 percentage point per year, and that the entry rate from some college to college also rises by 1 percentage point per year.

Foreign-born residents pose particular problems since they can enter at any time. But examination of CPS data showed very little difference in education attainment of immigrants by age. Thus, I treated immigrants in the same manner as I did other race-nativity groupings. Entering cohorts of twenty-five-year-olds were assigned the education rate of similar immigrants (plus growth under the high-growth assumption). They too were allowed to gain more education as they aged according to the SIPP transition matrices for their immigrant group.

The effect of these two assumptions can be seen in figure 9.6. With the level projections, the education attainment of thirty-year-olds stays roughly at current levels; with the high-growth projections, it rises significantly. Visually, the high-growth projection appears to suggest a return to the long-term trend in growing education attainment. In fact, it implies a quite dramatic rise in education attainment that is in part obscured by the changing racial mix. The high-growth assumptions imply that the fraction of twenty-five-year-old white natives with a college degree would rise from 30 percent to nearly 45 percent in the next two decades and that essentially all white natives would graduate from high school.

FIGURE 9.6 / Percentage Distribution of Education Among Thirty-Year-Olds by
Year–High-Growth and Level Projections

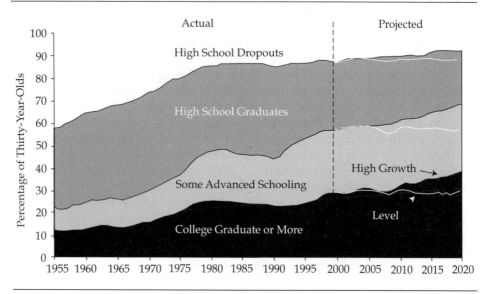

Source: Author's tabulations of March CPS data and author's projections (three-year centered moving averages).

This increase far exceeds the 10 percentage point rise in college attendance that occurred between 1983 and 1999, when there was a dramatic increase in the return to education. It is greater than that projected by the high-growth assumption in Day and Bauman (2000). The sharp projected growth in the Hispanic population, both native and immigrant, tends to slow apparent rises in education attainment. These groups on average currently receive far less education than do other groups.

The level projection is not as unreasonable as it may seem. Current trends do not suggest that a sudden spurt in education attainment of the sort projected in the high-growth model is likely. From 1994 to 1998 (the last year for which published data are available), the fraction of twenty- to twenty-one-year-olds enrolled in school remained level for both males and females. Moreover, the growing cohort size as the baby-boom echo is reaching college age seems likely to create crowding effects at schools. The post-secondary school-age population (eighteen to twenty-four) will grow by nearly 20 percent in the next decade. Indeed, the model of Card and Lemieux (2000) would seem to predict *declines* in the next few years because of cohort size absent a radical change in the rate of return to education. Gerald and Hussar (2000) of the Department of Education essentially predict a level-attainment pattern over the next decade. Still, if returns to education were to rise sharply, so might enrollment.

With these assumptions, one can project labor-force characteristics in the future. Table 9.1 shows the age and racial-nativity mix of the labor force and changes over time.[5] Several important conclusions emerge:

First, the labor force is projected to see far less growth in the next twenty years than it did in the previous twenty. While the labor force grew by over 38 million workers previously, it will grow by fewer than 20 million in the future. In percentage terms, the labor force grew by nearly 50 percent between 1980 and 2000, but, between 2000 and 2020, it is projected to grow just 16 percent. Moreover, I project that the so-called prime-age workforce will essentially stop growing altogether. After increasing by 35 million in the 1980s and 1990s, it will in-

TABLE 9.1 / Characteristics of the Labor Force Aged Twenty-Five and Over and Components of Change 1980, 2000, and 2020

	Labor Force in 1980	Growth, 1980 to 2000	Labor Force in 2000	Growth, 2000 to 2020	Labor Force in 2020
Age:					
Twenty-five to fifty-four	65.0	35.1	100.1	3.0	103.1
Fifty-five to sixty-four	11.8	2.2	14.0	12.5	26.5
Sixty-five and over	3.0	1.4	4.4	4.0	8.4
Total	79.8	38.7	118.5	19.4	137.9
Race-ethnicity-nativity					
White non-Hispanic, native born	63.0	21.5	84.5	2.6	87.1
Black non-hispanic, native born	7.6	4.6	12.2	2.8	15.0
Hispanic, native born	2.5	2.3	4.8	6.8	11.6
Other non-Hispanic, native born	.8	1.0	1.8	1.2	3.0
Hispanic, foreign born	1.8	4.5	6.3	2.8	9.1
Non-Hispanic, foreign born	4.1	4.8	8.9	3.3	12.2
Total	79.8	38.7	118.5	19.4	137.9
Summary					
Native-born white workers, twenty-five to fifty-four	50.8	19.3	70.1	−7.7	62.4
Native-born white workers, fifty-five and over	12.2	2.2	14.4	10.3	24.7
Workers of color, twenty-five to fifty-four	9.4	7.3	16.7	7.7	24.4
Workers of color, fifty-five and over	1.6	.5	2.1	3.0	5.1
Foreign-born workers	5.9	9.4	15.3	6.0	21.3
Total	79.8	38.7	118.5	19.4	137.9

Source: Author's tabulations of March CPS data and author's projections.

crease by just 3 million in the next twenty years. By contrast, the older workforce (those over age fifty-five) will nearly double in the next twenty years, rising by 16.5 million workers—a sharp contrast to the previous period, when only 3.6 million new workers were found.

The racial-nativity mix of new workers will also change radically. Whereas some 54 percent of net new workers in the past two decades were native-born whites, only 15 percent of new workers will be native-born whites in coming decades. The number of native-born white workers aged twenty-five to fifty-four will actually fall by 7.7 million—a decline of over 10 percent in the next twenty years. These workers will be replaced by older workers, persons of color (particularly Hispanics), and foreign-born workers.

Table 9.2 shows the striking projections of the education mix of the labor force under the level-attainment and high-growth assumptions: Even under the high-growth assumption, an assumption that I believe to be quite unrealistic, growth in the education attainment of the labor force will slow considerably. Between 1980 and 2000, the fraction of workers with college degrees more than doubled.

TABLE 9.2 / Education Level Attained by the Labor Force Aged Twenty-Five and Over, 1980, 2000, and 2020

	Labor Force in 1980	Growth, 1980 to 2000	Labor Force in 2000	Growth, 2000 to 2020	Labor Force in 2020
High-growth assumption					
Less than high school	17.3	−5.3	12.0	−1.1	10.9
High school only	31.5	6.3	37.8	1.5	39.3
Some schooling beyond high school	13.8	19.1	32.9	6.2	39.1
College degree or more	17.3	18.5	35.8	12.8	48.6
Total	79.8	38.7	118.5	19.4	137.9
Percentage with college degree	21.6		30.2		35.2
Level-attainment assumption[a]					
Less than high school	17.3	−5.3	12.0	.9	12.9
High school only	31.5	6.3	37.8	3.8	41.6
Some schooling beyond high school	13.8	19.1	32.9	6.2	39.1
College degree or more	17.3	18.5	35.8	7.7	43.5
Total	79.8	38.7	118.5	18.6	137.1
Percentage with college degree	21.6		30.2		31.7

[a]Subsequent cohorts have same education at age twenty-five as the cohort age twenty-five in 2000.

Source: Author's tabulations of March CPS data and author's projections.

In the next twenty years, it will rise by about one-third. Overall, the share of the labor force with a college degree rose from 21.6 percent in 1980 to 30.2 percent in 2000. At best, it appears that the share of college graduates will rise to just 35.2 percent over the next twenty years. Worse yet, under the level-attainment assumption, the share of college graduates in the labor force will hardly change at all, rising from 30.2 percent in 2000 to 31.7 percent in 2020.

It may seem surprising that even the high-growth assumption yields so little increase in the education attainment of the labor force. After all, entering cohorts still tend to have more education than departing ones. But the labor force is dominated by cohorts that entered during the 1970s and 1980s, when education attainment stagnated, and new cohorts take considerable time to age their way through. Moreover, the changing racial structure works against education gains.

The aging of the workforce has commanded a great deal of attention in the press and in scholarly work, particularly in debates over the funding of social security. And much has been made of the changing racial composition of the workforce. Far less attention has been paid to the sheer slowdown in the absolute number of workers and the nearly complete leveling off of prime-age workers. And even less attention has been paid to the sharp slowdowns in education attainment.

The obvious question that arises at this point is whether any of this matters. In traditional economic models in steady state, and with a constant saving rate, the overall rate of population and/or labor-force growth influences the total growth rate of the economy, and should increase capital per worker, with some rise in the real wage. Whether the projected short-term changes in demography would have much effect is harder to determine. In a more complex world, real effects can be felt. Fixed and sticky assets such as land and some forms of capital presumably are disadvantaged by a slowdown in population growth. Thus, one might generally expect wages to rise somewhat relative to capital returns. Short-run labor shortages raise Phillips curve concerns and may lead to tightened monetary policy.

It is also possible that an economy can make necessary adjustments to new technology and other economic demands more quickly in a context in which labor supplies are growing. Firms seeking additional workers do not need to bid them away from existing jobs. Labor shortages would seem to strengthen workers' hands. This might lead to new benefits and increased security. It may also lead to new demands that might reduce the flexibility of the market.

A slowdown in labor-force growth also implies profound changes in the age distribution of the population and the workforce that do create real problems. The best known is the problem that fewer workers will be available to finance the costs of pay-as-you-go social security and of Medicare. But the aging of the population also implies a sharp rise in the need for certain types of services. For example, home care and elder services have traditionally been provided by women under fifty-five. In the 1980s and 1990s, the over-sixty-five population grew by 9 million (or 38 percent), while the number of women aged twenty-five to fifty-four in the labor force grew by almost 20 million (or 71 percent). In the next two decades, the number of elderly persons will rise by 22 million (or 66 percent), and the number of prime-age female workers will rise by less than 2 million (or 3 percent). And the percentage growth in the population over 80 and even over 100 will be even larger.

Most important, as hinted in Card and Lemieux (2000), the slowdown in education-attainment growth would seem to imply a return to sharply rising inequality. The standard economic explanation for the rise in inequality rests heavily on the idea that education gains failed to keep up with the rising demands for skill in the labor force. But future education gains look small even under highly optimistic assumptions. The rise in inequality over the 1980s and 1990s occurred while education attainment grew by twice as much as it is projected to increase in the future under the high-growth assumption. Demand for educated workers seems even more likely to outstrip supply in the next twenty years.

Of course, all these projections depend on the assumptions of the model. One of the reasons that the aging of the baby boomers has such a profound effect is that labor-force-participation patterns fall off rapidly after age fifty-five and especially after age sixty-two. If baby boomers could be induced to work more at later ages, the labor-force picture could be brighter. Employers will likely seek ways to enhance the economic position of, and perhaps the appeal of the workplace for, older workers. Similarly, employers may also seek to upgrade the skills of existing workers if they cannot hire enough workers who already have the necessary skills. Thus, one interpretation is that the coming decades might be unusually bright for workers as employers fight to retain them and seek to upgrade their skills.

But there is an alternative. American employers may shift more and more of their work to other nations. Skilled work might be done abroad, while much of the service work that cannot be exported would remain.

Finally, immigration policy will certainly play a major role in the future. Already, skill shortages have led to greater numbers of skilled workers being granted visas. Given current projections, it seems inevitable that these numbers will continue to rise. Indeed, the census projections, which imply fewer new immigrants in the next decades than in past ones, look quite unrealistic. But immigration could move in different directions. Recent waves of immigrants tend to include a larger share of low-skilled workers and a somewhat larger share of more highly skilled workers than does a cross section of the native-born workforce. If immigration were uniformly expanded and the education mix remained the same as it is today, the labor force would be increased, but the deficits in skilled workers projected here would be only slightly alleviated.

This is not a paper about immigration or education policy, although these results strongly suggest that these will become increasingly critical issues. It is, rather, an examination of social policy. And, for that examination, three conclusions seem central: First, the slowing growth of the labor force implies that policies designed to encourage work by those receiving aid will become even more important. Second, the emerging education-attainment slowdown implies that policies that increase work by more-educated workers would contribute greatly to sustained growth and prosperity. Third, the aging of the potential workforce implies that social policies that increase employment among older workers would be particularly useful.

THE POTENTIAL FOR SOCIAL POLICY

Current American social policy might be thought of as consisting of three major elements: means-tested benefits; social-insurance programs; and work-support benefits.

Means-tested benefits are benefits where the level of aid is generally tied almost entirely to current circumstance and declines as income rises. There are four major national programs providing cash or near-cash benefits. The Aid to Families with Dependent Children (AFDC) program and its successor, Transitional Assistance for Needy Families (TANF), primarily serve low-income single mothers and their children. The supplemental security income (SSI) program aids low-income aged and disabled persons. The food-stamp program is available to virtually any low-income family or individual. Housing assistance is generally means tested and is available in various forms, but its funding structure leaves many eligible families without aid. In addition, states have various programs, notably general assistance, although these benefits have been sharply cut back in the past decade. In addition, Medicaid was typically provided to recipients of AFDC and SSI, and, in recent years, it has been expanded to cover all low-income children.

The benefits available under *social-insurance programs* are tied to past work and earnings, but the receipt of benefits is triggered by an event such as unemployment or retirement. Generally, benefits are tied to past earnings, although workers at the bottom of the income distribution often receive benefits that reflect a larger portion of past pay than do the better off. The big-three social-insurance programs are unemployment insurance, workers' compensation, and social security. Social security includes disability insurance and retirement benefits along with a variety of dependent, spouse, and survivor benefits. Medicare might also be grouped with these programs as it generally aids the aged and disabled who are eligible for social security.

Until the early 1990s, the United States offered relatively few *work-support benefits*—that is, targeted support for working families—a legacy no doubt of the origins of most current social policies in the Depression, when only the lucky few had jobs. But, today, the EITC, which aids low-income working families, is larger than the support provided by TANF/AFDC. Moreover, child care and medical coverage of various forms are far more readily available than they were in past decades to help support low- to moderate-income working families.

Means-tested and social-insurance programs unambiguously create incentives to reduce work. In the case of means-tested programs, the highest benefits are provided to the poorest families, and benefits are reduced as earnings rise. And these two factors reduce incentives to work. In the case of social-insurance programs, benefits are provided to the unemployed, the injured or otherwise disabled, and the retired. Since individuals have at least some control over these situations or their response to them, there is potential here for work reduction.

The work-support programs are more ambiguous. They often create strong incentives for one person in a family to enter work since benefits are typically available only to workers. But second and additional workers may face disincentives since benefits are eventually phased out as family income rises. And even the first family member to obtain work may face some disincentives to increase work hours beyond a certain point. Still, on net, these work-support programs seem to be increasing work thus far.[6]

There is a sizable literature on the effect of these government programs on work. To solve the inevitable sample-selection issues, many of the best and most recent offerings seek to exploit natural experiments—notably, significant policy changes—to infer effects. There is also a sizable literature testing specific experimental initiatives. I will turn to reviews of this literature shortly, but there are several features that somewhat limit its usefulness in assessing how much of an effect social policy could have on labor supply. Much of it tends to focus on one program at a time, but, within families, multiple program use is common. Often, the research is limited to testing a particular policy change or experiment. Few studies distinguish effects by level of education or age.

One can begin to get some sense of the potential adverse effect of these programs on labor supply by examining patterns of use. Table 9.3 provides information on the fraction of all persons who, according to the CPS, report receiving each of the means-tested benefits and social-insurance programs in 1999 by education and broad age classes. I do not include information on those over sixty-four as virtually all receive social security.

Even this simple tabulation gives a strong sense of both the potential and the limits of social policy. For one thing, nearly 13 percent of adults aged twenty-five to fifty-four and 27 percent of those aged fifty-five to sixty-four received some form of aid. The single most common was food stamps for the prime-age group and social security for the older category. Use differs enormously by level of education. Over 30 percent of twenty-five- to fifty-four-year-old high school dropouts receive some form of aid, while just 4 percent of college graduates do. Among those over fifty-four, 46 percent of dropouts, but only 14 percent of college graduates, receive aid.

The findings should not be particularly surprising. Food stamps is the only program available to virtually anyone under the age of sixty-two solely on the basis of income, so it should be the program most frequently utilized. Social security offers support for the disabled under sixty-five and for virtually all retirees over sixty-one, so it will inevitably be more widely used by those in the older group. And, since the incidence of inadequate income, unemployment, illness, or disability is unquestionably higher among the less educated, and since the difference between potential earnings and government benefits is also less for those with lower pay, one would certainly expect higher use of aid among

TABLE 9.3 / Proportion of Persons Aged Twenty-Five to Fifty-Four and Fifty-Five to Sixty-Four Receiving Various Types of Government Aid by Level of Education, 1999

	Public Assistance	SSI	Food Stamps	Housing Aid	UI	WC	Social Security	Received Any Aid
Twenty-five to fifty-four								
Less than high school	.044	.062	.148	.079	.047	.016	.064	.301
High school only	.016	.024	.053	.031	.043	.013	.032	.158
Some schooling beyond high school	.010	.013	.032	.020	.035	.014	.025	.113
College degree or more	.001	.003	.005	.004	.019	.004	.009	.040
All education levels	.013	.019	.044	.025	.035	.011	.027	.128
Fifty-five to sixty-four								
Less than high school	.014	.114	.108	.071	.032	.014	.299	.461
High school only	.005	.025	.025	.019	.028	.012	.212	.278
Some schooling beyond high school	.004	.020	.015	.013	.026	.015	.180	.233
College degree or more	.001	.009	.013	.008	.016	.007	.111	.138
All education levels	.006	.037	.035	.025	.025	.012	.197	.269

Source: Author's tabulations of March 2000 CPS data.

the less educated. Still, the magnitude of the differences by education class is striking. Even among the older group, among which most social security use is related to early retirement, when the less educated are compared to the more educated, three times as many of the former receive aid.

Before turning to specific estimates of what social policy can actually do, we can use the information on use to generate an extreme upper-bound estimate of what one might hope to accomplish by changing incentives in means-tested benefits and social-insurance programs. Suppose that within age, race, family-type, and sex groups, the employment rates for those who receive aid were somehow raised as high as the rates for those who did not receive aid. Of course, this sort of outcome is not in the least realistic. Aid is typically restricted to people who are in a weakened position to work because of some externally verifiable condition such as involuntary unemployment or disability. It is hard to imagine what combination of policies could push these individuals' employment rates up as high as those of nonrecipients. Nonetheless, such a calculation can provide an absolute maximum estimate of what might be achieved by altered social policies.

Tables 9.4 and 9.5 indicate both the actual employment rates of adults aged twenty-five to fifty-four and fifty-five to sixty-four, respectively, and what the rate would be if the employment patterns of current aid recipients were identical to those of current nonrecipients. They also show the number of new workers that would be implied in each category. To make these projections, I simply estimated a model of employment (separately by sex) in race dummies, detailed age groups, education dummies, family type (married, divorced, separated, widowed, never married), and number of children, confining the sample to the group of people who report receiving no aid. I then use this model to predict employment rates for the entire population regardless of whether aid was received.

The tables suggest the following: If employment rates of aid recipients were identical to those of nonrecipients, employment rates for twenty-five- to fifty-four-year-olds would rise by 4.3 percentage points, and 5 million more persons would be working, a rise of roughly 5 percent. By contrast, for the fifty-five- to sixty-four-year-olds, employment rates would rise by 12.3 percentage points, a 21 percent increase in the older labor force or a rise of roughly 3 million workers in 2000. This estimate represents an extreme upper bound to what could possibly be expected from policy change.

I want to emphasize that I am not suggesting that it would be possible to induce anything like this number to work or that it would be socially desirable to do so even if it were possible. Rather, I am seeking to bound the potential. That said, there are a few factors that may lead to some understatement in this estimate: there is significant underreporting of some benefits in the CPS, and it is possible that some work-support policies might induce people who are not now receiving aid to work more.

The fact that older workers have so much more hypothetical potential for increasing work is particularly important for the future. For, as we have seen, by the year 2020, the number of fifty-five- to sixty-four-year-olds in the population will have roughly doubled. Thus, the potential increase for that group could be

TABLE 9.4 / Actual and Predicted Employment Rates if Employment Rates for Persons Who Received Aid Equaled Employment Rates for Those Who Did Not Receive Aid, Ages Twenty-Five to Fifty-Four, 1999

	Actual Employment Rate	Predicted Employment Rate if Employment Rate of Those Who Received Government Aid Equaled Rate for Those Who Did Not Receive Aid[a]	Difference	Actual Number Employed (Millions)	Predicted Number Employed if Employment Rate of Those Who Received Government Aid Equaled Rate for Those Who Did Not Receive Aid (in Millions)[a]	Difference (Millions)
Less than high school	.618	.723	.105	8.4	9.8	1.4
High school only	.787	.838	.051	29.9	31.8	1.9
Some schooling beyond high school	.824	.862	.038	27.4	28.7	1.3
College degree or more	.866	.879	.014	29.6	30.1	.5
All education levels	.801	.843	.043	95.4	100.5	5.1

[a]Predicted employment based on a regression of employment rate (fraction of weeks worked in 1999) on age dummies, education dummies, race-nativity dummies, marital-status dummies, and number of children estimated only for persons who reported receiving no government aid. Models run separately by sex using March 2000 CPS data.

TABLE 9.5 / Actual and Predicted Employment Rates if Employment Rates for Persons Who Received Aid Equaled Employment Rates for Those Who Did Not Receive Aid, Ages Fifty-Five to Sixty-Four, 1999

	Actual Employment Rate	Predicted Employment Rate if Employment Rate of Those Receiving Government Aid Equaled Rate for Those Not Receiving Aid[a]	Difference	Actual Number Employed (Millions)	Predicted Number Employed if Employment Rate of Those Receiving Government Aid Equaled Rate for Those Not Receiving Aid (in Millions)[a]	Difference (Millions)
Less than high school	.414	.598	.184	1.8	2.6	.8
High school only	.565	.707	.142	4.7	5.9	1.2
Some schooling beyond high school	.641	.746	.105	3.4	3.9	.5
College degree or more	.714	.777	.063	3.9	4.3	.3
All education levels	.590	.712	.123	13.8	16.7	2.9

[a]Predicted employment based on a regression of employment rate (fraction of weeks worked in 1999) on age dummies, education dummies, race-nativity dummies, marital-status dummies, and number of children estimated only for persons who reported receiving no government aid. Models run separately by sex using March 2000 CPS data.

as high as 3 million in years to come. Shortly, we shall explore just how many workers might actually be moved into work with aggressive social-policy changes.

But one other fact is significant: It appears that social-policy changes are unlikely to do much to increase the more-skilled workforce, and, indeed, they are likely to reduce the overall average level of education among workers. The overwhelming majority of those who might enter the labor force as a result of social-policy changes are workers with a high school education or less. Moreover, even though high school dropouts represent less than 9 percent of current prime-age workers, they constitute nearly 18 percent of the potential new workers. Less-educated workers comprise an even larger share of the older group. College graduates represent less than 10 percent of the potential new workers.

If anything, these estimates probably understate the education skew among those who might be influenced to work more by social policy. The benefits received by more-educated workers are almost always much smaller in relation to their potential wage than are those received by less-educated workers. Therefore, since more-educated workers already face stronger incentives to work, one might surmise that they will be less sensitive to policy changes.

These upper-bound estimates are sizable, but they are not enormous relative to the changes in the workforce that have been experienced in the past twenty years. If one could induce half the potential five million prime-age workers into jobs, this would represent a one-time-only increase equivalent to just over one year's average annual increase in the prime-age labor force in the past twenty years. And, of course, the education mix would be vastly less favorable than the typical year's growth in the past twenty years.

It may be worth pausing to note that if the goal were to increase the number of low- to moderately skilled workers, increased immigration might be an easier, and potentially even less expensive, way to do so. And, given that the most serious concern in the labor market may be a shortage of more highly skilled workers, social-policy changes may not seem like the best way in which to entice additional workers into the labor force.

One other way of parsing the data can be helpful. Labor-supply decisions are sure to be influenced by family circumstances—namely, whether the adult in question is a single parent, a married parent, and so on. Thus, it may be appropriate to ask what the family status is of the prime-age persons who are not currently working. Table 9.6 gives that distribution by level of education. An examination of that table reveals that a sizable majority, 55 percent, of prime-age persons not currently working are married women. And married women constitute a larger share of the more-educated than of the less-educated nonworkers. Single parents constitute 12 percent of those not currently working and are concentrated disproportionately in the less-educated categories. The rest of the nonworkers are scattered among various categories.

It is obvious that nonworking married women, the vast majority of whom have children, constitute the largest group of nonworking adults under age twenty-five. Unfortunately, as we shall see, such persons already receive very

TABLE 9.6 / Percentage Distribution of Nondisabled Persons Aged Twenty-Five to Fifty-Four Who Were Not Employed in March 2000 by Education and Family Status

Level of Education	Married Men	Married Women	Single Parents	Grown Children and Others Living with Parents or Relatives	Single Individuals (Not Living with Relatives)	Total
Less than high school	2.2	9.2	4.0	1.8	2.1	19.3
High school only	3.4	18.5	4.2	3.0	3.9	33.0
Some schooling beyond high school	4.0	14.3	2.7	2.1	3.4	26.4
College degree or more	3.1	13.2	1.0	1.2	2.9	21.4
Total	12.7	55.2	11.8	8.0	12.3	100.0

Source: Author's tabulations of March 2000 CPS data.

little aid. So social policies would have to rely on carrots rather than sticks if the goal were to move them into work.

Next, I explore what might be realistically accomplished through social-policy change. Such an exploration will be facilitated if the policies are first broken down into four loose categories: means-tested benefits and work-support programs for nondisabled families and individuals; unemployment insurance and workers' compensation; disability programs; and retirement programs. This classification system has some real limitations because there is significant overlap among the categories—for example, persons collecting unemployment may also get food stamps or the EITC on the basis of earnings for part of the year, and some workers aged sixty-two to sixty-four may qualify for both disability and retirement benefits. But the classification is helpful in examining the literature, which tends to focus separately on one or another of these benefit types. In exploring these areas, I will seek to describe the nature of benefits and the changes therein over the past ten to twenty years, summarize what the existing literature suggests the effects of social policy are, and offer some estimate of what might realistically be achieved in the future.

Means-Tested Benefits and Work-Support Programs for Nondisabled Families and Individuals

In the United States, there has been in recent years a near revolution in the nature of support to low-income families, particularly single-parent families. Aid has been drastically cut for nonworking families but dramatically increased for low-income working families. The effect has been radically to change incentives facing parents. The unanimous conclusion of those economists who have examined the effects of these changes is that they, along with a remarkably strong economy, have led to an unprecedented increase in work among single parents. For certain other types of parents, notably married women with children, the incentive changes have been more ambiguous and the effect on work equally so. Thus, this "revolution" offers perhaps the best indication of what can and cannot be accomplished with social-policy reform.

The benefits described here differ from those discussed in other sections of this paper in three important and related respects. First, the population that these benefits target is generally low- to moderate-income people. Second, eligibility for these benefits is usually linked to family income and family characteristics, not individual circumstances; therefore, benefit receipt is likely to affect the behavior of more than one family member. Third, these programs' target populations often overlap significantly; for example, every family on AFDC/TANF gets food stamps, and many receive housing aid and even the EITC as well.

Finally, relative to their numbers, single mothers receive a highly disproportionate share of the aid provided by these programs, and they have been the target of an even more disproportionate share of policy reforms. Thus, I look separately at single mothers and all other types of aid recipients.

THE EFFECT OF POLICY CHANGE ON WORK BY SINGLE MOTHERS   Welfare reform as embodied in the Personal Responsibility and Work Opportunity Act of 1996 (PRWORA) was the culmination of several decades of changes in welfare policy. Since the 1970s, benefits in few states had been adjusted sufficiently to keep up with inflation. Committee on Ways and Means (2000, table 7–10, 390) indicates that real AFDC/TANF benefits for a family of three in the median state fell from roughly $580 in 1980 to $421 in January 2000.[7] Declining real benefits and other changes had significantly reduced the number of single parents receiving aid even before the current round of reforms. From 1972 to 1989, the fraction of single parents collecting aid fell from 0.85 to 0.55, before rising to 0.65 following the recession of the early 1990s (Ellwood 2000a, figure 1). During the 1990s, more and more states used "waivers" to create more work-oriented, more-demanding support programs.

Still, PRWORA, the national welfare-reform program, did represent a major departure, for it essentially gave states almost complete authority over TANF (which replaced AFDC), converting a program of matching aid to one of block grants, while including requirements that states ensure that a sizable fraction of the caseload be working or off aid altogether, and setting five-year time limits on aid for most persons. But perhaps far more important than statutory changes was a radical change in the climate surrounding welfare and attitudes toward recipients. States began aggressive campaigns to reduce welfare caseloads.

Since 1994, AFDC/TANF caseloads have essentially been in free fall, dropping by roughly 60 percent (Administration for Children and Families 2000). Just between June 1999 and June 2000, caseloads dropped 15 percent. Welfare reform seems certain to have played a central role in this decline, but other policy developments figured prominently as well.

Other means-tested aid (for those who are not disabled) fluctuated considerably less. Food-stamp-program benefits are automatically adjusted for inflation, and, while the program has at times been affected by changes in policy, those changes have in recent years been modest in comparison to those affecting AFDC/TANF. It is important to understand, however, that food stamps are determined "last." This means that changes in other program aid are partially offset by food-stamp benefits. The vast majority of those collecting AFDC/TANF also get food stamps, although there has been some reported drop in food-stamp receipt among AFDC/TANF recipients in recent years.[8]

Housing aid is a more complex story because such aid comes in several forms (including public housing and Section 8 vouchers for private rental housing), because it is administered locally, and because there is insufficient aid available to serve all those in need. Only about one-third of AFDC/TANF recipients received housing aid in recent years, although it should be noted that this figure represents an increase from the roughly 20 percent who received housing aid in the 1980s (Committee on Ways and Means 2000, table 15–3, 864).

Less well-known than changes in welfare are the dramatic expansions in aid to working families in recent years. The EITC expanded enormously. So did medical protection, particularly for children. Figure 9.7, drawn from Congressional Budget Office (1998), shows that the levels of support to low-income families not receiving cash aid—chiefly working families—rose in real terms from

FIGURE 9.7 / Federal Outlays on Low-Income Families Not Receiving Cash Assistance (Billions of 1999 Dollars)

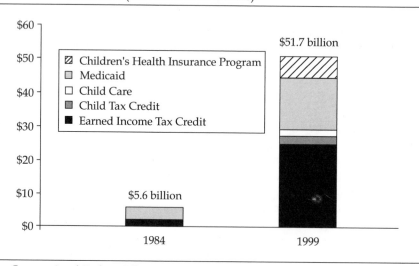

Source: Congressional Budget Office (1998).

less than $6 billion in 1984 to over $51 billion in 1999. Indeed, the United States spends more today on the EITC than it ever did on AFDC or TANF (in 1999 dollars). But almost equally large have been changes in medical benefits.

Not surprisingly, these radical changes have led to large changes in incentives. David Ellwood (2000b), for example, reports that, in 1986, a single parent with two children who was unemployed and receiving AFDC and food stamps could expect to collect $8,460 in benefits in the "average" state. If that same parent took a job paying $10,000, her net income would rise just $2,200 because of reductions in aid, and she and her children would likely lose Medicaid benefits, easily worth $2,200. By 1998, her benefits when not working had been cut to $7,717, assuming that she was even able to receive aid. But, if she went to work at a $10,000-a-year job, her income would rise to roughly $14,600—a gain of nearly $7,000—and her children would not lose Medicaid. Even she would be assured of Medicaid coverage for a transitional period.

One problem, however, with such a focus on benefit levels and effective marginal tax rates—an approach that is not unusual among economists—is that it does not fully capture the nature of recent reforms. Much of what has been done to the welfare system involves local bureaucratic initiatives more than state or national benefit or rule changes, initiatives that have often led to sharp caseload reductions.[9] Thus, it is far from clear that the unemployed single mother in the example just outlined would even get welfare in 1998.

Let me offer an alternative way to examine the changing patterns of aid. Ideally, one would like to explore the amount of aid for which persons in identical economic circumstances would qualify over time. Benefit levels alone are not very helpful here. But one can observe the amount of combined aid that persons actually received *conditional on their level of earnings.* If, for example, administrative procedures have tightened or the stigma attached to receiving aid has increased, persons with a given level of income may be less likely to receive aid and thus will be observed to collect a lower benefit. Moreover, by conditioning on earnings, one eliminates the single largest source of endogeneity in models of labor supply and benefit—the fact that benefits are themselves a function of income.[10]

Figure 9.8 offers this alternative method of determining the combined effect of various programs on single parents.[11] (For this exercise, earnings levels have been broken down as follows: no earnings; $1 to $7,500; $7,501 to $15,000; $15,001 to $30,000; and over $30,000.) Average benefits received by those with no earnings have fallen precipitously in recent years, moving from an average of over $7,000 to less than $5,000. By contrast, aid for those in the range $7,500 to $15,000 has, after falling in the early 1980s as a result of Reagan-era cuts, grown dramatically in recent years, from roughly $1,500 in the mid-1980s to nearly $3,500 today. This latter change is almost entirely the result of expansions in the EITC. Indeed, the difference in actual average benefits reported between those with no earnings and those with earnings in the range $7,500 to $15,000 has narrowed from $7,000 in the mid-1980s to only about $1,000 today. And it should be noted that this analysis still does not include Medicaid expansions for low-income working families, which would lower the gap even further.

FIGURE 9.8 / Real Mean Public Assistance, Food Stamps, Housing Aid, and EITC Benefits Reported by Nondisabled Single Parents by Level of Family Earnings

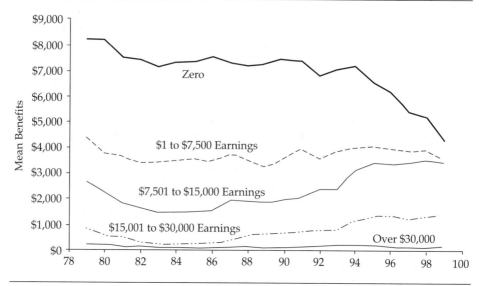

Source: Author's tabulations from March CPS data.

One critical note of caution should be sounded given the policy changes implied by figure 9.8: Social policy regarding low-income families is shifting from being strongly countercyclic to being far more procyclic. With benefits tied so closely to work and low earnings, low-income families may lose their jobs and their benefits during periods of recession.

There is a rapidly growing literature that examines the effect of these dramatic policy changes on work by single mothers. Some studies, including Thomas MaCurdy, David Green, and Harry Paarsch (1990), Robert Moffitt (1986), and Stacy Dickert, Scott Houser, and John Karl Scholz (1995), explicitly model the kinks and other features of the budget constraints created by the EITC and other programs using either assumed or estimated labor-supply elasticities. A second strategy is to quantify the various changed incentives facing potential workers and to use these to estimate a fairly straightforward reduced-form labor-supply model. The most sophisticated use of this strategy is Bruce Meyer and Dan Rosenbaum (1999). These authors go to considerable effort to parameterize the altered incentives created by both state and federal EITC policies and by changes in AFDC, including benefit-rule changes, time limits, some state Medicaid extensions, child care, and training.

Perhaps the most common approach is some form of difference-in-difference estimator comparing the change in labor supply of single mothers or low-skilled single mothers to changes in that of other groups over this period of policy change. The first authors to do this for the EITC were Nada Eissa and Jeffrey

Liebman (1996), and, since that time, work by Bruce Meyer and Dan Rosenbaum (1999, 2000), Rebecca Blank, David Card, and Philip Robbins (2000), David Ellwood (2000b), and Robert Schoeni and Rebecca Blank (2000) has used variations on this methodology.

All this literature—the clear consensus of which is that policy changes have sharply influenced the work behavior of single mothers—is nicely summarized in V. Joseph Hotz and John Karl Scholz (2001). A simple graph illustrates the basic findings. Figure 9.9 shows the level of work of single mothers by level of education. After roughly fifteen years with almost no change in work patterns, starting in the early 1990s, with the advent of welfare reform, sharp expansions in work supports such as the EITC, and a very strong economy, work by single parents began to rise sharply. And the greatest increases have been among single parents with the least education (that is, high school dropouts), rising from roughly 40 to nearly 60 percent in March 2000. Even among women with some schooling beyond high school, sizable increases occurred.

It has proved far more difficult to parse out the differential effect of different policies. Several authors, including Meyer and Rosenbaum (1999), argue that over half can be traced to the EITC changes alone. But, in previous work (Ellwood 2000b), I concluded that the interaction effects, the extreme difficulty of parameterizing state AFDC administrative changes, the failure to account for changes in Medicaid, housing, and child-care aid, and the strongly interactive effects of the economy (work incentives should have much different effects

FIGURE 9.9 / March Employment Rates Among Single Parents Who Are Not Disabled by Level of Education

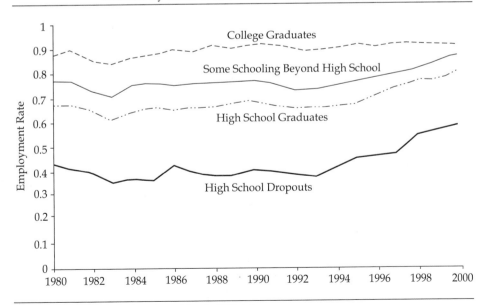

Source: Author's tabulations from March CPS data.

when jobs are plentiful) make it almost impossible to isolate the effect of one specific policy change.

A number of recent experimental programs use randomized control groups and thus can do a far better job of isolating specific incentives.[12] These programs confirm the power of incentives to increase work. The most dramatic increase in work incentives came in Canada's Self-Sufficiency Project, which guaranteed full-time workers half the difference between their current earnings and $30,000 to $37,000 and effectively increased the reward to working full-time by $3,000 to $7,000 as compared to the comparison system (Michalopoulos et al. 2000). Benefits were limited to families that had received welfare for at least a year and one member of which went to work full-time. The program raised the fraction who worked eighteen months later from 32 to 43 percent and boosted earnings by 50 percent. Minnesota's Family Investment Program (MFIP) raised work incentives by only $1,800 per year, but the fraction working eighteen months later still jumped from 36 to 53 percent among long-term recipients. But MFIP had other important elements (mandatory participation, counseling, and so on), and incentives alone seemed to account for perhaps one-third of the increase in work.

THE EFFECT OF POLICY CHANGE ON WORK BY OTHERS The evidence is overwhelming that social-policy changes can and do influence work by single mothers, particularly if these women have little education and have been collecting means-tested benefits. But single parents constitute just 7 percent of the population aged twenty-five to sixty-four, and only 20 percent of these are high school dropouts, for whom the effects seem to be largest. The potential effects of altered means-tested benefits and work supports on others may be far more limited.

It is rare for anyone other than single parents to receive means-tested benefits. Food stamps are the primary means-tested benefit available to two-parent families. Welfare benefits are available to some, but not to two-parent families where both parents are healthy and at least one adult is working. Only 2 to 3 percent of married couples with children report getting welfare in any given year between 1980 and today. By 2000, the numbers were down to 1.3 percent. But low-earning married couples can qualify for the EITC, and these benefits have expanded over the years.

Figure 9.10 shows the benefits for two-parent families in the same way that figure 9.8 did for nondisabled single parents. Figure 9.10 differs, however, in that the no-earnings and the $1 to $7,500 categories have been combined because only a tiny fraction of two-parent families (0.9 percent) where the husband is not disabled have no earnings for an entire year.[13] Comparing figures 9.10 and 9.8 one sees that two-parent families with no or extremely low earnings have always received much less in aid than single parents have, and what benefits they have received have fallen precipitously in recent years. But, just as with single parents, aid to two-parent families with earnings in the range $7,501 to $15,000 has (owing to the EITC expansions) risen sharply in recent years—so sharply, in fact, that it now exceeds aid to two-parent families with lesser earnings. Benefits

FIGURE 9.10 / Mean Public Assistance, Food Stamps, Housing Aid, and EITC
Benefits Reported by Nondisabled Two-Parent Families by Level of
Family Earnings in Given Year

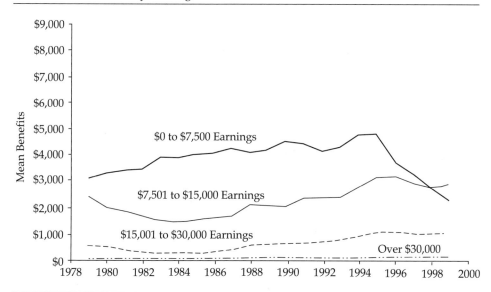

Source: Author's tabulations from March CPS data.

have also risen somewhat for those with earnings in the range $15,001 to
$30,000. But parents with earnings over $30,000 continue to receive essentially
nothing in aid.

Even more than with single parents, it is obvious that persons with low earnings—roughly the equivalent of full-year full-time minimum-wage workers—
have become increasingly advantaged as compared to those with almost no
earnings. In principle, work-support benefits such as the EITC should encourage
at least one person to work in such households, but, among those not reporting
a disability, employment rates for married men hover at 90 percent for this entire
period, and, among over 95 percent of married couples with children, at least
one person works now.

Figure 9.11 shows employment rates of married men with children over time.
Even among the high school dropouts in this group, employment rates typically
exceed 80 percent. It is this latter subgroup that might be induced to work if
EITC benefits were increased. Little work has been done on the effect of the
EITC on this subgroup, but a simple inspection of the figure suggests that, while
current work levels may be 1 or 2 percentage points higher than in other peak
years, the economic cycle seems to explain what little variation in work there is
over time. Generally, experimental designs such as MFIP have shown far more
mixed effects on work by men.

The story for married women is more complex. Married women are nearly
always one of two wage earners in a household if they work outside the home.

FIGURE 9.11 / March Employment Rates Among Married Men with Children Who Are Not Disabled by Level of Education

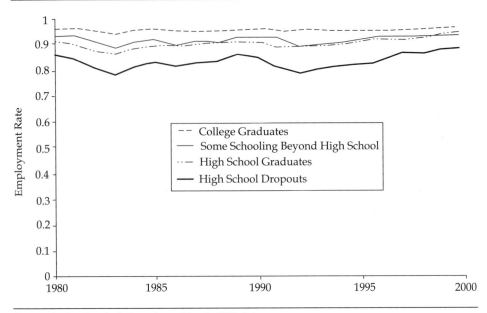

Source: Author's tabulations from March CPS data.

The current structure of aid shown in figure 9.10 actually creates *disincentives* working against a second low-wage worker entering the labor force. EITC benefits rise with earnings up to a point, but, after family income reaches $12,500, benefits begin to phase out. Thus, if a women is living with a man already earning $10,000 to $15,000, she often faces a very high marginal tax rate, including social security, federal and state income taxes, and EITC and even food-stamp-benefit reductions. Indeed, Ellwood (2000b) argues that, while the net gain for single mothers from taking a $10,000 job rose from $1,861 in 1986 to $6,876 in 1998, the net gain from working for married women with children whose husbands earn $15,000 fell from $4,665 to $3,329 over the same period.

The key insight is that targeted work supports advantage a family with low earnings relative to families with no earnings *and relative to families with slightly higher earnings*. Thus, they strongly encourage one family member to enter the labor market, but both income and substitution effects may discourage a second worker from entering.

These negative incentives really affect second wage earners only if the first member of a household to enter the labor force (typically the husband, but also sometimes the wife) has relatively low earnings. If one family member already earns more than $25,000 to $30,000, the household will not qualify for targeted work supports anyway whether or not a second wage earner brings in additional income. If women are commonly the second wage earner in a household, then only less-educated women (who are typically married to less-educated men) would be facing increased work disincentives as a result of the expanded work-support system.

Several authors, including Eissa and Hoynes (1999) and Ellwood (2000b), find evidence that the EITC has dampened work by married mothers in the least-educated groups. Figure 9.12 shows that work by the least-educated group is significantly lower than that for other groups and that the gap has grown in recent years.

Thus, it appears that the same incentives that pull more single parents into the labor market may also serve to discourage at least a few married women with children from participating. Given the fact that these women are perhaps the greatest source of potential new labor in the prime-age working group, these somewhat perverse incentives might be a source of concern.

Finally, we consider work by other adults—those who are not parents. Currently, the means-tested benefits available to healthy adults without children are extremely limited. Work supports are typically small as well. Employment rates are generally quite high among this group. There is little evidence that social-policy changes will significantly increase work by prime-age workers in this group.

HOW MUCH CAN ALTERED MEANS-TESTED BENEFITS OR WORK SUPPORTS DO TO IN-CREASE LABOR SUPPLY? There is abundant evidence that dramatic changes in social policies of the sort adopted by the United States in recent years can signif-

FIGURE 9.12 / March Employment Rates Among Married Women with Children Who Are Not Disabled by Level of Education

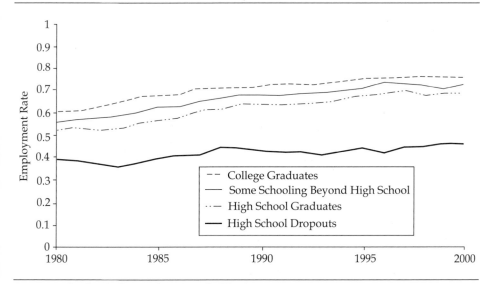

Source: Author's tabulations from March CPS data.

icantly increase work by those formerly receiving aid. Single parents work significantly more now than in the past, an increase that appears to be largely the result of policy change.

But there are also limits to what can be achieved by policy change. A comparison of the effects of policy changes on single parents with those on other groups illustrates these limits.

For single parents, it is hard to imagine a more extreme alteration of incentives: average benefits received when a single parent is not working have been reduced by nearly half, while aid for those who are working has gone up nearly as much. The economy has been remarkably strong. Employment rates among single mothers with at least a high school education now exceed 80 percent. Among college graduates, they exceed 90 percent. Much more could be done to support work. Expansions in aid may significantly help struggling families, but one has to wonder just how many more individuals with at least a high school education can realistically be expected to join the labor force.

Nonetheless, considerably more could be done to support single parents as they work. Expanded child care, especially high-quality care, might further accelerate movement into work and benefit future generations. Guaranteed medical protection regardless of work status might help as well. Finally, as states find ways to help those left on TANF, the so-called hard to employ, at least some of these women with children will move into the labor market.

I know of no way, however, in which to estimate just how much more might be accomplished. In the past five years, radical policy changes and an extraordinarily booming economy have reduced the number of nonworking men and women with children by 25 percent. Perhaps a reasonable upper-bound estimate of the amount by which the labor force can be increased might be 20 percent of the remaining single parents who are not now working outside the home—given the proper supports.

Table 9.7 illustrates that such an increase would raise the overall proportion of persons twenty-five and over who are working by 0.003 and increase total employment by slightly over 500,000 workers. The bulk of these new workers would be poorly educated women and/or have serious health or family problems.

We saw in table 9.6 that the largest group of persons not working among those aged twenty-five to fifty-four today are married women. Over 70 percent of these women have children. Very little attention has been paid to the question of whether government policies could effectively stimulate greater work by married women. In part, this lack of attention must reflect ambivalence about whether it is desirable to encourage women with children to work (although there seems to be little ambiguity about the position that the nation as a whole takes toward work by single mothers).

Other nations (for example, Sweden) have moved toward pro-employment policies when faced with serious labor shortages. Perhaps the United States will do so also. Such a move could sharply reduce the disincentives discouraging more than one individual in a household from entering the work force that are

TABLE 9.7 / Actual and Predicted Employment of Persons over Twenty-Four if Policy Reduced the Number of Nonemployed Single Parents by 20 Percent, 1999

	Actual Employment Rate	Predicted Employment Rate after Policy Change	Difference	Actual Number Employed (Millions)	Predicted Number Employed after Policy Change (Millions)	Difference (Millions)
Less than high school	.395	.402	.007	10.98	11.17	.20
High school only	.622	.625	.003	36.11	36.29	.18
Some schooling beyond high school	.716	.718	.003	31.79	31.91	.12
College degree or more	.774	.775	.001	34.70	34.74	.04
All education levels	.649	.652	.003	113.60	114.10	.54

Source: Author's tabulations of March 2000 CPS data predictions.

built into current work supports by expanding benefits further into the middle class. David Ellwood and Jeffrey Liebman (2000) and Robert Cherry and Max Sawicky (2000) offer strategies designed to increase child-related tax benefits for families above the EITC phaseout range and thereby significantly lower marginal tax rates for second wage earners.

One irony of the current direction of social policy is that the heavily targeted nature of work supports may have encouraged work by single parents while discouraging work by married men and women. It is obvious why aid is targeted: low-income working families are the most needy. But, if the goal is to increase work by married women with children as well, such benefits should probably not be so narrowly targeted since most such mothers are middle class. Support for child care could, for example, be significantly increased. Developmental day-care programs might improve prospects for future generations as well.

I am not aware of reliable estimates of what might be achieved by larger-scale child-care programs. There is some evidence that the availability of child care facilitates work by single parents. At a minimum, government-supported child care would reduce the cost of work. Several European countries offer far more supports to working mothers of all income classes, and work levels are sometimes higher in those countries than in the United States. Given that married women with children already work in large numbers and that many come from households whose incomes are sizable, perhaps it is unrealistic to expect work to increase by much more than 10 percent.

Table 9.8 simulates the effect of inducing an additional 10 percent of married women with children (of all education levels) to go to work. In that case, the result is that the labor force would grow by 850,000 workers and a sizable fraction of the group of new workers might be better.

Of course, any program designed to increase work by married women of all education levels would involve the expansion of work supports or child care into the middle class and beyond, and that is likely to be extremely expensive, partly because of the number of middle-class families to be found in the United States today, but also because of the cost of high-quality child care. Thus, any attempt to use social policies to encourage more married women to move into the labor force will likely carry a high price tag. Moreover, to the extent that the entry of married women requires an increase in the number of child-care workers, the net gain in the available workforce of activities other than childcare will be smaller than the increase in work by married women.

The level of means-tested aid available to other groups is much lower, and, in these groups, employment rates often exceed 80 or 90 percent. It therefore seems unlikely that government supports would change existing work patterns much.

Two strategies for moving remaining nonworkers into the labor market do, however, present themselves. The first is to require work of all those who receive food aid. (Such a proposal was in fact included in the PRWORA as it was initially established. Conditioning aid on work is, however, controversial, and the PRWORA has since been modified.) The second is to increase the rewards to be

TABLE 9.8 / Actual and Predicted Employment of Persons over Twenty-Four if Policy Reduced the Number of Nonemployed Married Women with Children by 10 Percent, 1999

	Actual Employment Rate	Predicted Employment Rate after Policy Change	Difference	Actual Number Employed (in Millions)	Predicted Number Employed after Policy Change (in Millions)	Difference (in Millions)
Less than high school	.395	.400	.005	10.98	11.12	.15
High school only	.622	.627	.005	36.11	36.37	.27
Some schooling beyond high school	.716	.721	.005	31.79	32.02	.23
College degree or more	.774	.779	.005	34.70	34.92	.21
All education levels	.649	.653	.005	113.60	114.40	.85

Source: Author's tabulations of March CPS.

gained from working—by, for example, expanding the EITC, which is currently limited primarily to those with children. But I doubt that this second strategy is likely to be very effective.

Unemployment Insurance and Workers' Compensation

Unemployment insurance and workers' compensation are considered together because both are linked closely to employment and both are administered by the states with some federal oversight. Both affect far fewer persons than do means-tested benefits and social security. Since both target the working population directly and both are specifically designed to provide aid during periods of unemployment, the potential for moral hazard is self-evident. And the incentive effects of both have been subject to careful economic analysis.

TRENDS IN UNEMPLOYMENT INSURANCE The UI system provides time-limited benefits to qualified workers who become unemployed—typically through "no fault of their own." In all states, persons who voluntarily leave a job without just cause and those who are fired receive delayed or reduced benefits, and they are often denied benefits altogether. Benefit recipients must be both able to work and available to work, and they cannot refuse suitable work, although what is considered suitable work varies by state and even by duration of unemployment (Committee on Ways and Means 2000, 288–90). Generally, benefits are limited to twenty-six weeks or less, although, at times of high unemployment, the federal government pays half the cost of a thirteen-week extension.

Benefits and eligibility are determined by a formula that varies state to state. Applicants must meet a minimum earnings requirement and have earnings in multiple quarters. Benefits are then typically calculated as a certain percentage of the applicant's wages, subject to a maximum and a minimum. As a result of the maximum, benefits as a fraction of actual wages—the replacement ratio—are typically lower for those in the higher wage groups. Many states have supplements if the applicant has dependents.

The two most common ways to measure the generosity of the system are to determine the fraction of unemployed persons who receive benefits and the replacement ratio for those who receive them. Aggregate data show a significant decline in the fraction of the unemployed who are covered. For example, Katherine Baicker, Claudia Goldin, and Lawrence Katz (1997) report that those claiming UI benefits as a fraction of all those unemployed fell from roughly 50 percent in the mid-1950s and early 1960s, to 40 to 45 percent in the 1970s and early 1980s, to 30 to 35 percent in the late 1980s and 1990s. Other series, including Committee on Ways and Means (2000, table 4–2, 285) and Blank and Card (1991), show similar patterns. There is also a strong cyclic component to the fraction of unemployment that is covered. In times of recession, coverage rates rise sharply, presumably because involuntary unemployment rises as a share of total unemployment and because of the traditionally high levels of unemployment among manufacturing workers, who are disproportionately represented among the cyclically unemployed.

The reasons for these coverage declines have been studied by several authors. Blank and Card (1991) conclude that almost none of the change in the fraction of unemployed covered by UI between 1977 and 1987 can be traced to changes in eligibility rules per se. They trace up to 50 percent of the decline to a geographic shift in the location of unemployment—with a larger share of unemployment being found in states where fewer of the unemployed have traditionally collected aid. A 1988 study by Mathematica Policy Research (as reported in Committee on Ways and Means 2000) reached somewhat different conclusions—tracing 22 to 40 percent of the decline to changes in state-program characteristics, 16 percent to geographic change, 4 to 18 percent to changing industry mix, and the rest to a variety of other changes, such as federal taxation of benefits and changes in measurement practices.

I found no published work that traces the way in which coverage has varied by skill-education level. As an alternative, I used March CPS data to determine the fraction of persons each year with more than four weeks of unemployment who report receiving UI during the previous year.[14] Figures 9.13 and 9.14 show the fraction collecting UI by gender and race. Three significant results are apparent: First, within genders, there is surprisingly little variation by education in the fraction of unemployed workers who report getting UI. High school graduates

FIGURE 9.13 / Fraction of Men with More than Four Weeks of Unemployment Who Reported Receiving Unemployment Benefits During the Year

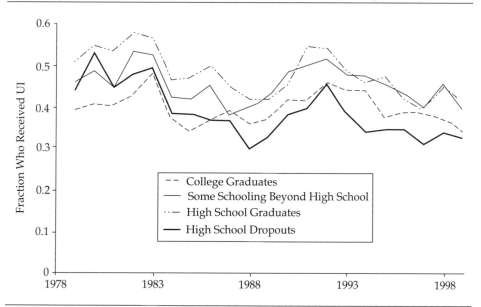

Source: Author's tabulations from March CPS data.

FIGURE 9.14   /   Fraction of Women with More than Four Weeks of Unemployment
Who Reported Receiving Unemployment Insurance Benefits
During the Year

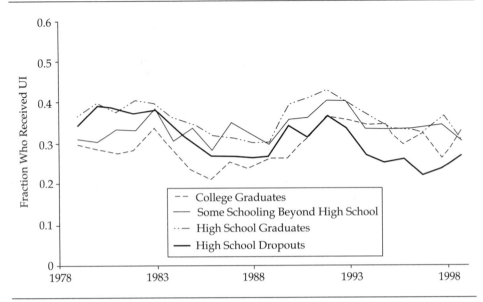

Source: Author's tabulations from March CPS data.

are somewhat more likely than either high school dropouts or college graduates
to get UI, presumably because of differences in their occupation-industry mix.
Second, the downward drift in UI receipt seems far more pronounced among
men than among women, perhaps because rising labor-force participation of
women has led more women to qualify for UI or because women are becoming
more aware of their eligibility to collect aid. Nonetheless, women are still significantly less likely to collect aid. Third, the downward drift in UI receipt is strongest among the least-educated workers.

There is much less information available on trends in replacement ratios for
those who do collect UI. Baicker, Goldin, and Katz (1997) report a series based
on average benefits and average wages that shows very little change. Committee
on Ways and Means (2000) and earlier years of the same publication include
tables on the replacement ratios for workers at different wage levels in each
state, but a consistent time series is not available. Thus, I used data on the rules
in each state in each year from 1980 to 2000 to project the replacement ratio for
workers at different wages. I used two different methods to determine wage
patterns: holding fixed real wages at a given level (say $5 or $10 per hour) and
using the actual wages observed for the median male worker and for workers at
the 33d and 67th percentiles of wages. This latter method is probably a better
measure of how incentives facing different workers have changed over time
since wage changes and benefit rules interact to influence actual replacement

ratios. I then weighted each of the state calculations by the fraction of all workers in the state in March 2000 to get a weighted national average. The results for male workers at different percentiles are shown in figure 9.15. As expected, replacement ratios are highest for low-wage workers and lowest for highly skilled workers. Replacement ratios for median-wage workers have drifted upward over the past twenty years, but those for workers in the top and bottom percentiles have not.

The slightly surprising differences are caused by two factors. Typically, the replacement ratio is 50 percent for someone not receiving the maximum benefit. In the 1980s, the maximums in many states were low enough that a median-wage worker (one who received roughly $14 per hour) got less than 50 percent. By the late 1990s, the maximums had risen in real terms in many states, and median wages had fallen slightly. At the high end, the higher maximum would also have pushed up benefits, but real wages rose more than the maximums, so the average replacement ratio remained unchanged.

INCENTIVE EFFECTS OF UNEMPLOYMENT INSURANCE Three features of UI have been the focus of particular attention: imperfect experience rating; the level of benefits as measured by the replacement ratio; and the time limits for collecting benefits.

UI is financed via taxes on firms. The taxes paid vary imperfectly with the past use of UI by workers who left the firm. Because there is imperfect experi-

FIGURE 9.15 / Replacement Ratios—Projected Weighted-Average UI Benefits as a Percentage of Wages for Men at Different Parts of the Wage Distribution

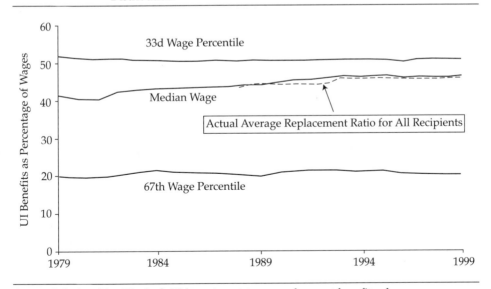

Source: Calculated by Elizabeth Welty using state unemployment-benefit rules.

ence rating, firms have an incentive to allow employment to fluctuate over the cycle and season more than they otherwise would because laid-off workers are partially insured. This may make it easier for firms to retain workers even after they are temporarily laid off, and it may even be welcomed as a quasi vacation by some workers. Martin Feldstein (1978), Robert Topel (1983, 1985), Patricia Anderson and Bruce Meyer (1994), David Card and Phillip Levine (1994), and Katherine Baicker, Claudia Goldin, and Lawrence Katz (1997) all find strong evidence that imperfect experience rating seems to increase cyclic or seasonal layoffs, thereby increasing unemployment. There is some evidence in Card and Levine (1994) that the effect of imperfect experience rating varies with the state of the economy, as these authors find significant results only during "recessionary" years. The differing methodologies and samples employed by these various studies makes it hard to convert these effects into effects on unemployment durations, but Topel (1983, 553) reports that the mean effect of imperfect experience rating is to increase the "average duration of layoffs by 1.3 weeks."

The second major influence on unemployment duration is the replacement ratio itself. This influence could operate in one of two ways. First, higher replacement ratios reduce the incentive to find a job quickly, increasing the duration and reducing the intensity of job search. Second, higher replacement ratios should heighten the consequences of imperfect experience rating for firms. Presumably, the greater the benefits laid-off workers will receive, the greater the incentives to allow "excessive" layoffs and seasonality in employment. Meyer (1990) finds that a 10 percentage point increase in replacement ratios might increase average spells by one and a half weeks. Robert Moffitt and Walter Nicholson (1982) find a one-week increase. Gary Solon (1985) reports an increase of one half to one week from a 10 percentage point rise.

The third element influencing behavior is maximum benefit durations. Numerous authors, including Moffitt and Nicholson (1982), Katz and Meyer (1990), Meyer (1990), and Card and Levine (1998), emphasize the sharp rise in the reemployment hazard as UI recipients approach their maximum durations, although Meyer (1990) somewhat discounts its significance since most unemployment spells have ended by that point. Katz and Meyer (1990) find that a thirteen-week extension of benefits would increase spell lengths by two to two and a half weeks. Card and Levine (1998) offer a particularly compelling test of the effect of duration limits when they examine the effect of an unexpected extension of benefits in New Jersey, concluding that a thirteen-week extension would raise durations by closer to one week.

HOW MUCH CAN ALTERED UNEMPLOYMENT INSURANCE INCREASE LABOR SUPPLY?

Clearly, evidence suggests that, by changing existing parameters, unemployment spells could be shortened. No one has examined what a combination of changes might accomplish. There are good reasons to expect mitigating or exacerbating interactive effects. For example, lowering the replacement ratio would tend to diminish the adverse incentives from imperfect experience rating. Nonetheless, loosely adding the estimated effects from the studies cited in the previous subsection, a very crude estimate is that the combination of increased experience rating, a 10 percentage point decline in replacement ratios, and shortening maximum durations by perhaps four weeks would reduce durations of unemployment by perhaps two to three weeks among the insured unemployed.

Such a combination would actually represent an extreme change in UI policy. The change in experience rating would be controversial, although it would not necessarily lead to decreased unemployment benefits. But the replacement-ratio cut represents almost a 25 percent decline, and the duration limitation would add to the effective reduction of aid. Meanwhile, given the declines in recent years, much of the recent discussion has been centered on ways in which to improve benefits and increase eligibility for UI, particularly since people are losing means-tested benefits as a result of welfare reform.

In the light of the fact that means-tested benefits and work-support programs are becoming more, not less, procyclic, there is serious reason for further examination of the implications of reducing UI support. Daron Acemoglu and Robert Shimer (1998) and many others emphasize that, in a world with risk-averse workers and no UI, the unemployed may engage in too little job search and, thus, that the UI system may in fact increase economic efficiency. Still, a few authors have called for more extreme changes than these to be explored. Jonathon Gruber (1999), for example, argues that many of the unemployed have adequate wealth to smooth expenditures, and he suggests that converting UI into a system of loans be considered.

There are other ways to reduce unemployment durations. There have been a series of experimental programs designed to do just that, many of which have been evaluated using randomized control methods. One experiment involved offering bonuses to workers who entered jobs before exhausting their benefits. Sometimes the level of the bonus was higher the quicker the person found work. Another set of experiments involved job-search requirements, intensive counseling, stricter monitoring, and the like. Meyer (1995) offers an excellent review of a sizable number of such experiments. He finds that, in experiments involving bonuses, unemployment was reduced by one half to one full week over the course of a year, although not all the results of these experiments were statistically significant. The job-search experiments also reduced durations by half to three-quarters of a week, with one exception: a 1977 experiment in Nevada that produced an apparent three and a half-week decline. Unfortunately, the Nevada program had one of the weakest and least-complete evaluations, and four other programs, all of which were completed after Nevada's, were shown to have smaller effects.

Whether through benefit reductions or bonus-job-search programs, it would seem that a realistic upper bound on what might be accomplished would be a reduction of unemployment durations by two weeks among the insured unemployed. Estimating the effect of such a change is straightforward if we assume that all those who reported receiving UI worked two weeks more—this represents a roughly 20 percent reduction in unemployment for these persons. The results are shown in table 9.9. Even a set of policies that reduces unemployment

TABLE 9.9 / Actual and Predicted Employment if Policy Changes Reduced Unemployment Durations by Two Weeks for Those Reporting Nonemployment Insurance, 1999

	Actual Employment Rate	Predicted Employment Rate after Policy Change	Difference	Actual Number Employed (Millions)	Predicted Number Employed after Policy Change (Millions)	Difference (Millions)
Less than high school	.395	.396	.001	10.98	11.01	.03
High school only	.622	.623	.001	36.11	36.18	.07
Some schooling beyond high school	.716	.717	.001	31.79	31.84	.05
College degree or more	.774	.775	.001	34.70	34.73	.03
All education levels	.649	.650	.001	113.60	113.80	.19

Source: Author's tabulations of March 2000 CPS data predictions. Assumes two weeks additional work for persons who reported receiving UI and who had more than two weeks of unemployment using March 2000 CPS data.

durations among the insured unemployed by 20 percent—something requiring a roughly 25 percent cut in aid or extremely large bonuses for getting a job—has a very small aggregate effect on the overall labor force, increasing the number of workers by just under 200,000.

While 200,000 workers is a significant number, it is a small portion of the labor force—equivalent to just two months' growth in the labor force over the past twenty years. The reason that effects are so small is easy enough to understand: if the unemployed represent 4 percent of the labor force and 30 percent of the unemployed get UI, a 20 percent reduced duration among UI recipients implies a change in employment of roughly $0.04 \times 0.30 \times 2$, or 0.24 percent. Of course, the effect would be larger in a time of greater unemployment. But, even in a period when unemployment rates were 9 percent, the change would be just 0.54 percent.

Thus, even though incentives matter a great deal in altering unemployment durations, simply too few people are affected for them to have much effect on the labor force overall.

EFFECTS AND OPTIONS FOR WORKERS' COMPENSATION The story for WC turns out to be much the same: sizable behavioral effects from policy change but such low levels of participation that aggregate effects are quite small.

There is far less information available on the trends in WC benefits and eligibility structures. Indeed, Committee on Ways and Means (2000, 997) reports that the historical data series providing information on "costs, benefits, and coverage of the workers' compensation system was discontinued by the Social Security Administration after publication of the 1993 data." The cost of the program itself is quite high—over $41 billion in 1996, with 40 percent going for medical costs and 60 percent in compensation. WC benefits are available for temporary total disability, permanent total disability, and permanent partial disability. According to Alan Krueger (1990a), 70 percent of claims are for temporary total disabilities.

As Bruce Meyer, W. Kip Viscusi, and David Durbin (1995, 332) argue: "Workers' compensation can influence incentives workers face in several ways. Higher benefits may decrease workers' incentives to avoid injuries, may increase incentives to file for compensation for any given job injury, and may foster more claims for nonwork injuries. In addition, higher benefits may make extending the duration of a claim more attractive." In addition, WC should presumably influence the behavior of firms, potentially making them more or less risk and/ or safety conscious, depending on whether they are at risk for the WC claims made by their own workers.

Increasingly, the literature distinguishes between the effect of WC benefits on the incidence of WC claims and that on the duration of disability. Generally, scholars track the effects of natural experiments using either administrative or micro data. Using CPS data, Krueger (1990b) reports that a 10 percent increase in WC benefits appears to be associated with a 7 percent increase in incidence or new receipt, or an elasticity of 0.7. Butler, Gardner, and Gardner (1997) offer frequency elasticity estimates—derived from significant benefit changes in three states—that range from 0.4 to 1.1 and average roughly 0.7 without regression adjustments. With regression adjustments for composition change, the variation in estimates grows considerably, averaging, however, around 1. Earlier work tends to result in somewhat lower estimates. For example, Richard Butler (1983) reports an elasticity of 0.3, James Chelius and Karen Kavenaugh (1988) an elasticity of 0.3, Richard Butler and John Worrall (1983) elasticities of 0.3 to 0.8, and John Ruser (1991) elasticities of 0.8 to 0.2 (depending on the size of establishment, with larger, more experience-rated firms having lower elasticities). Both Krueger (1990a) and Butler (1994) also find sizable effects of waiting periods on the incidence of benefits.

Using administrative data, Meyer, Viscusi, and Durbin (1995) use a variety of situations in which benefits were sharply increased to examine the effect of benefit levels on the *duration* of benefits. They find elasticities ranging from 0.3 to 0.6, with most clustered around the range 0.3 to 0.4. These estimates are higher than those of some earlier authors but lower than those of Krueger (1990b), who reports an elasticity of nearly 1.5—although his estimates are derived from a relatively small benefit increase of 8 percent in one state.

In principle, to determine the overall effect of benefit changes on WC spells, one needs simply to add these elasticities. The Krueger estimates lead to an estimated combined elasticity of over 2. Using a variety of incidence estimates from Butler and duration elasticities from Meyer, Viscusi and Durbin (1995) give an elasticity of closer to 0.6. Thus, a 25 percent reduction in WC benefits would tend to reduce aggregate weeks of WC claims from 15 to 50 percent. The upper end of this range seems implausibly large, but it is certainly reasonable to suggest that such a change might lead to a 25 to 30 percent reduction in aggregate weeks of WC.

One can roughly estimate the effect of a 25 percent change in benefits on employment rates using the CPS, but the procedure is more complicated than that for estimates involving UI. Reducing aggregate weeks of WC received does not necessarily imply that employment will rise equivalently. Moreover, the duration of WC receipt is not reported in the CPS—in contrast to unemployment duration. Finally, since the benefit changes affect both incidence and duration, one must factor in both effects.

I performed a simple estimate of potential effects in the following way. Assume, using Krueger's estimate of 0.7, that a 25 percent reduction in benefits reduces the incidence of WC receipt by 17.5 percent. This might be interpreted as meaning that the work level of 17.5 percent of existing WC recipients would become the same as others of the same age, race, and education level who received no benefits at all. This is clearly an upper-bound assumption. Then, using the 0.4 upper-end duration elasticity of Meyer, Viscusi, and Durbin, assume that the remaining 82.5 percent of WC recipients would reduce by 10 percent (25 percent × 0.4) the gap between their actual level of work and the level of work of others of the same age, race, and education level who received no benefits at all. The difference between actual and predicted benefits is the predicted effect of a 25 percent fall in benefits. The results are shown in table 9.10. The effect of

TABLE 9.10 / Actual and Predicted Employment of Persons over Twenty-Four if Workers' Compensation Benefits Were Reduced by 25 Percent, 1999

	Actual Employment Rate	Predicted Employment Rate after Policy Change[a]	Difference	Actual Number Employed (Millions)	Predicted Number Employed after Policy Change (Millions)[a]	Difference (Millions)
Less than high school	.395	.396	.001	10.98	11.00	.02
High school only	.622	.623	.001	36.11	36.16	.05
Some schooling beyond high school	.716	.716	.001	31.79	31.82	.02
College degree or more	.774	.774	.000	34.70	34.71	.01
All education levels	.649	.649	.001	113.60	113.70	.10

[a] Assumes 17.5 percent of WC recipients move to predicted employment based on a regression of employment rate (fraction of weeks worked in 1999) on age dummies, education dummies, race-nativity dummies, marital-status dummies, and number of children estimated only for persons who reported receiving no government aid. Remaining 82.5 percent reduce the gap between actual employment and predicted for those with no aid by 10 percent. Models run separately by sex using March 2000 CPS data.

even sizable reductions in WC would be modest, raising employment rates by less than 0.001 and increasing the labor force by approximately 100,000 workers.

Again, the logic is simple: On average, persons collecting WC have employment rates that differ from the employment rates of those who collect no aid at all by about 0.25. The changes reduce that gap by roughly 25 percent for the roughly 1 percent of workers who report collecting WC. The net effect, then, is 0.25 × 0.25 × 0.01, or 0.06 percent.

Note that the calculations shown in tables 9.8 and 9.9 should be seen as extremely rough. They may be downwardly biased both because of underreporting of benefits on the CPS and because of the effects of an unusually tight economy. On the other hand, the assumptions made in generating them tend to be close to upper-bound values. None of the changes shown here are considered remotely possible currently. Indeed, many argue that our UI system and, to a lessor degree, the WC system are far too restrictive in the current environment. Thus, it seems fair to conclude that little increase in the labor force can be expected from changes in UI and WC.

Disability Programs—Social Security and Supplemental Security Income

Persons with disabilities that render them unable to work (engage in "substantial gainful activity") for at least a year are eligible for two federal programs: social security disability insurance (DI) and supplemental security income (SSI). DI is a work-based program with benefits tied to past earnings, although benefits grow less than proportionately with past earnings. In addition, spouses and children sometimes qualify for a benefit as well. SSI is a means-tested program in which benefits are based entirely on current income. Earnings of other family members can be considered in determining the level of SSI, but they are not considered in determining DI benefits. Medical eligibility for both programs is determined through a process whereby state-based disability-determination units, under federal supervision but with considerable autonomy, use information supplied by the applicants' physicians and often conduct their own exams. The medical criterion is identical for both programs. Persons with low benefits from DI can also collect SSI.

There have been considerable changes in the standards and procedures for medical eligibility over the past twenty-five years. Concern about sharp growth in program utilization during the 1970s led first the Social Security Administration and then Congress to tighten standards and increase continuing disability reviews to look for persons whose condition now allows them to work. New DI awards per year fell from nearly 600,000 in 1975 to fewer than 300,000 in 1982. Then, in 1984, responding to intense criticism, Congress passed legislation that eased medical eligibility. Awards rose to 400,000 by the late 1980s. Eligibility rules were eased yet again in the early 1990s, and an SSI outreach program began. As a result, DI awards rose rapidly, from 468,000 in 1989 to 636,000 in

1992, and they remain at roughly that level today (Social Security Administration 2001a). Such large changes in flows naturally have a more modest effect on the stock of DI recipients, but, when inflows become large, the caseload does grow rapidly. The number of recipients was 2.86 million in 1980, fell to "only" 2.60 million in 1984 (during the big cutbacks of the early 1980s), but has now risen to nearly 5 million (Social Security Administration 2001b).

Needless to say, with such significant changes in awards, there is debate about exactly what constitutes a legitimate disability. Moreover, some with a disability that may limit work may still have some choice over whether to seek DI/SSI benefits or to keep working. Individuals presumably compare their opportunities in the labor market, given their medical condition, to what they might receive in disability benefits. The question is the extent to which changes in disability policy are reflected in changes in labor-force patterns.

Several different strategies have been used to examine the influence of DI on labor-force participation. The first is simply to compare patterns of work with patterns of benefit receipt. Figure 9.16 uses CPS data on men aged forty to sixty-one to track labor-force nonparticipation and the receipt of DI and/or SSI. The age range forty to sixty-one was selected because disabilities remain rare for people under thirty and because persons over the age of sixty-one who fail to qualify for social security by reason of disability can still qualify for retirement benefits, although at a somewhat reduced level.

Clearly, the trends in labor-force nonparticipation and in DI/SSI receipt track each other fairly well. The dip in DI/SSI receipt in the early 1980s does not seem

FIGURE 9.16 / Percentage Not in the Labor Force and Percentage Receiving DI/SSI Benefits Among Men Aged Forty to Sixty-One

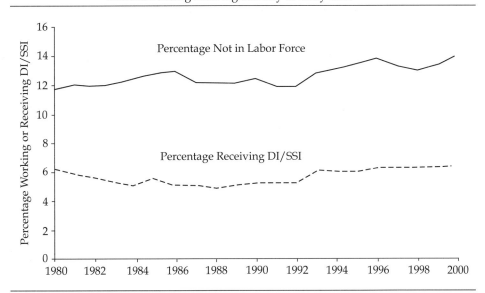

Source: Author's tabulations from March CPS data.

to be reflected in a comparable dip in labor-force participation, but the periods of growth in the 1990s are quite similar in both pattern and magnitude. The trends line up even more closely if one separates men by whether they report having a disability that limits work. Such data have been available in the CPS only since 1988. Figure 9.17 shows that, among those who report disabilities, receipt has risen sharply and almost completely in tandem with nonparticipation. Among those without reported disabilities, receipt is virtually unknown, and labor-force patterns have been quite stable.

John Bound and Timothy Waidmann (1992) raise the obvious point that self-reported disability status is in part endogenous. And, indeed, during the period 1988 to 2000, the fraction reporting a disability in the age group forty to sixty-one did rise slightly, from 10.2 to 10.7 percent, but this is small enough that the overwhelming growth in nonparticipation over this period must have come from the group already self-identifying as having a work-limiting disability.

Bound and Waidmann (1992, 2000) use a variant on this basic trend analysis to explore the potential contribution of DI to declining labor-force participation.[15] They conclude that roughly half the 4.9 percentage point drop in labor-force participation among men aged forty-five to fifty-four between 1949 and 1987, and perhaps a third of the 20 percentage point decline among men aged fifty-five to sixty-four, can be linked to DI. They also conclude that the "growth in the DI program can account for much of the decline in the relative employment position of the disabled" (Bound and Waidmann 2000, abstract) during the 1990s.

The question of causality is much harder to resolve or even to define. It is

FIGURE 9.17 / Percentage Employed and Percentage Receiving DI/SSI Benefits Among Men Aged Forty to Sixty-One by Disability Status

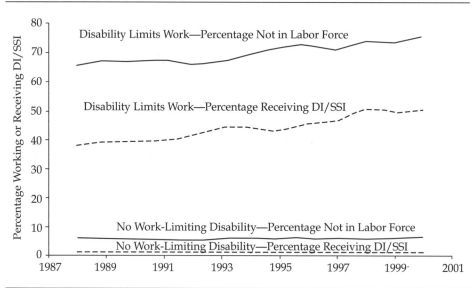

perfectly plausible that other factors reduced the rewards to working sufficiently that DI/SSI became a more attractive alternative. Thomas DeLeire (2000), for example, has argued that the sudden jump in nonparticipation starting around 1990 is more plausibly attributed to the Americans with Disabilities Act because that act may have raised the costs of hiring persons with disabilities. Presumably, persons facing a fall in demand for their services in the marketplace might choose instead to seek disability assistance. Under this or alternative scenarios, the decline in labor-force participation and the rise in DI/SSI were reflections of other forces, not things caused by policy changes themselves. But Bound and Waidmann (2000) argue that these programs still played a critical role in facilitating labor-force withdrawals. In the absence of the program, people would presumably have been far more likely to remain in the labor force even when demand for their services dropped.

A second method for assessing the effect of disability programs involves examining the effect of differentials in benefit levels or replacement ratios on labor-force participation. Donald Parsons (1980) found an elasticity of nonparticipation with respect to the replacement ratio of 0.63 for data in 1969 and argued that rising benefits could account for essentially all (actually, more than all) of the rise in nonparticipation among men aged forty-eight to sixty-two from 1948 to 1976. Bound (1989) points out that a serious limitation of this approach is that the structure of the DI system is such that persons with higher pay and greater labor-force attachment tend to have lower replacement ratios. Thus, the replacement ratio is likely to be spuriously negatively correlated with participation. In an attempt to deal with this problem, Robert Haveman, Philip de Jong, and Barbara Wolfe (1991) use a selection model and find an elasticity of 0.06, but there are questions about the exclusions needed to identify their model. Others, including Jonathan Leonard (1979) and Janice Halpern and Jerry Hausman (1986), have found elasticities in the range of 0.1 to 0.2.

Two other strategies have been used that rely on disability-denial patterns. Bound (1989) examined the likelihood that applicants denied DI return to work. He found that less than 50 percent of those denied benefits prior to 1978 were working eighteen months (or more) later and that many of those who were working were working part-time. Since one would anticipate that applicants denied DI would be healthier than those awarded DI, it would seem that, even at the margin, less than half of new enrollees would have been pulled from the labor market. Parsons (1991) claims that 75 percent of applicants denied DI who are living and not receiving government aid are working, while Bound (1991), rightly I think, notes that Parsons's sample is overly selected and proposes that 60 percent is a more accurate figure. Of course, all these results are from data that are nearly twenty-five years old and generated when vastly fewer people were collecting disability benefits.

Recently, a new strategy has been employed, one that relies on changes in denial rates over time and/or across states to identify effects. Jonathan Gruber and Jeffrey Kubik (1994) look at the effect of changes in state-level DI denial rates from 1977 to 1980 on changes in nonparticipation in the state over the same period. They conclude that a 10 percent increase in denial rates leads to a roughly 0.5 percentage point drop in participation rates (an elasticity of 0.27). David Autor and Mark Duggan (2000) are pursing a similar strategy and decomposing effects by level of education, although their work is not yet completed.

It is surprisingly difficult to draw straightforward conclusions from this literature about what might happen to participation patterns if the disability programs were cut back. The most obvious thought experiment is to consider what would happen if the number of disability recipients was reduced and then ask what fraction of those removed might be expected to work? The results of research on work patterns of applicants denied DI suggest that at most half might work, but this work is highly dated and reflects a time when disability standards were arguably more strict than they are today.

Another estimate can be taken from the estimated effects of a higher denial rate. A 20 percent rise in the denial rate should, over the long run, lead to at least a 20 percent fall in caseload (more if applications fall)—equivalent to 1.3 percent of the (male) population aged forty to sixty-one in the DI/SSI population. The Gruber-Kubik estimate implies that such a cut would reduce nonparticipation by 0.6 percent of the population, so the numbers seem to imply that half of those cut do not return to work. On the other hand, Jonathan Gruber and Jeffrey Kubik (1994) examine changes in participation in the short run. If one simply assumes that the entire change in participation in the two years that they examine comes from applicants denied DI in those years (that is, that theirs is a short-run, not long-run, estimate), their evidence could suggest that declines in work more than offset declines in beneficiaries.

Yet a third strategy is to consider what effect a 20 percent cut in benefits would have using the estimates of nonparticipation elasticities. Taking 0.3 as the elasticity, nonparticipation would grow by 6 percent, or from roughly 0.14 to 0.15, among persons aged 40 to 62. But what is unclear is how much the DI/SSI caseload would fall. If the only people to leave the program are those who go to work, this would imply a 17 percent fall in the caseload. But it is possible that others would choose not to receive aid.

A very rough guesstimate based on these findings is that, over the long run, perhaps 60 to 75 percent of persons who would be unable to get DI/SSI would instead be in the labor force. Numbers as low as 50 percent and as high as 100 percent are plausible given the current state of the literature, although it seems hard to believe that all the people at the margin would otherwise work.

But we are more interested in actual employment—not just being in the labor force. Autor and Duggan (2000) raise the question of whether a significant fraction of those denied DI return to the labor force but show up as unemployed. There is another way to generate an estimate. We have seen that most of the increase in DI/SSI use in the 1990s was among people who already claimed that a disability limited their ability to work. It turns out that, in 1990, roughly half of those who had a work-limiting disability but who received no government aid of any sort were working. Some of these probably had private sources of support, which might explain their not getting DI/SSI, but most are probably more able to work than are those who receive aid. Thus, a rough rule of thumb might be that 50 percent of those cut are actually able to work as much as those who receive no government aid at all.

Of course, strategies to get more people with disabilities working need not be draconian. Advocates for persons with disabilities strongly urge the nation to find supportive ways to increase work opportunities for those getting DI/SSI. Recently, changes have been considered—and some adopted—that are designed to remove barriers to work among DI/SSI recipients, including increased work disregards and the maintenance of health coverage if people go back to work. It is too early to judge the effect of such plans. On the basis of a simulation model, Hilary Hoynes and Robert Moffitt (1997) caution that many strategies, such as lowering tax rates and improving financial incentives, may, "contrary to perceived wisdom, possibly reduce work effort and increase the number of SSDI recipients" (abstract). They believe that employer subsidies hold more promise.

But suppose that one could move some workers with disabilities into work. Table 9.11 shows the effect of a 12.5 percent move into work, which might be accomplished via a 25 percent long-run reduction in disability rolls, assuming that 50 percent of those denied aid achieve work levels comparable to those of nondisabled people who receive no aid, or via new and as yet undeveloped support programs. From table 9.11, we see that a set of policies that moved 12.5 percent of DI/SSI recipients into work would increase employment rates overall by .003 and raise employment by 470,000 workers. Some 75 percent of these workers would be high school graduates or dropouts, and just 8 percent would be college graduates. Essentially all would have a physical or mental condition that limits their ability to work. And evidence from DeLeire (2000) and many other studies suggests that their wages would be low.

It is hard to imagine the nation adopting a policy that cut caseloads by 25 percent, given the outcry in the late 1970s when caseloads were cut by less than 20 percent and given that support programs remain to be developed. It thus remains to be seen what, if anything, might realistically be done to increase work among those currently receiving DI/SSI. It is clear, however, that, even in the best of circumstances, any new workers produced by policy change will be relatively poorly educated and at least partially disabled.

Social Security Retirement Benefits

Without question, the largest single force working to limit the size of the labor force from the 1960s to the early 1980s was the rapid decline in the labor-force participation among men over the age of fifty-five. As was shown in figure 9.2, the participation rate for men aged fifty-five to sixty-four fell from 87 percent to 67 percent before largely leveling off in the past fifteen years. Among those sixty-five and over, the rate fell from 31 percent in the early 1960s to roughly 17 percent from the 1980s through today. The overwhelming reason given for non-participation in both age groups is retirement.

TABLE 9.11 / Actual and Predicted[a] Employment of Persons over Twenty-Four: Move 12.5 Percent of DI/SSI Recipients Back to Work, 1999

	Actual Employment Rate	Predicted Employment Rate after Policy Change[a]	Difference	Actual Number Employed (Millions)	Predicted Number Employed after Policy Change[a] (Millions)	Difference (Millions)
Less than high school	.395	.401	.006	10.98	11.14	.16
High school only	.622	.625	.003	36.11	36.30	.19
Some schooling beyond high school	.716	.717	.002	31.79	31.87	.07
College degree or more	.774	.775	.001	34.70	34.74	.04
All education levels	.649	.651	.003	113.60	114.10	.47

[a]Assumes 12.5 percent of DI/SSI recipients aged twenty-five to sixty-one who report that a disability limits work move to predicted employment based on a regression of employment rate (fraction of weeks worked in 1999) on age dummies, education dummies, race-nativity dummies, marital-status dummies, and number of children estimated only for persons who reported receiving no government aid. Models run separately by sex using March 2000 CPS data.

No doubt, part of the reason for the rise in retirement has to do with rising incomes and wealth leading to increased consumption of leisure. There has been a nearly century-long trend toward earlier retirement. Still, several features of the social security system and changes over time likely contributed to the trend.

The simplest measure of the system's generosity is the replacement ratio. The structure of social security ensures that these ratios are much higher for those with low earnings than for those with high earnings, and these ratios have changed significantly over time. Peter Diamond and Jonathan Gruber (1999) report that, in the 1960s, replacement ratios for those with low earnings retiring at sixty-five averaged roughly 50 percent and that for those with moderate and higher earnings were closer to 30 percent. During the 1970s, benefits accelerated rapidly, and, by 1980, replacement ratios reached 70 percent for those with low earnings and 50 percent for those with moderate earnings. (Ratios did not change much for those with higher earnings.) Partly, these increases were the result of overindexation for inflation starting in 1972 that was not corrected until after 1977. In the early 1980s, replacement ratios fell rapidly, and they currently stand at roughly 60 percent, 40 percent, and 25 percent for those with low, moderate, and high earnings, respectively.

A second critical feature involves the link between benefits and retirement age. For most of its history, the normal retirement age was sixty-five, meaning that persons retiring at sixty-five got their "full" benefits. Starting in 1956 for women and 1961 for men, an early retirement age of sixty-two was established. Persons retiring between age sixty-two and age sixty-five receive a reduced benefit designed to be "actuarially fair" in the sense that the present value of benefits that they receive is the same on average as the value of benefits received by people who retire at age sixty-five. Persons retiring after sixty-five get delayed retirement credit that leads to higher payments in later years. As a result of legislation passed in 1983, the normal retirement age will be gradually extended, finally reaching sixty-seven for workers who turn sixty-two in 2022 or later. Because of the actuarial reduction for early retirement, the effect of this change is to lower benefits for sixty-two, currently reduced by 20 percent. With a normal retirement age of sixty-seven, they will be reduced by 30 percent.

A third feature of social security has to do with the treatment of earnings of people who are collecting social security. This test has changed considerably over time.[16] For example, in 1975, the benefits of all recipients were reduced $0.50 for each $1.00 earned over roughly $4,000 (in 1998 dollars). By 1983, the test was removed for persons over age seventy. It was liberalized considerably in subsequent years and was finally lifted for persons over the normal retirement age of sixty-five. Early retirees still face a 50 percent tax on earnings over $10,080.

Considerable progress has been made in recent years in determining the true marginal incentives for retiring at different ages. Early work tended to look at the retirement patterns of workers at different ages to infer the potential effect of social security. Gary Burtless and Robert Moffitt (1984), for example, show vividly a change in the retirement hazard after the adoption in 1961 of rules allowing early retirement.

According to Burtless and Moffitt, in 1960, there was no "spike" in the retirement rate at age sixty-two and a large spike at sixty-five. By 1970, a noticeable second spike had developed at sixty-two. By 1980, the spike at sixty-two was greater than it was at age sixty-five, and it remains so today.[17] There seems to be no plausible explanation for the shift of the retirement spike from sixty-five to sixty-two other than this change in social security rules. Note that the finding that retirement patterns closely mirror rules regarding normal and early retirement is vividly demonstrated country after country in Gruber and Wise (1999b). This is powerful evidence that social security rules influence behavior.

A sizable number of early and some recent studies have sought to relate retirement decisions to the level of social security benefits or wealth and pension benefits. Michael Hurd and Michael Boskin (1984), for example, suggest that much of the rise in retirement might be traced to rising social security. A sizable literature, however, including David Blau (1994), Peter Diamond and Jerry Hausman (1984), Alan Gustman and Thomas Steinmeier (1986), Gary Burtless and Robert Moffitt (1984), and Jerry Hausman and David Wise (1985), seems to conclude that, while social security has effects on retirement behavior, the magnitude of these effects is small enough that only a very modest portion of the decline in retirement age can be traced to social security.

Much of the early literature included fairly rudimentary estimates of incentives—often a simple replacement ratio. More recent work has recognized that a decision to retire also involves changing the entire future stream of benefits. Thus, Diamond and Gruber (1999) compute the change in social security wealth associated with working another year and the change in wealth as a percentage of the wage. And a number of authors, beginning with David Stock and David Wise (1984b, 1984a) and including most recently Andrew Samwick (1998) and Courtney Coile and Jonathan Gruber (2000b), have recognized that a decision to retire means forgoing the benefits associated with choosing a later retirement age and that one should incorporate the "options value" of postponing retirement as well. This later literature finds somewhat larger economic effects but still suggests only a modest role for social security in the long-run trends. Samwick (1998, abstract), for example, reports that expansions in pension and social security "in the early postwar period can account for one-fourth of the contemporaneous decline in labor force participation rates" and that the bulk of this effect is related to private pensions.

All this literature is subject to the criticism that benefits are in some sense a nonlinear combination of past earnings, family structures, and age and, thus, that the identification of an effect hinges critically on functional form. There are only a few studies that exploit natural experiments caused by unexpected changes in benefits. The most prominent, Krueger and Pischke (1992), found little labor-supply effect even of a sizable unanticipated jump in benefits.

There is a final strain in the literature, one that examines the effect of the earnings test. Not unlike the retirement literature, early work made much of a finding of earnings bunching right around the maximum. Gary Burtless and Robert Moffitt (1984), Wayne Vroman (1985), and, more recently, Leora Friedberg

(1999) have emphasized this point. Friedberg (1999) claims to find important effects if the earnings test is removed, but the magnitude is not large. As calculated in Jonathan Gruber and Peter Orszag (2000), the removal of the earnings test for sixty-five- to seventy-year-olds would increase their aggregate hours of work by just 3.4 percent. More recently, Gruber and Orszag (2000) found little net effect of the earnings test and even provide evidence that removing it may encourage more persons to take early retirement and be more likely to be poor later in life.

All in all, economists have had a remarkably difficult time showing that social security incentives had a major influence on the existing trends in retirement and work among the elderly, except in finding major spikes at early and normal retirement ages. In part, this is because many elements of the system, such as the reduction in benefits for early retirement, are designed to be actuarially fair, while other elements, such as earnings tests, that might reduce work are being eliminated.

The entirety of this literature is striking in its failure to find strong evidence that the massive social security program had much aggregate influence on retirement behavior. Perhaps this should not be too surprising. After all, Dora Costa (1998) reports that nearly 60 percent of the decline in labor-force participation of older men between 1880 and 1990 had occurred before the inauguration of social security.

Yet it seems certain that social security played some important role. One of the striking findings of the literature on incentives is that, for a typical worker with a normal time horizon without liquidity constraints, there is no particular incentive to retire at age sixty-two at all. Indeed, Diamond and Gruber (1999) and Coile and Gruber (2000b) both demonstrate that, for most workers, the current system actually creates some disincentives to early retirement. Of course, for some workers—those with short time horizons or those who expect to die at a younger age—there can still be financial benefits to early retirement. For most, however, the economic models provide no reason to withdraw early.

Still, we have seen that there is a sharp retirement spike at age sixty-two that arose only after the adoption of the early retirement age. The explanation may lie in the combination of myopia, credit constraints, and altered social norms. Social security does move income from the working years to the retirement years, and myopic or credit-constrained persons would respond to the income effect that it embodies. Moreover, a retirement decision may have as much to do with norms and expectations as incentives, and social security has clearly sent the signal that early retirement is acceptable.

CAN SOCIAL SECURITY BE USED TO ALTER WORK BEHAVIOR? Several proposals have been suggested that might alter retirement behavior. Removing the aforementioned earnings test is one proposal. But the test was already removed for those over sixty-five. And the most sophisticated work to date, Gruber and Orszag (2000), finds little evidence that removing it for early retirees will reduce retirement or increase labor supply. Indeed, doing so may have the opposite effect.

Two other prominent proposals are to increase the normal retirement age and to raise the delayed retirement credit. Coile and Gruber (2000a) investigate the effects of each of these proposals. They conclude that the current provisions of private pensions partially offset the effects of changed incentives.

Raising the normal retirement age to sixty-seven is predicted to have essentially negligible effects on work behavior. Currently, the delayed retirement credit penalizes retirement after age sixty-five. Over time, this penalty will be eliminated. Coile and Gruber (2000a) estimate that eliminating this penalty immediately would raise work somewhat, but by at most 1 or 2 percentage points when its effects peak around age sixty-five and sixty-six. This is a fairly sizable percentage rise on a base employment rate of 0.35, but its aggregate magnitude would be very small.

Clearly, only more radical changes will have a significant effect on labor supply of the elderly. Recently, the Committee for Economic Development released a report on creating new opportunities for older workers. Spurred both by the growing need for workers and by a desire to ensure future social security benefits, the committee made some bold proposals, including a call to extend the normal retirement age to seventy and to move the early retirement age to sixty-five (Committee for Economic Development 2000). Such a plan is unlikely to be politically popular. Citing Jacobs and Shapiro (1998), Gary Burtless and Joseph Quinn (2000, 18) report that "with rare exceptions solid majorities reject any proposed hike in the retirement age. The size of the majority opposing higher retirement age was higher in the 1990s than in the 1980s."

Nonetheless, political realities can change, so then the question is what effect such a plan would have. Given that current policies create limited direct incentives to retire early, it is possible that even changes this draconian would have a modest effect. But, keeping in mind the effects of credit constraints, myopia, and social norms, it seems certain that such a proposal would increase work. Of course, if the disability program remained unchanged, allowing workers to collect full benefits at any age, some might choose to enter that instead. Still, a recent paper by Olivia Mitchell and John Phillips (2000) suggests that the flows into work would be twice as large as the flows into DI.

There is no very reasonable way to model the long-term effect of such significant changes using the current literature. But suppose that, starting at age sixty-three, these changes shifted the pattern of work back a full two years. Thus, sixty-three-year-olds would now work as much as sixty-one-year-olds do, sixty-five-year-olds as much as sixty-three-year-olds, and so forth. This seems like an awfully large change, particularly since most models of social security predict far more modest changes from policy reforms. Moreover, the movement to disability programs is not considered directly. Thus, this estimate seems to be an upper bound on effects.

Table 9.12 provides the results. From it, we see that, if labor-force participation rates after age sixty-three could be retarded by two years, the aggregate employment rate would rise 0.005 and the employment overall would expand by nearly 1 million workers. This policy change, unlike any of the others, gener-

TABLE 9.12 / Actual and Predicted[a] Employment of Persons over Twenty-Four if Labor-Force-Participation Rates Starting at Age Sixty-Three Were Retarded Two Years So That Persons over Sixty-Three Began Participating as Much as Persons Two Years Younger Do Currently, 1999

	Actual Employment Rate	Predicted Employment Rate after Policy Change[a]	Difference	Actual Number Employed (Millions)	Predicted Number Employed after Policy Change (Millions)	Difference (Millions)
Less than high school	.395	.403	.009	10.98	11.22	.24
High school only	.622	.627	.005	36.11	36.41	.30
Some schooling beyond high school	.716	.720	.004	31.79	31.99	.19
College degree or more	.774	.779	.005	34.70	34.93	.22
All education levels	.649	.654	.005	113.60	114.50	.96

[a]Assumes labor-force-participation rates of persons over sixty-three would be equivalent to current rates for persons two years younger using March 2000 CPS data.

ates a significant number of new highly skilled workers. But that may not be realistic. Social security changes are likely to have a far smaller behavioral effect on the highly educated because their benefits are proportionately much lower and because they do not retire as early.

It is a bit hard to decide if this is a large or a small change. Surely, this is a considerably larger increase than that predicted by other policy changes. But the assumptions seem particularly strong, and the change is still less than a 1 percent expansion in the labor force.

The conclusion to be reached regarding changes in retirement behavior is decidedly mixed. On the one hand, the evidence is weakest that policy change can realistically alter behavior in a significant fashion. On the other hand, social security potentially affects a large number of people—including highly educated ones. Of course, that is also why social security changes face such large political hurdles.

CONCLUSIONS

In this chapter, I have sought both to explore what the future labor force might look like and to consider what social policy might do toward increasing labor supply. The broad conclusions were summarized in the opening section and will not be repeated here.

I have attempted to simulate the effects of some policy changes. In general, I have not tried to determine the exact effect of specific proposals, only to gauge what intensive policies that are still within the outside realm of plausibility might accomplish. Table 9.13 provides a summary of the projected effects of the various scenarios.

From table 9.13, we see that, if the goal is significantly to increase the number of workers and especially the number of more-educated workers, two proposals stand out as the most promising: get 10 percent more married women with children working and postpone retirement patterns by two years. But, sadly, these are probably the two most unrealistic proposals, and the former is extremely expensive. Even the policy changes underlying the other proposals were often extreme, assuming as they did either major benefit cuts or dramatic new programs of work support for highly disadvantaged persons. These policy changes do not increase the labor force a great deal, and most of the increase that does result is among the least-educated workers.

Thus, I generally would see each of these simulations as giving us a sense of what is the most that could be accomplished in the current climate. Overall, the numbers are sizable, but they are still not overwhelming. Collectively, they add up to roughly 3 million workers, a number equivalent to roughly 1.5 years of labor-force growth over the past twenty years, with nearly all the growth among lower-skilled groups. And there is no way in which one could achieve all these results.

Any discussion of using social policy to increase the workforce inevitably

TABLE 9.13 / Summary Table of Hypothetical Effects on Employment (Millions) of Various Policy Changes by Level of Education, 1999

	Reduce Unemployed Single Parents by 20 percent	Reduce Unemployed Married Women with Children by 10 percent	Reduce UI-Covered Unemployment Durations by Two Weeks	Reduce WC Benefits by 25 Percent	Move 12.5 Percent of DI/SSI Recipients Back to Work	Retard Retirement Patterns of Those Sixty-Three and Over by Two Years
Less than high school	.20	.15	.03	.02	.16	.24
High school only	.18	.27	.07	.05	.19	.30
Some schooling beyond high school	.12	.23	.05	.02	.07	.19
College degree or more	.04	.21	.03	.01	.04	.22
All education levels	.54	.85	.19	.10	.47	.96

Source: Summary of tables 9.7–9.12.

raises the larger question, Shouldn't the ordinary workings of the labor market be left to deal with any worker or skill shortages? If firms need more workers, they will bid up wages and automatically draw people into the labor market. It seems hard to justify prowork subsidies unless there is an additional reason to favor work.

Of course, there are often good and powerful reasons to support added aid for low-income workers, above and beyond the labor-supply effects. It may be that having working role models in the home is appropriate for children. The public may be more willing to give generous aid if people work to receive it. Subsidizing work will surely help the children in low-income working families. Providing more-universal child care might benefit children, and create community, and increase opportunities for women in the long run. And, thus, it may still make sense to encourage work with social policy.

But some ways of generating more work raise serious questions about security and dignity. Already, the move toward procyclic social policies raises questions about the loss of automatic stabilizers and the danger that people will be doubly disadvantaged during recessions—losing both work and benefits. The policy shifts transfer payments from less- to more-prosperous years. If work is further encouraged by reducing UI or tightening disability policy, some people will surely be hurt. A humane society protects its members from the insecurity of illness and unemployment and ensures dignity in old age. The challenge is to balance the goals of work, responsibility, and humanity. Programs like UI seem to be becoming more important as social policy shifts from being counter- to procyclic.

Two final issues arise from this discussion. Social-policy changes seem most suited to drawing less-skilled workers into the labor market. But the real need is for more-skilled workers. Perhaps a better direction for social policy is to seek to improve the skills of existing workers. Much more could be done to encourage new cohorts to enter and complete college. Moreover, if there is a need for more low-skilled workers, immigration offers a ready alternative.

This examination of workforce changes and the role for social policy, thus, indicated that more might be done to promote work through social policies. Incentives really do matter, and social policies can make a difference. Still, there are very real limits to what can be accomplished. The most important debates about what to do about the sputtering labor market may, thus, have little to do with social policy and much more to do with education, training, and immigration.

I gratefully acknowledge the generous support of the Century Foundation and the Russell Sage Foundation and additional support from the MacArthur Foundation. I thank Andrew Clarkwest, Sara Jung Edel, and Elisabeth Welty for their excellent research work and Seth Kirshenbaum for his careful editing and fine assistance. I benefited greatly from thoughtful comments from Alan Krueger, Jeff Liebman, Robert Moffitt, and Robert Solow.

NOTES

1. The Census Bureau puts emigration of natives out of the United States at 48,000 per year, an annual rate of 0.02 percent (Hollmann, Mulder, and Kallan 2000, 21).

2. "The new law increases the number of H-1B visas to 195,000 for each of the next three years, starting with the fiscal year that began Oct. 1. Without the law, the number would have been 107,500 for this fiscal year and 65,000 in subsequent years" (Associated Press 2000).

3. Another source of random error resulted from my desire to base initial projections on individual-level data. For each individual, I randomly assigned participation on the basis of a comparison of a random number with that person's projected participation rate. Again, the noise introduced by this procedure will generally average out in aggregate tabulations.

4. The projected figures are not entirely smooth after 2000 both because we are aging a population that is not quite smooth and because individuals were probabilistically assigned a labor-force status on the basis of the projected status for that group.

5. Since labor-force participation varies with education, even estimates of the size of the overall labor force depend slightly on the assumption regarding future educational attainment. For this table, however, I use the high-growth assumption. If the level-attainment assumption had been used, the projected 2020 over-twenty-four labor force would be 137.1 million instead of the 137.9 million shown.

6. For an excellent recent summary, see, for example, Hotz and Scholz (2001).

7. Benefit levels adjusted for inflation using the CPI-UX1.

8. Committee on Ways and Means (2000, table 15–3, 864) shows that 87 percent of AFDC recipients got food stamps in 1995 but that this figure dropped to 81 percent in 1997/1998.

9. Consider two examples: In Georgia, before she can even begin the application process, a woman seeking aid is required to get a form signed by six employers saying that she applied in good faith for a minimum-wage job and was turned down. Once enrolled, if she is penalized twice for failure to meet some key administrative or work requirement, she is barred for life from seeking aid in the state. In Wisconsin, no aid is provided *unless the person is already working.* When applicants claim that they really cannot find a job, the providers of TANF will, in some cases, provide a subsidized job for a limited duration, but aid remains tied to work. In both states, caseloads have dropped dramatically—nearly 80 percent in Wisconsin.

10. There are still important sources of potential bias. One can be found in the fact that, if work patterns change, the mix of persons in each earnings category will also change. For example, as more people go to work, fewer people—most likely only those with the most serious problems—will report no earnings. If aid is somehow conditioned on these unmeasured nonfinancial characteristics, changes over time in observed benefits received by those with no earnings may not reflect what others might receive if they experienced a loss of all earnings. This measurement problem would be most serious if one included disabled persons in the group. After a burst of work, all but the disabled would be transferred to a different category, one reflecting higher earn-

ings, and the disabled might then qualify for relatively high benefits. In this analysis, I omit those who report that they did not work in the past year because of illness or disability.

11. Disabled persons are defined as those reporting that the primary reason that they have not worked in the past year is illness or disability. This definition is not wholly satisfactory, but it is the only one available over the entire sample period.

  In determining family earnings, I used earnings of the immediate family or sub-family only. One concern with the no-earnings category is that it may reflect measurement error or include people who had high levels of income from other sources. For example, some of these people are those who live with relatives who are not members of their immediate family or subfamily, and some may simply have chosen not to receive aid. But, in recent years, some of those who have no earnings and receive no benefits may have been excluded from aid because of changing administrative practice, even time limits. Presumably, people who voluntarily refuse aid have other sources of income. Thus, I exclude from this figure anyone who does not receive benefits if the combined income from other sources of all the relatives in the household in question (including extended-family members) was greater than $5,000. Those with no earnings and no benefits who remain after this exclusion have very low levels of education (44 percent are high school dropouts). This methodology affects only the no-earnings category. If all those who by choice receive no benefits were excluded, the level of aid received by those with no earnings would be $9,200 in 1979 and $5,900 in 1999. If no one is excluded, the levels would be $6,700 in 1979 and $2,700 in 1999.

12. Unless specified otherwise, the information in the paragraph is drawn from Gordon Berlin (2000).

13. Indeed, only 2.6 percent fall in this combined category.

14. I used the four-week cutoff to eliminate the significant number of people who report having been unemployed for one week or two but who would be unlikely to have considered collecting UI. Results obtained when weighting by the number of weeks unemployed were very similar.

15. Strangely, and rather troublingly, these papers look at only DI patterns, not DI plus SSI, even though both would affect behavior and the populations only partially overlap. This is a flaw that plagues much of the disability literature.

16. For an excellent summary of changes in the earnings test over time, see Gruber and Orszag (2000).

17. For a comparison of all these hazards, see Gruber and Wise (1999a).

REFERENCES

Acemoglu, Daron, and Jorn-Steffen Pischke. 2000. "Changes in the Wage Structure, Family Income, and Children's Education." *NBER* working paper no. 7986. Cambridge, Mass.: National Bureau of Economic Research.

Acemoglu, Daron, and Robert Shimer. 1998. "Efficient Unemployment Insurance." *NBER* working paper no. 6686. Cambridge, Mass.: National Bureau of Economic Research.

Administration for Children and Families. 2000. "Temporary Assistance for Needy Families (TANF), 1936–1999." *http://www.acf.dhhs.gov/news/stats/3697.htm.* Accessed January 15, 2001.

Anderson, Patricia M., and Bruce D. Meyer. 1994. "The Unemployment Insurance Payroll Tax and Interindustry and Interfirm Subsidies." *Tax Policy and the Economy* 7: 111–44.

Associated Press. 2000. "Clinton Signs H1B Visas Bill." *http://www.usbc.org/info/jobs/1000signsh1b.htm.* Accessed January 7, 2001.

Autor, David H., and Mark G. Duggan. 2000. "Disability Recipiency and the Decline in Unemployment: Assessing the Contribution of the 1984 Disability Reforms." Paper presented to the National Bureau of Economic Research Summer Institute. Cambridge, Mass. (July 2000).

Baicker, Katherine, Claudia Goldin, and Lawrence F. Katz. 1997. "A Distinctive System: Origins and Impact of U.S. Unemployment Compensation." *NBER* working paper no. 5889. Cambridge, Mass.: National Bureau of Economic Research.

Berlin, Gordon. 2000. "Encouraging Work, Reducing Poverty: The Impact of Work Incentive Programs." Report. New York: Manpower Demonstration Research Corp., March.

Blank, Rebecca M., and David E. Card. 1991. "Recent Trends in Insured and Uninsured Unemployment: Is There an Explanation?" *Quarterly Journal of Economics* 106(4): 1157–89.

Blank, Rebecca, David Card, and Philip Robbins. 2000. "Financial Incentives for Increasing Work and Income among Low-Income Families." In *Finding Jobs: Work and Welfare Reform,* edited by Rebecca Blank and David Card. New York: Russell Sage Foundation.

Blau, David M. 1994. "Labor Force Dynamics of Older Men." *Econometrica* 62(1): 117–56.

Bound, John. 1989. "The Health and Earnings of Rejected Disability Applicants." *American Economic Review* 79(3): 489–503.

———. 1991. "The Health and Earnings of Rejected Disability Applicants: Reply." *American Economic Review* 81(5): 1427–34.

Bound, John, and Timothy Waidmann. 1992. "Disability Transfers, Self-Reported Health, and the Labor Force Attachment of Older Men: Evidence from the Historical Record." *Quarterly Journal of Economics* 107(4): 1393–1419.

———. 2000. "Accounting for Recent Declines in Employment Rates among the Working-Aged Disabled." *NBER* working paper no. 7975. Cambridge, Mass.: National Bureau of Economic Research.

Burtless, Gary, and Robert A. Moffitt. 1984. "The Effect of Social Security Benefits on the Labor Supply of the Aged." In *Retirement and Economic Behavior,* edited by Henry J. Aaron and Gary Burtless, 135–174. Washington, D.C.: Brookings Institution.

Burtless, Gary, and Joseph F. Quinn. 2000. "Retirement Trends and Policies to Encourage Work among Older Americans." Unpublished manuscript. Washington, D.C.: Brookings Institution, January.

Butler, Richard J. 1983. "Wage and Injury Rate Response to Shifting Levels of Workers' Compensation." In *Safety and the Work Force: Incentives and Disincentives in Workers' Compensation,* edited by John D. Worrall, 61–86. Ithaca, N.Y.: ILR Press.

———. 1994. "Economic Determinants of Workers' Compensation Trends." *Journal of Risk and Insurance* 61(3): 383–401.

Butler, Richard J., B. Delworth Gardner, and Harold H. Gardner. 1997. "Workers' Compensation Costs When Maximum Benefits Change." *Journal of Risk and Uncertainty* 15: 259–69.

Butler, Richard, and John Worrall. 1983. "Workers' Compensation: Benefit and Injury Claims Rates in the Seventies." *Review of Economics and Statistics* 65(4): 580–89.

Cameron, Stephen V., and James J. Heckman. 1999. "The Dynamics of Educational Attainment for Blacks, Hispanics, and Whites." *NBER* working paper no. 7249. Cambridge, Mass.: National Bureau of Economic Research.

Card, David, and Thomas Lemieux. 2000. "Dropout and Enrollment Trends in the Post-War Period: What Went Wrong in the 1970s?" *NBER* working paper no. 7658. Cambridge, Mass.: National Bureau of Economic Research.

Card, David, and Phillip B. Levine. 1994. "Unemployment Insurance Taxes and the Cyclical and Seasonal Properties of Unemployment." *Journal of Public Economics* 53(January): 1–29.

———. 1998. "Extended Benefits and the Duration of UI Spells: Evidence from the New Jersey Extended Benefits Program." *NBER* working paper no. 6714. Cambridge, Mass.: National Bureau of Economic Research.

Chelius, James, and Karen Kavenaugh. 1988. "Workers' Compensation and the Level of Occupational Injuries." *Journal of Risk and Insurance* 55: 315–23.

Cherry, Robert, and Max B. Sawicky. 2000. "Giving Tax Credit Where Credit Is Due: A 'Universal Unified Child Credit' That Expands the EITC and Cuts Taxes for Working Families." *EPI* briefing paper. Washington, D.C.: Economic Policy Institute.

Coile, Courtney, and Jonathan Gruber. 2000a. "Social Security and Retirement." *NBER* working paper no. 7830. Cambridge, Mass.: National Bureau of Economic Research.

———. 2000b. "Social Security Incentives for Retirement." *NBER* working paper no. 7651. Cambridge, Mass.: National Bureau of Economic Research.

Committee for Economic Development. 2000. "New Opportunities for Older Workers: Executive Summary." *http://www.ced.org/docs/executive/oldersummary.htm*. Accessed August 24, 2000.

Committee on Ways and Means. 2000. *2000 Green Book: Background Material and Data on Programs under the Jurisdiction of the Committee on Ways and Means*. Washington: U.S. Government Printing Office.

Congressional Budget Office. 1998. "Policy Changes Affecting Mandatory Spending for Low-Income Families Not Receiving Cash Welfare." Washington: U.S. Congress, September.

Costa, Dora L. 1998. *The Evolution of Retirement: An Economic History, 1880–1990*. Chicago: University of Chicago Press.

Day, Jennifer Cheeseman, and Kurt J. Bauman. 2000. "Have We Reached the Top? Educational Attainment Projections of the U.S. Population." *Population Division* working paper no. 43. Washington: U.S. Bureau of the Census.

DeLeire, Thomas. 2000. "The Wage and Employment Effects of the Americans with Disabilities Act." *Journal of Human Resources* 35(4): 693–715.

Diamond, Peter, and Jonathan Gruber. 1999. "Social Security and Retirement in the United States." In *Social Security and Retirement around the World*, edited by Jonathan Gruber and David A. Wise. Chicago: University of Chicago Press.

Diamond, Peter, and Jerry A. Hausman. 1984. "Retirement and Unemployment Behavior of Older Men." In *Retirement and Economic Behavior*, edited by Henry Aaron and Gary Burtless, 97–135. Washington, D.C.: Brookings Institution.

Dickert, Stacy, Scott Houser, and John Karl Scholz. 1995. "The Earned Income Tax Credit and Transfer Programs: A Study of Labor Market and Program Participation." In *Tax Policy and the Economy*, edited by James M. Poterba, 1–50. Cambridge, Mass.: MIT Press.

Eissa, Nada, and Hilary Hoynes. 1999. "The Earned Income Tax Credit and the Labor Supply of Married Couples." Mimeo. University of California, Berkeley.

Eissa, Nada, and Jeffrey B. Liebman. 1996. "Labor Supply Response to the Earned Income Tax Credit." *Quarterly Journal of Economics* 112(2): 605–37.

Ellwood, David T. 2000a. "Anti-Poverty Policy for Families in the Next Century: From Welfare to Work—and Worries." *Journal of Economic Perspectives* 14(1): 187–98.

———. 2000b. "The Impact of the Earned Income Tax Credit and Social Policy Reforms on Work, Marriage, and Living Arrangements." *National Tax Journal* 53(4, pt. 2): 1063–1106.

Ellwood, David T., and Thomas J. Kane. 2000. "Who Is Getting a College Education: Family Background and the Growing Gaps in Enrollment." In *Securing the Future,* edited by Sheldon Danziger and Jane Waldfogel. New York: Russell Sage Foundation.

Ellwood, David T., and Jeffrey B. Liebman. 2000. "The Middle Class Parent Penalty: Child Benefits in the U.S. Tax Code." In *Tax Policy in the Economy,* Vol. 15, edited by James Poterba. Cambridge, Mass.: MIT Press.

Feldstein, Martin. 1978. "The Effect of Unemployment Insurance on Temporary Layoff Unemployment." *American Economic Review* 68(December): 834–46.

Friedberg, Leora. 1999. "The Labor Supply Effects of the Social Security Earnings Test." *NBER* working paper no. 7200. Cambridge, Mass.: National Bureau of Economic Research.

Fullerton, Howard N., Jr. 1999. "Labor Force Participation: 75 Years of Change, 1950–98 and 1998–2025." *Monthly Labor Review* 122(12): 3–12.

Gerald, Debra E., and William J. Hussar. 2000. "Projections of Education Statistics to 2010." Unpublished manuscript. Washington: National Center for Education Statistics, U.S. Department of Education.

Gruber, Jonathan. 1999. "The Wealth of the Unemployed: Adequacy and Implications for Unemployment Insurance." *NBER* working paper no. 7348. Cambridge, Mass.: National Bureau of Economic Research.

Gruber, Jonathan, and Jeffrey D. Kubik. 1994. "Disability Insurance Rejection Rates and the Labor Supply of Older Workers." *Journal of Public Economics* 64(1): 1–23.

Gruber, Jonathan, and Peter Orszag. 2000. "Does the Social Security Earnings Test Affect Labor Supply and Benefits Receipt?" *NBER* working paper no. 7923. Cambridge, Mass.: National Bureau of Economic Research.

Gruber, Jonathan, and David A. Wise. 1999a. "Introduction and Summary." In *Social Security and Retirement around the World,* edited by Jonathan Gruber and David A. Wise, 1–35. Chicago: University of Chicago Press.

———, eds. 1999b. *Social Security and Retirement around the World.* Chicago: University of Chicago Press.

Gustman, Alan L., and Thomas L. Steinmeier. 1986. "A Structural Retirement Model." *Econometrica* 54(3): 555–84.

Halpern, Janice, and Jerry A. Hausman. 1986. "Choice under Uncertainty: A Model of Applications for the Social Security Disability Program." *Journal of Public Economics* 31(2): 131–61.

Hausman, Jerry A., and David A. Wise. 1985. "Social Security, Health Status, and Retirement." In *Pensions, Labor, and Individual Choice,* edited by David A. Wise. Chicago: University of Chicago Press.

Haveman, Robert, Philip de Jong, and Barbara Wolfe. 1991. "Disability Transfers and the Work Decision of Older Men." *Quarterly Journal of Economics* 106(3): 939–49.

Hollmann, Frederick W., Tammany J. Mulder, and Jeffrey E. Kallan. 2000. "Methodology and Assumptions for the Population Projections of the United States: 1999 to 2100." *Population Division* working paper no. 38. Washington: Bureau of the Census, U.S. Department of Commerce, 2000.

Hotz, V. Joseph, and John Karl Scholz. 2001. "The Earned Income Tax Credit." *NBER* working paper no. W8078. Cambridge, Mass.: National Bureau of Economic Research.

Hoynes, Hilary Williamson, and Robert Moffitt. 1997. "Tax Rates and Work Incentives in the Social Security Disability Insurance Program: Current Law and Alternative Reforms." *NBER* working paper no. 6058. Cambridge, Mass.: National Bureau of Economic Research.

Hurd, Michael, and Michael Boskin. 1984. "The Effects of Social Security on Retirement in the Early 1970s." *Quarterly Journal of Economics* 99(4): 767–91.

Jacobs, Lawrence R., and Robert Y. Shapiro. 1998. "Myths and Misunderstandings about Public Opinion toward Social Security." In *Framing the Social Security Debate: Values, Politics, and Economics,* edited by R. Douglas Arnold, Michael J. Graetz, and Alicia H. Munnell, 355–88. Washington D.C.: National Academy of Social Insurance.

Kane, Thomas J. 1994. "College Entry by Blacks since 1970: The Role of College Cost." *Journal of Political Economy* 102(5): 878–911.

———. 1999. *The Price of Admission: Rethinking How Americans Pay for College.* Washington, D.C.: Brookings Institution.

Katz, Lawrence F., and Bruce D. Meyer. 1990. "Unemployment Insurance, Recall Expectations, and Unemployment Outcomes." *Quarterly Journal of Economics* 105(4): 973–1002.

Krueger, Alan B. 1990a. "Incentive Effects of Workers' Compensation Insurance." *Journal of Public Economics* 41(1): 73–99.

———. 1990b. "Workers' Compensation Insurance and the Duration of Workplace Injuries." *NBER* working paper no. 3253. Cambridge, Mass.: National Bureau of Economic Research.

Krueger, Alan B., and Jorn-Steffen Pischke. 1992. "The Effect of Social Security on Labor Supply: A Cohort Analysis of the Notch Generation." *Journal of Labor Economics* 10(4): 412–37.

Leonard, Jonathan. 1979. "The Social Security Disability Program and Labor Force Participation." *NBER* working paper no. 392. Cambridge, Mass.: National Bureau of Economic Research.

MaCurdy, Thomas E., David A. Green, and Harry J. Paarsch. 1990. "Assessing Empirical Approaches for Analyzing Taxes and Labor Supply." *Journal of Human Resources* 25(3): 415–90.

Meyer, Bruce D. 1990. "Unemployment Insurance and Unemployment Spells." *Econometrica* 58(4): 757–82.

———. 1995. "Lessons from the U.S. Unemployment Insurance Experiments." *Journal of Economic Literature* 33(1): 91–131.

Meyer, Bruce D., and Dan T. Rosenbaum. 1999. "Welfare, the Earned Income Tax Credit, and the Labor Supply of Single Mothers." *NBER* working paper no. W7363. Cambridge, Mass.: National Bureau of Economic Research.

———. 2000. "Making Single Mothers Work: Recent Tax and Welfare Policy and Its Effects." *National Tax Journal* 53(4, pt. 2): 1027–62.

Meyer, Bruce D., W. Kip Viscusi, and David L. Durbin. 1995. "Workers' Compensation and Injury Duration: Evidence from a Natural Experiment." *American Economic Review* 85(3): 322–40.

Michalopoulos, Charles, David Card, Lisa Gennetian, Kristen Harknett, and Philip K. Robins. 2000. "The Self-Sufficiency Project at 36 Months: Effects of a Financial Work Incentive on Employment and Income." Report. New York: Manpower Demonstration Research Corporation.

Mitchell, Olivia S., and John W. R. Phillips. 2000. "Retirement Responses to Early Social Security Benefit Reductions." *NBER* working paper no. 7963. Cambridge, Mass.: National Bureau of Economic Research.

Moffitt, Robert. 1986. "The Econometrics of Piecewise-Linear Budget Constraints: A Survey and Exposition of the Maximum Likelihood Method." *Journal of Business and Economic Statistics* 4(3): 317–27.

Moffitt, Robert, and Walter Nicholson. 1982. "The Effect of Unemployment Insurance on Unemployment: The Case of Supplemental Federal Benefits." *Review of Economics and Statistics* 64(1): 1–11.

Parsons, Donald O. 1980. "The Decline in the Male Labor Force Participation." *Journal of Political Economy* 88(1): 117–34.

———. 1991. "The Health and Earnings of Rejected Disability Applicants: Comment." *American Economic Review* 81(5): 1419–26.

Ruser, John W. 1991. "Workers' Compensation and Occupational Injuries and Illnesses." *Journal of Labor Economics* 9(4): 325–50.

Samwick, Andrew A. 1998. "New Evidence on Pensions, Social Security, and the Timing of Retirement." *NBER* working paper no. 6534. Cambridge, Mass.: National Bureau of Economic Research.

Schoeni, Robert F., and Rebecca M. Blank. 2000. "What Has Welfare Reform Accomplished? Impacts on Welfare Participation, Employment, Income, Poverty, and Family Structure." *NBER* working paper no. W7627. Cambridge, Mass.: National Bureau of Economic Research.

Social Security Administration. 2001a. "Applications for Social Security Disability Benefits and Benefit Awards." *http://www.ssa.gov/OACT/STATS/table6c7.html*. Accessed January 19, 2001.

———. 2001b. "Table 5.A4—Number and Monthly Benefits, 1940–1991." *2001b. http://www.ssa.gov/statistics/Supplement/2000/html/t5a4.htm*. Accessed January 19, 2001.

Solon, Gary. 1985. "Work Incentive Effects of Taxing Unemployment Benefits." *Econometrica* 53 (1985): 295–306.

Stock, David, and David A. Wise. 1984a. "The Pension Inducement to Retire: An Option Value Analysis." In *Issues in the Economics of Aging,* edited by David A. Wise. Chicago: University of Chicago Press.

———. 1984b. "Pensions, the Option Value of Work, and Retirement." *Econometrica* 58(5): 1151–80.

Topel, Robert. 1983. "On Layoffs and Unemployment Insurance." *American Economic Review* 73(2): 541–59.

———. 1985. "Unemployment and Unemployment Insurance." In *Research in Labor Economics,* edited by Ronald Ehrenberg, 91–135. Greenwich, Conn.: JAI.

Vroman, Wayne. 1985. "Some Economic Effects of Social Security Earnings Test." In *Research in Labor Economics,* edited by Ronald Ehrenberg, 31–89. Greenwich, Conn.: JAI.

Part IV

The Benefits and Pitfalls of Tight Labor Markets

Chapter 10

Another Look at Whether a Rising Tide Lifts All Boats

James R. Hines Jr., Hilary W. Hoynes, and Alan B. Krueger

President John F. Kennedy made famous the saying, "A rising tide lifts all boats." The American experience of the 1960s and 1970s—decades during which periods of rapid economic growth were accompanied by improved living standards for the disadvantaged—amply supported this view. Subsequent decades, however, did not, and the steadily declining real earnings of low-wage workers during the economic expansions of the 1980s and early 1990s have led many to question the ability of economic growth to ameliorate economic and social ills for the disadvantaged and perhaps even for the median worker. This paper assembles evidence on the cyclic nature of a number of important economic and social indicators since the early 1970s. A bottom-line finding of our paper is that President Kennedy's shibboleth continues to hold true: the benefits of strong economic growth for the disadvantaged are at least as great as they are for the more advantaged, and the costs of a downturn are borne disproportionately by the disadvantaged.

Table 10.1 provides a brief summary of economic and social outcomes during the business-cycle peak of 1989, the labor-market trough of 1992, and the peak of 2000.[1] Although a number of factors contribute to the patterns revealed in table 10.1, the results provide a rough indication of the effect of the business cycle on economic and social outcomes for various groups. The table clearly indicates that good things tend to happen in good times. For example, the unemployment rate of African Americans fell to its lowest level ever recorded in the economic expansion that culminated in 2000. In addition, between 1992 and 2000, the average real income of the bottom 20 percent of households grew more rapidly (15 percent) than did that of the middle 20 percent (12 percent), while the income of the wealthiest 20 percent of households grew the fastest (25 percent). In the 1989 to 1992 downturn, families at the bottom experienced the greatest relative decline in income (8 percent). The poverty rate also rose in that recession and fell in the subsequent growth period. Extreme poverty—defined as having income less than half the poverty line for one's household size—also moves with the business cycle, although it is less sensitive to business conditions because individuals in extreme poverty are less connected to the labor market. Undesirable

TABLE 10.1 / Economic and Social Outcomes over Recent Business Cycles (Percent)

	Peak, 1989	Trough, 1992	Peak, 2000
Economic indicators:			
Unemployment rate (percent):[a]			
Overall	5.3	7.5	4.0
White	4.5	6.6	3.5
Black	11.4	14.2	7.6
Hispanic	8.0	11.6	5.7
Poverty rate (percent):[b,c]			
Overall poverty rate	12.8	14.8	11.8
Extreme poverty (less than half the poverty line)	4.9	6.1	4.6
Average household income ($):[b,d]			
Bottom 20 percent	9,433	8,654	9,940
Middle 20 percent	38,862	36,373	40,879
Top 20 percent	114,912	108,189	135,401
Federal surplus (+) or deficit (−) as a percentage of GDP[e]	−2.8	−4.7	1.7
Social indicators:			
Violent crimes per 1,000 people:[f]			
Household income < $7,500	...	84.7	57.5
Household income ≥ $75,000	...	41.3	22.9
Welfare-utilization rate (percent):[g]	4.4	5.3	2.1
High school dropout rate (percent):[h,i]	12.6	11.0	11.8
Single-parent rate (percent):[h,j]	24.4	26.7	27.7

[a]U.S. Bureau of the Census (1995).
[b]Income and poverty data for 2000 are not yet available, so 1999 data are used. Income is in 1999 dollars, deflated by the Consumer Price Index for All Urban Consumers.
[c]U.S. Bureau of the Census (2000).
[d]U.S. Bureau of the Census (2000).
[e]*Budget of the United States Government* (2001, tables 1.1 and 10.1). Surplus-to-GDP ratio for 2000 is an estimate.
[f]U.S. Department of Justice (2000). Criminal-victimization data are for 1993 and 1999 and pertain to people aged 12 and older.
[g]Committee on Ways and Means (2000); and U.S. Bureau of the Census (2000). Welfare-utilization figures for 2000 are for June.
[h]Data for 1998 are used, more recent data not being currently available.
[i]*Digest of Education Statistics* (1999, table 108). The high school–dropout rate is for sixteen- to twenty-four-year-olds.
[j]U.S. Bureau of the Census (1998) and earlier reports to be found at *http://www.census.gov/population/socdemo/ms-la/tabch-1.txt*.

social outcomes, such as criminal victimization and welfare participation, also appear to improve during expansions.

On the other hand, the high school dropout rate moves mildly counter-cyclically, perhaps in response to greater labor-market opportunities (see, for example, Card and Lemieux 2000), and the single-parent rate has been growing secularly. Nevertheless, the picture that emerges from table 10.1 is that of a rising tide continuing to lift all boats, the dinghies at least as much as the yachts, while a falling tide submerges many of the least seaworthy vessels.

The properties of employment, earnings, income, and real wages over the business cycle have been the most thoroughly studied in the literature. The first section reviews and extends the evidence on the cyclic pattern of employment, earnings, and real wages. The results point to a strong procyclic pattern of employment and work hours—lower-skilled individuals are particularly likely to find employment and work longer hours when the labor market tightens. In addition, real wages are mildly procyclic. We also find that changes in unemployment have a larger effect on family earnings and other outcomes at later stages of a recovery or recession, and we find some evidence of asymmetry over the cycle: the harmful effect of a 1 percentage point increase in unemployment during a downturn exceeds the helpful effect of a decline of equal magnitude during an upturn. Consequently, a less volatile economy (that is, one with fewer downturns) is predicted to lead to better long-run outcomes than a more volatile economy with the same average growth rate.

The cyclic pattern of wage data is difficult to interpret because the composition of employment changes over the course of a business cycle. In the second section, we use the Panel Study of Income Dynamics (PSID) to examine the cyclic pattern of real wages for a balanced sample of individuals, following earlier work by Gary Solon, Robert Barsky, and Jonathan Parker (1994). Like theirs, our findings suggest that real-wage gains accrue during a tight labor market even for a fixed set of workers; changes in the composition of the workforce tend to attenuate only slightly (if at all) the cyclic wage effect found in unbalanced samples. However, the responsiveness of wages to unemployment may have declined in the last two decades.

A more difficult question is whether the benefits of a high-pressure economy are lasting. Do they extend beyond the boundaries of a particular business cycle? If the benefits prove to be persistent—for example, by changing the long-run mix of jobs—then a high-pressure economy has even more going for it than is commonly appreciated. Arthur Okun (1973, 208), for example, presented evidence suggestive of "an upgrading of workers into more productive jobs in a higher-pressure economy." The discussant of Okun's paper was none other than Alan Greenspan, who was skeptical of the long-term benefits of a high-pressure economy. "It is by no means clear to me," Greenspan (1973, 257) remarked, "that class A employment [jobs with career ladders] can be promoted sustainably through high-pressure economic expansions." The results that we present in our second section provide suggestive evidence that a high-pressure economy makes it somewhat more likely that workers will move from dead-end jobs to jobs with upwardly sloping seniority profiles.

The third section broadens our examination of the importance of cycles by looking at the effects on crime, welfare participation, health, and education. Interestingly, work injuries, which are typically procyclic, declined considerably in the economic upturn of 1992 to 2000.

Finally, the effect of strong economic growth on government finances has received little attention in the literature. Table 10.1 suggests that the federal government's financial position is particularly buoyant when the economy grows. The federal-government budget deficit swelled to a seemingly intractable 4.7 percent of GDP at the depth of the 1992 downturn, while a surplus equal to 1.7 percent of GDP is estimated for 2000. Although cause and effect are difficult to distinguish, these figures suggest that the very strong procyclic nature of federal-government revenues may carry important implications for the economy. Indeed, the Treasury seems to be a major beneficiary of a strong economy.

In the fourth section, we consider the effect of the business cycle on the level and distribution of government expenditures across spending categories. We focus on the state- and local-government level to exploit regional variability in economic conditions. The evidence indicates that all components of state- and local-government spending are procyclic, with capital spending (for example, highways and parks and recreation) generally more procyclic than current spending (for example, health and education). An important, and striking, exception is welfare spending, levels of which are not only procyclic, but more strongly so than any other category of government spending. Since average individual needs for public assistance are countercyclic, the procyclic nature of total welfare spending indicates that public generosity per welfare recipient is powerfully procyclic. Hence, the cyclic nature of public finances reinforces the notion that the affluence associated with good economic times expands society's resources and thereby provides benefits to all income groups.

THE EFFECT OF THE BUSINESS CYCLE ON EMPLOYMENT, HOURS, AND EARNINGS

Previous Literature

The properties of employment, earnings, and wages have received the most attention in the literature. In particular, prior research has examined the effect of business cycles and local labor-market conditions on employment outcomes (Bartik 1991, 1993a, 1993b, 1996; Blanchard and Katz 1992; Holzer 1991; Hoynes 2000a), real wages (Bils 1985; Blank 1990; Keane, Moffitt, and Runkle 1988; Solon, Barsky, and Parker 1994), racial differences in labor-market outcomes (Bound and Holzer 1993, 1995), labor-market outcomes of disadvantaged youths (Acs and Wissoker 1991; Bound and Freeman 1992; Cain and Finnie 1990; Freeman 1982, 1991a, 1991b; Freeman and Rodgers 2000), and family income, poverty, and income inequality (Bartik 1994; Blank 1989, 1993; Blank and Blinder 1986; Blank and Card 1993; Cutler and Katz 1991; Freeman 2001). These studies almost universally find that labor-market outcomes are procyclic, with greater sensitivity among lower-skilled groups.

The studies of disadvantaged youths relate labor-market outcomes to local (typically, metropolitan statistical area, or MSA) unemployment rates. That literature has consistently found that higher local unemployment rates lead to reductions in employment and earnings (Acs and Wissoker 1991; Bound and Freeman 1992; Cain and Finnie 1990; Freeman 1982, 1991a, 1991b; Freeman and Rodgers 2000), with larger effects for blacks, younger workers, and less-educated workers (Acs and Wissoker 1991; Freeman 1991a). Using micro data, David Ellwood (1982) finds that extended spells of nonemployment among teenagers have a small effect on future employment prospects but a large, adverse effect on future wages.

Other studies have examined how MSAs' labor-market conditions affect employment and wages in the population (Bartik 1991, 1993a, 1993b, 1994, 1996; Bound and Holzer 1993, 1995). These studies estimate the effect of the growth and changing composition of MSA employment on area employment and earnings. The results differ somewhat across studies, but they generally show that changes in labor demand lead to larger changes for blacks, younger persons, and those with lower education levels. The patterns seem to hold for men and women. William Wilson (1996) carefully documents the decline in employment among low-skilled males since the late 1960s, a decline that he attributes to the fall in availability of jobs in central cities.

Hilary Hoynes (2000a) examines the effect of business cycles on the employment, earnings, and income of persons in different demographic groups defined by sex, education, and race. The business-cycle effects are identified using variation across MSAs in the timing and severity of shocks. The results consistently show that individuals with lower education levels, nonwhites, and low-skilled women experience greater cyclic fluctuation than do high-skilled men. The results are the most striking when examining comprehensive measures of labor-force activity, such as the likelihood of full-year, full-time work. Government transfers and the earnings of other family members decrease the differences between groups, as business cycles have more skill-group-neutral effects on family income than on individual earnings. The evidence further suggests that the 1992 recession led to more uniform effects across skill groups than did earlier cycles.

Studies of family income and poverty have typically used either national (Blank 1989, 1993; Blank and Blinder 1986; Cutler and Katz 1991) or regional (Blank and Card 1993) variation in unemployment rates or GNP as cyclic indicators. Such studies find a consistent negative relation between unemployment rates and inequality and poverty. In particular, Rebecca Blank (1989) disaggregates household income into many components and finds earnings and capital income to be procyclic and some transfer income to be countercyclic. Overall, she finds greater variation in income over the cycle for those who are young, male, and nonwhite. More recently, Richard Freeman (2001) used a pooled cross-state time-series model to examine the effect of earnings, unemployment, and inequality on poverty. He finds that decreases in unemployment or increases in real wages lead to declines in poverty.

Distinct from the literature on labor-market outcomes are empirical studies, dating back at least to John Dunlop (1938), that examine the cyclic nature of real wages. More recently, panel data have been brought to bear on this issue. This literature primarily uses aggregate measures of business cycles (national unemployment rates or GNP growth) and examines the degree to which real wages fluctuate with the business cycle and whether changes in the composition of the workforce over the cycle (for example, more low-paid new entrants during upturns) confound procyclic movements in wages. Katherine Abraham and John Haltiwanger (1995) provide a thorough review of this literature. A growing body of evidence uses panel data to hold the composition of the workforce constant over the cycle by focusing on a fixed sample of workers. Mark Bils (1985) uses the National Longitudinal Survey and concludes that composition changes have only a small effect on the cyclic nature of real wages, while Solon, Barsky, and Parker (1994, 3) use the PSID and conclude that "the apparent weakness of real wage cyclicality in the United States has been substantially exaggerated by a statistical illusion," namely, changes in the composition of the workforce. Solon, Barsky, and Parker attribute the difference between their conclusion and Bils's to his focus on young men, which misses changes in the age composition of the workforce. Our reading of the evidence is that real wages have moved slightly procyclically since 1970, although we agree with Abraham and Haltiwanger (1995, 1262) that "the cyclicality of real wages is not likely to be stable over time."

An important issue that arises throughout the literature is whether one should use national, regional, or metropolitan-area controls for business cycles. The main appeal of using the national cycle is that it is measured relatively precisely and reflects movements in the aggregate economy. However, there are two principal weaknesses of using an aggregate cycle measure: first, it may pick up the influences of unmeasured aggregate variables; second, it suffers from low power because the number of aggregate cycles is small. Furthermore, the use of an aggregate measure of the cycle does not exploit regional differences in the business cycle. In contrast, using regional or metropolitan-area variation in labor-market conditions leads to a substantial increase in the size of the estimation sample. This will, in general, lead to more precise estimates and allows for the estimation of models with unrestricted time effects. The time effects control for the unmeasured aggregate variables that are a concern in the aggregate models. Furthermore, some argue that labor-market outcomes are more influenced by local variables than by national variables (Blanchflower and Oswald 1994; Bartik 1994). However, using state or metropolitan areas introduces measurement error in the unemployment rate. In fact, the Current Population Survey (CPS), the main data set used in this area, is not designed for reliable estimates of most MSAs. Two other issues that argue against using metropolitan samples are that the boundaries of these areas change (perhaps endogenously) over time and that metropolitan areas do not cover the entire United States.

Another estimation issue that arises is whether the data should be specified as a Phillips curve or a wage-curve relation. The Phillips curve relates the *change* in the dependent variable (for example, log wages) to the *level* of the unemployment rate. The wage curve relates the level of the dependent variable to the level of the unemployment rate. In first-differences, the wage curve relates the growth of wages to the change in the unemployment rate over the corresponding time period. The wage-curve specification assumes that wages are higher when (or where) unemployment is low. The Phillips curve specification assumes that wages are growing when unemployment is low.

David Blanchflower and Andrew Oswald (1994) promote the wage-curve relation. David Card (1995) and Olivier Blanchard and Lawrence Katz (1997) test whether wage data are more consistent with the Phillips curve or the wage curve and conclude that a Phillips curve provides a better description of wage data. Interestingly, Blanchard and Katz interpret the Phillips curve as a wage curve, in which the wage in year $t - 1$ is proxying for the reservation wage. Because a wage-curve specification has a more natural theoretical interpretation and fits the data (hours as well as wages) that we use better than the Phillips curve specification does, in the subsequent analysis we estimate wage-curve specifications. Our main qualitative conclusions are likely to be similar if a Phillips curve specification were used instead.

Our findings for the labor market, presented in this section and the next, extend the literature by providing estimates through 1999—allowing us to analyze the effect of the sustained recovery and to examine whether this cycle is different from earlier cycles. We also examine the effect of cycles in more detail by exploring whether changes in unemployment have different effects in booms and busts or whether the length of the current boom or bust has an effect independent of the unemployment rate.

Estimating Effects of Cycles Using Time-Series Data

A natural starting point is to estimate the simplest model using annual time-series data on average annual hours worked and unemployment rates. We use a sample of persons aged twenty to fifty-five from the March CPS covering the years 1975 to 1999 to calculate average annual hours worked in each year and combine it with Bureau of Labor Statistics (BLS) data on annual unemployment rates. The March CPS is an annual demographic file that includes labor-market and income information for the previous year, at the individual and family levels. The sample size is approximately 150,000 persons per year.[2]

Annual hours worked is averaged over workers and nonworkers and thus reflects changes in the employment rate as well as in the intensity of work. We use this "prime-age" sample to minimize the effects of early-retirement and early-schooling decisions. We estimate a specification that regresses the year-to-year change in the log of average annual hours worked (ΔLNHRS) on the year-to-year change in the unemployment rate (ΔUR). We chose this specification after exploring several different ones. The first-differenced specification consistently provided a better fit to the data than did a Phillips curve specification (that is, change on level). We use the first-differenced specification throughout the paper. The coefficient estimates and standard errors for the time-series model are

$$\Delta LNHRS = 0.010 - 0.015(\Delta UR) - 0.0003(year), \quad R^2 = 0.87.$$
$$ (0.002) \quad (0.001) (0.0001)$$

A 3 percentage point decrease in the unemployment rate—about the size of the reduction experienced in the recovery since the 1992 trough—is associated with a 4.5 percent increase in average hours worked. To put this magnitude in perspective, note that annual work hours averaged 1,538 over this time period and ranged from a low of 1,378 to a high of 1,675. At the overall average, hours would increase by almost seventy, or two weeks of full-time work a year.

Using the National Bureau of Economic Research (NBER) national-business-cycle dating, we can allow the effect of the unemployment rate to differ in expansions (EXP) and contractions (REC). The coefficient estimates and standard errors are

$$\Delta LNHRS = 0.011 - 0.014(\Delta UR \times EXP) - 0.017(\Delta UR \times REC)$$
$$ (0.003) \quad (0.002) (0.002)$$
$$ - 0.0004(year), \quad R^2 = 0.87.$$
$$ (0.0002)$$

This suggests that a given change in the unemployment rate has a larger effect in a recession than in an expansion, although the differences are not statistically significant.[3]

To examine how stable the relation is over time, we add a dummy for POST89 and interact it with the change in the unemployment rate. The estimates for that model are

$$\Delta LNHRS = 0.005 - 0.009(POST89) - 0.015(\Delta UR)$$
$$ (0.003) \quad (0.004) (0.001)$$
$$ + 0.004(\Delta UR \times POST89) - 0.0003(year), \quad R^2 = 0.90.$$
$$ (0.003) (0.0003)$$

Although not precisely estimated, the results show that the effect of a change in the unemployment rate has decreased in the last cycle.

An alternative cyclic indicator to the unemployment rate is the Federal Reserve Board's capacity-utilization rate (CU). The capacity-utilization rate captures the concept of sustainable practical capacity and is equal to an output index divided by a capacity index. We were motivated to look at capacity utilization because James H. Stock and Mark W. Watson (1999) and others have highlighted the fact that the price Phillips curve is much more stable if one uses the capacity-utilization rate in place of the unemployment rate. The basic time-series first-difference model using capacity utilization yields the estimates:

$$\Delta LNHRS = \underset{(0.004)}{0.006} + \underset{(0.001)}{0.004}(\Delta CU) + \underset{(0.0003)}{0.0001}(\text{year}), \quad R^2 = 0.69.$$

A 3.5 percentage point increase in the capacity-utilization rate—the increase in the last recovery—is associated with a 1.4 percent increase in average annual hours. (We have divided the capacity-utilization rate by 100 in the regression, with the result that a 3.5 percentage point increase is equal to 0.035.) This suggests a weaker effect compared to that of a change in the unemployment rate.

Like the effect of a change in the unemployment rate, the marginal effect of a change in the capacity-utilization rate is larger in recessions:

$$\Delta LNHRS = \underset{(0.005)}{0.012} + \underset{(0.001)}{0.003}(\Delta CU \times EXP) + \underset{(0.001)}{0.006}(\Delta CU \times REC)$$

$$- \underset{(0.0003)}{0.0002}(\text{year}), \quad R^2 = 0.73.$$

Here, the coefficients are significantly different at the 10 percent level. Unlike the Phillips curve, however, the first-difference log of annual hours shows essentially the same degree of stability with either capacity utilization or the unemployment rate as the cyclic indicator. Adding the POST89 dummy and interaction to the model generates the following estimates:

$$\Delta LNHRS = \underset{(0.004)}{-0.001} - \underset{(0.006)}{0.017}(\text{POST89}) + \underset{(0.001)}{0.005}(\Delta CU)$$

$$- \underset{(0.002)}{0.002}(\Delta CU \times \text{POST89}) + \underset{(0.0004)}{0.001}(\text{year}), \quad R^2 = 0.80.$$

As with the unemployment rate results, we find that the effect of a change in the capacity-utilization rate has decreased in the last decade, although this change is insignificant.

While these results provide a simple summary of the data, the use of aggregate data is somewhat limiting. In particular, the cyclic indicators (unemployment rates and capacity-utilization rates) may, to some degree, pick up other unmeasured aggregate variables. In the next subsection, we extend our analysis by presenting models that take advantage of regional variation in the timing and severity of cycles. This increases the power of the empirical analysis and, by including year dummies, controls for the effect of unmeasured aggregate variables that cut across regions.

Employment, Earnings, and Wages and MSA-Specific Cycles

The aggregate regression will yield biased estimates if there are omitted factors that are correlated with the unemployment rate and that affect labor-market outcomes (for example, nationwide government-policy changes). We follow other recent papers in the literature (for example, Freeman and Rodgers 2000; Hoynes 2000a) by using MSA-level data to take advantage of the substantial variation in business cycles across regions in the United States and account for time effects. As previously, we start with a sample of persons aged twenty to fifty-five from the March CPS. The analysis uses data from the 1977 to 2000 CPS surveys, which cover the years 1976 to 1999. In each year, we calculate various labor-market outcomes for each MSA identified in the CPS sample. In particular, we calculate the fraction employed at some time during the year (called the annual EPOP, or employment-to-population rate) and mean values for hours worked, earnings, and hourly wages. Our measure of average wages is confined to workers, while the other outcome variables do not condition on work status. We also examine family outcomes, including mean family earnings, income, and poverty rates.[4]

Because we are ultimately interested in examining whether responsiveness to cycles varies across groups, we form demographic groups defined by education (less than twelve years, twelve years, thirteen to fifteen years, and sixteen or more years), race (white, nonwhite), and sex.[5] The regressions are based on cell-level data where the cells are defined by MSA, year, and demographic group. All regressions are estimated by weighted least squares, using as weights the number of observations in each cell.

We will rely on the unemployment rate as our main measure of the cycle. The MSA-level unemployment rates are available on an annual basis beginning in 1976 from the BLS Local Area Unemployment Statistics division.[6] Instead of using the national NBER dates of business cycles, we use the timing of the cycles at the census-division level. Specifically, we assigned cycle peaks and troughs for each of the nine regions by examining the local minimums and maximums in the division-level unemployment rates. Each MSA was assigned the cycle dates corresponding to the census division in which it is located.

These data allow us to estimate equations of the following form:

$$\Delta \log(y_{jmt}) = \alpha_j + \lambda_m + \theta_t + \gamma \Delta UR_{mt} + \varepsilon_{jmt},$$

where y_{jmt} is the mean labor-market outcome (such as mean real hourly wages) for demographic group j in MSA m in time t, and UR_{mt} is the unemployment rate in MSA m in period t. The regression also includes unrestricted effects for demographic group (α_j), MSA (λ_m), and time (θ_t). The identification of the key parameter, γ, comes from differences in the timing and severity of cycles across MSAs.

For comparability to the earlier aggregate analysis, we first relate the change in the log of average annual hours at the MSA-year-group level to the change in

TABLE 10.2 / Determinants of Change in MSA Log Average Annual Hours Worked, March CPS, 1976 to 1999

	(1)	(2)	(3)	(4)	(5)
ΔUR (national)	−.016	−.016			
	(.001)	(.001)			
ΔUR (MSA)			−.012	−.012	−.008
			(.001)	(.001)	(.001)
Additional controls (fixed effects)	None	Demographic group, MSA	None	Demographic group, MSA	Demographic group, MSA, year
Observations	44,773	44,733	44,733	44,733	44,733

Notes: Authors' tabulations of the 1977 to 2000 March CPS. The sample consists of persons aged twenty to fifty-five with positive CPS weights. The observations are MSA-demographic group-year cells. The demographic groups are defined by *race* (nonblack, black), *gender* (male, female), and *education* (< twelve, twelve, thirteen to fifteen, sixteen+). The dependent variable is the first-difference of log average annual hours worked in the MSA-demographic group-year cell. It is a weighted regression with the number of CPS observations in the cells as the weight. The unemployment rate, UR, is measured as a percentage of the labor force. Standard errors are in parentheses.

the aggregate unemployment rate. These results, shown in column 1 of table 10.2, utilize nationwide time-series variability in the cycle. The MSA cell-level analysis generates essentially the same estimates that we find for the country as a whole. Column 2 adds fixed effects for demographic group and MSA, which does not substantively change the estimates. Column 3 replaces the national unemployment rate with the MSA-level unemployment rate. The results show that the coefficient on the change in the unemployment rate is about one-quarter lower at the MSA level: a 3 percentage point reduction in the mean unemployment rate is associated with a 3.6 percent increase in average annual hours in an MSA. This smaller effect may be due to measurement error in the MSA unemployment rate or to different responses to local and national labor-market shocks. Column 4 adds fixed effects for demographic groups and MSAs, which does not alter the results. Adding time effects in column 5, however, reduces the effect of the unemployment rate by another third. This suggests that there are factors not being controlled for that are associated with higher unemployment rates and lower average annual hours worked.[7] All the remaining estimates in this section are from models that control for year, MSA, and demographic group.

Going beyond the use of annual hours as the labor-market measure, table 10.3 presents estimates for the full set of individual labor-market and family-outcome variables. The estimates in panel A are of the same specification as that used in column 5 of table 10.2. These estimates show that labor-market outcomes are strongly procyclic. The results indicate that annual earnings are more procyclic than are annual hours and that real hourly wages are less procyclic than are

TABLE 10.3 / Estimating the Effect of Cycles on Labor-Market Outcomes across MSAs Using the CPS, 1976 to 1999, Basic Specifications

Key Explanatory Variable	Change in Annual EPOP (Level)	Change in Log Annual Hours	Change in Log Real Annual Earnings	Change in Log Real Hourly Wage (Workers)	Change in Log Real Family Earnings	Change in Log Real Family Income	Change in Family Poverty Rate (Level)
A. Base case							
ΔUR	−.0030	−.0077	−.0097	−.0043	−.0121	−.0090	.0022
	(.0006)	(.0014)	(.0020)	(.0017)	(.0024)	(.0019)	(.0009)
B. Asymmetries in effect of unemployment rate							
ΔUR × recession	−.0043	−.0136	−.0144	−.0020	−.0173	−.0128	.0045
	(.0011)	(.0023)	(.0033)	(.0028)	(.0040)	(.0032)	(.0015)
ΔUR × expansion	−.0022	−.0040	−.0067	−.0057	−.0087	−.0066	.0008
	(.0008)	(.0018)	(.0026)	(.0022)	(.0031)	(.0025)	(.0012)
p-value for test of equal coefficients	.132	.001	.075	.310	.097	.141	.062

Note: Authors' tabulations of the 1977 to 2000 March CPS. The sample consists of persons aged twenty to fifty-five with positive CPS weights. The observations are MSA-demographic group-year cells. The demographic groups are defined by race (nonblack, black), gender (male, female), and education (< twelve, twelve, thirteen to fifteen, sixteen +). The dependent variable is the change in the (log or level) of the mean of the variable within the MSA-year-demographic cell. MSA unemployment rates are used. The model also includes fixed effects for demographic group, MSA, and year. It is a weighted regression with the number of CPS observations in the cells as the weight. The change in the unemployment rate, denoted ΔUR, is measured as a percentage of the labor force. Annual EPOP is the proportion of the population that worked during the year. Poverty rate is measured as a proportion of families. Standard errors are in parentheses.

wages or earnings. Average wages are particularly difficult to interpret when using pooled cross-sectional data since the mean is taken over a changing population if the composition of the workforce changes. We will address this issue in the next section using panel data from the PSID.[8]

The last three columns in table 10.3 examine the cyclic nature of family outcomes. An analysis of families may differ from one of individuals in that families contain varying numbers of potential workers with differences in propensities for intrafamily substitution of labor-market activity. Furthermore, family income and poverty status depend on government transfers, which are strongly procyclic. The basic estimates show that, as expected, family earnings and income are strongly procyclic and poverty rates countercyclic. Family income is less cyclic than family earnings (presumably owing to countercyclic transfers). The results suggest that the 3 percentage point reduction in unemployment rates in the economic recovery of the 1990s led to a 0.6 percentage point reduction in the poverty rate. The actual decline in the family-level poverty rate was 2.6 percentage points, so either other factors were at work, or the relation has become stronger over time.

Panel B of table 10.3 allows the effect of the unemployment rate to differ in recessions and expansions. As explained above, the cycles are dated using the nine census divisions. There seems to be an asymmetrical effect of unemployment in recessions and expansions. For employment, hours, and earnings, the effect of a change in unemployment rates is larger in recessions. The only exception is real hourly wages, which have a larger (but not statistically different) effect in expansions. These results imply that recessions tend to inflict a sharp amount of pain in a short period but that upswings lead to gradual improvements.

The models estimated in table 10.4 explore how the cyclic nature of labor market exerience varies across education groups and over time. Panel A of table 10.4 adds to the base model a set of interactions of the four education groups with the change in the unemployment rate. The results show that lower-education groups (especially those without a high school diploma) are much more responsive to cycles than are higher-education groups. For example, the results for annual earnings show that a 1 percentage point increase in unemployment leads to a 2.5 percent reduction in annual earnings for those with less than a high school education, compared to a 1 percent decline for those with a high school education, a 0.5 percent decline for those with some college, and a 0.1 percent decline for those with a college degree or more. In further results not shown here, nonwhites are more cyclic than whites, and women are less cyclic than men, the latter result due in part to women's behaving as added workers.

Referring back to table 10.3, in the sample as a whole, family income exhibits slightly less cyclic variation compared to family earnings (-0.012 versus -0.009). This tendency is present for all education groups but is much more pronounced for those with lower education levels. For example, among those with less than a high school education, a 1 percentage point increase in unemployment is associated with a 2.6 percent decline in family earnings but a 1.6

TABLE 10.4 / Estimating the Effect of Cycles on Labor-Market Outcomes in MSAs Using the CPS, 1976 to 1999, Exploring Differences across Education Groups and Time

	Change in Annual EPOP (Level)	Change in Log Annual Hours	Change in Log Real Annual Earnings	Change in Log Real Hourly Wage (Workers)	Change in Log Real Family Earnings	Change in Log Real Family Income	Change in Family Poverty Rate (Level)
A. Differences across education groups							
ΔUR × less than high school	−.005	−.020	−.025	−.005	−.026	−.016	.006
	(.001)	(.003)	(.004)	(.003)	(.005)	(.004)	(.002)
ΔUR × high school graduate	−.004	−.008	−.010	−.005	−.014	−.011	.003
	(.001)	(.002)	(.003)	(.002)	(.004)	(.003)	(.001)
ΔUR × some college	−.002	−.005	−.005	−.002	−.009	−.009	.003
	(.001)	(.002)	(.003)	(.003)	(.004)	(.004)	(.002)
ΔUR × college graduate or more	−.0002	.0004	−.001	−.005	−.002	−.001	−.001
	(.001)	(.002)	(.003)	(.003)	(.004)	(.004)	(.002)
B. Structural break in effect of unemployment rate							
ΔUR	−.003	−.008	−.012	−.005	−.013	−.010	.002
	(.001)	(.002)	(.003)	(.002)	(.003)	(.003)	(.001)
ΔUR × Post89	−.001	.001	.006	.002	.003	.002	.001
	(.001)	(.003)	(.004)	(.003)	(.005)	(.004)	(.002)

Notes: Authors' tabulations of the 1977 to 2000 March CPS. The sample consists of persons aged twenty to fifty-five with positive CPS weights. The observations are MSA-demographic group-year cells. Demographic groups are defined by *race* (nonblack, black), *gender* (male, female), and *education* (< twelve, twelve, thirteen to fifteen, sixteen +). The dependent variable is the change in the (log or level) of the mean of the variable within the MSA-year-demographic cell. MSA unemployment rates are used. The model also includes fixed effects for demographic group, MSA, and year. It is a weighted regression with the number of CPS observations in the cells as the weight. The change in the unemployment rate, denoted ΔUR, is measured as a percentage of the labor force. Annual EPOP is the proportion of the population that worked during the year. Poverty rate is measured as a proportion of families. Standard errors are in parentheses.

percent decline in family income, while, among those with a college degree, a 1 percentage point increase in unemployment leads to a 0.2 percent decline in family earnings and a 0.1 percent decline in family income. Thus, adding non-labor income to family earnings significantly reduces the differences in cyclic responses across demographic groups. This pattern was also found by Blank (1989), Blank and Card (1993), and Hoynes (2000a) and seems to be due to the effects of countercyclic income-transfer programs such as public assistance and unemployment compensation.

Panel B of table 10.4 tests for a structural break in the effect of unemployment rates. In particular, we examine whether the most recent cycle (captured by the dummy POST89) differs from the earlier period 1976 to 1989. As does the earlier aggregate regression, the point estimates here generally show that sensitivity to the cycle decreased slightly in the 1990s. However, these differences are not statistically significant. It is possible, of course, that our simple structural break in 1989 does not capture what is a more complicated time structure to the cyclic nature of unemployment. Our results are also consistent with those of Freeman (2001), who finds little change in the effect of the unemployment rate on poverty over time, conditional on changes in inequality and wage growth. These results suggest that the decline in the poverty rate in the 1990s is only partially a result of the tight labor market. Freeman's analysis suggests that factors such as declining inequality and the rising median wage in the latter part of the 1990s, apart from low unemployment, also played a role.

Does the Duration of the Recession/Expansion Have an Effect?

The specifications used earlier assume that a percentage point change in the unemployment rate has a uniform effect on labor-market outcomes independent of the tightness of the market or point in the expansion or recession. Table 10.5 extends the analysis by including two additional variables: the duration of the recession and the duration of the expansion. The duration of the recession is measured as the number of years since the most recent peak (if in a recession, 0 otherwise). The duration of the expansion is measured similarly as the number of years since the most recent trough (if in a expansion, 0 otherwise). These duration variables are constructed using business-cycle dates specific to each of the nine census divisions. This specification is a simple way in which to incorporate the dynamic effects of the business cycle on labor-market outcomes.

Panel A of table 10.5 repeats the estimates of the base-case specification in table 10.3 for comparison. Panel B adds the duration variables to the base-case specification. Adding these variables does not significantly change the importance of the unemployment rate. The point estimates on the duration variables show that, holding the change in unemployment rates constant, increasing the length of the recession by a year leads to a worsening of labor-market outcomes and that increasing the length of the expansion leads to an improvement in

TABLE 10.5 / Estimating the Impact of Cycles on Labor Market Outcomes Across MSAs Using the CPS, Exploring the Role of Length of Recession/Expansion

	Change in Annual EPOP (Level)	Change in Log Annual Hours	Change in Log Real Annual Earnings	Change in Log Real Hourly Wage (Workers)	Change in Log Real Family Earnings	Change in Log Real Family Income	Change in Family Poverty Rate (Level)
A. Base case							
ΔUR	−.0030	−.0077	−.0097	−.0043	−.0121	−.0090	.0022
	(.0006)	(.0014)	(.0020)	(.0017)	(.0024)	(.0019)	(.0009)
B. Adding duration of recession/expansion							
ΔUR	−.0028	−.0071	−.0094	−.0048	−.0108	−.0083	.0019
	(.0007)	(.0014)	(.0021)	(.0017)	(.0024)	(.0020)	(.0009)
Duration of recession (years)	−.0012	−.0025	−.0006	.0031	−.0039	−.0023	.0016
	(.0009)	(.0019)	(.0028)	(.0023)	(.0033)	(.0027)	(.0013)
Duration of expansion (years)	−.0002	.0003	.0008	.0007	.0017	.0009	.0000
	(.0005)	(.0011)	(.0016)	(.0013)	(.0019)	(.0015)	(.0007)
p-value for test of equal and opposite coefficients	.236	.380	.949	.207	.620	.313	.313
p-value for joint significance of duration variables	.43	.31	.22	.91	.20	.43	.38

C. Also interacting duration of recession/expansion with change in unemployment rate

ΔUR	−.0024	−.0039	−.0022	−.0033	−.0030	−.0000
	(.0014)	(.0029)	(.0042)	(.0035)	(.0050)	(.0041)
ΔUR × duration of recession (years)	−.0006	−.0034	−.0043	.0007	−.0051	−.0047
	(.0006)	(.0013)	(.0019)	(.0015)	(.0023)	(.0018)
ΔUR × duration of expansion (years)	.0000	−.0004	−.0019	−.0009	−.0024	−.0025
	(.0004)	(.0009)	(.0013)	(.0011)	(.0016)	(.0013)
p-value for joint significance of duration interactions	.39	.02	.08	.35	.08	.03

Notes: Authors' tabulations of the 1977 to 2000 March CPS. The sample consists of persons aged twenty to fifty-five with positive CPS weights. The observations are MSA-demographic group-year cells. The demographic groups are defined by *race* (nonblack, black), *gender* (male, female), and *education* (< twelve, twelve, thirteen to fifteen, sixteen +). The dependent variable is the change in the (log or level) of the mean of the variable within the MSA-year-demographic cell. MSA unemployment rates are used. Duration of recession and expansion corresponds to the cycles in the census division in which the MSA resides. The model also includes fixed effects for demographic group, MSA, and year. It is a weighted regression with the number of CPS observations in the cells as the weight. The change in the unemployment rate, denoted ΔUR, is measured as a percentage of the labor force. Annual EPOP is the proportion of the population that worked during the year. Poverty rate is measured as a portion of families. Standard errors are in parentheses.

labor-market outcomes. The recession effects are much larger than the expansion effects, probably reflecting the fact that recessions are typically shorter and more intense than expansions. The test statistics reported in the table, however, indicate that the duration variables are jointly and individually insignificant.

Panel C of table 10.5 presents estimates in which we include interactions between the change in the unemployment rate and the duration of the expansion and contraction (as well as including the main effect of the change in the unemployment rate). This specification allows the effect of a given change in the unemployment rate to differ with years into the expansion or recession. These results show important and statistically significant effects. Consider, for example, annual earnings. A 1 percentage point reduction in the unemployment rate in the second year into an expansion leads to a 0.6 percent increase in mean real earnings (0.002 + 2 × 0.0019), while the same reduction in the eighth year into an expansion leads to a 1.8 percent increase in mean real earnings (0.002 + 8 × 0.0019). These results could explain why such large improvements in earnings and family income were experienced toward the end of the 1990s.

COMPOSITION OF WORKFORCE AND JOBS OVER THE CYCLE

Balanced and Unbalanced Samples of Workers from the PSID

Employment of and hours worked by less-skilled workers in particular tend to rise during an upturn in the economy, as indicated by table 10.4. Even within narrowly defined demographic groups, the composition of the workforce could change over the business cycle. If lower-paid workers are induced to join the labor force during an upswing, then the cyclic wage effects estimated previously will be understated—that is, the average wage will be pulled down by lower-paid new entrants. To explore the effect of a change in the composition of the workforce on the cyclic behavior of real wages, we extend the analysis of Solon, Barsky, and Parker (1994) in tables 10.6 and 10.7. These researchers examined the cyclic nature of real wages for a *balanced* set of workers to prevent composition changes from affecting their results.

Table 10.6 uses the PSID to explore the cyclic nature of real wages for a balanced sample of individuals. Annual earnings data are currently available for 1967 to 1996, collected in the 1968 to 1997 waves of the survey. Following Solon, Barsky, and Parker, we initially restricted the sample to male household heads aged twenty-five to fifty-nine who were *continuously* employed at least one hundred hours each year from 1967 to 1987. Using this sample, we calculated mean log real hourly earnings each year, denoted $\ln(W_t)$.[9] We regressed the year-over-year change in $\ln(W_t)$ on the change in the national unemployment rate and a linear time trend.[10] Results are reported in column 1 of table 10.6. Column 2 reports the same estimated regression model but uses the change in log real GNP as a cyclic indicator instead of the unemployment rate. Because the sample

TABLE 10.6 / Aggregate First-Differenced Wage-Curve Estimates for Balanced Sample of Men, PSID, 1968 to 1987 and 1977 to 1996 (Dependent Variable: Annual Change in Mean Log Real Wage)

	Sample			
	1967/1968 to 1986/1987		1976/1977 to 1995/1996	
	(1)	(2)	(3)	(4)
Intercept	.241	.180	.155	.120
	(.038)	(.041)	(.080)	(.074)
Change in annual unemployment rate	− .013	. . .	− .006	. . .
	(.002)		(.006)	
Change in log real GNP	. . .	.572	. . .	.564
		(.128)		(.249)
Year	− .003	− .002	− .002	− .001
	(.0005)	(.0005)	(.0009)	(.0008)
Durbin-Watson statistic	1.34	1.93	2.65	2.59
R^2	.75	.70	.19	.33

Notes: Sample size is twenty years. Observations on 363 continuously employed male household heads born 1928 to 1942 were used to calculate mean log earnings each year from 1967 to 1987, and observations on 335 continuously employed male household heads born 1937 to 1951 were used each year from 1976 to 1996. Sample was limited to individuals who worked at least one hundred hours each year and did not have major assigned data for hours or labor income. The unemployment rate is measured as a percentage of the labor force. Standard errors are in parentheses.

of individuals underlying these regressions is fixed, any effect of composition changes over the business cycle is removed. Columns 3 to 4 extend this analysis for a similarly defined sample of men who were continuously employed from 1976 to 1996.

For comparison, table 10.7 presents analogous estimates for an unbalanced sample. In column 1, the dependent variable is the mean log real hourly wage. A varying, and less-restrictive, sample of men was used to calculate the dependent variable each year; to be included in the sample in year t, the individual needed to work 100 or more hours in year t and be older than age sixteen in year t. Column 2 also uses an unbalanced sample, but first-differences and regression adjusts the micro wage data. Specifically, we estimate the following model by weighted least squares:

$$\Delta \ln(W_{it}) = \theta_{68} + \ldots + \theta_{88} + \beta X_{it} + \varepsilon_{it},$$

where $\Delta \ln(W_{it})$ is the change in the log real wage from year $t - 1$ to t, $\theta_{68} \ldots \theta_{88}$ are coefficients on year dummies, and X_{it} is potential work experience (age

TABLE 10.7 / Aggregate First-Differenced Wage-Curve Estimates for an Unbalanced Sample of Men, PSID, 1968 to 1987 and 1977 to 1996 (Dependent Variable: Annual Change in Mean Log Real Wage)

	Sample			
	1967/1968 to 1986/1987		1976/1977 to 1995/1996	
	(1)	(2)	(3)	(4)
Intercept	.178	.120	−.011	−.028
	(.036)	(.029)	(.061)	(.054)
Change in annual unemployment rate	−.012	−.014	−.008	−.008
	(.002)	(.002)	(.005)	(.004)
Year	−.002	−.002	.0002	−.0002
	(.0004)	(.0004)	(.0008)	(.0006)
Regression adjusted	No	Yes	No	Yes
Durbin-Watson statistic	2.43	2.35	1.93	1.97
R^2	.71	.81	.14	.21

Notes: Sample size is twenty years. Sample each year includes all individuals aged sixteen or older who worked at least one hundred hours that year and did not have major assigned data for hours or labor income. In columns 1 and 3, the dependent variable is the change in the mean log hourly wage for the sample available in those years. Micro data sample size is 50,461 in column 1 and 47,914 in column 3. In columns 2 and 4, a two-step procedure was used. In the first step, the year-over-year change in each individual's log wage was regressed on year dummies and potential experience. In the second-step regression (reported here), the year dummies were regressed on the change in the unemployment rate and a time trend. The sample restrictions used in the first-step regression are identical to those used to calculate the dependent variable in columns 1 and 3, except that individuals were required to have worked in adjacent years. The unemployment rate is measured as a percentage of the labor force. Standard errors are in parentheses.

minus education minus 6). In the second-step regression reported in column 2, the coefficients on the year dummies are regressed on the unemployment rate in year t. Notice that, because the regression model uses wage growth as the dependent variable, any wage gains from entering the labor market (which may be due to changes in the composition of jobs or employees) is missed in this specification, although these effects would be reflected in the column 1 results. Columns 3 and 4 report analogous results for the period 1977 to 1996.

Preliminarily, it is reassuring to note that our point estimates for the period 1968 to 1988 are very close to those found by Solon, Barsky, and Parker, even though we made a few changes in the way in which we handled the data (for example, applying sample weights, trimming outliers).[11] A 3 percentage point decline in the unemployment rate—about the magnitude observed in the expansion of the 1990s—is associated with a 4 percent increase in real wages.

The results for the balanced sample indicate a slightly stronger wage response to unemployment than do the results for the raw means in the unbalanced sample, but the differences among all three estimates (balanced sample, unbalanced means, and regression adjusted) are trivial. These results suggest that the mildly procyclic pattern of real wages displayed in tables 10.3 and 10.4 is unlikely to be severely biased by a changing sample composition, especially in the light of the fact that those results condition on demographic groups and education.[12]

Solon, Barsky, and Parker, however, concluded that the balanced sample provides stronger support for procyclic wage behavior than do the unbalanced, unadjusted data. The reason for this difference is that they weighted the wage data by hours worked in the regression corresponding to the one in column 1 of table 10.7 because it is common to use total payroll divided by total hours worked as a measure of the hourly wage in macro models. We suspect that the hours weighting matters because, as shown previously, hours move with the business cycle, especially for less-skilled workers. Thus, changes in the composition of the workforce appear to be less important for the cyclic nature of real wages than are shifts in the share of hours worked by existing workers in different wage categories. For these models to be comparable to the types of models estimated in tables 10.3 and 10.4, however, we did not weight by hours. Moreover, the balanced data in table 10.6 are not weighted by hours worked. If we do weight the hourly wage by hours worked in the unbalanced sample, however, we find that wage movements are about 50 percent more procyclic in the balanced sample than in the unbalanced one, a finding similar to that of Solon, Barsky, and Parker.

A more important difference between Solon, Barsky, and Parker's results and ours is suggested by the regressions for the period 1977 to 1996. In the balanced panel, we find that the procyclic pattern of wages is statistically insignificant when the unemployment rate is used as the cyclic indicator and about half as large as that found for the period 1968 to 1988. When real GNP growth is used as the cyclic indicator, however, the responsiveness of wages to economic growth in the latter period is quite close to that found in the earlier period. If the change in capacity utilization is used as the cyclic variable (not shown here), the results are in between: the coefficient on capacity utilization falls by a quarter in the latter period.

The coefficient on the unemployment rate is on the margin of statistical significance in the unbalanced samples. Interestingly, in contrast to Solon, Barsky, and Parker's results, in this period unemployment has a smaller magnitude in the balanced sample than in the unbalanced one. These results suggest that unemployment is becoming a less effective measure of labor-market tightness and that composition effects might even move in the opposite direction. Since real-wage growth was particularly strong in the period 1997 to 2000, it would be interesting to see whether the results for the unemployment rate continue to hold when new wage data are available in the PSID. These results also highlight the added power obtained from identifying cyclic effects using regional differences in unemployment changes; the coefficient on unemployment in column 3 of table

10.6, for example, is about equal in magnitude to that found with the MSA-level data, but, here, it is statistically insignificant, whereas it was significant when the disaggregated data were used.

We have not reported the corresponding regressions for women because the number of continuously employed female household heads and married women over a twenty-year period in the PSID is fairly small (144 per year from 1968 to 1988 and 193 per year from 1977 to 1996). Nonetheless, when we estimated the analogous models for women, the results provided even less evidence of procyclic wage movement. For the balanced sample, for example, the coefficient on the unemployment rate was statistically insignificant, small, and *positive* in the period 1968 to 1988 and statistically insignificant, small, and *negative* in the period 1977 to 1996.[13] Likewise, if we estimate separate models by sex using the CPS data in the previous section, we find that wages move procyclically for men and neither pro- nor countercyclically for women.

Over the entire period 1968 to 1996, wages move procyclically in the PSID for men and acyclically (but not statistically significantly) for women. If we estimate the model in column 2 of table 10.7 for the pooled twenty-nine-year period, for example, the coefficient on the unemployment rate for men is -0.011 (SE $= 0.003$) and for women is -0.002 (SE $= -0.004$).

We should also note that we found relatively minor differences in the cyclic nature of wages for different education groups using the PSID data, similar to the findings of Solon, Barsky and Parker (1994) and Swanson (2001). In the period 1968 to 1988, male high school dropouts exhibited more cyclically sensitive wages than did those with a high school diploma or a college degree. In the period 1977 to 1996, however, change in unemployment was not significantly related to wage growth for any of the education groups we examined.

Composition of Jobs

To control for shifts in the composition of *jobs,* we estimated a wage curve using data from the BLS's employment cost index (ECI). Because the ECI is calculated for a fixed set of jobs, these results are unaffected by changes in the composition of jobs over the business cycle. Specifically, we regressed the proportionate change in the ECI (December to December) less the proportionate change in the Consumer Price Index for All Urban Consumers(CPI-UX1) on the change in the unemployment rate and a linear trend. We used data on the ECI for total compensation in the private sector in the years 1980 to 1999. The coefficient estimates (and standard errors) were as follows:

$$\Delta(\text{real ECI growth}) = -0.75 - 0.002\ \Delta(\text{UR}) + 0.0004(\text{year}), \quad R^2 = 0.16.$$
$$\phantom{\Delta(\text{real ECI growth}) = } (0.64) \quad (0.002) \phantom{\Delta(\text{UR}) + } (0.0003)$$

Changes in unemployment are notably uncorrelated with changes in the ECI less inflation. Abraham and Haltiwanger (1995) reach the same conclusion using quarterly ECI data from 1976 to 1993 and employment growth as a cyclic indicator.

On the one hand, these results suggest that whatever cyclicality does exist in wages is a result of changes in the mix of jobs. On the other hand, the PSID, the CPS, and the ECI suggest that real wages were not very sensitive to the unemployment rate in the 1980s and 1990s.

Do Workers Move to Jobs with Steeper Seniority Profiles in Good Times?

Okun (1973, 237–38) argued that, in a high-pressure economy, employers are more likely to provide jobs that offer "a schedule of wage increases at regular intervals, fringe benefits and seniority privileges" and paid vacation to improve worker attachment. His empirical support was based primarily on the fact that high-wage industries such as manufacturing and construction tend to have relatively strong procyclic employment swings. We use the PSID to test more directly the hypothesis that workers tend to gravitate toward jobs with rising seniority profiles in a tight labor market.

Specifically, for each of twelve major industries, we estimated a tenure slope by estimating a separate log wage equation that included years of tenure, potential experience and its square, sex, race, and years of schooling as explanatory variables, using the 1976 cross-sectional wave of the PSID.[14] The estimated tenure slopes ranged from virtually 0 in entertainment and recreational services, mining, and personal services to 2.8 percent higher pay per year of tenure in finance, insurance, and real estate. We computed separate wage regressions for seven major occupations as well. The resulting returns to tenure ranged from 0 for farmers to 2.2 percent per year for professional and technical workers. The estimated tenure slopes provide an indication of the extent to which jobs in particular industries and occupations offer upward-sloping seniority profiles.

We then assigned each individual in the PSID the tenure slope corresponding to his or her industry in year t and computed the change in each individual's industry-tenure slope between year t and year $t - 1$. We regressed this variable on the annual change in the national unemployment rate, sex, race, and potential experience and its square. The estimated coefficient on the change in the unemployment rate for the full sample is reported in column 1 of table 10.8, and columns 2 and 3 report separate estimates for workers broken down by whether they earned more or less than the median wage in year $t - 1$. Columns 4 to 6 provide the corresponding estimates using the change in the occupation-based returns to tenure as the dependent variable.

The results provide some suggestive evidence that workers tend to gravitate toward jobs in sectors with steeper tenure-earnings profiles when the labor market becomes tighter. The coefficient on the unemployment-rate change for the full sample is negative for both industry and occupation slopes, although only the former is statistically significant. Moreover, the significant shift in employ-

TABLE 10.8 / The Cyclic Nature of Seniority Profiles (Dependent Variable: Change in Tenure Slope Associated with Change in Industry or Occupation)

	Δ Industry-Based Seniority Returns			Δ Occupation-Based Seniority Returns		
	All (1)	High Wage (2)	Low Wage (3)	All (4)	High Wage (5)	Low Wage (6)
Change in unemployment rate (/1000)	−.016 (.009)	−.005 (.011)	−.031 (.017)	−.012 (.008)	−.014 (.008)	−.007 (.016)

Notes: Based on the PSID. Returns to seniority for each major industry and occupation were estimated from a standard human-capital log wage equation using the 1976 wave of the PSID. The year-over-year change in returns for each individual (based on industry or occupation) was then regressed on the change in unemployment rate, sex, race, and experience and its square (see the text). The coefficient on the change in the unemployment rate (times 1,000) is reported here. High wage is the subsample above the median wage in year $t − 1$; low wage is the subsample below the median wage in year $t − 1$. Occupation and industry refer to the current job, while wage (and median wage) refers to the preceding calendar year. Sample size for regressions using industry-level tenure returns is 115,751; sample size for regressions using occupation-level returns is 125,411. The industry analysis includes the years 1973 to 1997, and the occupation analysis includes the years 1970 to 1997. Standard errors are in parentheses.

ment toward industries with steeper tenure profiles in good times appears to be driven primarily by the behavior of lower-paid workers. The following calculation puts the magnitude of this effect in context and suggests that it is quite small in the aggregate. If the unemployment rate falls by 3 percentage points, the tenure profile is, on the basis of column 1, predicted to rise by 0.005 percent per year. The average industry-based tenure slope is 1.9 percent per year across the whole sample, so a tighter labor market would increase the average slope by only a trivial fraction. Because only a minority of workers change industrial sectors in a year, perhaps it is unreasonable to expect a very large effect in the aggregate. In any event, the results do suggest that workers tend to gravitate toward jobs in sectors with steeper earnings profile when the labor market tightens.

OTHER OUTCOMES

Crime

Crime rates dropped throughout the economic expansion of the 1990s. Between 1991 and 1997, the total crime index dropped 17 percent. As shown in table 10.1, violent crimes dropped by 32 percent in families with incomes less than $7,500 and by 45 percent in families with incomes over $75,000. Because crime rates are higher for those in lower income families, the number of violent crimes per thousand people fell more for lower income families. Studies have found that crime rates respond to labor-market opportunities, both changes in unemployment rates and changes in wage levels. This literature, summarized recently by Freeman (1999), shows that unemployment rates have a modest effect on crime but that wages may be more closely correlated with criminal activity. Richard Freeman and William Rodgers (2000) use the Uniform Crime Reports to create a state-level crime-rate series with which to explore the relation between crime rates and unemployment at the state level. They find that crime rates fell most rapidly in the states where unemployment fell the most. In particular, they find that a 1 percentage point decrease in unemployment is association with a reduction of 1.5 percent in the number of crimes per youth. Thus, the 3 percentage point reduction in the unemployment rate in this expansion would have reduced crime per youth by about 5 percent. H. Naci Mocan and Daniel Rees (1999), studying criminal activity among juveniles, find that a 1 percentage point reduction in unemployment rates leads to a 0.4 percent reduction in the probability of selling drugs and a 0.3 percent reduction in the probability of committing robbery.

Welfare Participation

The 1990s have seen unprecedented reductions in welfare participation in the United States. Looking back at table 10.1, the percentage of the population receiving welfare fell from 5.2 percent in 1992 to 2.9 percent in 2000, the lowest rate in over thirty years. Overall, the national welfare caseload has fallen by more than half since its peak in 1993. Welfare caseloads tend to be countercyclic, with increases in periods of higher unemployment rates. However, the correlation between the business cycle and welfare participation appears to be stronger in the current cycle. As discussed in the *Economic Report of the President* (Council of Economic Advisers 1999), significant changes in welfare programs and family structure may have masked the effect of cycles in the 1970s and 1980s.

A recent literature has explored the role that the strong labor market has played in the declining welfare caseload in the 1990s (for a survey, see Blank, forthcoming). Several studies use pooled cross-state data on welfare caseloads and economic conditions and estimate models that control for state fixed effects, time effects, and state-specific time trends. The estimates in these studies vary somewhat, but, overall, they find that labor-market conditions are important determinants of the welfare caseload (Blank 2001; Council of Economic Advisers 1997; Ziliak et al. 2000). The Council of Economic Advisers study estimates the relative contribution of the unemployment rate and welfare reform to the per capita welfare caseload and finds that a 1 percentage point decline in each of two successive years leads to a 4 percent decline in the caseload in the second year. Rebecca Blank and James Ziliak et al. find statistically significant but somewhat smaller effects of labor-market conditions than did the Council of Economic Advisers study. Hoynes (2000b) finds that improvements in local labor-market conditions lead to lower caseloads through increases in exits from welfare and reductions in recidivism.

We agree with Blank (forthcoming), who suggests that one should use caution in making conclusions that are based on the current research. She points out that many factors that could have affected welfare caseloads changed in the mid-1990s—including large expansions in the earned income tax credit, mini-mum-wage increases, welfare reform, and the strengthening of the labor mar-ket—and argues that our ability to determine the relative importance of these factors is limited by the fact that the changes were coincident.

Health and Work Injuries

A surge in work-related injuries is usually an undesired side effect of higher productivity growth in an expanding economy (Smith 1972). Injuries are ex-pected to rise when unemployment falls because work intensity increases and because many inexperienced workers are hired. The anticipated rise in work-related injuries has not occurred in the latest business cycle, however. Since 1992, the number of work-related injuries and illnesses fell by an impressive 25 per-cent, from 8.9 to 6.7 per 100 full-time-equivalent workers. All major types of injuries have declined. Since 1992, missed-workday cases are down by 36 per-cent for sprains and strains, 31 percent for broken bones, and 30 percent for carpal tunnel syndrome. Workplace fatalities are down by 13 percent, which suggests that the trend toward safer working conditions is not a mere reporting phenomenon.

A regression of the change in the overall injury and illness rate per one hun-dred workers on the change in the unemployment rate using data from 1973 to 1991 yields

$$\Delta(\text{injury rate}) = -0.11 - 0.35(\Delta\text{UR}), \quad R^2 = 0.83,$$
$$\quad\quad\quad\quad\quad (0.05) \quad (0.04)$$

which is remarkably similar to Smith's (1972) estimate of the cyclic nature of injury rates based on historical data. But, if the equation is estimated with the small number of post-1991 years, the correlation is positive and has a p-value of 0.12.

Figure 10.1 displays the injury and illness rate in each year and a prediction of the rate based on its pre-1992 relation with the unemployment rate. In 1998, the latest year for which data are available, there were 5.9 million cases of work-related injuries and illnesses in the private sector, the vast majority of which were injuries. If the pre-1992 relation between injuries and unemployment had held, one would have expected 3 million more injuries and illnesses in 1998 than the number actually recorded.

Interestingly, Leslie Boden and John Ruser (1999) find an inverse relation be-tween the state unemployment rate and work injuries across states in the 1990s,

FIGURE 10.1 / Actual and Predicted Work-Related Injury and Illness Rate

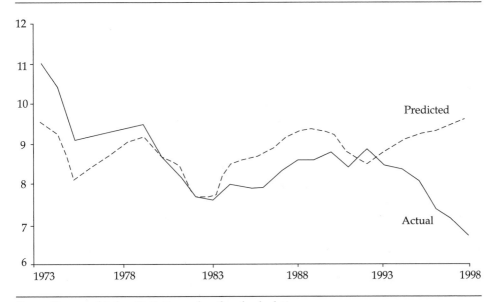

Source: Bureau of Labor Statistics and authors' calculations.

Note: The predicted rate is based on an OLS regression of the injury rate on the unemployment rate, using annual data from 1973 to 1991.

controlling for year and state fixed effects. This result suggests that injuries still move procyclically but that this effect is masked by an even stronger, nationwide downward trend in injuries in the 1990s.

The cause of the trend toward fewer work-related injuries is something of a mystery. The decline in injuries is not due to shifts in employment toward jobs in safer industries. Instead, injuries and illnesses declined within most industries. For example, the incidence rate fell by 22 percent in manufacturing, 33 percent in construction, and 27 percent in services. The decline also does not correspond well to the timing of changes in federal Occupational Safety and Health Administration (OSHA) policy and is just as strong in states that run their own OSHA programs as in those that are under federal OSHA programs.

Whatever the reason for the decline in injuries, the economic implications are sizable. W. Kip Viscusi's (1993) survey of compensating differentials finds that workers are willing to forgo at least $33,000 in earnings (in current dollars) to take a job that entails no risk of injury as compared with one that carries a certain risk of injury, all else equal. If this figure is correct, the 3 million fewer injuries and illnesses than predicted in 1998 would be implicitly valued by workers at around $100 billion—a bounty that is not included in the GNP. This amounts to a $1,000 raise per private-sector worker.

Education and Training

As indicated in table 10.1, the likelihood that youths will drop out of high school rises during the expansionary portion of the business cycle and falls during the contractionary portion. A countercyclic pattern of school enrollment has been carefully documented in studies by Alan Gustman and Thomas Steinmeier (1981), Audrey Light (1995), and David Card and Thomas Lemieux (2000), for example. This pattern likely arises because the opportunity cost of attending school is lower when the economy is depressed and good jobs are scarce. Likewise, the opportunity cost of attending school rises when jobs are plentiful. It is unclear, however, whether those who are induced to leave school early during good times return to school later on.

The cyclic pattern of job training is less well documented and mixed. For noncollege graduates, Lisa Lynch (1992) finds that, in the early 1980s, higher local unemployment increased the probability of participation in an apprenticeship program but decreased the probability of receiving on-the-job training from an employer. For a larger sample that included college graduates as well (again in the early 1980s), higher local unemployment increased the probability that young people who had completed school would take some off-the-job training.

PUBLIC FINANCES, THE BUSINESS CYCLE, AND THE DISADVANTAGED

The many beneficiaries of a strong economy include all levels of government. Rising incomes generate tax revenues that strengthen government finances, thereby facilitating expanded spending programs, tax cuts, debt reduction, or some combination of these three. Since the government may reasonably be expected to act as the agent of the citizenry, the benefits of government fiscal strength are received by citizens, although not necessarily in equal measure by all.

To the extent that economic expansion is associated with greater government spending, it follows that the disadvantaged are likely to receive many of the associated benefits. Government-funded activities provide services from which the disadvantaged benefit quite out of proportion to the tax obligations that they incur to finance them. There are two reasons why economic fluctuations over the business cycle may have particularly strong implications for the disadvantaged: governments with greater revenue sources tend to spend money on programs that particularly benefit the disadvantaged, and rising incomes generally trigger tax obligations that increase most rapidly among higher-bracket taxpayers. To put the same matter differently, economic downturns entail spending cuts that negatively affect the disadvantaged without providing commensurate tax relief.

This section considers evidence on the pattern of government activity over the business cycle and the likely effect of that activity on disadvantaged citizens. For this purpose, it is particularly useful to analyze data on American "states" (understood to include the District of Columbia) since states differ in the timing and magnitude of their economic cycles and thereby offer fifty-one separate glimpses into the effect of the business cycle on public finances. Moreover, state and local fiscal activity is important in its own terms, representing by now a significant fraction of the economy. Finally, there are interesting questions concerning the effect of economic cycles on the ability of subnational governments to pursue countercyclic policies, particularly insofar as these policies affect the disadvantaged.

The Scope of Government

It is useful to review the scope of government activity in order to identify the potential effect of cycle-induced fiscal-policy swings. Table 10.9 presents information on state- and local-government expenditures in the United States over the period 1952 to 1996. In 1996, state and local governments spent a total of $1.398 trillion, which represented 25.9 percent of personal disposable income in that year.[15] The largest single category of state- and local-government spending was that on public education, representing $399 billion, or 29 percent of the total. The next largest was welfare spending, at $193 billion, or 14 percent of the total, followed by health and hospitals, at $111 billion, or 8 percent of the total. Insurance-trust expenditures were also 8 percent of total spending in 1996, followed by highways at 6 percent and police and fire protection at 4 percent.

The U.S. federal government has somewhat different spending priorities that reflect its own political situation. Its on-budget 1996 spending of $1.260 trillion included $266 billion for national defense, $226 billion for income security (much of it transferred to the states and included in their totals), $174 billion for Medicare, $119 billion for health, $52 billion for education, training, employment, and social services, $40 billion for transportation, $22 billion for natural resources and the environment, $18 billion for justice, and, of course, numerous other categories of expenditure.

The effects of American business cycles are evident from the simple patterns revealed in table 10.9. Against a backdrop of steadily growing government, cyclic expansions are associated with growing state and local expenditures, while recessions are associated with spending slowdowns at the state and local level. For example, the recession of the early 1980s is reflected in the very modest growth ($36 billion, nominal) of total state and local expenditures between fiscal year 1981 and fiscal year 1982, a figure that is small compared to nominal growth in other years and striking in the light of the high rate of inflation during that time period. In order to identify more carefully the effect of business cycles on state and local fiscal activity, it is useful to examine the information available by comparing the experiences of American states over the cycle.

TABLE 10.9 / State and Local Expenditures by Function, Fiscal Years 1952 to 1996 ($Millions)

Year	Total	Public Education	Highways	Welfare	Health & Hospitals	Police & Fire Protection	Administration[a]	Insurance Trust[b]	Utility & Liquor Store[c]	Other[d]
1952	30,863	8,318	4,650	2,788	2,185	1,525	1,193	1,698	3,067	5,439
1953	32,937	9,390	4,987	2,914	2,290	1,636	1,263	1,711	3,316	5,430
1954	36,607	10,557	5,527	3,060	2,409	1,783	1,375	2,423	3,482	5,991
1955	40,375	11,907	6,452	3,168	2,524	1,923	1,452	2,764	3,886	6,299
1956	43,152	13,220	6,953	3,139	2,772	2,067	1,560	2,376	4,065	7,000
1957	47,553	14,134	7,816	3,485	3,119	2,278	1,725	2,749	4,429	7,818
1958	53,712	15,919	8,567	3,818	3,462	2,483	1,843	4,168	4,693	8,759
1959	58,572	17,283	9,592	4,136	3,724	2,624	2,003	4,784	4,901	9,525
1960	60,999	18,719	9,428	4,404	3,794	2,852	2,113	4,031	5,088	10,570
1961	67,023	20,574	9,844	4,720	4,086	3,104	2,237	5,299	5,523	11,636
1962	70,547	22,216	10,357	5,084	4,342	3,254	2,338	4,888	5,453	12,615
1963	74,698	23,729	11,150	5,420	4,638	3,398	2,439	4,987	5,736	13,201
1964	80,579	26,286	11,664	5,766	4,910	3,588	2,567	5,094	6,184	14,520
1965	86,686	28,563	12,221	6,315	5,361	3,855	2,773	4,950	7,058	15,590
1966	94,906	33,287	12,770	6,757	5,910	4,152	2,974	4,782	7,282	16,992
1967	105,978	37,919	13,932	8,218	6,640	4,548	3,313	5,278	7,350	18,780
1968	116,234	41,158	14,481	9,857	7,546	5,033	3,647	5,653	8,170	20,689
1969	131,600	47,238	15,417	12,110	8,520	5,694	4,105	6,053	8,820	23,643
1970	148,052	52,718	16,427	14,679	9,669	6,518	5,451	7,263	9,447	25,880
1971	170,766	59,413	18,095	18,226	11,205	7,531	6,243	9,793	10,300	29,960
1972	190,496	65,814	19,021	21,117	13,023	8,584	7,056	10,548	11,398	33,935
1973	205,466	69,714	18,615	23,582	13,844	9,584	7,934	11,074	13,035	38,084
1974	226,032	75,833	19,946	25,085	15,945	10,326	8,844	12,667	14,406	42,980
1975	269,215	87,858	22,528	28,155	18,846	12,048	10,154	21,209	17,285	51,132
1976	304,228	97,216	23,907	32,604	20,686	13,429	11,247	27,954	19,542	57,643

Year										
1977	324,554	102,780	23,058	35,905	23,039	14,857	12,453	26,149	24,190	62,123
1978	346,786	110,758	24,609	39,140	24,951	16,108	16,618	23,526	26,277	64,799
1979	381,867	119,448	28,440	41,898	28,218	17,354	18,448	23,504	30,845	73,712
1980	434,073	133,211	33,311	47,288	32,174	19,212	20,443	28,796	36,190	83,448
1981	487,048	145,784	34,603	54,121	36,101	21,283	20,001	36,583	43,016	95,556
1982	522,760	154,573	34,545	58,050	40,259	23,387	22,224	39,466	47,971	102,285
1983	566,567	163,876	36,655	60,484	44,118	25,516	24,508	47,335	52,811	111,264
1984	600,222	176,108	39,419	66,414	46,330	27,464	26,355	40,153	55,062	122,917
1985	657,888	192,686	44,989	71,479	49,581	29,873	28,890	44,191	59,798	136,401
1986	717,430	210,819	49,368	75,868	53,508	32,272	31,803	46,538	65,297	151,957
1987	775,318	226,658	52,199	82,520	56,972	35,594	34,896	50,815	68,440	167,224
1988	826,849	242,683	55,621	89,090	61,940	38,030	37,419	51,879	70,048	180,139
1989	890,863	263,898	58,105	97,879	67,757	39,703	40,923	54,994	73,510	194,094
1990	975,940	288,148	61,057	110,518	74,635	43,763	44,836	63,321	77,801	211,861
1991	1,063,270	309,302	64,937	130,402	81,110	46,568	48,461	74,159	81,004	227,327
1992	1,146,853	326,275	66,689	154,642	88,112	48,903	50,334	90,276	84,361	237,261
1993	1,207,125	342,595	68,134	167,046	94,651	51,943	52,402	98,908	84,361	247,085
1994	1,260,642	353,287	72,067	179,829	100,430	54,768	55,715	95,462	91,163	257,921
1995	1,347,763	378,273	77,109	193,110	105,946	58,064	60,018	107,340	94,235	273,668
1996	1,397,634	398,859	79,092	193,480	110,813	62,392	62,145	108,751	95,608	286,495

Source: Department of Commerce, Bureau of the Census.

Notes: Duplicative intergovernmental transactions are excluded.

[a]Includes financial, judicial and legal, general public building, and other government administration.

[b]Includes employee retirement, unemployment compensation, workers' compensation, and other social programs.

[c]Includes utility capital outlay, water supply, electric power, gas supply, transit, and liquor store.

[d]Includes interest, sewerage, utilities, and other categories.

Evidence of the Effect of Business Cycles

This section analyzes information on the spending activities of American state and local governments over the period 1977 to 1997. The following specification is useful in evaluating the effect of economic conditions on government fiscal activity:

$$S_{ijt} = Y_{jt}^{\beta_{1i}} N_{jt}^{\beta_{2i}} e^{\delta_{1ij} + \delta_{2it} + t\delta_{3ij} + u_{ijt}},$$

in which S_{ijt} is spending in category i by state j in year t, Y_{jt} is personal income in state j in year t, N_{jt} is the population of state j in year t, and β_{1i} and β_{2i} are parameters to be estimated. The dummy variable δ_{1ij} captures time-invariant state-specific effects on levels of spending in category i, δ_{2it} captures time effects, and δ_{3ij} captures state-specific growth rates in spending on i.

Taking first-differences of logs, the prior equation becomes

$$\Delta \ln S_{ijt} = \beta_{1i}\Delta \ln Y_{jt} + \beta_{2i}\Delta \ln N_{jt} + (\delta_{2it} - \delta_{2it-1}) + \delta_{3ij} + \varepsilon_{ijt},$$

in which ε_{ijt} is the residual, equal to $u_{ijt} - u_{ijt-1}$.

The first two rows of table 10.10 present estimates of the variant of this equation in which the S_{ijt} variable equals total spending by state and local governments. The data analyzed in this regression are drawn from the U.S. Census of Governments and consist of annual observations for the fifty states plus the District of Columbia over the period 1977 to 1997. The Census of Governments does attempt to verify that intergovernment transactions (such as spending by state governments that takes the form of transferring money to local governments) are counted just once in this tabulation. All the regressions include time dummy variables (not reported) to capture the $\delta_{2it} - \delta_{2i(t-1)}$ term. The regression reported in the first row of table 10.10 omits state dummy variables, thereby implicitly imposing the condition that the underlying expenditure growth rate δ_{3ij} be the same for all states, while the regression reported in the second row of table 10.10 includes state dummy variables and therefore does not impose this equality.

The results indicate that total spending responds positively to higher income and higher population levels. The estimated 0.18 coefficient in the first row of table 10.10 implies that a doubling of state income is associated (at a 1-year frequency) with 18 percent higher state spending. The 0.67 coefficient likewise indicates that a doubling of state population is associated with 67 percent greater spending. The inclusion of state dummy variables in the regression reported in the second row of table 10.10 changes these estimates only modestly.

It is hardly surprising that state- and local-government spending responds positively to personal-income growth since greater affluence is typically associated with demand for greater government services.[16] Furthermore, there is the widely documented "flypaper" effect—that government receipt of cash wind-

TABLE 10.10 / State and Local Expenditures and the Business Cycle

Dependent Variable	Δ ln Income	Δ ln Population	State Dummies	R^2
Δ ln total spending	.180	.670	N	.91
	(.045)	(.078)		
	.171	.670	Y	.91
	(.047)	(.098)		
Δ ln capital spending	.807	.870	N	.29
	(.166)	(.286)		
	.758	1.314	Y	.30
	(.173)	(.363)		
Δ ln direct spending	.154	.675	N	.90
	(.047)	(.081)		
	.141	.680	Y	.91
	(.048)	(.102)		

Notes: Data consist of annual observations of spending by a panel of U.S. states (plus the District of Columbia) over the period 1977 to 1997. All regressions have 1,020 observations. Dependent variables are first-differences of logs of indicated spending categories. All regressions include year dummy variables (not reported), and those with *Y* in the "State Dummies" column also include state dummy variables (likewise not reported). "Δ ln Income" is the first-difference of the log of state personal income, and "Δ ln Population" is the first-difference of the log of state population. Standard errors are in parentheses.

falls or other revenue sources tends to be accompanied by greater spending (Ladd 1993; Hines and Thaler 1995; Strumpf 1998). It is, however, instructive to compare the spending results in the first two rows of table 10.10 with those in rows 3 and 4, in which the dependent variable is the capital component of state- and local-government spending. In these regressions, income and population growth are again associated with greater spending, the difference being that the coefficients on income are now much larger. In the specification without state dummy variables, the estimated coefficient of 0.81 implies that a doubling of state income is associated with 81 percent greater capital expenditures. These results are consistent with the interpretation that governments fail to undertake worthwhile capital projects unless their finances are particularly strong and, in particular, that they cut back on capital projects in bad economic times.[17] Comparing the estimated income coefficients from the capital-spending regressions reported in rows 3 and 4 of table 10.10 with the estimated income coefficients from the equations for noncapital ("direct") spending reported in rows 5 and 6 makes this particularly apparent.

The results reported in table 10.10 are robust to a variety of alternative specifications of the estimating equations. In particular, replacing the change in personal income with the change in state unemployment rate yields results with opposite signs—that is, signs that again imply that state spending increases during strong economic times. Changing the dependent variable to the first-difference of the log of per capita spending (and omitting the population variable on the right-hand side) has only a small effect on the estimated coefficient on the change in log income. Inclusion of state dummy variables, but omission of year dummy variables, changes the results very little. Replacing OLS with a minimum-absolute-distance regression method, which is more robust to outliers, generates similar findings. And weighting the regressions by state population likewise had little effect on the results.

Further evidence of the effect of the business cycle on spending patterns is presented in table 10.11, in which five separate spending categories—health and hospitals, education, highways, police, and parks and recreation—are distinguished. All categories respond positively to personal-income growth, with the estimated short-run income elasticity highest for parks and recreation (0.95 in

TABLE 10.11 / Business-Cycle Effects on Major Spending Categories

Dependent Variable	Δ ln Income	Δ ln Population	State Dummies	R^2
Δ ln spending on health and hospitals	.260 (.107)	1.296 (.184)	N	.72
	.207 (.109)	1.732 (.229)	Y	.74
Δ ln education spending	.243 (.053)	.865 (.092)	N	.84
	.217 (.054)	1.053 (.114)	Y	.85
Δ ln highway spending	.415 (.138)	.879 (.238)	N	.23
	.383 (.144)	1.144 (.302)	Y	.24
Δ ln spending on police	.353 (.073)	.889 (.126)	N	.83
	.320 (.076)	1.081 (.159)	Y	.83
Δ ln spending on parks and recreation	.949 (.223)	1.582 (.386)	N	.67
	.823 (.230)	2.712 (.484)	Y	.68

Notes: Data consist of annual observations of spending by a panel of U.S. states (plus the District of Columbia) over the period 1977 to 1997. All regressions have 1,020 observations. Dependent variables are first-differences of logs of indicated spending categories. All regressions include year dummy variables (not reported), and those with Y in the "State Dummies" column also include state dummy variables (likewise not reported). "Δ ln Income" is the first-difference of the log of state personal income, and "Δ ln Population" is the first-difference of the log of state population. Standard errors are in parentheses.

the regression without dummy variables capturing state-specific growth trends) and lowest for education (0.24). The result that these spending categories respond positively to economic expansions is robust to replacing the change in income with the change in the state unemployment rate as well as replacing the dependent variables with per capita measures, weighting the regressions, using the minimum-absolute-distance regression method, and other straightforward specification checks.

Appendix table 10A.1 reports the results of reestimating the effect of the business cycle on major spending categories, using changes in state unemployment rates (in place of changes in log income) as indicators of business-cycle movements. As the results reported in the table indicate, higher unemployment rates are associated with reduced spending, the strongest effect appearing for welfare spending.[18] The standard errors for these regressions are rather large, in part reflecting the imprecision of using state unemployment figures in place of personal income as measures of desired demand for public spending. Nevertheless, the patterns are consistent with the procyclic nature of major government-spending programs evinced elsewhere. Other specification checks produced results that are similar to those reported in tables 10.10 and 10.11.[19]

The disadvantaged benefit (along with the rest of the population) from greater government expenditures in these major categories, although the extent to which various groups benefit from the services provided by marginal expenditures is difficult to assess. The evidence on welfare spending reported in table 10.12 suggests, however, that there may be a tendency to direct marginal resources in ways that benefit the disadvantaged.

Of perhaps the most consequence for the disadvantaged are government income-maintenance programs, and it is for this spending category that the results are the most striking and at first glance perhaps the most paradoxical. Table 10.12 presents these regressions. The results reported in the first two rows of table 10.12 indicate that total welfare spending responds positively to changes in local income, with a coefficient implying that a doubling of state personal income is associated with a 134 percent rise in total welfare spending. The relatively large standard errors make it impossible to reject the hypothesis that welfare spending is unaffected by changes in personal income, but the coefficient point estimates are positive. Similar results appear in other specifications, specifically, replacing changes in personal income with changes in state unemployment rates, defining dependent variables in per capita terms, removing year dummy variables, among others.

What makes these results striking is the countercyclic nature of caseloads in major welfare programs such as Aid to Families with Dependent Children (AFDC) since economic downturns are responsible for greater numbers of individuals eligible for, and receiving, welfare payments.[20] In order for total (major-program) welfare spending to respond positively to aggregate income growth, benefit levels per recipient must be strongly affected by the condition of local finances, in combination with the creation of new welfare programs at times when budgets make such initiatives feasible. Is it possible for benefit levels to exhibit such a strong dependence on local economic prosperity?

TABLE 10.12 / Welfare Spending and the Business Cycle

Dependent Variable	Δ ln Income	Δ ln Population	State Dummies	R^2
Δ ln total welfare spending	1.344	2.667	N	.12
	(1.404)	(2.417)		
	1.135	4.661	Y	.12
	(1.468)	(3.075)		
Δ ln spending on cash	2.157	2.139	N	.05
assistance	(1.662)	(2.861)		
	1.975	4.104	Y	.06
	(1.739)	(3.643)		
Δ ln spending on welfare	3.732	1.144	N	.02
institutions	(2.140)	(4.258)		
	3.656	3.039	Y	.04
	(2.295)	(6.361)		
Δ ln spending on categori-	1.246	2.338	N	.11
cal assistance	(1.592)	(.078)		
	1.113	3.724	Y	.11
	(1.665)	(3.489)		
Δ ln spending on other	.005	9.775	N	.07
public assistance	(3.881)	(6.170)		
	− .767	13.414	Y	.08
	(4.055)	(7.839)		

Notes: Data consist of annual observations of spending by a panel of U.S. states (plus the District of Columbia) over the period 1977 to 1997. All regressions have 1,020 observations. Dependent variables are first-differences of logs of indicated spending categories. All regressions include year dummy variables (not reported), and those with Y in the "State Dummies" column also include state dummy variables (likewise not reported). "Δ ln Income" is the first-difference of the log of state personal income, and "Δ ln Population" is the first-difference of the log of state population. Standard errors are in parentheses.

Were these purely cross-sectional regressions performed at an international level, one might not find the results so puzzling. A much smaller fraction of the population is living in poverty in the United States than in, say, India, yet per capita welfare spending in the United States vastly exceeds per capita welfare spending in India. The difference is obviously due to the much greater affluence of the United States and its ability therefore to afford generous transfer programs. Even within the United States, there are persistent differences between states in ability and willingness to pay for income-maintenance programs; these differences tend to be of the form that high-income states with smaller recipient populations nevertheless spend more per capita on income maintenance than do low-income states. The cross-sectional relation for the fifty states and the District of Columbia in 1997 is

$$\ln(\text{total welfare spending}) = 9.924 + 1.420(\ln \text{income})$$
$$(3.329) \quad (0.998)$$

$$- 1.313(\ln \text{population}), \quad R^2 = 0.06.$$
$$(1.020)$$

Further evidence can be obtained by examining categories of welfare expenditures, the determinants of which are estimated in the equations reported in rows 3 to 10 of table 10.12. Cash assistance, welfare institutions, and categorical assistance all appear to respond strongly to changes in state income.[21] In all these cases, the estimated coefficients on changes in log income exceed 1, although in none of these cases is the estimated coefficient significantly different from 0. Nevertheless, the positive sign pattern is striking. Other types of welfare assistance show very little association with state income.

One possibility is that the one-year nature of the first-differences of the spending equations imparts some kind of bias that obscures what might otherwise be the expected negative relation between welfare spending and state income. A long first-difference, covering the years 1977 to 1997 for the fifty states and the District of Columbia, produces

$$\Delta\ln(\text{total welfare spending}) = 0.232 + 1.332(\Delta \ln \text{income})$$
$$(2.869) \quad (2.667)$$

$$- 0.422(\Delta \ln \text{population}), \quad R^2 = 0.01,$$
$$(2.602)$$

which is reassuringly close to the panel results (although the standard errors are quite large).

One is left, therefore, with the impression that strong local economies contribute in a very important way to government spending and, therefore, economic outcomes for the disadvantaged. This analysis is necessarily somewhat imprecise about the magnitude of the associated benefits by income group, and it omits consideration of tax-rate cuts during economic expansions and other ways in which the disadvantaged benefit from strong government finances. But the central fact is that greater affluence is shared through government operations. This implies that the costs of economic downturns are likewise shared, which makes such downturns particularly burdensome for those who stand to lose the most from reduced government activity.

CONCLUSION

The results reported in this paper highlight the value of maintaining strong, steady macroeconomic growth. Although growth does not cure all social problems, it serves to alleviate many of them. Hours worked and family income, in particular, tend to rise when business conditions improve. The real-wage rate, however, is only weakly procyclic, although there is no evidence that wages tend to fall during periods of economic growth. Nevertheless, workers tend to gravitate toward jobs in sectors with steeper seniority-wage profiles when times are good and tend to gravitate toward dead-end jobs when times are bad. The main labor-market lift from a rising economic tide comes about by expanding opportunities to work more hours in better jobs, particularly for lower-paid individuals.

Why does a rising tide provide so many more marginal workers the opportunity to work? The most obvious interpretation is that many of those who are unemployed, out of the labor force, or underemployed are constrained: they would like to work (or work more hours) at the going wage but are unable to find employment. A cyclic upturn increases aggregate demand for labor. It also appears that wage rates are relatively sticky, both during a downturn and during an upturn. Consequently, for the most part, adjustments to employment and hours worked end up clearing the market rather than wages. This simple model of the economy is consistent with the "wage-curve" relations documented in this paper.

Freeman (2001) notes that, despite its benefits, a rising tide has important limits when it comes to reducing poverty. He estimates that, at the end of the 1990s, "close to 60% of adults in poor families were unlikely to be able to benefit much from the labor market" because they were disabled, retired, or had family obligations that prevented them from working enough to lift their families out of poverty. For this group, it is important to emphasize that the public provision of goods and services, including income transfers, also tends to rise with a rising tide. Thus, the potential exists to assist individuals who, for whatever reason, are not in the job market.

Two dark clouds associated with a sunny economy were noted. First, work injuries typically move procyclically—although the expansion of the 1990s is an exception to that pattern. Second, an upturn in the business cycle historically coincides with a slight increase in the high school–dropout rate. The latter tendency suggests that focusing public policy on dropout prevention and skill development—especially among those who are at a high risk of dropping out of high school—during an upturn could make a good deal of sense.

We thank David Ellwood, Jonathan Parker, and Robert Solow for helpful suggestions and Melissa Clark, Kenneth Fortson, Christian Jaramillo, and Justin McCrary for helpful research assistance.

APPENDIX

TABLE 10A.1 / Effect of the Unemployment Rate on Major Spending Categories

Dependent Variable	Δ Unemployment	Δ ln Population	State Dummies	R^2
Δ ln spending on	− .692	1.280	N	.15
health and hospitals	(.309)	(.192)		
	− .795	2.169	Y	.20
	(.309)	(.291)		
Δ ln education	− .149	1.220	N	.27
spending	(.160)	(.092)		
	− .206	1.771	Y	.30
	(.161)	(.152)		
Δ ln highway	− .747	1.452	N	.17
spending	(.430)	(.266)		
	− .769	2.119	Y	.19
	(.438)	(.413)		
Δ ln spending on	− .439	1.418	N	.21
police	(.222)	(.138)		
	− .487	1.933	Y	.23
	(.226)	(.213)		
Δ ln total welfare	− 2.106	.476	N	.09
spending	(4.507)	(2.803)		
	− 1.853	.565	Y	.10
	(4.644)	(4.378)		

Notes: Data consist of annual observations of spending by a panel of U.S. states (plus the District of Columbia) over the period 1977 to 1997. All regressions have 1,020 observations. Dependent variables are the first-differences of logarithms of indicated spending categories. All regressions include year dummy variables (not reported), and those with Y in the "State Dummies" column also include state dummy variables (likewise not reported). "Δ Unemployment" is the first-difference of the unemployment rate (where the unemployment rate is measured as a proportion rather than a percentage), and "Δ ln Population" is the first-difference of the log of state population. Standard errors are in parentheses.

NOTES

1. Although, according to the National Bureau of Economic Research, the recession officially ended in March 1991 (http://www.nber.org/March91.html), the unemployment rate did not peak until 1992. Consequently, we use 1992 as the trough year.

2. Specifically, we use the March CPS for survey years 1976 to 2000, which provides annual labor-market information for the following calendar year.

3. If cycles were symmetrical, in that the increase in unemployment rates in the recession equaled the decrease in unemployment rates in the expansion, then this estimated asymmetrical effect of unemployment rates would suggest that, after repeated cycles, average annual hours would be lower than at the beginning of the period. However, we are not observing such a steady-state economy; instead, we are looking at a finite slice of time, and, during this time period, unemployment rates have been trending downward.

4. Some standard adjustments to the data are implemented. The earnings data are top coded at $50,000 through 1981, $75,000 from 1982 to 1984, $100,000 from 1985 to 1988, and about $200,000 from 1989 on. Following Lawrence Katz and Kevin Murphy (1992), the earnings of top-coded individuals are adjusted to be 1.45 times the top-coded value. Beginning in 1996, instead of giving each top-coded observation the value of the top code, the CPS assigns the mean among the sample of top codes (by demographic group). The earnings figures can be as high as $600,000 in this period. We make no adjustment for top coding in these years. There is no apparent top coding of family earnings or family income. Real earnings and income are constructed using the deflator implied by the CPI-UX1.

5. The nonwhite group includes both blacks and white Hispanics.

6. The Federal Reserve provides an aggregate measure of only the capacity-utilization rate, so we cannot use this variable in the MSA-level analysis.

7. We also estimated models that included MSA linear time trends and unrestricted demographic group times year effects. Although including these variables improved the model fit considerably, they consistently had no significant effect on the estimated unemployment-rate effects.

8. Note that, for wages, earnings, and income, we use the change in the log of the mean outcome. It would be more consistent with an underlying individual model to take the mean of the log of the measure. However, since we are not, in general, conditioning on working, we cannot take the mean of log income or earnings owing to the prevalence of zeros.

9. For comparison to Solon, Barsky, and Parker (1994), earnings were deflated by the GNP deflator. Hourly earnings were derived as the ratio of annual labor income to annual hours worked. Individuals with assigned earnings or hours data were eliminated from the sample. Unlike Solon, Barsky, and Parker, we windsorized the hourly wage data (that is, rolled extreme values back) at $2.13 and $100 per hour in 1996 dollars and used sample weights to adjust for the low-income oversample; our results were not very sensitive to these changes.

10. When we tested the wage-curve specification against a Phillips curve specification, the PSID data preferred the wage curve; that is, if we include the current unemployment rate in the equations in table 10.6, it is statistically insignificant, while the change remains significant (in column 1).

11. For example, for column 1 of table 10.6, Solon, Barsky, and Parker find a coefficient of −.0135, and we find −.0129, and, for column 2 of table 10.7, we both find −.0140. The standard errors are also close.

12. If we use the log of the mean hourly wage (as was done in the previous section) in the model in column 1 of table 10.7 instead of the mean of the log hourly wage, the results are quite similar.

13. The coefficient (standard error) in the earlier period is 0.0046 (0.0054) and in the later period is −0.0033 (0.0063). The estimates for the unbalanced sample are similarly insignificant, as are estimates that use GNP growth as the cycle variable.

14. To check the robustness of our results, we also used the 1985 wave of the PSID and the May 1979 CPS Pension Supplement to estimate the tenure profiles. Our findings were qualitatively similar when the 1985 PSID sample was used but much less systematic when the CPS data were used.

15. Data reported in table 10.9 represent fiscal years, which for almost all states run from July 1 to June 30. Personal disposable income in the United States in the last two quarters of 1995 plus the first two quarters of 1996 was $5.398 trillion. Figures in table 10.9 are nominal, and therefore not adjusted for inflation.

16. See, for example, the estimated income coefficients in Anne Case, James Hines, and Harvey Rosen (1993), James Poterba (1994), and the studies surveyed by Daniel Rubinfeld (1987). It is for this reason that we use annual-income growth, rather than unemployment changes, as a measure of business-cycle conditions.

17. See the evidence provided in Poterba (1994, 1995).

18. Unlike in the preceding tables, the unemployment rate in these regressions is measured as a proportion, so a value of 0.01 corresponds to a 1 percentage point rise in state unemployment. Consequently, the estimates in the first column of table 10A.1 imply that a 1 percentage point rise in state unemployment (for example, the unemployment rate rising from 2.5 to 3.5 percent) corresponds to declines of 0.0069 percent in health and hospital spending, 0.0075 percent in highway spending, and 0.02 percent in welfare spending.

19. Other specification checks included adding additional lags of personal-income changes to the main regressions and (separately) distinguishing large from small personal-income changes to test for asymmetrical reactions over the business cycle. No consistently new patterns emerged from adding additional lags of personal-income changes to the main regressions, although estimated coefficients on lagged-income terms were often significant. When the sample is divided in half according to the size of income changes and the regressions run separately on each subsample, the results are similar to those reported for the whole sample. The estimated income coefficients tend to be somewhat larger for the sample with observations with slow income growth, suggesting that business-cycle downturns have a greater effect on the estimates than do periods of rapid economic growth, but the differences are not significant in a statistical sense.

20. In this context, it is noteworthy that AFDC and Transitional Assistance for Needy Families (TANF) represent relatively small fractions of total welfare spending by state and local governments. In fiscal year 1994, state and local governments spent $11.8 billion on AFDC, representing 12 percent of their total cash and noncash payments (of $98.6 billion) to persons with limited income. AFDC spending was roughly equal to the sum of total state and local spending on foster care, general assistance, and sup-

plemental security income (Burke 1996). Hence, business-cycle influences on AFDC expenditures might have a modest influence on total welfare spending by state and local governments.

21. Welfare institutions consist of the provision, construction, and maintenance of nursing homes and welfare institutions owned and operated by state and local governments for the benefit of needy persons; examples include public nursing homes, orphanages, homes for the elderly, and indigent-care institutions. Categorical-assistance programs include direct payments to beneficiaries under the supplemental security income program, AFDC or TANF, and Medicaid.

REFERENCES

Abraham, Katherine, and John Haltiwanger. 1995. "Real Wages and the Business Cycle." *Journal of Economic Literature* 33(3): 1215–64.

Acs, Gregory, and Douglas Wissoker. 1991. "The Impact of Local Labor Markets on the Employment Patterns of Young Inner-City Males." Mimeo. Washington, D.C.: Urban Institute.

Bartik, Timothy J. 1991. *Who Benefits from State and Local Economic Development Policies?* Kalamazoo, Mich.: W. E. Upjohn Institute for Employment Research.

———. 1993a. "Economic Development and Black Economic Success." *W. E. Upjohn Institute* technical report no. 93–001. Kalamazoo, Mich.: W. E. Upjohn Institute for Employment Research.

———. 1993b. "The Effects of Local Labor Markets on Individual Labor Market Outcomes for Different Demographic Groups and the Poor." *W. E. Upjohn Institute* working paper no. 93–23. Kalamazoo, Mich.: W. E. Upjohn Institute for Employment Research.

———. 1994. "The Effects of Metropolitan Job Growth on the Size Distribution of Family Income." *Journal of Regional Science* 34(4): 483–501.

———. 1996. "The Distributional Effects of Local Labor Demand and Industrial Mix: Estimates Using Individual Panel Data." *Journal of Urban Economics* 40(2): 150–78.

Bils, Mark. 1985. "Real Wages over the Business Cycle: Evidence from Panel Data." *Journal of Political Economy* 93(4): 666–89.

Blanchard, Olivier J., and Lawrence F. Katz. 1992. "Regional Evolutions." *Brookings Papers on Economic Activity* (1): 1–75.

———. 1997. "What We Know and Do Not Know about the Natural Rate of Unemployment." *Journal of Economic Perspectives* 11(winter): 51–72.

Blanchflower, David G., and Andrew J. Oswald. 1994. *The Wage Curve.* Cambridge, Mass.: MIT Press.

Blank, Rebecca. 1989. "Disaggregating the Effect of the Business Cycle on the Distribution of Income." *Economica* 56(2): 141–63.

———. 1990. "Why Are Wages Cyclical in the 1970s?" *Journal of Labor Economics* 8(1): 16–47.

———. 1993. "Why Were Poverty Rates So High in the 1980s?" In *Poverty and Prosperity in the Late Twentieth Century,* edited by Dimitri Papadimitriou and Edward Wolff. New York: St. Martin's.

———. 2001. "What Causes Public Assistance Caseloads to Grow?" *Journal of Human Resources* 36(1): 85–118.

———. Forthcoming. "Declining Caseloads/Increased Work: What Can We Conclude about the Effects of Welfare Reform?" Paper presented to the Federal Reserve Bank of New York conference, Welfare Reform Four Years Later. New York.

Blank, Rebecca, and Alan Blinder. 1986. "Macroeconomics, Income Distribution, and Poverty." In *Fighting Poverty: What Works and What Doesn't,* edited by Sheldon Danziger and Daniel Weinberg. Cambridge, Mass.: Harvard University Press.

Blank, Rebecca, and David Card. 1993. "Poverty, Income Distribution, and Growth: Are They Still Connected?" *Brookings Papers on Economic Activity* (2): 285–325.

Boden, Leslie, and John Ruser. 1999. "Choice of Medical Care Provider and Workplace Injuries." Mimeo. Washington: Bureau of Labor Statistics.

Bound, John, and Richard Freeman. 1992. "What Went Wrong? The Erosion of Relative Earnings and Employment among Young Black Men in the 1980s." *Quarterly Journal of Economics* 107(1): 201–32.

Bound, John, and Harry Holzer. 1993. "Industrial Shifts, Skill Levels, and the Labor Market for White and Black Males." *Review of Economics and Statistics* 75(August): 387–96.

———. 1995. "Structural Changes, Employment Outcomes, and Population Adjustments among Whites and Blacks: 1980–1990." *Institute for Research on Poverty* discussion paper no. 1057–95. Madison, Wisc.: Institute for Research on Poverty.

Budget of the United States Government, Fiscal Year 2001. 2000. Washington: U.S. Government Printing Office.

Burke, Vee. 1996. "Cash and Noncash Benefits for Persons with Limited Income: Eligibility Rules, Recipient and Expenditure Data, Fiscal Years 1992–1994." *Congressional Research Service* report no. 96–159 EPW. Washington: Congressional Research Service.

Cain, Glen, and Ross Finnie. 1990. "The Black-White Difference in Youth Employment: Evidence from Demand Side Factors." *Journal of Labor Economics* 8(1, part 2): S364–S395.

Card, David. 1995. "The Wage Curve: A Review." *Journal of Economic Literature* 33: 785–99.

Card, David, and Thomas Lemieux. 2000. "Dropout and Enrollment Trends in the Post-War Period: What Went Wrong in the 1970s?" *NBER* working paper no. 7658. Cambridge, Mass.: National Bureau of Economic Research, April.

Case, Anne C., James R. Hines Jr., and Harvey S. Rosen. 1993. "Budget Spillovers and Fiscal Policy Interdependence: Evidence from the States." *Journal of Public Economics* 52(3): 285–307.

Council of Economic Advisers. 1997. "Technical Report: Explaining the Decline in Welfare Receipt, 1993–1996." Mimeo. Washington: U.S. Government Printing Office.

———. 1999. *Economic Report of the President.* Washington: U.S. Government Printing Office.

Cutler, David M., and Lawrence F. Katz. 1991. "Macroeconomic Performance and the Disadvantaged." *Brookings Papers on Economic Activity* (1): 1–74.

Digest of Education Statistics. 1999. Washington: Department of Education, National Center for Education Statistics.

Dunlop, John. 1938. "The Movement of Real and Money Wages." *Economic Journal* 48(191): 413–34.

Ellwood, David T. 1982. "Teenage Unemployment: Permanent Scars or Temporary Blemishes?" In *The Youth Labor Market Problem: Its Nature, Causes, and Consequences,* edited by Richard Freeman and David Wise. Chicago: University of Chicago Press.

Freeman, Richard. 1982. "Economic Determinants of Geographic and Individual Variation in the Labor Market Position of Young Persons." In *The Youth Labor Market Problem: Its Nature, Causes, and Consequences,* edited by Richard Freeman and David Wise. Chicago: University of Chicago Press.

———. 1991a. "Employment and Earnings of Disadvantaged Young Men in a Labor Shortage Economy." In *The Urban Underclass,* edited by Christopher Jencks and Paul Peterson. Washington, D.C.: Brookings Institution.

———. 1991b. "Labour Market Tightness and the Mismatch between Demand and Supply of Less-Educated Young Men in the United States in the 1980s." In *Mismatch and Labour Mobility,* edited by P. Schioppa. Cambridge: Cambridge University Press.

———. 1999. "The Economics of Crime." In *Handbook of Labor Economics,* vol. 3c, edited by Orley Ashenfelter and David Card. Amsterdam: North-Holland.

———. 2001. "The Rising Tide Lifts . . . ?" *NBER* working paper no. 8155. Cambridge, Mass.: National Bureau of Economic Research.

Freeman, Richard, and William Rodgers III. 2000. "Area Economic Conditions and the Labor Market Outcomes of Young Men in the 1990s Expansion," In *Prosperity for All,* edited by Robert Cherry and William Rodgers III, 50–87. New York: Russell Sage Foundation.

Greenspan, Alan. 1973. "Comment on Okun." *Brookings Papers on Economic Activity* (1): 256–57.

Gustman, Alan, and Thomas Steinmeier. 1981. "The Impact of Wages and Unemployment on Youth Enrollment and Labor Supply." *Review of Economics and Statistics* 63(4): 553–60.

Hines, James R., Jr., and Richard H. Thaler. 1995. "The Flypaper Effect." *Journal of Economic Perspectives* 9(4): 217–26.

Holzer, Harry J. 1991. "Employment, Unemployment, and Demand Shifts in Local Labor Markets." *Review of Economics and Statistics* 73(1): 25–32.

Hoynes, Hilary W. 2000a. "The Employment and Earnings of Less Skilled Workers over the Business Cycle." In *Finding Jobs: Work and Welfare Reform,* edited by Rebecca Blank and David Card, 23–71. New York: Russell Sage Foundation.

———. 2000b. "Local Labor Markets and Welfare Spells: Do Demand Conditions Matter?" *Review of Economics and Statistics* 82(3): 351–68.

Katz, Lawrence, and Kevin Murphy. 1992. "Changes in Relative Wages, 1963–1987: Supply and Demand Factors." *Quarterly Journal of Economics* 107(1): 35–78.

Keane, Michael, Robert Moffitt, and David Runkle. 1988. "Real Wages over the Business Cycles: Estimating the Impact of Heterogeneity with Micro Data." *Journal of Political Economy* 96(6): 1232–66.

Ladd, Helen F. 1993. "State Responses to the TRA86 Revenue Windfalls: A New Test of the Flypaper Effect." *Journal of Policy Analysis and Management* 12(1): 82–103.

Light, Audrey. 1995. "Hazard Model Estimates of the Decision to Re-Enroll in School. *Labour Economics* 2(4): 381–406.

Lynch, Lisa. 1992. "Private Sector Training and Earnings." *American Economic Review* 82(1): 299–312.

Mocan, H. Naci, and Daniel Rees. 1999. "Economic Conditions, Deterrence, and Juvenile Crime: Evidence from Micro Data." *NBER* working paper no. 7405. Cambridge, Mass.: National Bureau of Economic Research.

Okun, Arthur M. 1973. "Upward Mobility in a High-Pressure Economy." *Brookings Papers on Economic Activity* (1): 207–52.

Poterba, James M. 1994. "State Responses to Fiscal Crises: The Effects of Budgetary Institutions and Politics." *Journal of Political Economy* 102(4): 799–821.

———. 1995. "Capital Budgets, Borrowing Rules, and State Capital Spending." *Journal of Public Economics* 56(2): 165–87.

Rubinfeld, Daniel L. 1987. "The Economics of the Local Public Sector." In *Handbook of*

Public Economics, vol. 2, edited by Alan J. Auerbach and Martin Feldstein, Amsterdam: North-Holland.

Smith, Robert S. 1972. "Intemporal Changes in Work Injury." *Industrial Relations Research Association Proceedings*: 167–74.

Solon, Gary, Robert Barsky, and Jonathan Parker. 1994. "Measuring the Cyclicality of Real Wages: How Important Is Composition Bias?" *Quarterly Journal of Economics* 109(1): 1–26.

Stock, James H., and Mark W. Watson. 1999. "Forecasting Inflation." *Journal of Monetary Economics* 44(2): 293–335.

Strumpf, Koleman S. 1998. "A Predictive Index for the Flypaper Effect." *Journal of Public Economics* 69(3): 389–412.

Swanson, Eric. 2001. "Real Wage Cyclicality in the PSID." Working paper. Washington: Federal Reserve Board of Governors.

U.S. Bureau of the Census. 1993. "Income and Poverty: 1993." CD-ROM. Available at *http://www. census.gov/hhes/income/incpov93/povtab2.html.*

———. 1998. "Marital Status and Living Arrangements: March 1998 Update." *Current Population Reports* series no. P20-514. Washington: U.S. Government Printing Office.

———. 2000. Income Statistics Branch/HHES Division. Current Population Survey. Available at *http://www.census.gov.hhes.income/histinc/h03.html.*

———. 2000. Poverty and Health Statistics Branch/HHES Division. Current Population Survey. Available at *http://www.censusgov/hhes/poverty/histpov/hstpov22.html.*

U.S. Department of Justice, Bureau of Justice Statistics. 2000. *Criminal Victimization 1999: Changes in 1998–1999 with trends 1993–1999.* Washington: U.S. Department of Justice.

U.S. House of Representatives, Committee on Ways and Means. 2000. *Background Material and Data on Programs within the Jurisdiction of the Committee on Ways and Means.* Washington: U.S. Government Printing Office.

Viscusi, W. Kip. 1993. "The Value of Risks to Life and Health." *Journal of Economic Literature* 31(4): 1912–46.

Wilson, William J. 1996. *When Work Disappears: The World of the New Urban Poor.* New York: Knopf.

Ziliak, James, David Figlio, Elizabeth Davis, and Laura Connelly. 2000. "Accounting for the Decline in AFDC Caseloads: Welfare Reform or Economic Growth?" *Journal of Human Resources* 35(3): 570–86.

Chapter 11

Rising Productivity and Falling Unemployment: Can the U.S. Experience Be Sustained and Replicated?

Lisa M. Lynch and Stephen J. Nickell

T he economic expansion of the U.S. economy over the past decade was quite exceptional, if not "fabulous," as Alan Blinder and Janet Yellen (chapter 3 in this volume) label it. Growth was at its highest level, and unemployment fell to its lowest level in a generation. Our purpose in this paper is to look at some of the forces underlying these dramatic changes.

We begin in the first section by looking at the sharp increase in the growth rate of potential output, which we split up into trend-productivity growth, the growth in the population of working age, falls in the equilibrium-unemployment rate, and the rate of inactivity. In the second section, we speculate on the reasons why trend-productivity growth rose in response to the rapid fall in the price of information-and-communication-technology (ICT) capital when no such shift was observed in the other industrialized countries despite their facing exactly the same decline in ICT prices. Particular issues that we highlight include the extensive workplace innovations and reorganization that took place in the 1990s and the lower regulatory burdens faced by U.S. firms, particularly with regard to business start-ups. However, we feel that there is some doubt as to whether the U.S. economy has the capacity to ensure that the skills of the workforce keep pace with the demands of information technology (IT) and new workplace practices.

In the third section, we analyze the fall in equilibrium unemployment, looking particularly at age-composition effects, the efficiency of job matching, and the unexpected rise in total-factor-productivity (TFP) growth. Then, in the fourth section, we focus on the inactivity rate, noting first that it fell only marginally during the boom of the late 1990s despite buoyant labor demand and rising real wages. In the light of this, we look at policies that might enhance labor-supply growth and lower the inactivity rate. These include improving job matching, providing wage subsidies, overcoming spatial mismatch, reducing disability, and improving labor supply among ex-prisoners. The paper concludes with a summary of policy recommendations.

RECENT EVENTS IN THE U.S. ECONOMY

The behavior of the U.S. economy has been startling—especially in the second half of the 1990s. Comparing averages over the periods 1986 to 1995 and 1996 to 1999 (inclusive), we find, as shown in figures 11.1 to 11.3, that average annual GDP growth has risen from 2.8 to 4.2 percent, that the average CPI inflation rate has fallen from 3.6 to 2.4 percent, and, most interestingly, that real-wage growth has increased from 0.3 to 1.7 percent. Indeed, average real wages have started to grow significantly for the first time in a generation. So what we have seen is a substantial and sustained increase in both GDP and real-wage growth at low and stable levels of inflation.

In order to see what underlies this dramatic shift, it is useful to look at the rate of growth of potential output, γ^*. First, we define potential output, Y^*, as

$$Y^* = \Theta^* \times \text{Pop} \times (1 - a) \times (1 - u^*) \times H^*, \qquad (11.1)$$

where Θ^* is "trend" productivity, Pop is the population of working age, a is the equilibrium rate of inactivity, u^* is the equilibrium-unemployment rate, and H^* is equilibrium hours. So potential output growth is given by

$$\gamma^* = \theta + \dot{\text{Pop}} - \dot{a} - \dot{u}^* + \dot{h}^*, \qquad (11.2)$$

FIGURE 11.1 / Real GDP

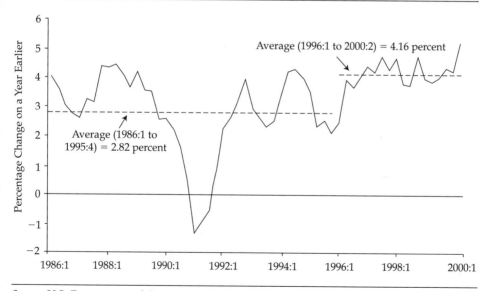

Source: U.S. Department of Commerce, Bureau of Economic Analysis.

where θ is trend-productivity growth, Pop, $\dot{h}^*$ are population- and equilibrium-hours-growth rates, and $\dot{a}$, $\dot{u}^*$ are rates of change of equilibrium inactivity and unemployment. The units are percentages per annum for the growth rates and percentage points per annum for the rates of change.

The next step is to investigate what has happened to the different elements of potential output growth in recent years. Here, we focus on average growth rates over the period 1996 to 2000 relative to 1986 to 1995.[1] We take each element of equation 11.2 in turn.

Trend-Productivity Growth

Over the period 1975 to 1995, U.S. labor-productivity growth (nonfarm-business sector) was 1.5 percent per annum, and there was no noticeable shift in the second half of this period, which we may take as the trend rate of productivity growth over the period 1986 to 1995. What has happened since? The changes are summarized in table 11.1, which is adapted from Stuart Berry and David England (2000, table 1). Robert Gordon (2000) suggests that trend-productivity growth has increased by 0.8 percentage points. Gordon's work reflects perhaps the most comprehensive attempt to eliminate the effects of the cycle, although

FIGURE 11.2 / The CPI

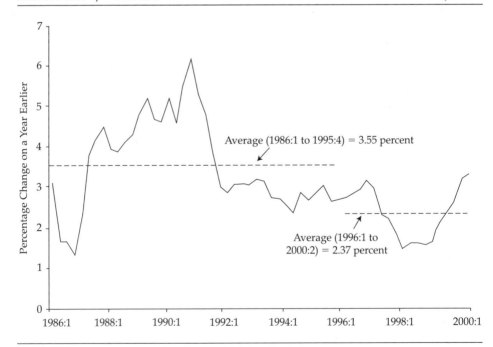

Source: U.S. Department of Labor, Bureau of Labor Statistics.

FIGURE 11.3 / Real Wages

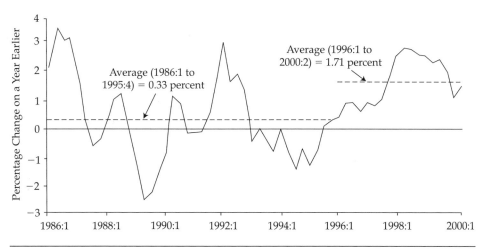

Source: U.S. Department of Labor, Bureau of Labor Statistics.

his estimates are thought by many to be conservative. This suggests a trend-productivity-growth rate in 1996 to 2000 of at least 2.3 percent.

The overall impression given by table 11.1 suggests that capital deepening focused on IT and TFP growth in IT production are crucial elements. The whole investment process is driven, at least in part, by the rapidly declining real price of IT capital, while improvements in labor quality appear to play no significant role. But there remains the mystery of what is driving TFP growth. Part of this may be some degree of TFP spillover into other sectors arising from the use of IT. This last point is less widely accepted, and we will return to this and other possible explanations later.

Population of Working Age

The average growth of the population of working age moved up from around 0.8 percent per annum in the period 1986 to 1995 to 1.3 percent per annum in 1996 to 2000.[2] Some of this growth is the result of pure demographics, but there has been a rise in the rate of net immigration over this period that has also contributed to this increase.

Inactivity Rate

Inactivity—and by *inactivity* we mean being out of the labor force—has been falling very slowly since the mid-1980s as steadily falling inactivity among women has been offset by very gradually rising inactivity among men. Over the period from the mid-1980s to the mid-1990s, inactivity has declined at a rate of

TABLE 11.1 / Sources of the Acceleration in Labor-Productivity Growth in the United States, 1974 to 1999

	Study 1	Study 2	Study 3	Study 4	Study 5
Acceleration in labor productivity	1.0	1.0	1.0	1.5	.8[a]
Of which					
Capital deepening	.5	.5	N.A.	.5	.3
IT sector	.3	.5	.5	N.A.	N.A.
Other sectors	.2	0	N.A.	N.A.	N.A.
Labor quality	−.1	−.1	N.A.	.1	.1
TFP	.6	.7	N.A.	.9	.3
IT production	.2	.4	.3	.2	.3
Other	.4	.3	N.A.	.7	.0
All other factors	N.A.	N.A.	.3	N.A.	.1[b]

Sources: Jorgenson and Stiroh (2000), Oliner and Sichel (2000), Whelan (2000), Council of Economic Advisers (2000), and Gordon (2000).

Notes: Study 1 (Jorgenson and Stiroh 2000) covers the periods 1990 to 1995 and 1995 to 1999; study 2 (Oliner and Sichel 2000) the periods 1990 to 1995 and 1995 to 1998; study 3 (Whelan 2000) the periods 1974 to 1995 and 1996 to 1998; study 4 (Council of Economic Advisers 2000) the periods 1973 to 1995 and 1995 to 1999; and study 5 (Gordon 2000) the periods 1972 to 1995 and 1995 to 1999. N.A. = not available.

[a]Structural acceleration in labor productivity, which eliminates the increases associated with cyclic effects.

[b]Includes the contribution of price-measurement changes.

around 0.14 percentage points per year. Then, in the most recent period, the overall rate of decline has slowed to a mere 0.03 percentage points per annum, which is quite surprising given the growth in real wages and the booming demand for labor.[3] Given that these rates are so minuscule, there seems to be no harm in assuming that they reflect trend rates.

Equilibrium-Unemployment Rate

Actual unemployment in 1985 was 7.4 percent. By 1995, it had fallen to 5.6 percent, and it fell to 4.1 percent in 2000.[4] This latter number reflects the lowest rate of unemployment that the United States has seen for a generation. The numbers also suggest, given low and relatively stable levels of inflation, that equilibrium unemployment has fallen, and this impression is confirmed by the estimates presented in OECD (1999b, table B3), which suggest that U.S. equilibrium unemployment fell from 6.3 percent in 1986 to 5.7 percent in 1995, a rate of decline of 0.067 percentage points per annum, and that it experienced a more rapid rate of decline of 0.2 percentage points per annum in the late 1990s. More recent estimates derived from Douglas Staiger, James Stock, and Mark Watson (chapter 1 in this volume) suggest a somewhat faster rate of decline in the earlier period of 0.13 percentage points per annum, rising to the same rate of 0.2 percentage points per annum in the late 1990s.[5] We shall use these estimates in table 11.2.

Working Hours

Average annual hours worked per employed person have been very stable in the United States since the 1970s (see OECD 1999a, table F), aside from some small cycle effects, so we feel that it is best to suppose that long-run potential hours have remained unchanged throughout.

Summarizing Potential Output Growth

The preceding discussion suggests the following breakdown of potential output growth over the two periods (see table 11.2). The first point to note is the substantial rise of over 1.3 percentage points in the second period. This increase in the rate of growth of potential supply is the force underlying the benign outcome of increased GDP growth at low and stable levels of inflation noted at the outset. Of course, the key macroeconomic policy problem that arises when there is a surge in the growth rate of potential supply is to allow monetary policy to be loose enough to enable aggregate demand to keep pace, despite the fact that, looking backward, such a monetary policy would appear dangerously expansionary. This seems to have been achieved in the mid-1990s in the United States, an achievement that has, presumably, contributed to the mythical status of the chairman of the Federal Reserve.

Also apparent from table 11.2 is the fact that the major part of the increase in potential GDP growth is due to the rise in labor-productivity growth and the growth of the population of working age. Contributions from changes in the employment rate are negligible, with a faster rate of decline in equilibrium unemployment being offset by a slower rate of fall in inactivity.

Having identified the factors underlying the dramatic change in the U.S. economy in the late 1990s, we look more closely at each in turn. First, we discuss certain aspects of the rise in trend productivity, including the factors that have contributed to this growth and what might undermine future growth potential. Then we analyze the fall in equilibrium unemployment and the very slow decline in inactivity. In the light of this final point, we then discuss policies that might improve the operation of the labor market and enhance the growth of labor supply. Although the change in the growth rate of the population of working age plays a key role in table 11.2, we shall not have much more to say on the subject. Aside from demographics, the key factor here is immigration, which is a major issue and one that we do not have the space to tackle. David Ellwood (chapter 9 in this volume) provides a full treatment of the population question.

TABLE 11.2 / Contribution to Potential Output Growth, 1986 to 2000

	1986 to 1995	1996 to 2000
Productivity	1.50	2.30
Population of working age	.80	1.30
Inactivity	.14	.03
Equilibrium unemployment	.13	.20
Hours	0	0
Total	2.58	3.83

Source: Authors' tabulations.

THE RISE IN TREND PRODUCTIVITY

The rise in trend-productivity growth in the United States in the second half of the 1990s is remarkable because, for the first time since the Second World War, trend-productivity growth is now higher in the United States than in most of the developed OECD countries.[6] Prior to 1995, trend-productivity growth in the United States was consistently below that in nearly all OECD countries. This fact was consistent with a steady convergence of these countries toward the frontier country (the United States) (see Crafts and Toniolo 1996).

With average annual productivity growth in the United States during the 1990s at 2.7 percent for nonfinancial corporations (the preferred measure of the chairman of the Federal Reserve) and 4 percent for manufacturing firms, many have argued that a "new economy" is being created in the United States. This new economy is characterized, as we have already noted, by capital deepening, mainly in IT capital, with increases in TFP growth in the IT sector and some spillovers into other sectors. As we have also already noted, a major driving force behind this investment has been the rapid decline in the real price of IT capital. But this price decline has occurred in all other countries as well. So why has the United States experienced this surge in technological change and, hence, in labor demand and, ultimately, in real wages, a surge that has not really been visible elsewhere? The surge has probably not been due simply to large differences in ICT expenditure because, as we can see from table 11.3, the relevant expenditures are not that dissimilar. Nor is it due to any dramatic differences in research and development, for, while the United States has a relatively high research-and-development intensity, it is not exceptional, being lower than that in Japan, for example (see OECD 1999c). Furthermore, the significance of domestic research and development is diminished by the diffusion of new technology via foreign transplants.

So what might be some possible explanations? We propose two. The first relates to regulatory barriers, which, we suspect, have played a role in cross-country differences in productivity growth in recent years. The second has to do with another dimension of the so-called new economy—workplace reorganization.

TABLE 11.3 / ICT Expenditure as a Percentage of GDP, 1997

	IT Hardware	IT Service and Software	Telecommunications	Total
United States	1.7	3.4	2.7	7.8
France	.9	3.3	2.2	6.4
Germany	.9	2.4	2.3	5.6
United Kingdom	1.5	3.4	2.7	7.6
Japan	1.1	2.7	3.6	7.4
OECD	1.3	2.8	2.8	6.9

Source: OECD (1999c, table 2.3.1).

Regulatory Burdens

The idea that we pursue here is that the United States is able to generate and, more important, to absorb new technologies more rapidly than other countries because firms face relatively modest regulatory barriers. With the rise of ICT at a rapidly declining cost, what is required is the necessary flexibility both to generate practical new ideas and to absorb these into production and distribution. And, of course, the more easily new ideas can be absorbed, the greater the incentive to produce them. What is the evidence on this issue? As we have already noted, a surge in productivity growth has a direct effect on labor demand. Robert Haffner et al. (2000) provide a cross-country analysis of the relation between product-market regulations and employment rates. As a first step, the employment rates of all the countries analyzed are purged of the effect of labor-market institutions using panel-data analysis with country dummies (see Haffner et al. 2000, table 3.2). At the second stage, the residual cross-country variation in employment rates is related to various types of business regulation (see Haffner et al. 2000, table 3.3). Two particular types stand out as being of vital importance— state interference in private firms and administrative burdens on both corporations and business start-ups. Both factors are associated with low levels of employment, having already controlled for standard differences in labor-market regulation.[7]

In table 11.4, we present indicators for these different factors across the OECD, and it is immediately clear that the United States had relatively low levels of interference and administrative burden, particularly as far as start-up companies are concerned. It is especially noteworthy that both Ireland and Denmark, two European success stories of the 1990s, also have low levels of regulation. By contrast, the major countries of Continental Europe—France, Germany, Italy, and Spain—are highly regulated, so it is less than surprising that they respond more sluggishly to the new opportunities generated by ICT. However, although they will absorb the new technology more slowly because of their high entry barriers, there is, on the basis of past evidence, every reason to assume that France and Germany will eventually catch up. And, once having done so,

TABLE 11.4 / Summary Indicators of Regulations of the Private Sector

	State Interference in Private Firms	Administrative Burdens on Business Start-Ups	Corporations
United States	.9	.8	.5
Australia	1.8	1.0	1.0
Austria	1.8	2.4	2.8
Belgium	3.8	2.6	1.5
Canada	1.4	1.3	1.5
Denmark	2.7	.4	.5
Finland	1.9	1.7	1.5
France	3.0	3.4	3.3
Germany	2.5	2.5	2.5
Ireland	.5	.9	1.5
Italy	3.3	4.5	5.3
Japan	2.1	2.0	2.3
The Netherlands	1.9	1.6	1.8
Norway	2.5	1.6	1.9
New Zealand	1.8	.9	1.0
Portugal	3.0	1.8	2.5
Spain	3.4	2.8	3.8
Sweden	.6	1.0	1.3
Switzerland	1.8	2.2	3.3
United Kingdom	1.2	.8	.8

Source: Nicoletti, Scarpetta, and Boyland (2000, tables A3.1, A3.2, A2.2.2).

they will then be able to sustain solid rates of productivity growth as the technology matures because of their effective systems of labor-force training at all levels of the ability range (see, for example, Steedman 1999). An interesting issue is, thus, the extent to which training systems in the United States can help maintain the newfound momentum on the productivity front. This is the topic of our next subsection.

The Knowledge Economy

In addition to investments in ICT, firms have also during the 1990s been adopting "knowledge-based" work processes, in which an increasing proportion of nonmanagerial workers are involved in problem solving and identifying opportunities for innovation and growth. Some have argued that this new focus on quality management, continuous innovation, incentive-based compensation, and employee-involvement programs has in turn raised the productive capacity of our economy. Recent studies by Stephen Oliner and Daniel Sichel (2000) and Dale Jorgenson and Kevin Stiroh (2000) find that, while slightly less than half the growth in output in U.S. private nonfarm business during the 1990s can be explained by changes in inputs (especially capital), more than half is due to multi-factor-productivity growth. And figure 11.4 shows that multifactor-productivity growth was an extremely important component of output growth in the manu-facturing sector during the 1990s.

So what might explain the growth in multifactor productivity? One possible explanation is technology spillover. A second concerns the effect of workplace innovation on productivity. Recent work by Sandra Black and Lisa Lynch (2001a) uses estimates of the effect of workplace practices on labor productivity in the manufacturing sector to examine how different types of workplace innovation can account for changes in manufacturing output over the period 1993 to 1996. Black and Lynch find that workplace practices accounted for approximately 30 percent of output growth in manufacturing, or 89 percent of multifactor-produc-tivity growth.

What are some examples of these workplace innovations? As detailed in Black and Lynch (2001b), in a nationally representative survey of U.S. employers in 1997, 41 percent of manufacturers and 54 percent of nonmanufacturers re-ported that 50 percent or more of their nonmanagerial employees met on a regu-lar basis to discuss workplace issues. Nineteen percent of manufacturers and 16 percent of nonmanufacturers had a quarter or more of their employees in self-managed teams. Slightly more than 25 percent of all businesses (both manufac-turing and nonmanufacturing) underwent some type of reengineering activity over the period 1993 to 1996. Finally, more than 40 percent of employers offered profit sharing or stock options to their employees. Given the extent of computer-

FIGURE 11.4 / Annual Output Growth in Manufacturing, 1990 to 1998: Contributions from Combined Inputs and Multifactor Productivity

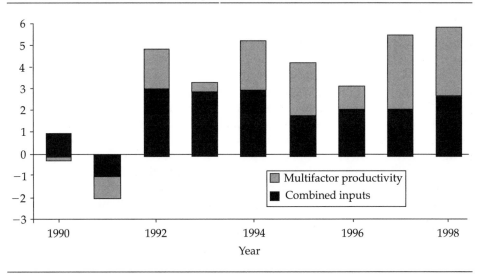

Source: U.S. Bureau of Labor Statistics (2000).

Note: Output growth is composed of changes in multifactor productivity and combined input.

ization and changing work organization, it is not surprising to see that 53 percent of nonmanufacturing and 46 percent of manufacturing employers in the United States reported that skills associated with the work of production or frontline employees increased over the period 1993 to 1996.

So the good news is that workplace innovations may go some way toward explaining the recent growth in multifactor productivity. But, if these workplace practices are so good, why haven't they been adopted by all firms? There are a variety of possible explanations. First, many firms may be ignorant of the potential benefits of adopting such practices. There is certainly a thriving management-consulting sector in the U.S. economy that has tried to bridge this information gap. Second, while these practices may raise productivity, they are not costless. As a result, after tallying the costs of adopting them (including management-consulting fees, lost output, and wage premiums to get workers to participate), some firms may decide that they are too expensive (for a discussion of the effect of these practices on compensation costs, see Black and Lynch 2001a). Finally, new technologies and greater employee involvement in problem solving and decision making require higher skill levels of workers. If current workers are not sufficiently prepared to utilize new technologies or other types of workplace innovations, then firms may find that training costs are too high to bring their workforce up to speed.

In other words, skill shortages in the tight U.S. labor market can take two forms—a scarcity of labor and a scarcity of skills. The first manifests itself in labor shortages, and policies to address it will be addressed in the next section. The second manifests itself in a lack of preparation on the part of currently employed workers. For example, in 1997, more than one-third of U.S. employers reported that 25 percent or more of their workers were not fully proficient at their current job. This is slightly up from 1994, when 32 percent of employers reported that a quarter or more of their workers were not fully proficient (see Black and Lynch 1996, 2001b). A 1999 American Management Association survey reported that over 38 percent of job applicants tested for basic skills by U.S. corporations lacked the necessary reading, writing, and math skills to do the jobs they sought—up from 35.5 percent in 1998 and 22.8 percent in 1997. It is not just employers who say that workers are not prepared for their jobs. Workers recognize this as well. For example, a recent study by Edwin Leuven and Hessel Oosterbeek (1999) found that one in four workers in the United States reported being undertrained. Part of the reason why employers may be facing more skills-deficient applicants is because they are hiring further down in the distribution of skills given the overall strength of the economy.

While this skills shortage seems not to have stalled or limited the growth associated with the new economy so far, it may do so in the future. Therefore, it is important to understand the current distribution of skills in the economy and the ability of existing institutions to provide skills upgrading support. Let us begin with the preparedness of workers entering the workforce. As shown in table 11.5, there is significant variation across countries in terms of the basic preparation of youths entering the labor force. For example, among those aged

TABLE 11.5 / Percentage of Sixteen- to Twenty-Five-Year-Olds with Low Literacy Skills

Sweden	3.1	Australia	9.7
Germany	5.2	Canada	10.4
Belgium	5.8	Ireland	17.0
The Netherlands	6.1	United Kingdom	17.8
Switzerland (German speaking)	7.1	New Zealand	18.3
Switzerland (French speaking)	8.7	United States	24.7

Source: OECD (1997b).

sixteen to twenty-five, 25 percent in the United States but only 3 percent in Sweden suffer from low literacy skills.

The recently released TIMMS (2000) international study on student achievement in mathematics in the eighth grade gives us even more reason to worry. In 1995, when students in the fourth and eighth grades were tested on their mathematics abilities, American fourth graders were at, but American eighth graders were well below, the international average. The hope was that the education reforms instituted in the second half of the 1990s would improve the performance of U.S. eighth graders considerably. However, when students were tested again in 1999, the relative position of the United States remained well below the international average, just as in 1995. Given that, in the United States, less-educated workers are less likely to obtain on-the-job skills training (see Lynch 1992, 1994), a vicious circle is created for those young people who enter the labor market poorly prepared to work with most technologies, let alone ICTs.

There are many strategies that one could pursue to equip young workers with the skills that they need to face the changing labor market. In the United States, where there is less emphasis on vocational education than there is in countries such as Germany, the dropout-prevention effort has included attempts to keep at-risk youths in school longer as well as bringing work-based learning within schools. Unfortunately, when one evaluates programs targeting unemployed and disadvantaged youths, the results are mixed. For example, programs funded by the Job Training Partnership Act (JTPA) have had little effect on subsequent employment or earnings (see U.S. Department of Labor 1995). Funding for youth training has fallen sharply on the basis of the resulting perception that such intervention does little good. More generally, as detailed in Donahue, Lynch, and Whitehead (2000), total federal outlays for education and training peaked at a bit more than 1 percent of GDP in 1977 but declined to just over half the 1977 level by 1997. Inflation-adjusted JTPA training funds per civilian labor-force member declined from almost $9 in 1993 to around $7 in 1999. Fewer than 1 percent of eligible American adults actually participated in JTPA programs in the mid-1990s, and fewer than three-fourths of those who participated received any actual training (as opposed to skills assessment and other placement services)—most of which, moreover, was very short term.

But there are successful programs. One such is the Job Corps. Each year, at

121 sites across the United States, the Job Corps enrolls about seventy-three thousand young people—most of whom are high school dropouts who have never held jobs—in a twelve-month, highly intensive residential program that combines education with training in vocational skills and provides a range of other support services as well. While this is an expensive program—the average cost per individual enrollee is $19,000—an early evaluation (Mallar et al. 1982) concluded that, when one compared its upfront costs with the value of the output—reduced government assistance, increased earnings, and reductions in serious crime—its lifetime benefits exceeded its costs by 45 percent. The recent random-assignment evaluation in Peter Schochet, John Burghardt, and Steven Glazerman (2000) suggests that the Job Corps continues to generate positive employment and earnings effects. For example, as shown in table 11.6, thirty months after program completion, the gain in average weekly earnings per participant was 11 percent.

A second success story has been the Center for Employment Training in San Jose (see U.S. Department of Labor 1995). This program provides three to six months of nonresidential vocational training to disadvantaged youths and adults. Most of the enrollees are high school dropouts, most are Hispanic, and over half are limited in their ability to speak English. After completion of the program—which for youths on average involves 335 hours of training over a 4.1-month period—earnings of participants are 40 percent higher than those of similar workers who have not completed the program. What seems to have made the program so successful are the close connections that the staff have with local employers, the fact that programs and counseling services are tailored to individual needs, and the fact that basic skills training is provided in the context of job training. It should also be noted that this program is much less

TABLE 11.6 / Effect of Job Corps Using Random Assignment

	Program Group	Control Group	Effect per Eligible Applicant	Effect per Participant
Average weekly earnings by quarter after random assignment ($)				
8 quarters	161.90	153.9	8.0*	10.9*
10 quarters	180.6	167.7	12.9*	17.7*
Percentage employed by quarter				
8 quarters	59.9	58.4	1.6*	2.1*
10 quarters	66.9	64.8	2.1*	2.8*
Sample size	7,311	4,476	11,787	

Source: Schochet, Burghardt, and Glazerman (2000).

*Significantly different from 0 at the .05 level, two-tailed test.

expensive than the Job Corps, with an average cost of $4,200 per enrollee in the early 1990s. (For more details on this and other programs, see Cave et al. 1993.)

New ICTs (the Internet in particular) may provide important tools with which to meet the skill deficiencies of disadvantaged youths. Not everyone can take advantage of these developments, however, since not everyone has equal access to computers. Advantaged families are much more likely to have computers at home than are disadvantaged families. As a result, children from advantaged households become more proficient with the technology and proficient earlier than do children from disadvantaged households. Also, schools and libraries in affluent communities (or countries) are much more likely to have computers than are schools and libraries in poor areas, with the same result—greater proficiency among the affluent.

It is clear that the transition of a young worker from formal education into the workplace will be more complicated in the years to come than it was in the past. It is also clear that learning will not stop the moment a student leaves the classroom. It is, therefore, important to ensure that initial education provides a solid basis on which workers can build as they acquire new skills in the workplace.

Resolving to give our young people a better education in the future is all well and good, but what about those individuals already in the workforce, 40 percent of whom have only a high school diploma or less? What innovative technologies and workplace practices have highlighted is the necessity of acquiring new skills after completing formal education. Where can such skills be acquired?

One option is federal-government-funded training programs for those workers who lose their jobs or have been out of work for a significant amount of time. Random-assignment evaluations of job-training programs for disadvantaged adults (see Bloom et al. 1993) have found higher earnings among those who participated in federally funded JTPA programs, especially when those programs involved on-the-job training. Unfortunately, few studies have evaluated programs targeting dislocated workers, such as those provided under the Trade Adjustment Assistance Program. However, one study of Pennsylvania's Displaced Workers Employment and Training Program (see Jacobson, LaLonde, and Sullivan 1994) found that workers who received one to two years of community college training showed earnings gains of 6 to 7 percent per year of education received. More generally, gains for workers from these types of federally funded training programs appear to grow with time.

In spite of the evidence that government training programs can make a difference in the employment and earnings experience of adult workers, it is unlikely that, in the near future at least, displaced or low-wage adult workers will obtain much retraining through federally funded programs. The formulas for allocating each year's Workforce Investment Act appropriations among the states have been inherited from the JTPA. As a result, a state's share of funding is based mostly on unemployment rates and concentrated joblessness, which works against states that are plagued more by earnings shortfalls among the working poor than by high pockets of unemployment. In fact, in President Bush's proposed budget for 2002, there is a cut of over $500 million in funding for training adult dislocated workers (a 10 percent reduction from fiscal year 2001), a cut justified in part because so many states in the past were not able to draw federal funds for training because their unemployment rate had fallen too low.

A second option for workers seeking to acquire new skills is state-funded training programs. The National Governors' Association (1999) recently completed a survey of state training initiatives. It was calculated that, in 1998, over $575 million was spent by states on employer-focused job-training programs. The four states with the largest programs on a per capita basis—California, Iowa, Rhode Island, and Texas—spent well over $1,000 per trainee, while the state ranked twenty-fifth, Utah, spent just $300 per trainee. While most states pay for such programs out of general-fund appropriations, ten states fund employer-focused training through a levy on employers linked to the unemployment-insurance tax. Three other states (Iowa, Kansas, and Missouri) have developed special debt instruments to finance such training programs.

But workers are still most likely to acquire retraining in the workplace. This is especially true for training associated with ICT, which may be proprietary or too new for training to be available outside the firm that developed the technology. Workplace training differs from other forms of human-capital investment such as education and government training programs in that there are at least two parties to the training decision—the worker (who may or may not be represented by a union) and the firm. Firms concerned with upgrading employees' skills are constantly facing two possible strategies—"make" the skills in house or "buy" them from outside. If employee turnover is high, firms may be reluctant to train workers in house. If new skills such as those associated with IT are valuable to other employers, firms run the risk of having a newly trained worker hired away by another employer and, as a result, may be less likely to provide these skills. Consequently, investments in nonportable firm-specific training are more attractive investments to firms than is more general training. In addition, smaller firms often face higher training costs per employee because they cannot spread fixed training costs across a wider group of employees. The end result is that rational employers may wind up investing in a suboptimal level of training.

Since the training investment is two-sided, there is still no guarantee that workers who want and need training will actually be able to obtain it. Research has shown that it is the more educated employees who are the most likely to be retrained by their firms (see, for example, Lynch 1992). This results in the creation of both a "virtuous" circle and a "vicious" circle of human-capital accumulation. Individuals who acquire more schooling are also more likely to receive postschool employer-provided training (the virtuous circle), while those with minimal education find it extremely difficult to make up this deficiency in human capital once they enter the labor market (the vicious circle). In addition, as summarized in Lynch (1994), workers typically less likely to receive employer-sponsored training include women, minorities, and those employed in smaller firms. Table 11.7 shows how the probability of receiving employer-provided training varies by occupation and firm size.

TABLE 11.7 / Who Gets Employer-Provided Job-Skills Training? (Percentage)

Category of Worker	All Employers	Smaller Employers	Larger Employers
Management	50	46	80
Professional or technical	38	38	42
Computer	53	51	71
Sales	58	56	69
Clerical	35	33	48
Services	17	16	29
Production	36	34	47

Source: U.S. Bureau of Labor Statistics (1993).

None of these issues would necessarily result in underinvestment in training if capital markets were perfect and workers could therefore borrow to finance more general training, assuming that the government subsidized general training or that workers accepted lower wages during training spells. However, capital markets are far from perfect, and workers differ from employers in their attitudes toward risk and time horizons. As a result, there may be a market failure in the provision of general training and the proportion of workers trained in more general skills.

Not surprisingly, one reason cited for the increased demand for learning by workers is the rapid rate of technological change. One group particularly vulnerable to change associated with IT is older workers. If IT increases the depreciation rate of both physical and human capital because it makes older, non-IT technology and skills obsolete, and if the payoff period to investment in human capital is shortened, older workers may become more marginalized in the workforce. In an increasingly skills-driven economy, a key issue is the extent to which the growing number of mid- and late-career workers are able to refresh, expand, and redeploy their job skills.

Innovation in ICT could, in principal, be a powerful tool to help workers acquire the skills needed to keep pace with changes in technology. For small firms, the development of distance learning may go some way toward lowering the marginal costs of training workers. Computer-based learning can also potentially address a second deficit that many unskilled workers face—the time deficit. In the face of falling hourly wages, many unskilled workers have taken on second jobs or increased their hours of work to try to maintain standards of living. What this means, however, is that they have little time outside work to engage in new learning activities. For women, this can be especially difficult as many finish the paid workday and return home to start the "second shift." So a pressing policy issue seems to be how to get unskilled workers who are not computer literate sufficiently skilled to take advantage of additional training through the Internet. At the moment, IT is more likely to play a role in refining and extending existing skills than in developing basic skills, a process that will probably remain more interpersonal.

In sum, the dramatic increase in productivity growth in the United States during the second half of the 1990s seems to be due to investments in new ICTs. In addition, workplace innovations and reorganization (including spillovers from these IT investments) appear to have contributed to the rise in TFP growth over this period. It also appears to be the case that, owing to lower regulatory burdens, U.S. firms have been able to leverage new technology and workplace innovations better than many of their European counterparts. But the capacity of the U.S. economy to ensure that the skills of its workforce keep pace with the demands of IT and new workplace practices seems suspect—unless we see drastic changes in business practices.

THE FALL IN EQUILIBRIUM UNEMPLOYMENT

There are many models of equilibrium unemployment based on both stock and flow foundations (for a basic example of the former, see Blanchard and Katz 1997; for an example of the latter, see Pissarides 1990). Luckily, nearly all have the same broad implications. Several things are notable. First, actual unemployment is determined by real demand. Indeed, it does little harm to think of these as one and the same thing. Second, in the long run, real demand and thus unemployment generally tend toward the level required to stabilize inflation, that is, the equilibrium level. These days, across most OECD countries, the way in which monetary policy is set typically assists this process. Third, the equilibrium level of unemployment is determined by a group of factors that may be conveniently divided into two groups: those that tend to shift the Beveridge curve (the steady-state unemployment-vacancy [UV] locus) and those that tend to raise wages despite excess supply in the labor market. These latter will not, generally, shift the Beveridge curve. The former set of factors includes benefit systems, exogenous factors influencing inflow rates (from employment [E] to unemployment [U]), mobility barriers, and job-matching efficiency. The latter factors include wage-bargaining systems and real-wage resistance. This last reflects situations where wage outcomes sustain or attempt to sustain past levels of real-wage growth when the level of real-wage growth consistent with stable employment levels unexpectedly falls or rises. This happens when, for example, there are changes in employment taxes, the terms of trade, or trend rates of productivity growth (see Ball and Moffitt, chapter 2 in this volume).

In the light of this, what has happened in the United States over the 1990s? Many of the important issues have been discussed in Lawrence Katz and Alan Krueger (1999), and we consider, in turn, the Beveridge curve, demographics and other composition effects, improvements in job matching, increases in product-market competition, and the effect of the rise in trend-productivity growth.

Shifts in the U.S. Beveridge Curve

In figure 11.5, we present a picture of the shifting Beveridge curve since 1960, where vacancies are based on the "help wanted" index. We also show the cubic trend (figure 11.6) based on the following estimated curve (1961 to 1999):

$$\ln u_t = \underset{(6.8)}{0.45} \ln u_{t-1} - \underset{(10.5)}{0.76} \ln v_t + \underset{(4.4)}{0.047}\, t - \underset{(1.6)}{0.11 \times 10^{-2} t^2} - \underset{(0.4)}{0.47} \underset{(11.3)}{}$$
$$\times 10^{-5} t^3 + \text{constant}, \quad T = 39, \ \overline{R}^2 = 0.93.$$

It seems clear that there has been a significant move to the left since the early 1980s, which is consistent with a fall in equilibrium unemployment over this period and, furthermore, suggests an important role for the group of variables that are liable to move the Beveridge curve. Unfortunately, this evidence is not decisive because the vacancy data rely on the use of the help-wanted index, which is based on newspaper advertisements. The secular relation between the number of vacancies and the volume of job advertisements is unlikely to be stable, and, while Katherine Abraham (1987) has provided some adjustments to the help-wanted index prior to 1985, nothing that corrects the index after 1985 is available. A glance at figure 11.5 reveals that vacancies in the late 1990s seem

FIGURE 11.5 / The U.S. Beveridge Curve, 1960 to 1999

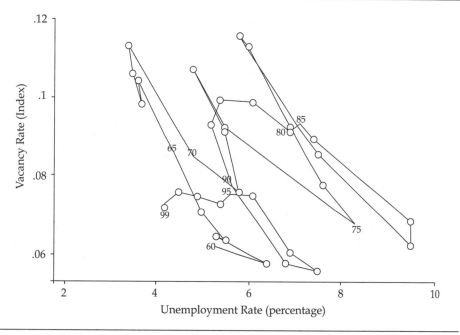

Sources: U.S. Department of Labor, Bureau of Labor Statistics and The Conference Board.

FIGURE 11.6 / Trend for the United States, 1961 to 1999

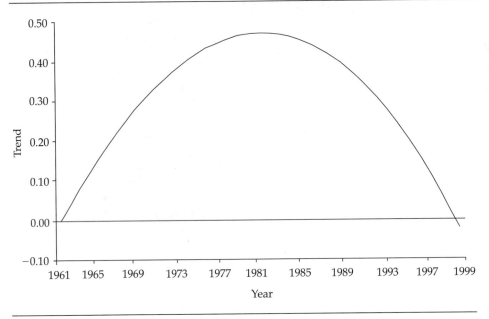

Source: Authors' calculations.

low given the tightness of the labor market, and this may well be due to job recruiters making relatively less use of newspapers and more use of electronic media. As a consequence, we need to look for more specific evidence.

Changes in the Age Structure of the Labor Force and Other Composition Effects

As is well-known, young workers have higher unemployment rates than do prime-age workers, largely because they have higher inflow rates. Furthermore, the proportion of young workers (those aged sixteen to twenty-four) in the labor force has declined steadily since the late 1970s as the baby-boom generation has aged, falling from around 24 to 16 percent in the late 1990s. The contribution of this decrease to the decline in equilibrium unemployment since the mid-1980s is, according to Katz and Krueger (1999), around 0.4 percentage points. Katz and Krueger also note the potential contribution made by the dramatic rise in the prison population since the early 1980s (from around 0.3 percent of the population of working age in 1980 to close to 1 percent in the late 1990s). Since the potential unemployment rate among those incarcerated is likely to be far higher than average, their removal from circulation has an effect on the equilibrium-unemployment rate equal to close to 0.2 percentage points (see Katz and Krueger 1999, table 13).

Improvements in the Efficiency of Job Matching

Various changes in the U.S. labor market point in the direction of improving job-matching efficiency. First, the benefit system took on a more active role in helping difficult-to-place workers into jobs, with the introduction of Worker Profile and Re-Employment Services programs in the mid-1990s. While this is only a small step relative to the changes introduced in, for example, Denmark or the Netherlands (discussed subsequently), it seems to be one in the right direction. Second, and much more significant in terms of matching efficiency, is the rapid growth of private-sector-employment intermediaries in the 1990s. By December 2000, no less than 2.5 percent of U.S. employment was in the temporary-help-services industry, up from around 0.5 percent in 1982. The evidence suggests that these intermediaries lower hiring costs and facilitate better job matches, which would tend to shift the Beveridge curve to the left. Katz and Krueger (1999) suggest that these changes may have reduced equilibrium unemployment by as much as 0.4 percentage points.

In recent years, the Internet has also had a large effect on the job-matching process. As described in a recent study by Merrill Lynch (2000), numerous on-line job sites have emerged that enable job seekers to have much greater access to information about the labor market and employers to have direct contact with job seekers in a less expensive manner. Merrill Lynch reports that the average cost per Internet hire is around $1,000 but that the cost of hiring through job fairs is about $3,000, through newspaper ads $5,000, and through a headhunter $12,000. In 1996, the U.S. Department of Labor launched America's Job Bank (*www.ajb.org*) to promote improved access to information on job availability and training. There are currently over 1.2 million jobs listed with America's Job Bank and close to 500,000 résumés. The private sector has also become very active in the use of the Internet for job placement. One such site is monster.com, launched in 1999. By the end of 2000, monster.com had 7.2 million résumés and over 250,000 employers registered on its site. This is up from 2.5 million résumés and approximately 60,000 employers in 1999. As discussed in David Autor (2000), one of the implications of the increasing reliance by employers on the Internet for job matching is that use of only the Conference Board's help-wanted index as an indication of job vacancies may miss out on other important sources of job listings.

Increases in Product-Market Competition

It is sometimes argued that product-market competition has increased through the 1990s as a result of deregulation and increased international trade. In general equilibrium, an overall increase in product-market competition will typically lead to lower equilibrium unemployment as well as higher wages[8] and a higher wage share (for a summary of theory and evidence, see Nickell 1999). For example, in the standard Cobb-Douglas case, the share of labor is the employment exponent in the production function divided by the price markup on marginal cost. The latter, of course, tends to fall as product-market competition rises. However, since there is no strong evidence of any secular rise in labor's share in the United States since the 1980s (see Bentolila and Saint-Paul 1999), this is not a very persuasive reason for falling equilibrium unemployment.

The Unexpected Rise in TFP Growth

As we can see from table 11.1, the trend rate of TFP growth rose unexpectedly, by between 0.3 and 0.9 percentage points per annum. This could lead to a temporary reduction in equilibrium unemployment if workers continue to base target real-wage growth on previous lower rates of increase of trend productivity.[9] The effect is, of course, only temporary because target real-wage growth will eventually converge on the new higher rate of trend productivity. Recent results based on a panel of OECD countries and reported in Nickell et al. (2001) reveal that favorable shocks to TFP growth will tend to have a negative effect on real wages relative to trend productivity and on equilibrium unemployment. The full effect of an unexpected rise in TFP growth of 1 percentage point is between 0.6 and 1 percentage point off equilibrium unemployment (for details, see the appendix). So, in the situation of the late 1990s, the effect of the (average) unexpected rise of 0.6 percentage point in TFP growth after 1995 might temporarily pull down equilibrium unemployment by between 0.36 and 0.6 percentage point. These numbers are broadly consistent with the results reported in Laurence Ball and Robert Moffitt (chapter 2 in this volume).

In summary, the combination of demographics, the rise in the prison population, the rise in employment intermediaries, and the surge in TFP growth could explain a fall in equilibrium unemployment since the mid-1980s of up to 1.5 percentage points. A part of this would, however, be only temporary.

POLICIES TO ENHANCE LABOR SUPPLY

With the sharp fall in U.S. equilibrium unemployment since the mid-1980s, where and how can employers get the labor that they need to ensure continued growth without triggering rapid inflation? One solution is to rely on immigrants as a source of skilled labor. In fact, we have seen a dramatic increase in the allotment of H1B visas from 65,000 to 195,000 per year. These visas allow employers to hire skilled workers from abroad on a temporary basis (usually for a period of three to six years). Employers must pay prevailing wages and a $500 fee that goes toward training workers in the United States. (The use of immigrants to enhance the labor supply is discussed in more detail in Ellwood, chapter 9 in this volume.)

A second strategy is to tap into the pool of nonworking adults. As of April

2001, there were 6.4 million unemployed workers. But the unemployed are disproportionately unskilled compared to the workforce as a whole. Unemployment rates for those with less than a high school education are approximately four times those for college graduates. Almost 60 percent of the unemployed aged twenty-five and over have only a high school education or less, and, as shown in figure 11.7, the percentage of the unemployed who have been out of work for more than six months is relatively high, adjusting for the cycle. Some of this increase may be due to the changes in the demographic composition of the workforce, as outlined in Katherine Abraham and Robert Shimer (chapter 8 in this volume). Nevertheless, when employers look at those out of work, they are seeing a pool that is less skilled and with relatively longer spells of unemployment (although certainly nothing like the European situation). As discussed earlier, the opportunities available to this group of workers to obtain the skills training that will make them more competitive in the labor market are limited.

Another potential source of labor is workers who say that they are interested in working but have not looked for work in the past four weeks—the so-called discouraged workers. Figure 11.8 shows the time-series trend in the unemployment rate when this group is added into the unemployment figures—the U4 series. In December 2000, this group added only two-tenths of a percentage point to the overall unemployment rate, and the number of discouraged workers has declined sharply as the overall rate fell during the 1990s. As shown in figure 11.8, the Bureau of Labor Statistics also calculates a labor-underutilization rate

FIGURE 11.7   /   The Percentage Long-Term Unemployed Compared with the Unemployment Rate

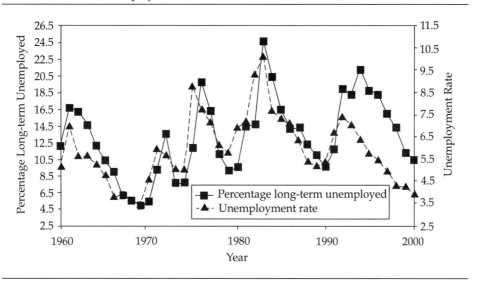

Source: U.S. Bureau of Labor Statistics, Current Population Series. Data are seasonally adjusted and refer to April of each year.

FIGURE 11.8 / Alternative Unemployment Rates

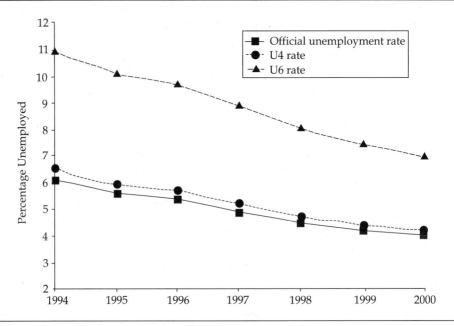

Source: U.S. Bureau of Labor Statistics, Current Population Series.

Note: These data are *not* seasonally adjusted. They refer to the annual rate for each year. The U4 unemployment rate is the total unemployed plus discouraged workers as a percentage of the civilian labor force plus discouraged workers. The U6 rate is the total unemployed plus all marginally attached workers plus total employed part-time for economic reasons as a percentage of the civilian labor force plus all marginally attached workers. Marginally attached workers are persons who currently are neither working nor looking for work but indicate that they want to work, are available to work, and have looked for work at some point in the recent past. Discouraged workers, a subset of the marginally attached, have given a job-market-related reason for not currently looking for a job. Persons employed part-time for economic reasons are those who want to work and are available to work full-time but have had to settle for part-time work.

called the U6 that includes all the unemployed, discouraged workers, individuals who say that they are available to work but have stopped searching for other reasons, and those who are working part-time. This series shows that, by the year 2000, the labor-underutilization rate was close to 7 percent, again down sharply from almost 11 percent in 1994. So, while a pool of underutilized workers does remain, it shrank rapidly during the 1990s.

In table 11.8, we present the U.S. inactivity rate since 1990. We see that, in the late 1990s, the overall rate changes imperceptibly as the gradual rise in inactivity among men is offset by the gradual fall in inactivity among women. For the sake of comparison, we show in table 11.9 the 1999 inactivity rates in a standard European country (Germany), a country with very high inactivity (Italy), and a country with much lower inactivity (Denmark). From this comparison, we can

TABLE 11.8 / U.S. Inactivity Rates, Ages Sixteen to Sixty-Four (Percentage), 1990 to 1999

	1990	1995	1996	1997	1998	1999
Total	23.5	23.1	22.9	22.6	22.6	22.8
Men	14.4	15.7	15.7	15.8	15.8	16.0
Women	32.2	30.3	29.9	29.3	29.3	29.3

Source: OECD (2000, table B).

see that, relative to most of the OECD, the United States has a low level of inactivity, but Denmark (and other Scandinavian countries) illustrates that it is possible for a wealthy market economy to have considerably higher activity rates, particularly among women. The big difference here is among prime-age and younger women since the participation rates among older women are much the same in the United States and Denmark.

Overall, then, while the boom conditions of the late 1990s have seen U.S. unemployment fall to its lowest level in a generation (around 4 percent), inactivity rates have hardly moved despite the novelty of rising real wages and booming demand. In the light of this, we now consider a variety of policies that might improve the operation of the labor market and enhance labor-supply growth. In particular, we examine the use of community-based organizations, training for welfare recipients, wage subsidies, and programs to reduce spatial mismatch as possible strategies for lowering inactivity rates. We then look at workers whose employment experience during the 1990s has moved in the opposite direction of the overall trend—the disabled and ex-inmates.

Job Matching

As discussed earlier, during the 1990s, there was a sharp increase in the use of private-sector temporary-help firms, and this appears to have improved the efficiency of labor-market matching. But an increasing number of not-for-profit organizations have also become involved in job matching. For example, in San Jose, California Working Partnerships was established in 1995 as a collaboration between community-based organizations and the AFL-CIO to act as a labor-market intermediary for local temporary-help workers employed in clerical jobs

TABLE 11.9 / Inactivity Rates for Selected Countries, Ages Fifteen to Sixty-Four, 1999

	Germany	Italy	Denmark	OECD (Average)
Total	28.8	40.4	19.4	29.6
Men	20.3	26.3	15.0	18.5
Women	37.7	54.4	23.9	40.5

Source: OECD (2000, table B).

in Silicon Valley. More generally, with the passage of welfare reform in 1996, more community-based organizations have become involved in training low-wage underemployed workers and former welfare recipients and supporting their search for better career paths.

At the same time, these organizations help employers access potential employees outside their traditional recruiting channels. One such organization is Workforce Staffing Partnerships, established in 1995 in Boston (for other examples, see Lynch 2000). This organization acts as an intermediary between three hundred community-based organizations in Boston (especially immigrant groups) and employers primarily in the health-care services. It provides pre-screening of workers for employers, worker training, postplacement follow-up (including counseling), and support for child-care and transportation issues.

The ability of these types of intermediaries to succeed within the employer community will ultimately depend on their ability to establish a reputation for identifying and preparing motivated and work-ready employees beyond what private-sector intermediaries are able to do. Their ability to succeed with workers will be a function of their employer networks and the quality of the training and postplacement services that they provide. But, before we conclude that a new type of labor-market intermediary has been established in the United States, there needs to be much more research that evaluates the ability of these types of organizations to secure funding and go to scale.

Training Welfare Recipients

The late 1990s welfare reform certainly helped contribute to an increase in the labor supply. But, if welfare recipients are not job ready, then pushing them into the labor market does not necessarily make it easier to sustain low unemployment without wage inflation. As part of welfare reform, many states switched from emphasizing skills development through education and training to a "work first" strategy. In other words, they moved welfare recipients into unsubsidized employment as quickly as possible without having made a prior human-capital investment.

As detailed in two recent papers (Hotz, Imbens, and Klerman 2000; Dehejia 2000), this switch in strategy was based on the results of welfare-to-work programs developed in California in the late 1980s. In 1986, California had established the Greater Avenues to Independence (GAIN) program to facilitate the transition from welfare to work. While GAIN provided guidance and funding, it left individual counties free to develop their own programs. As part of GAIN, the state conducted a randomized evaluation of implementation efforts in six counties, finding significant differences in emphasis among programs—Riverside County, for example, bypassed education and training, focusing on moving welfare recipients into jobs as quickly as possible (a work-first emphasis), whereas Alameda and Los Angeles Counties focused on vocational education and remedial adult education first, moving clients into the labor market only after training has been completed (a human-capital-development emphasis). An independent evaluation conducted by the Manpower Demonstration Research Corporation (see, for example, Riccio and Friedlander 1992; and Riccio, Friedlander, and Freedman 1994) showed that those who had gone through the Riverside program experienced the greatest gains in terms of both employment and earnings three years after enrollment.

The results of the Manpower evaluation convinced Los Angeles and other counties to refocus their programs on a work-first approach. But as shown in Joseph Hotz et al. (2000) this finding is stood on its head when one follows enrollees over a longer period of time and after taking into account differences in the composition of the participant populations across countries. They conclude that, although work-first programs were initially more successful than human-capital-development programs, this relative advantage disappears and is, in fact, reversed in later years. This suggests that, in terms of sustainability, human-capital investment plays a critical role in the transition from welfare to work.

Wage Subsidies

Another way in which to get more people into the labor market is through tax policy. The effect of the earned income tax credit, for example, has been to increase labor-force-participation rates (see Ellwood, chapter 9 in this volume), especially among single mothers (see Eissa and Liebman 1996; Meyer and Rosenbaum 2000; and Hotz and Scholz 2001). But tax policy has also been used to create incentives for employers to seek out and hire former welfare recipients and other disadvantaged workers. Tax credits established during the 1990s include the welfare-to-work tax credit (WTWTC); the work-opportunities tax credit (WOTC); a 20 percent tax credit on the first $15,000 of wages and training expenses for employees who live and work in areas designated as *empowerment zones* (there are currently twelve, including the District of Columbia); a Native American wage credit that provides a 20 percent credit on the first $20,000 of wages and health-insurance costs for Native Americans employed on or near a reservation; and an employment tax credit that essentially revamps Section 936 corporate tax incentives to locate in Puerto Rico.

The WOTC, enacted in 1996, replaces the targeted-jobs tax credit, which had been in place from 1978 to 1994. Under the WOTC, an employer can claim a tax credit for employing workers who are members of certain targeted groups. The tax credit is 25 percent for workers employed for between 120 and 399 hours and 40 percent for workers employed for 400 hours or more, up to $6,000 of wages may qualify for the credit, and the maximum credit is $2,400 per eligible employee. The WTWTC, enacted in 1997, is meant to encourage employers to hire long-term welfare recipients. It provides a credit of 35 percent of the first $10,000 of qualified wages in the first year of employment and 50 percent of the first $10,000 of qualified wages in the second year. The maximum credit for 2 years is $8,500, and the employee must work for the employer for at least 180 days or 400 hours.

In the past, one of the problems with these types of wage-subsidy programs was that they created an incentive for employers to churn eligible employees and thereby collect the subsidy again. However, both the WOTC and the WT-WTC were designed with an eye toward minimizing churning—first through Department of Labor oversight and second, in the case of the WTWTC, by making the subsidy even more generous in the second year. Unfortunately, the WOTC is scheduled to expire on December 31, 2001, and the president's budget proposal of April 2001 included no additional funding beyond this year for the WTWTC. The current administration's lack of interest in these programs is certainly not due to a lack of demand for them. In 1997, 126,000 wage-subsidy certifications for disadvantaged workers were granted by the Department of Labor, and, by 2000, this number had increased to 525,000.

While there have been no studies of the effect of these most recent tax credits on inactivity rates during the 1990s, the justification for introducing these taxes was based in part on previous experience with wage subsidies for the disadvantaged. As reviewed by Katz (1998), wage subsidies to private employers meant to encourage the hiring of disadvantaged workers present a relatively flexible and efficient method of improving the earnings and employment of the less skilled. Subsidies to private-sector employment accounted for 11 percent on average of total spending on active measures in the OECD in 1996. Katz concludes that stand-alone wage subsidies that target specific groups appear to be somewhat less effective than more broadly targeted subsidies are—although narrowly targeted programs that operate through an intermediary (for example, a public employment agency or not-for-profit organization) and combine job development, job-search assistance, training, and wage subsidies appear to be more successful than narrowly targeted programs designed differently. But, while wage subsidies may improve the labor-market position of disadvantaged workers in the short run, they are no substitute for investing in education and training. Failure to make such an investment amounts to a cynical write-off of a nontrivial part of the population.

Spatial Mismatch

Another possible reason for inactivity is that nonworking poor individuals are increasingly concentrated in high-poverty areas. As detailed in Paul Jargowsky (1997), between 1970 and 1990, the percentage of poor persons in metropolitan areas living in census tracts with a poverty rate of 40 percent or more increased from 12 to 18 percent. As poverty has become concentrated in central cities, more employment is located in suburban areas. In addition, recent work by Bruce Weinberg, Patricia Reagan, and Jeffrey Yankow (2000) finds that a 1-standard-deviation increase in social characteristics of a neighborhood increases annual hours worked by 6 percent and that a similar increase in job proximity raises hours by 4 percent.

Given the increasing segregation by income, a series of demonstration projects have been funded to address the problem of spatial mismatch. There are two general types of strategies that have been pursued. The first is to provide transportation assistance to welfare recipients and other low-income job seekers so that they can reverse commute to jobs in the suburbs. The second is to move the people themselves out of the central city and into suburban communities. The initial evidence suggests that both strategies have a limited effect on the employment prospects of poor inner-city residents.

Let us begin with the first strategy, facilitating a reverse commute. Stephen Raphael and Michael Stoll (2000) examine whether boosting minority car-ownership rates would narrow interracial employment-rate differentials. They conclude that raising minority car-ownership rates to the white ownership rate would eliminate 45 percent of the African American–white employment-rate differential and 17 percent of the comparable Latino-white differential. These effects are large, but the analysis rests on the very strong assumption that the skill differentials (both observed and unobserved) between car owners and non–car owners are equal across race and ethnicity. While Raphael and Stoll attempt to control for observed skill differentials, their work is still subject to omitted-variables bias, which weakens the strength of their overall findings.

This unobserved heterogeneity-bias problem is addressed in a recent demonstration project funded by the U.S. Department of Housing (HUD). HUD developed a five-city Bridges to Work demonstration project to serve forty-six hundred people over the period 1996 to 2000 and included as part of the project a random-assignment evaluation in four of the cities. As discussed in Mark Elliott, Beth Palubinsky, and Joseph Tierney (1999), Bridges to Work was designed to test whether information, job-placement assistance, and transportation could connect job-ready inner-city workers to suburban employment. The program assumed, not only that there was a large potential supply of would-be workers and employers, but also that transportation was the main hurdle facing the would-be workers and that training, therefore, need not be provided. But, as Elliott, Palubinsky, and Tierney point out, while "the logistics of taking people from point A to point B is an inherently solvable problem," what remains an "ongoing challenge" is "the basics of employment—recruitment, assessment, preparation, placement, and support of job seekers." They conclude that, "in the end, unless organizations are good at the job-matching process, there will be lots of empty seats on the bus."

What is striking in reviewing the first field report written by Elliott, Palubinsky, and Tierney (1999) on this project is that one of the difficulties encountered in making the random assignments was finding enough workers to participate. Many local public and not-for-profit employment organizations were reluctant to refer their clients to the Bridges program. One of the reasons cited for this reluctance was the fear that those who were assigned to the control group would wind up resenting the fact that they had been referred to the Bridges program in the first place!

Let us now turn to the second strategy, moving low-income inner-city families to low-poverty areas (a census tract with under 10 percent poverty rate in 1990). In the 1990s, HUD undertook another experimental, random-assignment evaluation program called Moving to Opportunity (MTO), this time focusing on housing mobility. According to an extensive analysis of the MTO demonstration in Boston (see Katz, Kling, and Liebman, forthcoming), two years after program enrollment, households (over 90 percent female headed) in the treatment group experienced increased safety, improved health among household heads, fewer asthma attacks among children, fewer behavior problems among boys, and reduced victimization (both crime and injury) among children. These results are consistent with those obtained in the Jens Ludwig, Helen Ladd, and Greg Duncan (2000) analysis of the Baltimore MTO demonstration, where it was found that providing an opportunity for public-housing residents to move from high-poverty to low-poverty neighborhoods improved children's reading and math scores by about one-quarter of a standard deviation compared to those of the control group. However, Lawrence Katz, Jeffrey Kling, and Jeffrey Liebman found that the Boston MTO had no significant short-run effects on parents' employment, earnings, or welfare receipt. So offering housing vouchers to residents of inner-city housing projects improves the well-being of residents interested in moving out of public housing, but the reduction in spatial mismatch alone does not appear to be sufficient to overcome the labor-market difficulties of inner-city single mothers.

In sum, there seems to be a growing role for both private and not-for-profit labor-market intermediaries in job matching, especially as the labor market tightens and employers need to move beyond their traditional methods of finding new employees. Not only can these intermediaries match employers with workers, but they can also provide workers with important job-readiness training and postemployment support, services that seem to be critical to successful matches. More generally, training workers who have been out of the labor force for an extended period of time seems to pay off in the medium and longer term as these retrained workers experience better employment and earnings than those who have been moved into the labor market with little or no skills training. Wage subsidies can be a relatively flexible and efficient way in which to improve the earnings and employment of the less skilled, but the subsidies that were introduced in the 1990s to promote the hiring of long-term welfare recipients have yet to be evaluated. Finally, initial evaluations indicate that programs that are meant to reduce spatial mismatch in the labor market seem to have large effects on the quality of family life, health, and the education of children but little effect on the employment experience of single mothers.

Ellwood (chapter 9 in this volume) discusses how the supply of workers in the 1990s has been affected by the introduction of the Americans with Disabilities Act and changes in disability-insurance benefits. The net effect appears to have been a sharp decline in employment rates for the disabled through the

1990s. We now turn to a second group of potential workers who have also seen their inactivity rates rise during the 1990s.

The Role of Prisons in the Labor Market

One of the advantages of the tight 1990s labor market is that, along with increases in reported employment-population ratios and declines in unemployment, we have seen a sharp decline in crime. Causality is not easy to determine, but Freeman and Rodgers (1999) discuss how the improved labor market has been especially beneficial for young non-college-educated African Americans during the 1990s. In addition, they find that youths have higher earnings and employment in low-crime states and poorer labor-market outcomes in states where incarcerations are high.

The link between labor-market outcomes and crime is an important one, especially since the incarceration rate had, by 1996, risen to more than 1.5 million in federal, state, and local jails or prisons, its highest level in U.S. history. As discussed earlier, the increase in the prison population contributed in part to the decline in the equilibrium-unemployment rate. But, when incarceration is taken into account in employment-population ratios or overall inactivity rates in the 1990s, one sees a disturbing trend.

Bruce Western and Becky Pettit (1998) have undertaken the herculean task of combining surveys on prisons and jails with the Current Population Survey to estimate employment-population ratios for black and white men over the period 1982 to 1996. Examining these ratios, they find that, on average, adjusting for incarceration rates does little to alter the standard labor-force data for whites over this time period. However, the picture changes dramatically when the incarceration adjustment is made for black men. During the 1990s, the size of the black prison population reduced the conventional black employment-population ratios by more than 4 percentage points overall and by more than 13 percentage points for young (twenty- to thirty-five-year-old) black male high school dropouts. For this latter demographic group, the conventional reported values for employment-population ratios rose from 41.2 percent in 1991 to 46 percent in 1996, while ratios incorporating the prison population slightly decreased from 30.6 to 29.3 percent over the same period.

It is important to note that this exercise is not the same thing as trying to predict what the employment-population ratio would have been had there not been such a sharp rise in incarceration rates over the 1990s. Nevertheless, it highlights how the official improvement in the employment-to-population ratio for African American men reflects both the fact that more of them are employed and the fact that more of them are incarcerated and, thus, do not figure in employment calculations.

In order to try to predict what would happen if the percentage of those in prison decreased sharply, we would need to have a better understanding of the labor-market prospects of those in jail. And, for this, we would need to understand something about the labor-market characteristics of those who are incarcerated and the effect of time in prison on subsequent employment. As detailed in Bernstein and Houston (2000), the incarcerated are disproportionately young minority men with low skills (see table 11.10). Especially striking is the high percentage of released prisoners in 1996 who do not have a high school degree. Since we know that, during the 1980s and 1990s, this group was especially hard hit by technological change, it appears that the recently released prison population faces the dual problem of being stigmatized as ex-cons and entering an economy for which they are increasingly ill prepared.

The effect of jail time on labor-market prospects appears to be quite negative, although detailed research following individuals over time is still limited. Richard Freeman (1992), using data from the National Longitudinal Survey of Youth, found that young men who had ever been in a juvenile or adult correctional facility by 1980 had lower subsequent earnings and worked about 25 percent less in the ensuing 8 years than those who had not experienced prison time. Western and Beckett (1998), again using the NLSY but controlling for adult incarceration that occurred after 1980, found small but negative effects of juvenile prison experience on employment, effects that persist over time.

For adults, the picture appears to be more mixed. Western and Beckett (1998) find that adult incarceration has large negative effects on the employment of ex-inmates immediately after release but that these effects go away after three to four years. Kling (2000) has argued that spending more time in jail does not significantly affect the postprison labor-market experience of adults. But one explanation for this finding (which Kling himself cites) is that former inmates are all viewed in the same way in the labor market no matter how long their prison

TABLE 11.10 / Characteristics of Released Prisoners Compared to All Workers, 1996

	All Workers	Federal and State Prisoners Released
Male	52.6	90.3
Female	47.4	9.7
White	74.8	36.0
African American	11.4	49.6
Hispanic	9.8	13.2
16 to 24 years of age	11.2	18.9
25 to 34 years of age	28.0	42.2
35 to 54 years of age	50.8	37.2
55 years of age and over	10.0	1.7
Less than high school education	11.5	58.7
High school graduate/GED	33.8	33.6
Some college	28.2	6.2
College	26.5	.9

Source: Bernstein and Houston (2000).

sentence. As a result of such stigmatization, length of time in prison has little effect on subsequent employment. Kling also finds that earnings are strongly and negatively affected by prison time. In percentage terms, he finds that the earnings losses experienced by ex-inmates are similar to the 25 percent earnings losses experienced by displaced workers 6 years after in mass layoffs.

In sum, accounting for the incarcerated population can reverse some of the "good news" reported for certain demographic groups during the 1990s expansion. In addition, time in prison worsens subsequent employment and earnings, especially for young offenders. Given this, the decision in the late 1990s to deny inmates Pell grants to pursue higher education and calls to shut down adult and vocational-education programs for prisoners (supposedly to reinforce the fact that they are being punished) seem ill advised. More extensive research on the effect on the labor market that the dramatic increase in the prison population has had and will continue to have is certainly in order.

CONCLUSIONS

During the 1990s, we have seen a rise in trend-productivity growth in the United States so rapid that, for the first time since the Second World War, productivity growth is now higher in the United States than in most of the developed OECD countries. This growth has been spurred by investments in ICTs, the growth of which has in turn been spurred by the rapid decline in the real price of IT capital and workplace innovation and reorganization. Although we do not have comparable cross-country data on workplace innovation, we do know that the ICT price decline has occurred across the board, not just in the United States. We argue that part of the reason why the U.S. experience differs from that of other countries is cross-country differences in regulatory barriers. The United States is able to generate and, more importantly, to absorb new technologies more rapidly than other countries because U.S. firms face relatively modest regulatory barriers. This is an important lesson for other countries. But it is unlikely that the skills of American workers will be able to keep pace with the demands of IT and new workplace practices unless current education and training practices are radically overhauled in the face of the needs of the new economy.

We argue that the combination of demographics, the rise in the prison population, the rise in employment intermediaries, and the surge in TFP growth could explain a fall in equilibrium unemployment since the mid-1980s of up to 1.5 percentage points. A part of this could, however, be only temporary. In addition, while the boom conditions of the late 1990s have seen the U.S. unemployment rate fall to its lowest number for a generation (around 4 percent), inactivity rates have hardly moved despite the novelty of rising real wages and booming demand. We argue that the use of community-based organizations, training, and wage subsidies may have some effect on further reducing these inactivity rates. However, the evidence on the effect of programs meant to reduce spatial mismatch suggests that, while these programs have large effects on health, safety, and the education outcomes of children, their effect on the employment experience of single mothers is not significant, at least early on in the program. The experience of such demonstration projects as Bridges to Work suggests that, while transportation is a problem that is easily solved, that of the recruitment, assessment, preparation, placement, and support of job seekers is much more challenging. Finally, we examine the effect of incarceration rates on employment trends and find that the progress made during the 1990s by young African American workers looks less promising when incarceration effects are taken into account. Ex-inmates represent some of the most disadvantaged low-skilled workers in the U.S. labor market. Addressing the skill shortage and labor-market difficulties encountered by this group of workers will become an increasing challenge given the large increase in the prison population in recent years.

Throughout this paper, we have pointed to the need for greater investment in worker skills training in order to sustain low unemployment without wage inflation. What innovations in technologies and workplace practices have highlighted is the necessity of acquiring new skills after formal education has been completed. But what do we see in terms of a commitment to investing in training? In terms of numbers of adults served by federally funded training programs, the president's proposed budget for the Department of Labor for fiscal year 2002 sets the total number of adult to receive government training assistance equal to the number who did so in 2001 in spite of a slowing economy and an expanding workforce. Over $60 million set aside to run pilot programs and conduct demonstration and research projects on the effectiveness of adult training programs has been dropped from the budget. Because of funding formulas, many states in fiscal year 2001 were unable to tap into all allocated funds for youth or adult training. While many state-sponsored employer-focused training programs were expanded in the 1990s, as the economy slows and state revenues fall, some states have had difficulty finding the continued funding needed by these programs. A reexamination of the funding formulas for federal training programs under the Workforce Investment Act that took into account the presence of low skills/ wages in local labor markets in addition to the unemployment rates would be useful. This would encourage the training of low-skilled workers during periods when there are employers ready to take on job-ready employees. To wait to fund training programs until the unemployment rate is high seems misguided. More generally, to spend less today on worker education and training than what was spent twenty years ago is incomprehensible.

To encourage employers to provide more training to low-wage workers, the government should also consider removing federal policy barriers that discourage technology-enabled learning and that limit access to and financing for nontraditional learning approaches. In particular, the ability of adult students to take out student loans to participate in the growing market of E-learning providers is severely limited given regulations that were set up, quite rightly, in the 1970s to limit fraud in for-profit proprietary schools. In addition, federal and state governments could broaden tax incentives that encourage businesses to expand learning opportunities to those workers who are less likely to receive employer-financed training. For example, the federal government could provide additional tax credits for employers who provide such workplace programs as English as a second language, adult basic education, and basic computer skills to their employees.

Our work suggests a number of areas for future research and evaluation. We have identified regulatory barriers and workplace innovation as potentially important determinants of the productivity differences across the United States and Europe in spite of similar price declines in IT. Therefore, cross-country comparisons of the role of regulatory barriers in inhibiting the adoption and diffusion of new technologies, along with cross-country comparisons of workplace innovation and its effect on productivity, would be useful. In addition, in the light of our discussion of the need to train incumbent workers to meet the changing skill demands of the new economy, current attempts to eliminate research on and evaluation of federally funded government training programs seem shortsighted. Finally, as policy makers continue to develop ways to enhance the labor supply of workers with those who are currently out of the labor force, research that examined the role of private and not-for-profit labor-market intermediaries in job matching and workforce development, programs to aid the transition from prison to work, and the effectiveness of wage subsidies would be especially beneficial for policy makers.

APPENDIX

In tables 11A.1 and 11A.2, we report equations based on data from twenty OECD countries over the period 1961 to 1992. From table 11A.1, we see that holding constant real labor cost relative to trend productivity, a positive 1 percentage point TFP shock will tend to reduce unemployment by $0.31/0.64 = 0.5$ percentage points. Alternatively, in the unemployment equation in table 11A.2, the long-run effect of a 1 percentage point rise in TFP growth (0.01 in this equation) is to reduce unemployment by around 1 percentage point. These are only temporary effects since the shock variables are stationary with a mean of 0.

TABLE 11A.1 / Explaining Real Labor Cost, 1961 to 1992 (Dependent Variable: Log Real Labor Cost$_{it}$)

Log real labor cost$_{it-1}$	.73	Coordination$_{it}$	.014
	(31.7)		(1.1)
u_{it}	−.64	Total employment-tax rate$_{it}$	.080
	(8.5)		(2.3)
Δu_{it}	−.10	Coord.$_{it}$ × total	−.21
	(.2)	employment-tax rate$_{it}$	(5.3)
Coord.$_{it}$ × u_{it}	−.49	Trend productivity	.44
	(6.0)		(11.3)
Benefit-replacement ratio$_{it}$	.59	TFP shock	−.31
× u_{it}	(2.4)		(3.2)
Union density$_{it}$ × u_{it}	.79	Real-import-price shock	.37
	(3.4)		(6.9)
Employment protection$_{it}$	.042		
	(5.2)	NT Number of coun-	
Coord.$_{it}$ × employment	−.039	tries × time periods	
protection$_{it}$	(4.0)	observed.	507
Benefit-replacement ratio$_{it}$	.061	N number of countries.	20
	(3.8)		
Benefit duration$_{it}$	.016		
	(1.8)		
Benefit duration$_{it}$ × benefit	.026		
replacement ratio$_{it}$	(.6)		

Source: Authors' Calculations.

TABLE 11A.2 / Explaining Unemployment, 1961 to 1992 (Dependent Variable: u_{it} [Percentage])

u_{it-1}	.89	Labor-demand shock$_{it}$	−27.9
	(55.0)		(19.7)
Employment protection$_{it}$	.49	TFP shock$_{it}$	−11.3
	(2.3)		(10.5)
Coord.$_{it}$ employment protection$_{it}$	−.57	Real-import-price shock$_{it}$	5.76
	(2.3)		(3.7)
Benefit-replacement ratio$_{it}$	1.36	Money-supply shock$_{it}$	.13
	(3.8)		(.5)
Benefit duration$_{it}$	.81	Real interest rate$_{it}$	−.19
	(3.4)		(.2)
Benefit duration$_{it}$ × benefit replacement ratio$_{it}$	3.30		
	(3.7)		
Union density$_{it}$	.39	NT Number of countries × time periods observed.	
	(.5)		552
Coordination$_{it}$	−1.28	N number of countries.	20
	(5.0)		
Coord.$_{it}$ × union density$_{it}$	−4.12		
	(3.7)		
Total employment-tax rate$_{it}$	1.86		
	(2.3)		
Coord.$_{it}$ × Total employment-tax rate$_{it}$	−4.22		
	(4.0)		

Source: Authors' calculations.

Note: Equations contain country dummies, country-specific time trends, time dummies. Estimation allows for heteroskedasticity, country-specific first-order serial correlation.

We are most grateful to George Johnson, Alan Krueger, Bob Solow, and David Weiman for helpful comments on an earlier draft of this paper.

NOTES

1. To make this absolutely clear, we refer to the average annual growth rates from 1995/1996 to 1999/2000 and from 1985/1996 to 1994/1995.

2. These data come from OECD (1997a), OECD (1998, table C), and OECD (1999, table 1.2 plus projections).

3. The data for 1983 come from OECD (1997a, table B); those for 1995 and 1999 come from OECD (1999a, table B).

4. These data come from OECD (1998, table 1.6) and OECD (2000, tables 1.3 for the projection and A).

5. The OECD results for the late 1990s reflect an average of the rates of decline generated by the Kalman filter measure (0.3) and the Secretariat estimates (0.1) reported in OECD (1999b, tables B1 and B3, respectively). The Staiger, Stock, and Watson (chapter 1 in this volume) results are taken from the price-equation NAIRU illustrated in their figure 1.4.

6. That is, all the OECD countries except the Czech Republic, Greece, Hungary, Korea, Mexico, and Turkey.

7. That is, government-sector employment, unemployment benefits, union density, employment protection, and the labor-tax wedge.

8. In partial equilibrium, wages will typically fall as the firm's rents, and hence the workers' share, are squeezed. However, if product-market competition increases across the board, the marginal-revenue product of labor and, hence, labor demand tends to increase, and this will typically outweigh the effect of rents on wages.

9. This is, of course, the reverse of the well-documented effect of the adverse productivity and terms-of-trade shocks in 1974 (see, for example, Layard et al. 1991, chapter 9).

REFERENCES

Abraham, Katherine G. 1987. "Help Wanted Advertising, Job Vacancies, and Unemployment." *Brookings Papers on Economic Activity* (1): 207–48.

Autor, David. 2000. "Wiring the Labor Market." *NBER* working paper no. 7959. Cambridge, Mass.: National Bureau of Economic Research, October.

Bentolila, Samuel, and Gilles Saint-Paul. 1999. "Explaining Movements in the Labor Share." *CEMF* working paper no. 9905. Madrid: Centro de Estudios Monetarios y Financiero.

Bernstein, Jared, and Ellen Houston. 2000. *Crime and Work: What We Can Learn from the Low-Wage Labor Market.* Washington, D.C.: Economic Policy Institute.

Berry, Stuart, and David England. 2000. "Has There Been a Structural Improvement in U.S. Productivity?" London: Bank of England, Monetary Analysis (HO-2), International Economic Analysis Division.

Black, Sandra E., and Lisa M. Lynch. 1996. "Human Capital Investments and Productivity." *American Economic Review* 86(May): 263–67.

———. 2001a. "What's Driving the New Economy? The Benefits of Workplace Innovation." *Federal Reserve Bank of New York* staff report no. 118. New York: Federal Reserve Bank of New York, March.

———. 2001b. "How to Compete: The Impact of Workplace Practices and Information Technology on Productivity." *Review of Economics and Statistics* 83(August): 434–45.

Blanchard, Olivier, and Lawrence F. Katz. 1997. "What We Know and Do Not Know about the Natural Rate of Unemployment." *Journal of Economic Perspectives* 11(winter): 51–72.

Bloom, Howard S., Larry L. Orr, George Cave, Stephen H. Bell, Fred Doolittle, and Winston Lin. 1993. "The National JTPA Study, Overview: Impacts, Benefits, and Costs of Title II-A." Bethesda, Md.: Abt Associates, November.

Cave, George, H. Bos, Fred Doolittle, C. Toussaint. 1993. "JOBSTART: A Final Report of a

Program for High School Dropouts." New York: Manpower Demonstration Research Corporation, October.

Council of Economic Advisers. 2000. *Economic Report of the President: 2000.* Washington: U.S. Government Printing Office.

Crafts, Nicholas, and Gianni Toniolo. 1996, "Postwar Growth: An Overview." In *Economic Growth in Europe since 1945,* edited by N. Crafts and G. Toniolo. Cambridge: Cambridge University Press.

Dehejia, Rajeev. 2000. "Was There a Riverside Miracle? A Framework for Evaluating Multi-Site Programs." *NBER* working paper no. 7844. Cambridge, Mass.: National Bureau of Economic Research, August.

Donahue, Jack, Lisa M. Lynch, and Ralph Whitehead. 2000. *Opportunity Knocks: Training the Commonwealth's Workers for the New Economy.* Boston: MASSINC.

Eissa, Nada, and Jeffrey B. Liebman. 1996. "Labor Supply Responses to the Earned Income Tax Credit." *Quarterly Journal of Economics* 111(2): 605–37.

Elliott, Mark, Beth Palubinsky, and Joseph Tierney. 1999. *Overcoming Roadblocks on the Way to Work: Bridges to Work Field Report.* Philadelphia: Public/Private Ventures.

Freeman, Richard B. 1992. "Crime and the Employment of Disadvantaged Youth." In *Urban Labor Markets and Job Opportunity,* edited by George Peterson and Wayne Vroman, 201–37. Washington, D.C.: Urban Institute.

Freeman, Richard B., and William M. Rodgers III. 1999. "Area Economic Conditions and the Labor Market Outcomes of Young Men in the 1990s Expansion." *NBER* working paper no. W7073. Cambridge, Mass.: National Bureau of Economic Research, April.

Gordon, Robert J. 2000. "Does the New Economy Measure Up to the Great Inventions of the Past?" *Journal of Economic Perspectives* 14(4): 49–74.

Haffner, Robert C. G., Stephen J. Nickell, Giuseppe Nicoletti, Stefano Scarpetta, and Gylfi Zoega. 2000. "European Integration, Liberalisation, and Labor Market Performance." In *Welfare and Employment in a United Europe,* edited by Giuseppe Bertola, Tito Boeri, and Giuseppe Nicoletti. Cambridge, Mass.: MIT Press.

Hotz, Joseph V., Guido W. Imbens, and Jacob Klerman. 2000. "The Long-Term Gain from GAIN: A Re-Analysis of the Impacts of the California GAIN Program." *NBER* working paper no. 8007. Cambridge, Mass.: National Bureau of Economic Research, November.

Hotz, Joseph V., and John Karl Scholz. 2001. "The Earned Income Tax Credit." *NBER* working paper no. 8078. Cambridge, Mass.: National Bureau of Economic Research, January.

Jacobson, Louis S., Robert J. LaLonde, and Daniel G. Sullivan. 1994. "The Returns from Classroom Training for Displaced Workers." *Macroeconomic Issues* working paper no. 94–27. Chicago: Federal Reserve Bank of Chicago.

Jargowsky, Paul A. 1997. *Poverty and Place.* New York: Russell Sage Foundation.

Jorgenson, Dale, and Kevin J. Stiroh. 2000. "Raising the Speed Limit: US Economic Growth in the Information Age." *Brookings Papers on Economic Activity* (1): 125–211.

Katz, Lawrence F. 1998. "Wage Subsidies for the Disadvantaged." In *Generating Jobs,* edited by Richard Freeman and Peter Gottschalk, 21–53. New York: Russell Sage Foundation.

Katz, Lawrence, Jeffrey Kling, and Jeffrey Liebman. Forthcoming. "Moving to Opportunity in Boston: Early Results of a Randomized Mobility Experiment." *Quarterly Journal of Economics.*

Katz, Lawrence F., and Alan B. Krueger. 1999. "The High Pressure U.S. Labor Market of the 1990s." *Brookings Papers on Economic Activity* (1): 1–87.

Kling, Jeffrey. 2000. "The Effect of Prison Sentence Length on the Subsequent Employment and Earnings of Criminal Defendants." Mimeo. Princeton University, Department of Economics, August.

Layard, Richard, Stephen Nickell, and Richard Freeman. 1991. *Unemployment, Macroeconomic Performance and the Labor Market.* Oxford, U.K.: Oxford University Press.

Leuven, Edwin, and Hessel Oosterbeek. 1999. Demand and Supply of Work-Related Training: Evidence from Four Countries. *Research in Labor Economics* 18: 303–30.

Ludwig, Jens, Helen F. Ladd, and Greg J. Duncan. 2000. "The Effects of Urban Poverty on Educational Outcomes: Evidence from a Randomized Experiment." Mimeo. Georgetown University, Public Policy Institute, October.

Lynch, Lisa M. 1992. "Private Sector Training and Its Impact on the Earnings of Young Workers." *American Economic Review* 82(March): 299–312.

———, ed. 1994. *Training and the Private Sector: International Comparisons.* Chicago: University of Chicago Press.

———. 2000. "Labor Market Intermediaries for the Training of Low Wage Workers." Paper presented to the National Bureau of Economic Research conference "Emerging Labor Market Institutions for the Twenty-first Century." Cambridge, Mass. (August 20).

Mallar, Charles, Stuart Kerachsky, Craig Thornton, and David Long. 1982. *Evaluation of the Impact of the Job Corps Program: Third Follow-Up Report.* Princeton, N.J.: Mathematica Policy Research.

Merrill Lynch & Co. 2000. *The Knowledge Web: People Power—Fuel for the New Economy.* New York.

Meyer, Bruce, and Dan Rosenbaum. 2000. "Making Single Mothers Work: Recent Tax and Welfare Policy and Its Effects." *NBER* working paper no. 7491. Cambridge, Mass.: National Bureau of Economic Research, January.

National Governors' Association Center for Best Practices. 1999. *A Comprehensive Look at State-Funded Employer-Focused Job Training Programs.* Washington, D.C.: National Governors' Association.

Nickell, Stephen J. 1999. "Product Markets and Labor Markets." *Labor Economics* 6(March): 1–20.

Nickell, Stephen J., Luca Nunziata, Wolfgang Ochel, and Glenda Quintini. 2001. "The Beveridge Curve, Unemployment, and Wages in the OECD from the 1960s to the 1990s." Unpublished manuscript. London: Centre for Economic Performance, London School of Economics.

Nicoletti, Giuseppe, Stefano Scarpetta, and Olivier Boylaud. 2000. "Summary Indicators of Product Market Regulation with an Extension to Employment Protection Legislation." Economics Department working paper no. 226. Paris: OECD.

OECD. 1997a. *Employment Outlook.* Paris.

———. 1997b. *Literacy Skills for the Knowledge Society.* Paris.

———. 1998. *Employment Outlook.* Paris.

———. 1999a. *Employment Outlook.* Paris.

———. 1999b. *Implementing the OECD Jobs Strategy: Assessing Performance and Policy.* Paris.

———. 1999c. *OECD Science, Technology, and Industry Scoreboard: Benchmarking Knowledge Based Economies.* Paris.

———. 2000. *Employment Outlook.* Paris.

Oliner, Stephen, and Daniel E. Sichel. 2000. "The Resurgence of Growth in the Late 1990s: Is Information Technology the Story?" *Journal of Economic Perspectives* 14(4): 3–22.

Pissarides, Christopher A. 1990. *Equilibrium Unemployment Theory.* Cambridge, Mass.: MIT Press.

Raphael, Steven, and Michael Stoll. 2000. "Can Boosting Minority Car-Ownership Rates

Narrow Inter-Racial Employment Gaps?" Mimeo. University of California, Berkeley, Goldman School of Public Policy.

Riccio, James, and Daniel Friedlander. 1992. *GAIN: Program Strategies, Participation Patterns, and First-Year Impacts in Six Counties.* New York: Manpower Demonstration Research Corp.

Riccio, James, Daniel Friedlander, and Stephen Freedman. 1994. *GAIN: Benefits, Costs, and Three-Year Impacts of a Welfare-to-Work Program.* New York: Manpower Demonstration Research Corp.

Schochet, Peter, John Burghardt, and Steven Glazerman. 2000. "National Job Corps Study: The Short-Term Impacts of Job Corps on Participants' Employment and Related Outcomes." Princeton, N.J.: Mathematica Policy Research.

Steedman, Hilary. 1999. "Looking into the Qualifications 'Black Box': What Can International Surveys Tell Us about Basic Competence?" *CEP* discussion paper no. 431. London: London School of Economics, Centre for Economic Performance.

TIMMS. 2000. *TIMMS 1999 International Mathematics Report.* Boston: Boston College, Lynch School of Education, International Study Center. *http://isc.bc.edu/timss1999i/math_achievement_report.html.*

U.S. Bureau of Labor Statistics. 1993. *Employer Training Survey.* Washington: U.S. Bureau of Labor Statistics.

———. 2000. *Multifactor Productivity Trends, 1998.* Washington: U.S. Bureau of Labor Statistics.

U.S. Department of Labor. 1995. *What's Working (and What's Not).* Washington: Office of the Chief Economist.

Weinberg, Bruce A., Patricia B. Reagan, and Jeffrey J. Yankow. 2000. "Do Neighborhoods Affect Work Behavior? Evidence from the NLSY79." Mimeo. Ohio State University, Center for Human Resource Research, September.

Western, Bruce, and Katherine Beckett. 1998. "How Unregulated Is the U.S. Labor Market? The Penal System as a Labor Market Institution." Mimeo. Princeton University, Department of Sociology, March.

Western, Bruce, and Becky Pettit. 1998. "Incarceration and Employment Inequality among Young Unskilled Men." Mimeo. Princeton University, Department of Sociology, August.

Whelan, Karl. 2000. "Computers, Obsolescence, and Productivity." *Finance and Economics* discussion paper no. 2000-06. Washington: Federal Reserve Bank, Board of Governors, February.

Index

Numbers in **boldface** refer to figures or tables.

Abowd, John, 412, 413
Abraham, Katherine, 224, 226, 498, 555, 559
Acemoglu, Daron, 430, 463
ADA (Americans with Disabilities Act), 566
AFDC (Aid to Families with Dependent Children), 437, 445–50, 527
AFL-CIO, 561
age: baby boomers and unemployment duration, 369, 384–85, **386–88**; earnings growth across business cycles, **320–21**, 322, **325**, 326, 341, 342, **343**, **346**, **350**, **354**, **357**, **361**; by employment and social insurance use, 440, **441**, **442**; job training and retraining, 553; labor force changes in, 556; labor force participation, **325**, 326, 329, **330**, 424, 429; prime-age workforce and labor force projections, 422–23, 425, 427, 433–36; social insurance utilized, 438–40, **439**. *See also* youth
Aid to Families with Dependent Children (AFDC), 437, 445–50, 527
Akerlof, George, 5, 54, 62
AMA (American Management Association), 95–96, 548
American Management Association (AMA), 95–96, 548
Americans with Disabilities Act (ADA), 566
America's Job Bank, 557
Anderson, Patricia, 462
Appelbaum, Eileen, 232
armed forces, earnings growth composition, 332
Asian financial crisis, 129
Autor, David, 40, 41, 230, 231, 234, 472, 557

baby boomers: labor force participation, 424; unemploy-
ment duration, 369, 384–85, **386–88**. *See also* age
Baicker, Katherine, 458, 460, 462
balanced-growth model, 312, 335–39
Baldwin, Robert E., 276, 278
Ball, Lawrence, 82, 164, 196–97, 204, 558
banking system. *See* Federal Reserve Bank
Barsky, Robert, 495, 498, 510, 512, 513, 514
Basu, Susanto, 66, 313
Batt, Rosemary, 232
Bauman, Kurt, 431, 432
BEA (Budget Enforcement Act of 1990), 94, 147, 315, 336
Becker, Gary, 375
Beckett, Katherine, 568
benefits: benefit shock, 118, **126**, **127**; cost decline, 220; cost of, WUMM and FRB-US models, 120; health care, 118–21, **126**, **127**, 130–31, 220; inflation, 118–21, 130–31; temporary workers, 254n21
Bentsen, Lloyd, 103
Berman, Eli, 278
Bernstein, Jared, 568
Berry, Stuart, 540
Bertola, Guiseppe, 198
Beveridge curve: equilibrium unemployment, 554–56; HPWO adoption, 233; job matches, 557; labor rents, erosion of, 241, **242**, 243, 250; and NAIRU, 220, 221, 223–25, 231; vacancy-unemployment, 249
Bewley, Truman, 63
Bhagwati, Jagdish, 276, 278
Bils, Mark, 66, 498
Black, Sandra, 234, 547
Blanchard, Olivier: human resource management practices and sustainable employment, 224; interna-
tional labor-market outcomes, 160, 161, 165, 166, 173, 174, 176, 178, 179, 185, 188, 189, 192, 193, 198, 201, 202, 205–6, 207, 208; international trade effects on U.S. labor markets, 295; NAIRU, prices and wages, 15; productivity growth and Phillips curve, 62, 63, 65; wage-curve relations, 499
Blanchard-Katz model, 295–97
Blanchard-Wolfers data set and models, 165, 166, 173, 174, 176, 178, 179, 181, 188, 192, 193, 198, 202, 205–6, 207–9, **210**
Blanchflower, David, 499
Blank, Rebecca, 449, 458, 459, 497, 507, 517, 518
Blau, David, 476
Blau, Francine, 172, 198, 407
Blinder, Alan, 61, 62, 538
BLS. *See* Bureau of Labor Statistics (BLS)
Blue Chip forecasters, 103, 106, 115, 128
Boden, Leslie, 518
bonus-job-search program, 463, 465
Borjas, George, 271, 279
Boskin, Michael, 125, 476
Bound, John, 278, 470, 471
Bresnahan, Timothy, 234
Bridges to Work, 570
Browning, Martin, 372
Brynjolfsson, Erik, 234
budget agreement, federal (1990,1993,1997), 93–94, 100–108, 140–41
budget deficit. *See* federal deficit reduction
Budget Enforcement Act of 1990 (BEA), 94, 147, 315, 336
Bureau of Economic Analysis, 41
Bureau of Labor Statistics (BLS): annual unemployment data, 499; CPS redesign, 124, 369;

Bureau of Labor Statistics *cont.*
employment-population ratio, 379; job composition, 514; labor force participation rate, 428; labor supply enhancement, 559; MSA-level unemployment data, 502; unemployment and inflation, 65

Burgess, Simon, 233

Burghardt, John, 550

Burtless, Gary, 225, 227, 475, 476, 478

Bush, George H. W., 93, 97, 99, 100, 103, 106, 551

Bush, George W., 143

business. *See* industry

business cycle: decomposition of earnings and productivity, 310–14; earnings, productivity and capital accumulation, 335–40, **343–64**; earnings and demographic composition of growth, 316–18, **319, 320–21, 323, 324, 325,** 326, **327, 328**; during economic expansion, 496–510, **504, 506, 508–9,** 520–29, **522–** 23; and gross national product (GNP), 497–98, 513; HPWO adoption and Beveridge curve, 243; workforce composition over, 510–16. *See also* economic growth, effects on advantaged and disadvantaged

Butler, Richard J., 465, 466

Cain, Glen G., 276, 278

California Working Partnerships, 561

Campbell, John, 129

capacity-utilization rate (CU), 500–501

capital: accumulation, earnings and productivity, 335–40, 340–41, 342, **343–64**; and labor, data on, 315–16; labor force projections, 435; sustainable technological growth, 312

capital, human. *See* human capital

Caplin, Andrew, 375

Card, David, 429, 430, 431, 436, 449, 458, 459, 462, 495, 499, 507, 520

CBO (Congressional Budget Office), 103, 104, 141–42, 143, 446

Census Bureau, 427

Census of Governments, 524

Center for Employment Training (San Jose, CA), 550–51

Chelius, James, 466

Cherry, Robert, 456

children, mothers with. *See* single parents

Chilean productivity miracle, 81–84, **83**

Cho, Jang-Ok, 66

Clinton, Bill: balancing the budget, 143; deficit-reduction plan, 100–101, 103–4, 105, 106, 107, 140, 141; and Federal Reserve Bank monetary policy, 99, 109, 144–45; and Fed interest rate hikes, 109; healthcare initiative, 119; inauguration macroeconomic success, 97; Presidential campaign slogan, 92, 93; and tax hikes, 106

Cobb-Douglas case, 558

Cogley, T., 6

Cohen, Jessica, 244, 246, 247

Coile, Courtney, 476, 477, 478

collective bargaining and coordination: institutional roles, 185, 189, **190,** 192, 193–94; marketing-equilibrium model, 245–49; role in U.S. vs. non-U.S., 163, **175**. *See also* unions

college. *See* education and educational attainment

Committee for Economic Development, 478

Committee on Ways and Means, 445, 458, 460

compensation. *See* wages

computers: for distance retraining, 553; family availability, 551; Internet jobs, 557, 570; prices and productivity growth, 131–38. *See also* information technology (IT)

cone of diversification, 274, 286–90

Conference Board, 224, 557

Congressional Budget Office (CBO), 103, 104, 141–42, 143, 446

consumer price index (CPI): budget agreement (1993), 103; Federal Reserve forbearance, 114–17; inflation rate, 65, 97, **98,** 539; macro-level data for NAIRU, **8, 22–** **23,** 30, **33**; price shocks and Federal Reserve policy, 122, 124–25, **126, 127**

Consumer Price Index for All Urban Consumers (CPI-UX1), 514

contract workers, 219, 226–31, **228,** 239, 244–49. *See also* temporary workers

contradictory fiscal policy and economic growth, 146–47

Costa, Dora, 477

Council of Economic Advisors, 61, 102, 267, 517

CPI. *See* consumer price index (CPI)

CPI-UX1 (Consumer Price Index for All Urban Consumers), 514

CPS. *See* Current Population Survey (CPS)

crime: economic growth, effects on advantaged and disadvantaged, 516–17; prison, role in labor market, 567–69

Crossley, Thomas, 372

CU (capacity-utilization rate), 500–501

Current Population Survey (CPS): business cycle measurements, 498–99, 502–3, **504;** labor force and earnings, ORG data, 314–16, 331; labor force projections, 427; MORG data, 39, 40–43, 45; parallel survey analysis and CPS redesign, 407–11, **410;** price, wages and NAIRU, 37, 39, 40–41; prison, role in labor market, 567–69; productivity growth and Phillips curve, 84–87; trade liberalization, 289–90; unemployment duration measurement and CPS redesign, 369, 376–79, **380–83,** 384, 393; workers' compensation effect, 422, 437, 465–68, **467;** worker-transition data construction, 411–13, **414–15**

cyclic factors. *See* business cycle

Danninger, Stephen, 225, 235
Davis, Donald, 278
Day, Jennifer, 431, 432
Deardorff, Alan, 304
Deavers, Kenneth, 202
decomposition of labor, earnings and productivity, 310–14, 315
deficit reduction. *See* federal deficit reduction
deflator, personal-consumption-expenditure (PCE), **4**, 8, 9, **22**, 30, **32**. *See also* GDP deflator
Dehejia, Vivek, 278278
de Jong, Philip, 471
DeLeire, Thomas, 471, 473
DeLong, J. Bradford, 62
demand: globalization and labor market performance, 268–90; labor market, 173, 176, **177**, 269; RD (relative demand) trade model, 268, 270–71, 273–76, 279, 281, 288–90; shocks, 128–30; skill demand, 233–34
demographics: capital intensity and labor, 338–39; earnings growth composition, 316–18, **319**, **320–21**, **323**, **324**, **325**, 326, **327**, **328**, 329–32; labor force participation, **323**, 329–32; labor market (1980–2000), 422–26; labor-market outcomes, comparative international, 162, 178–85, **180**, **183–84**; labor market projections, 426–37; population of working age, 541, **544**; state evidence on NAIRU structural shifts, 49–50. *See also* gender differences; race and ethnicity
Department of Housing and Urban Development (HUD), 565, 566
Department of Labor, 557, 564, 570
Diamond, Peter, 224, 475, 476, 477
Dickens, William, 5, 54, 241, 244, 246, 247
Dickert, Stacy, 448
disability insurance, 468–73, **474**
disability programs, 468–73, **474**, 484*n*11
discouraged workers, 559

disincentives through means tested programs, 437–38, 452–53
Displaced Workers Employment and Training Program (PA), 551
Displaced Workers Survey, 96
diversification, cone of, 274, 286–90
dollar, value of: global competitiveness, 95; policy of forbearance, 130; price shocks and Federal Reserve policy, 121–23
Donahue, Jack, 549
Dornbusch, Rudiger, 82
downsizing, 94, 95–96, 176, 225, 227
DRI Basic Economics Database, 55, **56–57**
dropouts. *See* education and educational attainment
Duggan, Mark, 41, 472
Duncan, Greg, 566
Dunlop, John, 498
Dunne, Timothy, 234
duration of unemployment. *See* unemployment duration
Durbin, David, 465, 466

earned income tax credit (EITC), 429, 437, 444–53, 445–53, 450, 456, 458
earnings: business cycle effects, 496–510, **504**, **506**, **508–9**; decomposition of, 310–13; demographic composition of growth, 316–18, **319**, **320–21**, **323**, **324**, **325**, 326, **327**, **328**; during economic expansion, 493, **494**, 495; EITC (earned income tax credit), 429, 437, 444–53, 456, 458; inequalities in, 333–35, **334**; labor force, 314–15; and labor quantity, **319**, **323**, **324**, **325**, 326, **327**, **328**, 329–32; productivity and capital accumulation, 335–40, **343–64**; skills inequality, 263–65; wage distribution, 332–35, **334**. *See also* wages
ECI (employment cost index), 9, 30, **118**, 514–15
economic expansion, sustainability and replicability

of, 538–77; about, 538; duration, effects of, 507, **508–9**, 510; equilibrium unemployment fall, 554–58; recent U.S. economic events, 539–44; trend productivity rise, 544–54
economic growth, effects on advantaged and disadvantaged, 493–537; about, 493–96, **494**, 529–30; business cycle effects, 496–510, **504**, **506**, **508–9**; crime, 516–17; education and training, 520; health and work injuries, 518–19; public finance, business cycle and disadvantaged, 520–29, **522–23**; welfare participation, 517–18; workforce composition over business cycle, 510–16
Economic Report of the President (Council of Economic Advisors), 102, 267, 517
economics and new economy: business cycle and government spending, 496–510, **504**, **506**, **508–9**, 529; globalization and labor market performance, 268–90; government, scope of, 521, **522–23**; Greenspan on, 127–28, 131; immigration policy, 278–80; industry reallocation in, 313–14, 339–40, **343–64**; knowledge-based, 546–54; SBTC policy, 277–78, 286, 298. *See also* macroeconomic perspectives on "Fabulous Decade"; shocks, economic
economic shocks. *See* shocks, economic
education: index of trade sensitivity, 289–90, **291–92**
education and educational attainment: business cycles and government spending, 521, **522–23**, 524–29; capital intensity and labor, 338–39; current student achievement, 549–50; earnings growth across business cycles, **320–21**, 322, **324**, 341, **344**, **346–47**, **350–51**, **355**, **358**, 362; during economic expansion, 493, **494**, 495; employment and social insurance, 440, **441**, **442**, 443; employment and social pol-

education and educational attainment *cont.*
icy changes, 480–82, **481**; family status and unemployment, 443–45; food stamps use, 438–40, **439,** 446; of immigrant men, 279–80; immigration and labor market performance, 280; labor force participation, **330,** 429–30; labor force projections, 421, 423, 425, 426, 427, 429–33, 434–35, 436–37; labor supply enhancement, 558, 559; productivity and Phillips curve, 84–87; real-wage growth, 267; retraining long-term unemployed, 374–75; skill premium, 264, 281; state evidence on NAIRU structural shifts, 49–50; for temporary workers, 230–31; trade liberalization, 288–89, 299; unemployment and earnings, 505–7, **506**; unemployment insurance, 459–60. *See also* training and retraining

efficiency: job-matching, 557, 561–62; labor-matching, 220, 227, 229, 250
Eissa, Nada, 448, 453
EITC (earned income tax credit), 429, 437, 444–53, 445–53, 450, 456, 458
Elliott, Mark, 565
Ellwood, David, 271, 289, 342, 449, 452, 453, 456, 497, 543, 566
empirical state wage Phillips curves, 42–43, **44,** 45–47
employment: by age and social insurance use, 440, **441, 442**; benefits and inflation, 118–21, 130–31; business cycle effects, 496–510, **504, 506, 508–9**; education and social policy changes, 480–82, **481**; growth rates, 317, **318**; layoffs, 225–26, 233, 238; pro-employment social policies, 454, 456; protection of, **175,** 185, 187–88, 189, 210*n*2, 212*n*24; spatial mismatch, 564–67; steeper tenure profile during economic expansion, 515–16; workplace innovation, 547–48. *See also* jobs; training and retraining; unemployment

employment cost index (ECI), 9, 30, **118,** 514–15
employment-protection legislation (EPL), **175,** 185, 187–88, 210*n*2
employment-to-population (EPOP) rate, 502
empowerment zones, 563
energy prices, 5, 123–24, **126, 127,** 130, 220
England, David, 540
equilibrium model for labor market, 269–71
equilibrium unemployment: fall of, sustainability, 542–43, **544,** 554–58; foreign price change impact on, 294–97; and labor supply enhancement, 558; product-market competition increase, 557–58. *See also* unemployment
equilibrium wages and globalization, 269
Estevao, Marcello, 230
ethnicity. *See* race and ethnicity
expansion duration, effects of, 507, **508–9,** 510
expected utility of worker and unemployment duration, 372–74
exports, international. *See* labor market, international trade effects on U.S.
export sensitivity, index of, 289–90, **291–92**

"Fabulous Decade." *See* macroeconomic perspectives on "Fabulous Decade"
factor-price-insensitivity (FPI) theorem, 273, 282, 285, 286, 289
family structure. *See* marital status; single parents
FDI (foreign-direct-investment), 261–63
federal deficit reduction: Clinton's plan for, 100–101, 103–4, 105, 106, 107, 140, 141; deficit (early 1990s), 92–93, 97; Greenspan and, 101, 102, 107; success of, 139–44
federal government: budget agreement (1990,1993,1997), 93–94, 100–108, 140–41; public finance during economic expansion, 520–29, **522–23**; scope of, 521, **522–23**; spending and business cycles, 496–510, **504, 506, 508–9,** 529; training and retraining programs, 551–54. *See also* policy issues
Federal Open Market Committee (FOMC), 105–12, 127–30, 138–39
Federal Reserve Bank: fall of equilibrium unemployment, 554–58; forbearance and Phillips curve, 114–31; inflation control, 5; investment and monetary policy, 146–48; monetary policy easing, 97–100; potential output growth, 543, **544**; soft landing engineering, 108–14
Feenstra, Robert, 276, 278, 289
Feldstein, Martin, 462
Fernald, John, 313
Fine-tuning economy and monetary policy, 147
Fischer, Stanley, 82
flexible specialization, 220, 221, 237, 244
FOMC (Federal Open Market Committee), 105–12, 127–30, 138–39
food stamp program, 438–40, **439,** 446, 447, 450
forbearance by Federal Reserve Bank, 115
foreign born. *See* immigration
foreign-direct-investment (FDI), 261–63
FPI (factor-price-insensitivity) theorem, 273, 282, 285, 286, 289
FRB-US model. *See* WUMM and FRB-US models
Freeman, Richard, 267, 271, 279, 497, 507, 517, 530, 567
Friedberg, Leora, 476–77
Fullerton, Howard, 428–29

GAIN (Greater Avenues to Independence), 562–63
gains from trade, theory of, 276
gap construction, macro-level data trends, 7, 8
Gardner, B. Delworth, 485
Gardner, Harold H., 485

GATT (General Agreement on Tariffs and Trade), 286–87

GDP. *See* gross domestic product (GDP)

GDP deflator: budget agreement (1993), 103; prices, wages and NAIRU, 3, 8–10, 13; productivity growth and NAIRU, **22–25**, 30, **31–35**

gender differences: earnings growth and capital across business cycles, 318, **319, 320–21,** 322, 338, 341, **343, 346, 350, 354, 357, 361**; education and index of trade sensitivity, 289–90, **291–92**; inactivity rate, labor force, 560–61; labor force participation, 329–31, **330,** 342, 429; labor force projections, 427; prison, role in labor market, 567–69; second shift work, 553; unemployment duration and labor-force attachment, 369, 372, 388–89, **392, 394–95, 396–97,** 403–7, **404–5**; wages, international vs. U.S., 160, 161, **198,** 198–201

General Agreement on Tariffs and Trade (GATT), 286–87

general skills, desirability of, 230–31, 233–34, 237, 244–49; 250–51

Gerald, Debra, 431, 432

Gingrich, Newt, 140

Glazerman, Steven, 550

globalization. *See* labor market, international trade effects on U.S.

GNP. *See* gross national product (GNP)

Goldin, Claudia, 458, 460, 462

Gordon, Robert: computers and TFP, 134; Nixon price controls, 75; prices. labor and NAIRU, 5, 6, 9, 13, 14, 16, 19, 26; on productivity cycles, 313, 540–41; wage Phillips curve, 42

Gore, Al, 101

government. *See* federal government; states

government aid. *See* social insurance

Gramm-Rudman-Hollings (GRH), 94

Greater Avenues to Independence (GAIN), 562–63

Green, David, 448

Greenspan, Alan: Bush election loss, 97; deficit reduction, 101, 102, 107; interest rate easing, 97, 99, 102, 112, 148; interest rate hikes, 108, 109, 110, 111, 128; loose monetary policy, 144–45; as macroeconomic magician, 113, 147; NAIRU approach, 138; and new-economy thinking, 127–28, 131; and productivity, 116; on sustainable employment, 495; traumatized-worker hypothesis, 117–18

gross domestic product (GDP): budget agreement (1993 and 1997), 104–5, 142; computer prices, 136; globalization, 261–63; growth in real, 539, 543; imports and exports, 299; and price shocks, 123, 124; soft landing by Federal Reserve Bank, **109,** 113, 114. *See also* GDP deflator

gross national product (GNP): business cycle effect, 497–98, 513; and injuries on the job, 519; and trade theory, 272

gross state product (gsp), 41

Grubb, Dennis, 61, 81

Gruber, John, 372

Gruber, Jonathon, 463, 471, 472, 475, 476, 477, 478

Gruber-Kabik estimate, 472

gsp (gross state product), 41

Gustman, Alan, 476, 520

Haffner, Robert, 545

Hakura, Dalia, 304

Hall, Robert E., 6, 338

Halpern, Janice, 471

Haltiwanger, John, 498

Hanson, Gordon, 276, 278, 279, 286

"hard to employ," 454

Haskel, Jonathan, 278, 284, 286

Hattiangadi, Anita, 202

Hausman, Jerry, 471, 476

Haveman, Robert, 471

health: business cycles and government spending, 521, **522–23,** 524–29; economic growth, effects on advantaged and disadvantaged,

518–19; health care, 118–21, **126, 127,** 130–31, 220

Heckscher-Ohlin (HO) trade model: globalization and labor market performance, 268–69, 272, 274–76, 279; relevancy of, 281–86, **283**

Heilbroner, Robert, 159

Heller, Walter, 147

Helpman, Elhanan, 285

high-performance work organization (HPWO): adoption of, 232–35, 236, 237, 241, 243, 251; defined, 220; deployment of, 222, 223; and outsourcing, 240

high school. *See* education and educational attainment

Hitt, Lorin, 234

Hodrick-Prescott (HP) filter, 67, 79, 379

Hollmann, Frederick, 427, 428

Hotz, Joseph V., 563

Hotz, V. Joseph, 449

hours worked: business cycle effects, 496–510, **504, 506, 508–9,** 529; "second shift" for women, 553; sustainability and replication of economic expansion, 543, **544**; unemployment duration and risk, 372–74

Houseman, Susan, 229

Houser, Scott, 448

Housing and Urban Development, Department of (HUD), 565, 566

Houston, Ellen, 568

Hoynes, Hilary Williamson, 453, 473, 497, 507, 517

HP (Hodrick-Prescott) filter, 67, 79, 379

HPWO. *See* high-performance work organization (HPWO)

HUD (Department of Housing and Urban Development), 565, 566

human capital: flexible production, 221; market-equilibrium model, 244–49; skill demands, 233–34; training and retraining, 549–54

human resource management practices and sustainable unemployment, 219–59; about, 219–23, 249–52; interviews with HR managers, human resource management practices and sustainable unemployment *cont.* 236–40; labor market changes and NAIRU, 244–49; labor rent erosion, 240–44, **242**, 250; U.S. labor market changes, 223–36, **228**

human-resource managers, interviews with, 236–40

Hurd, Michael, 476

Hussar, William, 431, 432

hysteresis and unemployment, 368, 374–76

ICT (information-and-communication-technology), 538, 544–45, 551, 552, 553–54

Idson, Todd, 226

immigration: earnings growth composition, 331–32; future labor projections, 421, 423, **424,** 426, 431–32, **433,** 434, 436; globalization and economy, 261, **262**; labor force participation, 330–32, 341; labor force projections, 427; labor supply enhancement, 558–59; policy and the new economy, 278–80; population of working age, 541, **544**

Immigration Reform and Control Act (1986), 427

import sensitivity, index of, 289–90, **291–92**

inactivity rate, labor force, 538, 541–42, **544,** 560–61

incarceration, role in labor market, 567–69, 570

income: family, vs. family earnings, 505, 529; globalization and changes in U.S, 263–67. *See also* earnings

index of export sensitivity, 289–90, **291–92**

index of trade sensitivity, 289–90, **291–92**

index of unemployment pressure, 376, **377**

individual-level data, MORG from CPS, 40–41

industry: characteristics and state evidence on NAIRU structural shifts, 50, **51**; factor intensity in U.S, 282, **283–84**; new economy reallocation, 313–14, 339–40,

344–45, 347–49, 351–53, 355–56, 358–60, 362–64; restructuring and budget agreements, 94–96

inflation: CPI indication of, 65, 97, **98,** 539; forecasts, and Philips curve, 70, **71, 72,** 73, 75, 77, **78**; and health care, 118–21, 130–31; lessons learned and fiscal policy, 147–48; macroeconomic shocks, 174, **175**; macroeconomic shocks, international comparison, 196–97; and NAIRU decline, 219; price and wage, 12; in sustained expansion, 3–8, **4**; and unemployment, 65, 70, 223; unemployment and earnings growth, 340; wage and productivity growth, 61–62. *See also* NAIRU (nonaccelerating inflation rate of unemployment)

information-and-communication-technology (ICT), 538, 544–45, 551, 552, 553–54

information technology (IT): advances in, 284; human resource management practices, 225, 234–37, 238, 240, 250, 251; and productivity growth, 131–38, 145, 220; sustainability and replicability of economic expansion, 538, 541, 544, 552, 553–54, 571; wage effects in HO model, 278

Information Technology Support Center, 41

injuries, on the job, during economic expansion, 518–19

innovation, workplace, 547–48

institutions: globalization and labor market performance, 268–90; labor-market outcomes, comparative international, 162–65, 185–97, **190–91**; time-invariant, institutions and shocks, 188–93, **190–91**; and unemployment, 163–64, 210n2, 212n24

instrumental-variables (IV) estimation, 8, 42, 45, 52

insurance, social. *See* social insurance

interest rates: budget agreement (1993), 103, 105; easing, by Fed, 97, 99, 102, 112,

148; economic expansion, 114–21; hikes, by Fed, 108, 109, 110, 111, 128; and macroeconomic shocks, 173, 174, **175, 177,** 178; soft landing by Federal Reserve Bank, 108–14

international trade and labor markets. *See* labor market, international trade effects on U.S.; labor-market outcomes, comparative international

Internet: jobs, 557, 570; price competition, 5. *See also* information technology (IT)

investment and monetary policy, 146–48

IT. *See* information technology (IT)

Jackman, Richard, 61, 81

Jacobs, Lawrence R., 478

jail in labor market, 567–69

Jamaica, productivity in, 81

Jargowsky, Paul, 564

Job Corps, 549–50

jobs: composition of, 514–16; creation of, international vs. U.S., 161; decreasing stability and security, 225–26; downsizing, 94, 95–96; matching efficiency, 557, 561–62; in recession recovery, 92; turnover, 225–26; unemployment duration and hysteresis, 374–76; vacancy rates and unemployment, 222, **224,** 249. *See also* employment; training and retraining

Job Training Partnership Act (JTPA), 549, 551

Johnson, George, 278278

Jordan, Jerry, 107

Jorgenson, Dale, 546

JTPA (Job Training Partnership Act), 549, 551

Juhn, Chinhui, 305

Kahn, Lawrence, 172, 198, 200–201, 407

Kahneman, Daniel, 84

Kallan, Jeffrey, 427, 428

Kalman smoother and filter, 17, **18,** 21, 26, 38, 47, 73

Katz, Lawrence: human resource management practice, 225, 226, 227, 231; international trade effects on U. S. labor market, 271, 279, 295; NAIRU, prices and wages, 5, 15, 48, 52; productivity and Phillips curve, 62, 63, 65, 84; social policy and labor force, 458, 460, 462; sustainability and replicability of economic expansion, 554, 556, 557, 564, 566; wage-curve relations, 499; youth unemployment, 179
Kaufman, Roger, 159
Kavenaugh, Karen, 466
Kennedy, John F., 493
Keynesian economics, 99, 101
Kimball, Miles, 66
King, Robert, 13, 16
Kling, Jeffrey, 566, 568–69
Knetsch, Jack, 84
knowledge-based economy, 546–54. *See also* information technology (IT)
Korenman, Sanders, 179
Krueger, Alan: human resource management practice, 225, 227, 231, 241; international trade and U.S. skill premium, 276; NAIRU, prices and wages, 5, 48, 52; productivity and Phillips curve, 63, 65, 84; social policy and labor force, 465, 466, 476; sustainability and replicability of economic expansion, 554, 556, 557; youth unemployment, 179
Krugman, Paul, 267, 278, 285
Kubik, Jeffrey, 471, 472

labor, output sustainability and productivity growth, 309–66; about, 309–10, 340–42; analytic framework, 310–14; data, 314–16; earnings, productivity and capital accumulation, 335–40, **343–64**; earnings growth composition, 316–18, **319, 320–21, 323, 324, 325,** 326, **327, 328**; wages and distribution, 332–35, **334**
labor demand, 173, 176, **177,** 269

labor force and labor-force attachment: age changes in, 556; composition over business cycle, 510–16; earnings, 314–15; gender and labor-market outcomes, 388–89, **392, 394–95, 396–97, 404–5**; and globalization, 280–81; in high-productivity industries, 339–40, **343–64**; labor-market transitions, 389, **398–99, 400–401,** 402–3, **404–5**; participation changes and demographics, **323,** 329–31, 429; skill shortage, 548; unemployment duration, 369, 372; worker-transition data construction, 411–13, **414–15**
labor force projections and social policy, 421–90; about, 421–23, 480, **481,** 482; changing of (1980–2000), 422–37; disability programs, 468–73, **474,** 484n11; means-tested programs, 437–58, **439, 441–42, 455, 457**; potential for policy, 437–80, **439, 441–42, 455, 457, 464, 467, 474, 479, 481**; social-insurance programs, 437, 458–68, **464, 467**; social security retirement benefits, 422, **439,** 473, 475–80, **479, 481**; work-support benefits, 437–58, **439, 441–42, 455, 457**
labor market: demand, 173, 176, **177,** 269; demographics and demographic projections, 422–26, 426–37; equilibrium model, 269–71; globalization and labor market performance, 269–71, 277–81; institutions and unemployment, 210n2, 212n24; labor mobility, 284; role of prison in, 567–69. *See also* economic expansion, sustainability and replicability of; economic growth, effects on advantaged and disadvantaged; human resource management practices and sustainable unemployment
labor market, international trade effects on U.S., 260–306; about, 260, 299–300; human resource management practices and sustainable unemployment, 223–26,

228; performance, long-term, 268–90; price shocks and Federal Reserve policy, 121–23; trade and employment, 290–98, **291**; wage impacts, 264–68
labor market equilibrium model, 269–71
labor-market outcomes, comparative international, 159–218; about, 159–62, 206; cross-country time-series data for, 165–73; data appendix, 207–9, **210**; institutional differences and outcomes, 162–65; institutional role, 185–97, **190–91**; macroeconomic shocks, role of, 162, 173–78, **175**; performance in disaggregated labor-market, 197–201, **199**; regulatory burden and productivity, 545–46; U.S. labor market dynamics and robustness, 201–5, **203**; youth in demographic developments, 178–85, **180, 183–84,** 189, **190,** 192, **198,** 198–201, 204
labor rents, erosion of, 240–44, **242,** 250
labor supply: enhancement policies, 558–69; and globalization, 269; globalization and labor market performance, 268–90; matching efficiency, 220, 227, 229, 250; means tested programs, 453–58, **455, 457**; and unemployment insurance, 462–65, **464**
labor unions. *See* unions
Lach, Saul, 230
Ladd, Helen, 566
lag dynamics, prices and wages, 13–15, 37
Lane, Julia, 233
LaWare, John, 107
Lawrence, Robert, 276
Layard, Richard, 61, 81
layoffs, 225–26, 233, 238
Leahy, John, 375
Leamer, Edward, 273, 276, 278
Lemieux, Thomas, 429, 430, 431, 436, 495, 520
Leonard, Jonathon, 471
Lerman, Robert, 50
Leuven, Edwin, 548
Levine, Phillip B., 462
Levinsohn, James, 273

Levy, Frank, 234
liberalization of trade, 286–90
Liebman, Jeffrey, 449, 456, 566
Light, Audrey, 520
Lindbeck, Assar, 234, 235
Long Term Capital Management, 130
lowest sustainable rate of unemployment (LSRU), 252n2
LSRU (lowest sustainable rate of unemployment), 252n2
Lucas, Robert, 372
luck, and economic expansion, 5–6, 27, 91, 121–26, **127**, 137
Ludwig, Jens, 566
Lynch, Lisa, 234, 520, 547, 549, 552
Lyons, Max, 202

Machin, Steve, 278
Macroeconomic Advisors (St. Louis, MO), 99
macroeconomic perspectives on "Fabulous Decade," 91–156; about, 91; budget agreements, 93–94, 100–108; deficit reduction, 139–44; Federal Reserve forbearance and Phillips curve, 114–31; Federal Reserve's monetary policy, 97–100, 138–39; Federal Reserve's soft landing engineering, 108–14; policy lessons, 144–48; productivity growth, 131–38, 543, **544**; setting for, 91–97; shocks, role of, 162, 173–78, **175**. *See also* prices, wages and NAIRU; productivity growth
macro estimates of price and wage Phillips curves, 17–36; benchmark price regressions, **17**, 17–21, **20**, 27–29; sensitivity analysis, 21, **22–25**, 26, 36; summary of findings, 26–27, 36
macro-level data trends for prices, wages and NAIRU, 8–13; aggregate U.S. data description, 8–9; estimation methods and gap construction, 7, 8; properties of low-frequency data, 9–13
MaCurdy, Thomas, 448
Manpower Demonstration Research Corporation, 563

marital status: earnings growth across business cycles, **320–21**, 326, **327**, **345**, **349**, **353**, **356**, **360**, **364**; education and unemployment, 443–45; labor force participation rate, 424–25; social insurance program changes, 451–53
market-equilibrium model, 244–49
Markov transition matrix, 393, 402, 413
matching efficiency: jobs, 557, 561–62; labor, 220, 227, 229, 250
Mathematica Policy Research, 459
McDonough, William, 110
means tested programs: disability programs, 468–73, **474**; labor force projections, 437–38; labor supply, 453–58, **455**, **457**; reform effects, 444–58, **455**, **457**
Medicaid, 437
Merrill Lynch, 557
Mexican financial crisis, 112
Meyer, Bruce D., 226, 448, 449, 462, 463, 465, 466
Meyer, Laurence, 127, 128
MFA (Multi-Fiber Agreement), 287
MFIP (Minnesota's Family Investment Program), 450
micro evidence of productivity growth and Phillips curve, 84–87
military, earnings growth composition, 332
Milkovich, George, 62–63
Miller, Stephen, 226, 407–9, 411, 413
Mincer, Jacob, 225, 235
minimum-wage levels, 163, 188, 206
Minnesota's Family Investment Program (MFIP), 450
Mitchell, Olivia, 478
Mocan, H. Naci, 517
Moffitt, Robert, 164, 204, 448, 462, 473, 475, 476, 558
monetary policy. *See* Federal Reserve Bank
monster.com, 557
Monthly Labor Relations Review, 41
Moore's law, 134

MORG data, CPS, 39, 40–43, 45
mothers, single. *See* single parents
Moving to Opportunity (MTO), 566
Moynihan, Patrick, 125
MSA-specific business cycles, 497, 502–7, **504**, **506**
MTO (Moving to Opportunity), 566
Mulder, Tammany, 427, 428
Mullins, David, 107
Multi-Fiber Agreement (MFA), 287
Murnane, Richard, 234
Murphy, Kevin, 305

NAIRU (nonaccelerating inflation rate of unemployment): and Beveridge curve, 220; decline in, and HRM practice, 219–20, 226, 251; defined, 3, 8; economic expansion, 114–17, 142; human resource management practices and sustainable unemployment, 244–49; Phillips curve and productivity growth, 63–65, 70, 81; structural changes over time, 49–50; time-varying, 77, 79, **80**; wages and unemployment duration, 376. *See also* prices, wages and NAIRU; TV-NAIRU
National Bureau of Economic Research (NBER), 289, 314, 500
National Governors' Association, 552
National Longitudinal Survey, 498
National Longitudinal Survey of Youth, 568
Native American wage credit, 563
nativity. *See* immigration
NBER (National Bureau of Economic Research), 289, 314, 500
Neumark, David, 179, 226
new economy. *See* economics and new economy
Newman, Jerry, 63
Nicholson, Walter, 462
Nickell, Stephen, 185, 208, 558

Nixon price control, 75
nonaccelerating inflation rate
of unemployment (NAIRU).
See NAIRU (nonaccelerating
inflation rate of unemployment)
nonaccelerating wage rate of
unemployment (NAWRU),
3, 8

Occupational Safety and
Health Administration
(OSHA), 519
OECD (Organization for Economic Co-operation and Development): Chilean miracle,
81–82; databases from, 207–
9, **210**; fall of equilibrium
unemployment, 554–58; in-
activity rate, labor force,
560–61; institutional roles,
189, 192–97; macroeconomic
shocks, 173–78, **175**; regulatory burden and produc-
tivity, 545–46; sustainability
and replicability of eco-
nomic expansion, 571, **572,
573**; TFP growth, 558; unemployment and wages, 201–6,
203; "unified theory" of
labor-market outcomes, 161–
65; wages, international vs.
U.S., 161; wage subsidies,
564
oil prices, 123–24, **126, 127,**
130, 220
Okun, Arthur, 495, 515
Okun's law, 310
Oliner, Stephen, 134, 165, 546
OLS (ordinary least squares)
model, 42, 45, 176, 177,
178
O'Neill, June, 407
Oosterbeek, Hessel, 548
OPEC (Organization of Petroleum Exporting Countries),
130
openness, economic. *See* labor
market, international trade
effects on U.S.
Organization of Petroleum Exporting Countries (OPEC),
130
ORGs (outgoing rotation
groups) data, CPS, 314–16,
331
Orszag, Peter, 477

OSHA (Occupational Safety
and Health Administration),
519
Osterman, Paul, 232–33,
234
Oswald, Andre, 499
Otoo, Maria Ward, 227
outgoing rotation groups
(ORGs) data, CPS, 314–16,
331
output sustainability. *See* labor,
output sustainability and
productivity growth
outsourcing, 239–40

Paarsch, Harry, 448
Palubinsky, Beth, 565
Panel Study of Income Dy-
namics (PSID), 495, 505,
510–16
parallel survey analysis and
CPS redesign, 407–11, **410**
Parker, Jonathan, 495, 498, 510,
512, 513, 514
Parry, Robert, 107
Parsons, Donald, 471
pay-as-you-go (PAYGO) pool,
94, 147
PAYGO (pay-as-you-go) pool,
94, 147
PCE (personal-consumption-
expenditure) deflator, **4, 8,** 9,
22, 30, **32**
performance, labor market:
disaggregated, comparative
international trade, 197–201,
199; future trade and immigration liberalization,
286–90; and globalization,
268–90; HO trade model relevance, 281–86, **283**; labor
perspective, 269–71; policy
and wage implications, 277–
81; trade perspective, 272–
77. *See also* labor-market
outcomes, comparative in-
ternational
Perot, Ross, 101
Perry, George, 5, 54
personal consumption expenditure (PCE), 115
personal-consumption-
expenditure (PCE) deflator,
4, 8, 9, **22,** 30, **32**
Personal Responsibility and
Work Opportunity Act of
1996 (PRWORA), 445, 456

Pettit, Becky, 567
Phelps, Edmund, 295
Phillips, John, 478
Phillips curves: business cycle
measurements, 499; conventional, 70, **71**; derivation of,
63–64; economic expansion
interpretation, 3–8, **4**; empirical state wage, 42–47, **44**;
Federal Reserve forbearance,
114–31; price, derivation of,
64; price, macro estimates
of, 13–15, 17–27, 53; price-
price Phillips curve, 116,
117; productivity growth,
61–90; stability of, 48; θ–A,
70–73, 72, 79, **80**; wage, derivation of, 64; wage, macro
estimates of, 13–15, 27–36;
wage, specification and estimation of state-level, 36–39;
wage, time-series analysis
extensions, 74–77, **76**; wage
aspirations and NAIRU, 63–
65; wages and unemploy-
ment duration, 369, 376. *See
also* productivity growth
Pischke, Jorn-Steffen, 430, 476
Polachek, Solomon, 407–9
policy issues: Federal Reserve
macroeconomic perspec-
tives, 144–48; globalization
and labor market perfor-
mance, 277–81; government
and state evidence on
NAIRU structural shifts, 50,
51; labor supply enhancement, 558–69; macro-
economic perspectives and
history, 144–48; policy
changes, employment and
education, 480–82, **481**; pro-
employment, 454, 456; re-
training long-term
unemployed, 374–75; trade
liberalization, 286–90. *See
also* labor force projections
and social policy
Polivka, Anne, 226, 229, 407–9,
411, 413
poverty rate and economic expansion, 493, **494,** 495
Presidential election (1992),
92–93, 97, 100, 144
price: competition, 5, 6; foreign price changes and unemployment, 294–97;
Phillips curve derivation, 64;
Phillips curves, macro esti-

price *cont.*
mates of, 13–15, 17–27;
price-price Phillips curve,
116, 117; price shocks and
Federal Reserve policy, 121–
26, **127**
prices, wages and NAIRU, 3–
60; about, 3–8, **4,** 53–54, **55**;
data appendix, 55, **56–57**;
macro-level data trends, 8–
13; macro price and wage
equations, specification and
estimation of, 13–17; Phillips
curves, empirical state
wage, 42–47, **44**; Phillips
curves, macro estimates of
price, 13–15, 17–27; Phillips
curves, macro estimates of
wage, 13–15, 27–36; Phillips
curves, specification and estimation of state-level wage,
36–39; state evidence on
NAIRU structural shifts, 47–
52, **51**; state-level data set,
39–40
prison, role in labor market,
567–69
product cycles, 244–49, 250
productivity: and labor, data
on, 315–16; output and capital accumulation, 335–40,
343–64; output decomposition, 310–13; prices, wages
and NAIRU, 9–13, 53–54;
product cycles, 244–49, 250;
and real wages, 267; shocks,
135. *See also* economic expansion, sustainability and
replicability of
productivity growth: about,
61–62, 87; balanced, 335–39;
Chilean miracle, 81–84, **83**;
and computer prices, 131–
38; data and measurement,
65–69; and macroeconomic
shocks, 173–78, **175**, 204;
micro evidence of, 84–87;
and Phillips curve, 61–90;
Phillips curve and NAIRU,
63–65; Phillips curve estimates, 69–74, **72**; rate of, 91;
sustainability and replication of economic expansion,
538, 543, 544–54, 554, 569;
time-series analysis extensions, 74–84, **76, 78, 80, 83**;
wage aspirations, 62–63, 66–
69; and wage growth, 65,
220. *See also* labor, output

sustainability and productivity growth
product-market competition,
557–58
pro-employment social policies, 454, 456
PRWORA (Personal Respon-
sibility and Work Oppor-
tunity Act of 1996), 445,
456
PSID (Panel Study of Income
Dynamics), 495, 505, 510–16
public assistance. *See* social insurance
public finance during economic expansion, 520–29,
522–23

quality control. *See* high-
performance work organization (HPWO)
Quinn, Joseph, 478

race and ethnicity: earnings
growth and capital across
cycles, **320–21,** 322, **323, 343,
346, 350, 354, 357, 361**; labor
force participation, 330–32,
429; labor force projections,
421, 423, **424,** 426, 427, 431–
32, **433,** 434, 436; prison,
role in labor market, 567–69,
570; training and retraining
programs, 550; unemploy-
ment rate during economic
expansion, 493, **494,** 495
random-walk specification, 16
Raphael, Stephen, 565
RD (relative demand) trade
model, 268, 270–71, 273–76,
279, 281, 288–90
Reagan, Patricia, 564
Reagan, Ronald, 106
recession duration, effects of,
507, **508–9,** 510
Rees, Daniel, 517
reference groups and wage
fairness, 84
reference transactions, 63
region, earnings growth across
business cycles, **320–21,** 326,
**328, 343, 346, 350, 354, 357,
361**
regulatory burden and productivity, 545–46

relative demand (RD) trade
model, 268, 270–71, 273–76,
279, 281, 288–90
relative supply (RS) trade
model, 268, 270–71, 273–76,
279, 281, 288–90
rents, labor, erosion of, 240–44,
242, 250
replacement ratio, 462, 475
reservation wage, 245–46
retirement benefits from social
security, 422, **439,** 473, 475–
80, **479, 481**
retraining. *See* training and retraining
Ricardo-Viner models, 282
Richardson, J. David, 278
"rising tide lifts all boats." *See*
economic growth, effects on
advantaged and disadvan-
taged
risk and unemployment, 372–
74
Robbins, Phillip, 449
Rodgers, William, 517, 567
Rodrik, Dani, 268, 297
root-canal economics, 103
Rosenbaum, Dan, 448, 449
Rothschild, Michael, 374
RS (relative supply) trade
model, 268, 270–71, 273–76,
279, 281, 288–90
Rubin, Robert, 129
Ruser, John, 466, 518
Russian financial crisis, 130
Rybczynski theorem, 273, 279,
282, 285

Sachs, Jeffrey, 276
Samuelson, Paul, 276, 281
Samwick, Andrew, 476
Sargen, J. D., 15
Sargent, T., 6
Sawicky, Max, 456
SBTC (skill-biased technologi-
cal change), 270, 277–78,
286, 298
Schmidt, Stefanie, 50
Schochet, Peter, 550
Schoeni, Robert, 449
Scholz, John Karl, 448, 449
schooling. *See* education and
educational attainment
"second shift" for women, 553
Segal, Lewis, 40, 229, 230
Self-Sufficiency Project of Can-
ada, 450

sensitivity analysis: price Phillips curves, macro estimates of, 8, 21, **22–25,** 26; wage Phillips curves, empirical state, 43, **44,** 45; wage Phillips curves, macro estimates of, 29–30, **31–35, 36,** 38
sex. *See* gender differences
Shapiro, Matthew, 313
Shapiro, Robert Y., 478
Shatz, Howard, 276
Shiller, Robert, 129
Shimer, Robert, 49, 179, 181, 225, 385, 463, 559
shocks, economic: benefit, 118, **126, 127;** demand, 128–30; foreign, 260; inflation, international comparison, 196–97; price, and Federal Reserve policy, 121–26, **127;** productivity, 135; role of macroeconomic, 173–78, **175;** shock variables and international comparison, 201–6, **203;** time-invariant institutional measures, 188–93, **190–91;** time-variant institutional measures, 193–95; wage, 117; wage-price, 125–26, **127.** *See also* supply shocks
Sichel, Daniel, 134, 165, 224, 546
single parents: earnings growth, 326, **327,** 341, **353, 364;** during economic expansion, 493, **494,** 495; education and employment rate, 443–44; labor force participation rate, 424–25; labor force projections, 421–22; preemployment policies, 454–56, **455;** social policy and less educated, 421. *See also* means tested programs
SIPP (Survey of Income and Program Participation), 431
SI (supplemental security income), 437, **439,** 468–73, **474**
skill-biased technological change (SBTC), 270, 277–78, 286, 298
skills: desirability of general, 230–31, 233–34, 237, 244–49, 250–51; earnings growth, **323,** 329–31, 341–42; flexible production, 221; immigration and globalization, 262–65, 280; immigration and la-

bor force projections, 428; inequality and globalization, 263–65, 300; policies and mix of, 280–81; premium on, 264, 281; real-wage growth, 266–68; shortages, and new economy, 548–49; tariffs and industry skill intensity, 287–88; training and retraining, 549–54
Slaughter, Matthew, 276, 278, 279, 284, 286, 298
small country assumption, 285–86
Smith, Robert S., 518
Snower, Dennis, 234, 235
social insurance: by age and employment, 440, **441, 442;** business cycles and government spending, 521, **522–23,** 524–29; disability insurance, 468–73, **474;** duration of, 466; during economic expansion, 493, **494,** 495; labor force projections, 437–38; social security retirement benefits, 422, **439,** 473, 475–80, **479, 481;** worker's compensation, 422, 437, 465–68, **467.** *See also* unemployment insurance (UI)
social security disability insurance (DI), 468–73, **474**
social security retirement benefits, 422, **439,** 473, 475–80, **479, 481**
soft landing by Federal Reserve Bank, 108–14
Solon, Gary, 462, 495, 498, 510, 512, 513, 514
Solow, Robert M., 312
Solow model, 312
"Solow's paradox," 131
spatial mismatch, 564–67
specific-factor model, 282
spending control and fiscal policy, 147
SSI (supplemental security income), 437, **439,** 468–73, **474**
stability, state evidence on NAIRU structural shifts, 48
Staiger, Douglas, 6, 7, 13, 16, 543
states: business cycles and government spending, 496–510, **504, 506, 508–9,** 529; data for prices, wages and NAIRU, 40–41; evidence on NAIRU structural shifts, 47–

52, **51;** government, scope of, 521, **522–23;** regional earnings growth across business cycles, **320–21,** 326, **328, 343, 346, 350, 354, 357, 361;** unemployment insurance, 458; wage Phillips curves, empirical state, 42–47, **44;** wage Phillips curves, specification and estimation of, 36–39
Steinmeyer, Thomas, 476, 520
Stevens, David, 233
Stiglitz, Joseph, 62, 68, 374
Stiroh, Kevin, 546
Stock, David, 476
Stock, James H., 6, 7, **12,** 13, 16, 19, 501, 543
Stoll, Michael, 565
Stolper, Wolfgang, 276, 281, 289
Stolper-Samuelson theorem, 282, 285, 286
Sullivan, Daniel, 40, 229, 230
Summers, Lawrence, 241
supplemental security income (SSI), 437, **439,** 468–73, **474**
supply: RS (relative supply) trade model, 268, 270–71, 273–76, 279, 281, 288–90; small country assumption, U. S., 285–86. *See also* labor supply
supply shocks: Federal Reserve and, 127–28, 137–38, 145; labor and wage sensitivity analysis, 9, 27; NAIRU, 65, 220; Phillips curve, 65, 75, 77. *See also* shocks, economic
Survey of Income and Program Participation (SIPP), 431
Swanson, Eric, 514

TANF (Temporary Assistance for Needy Families), 437, 445–49, 454
tariffs, U.S., 286
tax issues: budget agreement (1997), 143–44; credits as wage subsidies, 563–64; earned income tax credit (EITC), 429, 437, 444, 445–53, 450, 456, 458; hike, and budget agreement (1993), 103; unemployment insur-

Index

tax issues *cont.*
ance, 461–62; welfare-to-work tax credit (WTWTC), 563–64; work-opportunities tax credit (WOTC), 563–64
Taylor, John, 5, 54
Taylor, Susan, 226
technology: information-and-communication-technology (ICT), 538, 544–45, 551, 552, 553–54; sustainable growth in, 312; wage effects in HO model, 278. *See also* information technology (IT)
Temporary Assistance for Needy Families (TANF), 437, 445–49, 454
temporary workers: compensation of, 254*n*21; growth of, 222, 226–31, **228**, 244–49, 250–51; and layoff levels, 238–40; state evidence on NAIRU structural shifts, 50
TFP. *See* total-factor-productivity (TFP)
Thailand, productivity in, 81
Thayler, Richard, 84
theory of gains from trade, 276
θ–A Phillips curves, **70–73**, **72**, 79, **80**
Thurow, Lester, 159
Tierney, Joseph, 565
time-series data and analysis: business cycle effects, 499–501; extensions, productivity growth and Phillips curve, 74–84, **76**, **78**, **80**, **83**; index of unemployment pressure, 376, **377**; job procurement and unemployment duration, 374, **375**; labor force transition rate, **398–99**, **400–401**; labor-market outcomes, comparative international, 165–73; parallel survey analysis and CPS redesign, 407–11, **410**; Phillips curve, 74–77, **76**; price inflation, 9, **10**, 15; sensitivity analysis, 29, **30**; time-invariant, institutions and shocks, 188–93, **190–91**; time-variant, institutions and shocks, 193–95; time-varying NAIRUs, 77, 79, **80**; unemployment duration, 367, **370–71**, 374, **375**, **380–81**, **382–83**, **386–87**, **390–91**, **394–97**, **400–401**, **404–5**; unemployment rate,

367, **368**, **370–71**, **388**, **390–91**, **392**, **394–97**
TIMMS study, 549
Topel, Robert, 298, 462
total-factor-productivity (TFP): annual in OECD, 164–65; computer sector, 133–34, 145; HO trade theory, 275, 278; international trade, 275; macroeconomic shocks, 173–74, **175**, 176, 177, 202, **203**; SBTC in new economy, 278; sustainability and replicability of economic expansion, 538, 541, 544, 554, 558, 569, 571, **572**, **573**
total quality management (TQM). *See* high-performance work organization (HPWO)
TQM (total quality management). *See* high-performance work organization (HPWO)
trade, international. *See* labor market, international trade effects on U.S.
Trade Adjustment Assistance Program, 551
trade perspective on globalization and labor market performance, 272–81
trade sensitivity, index of, 289–90, **291–92**
trade theory. *See* Heckscher-Ohlin (HO) trade model
training and retraining: retraining long-term unemployed, 374–75; for skill improvement, 549–54; wage effects of training, 281; of welfare recipients, 562–63. *See also* education and educational attainment
transitions: labor-market, 389, **398–99**, **400–401**, 402–3; **404–5**, 411–13, **414–15**; worker-transition data construction, 411–13, **414–15**
traumatized-worker hypothesis, 117–18
trend-productivity growth, 538, 540–41, 569
TV-NAIRU: estimation and NAIRU, 15–17, 19, 21, 38–39, 45–47; state evidence on structural shifts in, 47–52, 51. *See also* NAIRU (nonaccelerating inflation rate of unemployment)

UI. *See* unemployment insurance (UI)
unemployment: business cycle effects, 499–501; earnings growth, 316–17, 340, 342; equilibrium, foreign price change impact on, 294–97; foreign price effects on, 260; and inflation, 65, 70, 223; injuries, on the job, during economic expansion, 518–19; institutional involvement, 163–64, 210*n*2, 212*n*24; insurance against, 437, 458–65, **464**; international transmission of, 292–97, 298; international vs. U.S. (1970s–1990s), 159–61, 166–67, 169–73, 201–6, **203**; job turnover and layoffs, 225–26; labor market institutions and, 210*n*2, 212*n*24; labor supply enhancement policies, 558; lessons learned and fiscal policy, 147–48; marital status and education, 443–45; NAWRU, 3, 8; Phillips curve and sustainability of low, 73–74; by race and ethnicity, during economic expansion, 493, **494**, 495; rate, in sustained expansion, 3–8, **4**, 53–54, 91, 114, 367; role of macroeconomic shocks and, 173–78, **175**; and wages, 222; youth in labor-market outcomes, comparative international, 178–85, **180**, **183–84**, 189, **190**, 192, **198**, 198–201, 204. *See also* economic expansion, sustainability and replicability of; equilibrium unemployment; human resource management practices and sustainable unemployment; NAIRU (nonaccelerating inflation rate of unemployment)
unemployment duration, 367–420; about, 367–72, **370–71**, 403–7; baby boom aging, 384–85, **386–88**; bonus-job-search program, 463–65, **464**; CPS redesign, parallel survey analysis of, 407–11, **410**; institutional role in, **175**, 185, 189; measurement issues, 376–84, **380–83**; pol-

icy changes by education, 463–65, **464**; rates, 367–72, **370–71**, 403–7, **404–5**; theory of, 372–76; and unemployment insurance, 461–62
unemployment insurance (UI): by age and education, **439**; changes in, and labor supply, 462–65, **464**; incentive effect, 461–62; institutional role of, international vs. U.S, 163, **175**, 185, 189, 193; trends in, 422, 437, 458–61, 458–65, **464**
unemployment pressure, index of, 376, **377**
"unified theory" of labor-market outcomes, 161–65, 185
Uniform Crime Reports, 517
unions: collective bargaining and coordination, 163, **175**, 185, 189, **190**, 192, 193–94; declines in private-sector, 284; density and labor-market outcomes, **175**, 185, 189, 193, 194; and outsourcing, 239–40; and unemployment, 210n2, 212n24; wage compression, 231; youth employment, 200–201. *See also* collective bargaining and coordination
university. *See* education and educational attainment
USA Today, 93

vacancy rates and unemployment, 222, **224**, 249
Valletta, Robert, 226
vicious circle, employer-provided training, 552
virtuous circle, employer-provided training, 552
Viscusi, W. Kip, 465, 466, 519
Visser, Jelle, 193
Volcker, Paul, 107
Vroman, Wayne, 476

wage-curve relation, 499
wage-price shocks, effect of, 125–26, **127**
wages: aspirations, 62–63, 66–69, 135; business cycle ef-

fects, 502–7, **504**, **506**; and computer prices, 135; decline in manufacturing, 296; decompression of, U.S. labor market changes, 231; distribution of, 332–35, **334**; downward pressure unemployment duration, 376; early 1990s, 92; earned income tax credit (EITC) effects, 429, 437, 444–53, 456, 458; equilibrium wages and globalization, 269; Federal Reserve policy and inflation of, 117–21; gender differences, international vs. U.S., 160, 161, **198**, 198–201; globalization and U.S., 264–68; growth of real wages, 265–68, 539; in HO model, 274, 275; human capital, 221; immigration and trade globalization, 279; and international trade, 260; international vs. U.S., 160–61, 166–73, 195–96, 201–7; labor rents, erosion of, 240–44, **242**, 250; market-equilibrium model, 244–49; and outsourcing, 239; Phillips curve, specification and estimation of state-level wage, 36–39; Phillips curve derivation, 64; Phillips curves, empirical state, 42–47, **44**; Phillips curves, macro estimates of, 13–15, 27–36; Phillips curves and time-series analysis extensions, 74–77, **76**; pressure and trade liberalization, 288, 297–98; and productivity, 65, 220; product-market competition increase, 557; subsidies, 563–64; temporary workers, 254n21; trade perspectives, 277–81; and unemployment duration, 369; unemployment insurance, 460–61. *See also* earnings; NAIRU (nonaccelerating inflation rate of unemployment); prices, wages and NAIRU
wage shocks, 117
Waidmann, Timothy, 470, 471
Wall Street Journal/NBC News poll, 93
Watson, Mark W., 6, 7, 13, 16, 19, 501, 543

Weinberg, Bruce, 564
welfare: business cycles and government spending, 521, **522–23**, 524–29; job matching efficiency, 562; job training for recipients, 562–63; participation during economic expansion, 517–18; reform effects, 444–58, **455**, **457**; wage effects of reform, 281. *See also* social insurance
welfare-to-work tax credit (WTWTC), 563–64
Western, Bruce, 567, 568
Whitehead, Ralph, 549
Wilson, William, 497
Wise, David A., 476
Wolfe, Barbara, 471
Wolfers, Justin, 160, 161, 164, 165, 173, 174, 176, 178, 185, 188, 189, 192, 193, 198, 201, 202, 205–6, 207, 208
women. *See* gender differences
Wood, Adrian, 271
work behavior: means tested programs, 437–38, 452–53; social security, 477–80, **479**
Worker Profile and Re-Employment Services program, 557
workers. *See* labor force; labor force and labor-force attachment
workers' compensation (WC) insurance, 422, 437, **439**, 465–68, **467**
Workforce Investment Act, 551, 570
Workforce Staffing Partnerships (Boston, MA), 562
working hours. *See* hours worked
work-opportunities tax credit (WOTC), 563–64
workplace innovation, 547–48
work-support benefits, 437
World Development Indicators, 81
World Trade Organization (WTO), 287–88
Worrall, John, 466
WOTC (work-opportunities tax credit), 563–64
WTO (World Trade Organization), 287–88
WTWTC (welfare-to-work tax credit), 563–64
WUMM and FRB-US models: benefit costs, 120; and price

WUMM and FRB-US models *cont.*
shocks, 121, 122, 124, 125–26, **127**; productivity growth and computer prices, 136–37, **138**; supply shock effects, 137–38; sustained easy-money policy by Federal Reserve, 99–100, 104, **105**, 138–39

Yankow, Jeffrey, 564
Yellen, Janet, 62, 538
youth: labor-market outcomes, comparative international, 178–85, **180**, **183–84**, 189, **190**, 192, **198**, 198–201, 204; unemployment rate, 384, 497

Zellner, Arnold, 412, 413
zero-profit conditions, trade theory, 274, 279
Ziliak, James, 449, 458, 459, 507, 517